THE LEGAL ENVIRONMENT OF BUSINESS

Jethro K. Lieberman
New York Law School

George J. Siedel
University of Michigan

HBJ
HARCOURT BRACE JOVANOVICH, PUBLISHERS
San Diego New York Chicago Austin Washington, D.C.
London Sydney Tokyo Toronto

Cover Photo: Justice Holding Scales. Photo © Eric Carle, New York/ FourByFive.

ISBN: 0-15-550503-3
Library of Congress Catalog Number: 88-80613
Printed in the United States of America

ILLUSTRATION CREDITS p. **73** HBJ Collection; **301** HBJ Collection; **306** courtesy of TRW Information Systems Group; **357** HBJ Collection; **552–54** HBJ Collection; **685** courtesy of Xerox Corporation.

Preface

Most chief executive officers in U.S. corporations devote between 5 and 25 percent of their time to legal problems, according to a survey conducted by the *Harvard Business Review*. In certain corporations the percentage is much higher; as the chairman of General Motors once noted (in referring to the company's general counsel): "Mr. Malone and I go pretty steady." The percentage is also likely to be higher in any company faced with a crisis. The board chairman of Westinghouse Corporation, for instance, once turned over company operations to subordinates so that he could concentrate on resolving uranium contract litigation that threatened to bankrupt the company. According to an article in the *Wall Street Journal,* however, even in companies that are not facing crises, "More and more, the solutions to corporate problems aren't found in business school textbooks. The fate of big corporations frequently rests in their lawyers' hands." (Reed, 1985, xi)

Management first became extensively involved with legal issues in the early 1970s. A 1973 article in *Fortune* entitled "The 'Legal Explosion' Has Left Business Shell-Shocked" pinpointed the reasons for this involvement. Based on a survey of a cross section of leading U.S. corporations, the article concluded that "on balance, it seems clear that five areas—**antitrust, securities and stockholder matters, consumerism, environment, and fair employment practices**—are matters of serious and widespread concern." (Carruth, 1973, 68) (emphasis supplied)

Today these five areas continue to play an important role in business. As noted in a *Harvard Business Review* article:

> A decade of growth in the scope, nature, and complexity of government regulation has catapulted attorneys into daily business operations to an unprecedented degree. The equally rapid rise in consumer, shareholder, employee, and competitor litigation has forced prudent managers to include legal advice as an essential element of business planning and decision making. (Chayes, Greenwald & Winig, 1983, 84)

In recent years a sixth area—**international business**—has been added to the list. The influential 1988 report by Porter and McKibbin on management education observed that "the international aspects of business have grown increasingly crucial in recent years." In the report they cite the expectation of the American Assembly of Collegiate Schools of Business that "every student should be exposed to the international dimension." (Porter and McKibbin, 1988, 66)

The organization of this book is based on the six areas that dominate management decision making. The book opens with two units designed to introduce students to the relationship between business and the legal system (Part I) and the foundations of business law: contracts and torts (Part II). The six areas are then covered in the following sequence:

- **Consumerism** (including, as did the *Fortune* article, product safety)—Part III
- **Employment Relationships**—Part IV
- **Investors and Securities Regulation**—Part V
- **Government Regulation** (with emphasis on antitrust)—Part VI
- **Property Rights and the Environment**—Part VII
- **The International Business Environment**—Part VIII

International Perspectives and the Public-Private Interface

Two underlying considerations have guided the organization of materials within each unit. First, recognizing that U.S. and international business have become inextricably entwined, we do not confine international issues to Part VIII but, instead, emphasize them throughout the text. The introductory units, for example, include coverage of other legal systems, a cross-cultural view of contracts, and differing concepts of duty in tort law. Elsewhere the text provides international perspectives on a variety of topics ranging from the European Economic directive on product liability to antitrust enforcement abroad.

The second underlying consideration relates to the relationship between the external environment and the internal organizational environment. The 1988 Porter-McKibbin report concluded that business schools place too much emphasis on the internal organizational environment (which, in law, would be called "traditional business law" or private law) to the exclusion of the external environment (in law, the "legal environment" or public law). The report therefore recommends "a proportionate increase in attention to the external environment—governmental relations, societal trends, legal climate, international developments, among other areas—for the obvious reason that these events 'outside' the organization are increasingly penetrating into the internal operations of the firm and affecting its core efficiency and effectiveness." (Porter and McKibbin, 1988, 318)

We agree wholeheartedly with this recommendation. However, we also recognize that the report recommends a "proportionate increase" in external environment topics. In other words, increasing emphasis on the external environment (the "legal environment" or public law) does not imply elimination of internal organizational environment coverage ("traditional business law" or private law) but does suggest the importance of the interface between the external and internal environments.

We strive in this text, therefore, to emphasize this interface. The law is a seamless web, and a course of study that focuses exclusively on public or private law does not provide students with the balanced approach offered here. For instance, the text covers not only the public law of antitrust and unfair trade practices, but also private law tort and contract principles relating to unfair competition and illegality. Although many other illustrations could be given (such as the combination of labor–management relations and agency law in Part IV, and private and public regulation of land use in Part VII), perhaps the best example of the interaction between public and private law is found in the franchising chapter (Chapter 22), which brings together a wide variety of antitrust, product liability, agency, and other issues.

Other Features

In addition to its international perspectives and emphasis on the interface between public and private law issues, the book offers the following features:

- A chapter devoted to relations with lawyers and alternative dispute resolution. The chapter includes a basic introduction to decision tree analysis, a technique now taught in law schools and increasingly used by attorneys and management in making legal decisions.
- A chapter on business ethics and social responsibility. Rather than focus on abstract philosophical concepts, the chapter emphasizes the relationship between law and ethics in real-life situations, including cases where the law and ethics may conflict.
- In-depth coverage of topics frequently omitted from legal environment texts. In addition to the chapters on international business and franchising discussed above, we include a lengthy chapter on contract law as well as separate chapters covering torts, bankruptcy, and intellectual property.

Cases and "Boxes"

Cases are a powerful tool for imparting to students the complexity of the law and the underlying policies that account for the complexity. The cases reprinted in this book have been edited rather than summarized in order to provide students with the full flavor of how judges develop the law and to demonstrate the importance of specific facts in applying the law. Many of the cases are schoolroom classics, but others, especially in areas where law has undergone substantial change, are from the most recent advance sheets.

Whenever possible, the cases illustrate the principle of law adopted by most courts—that is, the majority view—and also illustrate the application of the law in business practice. With the instructor's guidance, students who study the cases can develop analytical skills that will be exceedingly useful when they enter the business world.

Supplementing the cases are numerous "boxed" items from newspapers, magazines, and journals. These "boxes," by relating law to life in the business community, bring flavor and context to class discussions.

Cross-References

Within the eight units of this book, a vast mix of topics and concerns from everyday headlines is discussed: product liability law, workers' right to strike, bankruptcy, commercial zoning, copyright and patent law, crimes, antitrust, and dozens of others. Recognizing that the law is a "seamless web," so that sooner or later every part connects to every other part, we have included scores of cross-references to permit the student to move forward or back to locate the point at which a topic is discussed most fully.

Supplementary Materials

A detailed Instructor's Manual has been prepared by James Jurinski and Gretchen A. Brevig. In addition to case briefs and solutions to the problems that follow each chapter, the manual includes numerous suggestions and supplementary materials for instructors whose preparation time is limited. A Test Book by Jurinski and Brevig is also available to instructors.

For students, a Study Guide has been prepared by Alvin Stauber and Patrick Maroney, both of Florida State University. The Study Guide features chapter reviews as well as true–false, matching, multiple choice, and essay questions in a self-test format.

Acknowledgments

We wish to thank the following reviewers for their helpful comments and suggestions: Dudley Buffa, Oregon State University; Tracy Dobson, Michigan State University; Mary Jane Dundas, Arizona State University; and June Horrigan, California State University—Sacramento. We also wish to thank the following members of the production team at Harcourt Brace Jovanovich: Ken Rethmeier, Executive Editor; Mickey Cox, Acquisitions Editor; Jan Duffala, Associate Editor; Cindy Simpson, Production Editor; Merilyn Britt, Designer; Lesley Lenox, Production Manager; and Paulette Russo, Art Editor. Last, but certainly not least, we wish to acknowledge the research and proofreading assistance of Brian L. Jefferson, Jaime E. Kent and Elizabeth K. Lieberman.

Jethro K. Lieberman
George J. Siedel

To the Student

This book presents the law in two ways—through discussion in plain English of the major themes and rules, and through edited cases that discuss many of the major points in the judges' own words. The cases are integrated with the text, so that you will find each case at the appropriate place in the discussion. You should be aware that every case has been abridged, many considerably abridged (deletions within case opinions are indicated by asterisks and ellipses). If you are interested in reading any case in its entirety, the citations at the head of the case will enable you to find it in any law library.

The Study of Law

As you plunge into the study of law, you will quickly discover some disconcerting features of the subject. The law is not always easy to understand. It requires a good deal of concentration and attention to murky statements sometimes written in an appallingly opaque style. Most of the time your sense that the writing is dense will not be a reflection on you, but on the law. Those who "write the law" are not always the best writers, and half the difficulty of the subject is getting through their prose. We have done our best to simplify and clarify.

Detail

The law, you will discover, is extremely detailed and often at least seemingly fussy and picky. Qualifications pile upon exasperating qualifications, so that some sentences—judges' sentences, not ours, we hope!—are choked with sharp twists and often unfathomable turns. This is not just an idiosyncracy of the writers of the law. The law corresponds to the myriad ways people go about organizing their world, and it would not be useful if it could not distinguish between two similar, but different, situations.

Consider, for example, the ordinary distinctions between interests in property. You may give away your car, or sell it, or loan it, or retain an interest in it. Merely to memorize these distinctions may seem boring, but to understand them is to understand the way in which we organize our lives. What does it mean, for instance, to say that you "own" an automobile? You may have arranged a loan from a bank to pay for it. If you fail to pay off the loan, the bank may repossess it. Do you "own" the car under those circumstances? You may loan the car to a friend for a day or park it in a garage. You may decide to give it away to a friend or to sell it. Does the friend to whom you have given it free as a gift "own" it in the same sense as the stranger to whom you sold it? Does the friend "own" it if you promise to give, but later renege on the promise? When you put your car in a garage, you are surrendering temporary possession but not title. When you sell the car, but agree to keep it in your garage for a month (with permission to use it), you are surrendering title, but not possession. When you borrow to purchase it, your bank or dealer may hold a security interest.

In all these cases, either you or the person to whom you sold or gave it owns the car, but differing consequences may flow from the way in which you disposed of it. These differences are captured in law, and a major part of your study will be to attend to the meaning and utility of the distinctions. And always bear in mind that although the law seems to create these distinctions, in reality it is the necessities of human existence that create them—and that also create the law to deal with them.

The Logic (or Illogic) of the Law

"The life of the law has not been logic; it has been experience," said the often-quoted Justice Holmes. You may find much apparent irrationality in the law—for example, an antitrust policy that forbids actions that injure competition, side-by-side a price-discrimination law that itself appears to injure competition. Law is not a monolith; it is a series of customs, conventions, rules, and aspirations that have been recognized in different places at different times for different circumstances. The law is not always consistent, in part because different judges interpret the law differently, in part because circumstances change, in part because different political majorities can persuade legislators to draw different lines in legislation at different times.

Nevertheless, a deep strain of *reasonableness* undergirds much of American law. Certain laws may be irrational or inconsistent with other laws, but as a whole the enterprise of law, at least as carried on in our time, is fundamentally built on reason. What your common sense tells you ought to be usually is. The difficulties start when the situations become too complex for common sense to guide. Then it is necessary to spend most of your energy trying to understand the situation. The facts are the most important element of any case. Once you understand them—and not until you understand them—will you be able to appreciate the law that is applied to them and to discern whether it makes sense or not.

The Complexity of Legal Relations

Legal relations are complex because law serves more than one purpose simultaneously. A given law or legal policy is directed toward certain people, not toward everyone. It controls certain behavior, not all behavior. It provides for remedies or sanctions. It may be superseded by other law, depending on the circumstances. If applied by a court, the judge's ruling can be appealed, because law is liable to be misinterpreted. There must always be a way to change the law, so no legal policy is ever final and unalterable. All these considerations complicate the study of law.

The Uncertainty of Law

For all the foregoing reasons, in the final analysis, law is never certain. Although statutes appear to be definitive, they are always subject to interpretation. Precedents of the courts are almost always ambiguous because they are couched in language that is capable of an infinite variety of meaning—"reasonable," "substantial," "unconscionable," "restraint of trade." Beware of those who claim to know definitively what the law is, for a simple change of circumstances can change the result when even the plainest law is applied. And much of the law is written in open-ended language that takes on meaning only from case to case. As Justice Holmes said: "General propositions do not decide concrete cases." Moreover, the enterprise of law is so immense—there is so much law—that for every apparently certain statement that one can make about the law (for example, "The contract of a person who is not yet eighteen years old is not binding"), it is usually possible to find another statement of law that will contradict it under some set of facts ("The minor's contract is binding if ratified after becoming eighteen"). Never say never.

The foregoing facets of the law—excessive detail, apparent illogic, complexity, and uncertainty—might appear to make the study of law dismal. They certainly may make the study frustrating. Yet these facets of law are also its great strength, for they mean that the law lives and breathes and is not forever frozen, unable to adapt to changing circumstances. Although we do not always make this point explicitly, it underlies virtually every page in this book.

Four Tips on Studying Law

Don't Argue with the Facts

Throughout this book, you will be presented with both real and hypothetical cases containing certain circumstances, but not others. The purpose of these cases is to study how the law is to be applied. *Don't argue with these facts.* Don't say: "But what if he didn't really agree with the terms of the contract?" (if in the example he did agree) or, "But what if he wasn't driving recklessly?" (if the example requires that he was). The result may certainly be different if the same law is applied to different facts, but the purpose of each example is to understand the law with reference to the facts presented. Once you understand the particular rule, then you may ask yourself—indeed, you ought to ask yourself—"Yes, but suppose the facts were different, what then? Would the rule apply or must the rule be modified?"

Don't Confuse the Legal Rule with the Proof of the Case

Frequently you may be tempted to substitute evidence for law. Don't succumb. Because a case may be difficult to prove does not mean that the law does not really apply as stated to the given facts. This is a corollary of the tip above. For example, a rule of law says that oral contracts for the sale of goods valued at less than $500 are binding. You might be tempted to think: "That's all to the good, but anyone can lie about making a deal, so how can such a contract be binding, for how can the oral agreement be proved?" This book deals in the main with the law, not with the lawyer's practical job of proving a case, although we frequently point out how attention to the practicalities can reap rich dividends. Therefore, if the case example states that an oral agreement was made, do not quarrel with that fact or reject it in your mind, and do not confuse the rule that says the agreement is binding with the admittedly difficult problem of proving at trial that an oral agreement was made. The meaning and application of the law does not depend on the existence of evidence, although winning a case in court usually does. In this book, you can assume that the facts we give are the truth, so that in most of the discussion throughout the text, the evidentiary problem does not arise.

Don't Confuse the Difficulty of Creating Factual Conditions with the Legal Relations That Govern Them

Many of the rules that you will study in this book depend on the existence of certain conditions. To take a simple illustration, the federal Arbitration Act recognizes the validity of a clause in a contract that binds the parties to take a dispute arising out of the contract to a private arbitrator for resolution, rather than to a court. The application of the Arbitration Act obviously depends on the existence of the clause in the contract. Now it may prove impossible for one party to negotiate the clause. The other party may be adamantly against it. Does that mean that the law itself is somehow invalid or not worth studying? Obviously not. We attempt to examine the whole panoply of law that affects business. But quite obviously not every business and not every person will be able to take advantage of every law and legal policy, just as not every business and not every person will be affected by them. The difficulty of conducting a particular business, the inequality of bargaining power, the different situation from which each person starts, do not invalidate the general rules of the law.

Don't Confuse Certain Laws with Rules People Can Write for Themselves

This tip is a bit different from the others. Certain laws—most prominently, the Uniform Commercial Code—impose obligations *only in the absence of agreement between the parties*. Although we restate this principle at different points in the text, try to bear in mind as you read that not all law is always obligatory. Some law governs regardless of what people have provided for themselves. Two corporate marketing managers may agree not to be bound by the antitrust laws, but that agreement will not avail them one whit when they are prosecuted and thrown in jail for fixing their retail prices. Some law, on the other hand, governs only those situations in which people have not provided for their own rules. For example, the Uniform Commercial Code tells manufacturers that when they sell their goods they extend an implied warranty of fitness—that is, that the goods will be fit for a particular purpose to which they will be put. But the manufacturer may disclaim that warranty—for example, by stating that the goods are sold "as is." If the parties agree to the disclaimer, the Uniform Commercial Code does not apply. If the contract is silent—that is, does not disclaim the warranty—then the Code does apply. The law is not changed, only its application. It is rather like the set of instructions accompanying the board game *Monopoly*. The instructions tell you what the rules are, unless all the players agree to deviate from them.

In the end, these tips are only that. Ultimately, you will need to find your own way, the way that suits you best in mastering the manifold materials of the law. The law is unlike anything you have ever studied before. You may think it at times exasperating and frustrating. But it can also be fascinating and exhilarating. Whatever else it is, it is always very real.

Be patient, and the study will reward each hour you devote to it many times over.

About the Authors

Jethro K. Lieberman is a professor at New York Law School. As a lawyer, journalist, and author, he has devoted his career to writing about law and the legal system. He is a cum laude graduate of both Yale College and Harvard Law School and is a member of the New York and District of Columbia bars. He practiced law for more than five years (first as a Navy lawyer during the Vietnam War, then with a large Washington law firm doing antitrust and trade regulation law, and then as general counsel of a closely held New York publishing company). Thereafter he served for nine years as legal affairs editor of *Business Week* magazine (1973–1982), where he was responsible for national legal coverage. He taught for three years at Fordham University School of Law in New York, while serving as founding editor of *Alternatives to the High Cost of Litigation,* a monthly newsletter for corporate counsel on alternative dispute resolution. He has been a consultant to law firms and to various nonprofit law-reform groups. He is the author, coauthor, or editor of more than twenty books, including *The Enduring Constitution* (1987), which won the American Bar Association's prestigious Silver Gavel Award in 1988; *Milestones! 200 Years of American Law* (1976); and *The Litigious Society* (1981), which won the Silver Gavel Award in 1982.

George J. Siedel is a professor of business law at the School of Business Administration of the University of Michigan. He holds a B.A. degree from the College of Wooster, a J.D. degree from the University of Michigan, and a diploma in comparative legal studies from Cambridge University, where he studied under a Ford Foundation fellowship. He has been an associate attorney in a professional corporation and an officer and member of the board of directors of an international corporation. Professor Siedel has been admitted to practice before the United States Supreme Court. He is the chief editor of the *Michigan Real Property Review* and has served as staff editor of the *American Business Law Journal.* He is the editor, author, or contributing author of ten books and has published over twenty articles in law reviews and journals. In 1980 he was elected a visiting fellow at Wolfson College, Cambridge University, and in 1981 he received the University of Michigan Faculty Recognition Award for teaching and research. He also served as Visiting Professor of Business Law at Stanford University in 1985.

Contents

PART ONE

BUSINESS AND THE LEGAL SYSTEM: INTRODUCTORY THEMES

1

Law and the Legal System

> The law touches every interest of man. Nothing that is human is alien to it.
>
> —JUSTICE FELIX FRANKFURTER

> The law is the witness and external deposit of our moral life. Its history is the history of the moral development of the race. The practice of it, in spite of popular jests, tends to make good citizens and good men.
>
> —JUSTICE OLIVER WENDELL HOLMES, JR.

What Is Law?

The Nature of Law

Law is the instrument that people use to regulate their conduct in civilized society. It is a complex of rules, institutions, and ways of thinking about and interpreting those rules and institutions, that permits civilization to exist and people to live orderly lives. A more precise definition of law is difficult, if not impossible, to give. Philosophers have been debating the nature of law for thousands of years. One line of thought—that of the "positivists"—holds that law is simply the rule-like pronouncements of the sovereign, whether king or a democratically elected legislature. According to another approach—that of the "natural law" philosophers—law is a system of reason, a set of deductions from principles of ethics, morals, or justice. Let us consider an actual case to see where the truth might lie.

Back in the 1840s in Illinois, a farmer named Seeley raised hogs on land next to that of a wheat farmer named Peters. Seeley's farm had no fences, and his hogs were free to roam the countryside. Peters fenced his own property, but poorly, and Seeley's hogs entered through breaks, trampling the crop. Peters sued Seeley, demanding that the court award him **damages** (a legal term meaning a sum of money that will recompense the victim for the injury he has suffered).

The question for the court was what law applied to the circumstances of this case. Now it should seem clear that some law would apply. If your neighbor breaks down your front door and walks out with your television set, common sense says that you should have a legal means of recovering for the damage done to your door and for the theft of your television. Common sense is right, of course; you are entitled to recover your legal damages. As the ancient maxim had it: for every (legal) wrong there is a remedy.

The case of *Peters* v. *Seeley,* however, was a bit more complex. A law could rationally put liability on the keeper of animals. Equally logically, however, the law could require a wheat farmer to fence his land. The trouble was that no clearly written law expressly declared one rule or the other. Instead, a law of Illinois enacted in the early part of the nineteenth century declared that the "common law" of England was thenceforth the law in Illinois as well. We consider the nature of common law in some detail later on (pp. 14–15); for now it is sufficient to say that **common law** is the body of court rulings that governs the legal relationships among people in the absence of explicit legislative enactment. The "reception statute"—so called because the law *received* the common law of England into Illinois—did not spell out the rights and duties of hog farmers and wheat farmers toward one another.

To resolve the case, the Illinois Supreme Court began as you would begin. It asked: What is the common law with respect to the mutual obligations of hog and wheat farmers? The English common law had no specific rule relating to hog and wheat farmers, but it did have a firm rule that if the owner of animals fails to fence them in, he is liable for damages done by them to the property of others. Peters, the wheat farmer, thought that should be the end of the case, for the legislature had declared that the law to be used in Illinois was the common law of England, and by the common law of England, Peters was entitled to damages.

But the court went further with its analysis. The English common law rule had developed in a country where land was scarce and people lived close by one another. In the United States, however, the situation was quite the reverse, and the custom of fencing in animals had never taken hold. The court gave as the reason for this difference in custom the boundless land that the people of Illinois enjoyed. So much land and so little timber was available that "it must be many years yet before our extensive prairies can be fenced," and the grain would rot unless the cattle could feed on it. [Seeley v. Peters, 10 Ill. 130 (1848)][1] The court thus overrode the legislature's law and substituted its own judgment in order to conform law to the conditions and customs of the people in the state. Peters had to fence in his wheat, not Seeley his hogs.

We can see in this example a notion that law is not only the commandment of political authority, but a statement of rule that must comport in some way with reason and common sense. You might object that the example proves no such thing—that the political authority, in this case, was the court itself and that the law is whatever the court says it is. The noted jurist Oliver Wendell Holmes, Jr., a member of the Massachusetts Supreme Judicial Court for more than twenty years and of the United States Supreme Court for thirty (1902–1932), was of this view. In a lecture given in 1897, he declared (in a passage often quoted):

> Take the fundamental question, What constitutes the law? You will find some text writers telling you that it is something different from what is decided by the courts of Massachusetts or England, that it is a system of reason, that it is a deduction from principles of ethics or admitted axioms or what not, which may or may not coincide with the decisions. But if we take the view of our friend the bad man we shall find that he does not care two straws for the axioms or deduction, but that he does want to know what the Massachusetts or English courts are likely to do. I am much of his mind. *The prophecies of what the courts will do in fact, and nothing more pretentious, are what I mean by the law.* (emphasis added)

Holmes's view was adopted by an influential school of American scholars known as the "legal realists." They wanted to dispense with metaphysical notions of law and study what lawmaking bodies such as legislatures and courts really do.

The difficulty with this viewpoint is that if law is a prophecy of what courts do, then there must be some basis on which to make the prophecy, some underlying set of rules, or else the law is simply the outpouring of a dictator acting on whim. Suppose Seeley's lawyer had told his client: "Your case looks bad, because the common law of England clearly requires you to fence in your hogs. But here in this country the law is really what I can prophesy the courts will do. And I predict that the Illinois Supreme Court will rule in your favor because I am going to transmit to them a large bribe, which you will pay, and it is well known that they rule in favor of bribers." Obviously, this view of the law—that it is whatever anyone can cajole out of a court by any means, fair or foul—is not sustainable. There must be some set of social, political, and moral norms on which law and lawmaking are based. These norms will occupy us throughout most of this chapter and will be reflected in much of the discussion throughout the text.

[1] For a description of legal citations and how to read them, see Appendix A at the end of this book.

Law Distinguished from Morals and Justice

In exhorting his listeners to think about what courts actually do, Holmes was not speaking nonsense. He was attempting to clarify an important point in the debate about the nature of law—namely, that law is not the same as "what is right" or "what is just." To be sure, legal principles and principles of morality and justice overlap. Most, but not all, of the Ten Commandments are also legal precepts as well. It is morally wrong to steal and kill; it is also illegal to do so. But it is not unlawful to take the Lord's name in vain, though it may be blasphemous, and the sin of envy is no crime.

Immorality is not always unlawful, and neither is illegality always immoral. The law requires us to drive on the right side of the road, but nothing is intrinsically evil about driving on the left, and the British are not an immoral nation because they follow a different rule.

In general, the law concerns itself with the lowest common denominator of human conduct, not the highest. Law imposes on all of us certain duties and obligations to refrain from interfering with others and from injuring them by our own actions. But it does not require us to act to prevent any harm from befalling another. A common example is that of the drowning person. A child who cannot swim is thrashing about close to shore in a lake next to which you are walking. The child is a stranger to you, and you have nothing to do with the child's being in the water. You could probably save the child simply by wading several feet out, and in any event you are a strong swimmer. But you prefer not to get your Sunday clothes wet, so you walk on, and the child dies. Your failure to rescue the child would rightly be condemned as immoral, but there is no legal duty to save him. In short, the law does not tell us so much to do our best as it does to refrain from doing our worst. However, as Box 1-1 indicates, one state has changed this ancient rule.

Likewise, law and justice overlap frequently, but not always. It is unjust to punish a man for an act that was not illegal when he committed it, and the law prohibits the government from doing so. But a law that imposes a penalty of ten years' imprisonment on a starving man who stole a shopping cart full of groceries may be woefully unjust, yet it is nevertheless the law. Legislatures enact many laws that someone thinks are unjust, and courts do not invalidate laws or refuse to enforce them simply because one or more people demonstrate that they are harsh or unfair as applied.

The Language of Law

The law is frequently couched in obscure terms, jargon, and mystifying phraseology. Lawyers like to claim that this is because they write precisely, that their special words are required in order to state exactly the necessary qualifications, exceptions, and distinctions that make up so complex a subject as the law. In part this is true. Every discipline has its special language,

Box 1-1 A Statutory Duty to Act

Minnesota Law Mandates Bystander Help in Crises

ST. PAUL, Aug. 2 (AP)—Being a "Good Samaritan" is now a duty, not an option, in Minnesota, where a new provision in state statutes provides up to a $100 fine for people who fail to aid in an emergency.

The amendment to an older law went into effect Monday. It is designed to prevent incidents such as one last week in St. Louis, where a 13-year-old girl was raped over 40 minutes by two youths as several people stood by. Police finally were summoned by an 11-year-old boy.

Previously, an expert lifeguard "could watch a 6-month-old baby crawl into the river and drown and sit by and do nothing about it and nothing would happen," said State Representative Randy Staten, an author of the measure. "That is totally unacceptable conduct for civilized society."

Many states have "Good Samaritan" laws that relieve a person of liability when they render aid in an emergency. The amendment to Minnesota's law goes a step further by making it a duty to assist.

Linda Close, division manager of public safety and litigation in the Minnesota Attorney General's office, said the amended statute "creates a duty to help somebody if a person is exposed to 'grave physical harm.' "

Mr. Staten, a Minneapolis Democrat, says he believes the statute is the first of its kind in the country, and he said officials from other states appear interested in enacting similar laws. The amendment was prompted by incidents far from Minnesota, he said, citing the rape of a woman on a pool table in New Bedford, Mass., as a group of people watched, and the Kitty Genovese case of many years ago, in which the Queens, N.Y., woman was fatally stabbed as people watched from apartment windows.

Source: *New York Times*, August 3, 1983

and much of it is useful to the initiate. And the language of American law—a curious mixture of Old English, Old French, and a little Latin—is a lot less mystifying, a lot less given to archaisms, than it was even a few decades ago.

Nevertheless, mystifying words continue to abound. Lawyers' prose is often bad. The student who reads through judicial opinions and lawyers' briefs will find much to satisfy a taste for fuzziness. One reason is that, contrary to the usual assertion, the language of law is not so precise. Another is that words are beguiling; unfamiliar words that seem to have a fixed meaning can seduce the lazy or unwary into believing they say more than they do.

One reason for this is that much law is the product of political compromise. Legislators can be cajoled into backing each other's bills if the bills contain language ambiguous enough to let each side suppose it is securing what it wants. In addition, no rule can possibly anticipate every possible set of circumstances. Therefore, lawmakers must resort in most instances to language that is inherently fuzzy: "deceptive," "unreasonable," and "substantial."

Even words that seem to have a fixed meaning can be shown, on close inspection, to be susceptible to varying interpretations. Suppose that you are a legislator who wants to punish those who use guns and other weapons during the commission of a crime. You could specify each type of weapon of which you disapprove: handguns, rifles, shotguns, machine guns, bazookas, and so on. Since it is easy to omit a type you wished to include, you would probably add a phrase such as "and other dangerous weapons." But what is a weapon? Is a stick a weapon? A heavy-duty flashlight? It depends on why you were carrying the item and to what use it was put. No definitive list can be given.

Ultimately, any attempt to define with precision conduct that is to be outlawed must fail. A society in which all rules were absolute, stated without room for maneuver, would be an intolerable place to live for any who value freedom because the rules would almost invariably be overinclusive and restrictive. As Judge Jerome Frank noted in *Law and the Modern Mind* (1963, p. 7), "Much of the uncertainty of law is not an unfortunate accident: it is of immense social value."

Nevertheless, the uncertainty that arises through sheer linguistic sloppiness and unconscious semantic confusion is not of immense social value; to the contrary, it is of no value. Beginning in the late 1970s, a move to overcome the purely linguistic mystification of law gathered some steam. This is the "plain English" movement. Under an executive order of President Jimmy Carter in 1977, federal regulators were required to draft rules and regulations in simple English. Some simplification has resulted, though far from enough. Beginning with New York, a few states at the same time began to pass laws requiring contracts with consumers—insurance policies and leases, for example—to be written in straightforward language.

Classification of Types of Law

Because the "law" has so many different connotations, there is no one way to classify the different types of law. What follows is a simple fourfold classification scheme that presents law along its major dimensions: substantive, jurisdictional, governmental type, and procedural.

The Major Types of Substantive Law

Substantive law deals with the different ways people interact. On a family tree of law the broadest "kingdoms" are criminal and civil law. These are substantive branches of law because they deal with human conduct. **Criminal law** (Chapter 7) is that body of law that deals with violations of public order, including violent crimes (such as murder, rape, assault, and robbery), crimes against property (larceny, embezzlement), and crimes consisting of infractions of regulatory codes (income tax fraud, securities fraud, and the like). Penalties for violation of the criminal law include death, imprisonment, and monetary fines. Serious crimes, usually those punishable by imprisonment of more than one year, are called *felonies;* less serious crimes are *misdemeanors.*

Civil law governs the private relations among individuals. It might also be defined as all branches of the law not included within the criminal law. ("Civil" has a different connotation in legal systems outside the Anglo-American tradition—in those countries, the civil law refers to codes enacted by the national legislatures.

Civil law can be divided into two main branches. One is **public law**—for example, constitutional law (pp. 15–23 and Chapter 2) and administrative law (Chapter 5)—so called because this branch (along with criminal law) deals with the relations between government and private citizens and organizations. The most significant development in twentieth-century American law is the growth of administrative or regulatory law. Examples in this category include *labor law*—the relations between unions, their members, and their employers (Chapter 15); *antitrust law*—the appropriate form of competition (Chapters 19–20); *securities law*—the code governing trading in corporate stocks (Chapter 18); and *tax law*—how the government raises money to pay for its activities.

The other principal branch is **private law**, which is the set of laws that spell out the duties, obligations, and responsibilities that individuals and organizations owe to each other. Within the sphere of private law are the following:

Tort Law The word "**tort**" derives from Old French, meaning a wrong or injustice, substantially the connotation it carries today. Tort law spells out the duties of care that one person owes to another. Many *intentional* torts are also crimes: murder, assault, rape, and robbery are torts, and the victim or family can legally sue to recover damages. Other torts include false imprisonment (akin to kidnapping), trespass on property, theft (including the stealing of business, known as *unfair competition*), defamation of character, invasion of privacy—indeed, most acts that you would consider injurious to another are probably torts. A tort need not be intentional. The biggest class of tort lawsuits today—automobile accident litigation—involves *negligent,* or careless, actions that harm another. (Another type of negligent tort is the *malpractice* action against a doctor or other professional.) During the 1970s, a third type of tort involving neither intentional nor negligent conduct—*strict liability*—began to gain ground in the courts as a means of redressing injuries resulting from all sorts of defective products. Unlike criminal law, which serves at least in part to punish the wrongdoer, tort law serves to compensate the victim. We will consider tort law in more detail in Chapters 9 and 10.

Contract Law Tort law spells out the rights that individuals have to remain unharmed by wrongful acts of others. It is the law that creates the duty to refrain from wrongful conduct. But people may also create their own sets of obligations toward each other by entering into contracts. A contract may impose upon an individual a liability that he would not otherwise legally have. Sometimes a contract can relieve an individual from a liability that he would have under tort law. Contract law is discussed in Chapter 8.

Property Law A third category of private law is that which deals with property. In a narrow sense, the law of property deals with land and buildings (called *real property*) and personal possessions (called *personal property*). The law of real property concerns the rights of buyers, sellers, lessors, and lessees of land, houses, and other buildings (Chapter 23). The law of personal property deals with a range of issues that arise from the way we use our belongings—for example, the temporary possession of an automobile by a parking garage (bailment), the way we give control of money or other assets to family members or others (trusts), how we dispose of property after a death (wills and estates), and how we protect the fruits of an invention (patent, trademark, and copyright, Chapter 24).

In a broader sense, property law deals with a host of issues that are also affected by other types of law. It is usually closely bound up with contract law, because much of what we contract about has to do with property. Control and operation of the myriad organizations that make up modern industrial life are steeped in property law but also are intimately bound up in law that developed specifically for this purpose; these include *agency*, *partnership*, and *corporation law*.

Agency Law Agency law treats the relations among individuals who undertake to act on behalf of others—employees, agents, corporate officers, and the like. Without agency law, no industrial life would be possible. We study it in Part Four.

Partnership and Corporation Law The predominant forms of business enterprise are the partnership and the corporation. Each is governed by a complex set of laws that we study separately in Part Five.

Jurisdictional Classification: Federal, State, Local, and International

Law, as we use the term, is not a monolith. It does not spring whole from a single source, like the pronouncements of some autocratic king. Modern law is a complex affair that comes from a variety of political entities, defined both geographically and institutionally.

Geographically, law comes from several types of "jurisdictions"—that is, governments. In the United States, with its complex form of federalism, there are three types of government: federal, state, and local. The first two are semi-sovereign; the last, local government, is dependent on the other two.

Federal Law The **federal** government is the national government, with the power to make law for the country as a whole, though its lawmaking power does not extend to everything over which government is capable of making law. The federal government consists of Congress, which functions as the national legislature; the executive branch, headed by the president and including governmental departments and administrative agencies; and the federal courts, or judicial branch. Within its sphere, federal law is superior to that of state and local law.

State Law The second semi-sovereign form of government is that of **state** government. The states also have legislative, executive, and judicial branches. Their legal power does not spring from the federal government but is rooted independently in the Constitution. Both federal and state governments are said to be "semi-sovereign" because, despite the persistence of the myth, there simply is no such thing as sovereignty in the United States—no law need forever be so, no person or institution is supreme. In our system of checks and balances, there is always a means of challenging law and political action.

Local Law The third form of government is not, however, even semi-sovereign. This is **local** government: cities, towns, villages, counties, and other political districts within the states. The powers of these governments are delegated by the states and may be modified, limited, or removed by the states. To the extent that it is authorized to do so, local government also creates law (in the form of municipal ordinances and regulations).

International Law This law is created by international organizations, by the customs and practices that prevail among nations, and by agreement. However, to the extent that international law is applicable within the United States, it is so generally because the nation has entered into *treaties* with other countries and the treaties are enforceable as part of federal law.

Law Classified by Governmental Branch Creating It

For historical as well as legal reasons, there are differences between law that comes from a legislature and law that emanates from other governmental bodies. Implicit in much of the discussion in this book is the relationship between the courts and the other branches and how that relationship affects the meaning and enforcement of law.

Statutes A law enacted by a legislature is called a *statute*. It is written and published in various forms.

Regulations Laws emanating from the executive branch—the source of administrative law—are called *regulations* or *rules;* they too are written and published. The executive branch generally derives its power to promulgate regulations and rules from the legislature. Neither statutes nor regulations stand alone. They must often be interpreted by the courts. A judicial gloss on a statute or regulation rendered in the course of a lawsuit is in effect the meaning of the statute or regulation. In most cases, members of the legislature or executive agency can always amend the statute or regulation after the court has ruled, if they are dissatisfied with the court's interpretation. The amendment will then apply to future cases.

Common Law The courts also produce a third kind of law, known as the *common law* or *unwritten law*. "Unwritten" is a misnomer: in fact, the common law has always been written down more or less, in the reports of the courts' decisions in individual cases. The vast body of judicial *opinions* constitutes the written record of the common law. Shortly, we will explore in some detail the authority of the courts to fashion the common law. For now it is enough to note that the authority is not a delegated one; it is inherent and assigned by the Constitution to the judiciary. The common law is not the exclusive province of the courts, however. The legislature may intrude and enact legislation modifying or even abolishing common law rules laid down by courts. The courts in turn have the authority to interpret the statutes that do so.

Substantive vs. Procedural Law

Still another way to classify law is by the person, group, organization, or institution to which it is addressed. Law addressed to actions and relationships among people is **substantive law.** Law that structures government by laying down procedures on how it must act—especially that which relates to the courts themselves—is known as **procedural law** or **adjective law.** For the most part, we will be concerned with that part of procedural law that shapes the legal-judicial process: how lawsuits begin and move through the courts. Every court system has its own rules of procedure, and there are often significant differences in procedure among different courts within the same system. Thus, the Federal Rules of Civil Procedure, promulgated by the Supreme Court and approved by Congress, apply to all federal courts. But each local federal court has its own set of supplementary rules with which lawyers—but not their clients—must be familiar.

Sources of Law

However law is defined and classified, it is a product of human institutions. At different times, different institutions—legislatures, courts, regulatory bodies, ad hoc conventions—create or shape laws that have varying imports and impacts on the population. Amid all this lawmaking, there are four general sources of law.

Constitutional Law

The United States Constitution is the supreme law of the land. No other law takes precedence over it, and any law that is inconsistent with it is invalid and void. In legal theory, the Constitution derives from "the people," though of necessity it was drafted by a committee of the people—those who attended the Constitutional Convention of 1787—and ratified by the people through special conventions in each state called for that purpose. We examine the Constitution in more detail later.

Although the federal Constitution is supreme, it is not the only constitution. Each state has its own. State constitutions play precisely the same role within the state that the federal Constitution plays nationally. Cities and certain other forms of municipal government have "charters" granted by the states. These charters are akin to constitutions for the municipalities.

Statutes

Statutes—the enactments of legislatures—have become our most fertile source of law during the twentieth century. Congress, the state legislatures, and city councils (whose ordinances are akin to statutes) have legislated on virtually every imaginable subject, including the conduct of war, the structure of government, national price controls, environmental protection, economic relations, retirement benefits, civil rights, rent control—the list is endless.

In general, there are four types of statutes. A legislature may declare a particular act or type of conduct to be unlawful and subject to severe sanctions, such as imprisonment and substantial fines. Such statutes fall within the criminal law. A statute may establish standards for judging conduct or spelling out relations between individuals and groups. For example, the legislature may decide that in automobile accident lawsuits, the negligence of the defendant must be weighed against that of the plaintiff. Such statutes fall within the realm of civil law. Or a statute may establish a governmental body or restructure an existing one and delegate to it the power to promulgate specific rules for the regulation of an industry or type of activity. Frequently, all three types of enactment are combined within a single statute—for example, environmental-protection statutes prescribe standards that people and companies must follow, permit certain classes of people to sue civilly if the standards are not followed, prescribe criminal penalties for some violations, and grant existing and new agencies the power to police the environment. The fourth type of statute is that which raises tax revenues and spends the public monies.

Administrative Law

As we have seen, administrative agencies of the executive branch of the federal and state governments promulgate rules and regulations, pursuant to power delegated by the legislatures. From at least the middle of this century, administrative law has probably been the most voluminous. Unless the agencies go beyond the scope of the power delegated to them, the rules they announce have the full force of law and are entitled to equal weight with statutes when the courts are called upon to enforce them.

Unwritten Law: The Common Law

The Constitution, statutes, and administrative law are all "written." The exact text of the rules can be consulted because they have all been published and are more or less easily accessible. But there is a vast body of law that has been called "unwritten" because it is not embodied in statutes and regulations. As we have noted, this is the *common law,* the body of law that emanates from courts. To understand why there is common law, let us consider three basic functions that courts perform.

The first function is "fact-finding." Did the accused kill the victim, as charged by the prosecutor? Did the defendant promise to complete construction on the plaintiff's house by June 30? The courts sift lies from truth and attempt to sort through the ambiguities. Someone has to perform this critical function; the courts, with their elaborate procedural protections for the claimants who appear before them, do so.

The second function is "law-applying." Suppose the plaintiff, a wholesale buyer of canned tomatoes, claims that a statute gives him the right to return a defective shipload to the seller. The seller retorts that the plaintiff's interpretation of the statute is incorrect and demands the purchase price. The court must decide what the statute means and whether it applies in the circumstances of the case before it.

In most cases, both fact-finding and law-applying are required. When there is a jury, it will be responsible not only for determining what the true state of affairs was but also for applying the law to the facts. It does this by following the judge's instructions on the law. After most jury verdicts, the case is at an end. The result is a decision for one side or the other, without elaboration of the reasons. But when there is no jury, or when a case is appealed to a higher court, there will usually be a written opinion by the judge. This opinion will often be published and will usually contain a statement about the meaning of the statute in question. This opinion is significant, because it too is a source of law.

By placing its own interpretation on the literal language of a statute, the court is adding something to the law and saddling it with a meaning for the future—unless the legislature chooses to amend the statute in view of the court's decision. Those who would "look up" a statute should be wary: rarely can anyone know what the law means simply by perusing the language in the statute books, because anywhere from a handful to hundreds of published judicial opinions may interpret a particular statutory provision. These decisions cannot be disregarded, for in future cases judges will look to them as precedents to be followed.

The third type of judicial function does not involve a statute: it involves deciding whether a plaintiff's common law rights have been violated. As noted earlier, the common law is a body of legal principles enunciated by courts in the absence of statute during the past several centuries. It is not written in the statutory sense because each principle, with its corollaries and exceptions, is not set forth in one place. Rather, each principle is stated, often in lengthy prose, in judicial opinions discussing a particular case.

Where do these principles come from? The debate has been long, learned, and unending. Some say they come from God, others from reason. Still others suppose that the principles derive from the "character of the people." It seems rather more likely that the common law is a tapestry woven from age-old customs, modified by experience and new conditions, and tempered by the dictates of reason and the promptings of moral concern—and sometimes by the biases and prejudices of judges, who, after all, are the oracles of the common law.

In short, judges make law. They have made most of tort law and contract law, although large portions of contract law have been superseded by the Uniform Commercial Code and other statutes. Many rules embodied in statutes are simply articulations of common law principles. Equally important, the rules that courts use to guide them in interpreting statutes are common law rules. Inherent in the judicial power of the courts is the power to determine how to interpret.

Because the courts over the years have written millions of opinions, the search for common law principles in library stacks would be arduous. To overcome this difficulty, and to help bring order and rationality to the many conflicting decisions (for judges frequently disagree with each other), a group of lawyers and academicians—members of a private group called the American Law Institute—sat down in the 1920s to write what has become a series of "Restatements." The first was the *Restatement of the Law of Contracts,* published in 1932 after years of drafting and redrafting. Work began on its successor, *Restatement (Second) of Contracts,* in 1964; it was finally completed and published in 1981. Other Restatements include those on torts, agency law, remedies, and trusts.

The Restatements are not the law. They are statements of the law, in statutelike form, written by private citizens. But they have been extremely influential in helping to spark debate and to shape the law. They are frequently cited by judges in their opinions, and we will encounter their provisions frequently in this book.

Purposes of the U.S. Constitution

"The American Constitution is the most wonderful work ever struck off at a given time by the brain and purpose of man," British Prime Minister William Ewart Gladstone is reputed to have said, and so it very well might be. It is short, readable, and durable. Its seven articles and the Bill of

Rights, as supplemented by sixteen other amendments, have endured for nearly two centuries, making it the oldest living written constitution in the world.

The Constitution performs two fundamental legal tasks: it structures the government, and it imposes limitations on the government's power to act.

The Structure of the Government

Articles I, II, and III of the Constitution set forth the structure and powers of the three branches of the federal government, as well as methods of electing or appointing officials to offices within these branches.

The first article, reflecting the Founding Fathers' belief in its paramountcy, deals with Congress, the national legislature. To Congress are given "all legislative powers herein granted." Among other powers, Congress has the authority to regulate money, enact uniform bankruptcy laws, borrow on the credit of the United States, regulate interstate and foreign commerce, and "make all laws which shall be necessary and proper for carrying into execution the foregoing powers, and all other powers vested by this Constitution in the government of the United States, or in any department or officer thereof." Not surprisingly, this "necessary and proper" clause has been called the "elastic clause."

The second article of the Constitution vests the "executive power" in the president, spells out certain functions the chief executive must perform, and enumerates a few specific roles he must play (for example, commander in chief of the military).

The third article vests "the judicial power" in the Supreme Court and "in such inferior courts as the Congress may from time to time ordain and establish."

In vesting the legislative, executive, and judicial powers in separate branches of government, the makers of the Constitution gave the most precise expression ever made of the principle of "separation of powers." The theory, derived from the writings of the French social philosopher Baron de Montesquieu, is that freedom can be preserved by separating the types of governmental authority among the branches of government, which will check and balance each other, preventing any one branch from becoming too strong. It is noteworthy that the Constitution does not define "legislative," "executive," or "judicial" power. We could say that the legislative power is the power to make law, the executive power the power to carry it out, and the judicial power the power to decide cases arising under the laws. But that is too simple a view. The fact is that the powers overlap. Each branch has influence over the others. The president can veto congressional enactments and appoint judges. Congress can create executive departments. The courts can, in effect, make laws through statutory interpretation. Nor is it easy to see how it could be otherwise. But this fact makes the statement and understanding of law difficult because the law is subject to so many pressures and changes from so many directions.

The fourth article of the Constitution deals briefly with the states. It does not create the states; it accepts them as given. Under the terms of this article, each state must give "full faith and credit" to the "public acts, records, and judicial proceedings" in all the other states.

The fifth article deals with methods of amending the Constitution.

The sixth article embodies the Supremacy Clause, stated here in full: "The Constitution, and the Laws of the United States which shall be made in Pursuance thereof; and all Treaties made, or which shall be made, under the Authority of the United States, shall be the supreme Law of the Land; and the Judges in every State shall be bound thereby, any Thing in the Constitution or Laws of any State to the Contrary notwithstanding." This critical clause establishes a hierarchy of law and permits some order to be fashioned out of a republic in which dual jurisdictions frequently clash.

The seventh article provided for the ratification of the Constitution and is no longer operative.

Since 1789, when these original seven articles became effective, twenty-six amendments have been adopted. The first ten, the Bill of Rights, were adopted in 1791, in response to cries during the ratification debate that the articles insufficiently protected individual freedom. Most others deal with the structure of government, specifically concerning the right to vote and election of the president. The Thirteenth Amendment abolished slavery. The Sixteenth gave Congress the power to enact an income tax. The Eighteenth—Prohibition—was repealed by the Twenty-first. Of all the subsequent amendments, only the Fourteenth has had an immense legal as well as political impact on the nation, as will be explored later in this chapter.

Constitutional Limitations

In the United States, government is not sovereign; in legal theory the people are. The Constitution establishes several important limitations on the powers of government, both federal and state, to enact and enforce laws that would interfere with individual liberty.

Article I prohibits both federal and state governments from enacting any "bills of attainder" or "ex post facto" laws. A bill of attainder is a statute that imposes a penalty on a named individual. It is a means that was exercised by British monarchs to avoid trial and was universally condemned. An ex post facto law is one outlawing a particular act already performed. It too was a means of jailing persons whom the government disliked, and was likewise condemned. (A retroactive tax law, changing the tax rates or imposing new taxes on income, sales, or other activities that have already taken place, is not considered ex post facto and is not barred by the Constitution.) Article I also prohibits the federal and state governments from preferring one port of entry to another. Interstate shipments of goods are not subject to import duties, nor are foreign imports or exports subject to duties by the states. Finally, the states—but not the federal government—are prohibited from "impairing the obligation of contracts."

Article VI prohibits any religious test from being administered to any official of the federal or state governments.

The remainder of the significant limitations on government appear in the Bill of Rights and the Fourteenth Amendment. Most of these limitations are concerned with rights of the accused in criminal trials and are explored in Chapter 7. The rest—the "preferred freedoms" of the First Amendment and the important principles of due process and equal protection of the law—we consider shortly.

Judicial Review

Before turning to these critical constitutional rights, it will be useful to consider the mechanisms by which they are secured to us as individuals. The Constitution is, after all, but a piece of paper, preserved in chemicals and under glass at the National Archives in Washington, D.C. Suppose Congress enacts a law that conflicts with a provision in the Constitution. What then?

The short answer is that we possess the right to challenge actions of the government in lawsuits—either by raising constitutional objections if we are defendants or by pleading constitutional rights as plaintiffs. If the courts conclude that the constitutional provision and the statute conflict, they are required to invalidate the statute and give priority to the Constitution. This authority is known as **judicial review**, and it distinguishes the legal system of the United States from that of every other nation in the world. Through its power to review, the U.S. Supreme Court becomes embroiled to an extent unknown by courts outside the United States in the most difficult and delicate questions of public policy. As Alexis de Tocqueville noted in a celebrated line in his *Democracy in America* (1835): "There is hardly a political question in the United States which does not sooner or later turn into a judicial one."

How the federal courts, and the Supreme Court in particular, came to claim and use this power is an oft-told tale, but one that bears repeating. In 1800, John Adams, a Federalist and advocate of strong central government, was defeated for reelection by Thomas Jefferson, an anti-Federalist whose sympathy lay toward local government. In January 1801, when the Chief Justice's seat on the Supreme Court opened up, President Adams appointed John Marshall, then secretary of state, and the Federalist Senate promptly confirmed him. Five days before the end of Adams's term,

Congress rushed through a bill creating judgeships in the District of Columbia, and Adams appointed forty-two justices of the peace. The Senate confirmed the nominees on Adams's last day of office. Commissioning papers needed to be signed by the President to make their appointments official, and so into the evening Adams signed the documents (thus the term "midnight judges"). In the rush, four commissions were never dispatched. Thomas Jefferson found them the next day and forbade them to be delivered.

One of the disappointed men, William Marbury, went to the Supreme Court in December 1801 and filed suit, asserting that he was entitled to his office. He sought a *writ of mandamus,* a judicial order directing a government official to take a specific action—in this case, an order to James Madison, then secretary of state, to hand over the commission to Marbury.

The Supreme Court's answer in the case of *Marbury* v. *Madison,* in an opinion by Chief Justice Marshall, was a bombshell and remains both the classic statement of the principle of judicial review and the classic example of judicial statesmanship. Marshall said that three questions had been raised. (1) Did Marbury have a right to the judicial commission he demanded? (2) If Marbury had a right to it and that right was violated, did the laws of the United States afford him a remedy? (3) If they did afford him a remedy, was it by a "mandamus issuing from the Supreme Court"?

The first two questions Marshall answered in the affirmative: (1) Marbury had been properly nominated and confirmed by the Senate, and nothing more was necessary to make Marbury a judge. (2) "The very essence of civil liberty certainly consists in the right of every individual to claim the protection of the laws, whenever he receives an injury." The law required Madison to deliver the commission, and officers of the government are bound by the law. The proper method of compelling a government official to obey the law is by a writ of mandamus.

The third question, however, Marshall answered in the negative. Marbury had a legal remedy, but the *Supreme Court* could not *constitutionally* provide it. The Judiciary Act of 1789 authorized the Supreme Court to issue writs of mandamus "in cases warranted by the principles and usages of law . . . to persons holding office under the authority of the United States." That law certainly would permit the Court to mandamus Madison, unless the law itself was invalid. The problem, Marshall said, was that Article III of the Constitution did not give the Supreme Court **original jurisdiction** over such a case. That is, in all but a rare category of cases the Constitution prohibits the Supreme Court from conducting trials, determining the facts, and applying the law to them; it can only hear appeals from trials conducted by lower courts. This prohibition certainly applied to Marbury's case. Yet here was Marbury appearing before the Supreme Court, asking it to hold a trial and issue a remedy. This, Marshall said, the Supreme Court could not do. Marbury would have to find another court to issue the writ of mandamus.

MARBURY v. MADISON[2]
5 U.S. (1 Cr.) 137 (1803)

* * *

The act to establish the judicial courts of the United States authorizes the supreme court, "to issue writs of *mandamus,* in cases warranted by the principles and usages of law, to any courts appointed or persons holding office, under the authority of the United States." The secretary of state, being a person holding an office under the authority of the United States, is precisely within the letter of this description; and if this court is not authorized to issue a writ of *mandamus* to such an officer, it must be because the law is unconstitutional, and therefore, absolutely incapable of conferring the authority, and assigning the duties which its words purport to confer and assign.

* * *

The question, whether an act, repugnant to the constitution, can become the law of the land, is a question deeply interesting to the United States; but, happily, not of an intricacy proportioned to its interest. It seems only necessary to recognize certain principles, supposed to have been long and well established, to decide it. That the people have an original right to establish, for their future government, such principles, as, in their opinion, shall most conduce to their own happiness is the basis on which the whole American fabric has been erected. The exercise of this original right is a very great exertion; nor can it, nor ought it, to be frequently repeated. The principles, therefore, so established, are deemed fundamental. And as the authority from which they proceed is supreme, and can seldom act, they are designed to be permanent. This original and supreme will organizes the government, and assigns to different departments their respective powers. It may either stop here, or establish certain limits not to be transcended by those departments. The government of the United States is of the latter description. The powers of the legislature are defined and limited; and that those limits may not be mistaken, or forgotten, the constitution is written. To what purpose are powers limited, and to what purpose is that limitation committed to writing, if these limits may, at any time, be passed by those intended to be restrained? The distinction between a government with limited and unlimited powers is abolished, if those limits do not confine the persons on whom they are imposed, and if acts prohibited and acts allowed, are of equal obligation. It is a proposition too plain to be contested, that the constitution controls any legislative act repugnant to it.

* * *

It is emphatically the province and duty of the judicial department to say what the law is. Those who apply the rule to particular cases, must of necessity expound and interpret that rule. If two laws conflict with each other, the courts must decide on the operation of each.

So if a law be in opposition to the constitution; if both the law and the constitution apply to a particular case, so that the court must either decide that case conformably to the law, disregarding the constitution; or conformably to the constitution, disregarding the law; the court must determine which of these conflicting rules governs the case. This is of the very essence of judicial duty.

If, then, the courts are to regard the constitution, and the constitution is superior to any ordinary act of the legislature, the constitution, and not such ordinary act, must govern the case to which they both apply.

Those, then, who controvert the principle that the constitution is to be considered, in court, as a paramount law, are reduced to the necessity of maintaining that courts must close their eyes on the constitution, and see only the law.

This doctrine would subvert the very foundation of all written constitutions. It would declare that an

[2] Many court decisions discuss more than one issue of law; in order to focus specifically on the issues at hand, all cases in this text have of necessity been abridged. Asterisks within cases indicate that a paragraph or more has been deleted; deletions of less than a paragraph are indicated by ellipses. Many court opinions cite extensively to the decisions of previous courts; except where necessary to an understanding of the case, such citations and footnotes are deleted in this text, without indication of where the citations occurred.

act which, according to the principles and theory of our government, is entirely void, is yet, in practice, completely obligatory. It would declare that if the legislature shall do what is expressly forbidden, such act, notwithstanding the express prohibition, is in reality effectual. It would be giving to the legislature a practical and real omnipotence, with the same breath which professes to restrict their powers within narrow limits. It is prescribing limits, and declaring that those limits may be passed at pleasure.

That it thus reduces to nothing what we have deemed the greatest improvement on political institutions, a written constitution, would of itself be sufficient, in America, where written constitutions have been viewed with so much reverence, for rejecting the construction. But the peculiar expressions of the constitution of the United States furnish additional arguments in favour of its rejection.

The judicial power of the United States is extended to all cases arising under the constitution.

Could it be the intention of those who gave this power, to say that in using it the constitution should not be looked into? That a case arising under the constitution should be decided without examining the instrument under which it arises?

This is too extravagant to be maintained.

In some cases, then, the constitution must be looked into by the judges. And if they can open it at all, what part of it are they forbidden to read or to obey?

There are many other parts of the constitution which serve to illustrate this subject.

It is declared that "no tax or duty shall be laid on articles exported from any state." Suppose a duty on the export of cotton, of tobacco, or of flour; and a suit instituted to recover it. Ought judgment to be rendered in such a case? Ought the judges to close their eyes on the constitution, and only see the law?

The constitution declares "that no bill of attainder or ex post facto law shall be passed."

If, however, such a bill should be passed, and a person should be prosecuted under it; must the court condemn to death those victims whom the constitution endeavors to preserve?

"No person," says the constitution, "shall be convicted of treason unless on the testimony of two witnesses to the same overt act, or on confession in open court."

Here the language of the constitution is addressed especially to the courts. It prescribes, directly for them, a rule of evidence not to be departed from. If the legislature should change that rule, and declare one witness, or a confession out of court, sufficient for conviction, must the constitutional principle yield to the legislative act?

From these, and many other selections which might be made, it is apparent, that the framers of the constitution contemplated that instrument as a rule for the government of courts, as well as of the legislature.

Why otherwise does it direct the judges to take an oath to support it? This oath certainly applies in an especial manner, to their conduct in their official character. How immoral to impose it on them, if they were to be used as the instruments, and the knowing instruments, for violating what they swear to support!

* * *

It is also not entirely unworthy of observation, that in declaring what shall be the supreme law of the land, the constitution itself is first mentioned; and not the laws of the United States generally, but those only which shall be made in pursuance of the constitution, have that rank.

Thus, the particular phraseology of the constitution of the United States confirms and strengthens the principle, supposed to be essential to all written constitutions, that a law repugnant to the constitution is void; and that courts, as well as other departments, are bound by that instrument.

The rule must be discharged.

Although the Supreme Court would not strike down another federal statute for fifty-four years (and when it did, in *Dred Scott* v. *Sandford,* 19 How. 393 [1857], it foreordained the Civil War), judicial review became a fixed legal principle from which the courts have never deviated.

However, not every constitutional question pressed upon the courts, especially the Supreme Court, will receive an answer. There are a number of limitations, some constitutional and some prudential, on the power and willingness of the courts to decide constitutional issues. As summarized by Supreme Court Justice Louis D. Brandeis, here is a series of rules by which the courts try to avoid the necessity of making declarations about constitutionality:

1. The Court will not pass upon the constitutionality of legislation in a friendly, nonadversary proceeding.
2. The Court will not anticipate a question of constitutional law in advance of the necessity of deciding it.
3. The Court will not formulate a rule of constitutional law broader than is required by the precise facts to which it is to be applied.
4. The Court will not pass upon a constitutional question although properly presented by the record, if there is also present some other ground upon which the case may be disposed of.
5. The Court will not pass upon the validity of a statute upon complaint of one who fails to show that he is injured by its operation.
6. The Court will not pass upon the constitutionality of a statute at the instance of one who has availed himself of its benefits.
7. When the validity of an act of the Congress is drawn in question, and even if a serious doubt of constitutionality is raised, it is a cardinal principle that this Court will first ascertain whether a construction of the statute is fairly possible by which the question may be avoided. [Ashwander v. Tennessee Valley Authority, 297 U.S. 288 (1937)]

These principles have their roots in *Marbury* v. *Madison*. Note that Chief Justice Marshall decided the other legal questions before passing on to the constitutional question of mandamus.

The Fourteenth Amendment

In the 1780s when the Constitution was adopted, the people did not so much fear government power as they did *central* government. Hence limitations in the Constitution, which established the national government, were for the most part applicable only to the national government. This was particularly true of the Bill of Rights, the first ten amendments adopted for the specific purpose of limiting central power. Thus the Fifth Amendment says that no person shall be denied life, liberty, or property without due process of law, but that provision did not bar the states from doing so. Many, but not all, of the states had substantially similar constitutional provisions.

This situation changed dramatically after the Civil War. In its 1857 *Dred Scott* decision, the Supreme Court had ruled that blacks could not become citizens of the United States. In 1868, with the ratification of the

Fourteenth Amendment, this historical injustice was cured. Thenceforth, all persons born in the United States were automatically citizens.

The Fourteenth Amendment did not stop there. It went on to impose a significant restraint on state governments. The amendment says that no state may "deprive any person of life, liberty, or property, without due process of law; nor deny to any person within its jurisdiction the equal protection of the laws." These words heralded an immense shift in the relationship of the states and federal government, and in time gave significant power to the federal courts, for the law meant that sooner or later people could bring suit in federal court testing the actions of state governments under the amendment.

That testing began in the 1870s and has not abated. The twists and turns of the legal doctrines that have developed fill several hundred volumes. All that we will note here is that during the past century the Supreme Court has gradually incorporated into the Fourteenth Amendment most of the various protections in the original Bill of Rights, so that the restraints that operate against the federal government for the most part operate as well against the states.

The Development of the Common Law

The Function of Courts

One modern criticism of courts is that they are usurping lawmaking authority, that as the third branch of government they have become too involved in setting policy. However, both the anthropological and historical literature suggest that this role is hardly new, having emerged from the early desire for peace in the community.

In most primitive communities without a formal political order, every person, family, or clan believed it had a right to redress wrongs done to one of them, and a single act of killing by a hot-headed individual would often lead to a blood feud that spread geographically and persisted over time. The need to suppress the free exercise of this desire to repay one killing with another gave birth to the political ruler, whose first duty was to settle disputes. Anthropological evidence suggests that the need to resolve disputes is what motivates a political order among peoples whose relations theretofore have been merely familial or neighborly.

Certainly this was true in the society that contributed most directly to our judicial system: England. Though English society before the twelfth century was scarcely primitive, the center of political activity, where it existed, was predominantly local; there was no nation-state in the modern sense. Courts did exist, but they were virtually the private property of the nobility. The great property owners exercised a crude and self-interested justice to put down insurrection and to settle disputes among serfs, vassals, and others beholden to them. In so doing, the nobles consolidated their power as petty sovereigns. The nobles warred with each other, however, and until the kings established royal courts and substituted public sanctions and a system of compensation for blood feuds, warfare and violence reigned.

The Royal Writs

From the time of the Norman Conquest in A.D. 1066, the kings professed to be the guarantors of justice. One of the most noteworthy developments was that of the royal judicial "writs," an innovation of Henry II in the twelfth century. The writ was a formal document commanding someone to appear in the royal courts. Originally, a writ was issued to the sheriff, whose job was to summon the defendant to court. In time, plaintiffs purchased these writs—a handy source of revenue for the king. In essence, the writs permitted lawsuits to be instituted in court. Different writs were issued for different types of complaints, and within two centuries of the Conquest they swept away the private courts that had dispensed justice on the manors.

Law and justice thus became public, and as they diffused throughout the countryside they gave birth to the nation. The royal courts were the beneficiaries of a nice symbiosis: On the one hand, the king increased his revenues by selling writs, and he consolidated his power over owners and possessors of land—the most valuable commodity in the country—by insisting that real property cases be heard in his courts. On the other hand, the people generally benefited from the steady march of royal jurisdiction. As the historian Joseph R. Strayer has written:

> Kings were quite ready to accept the idea that justice was all-important, since it was a sign of their authority and a weapon by which they might achieve supremacy in their realms. For the common folk, and even for many members of the lesser aristocracy, justice meant protection against violence and loss of lands. Thus rulers who tried to create regularly functioning law courts were assured of almost universal approval. The most warlike barons could not object to the existence of courts, though they might be very slow to obey their orders. (Strayer, 1970, p. 32)

As early as 1215, in Magna Carta—the charter of basic rights that King John was forced to grant at Runnymede—the barons themselves were insisting on a fixed place for regular courts of justice (to avoid the difficulties attendant on the peregrinations of their monarch).

The writs served as the basis for the substantive law. Writs were individual: there was one for trespass, for taking of property, for assault, and so on. The decision of the king's ministers to issue a new writ was in essence a decision that the act complained of was a legal wrong.

Stare Decisis

But by themselves, the writs were not the law. The common law ultimately was to be found in the decisions of judges in the cases that came before them. Their decisions were recorded from early days; records of judicial decisions date back to at least the thirteenth century. When questions of law arose, the judges relied on the pronouncements of their predecessors. Earlier cases served as precedent, and the great principle of **stare decisis** emerged, which means "to stand by decided cases." *Stare decisis* is the source of the stability and conserving strength of the common law: once a legal principle is enunciated by a court, it is the law and is not to be overturned.

Of course, if legal judgments were too sweeping, a legal system that did not permit modifications could become inflexible and break down as social and economic conditions changed. The common law system accommodated this difficulty by requiring judges to consider only the case that was before them and to announce a principle no broader than was required by the case. If a later case presented different factual circumstances, a variant of the rule was possible. Thus lawyers became adept in the art of *distinguishing*—pointing to the vital but often subtle differences that made an earlier, unfavorable ruling inapplicable.

The Jury System

One reason for the relatively speedy acceptance of the king's justice was the change in the method of determining disputed facts. Certainly the mass of common folk welcomed procedures that substituted the knowledge of local jurors for the dreaded trials by "ordeal." Early justice did not contemplate dispassionate fact-finding, such as occurs (in theory at least) in our courts today. Instead, various methods relied on force and superstition. In the ordeal, people were forced to hold burning coals or were thrown into water; if they did not burn or sink, they were presumed innocent. This sadism was reserved for the lower classes. The aristocracy had a less painful method: **compurgation**, or swearing. After protesting his innocence, the defendant produced a number of people who swore to his good reputation. But they had to do it in a highly formal manner, and the defendant had to have a proper number of compurgators. If he did not have enough, or if they stumbled over the ritualistic formula, he was guilty. If they sailed through their set speech, however, he was free. The theory was that God tripped up those who were swearing on behalf of a guilty man. A third method was trial by battle, in which the parties fought, often to the death (the parties later were permitted to use stand-ins—hired lances, so to speak). By the thirteenth century, a jury of witnesses was well on its way to replacing these barbarisms.

Equity

As time passed, the form of the writs tended to harden. A case had to fall within the four corners of a writ's formula, or it would be dismissed without further hearing. As the economy grew and society became more complex, many types of disputes did not easily fall within the confines of the writ system. Although the common law jurists intoned that "every wrong has a remedy," that was not always true. So people petitioned the kings for relief, and gradually a new system of law developed: **equity.** The king delegated the job of hearing these petitions to the chancellor, keeper of the royal seal and head of the king's council.

Equity removed the hard edges of the common law, softening its rigidities. Informally at first, the chancellor would do justice in individual cases for which the writs were unsuitable. For example, under common law virtually the only possible remedy was an award of money or a return of goods taken. If a seller of land reneged on his contract, the common law courts could not order transfer of title. Similarly, an **injunction**, an order to force someone to discontinue a harmful course of conduct, was not within the power of the common law courts. But the chancellor, acting from his office, known as the chancery, could decree **specific performance** of real estate contracts (direct the parties to carry them out), issue injunctions, and provide other forms of relief.

In theory, a litigant did not have a legal entitlement to equitable relief; the grant of relief was at the discretion of the chancellor, exercising the king's conscience. But in time, the courts of **chancery** developed equity into a full-fledged system of justice. Equity gave relief when there was no "adequate remedy at law."

Today, common law and equity have been merged into a unified court system, although in a few states, chancery courts or chancery divisions of the trial court still exist in name (see Box 1-2). A major legacy of the former division between the two concepts concerns the right to jury trial. Juries did not sit in chancery, since the chancellor was doing justice by making an exception to the hard rules of the common law. This meant that if a plaintiff sought an equitable remedy, such as an injunction or specific performance, he was not entitled to a jury trial. That distinction remains today. Cases seeking equitable relief are for judges; only in cases that were once within the jurisdiction of common law courts are the parties entitled to a jury.

Common law and equity were not the only systems of law. In the seventeenth century, one jurist counted fifteen separate systems. These included maritime law, the law merchant (an international commercial law), and ecclesiastical law (the church courts until Henry VIII's split with the Catholic Church had jurisdiction over what today we call family law, including matrimonial law). In time, equity absorbed much of these other systems.

Box 1-2 Chancery: Old-Fashioned Court with Very Modern Tasks

Delaware's Sedate Chancery Court Is a Major Corporate Battlefield
By Mary Williams

Wilmington, Del.—The lawyer for Shell Oil Co. shareholders fumbled as he argued for a preliminary injunction blocking Royal Dutch/Shell Group's $5.49 billion tender offer. He said million when he meant to say billion, then joked that the amounts were so vast he could hardly grasp them.

The judge was not amused. "We deal with that all the time," he said curtly.

It's true—despite appearances. Delaware's Court of Chancery is a small, quiet pair of courtrooms tucked at the back of a building on the Wilmington town square. Most of the time its officials handle humdrum squabbles like divvying up deceased aunts' dishes and ordering bird lovers to clean up their coops because the neighbors are complaining.

But the chancery court, a holdover from 12th-century England, has also become a major battleground in corporate fights.

* * *

A disproportionate number of the biggest merger and takeover battles turn up here because of the laws of Delaware, which are designed to lure as many corporations as possible to the state. Delaware's low franchise fees, lenient business tax structure and do-as-you-please corporate code have already persuaded about half of the Fortune 500 companies and a third of the concerns listed on the New York Stock Exchange to incorporate here. More come every year, and with them come lawsuits. In Delaware, criminal cases and those involving monetary judgments go to superior court. But when individuals or companies sue the directors of a company incorporated in Delaware, they're usually seeking equitable relief, such as an injunction or a temporary restraining order. And those fall under the jurisdiction of the Court of Chancery.

That dual system isn't the only thing that sets the chancery court apart. It is militantly informal, and small. The whole place consists of four judges—called the chancellor and vice chancellors—two clerks, two court reporters and a half-dozen clerical workers who crank out opinions on an old hand-fed copy machine. When there's a big case, the judges have to help collate the opinions, walking round and round a table along with their secretaries.

* * *

Delaware officials assure companies that, if hauled into chancery, they aren't likely to get any rude surprises. The judges are experienced, and the past cases plainly lay out the law. Delaware lawyers can often predict which way the case will swing, the argument goes.

That's one reason so many big cases are filed in Delaware, even though cases against large companies can usually be filed just about anywhere. Another reason is that the chancery court, which never empanels jurors, decides major cases quickly.

* * *

[According to] Richard Greenfield, a Pennsylvania lawyer who specializes in shareholder suits, . . . "The judges act very often from the heart. . . . They'll listen to you, rather than the strict letter of the law."

That may be because chancery courts were set up in medieval England to help people who couldn't get justice in the common-law courts. Chancery courts back then didn't bother with formal rules or documents penned in Latin. The British imported the chancery system to America in colonial times, but most states rejected chancery courts as signs of imperial authority. Delaware, an oddball, set up a chancery court in 1792.

* * *

Source: *Wall Street Journal*, May 10, 1984

Preexisting Law vs. Judge-made Law

In the early years, the prerogative of dispensing justice was assumed to be personal to the king; it was an attribute of kingship. By the fifteenth century, however, the press of judicial business was too large, and the kings left the administration of justice to the cadre of judges who increasingly were specially trained in law. By then, kings had become true monarchs, and the coming battles over royal sovereignty would center on the extent of their legislative and executive authority.

What was this judicial power that emanated from the king? Though King James I would insist in 1608 (and thereafter) that the king was superior to the law ("The King protecteth the law, and not the law the King," he said), his predecessors had supposed, at least since 1215, that they were bound by the law. Magna Carta, say Pollock and Maitland, the great historians of medieval English law, "means this, that the king is and shall be below the law." In short, the law—the body of rules that had become the common law—was superior and existed prior to any conscious human creation by judges hearing cases. The law simply *was,* and it was the function of judges to ascertain it, not to make it up. For a time considerably beyond the seventeenth century, even legislation was asserted to be a restoration of the old law, not a breaking of new ground, a reconfirmation of old rights, not a creation of new ones. In this, the kings and judges acted in accordance with a universal belief of the middle ages, that law was permanent and unchanging. As Fritz Kern, the historian of medieval Europe, put it:

> Modern law is always, in one way or another, enacted by the State. Mediaeval law simply exists; it was accepted by mediaeval opinion not as being enacted by men, but as part of the Just and the Good, which are eternal. . . . Mediaeval law, . . . being neither enacted nor annulled, was not so much actual as timeless. Only good law was real law, no matter whether human law-givers or judges recognized it or ignored it, no matter whether it were positive or "only" ideal law. The attitude of law-givers and judges towards the law was only like a shadow that fell over it; it might obscure the law, but could not set it aside. (Kern, 1970, p. 156)

For several centuries, the theory of law thus developed at odds with its practice. The judges held that they were merely discovering law, even as they grandly created a huge body of common law dealing with subjects unknown to their ancestors. Precisely because it was not of human origin, this law was not to be trifled with.

This notion, that the courts sit to resolve disputes by applying preexisting law, passed into fundamental American law via Montesquieu, who articulated clearly the great principle of the separation of powers—that each of the three branches of government should be confined to its proper sphere. If separation of powers were truly observed, Montesquieu said, the judges would pose no threat: "[T]he national judges are no more than the mouth that pronounces the words of the law, mere passive beings, incapable of moderating either its force or rigour." The delegates to the Constitutional Convention studied Montesquieu; the first three articles of the Constitution owe their general structure to him. The nub of the position is that which any schoolchild can recite: rule-making is for legislators; the courts, when they try cases, are merely interpreting. This textbook view, still devoutly held by many, shades the truth considerably. Though lawmaking troubled the early judges and they frequently created extravagant fictions to persuade themselves or others that they were not deviating from the ancient customs, the courts virtually from the outset were making law. Often substantive changes were cloaked in procedural reform.

Anglo-American courts have always been rule-making institutions. The types of disputes that the common law and equity courts heard gave birth to a huge corpus of rules governing all sorts of private relations. In time these became unexceptionable, and many fields of law down to the present day are articulated largely at the hands of the judges.

Federal vs. State Common Law

The need to parse the nature of common law flows from quite practical considerations. Perhaps the clearest example of the consequences that follow from defining it one way or another is the conundrum of which "law" federal courts should apply when hearing cases based on state legal issues. As we will see in Chapter 3, the Constitution permits federal courts to hear disputes arising between citizens of different states even though no federal claims are involved. These suits would have to be lodged in state courts if the parties were citizens of the same state. Should state or federal law apply in such cases?

Under the 1789 federal Judiciary Act, federal courts are required to apply state "law." The act says: "The laws of the several States, except where the Constitution, treaties, or statutes of the United States shall otherwise require or provide, shall be regarded as rules of decision in trials at common law in the Courts of the United States in cases where they apply." Although somewhat obscure, this language was taken to mean that federal courts must look to state law. On a number of occasions during the early nineteenth century, the U.S. Supreme Court had ruled that there was no "common law of the United States." The common law exists only within each state, and the common law of each state may be different. Then, in 1842, Supreme Court Justice Joseph Story wrote an opinion that radically changed this understanding. [Swift v. Tyson, 41 US. 1 (1842)]

The case arose in New York and raised the question of whether the payment of a negotiable bill in return for a promise to cancel a preexisting debt constituted a valid contract. The parties were citizens of different states, so the case was brought in federal court. New York had no statute governing the question. State judicial decisions did not clearly spell out the law. So to what state law should the federal court look?

The answer turned on the fundamental meaning of "law" itself. Justice Story said that only statutes are law, not court decisions, and consequently federal courts could decide independently what the common law of a state should be. The philosophy that common law is some preexisting metaphysical concept that judges somehow discern through right reasoning has claimed the better part of Anglo-American legal history. But it was not without its detractors, and by the turn of the twentieth century critics more emphatically and cogently showed that common law is not found but made—by judges. In a characteristically acerbic and celebrated aside, Justice Oliver Wendell Holmes, dissenting in a 1917 Supreme Court case, declared that "law is not a brooding omnipresence in the sky." [Southern Pacific Co. v. Jensen, 244 U.S. 205 (1917)]

Finally, in 1938, the force of criticism by the so-called "legal realists" caught up to the Supreme Court, and Justice Story's conclusion was rejected in the next case. The ninety-six-year-old precedent was reversed. There is no general federal common law, the Court declared. In deciding a case based on diversity of citizenship, the federal judges must look to both state statutes and state court decisions, not to their own conception of "general commercial law," or some other general law.

ERIE RAILROAD CO. v. TOMPKINS
304 U.S. 64 (1938)

MR. JUSTICE BRANDEIS delivered the opinion of the Court.

The question for decision is whether the oft-challenged doctrine of Swift v. Tyson shall now be disapproved.

Tompkins, a citizen of Pennsylvania, was injured on a dark night by a passing freight train of the Erie Railroad Company while walking along its right of way at Hughestown in that state. He claimed that the accident occurred through negligence in the operation, or maintenance, of the train; that he was rightfully on the premises as licensee because on a commonly used beaten footpath which ran for a short distance alongside the tracks; and that he was struck by something which looked like a door projecting from one of the moving cars. To enforce that claim he brought an action in the federal court for Southern New York, which had jurisdiction because the company is a corporation of that state. It denied liability; and the case was tried by a jury.

The Erie insisted that its duty to Tompkins was no greater than that owed to a trespasser. It contended, among other things, that its duty to Tompkins, and hence its liability, should be determined in accordance with the Pennsylvania law; that under the law of Pennsylvania, as declared by its highest court, persons who use pathways along the railroad right of way—that is, a longitudinal pathway as distinguished from a crossing—are to be deemed trespassers; and that the railroad is not liable for injuries to undiscovered trespassers resulting from its negligence, unless it be wanton or willful. Tompkins denied that any such rule had been established by the decisions of the Pennsylvania courts; and contended that, since there was no statute of the state on the subject, the railroad's duty and liability is to be determined in federal courts as a matter of general law.

The trial judge refused to rule that the applicable law precluded recovery. The jury brought in a verdict of $30,000; and the judgment entered thereon was affirmed by the Circuit Court of Appeals, which held that it was unnecessary to consider whether the law of Pennsylvania was as contended, because the question was one not of local, but of general, law, and that "upon questions of general law the federal courts are free, in absence of a local statute, to exercise their independent judgment as to what the law is; and it is well settled that the question of the responsibility of a railroad for injuries caused by its servants is one of general law. . . . Where the public has made open and notorious use of a railroad right of way for a long period of time and without objection, the company owes to persons on such permissive pathway a duty of care in the operation of its trains. . . . It is likewise generally recognized law that a jury may find that negligence exists toward a pedestrian using a permissive path on the railroad right of way if he is hit by some object projecting from the side of the train."

* * *

Because of the importance of the question whether the federal court was free to disregard the alleged rule of the Pennsylvania common law, we granted certiorari.

Swift v. Tyson, 16 Pet. 1, 18, held that federal courts exercising jurisdiction on the ground of diversity of citizenship need not, in matters of general jurisprudence, apply the unwritten law of the state as declared by its highest court; that they are free to exercise an independent judgment as to what the common law of the state is—or should be.

* * *

Experience in applying the doctrine of Swift v. Tyson, had revealed its defects, political and social; and the benefits expected to flow from the rule did not accrue. Persistence of state courts in their own opinions on questions of common law prevented uniformity; and the impossibility of discovering a satisfactory line of demarcation between the province of general law and that of local law developed a new well of uncertainties.

On the other hand, the mischievous results of the doctrine had become apparent. Diversity of citizenship jurisdiction was conferred in order to prevent apprehended discrimination in state courts against those not citizens of the state. Swift v. Tyson introduced grave discrimination by noncitizens against citizens. It made rights enjoyed under the unwritten "general law" vary according to whether enforcement was sought in the state or in the federal court; and the privilege of selecting the court in which the right should be determined was conferred upon the noncitizen. Thus, the doctrine rendered impossible equal protection of the law. In attempting to promote uniformity of law throughout the United States, the doctrine had prevented uniformity in the administration of the law of the state.

The discrimination resulting became in practice far-reaching. This resulted in part from the broad province accorded to the so-called "general law" as to which federal courts exercised an independent judgment. In addition to questions of purely commercial law, "general law" was held to include the obligations under contracts entered into and to be performed within the state, the extent to which a carrier operating within a state may stipulate for exemption from liability for his own negligence or that of his employee; the liability for torts committed within the state upon persons resident or property located there, even where the question of liability depended upon the scope of a property right conferred by the state; and the right to exemplary or punitive damages. Furthermore, state decisions construing local deeds, mineral conveyances, and even devises of real estate, were disregarded.

* * *

The injustice and confusion incident to the doctrine of Swift v. Tyson have been repeatedly urged as reasons for abolishing or limiting diversity of citizenship jurisdiction. Other legislative relief has been proposed. If only a question of statutory construction were involved, we should not be prepared to abandon a doctrine so widely applied throughout nearly a century. But the unconstitutionality of the course pursued has now been made clear, and compels us to do so.

Except in matters governed by the Federal Constitution or by acts of Congress, the law to be applied in any case is the law of the state. And whether the law of the state shall be declared by its Legislature in a statute or by its highest court in a decision is not a matter of federal concern. There is no federal general common law. Congress has no power to declare substantive rules of common law applicable in a state whether they be local in their nature or "general," be they commercial law or a part of the law of torts. And no clause in the Constitution purports to confer such a power upon the federal courts. . . .

The fallacy underlying the rule declared in Swift v. Tyson is made clear by Mr. Justice Holmes. The doctrine rests upon the assumption that there is "a transcendental body of law outside of any particular State but obligatory within it unless and until changed by statute," that federal courts have the power to use their judgment as to what the rules of common law are; and that in the federal courts "the parties are entitled to an independent judgment on matters of general law":

"But law in the sense in which courts speak of it today does not exist without some definite authority behind it. The common law so far as it is enforced in a State, whether called common law or not, is not the common law generally but the law of that State existing by the authority of that State without regard to what it may have been in England or anywhere else. . . .

"The authority and only authority is the State, and if that be so, the voice adopted by the State as its own [whether it be of its Legislature or of its Supreme Court] should utter the last word."

Thus the doctrine of Swift v. Tyson is, as Mr. Justice Holmes said, "an unconstitutional assumption of powers by the Courts of the United States which no lapse of time or respectable array of opinion should make us hesitate to correct."

* * *

Reversed.

Nature of the Judicial Process

On what basis do judges interpret and declare law? Judges certainly are not free to pluck from thin air any policies they would like and simply declare them as law. Of course judges may rationalize their decisions, as a dictator cloaks his arbitrary actions in the guise of reasonableness. There is no one to stop them from doing so, except a higher court or a legislature aroused enough to enact a new law. But if they are adhering faithfully to the judicial process, how do they make their decisions?

Many judges and scholars have wrestled with this question. It is not possible to give a short or definitive answer. Judging is at bottom an art. Judges will naturally look at constitutions and statutes, and a variety of principles govern the interpretation of statutory language. (For example, an interpretation that renders consistent two provisions in a statute is to be preferred to an interpretation that makes them contradictory.) If the language of the statute does not help, judges will naturally look to precedent: *stare decisis* remains a guiding principle of our law. When the previous cases fit the facts of the present one, the decision will be easy. But few cases are so simple; when the law is clear, the parties rarely argue very long about it.

Even a precedent itself is subject to questioning, retesting, and reformulating. As Justice Benjamin N. Cardozo wrote in *The Nature of the Judicial Process:*

> Fifty years ago [around 1870], I think it would have been stated as a general principle that A. may conduct his business as he pleases, even though the purpose is to cause loss to B., unless the act involves the creation of a nuisance.

> Spite fences were the stock illustration, and the exemption from liability in such circumstances was supposed to illustrate not the exception, but the rule. Such a rule may have been an adequate working principle to regulate the relations between individuals or classes in a simple or homogenous community. With the growing complexity of social relations, its inadequacy was revealed. As particular controversies multiplied and the attempt was made to test them by the old principle, it was found that there was something wrong in the results, and this led to a reformulation of the principle itself. Today, most judges are inclined to say that what was once thought to be the exception is the rule, and what was the rule is the exception. A. may never do anything in his business for the purpose of injuring another without reasonable and just excuse. There has been a new generalization which, applied to new particulars, yields results more in harmony with past particulars, and, what is still more important, more consistent with the social welfare. This work of modification is gradual. It goes on inch by inch. Its effects must be measured by decades and even centuries. Thus measured, they are seen to have behind them the power and the pressure of the moving glacier. (Cardozo, 1921, pp. 24–25)

Because the process of modification is gradual, few judicial opinions crystallize the moment when change has occurred. It is usually only afterward that one can look back and see how much ground has been covered. The following case, decided by the Minnesota Supreme Court, is remarkable for the way in which it reflects on the necessity for change, and even more remarkable for announcing a new rule that would apply thereafter, but not to the case in which it was decided. The opinion is a useful guide to and summary of the process of judicial reasoning and the nature of law.

The facts were simple. A five-year-old boy was injured on a slide in his kindergarten classroom. His father brought suit against the public school district, the school principal, and the boy's teacher, alleging that they were negligent in permitting the children to play on a defective slide. The lower court dismissed the lawsuit without trial on the grounds that a well-established legal doctrine—that of "sovereign immunity"—barred lawsuits against public agencies or its employees.

SPANEL v. MOUNDS VIEW SCHOOL DISTRICT NO. 621
264 Minn. 279, 118 N.W.2d 795 (1962)

OTIS, JUSTICE.

Plaintiff sues on behalf of his 5-year-old son to recover damages from a school district and a teacher and principal employed by it for injuries resulting from the alleged negligence of defendants in permitting a defective slide to remain in the kindergarten classroom of an elementary school.

Plaintiff appeals from an order granting a motion to dismiss the action as to defendant school district on the ground the complaint fails to state a claim upon which relief can be granted against it.

The only issue before us is whether the doctrine of governmental tort immunity shall now be overruled by judicial decision.

* * *

We hold that the order for dismissal is affirmed, with the caveat, however, that subject to the limitations we now discuss, the defense of sovereign immunity will no longer be available to school districts, municipal corporations, and other subdivisions of government on whom immunity has been conferred by judicial decision with respect to torts which are committed after the adjournment of the next regular session of the Minnesota Legislature.

All of the paths leading to the origin of governmental tort immunity converge on Russell v. The Men of Devon, 100 Eng.Rep. 359, 2 T.R. 667 (1788). This product of the English common law was left on our doorstep to become the putative ancestor of a long line of American cases beginning with Mower v. Leicester, 9 Mass. 247 (1812). Russell sued all of the male inhabitants of the County of Devon for damages occurring to his wagon by reason of a bridge being out of repair. It was apparently undisputed that the county had a duty to maintain such structures. The court held that the action would not lie because: (1) To permit it would lead to "an infinity of actions," (2) there was no precedent for attempting such a suit, (3) only the legislature should impose liability of this kind, (4) even if defendants are to be considered a corporation or quasi-corporation there is no fund out of which to satisfy the claim, (5) neither law nor reason supports the action, (6) there is a strong presumption that what has never been done cannot be done, and (7) although there is a legal principle which permits a remedy for every injury resulting from the neglect of another, a more applicable principle is "that it is better that an individual should sustain an injury than that the public should suffer an inconvenience." The court concluded that the suit should not be permitted *"because the action must be brought against the public."* (Italics supplied.) There is no mention of "the king can do no wrong," but on the contrary it is suggested that plaintiff sue the county itself rather than its individual inhabitants. Every reason assigned by the court is born of expediency. The wrong to plaintiff is submerged in the convenience of the public. No moral, ethical, or rational reason for the decision is advanced by the court except the practical problem of assessing damages against individual defendants. The court's invitation to the legislature has a familiar ring. It was finally accepted as to claims against the Crown in 1947, although Russell had long since been overruled.

In 1812 when Mower's horse was killed by stepping in a hole on the Leicester bridge, counsel argued that "Men of Devon" did not apply since the town of Leicester was incorporated and had a treasury out of which to satisfy a judgment. The Massachusetts court nevertheless held that the town had no notice of the defect and that quasi-corporations are not liable for such neglect under the common law. On the authority of "Men of Devon" recovery was denied. It was on this shaky foundation that the law of governmental tort immunity was erected in Minnesota and elsewhere.

* * *

Very recently a number of American jurisdictions have met sovereign immunity head on. In 1957 Colorado permitted an action against the State Racing Commission for "breakage" in a decision which coined the much-quoted phrase, "In Colorado 'sovereign immunity' may be a proper subject for discussion by students of mythology but finds no haven or refuge in this Court."

* * *

California undertook to abolish tort immunity in a suit against a public hospital district. Mr. Justice Traynor in a carefully documented and thoroughly considered opinion adverted to Borchard's comment in his classic treatise on the subject:

> Nothing seems more clear than that this immunity of the King from the jurisdiction of the King's courts was purely personal. How it came to be applied in the United States of America, where the prerogative is unknown, is one of the mysteries of legal evolution.

* * *

Our consideration of the origins of tort immunity persuade us that its genesis was accidental and was characterized by expediency, and that its continuation has stemmed from inertia. The development of governmental liability for proprietary functions was an acknowledgment that the original rule was unduly restrictive, and reflected an uneasiness in the corporate conscience. No student of the law has suggested any explanation for the arbitrary assumption of legal responsibility for negligence in the maintenance of municipal streets and sidewalks and contemporaneously a rigid adherence to immunity with respect to those maintained by towns and counties. It has been argued on behalf of defendants that if immunity is abolished public schools will be deluged with claims for injuries resulting from inadequate supervision, from frostbite while waiting for buses, from blows struck by other children, from forbidden and mischievous activities impulsively and foolishly inspired, and from a host of other causes. School children have a special status in the eyes of the law, and in view of the compulsory attendance statute deserve more than ordinary protection. Operating an educational system has been described as one of the nation's biggest businesses. The fact that subdivisions of government now enjoy no immunity in a number of areas of activity has not noticeably circumscribed their usefulness or rendered them insolvent.

Nor have our privately endowed schools and colleges been forced to close their doors or curtail their academic and extracurricular programs because the law has imposed on them liability for the negligence of their employees in dealing with students and the public. . . .

* * *

While the court has the right and the duty to modify rules of the common law after they have become archaic, we readily concede that the flexibility of the legislative process—which is denied the judiciary—makes the latter avenue of approach more desirable.

* * *

Counsel has assured us that members of the bar, in and out of the legislature, intend to draft and secure the introduction of bills at the forthcoming session which will give affected entities of government an opportunity to meet their new obligations. A number of procedural and substantive proposals for the orderly processing of claims have been suggested. Among them are: (1) A requirement for giving prompt notice of the claim after the occurrence of the tort, (2) a reduction in the usual period of limitations, (3) a monetary limit on the amount of liability, (4) the establishment of a special claims court or commission, or provision for trial by the court without a jury, and (5) the continuation of the defense of immunity as to some or all units of government for a limited or indefinite period of time.

The technique of prospective overruling has the sanction not only of legal scholars and commentators but of the United States Supreme Court as well.

* * *

On this subject Mr. Justice Cardozo has stated (109 Pa.L.Rev. 13):

> The rule that we are asked to apply is out of tune with the life about us. It has been made discordant by the forces that generate a living law. We apply it to this case because the repeal might work hardship to those who have trusted to its existence. We give notice, however, that any one trusting to it hereafter will do so at his peril.

It may appear unfair to deprive the present claimant of his day in court. However, we are of the opinion it would work an even greater injustice to deny defendant and other units of government a defense on which they have had a right to rely. We believe that it is more equitable if they are permitted to plan in advance by securing liability insurance or by creating funds necessary for self-insurance. In addition, provision must be made for routinely and promptly investigating personal injury and other tort claims at the time of their occurrence in order that defendants may marshal and preserve whatever evidence is available for the proper conduct of their defense.

Affirmed.

Chapter Summary

Law is the set of rules and institutions that permit us to lead a civilized and orderly life. In a democratic society, laws must be known and understood, but complete certainty in law is not merely impossible, it is undesirable. The study of law is not like the study of chemistry or some other science; it is a discipline that requires interpretation, that calls for an understanding of human nature, philosophy, logic, and common sense. Law is a means of fixing in written form our present values and social goals.

Law can be categorized by both its substantive and its procedural aspects. One of the broadest divisions is between criminal and civil law—rules barring acts offensive to society as a whole and rules and regulations that govern our private relations.

In the United States there are several sources of law: legislative enactments, administrative regulations, and judicial decisions. These different types of law emanate from various levels: federal, state, and local. Underlying all American law is the Constitution, which regulates the relationships among the different branches of government and puts limits on their powers.

Courts play three essential roles: (1) They are the forum in which the facts of a case can be determined, (2) they apply the law to the facts, and (3) they interpret the law. The latter function gives the judiciary considerable power, for through judicial review they can void statutes that conflict with the Constitution.

The Constitution deals almost exclusively with powers of and limitations on government, rather than with private conduct. The civil liberties embodied in the First and Fourteenth Amendments have given the courts a large role to play in preserving freedoms against state intrusion. But the Constitution is not the only source of judicial authority. Courts have long independently developed the common law.

Problems

1. A municipal hospital had failed for many years to repair its stairways. One day a visitor caught her shoe on a particularly large crack and fell down a flight of stairs, seriously injuring herself. She sued the hospital which defended itself by invoking the doctrine of "sovereign immunity." What is that doctrine? How could the courts abolish sovereign immunity? How could the legislature abolish it?
2. Name the principal branches of substantive law and describe them briefly.
3. Under what circumstances may a federal court declare a state law unconstitutional? Under what circumstances may a state court declare a state law unconstitutional? Under what circumstances may a state court declare a federal law unconstitutional?
4. What is the common law? Where do the courts get the authority to interpret it and to change it?
5. Ten years ago, the state's highest court announced as a rule of law that a mother who sees her child run over by an automobile may not recover money damages for the acute mental distress she suffered. This year, a jury has awarded a mother damages under these circumstances.

The driver appeals the jury award to the state's highest court. Different judges are now sitting on that court. How must they rule? Must they throw out the jury's award? May they do so? What arguments can you find for reversing the jury? Sustaining it?

6. You hear screams coming from your neighbor's apartment. You suspect that her husband is beating her up. However, you are afraid to become involved since her husband is large and menacing. Do you have a legal obligation to call the police? Why or why not?

2

Business and the Constitution

Introduction

As we saw in Chapter 1, the United States Constitution is our fundamental source of law and liberties. It structures the federal government, sets out the relationship between the federal government and the states, and limits the exercise of power by both the federal government and the states. Much of the contemporary debate over constitutional law, reflected in frequent headlines, centers on the extent of the powers the President and Congress share, limits on the power of the courts to interpret the Constitution, and rights of women, minorities, and criminal defendants. The constitutional relationship between business and the state is also an important issue. In this chapter, we will explore the modern interpretation of the Constitution as it affects commercial affairs and the powers and rights of the business corporation.

Regulating Business: Federal Regulation of Interstate Commerce

The federal Constitution was written in large part because the states proved inept, after the Revolution, at regulating commerce. Each state looked to its own advantages—imposing export duties and other taxes, creating monopolies for local industry, and otherwise interfering with a truly national market. To overcome the petty jealousies of the states and their natural incentives to legislate on behalf of their own industries, the Constitution gives to Congress the power to regulate interstate and foreign commerce. This power is located in the *Commerce Clause* of Article I, which reads: "The Congress shall have Power: . . . To regulate Commerce with foreign Nations, and among the several States, . . ."

In the early years of the nation, the states originated the only business regulations, which were minimal. But in two important cases, Chief Justice Marshall embraced a nationalistic interpretation of Article I that opened the way to a broad federal power. In the first, *McCulloch* v. *Maryland* [4 Wheat. 316 (1819)], Marshall held that Congress had the power to incorporate a national bank, even though the Constitution does not spell out the power in so many words. Pointing to the clause in Article I that allows Congress to enact laws that are "necessary and proper," Marshall reasoned that Congress had great leeway in determining how it would carry out any of the powers the Constitution had given it: "Let the end be legitimate, let it be within the scope of the constitution, and all means which are appropriate, which are plainly adapted to that end, which are not prohibited, but consistent with the letter and spirit of the constitution, are constitutional."

Five years later, in *Gibbons* v. *Ogden* [6 Wheat. 1 (1824)], Marshall ruled that New York State could not grant a monopoly to operate steamboats on the state waterways. The grant (copied in other states that sought to retaliate) was intended to prevent shippers from delivering goods to and from New Jersey without securing a license from the monopolists.

The state made two arguments: first, that navigation was not part of "commerce," and, therefore, Congress could not regulate it, and second, that even if navigation were "commerce," it was not part of commerce "among the states."

The first argument was that the term "commerce" is limited to buying and selling. "Navigation" is not a commerce activity itself but implies the mere carrying of commodities. Marshall responded that there was no warrant in the Constitution for narrowly reading the term "commerce" and that, indeed, the federal power to regulate navigation was "one of the primary objects for which the people of America adopted their government."

New York argued also that navigation was a local matter, not within the interstate commerce power, because navigation begins entirely within the state. Marshall responded that all commerce begins that way; there are no spaces between the states. Federal regulation of commerce may reach into local matters as long as the regulation is aimed at commerce that is not itself purely local but involves trade among the states.

In the steamboat case, Marshall pointed to a congressional enactment providing for licensing of those engaged in plying the coastal waterways. The Chief Justice ruled that the federal law was well within the federal interstate commerce power, and since there was a federal law on the subject, state laws that conflicted with it (by establishing state monopolies) were unconstitutional by virtue of a clause in Article VI that gives supremacy to U.S. laws. This ruling in *Gibbons* and in other cases kept open the flow of commerce among the states by barring state restrictions that conflicted with federal law.

With the explosive growth of industry, transportation, and national commerce in the late nineteenth century, a considerable constitutional problem arose as Congress sought to control the effects of industrial combinations and monopolies. How far does the federal commerce power extend into matters that have always been considered local? At first, the Supreme Court was inclined to narrow the scope of federal power. For example, in 1895 in an important test of the Sherman Antitrust Act, the Court dismissed a federal prosecution of the giant American Sugar Refining Company, even though the company, by acquiring other companies, controlled 98 percent of the nation's sugar refining capacity. The Court reasoned that "manufacturing" was a local activity and could never be part of interstate "commerce." [United States v. E. C. Knight Co., 1956 U.S. 1 (1985)]

But the Court soon bowed to the necessity for federal antitrust and other laws regulating the economy, justifying Congressional enactments on a number of grounds. For example, early in the twentieth century, the Court held that federal agencies had power to control state activities that interfered with prices on the national market. [The Shreveport Rate Case, 234 U.S. 342 (1914)] It also held that federal agencies could regulate charges and practices of such activities as stockyards because they were not the final resting place of commodities but "a throat through which the current [of commerce] flows." [Stafford v. Wallace, 258 U.S. 495 (1922)] The Court also held that Congress could prohibit the flow across state lines of illicit goods—for example, lottery tickets and adulterated foodstuffs. [Champion v. Ames, 188 U.S. 321 (1903); Hipolite Egg Co. v. United States, 220 U.S. 45 (1911)]

By the first third of this century, the immense growth in the American economy and the almost miraculous development of technology made it difficult to find any purely local commerce. With the Depression, Congress began to realize how interdependent the American economy had become and increasingly asserted jurisdiction to regulate a host of commercial interests—including transportation, trade, production, and employment—and competitive practices generally.

By the 1940s, a new theory had emerged from the cases: if a business action "affected" interstate commerce, Congress could regulate it. Large numbers of employees, for example, worked for companies that sold goods throughout the country. Was this connection sufficient to give Congress jurisdiction to enact national wage and hours standards? In the Fair Labor Standards Act of 1938, Congress set up a comprehensive scheme that prevented manufacturers from shipping certain products in interstate commerce unless they complied with minimum wage and maximum hour standards. In 1941, the Supreme Court dismissed a constitutional challenge to the law: "Congress may . . . by appropriate legislation regulate intrastate activities where they have a substantial effect on interstate commerce." [United States v. F. W. Darby Lumber Co., 312 U.S. 100 (1941)]

In the very next year, the Court upheld an application of the Agricultural Adjustment Act of 1938 to a farmer who harvested 239 bushels of wheat more than he was allotted under the act. Most of the excess wheat was consumed on the farm as food for his family and animals and was used as seed for the next year's crop. The farmer asserted that his use of the wheat was purely local, hence not within the power of Congress to reach. The Court disagreed: "Even if [the farmer's] activity be local and though it may not be regarded as commerce, it may still, whatever its nature, be reached by Congress if it exerts a substantial economic effect on interstate commerce, and this irrespective of whether such effect is what might at some earlier time have been defined as 'direct' or 'indirect'." [Wickard v. Filburn, 317 U.S. 111 (1942)] Neatly summing up the congressional commerce power in 1949, Justice Robert H. Jackson said: "If it is interstate commerce that feels the pinch, it does not matter how local the operation that applies the squeeze."

Today, the commerce power is nearly coextensive with the desire of the federal government to regulate private economic activity. Through dozens of agencies, the federal government oversees the national markets in securities and commodities; regulates rates and practices in communications, transportation, power generation and transmission; and sets national minimum wages and standards for millions of employees in interstate businesses. So broad is the commerce power that it has even been used to reach into the civil rights arena, once though to be within the exclusive domain of the states by virtue of the *Civil Rights Cases* of 1883. The Court had ruled that Congress had no constitutional power to ban private acts of discrimination. But in the 1960s, finally moved to end the ancient indignities heaped upon Blacks in America, Congress enacted a series of civil rights laws. One of them prohibited discrimination in public accommodations—the very subject of the law that the Court had struck down in 1883. This time Congress rested its power on the Commerce Clause, and the Supreme Court upheld the law, thus confirming congressional power to deal with private acts of racial discrimination in the economic arena. [Heart of Atlanta Motel v. United States, 379 U.S. 241 (1964)]

In the 1980s, the Court demonstrated anew that little commercial activity can escape the regulatory power of Congress. At issue in the following case was the power of Congress to outlaw arson, usually considered a purely local crime. The law under which the defendant had been convicted banned arson and attempted arson in any building used in interstate commerce or in any activity affecting interstate commerce. The defendant had tried to burn down a two-unit Chicago apartment.

RUSSELL v. UNITED STATES
471 U.S. 858 (1985)

JUSTICE STEVENS delivered the opinion for the Court.

The question presented is whether 18 U.S.C. § 844(i) applies to a two-unit apartment building that is used as rental property.

Petitioner owns an apartment building located at 4530 South Union, Chicago, Illinois. He earned rental income from it and treated it as business property for tax purposes. In early 1983, he made an unsuccessful attempt to set fire to the building and was consequently indicted for violating § 844(i). Following a bench trial, petitioner was convicted and sentenced to 10 years' imprisonment. The District Court and the Court of Appeals both rejected his contention that the building was not commercial or business property, and therefore was not capable of being the subject of an offense under § 844(i).

Section 844(i) used broad language to define the offense. It provides:

> Whoever maliciously damages or destroys, or attempts to damage or destroy, by means of fire or an explosive, any building, vehicle, or other real or personal property used in interstate or foreign commerce or in any activity affecting interstate or foreign commerce shall be imprisoned for not more than ten years or fined not more than $10,000, or both. . . .

The reference to "any building . . . used . . . in any activity affecting interstate or foreign commerce" expresses an intent by Congress to exercise its full power under the Commerce Clause.

The legislative history indicates that Congress intended to exercise its full power to protect "business property." Moreover, after considering whether the bill as originally introduced would cover bombings of police stations or churches, the bill was revised to eliminate the words "for business purposes" from the description of covered property. Even after that change, however, the final Report on the bill emphasized the "very broad" coverage of "substantially all business property." In the floor debates on the final bill, although it was recognized that the coverage of the bill was extremely broad, the Committee Chairman, Representative Celler, expressed the opinion that "the mere bombing of a private home even under this bill would not be covered because of the question whether the Congress would have the authority under the Constitution." In sum, the legislative history suggests that Congress at least intended to protect all business property, as well as some additional property that might not fit that description, but perhaps not every private home.

By its terms, however, the statute only applies to property that is "used" in an "activity" that affects commerce. The rental of real estate is unquestionably such an activity. We need not rely on the connection between the market for residential units and "the interstate movement of people," to recognize that the local rental of an apartment unit is merely an element of a much broader commercial market in rental properties. The congressional power to regulate the class of activities that constitute the rental market for real estate includes the power to regulate individual activity within that class.

Petitioner was renting his apartment building to tenants at the time he attempted to destroy it by fire. The property was therefore being used in an activity affecting commerce within the meaning of § 844(i).

The judgment of the Court of Appeals is affirmed.

Federal Limitations on State Power over Commerce

Due Process Limitations

The Commerce Clause speaks only of the power of Congress to regulate commerce among the states and with other nations. It does not deny the power to states to regulate their own commerce, and from the earliest days the states were actively engaged in economic legislation—allowing construction of canals and railroads, regulating banks, and, increasingly, forbidding numerous private economic activities thought to be deleterious to the commonweal. By 1881 in Indiana, for example, the criminal code contained dozens of prohibitions against economic crimes: shooting prairie hens out of season, falsely weighing and selling coal, using nets to prevent fish from swimming into or out of any creek emptying into the Ohio River, advertising or selling any drug that cautioned pregnant women against using it. In 1891, the state made it a punishable offense for railroads to fail to employ flagmen at crossings. In 1898, the New York Legislature prohibited labeling commodities as "sterling silver" unless they were 92.5 percent pure. Many states began to enforce dormant Sunday closing laws to give workers a day of rest.

States enacted these laws under their general "police powers"—the power to ensure the public health, safety, and morals. Unless these laws conflicted with federal commercial legislation, they were considered, almost to the end of the nineteenth century, well within the constitutional powers of the states. But for several decades, commercial lawyers had been pressing a novel argument on the Supreme Court: a state that "unreasonably" interfered with a business corporation's economic activity was violating the clause in the Fourteenth Amendment that provides: "No State shall . . . deprive any person of life, liberty or property without due process of law. . . ."

Due process of law is one of the two or three most significant concepts in our constitutional law. Although due process is capable of no precise definition—if it were, it would have exhausted its utility long ago—it connotes in general *fairness* and *freedom from arbitrary official action*. The due process clauses of both the Fifth and Fourteenth Amendments mean that the state may not execute, imprison, or fine a person without first having provided him a fair trial: the right to be heard, to have counsel, to cross-examine witnesses. In Chapter 7, on criminal law, we examine the procedural requirements of due process in greater detail.

Due process also has an important role to play in the context of civil law. The issue centers on the word "property." As we see below (pp. 61–64) the state may not take a citizen's land without compensating him for it. In addition, under the Fifth Amendment, a separate clause explicitly provides that when the federal government exercises its power of *eminent domain* (the taking of private property for public purposes—for example, to build a road), the owner must be given "just compensation." The just-compensation principle applies to the states through the Fourteenth Amendment's due process clause. But "property" is not restricted to land and tangible physical possessions. Over the years the word has become freighted with a vast number of other meanings and at times has practically merged with the term "liberty."

Beginning in the 1870s, businesses argued that many state economic regulations were arbitrary deprivations of property without due process. For example, in 1869 Louisiana gave a monopoly of the slaughtering trade in New Orleans to a particular company it created for the purpose. Dozens of other butchers complained that in being deprived of their livelihood (they could no longer run their own businesses), Louisiana had violated the due process clause of the Fourteenth Amendment. The Supreme Court at first said that the due process clause had no application to merely economic matters. [Slaughterhouse Cases, 16 Wall. 36 (1873)] When the operators of grain elevators protested an Illinois law regulating their rates, the Court again rejected the argument, holding that the police power permitted states to regulate the use of private property "when such regulation becomes necessary for the public good." [Munn v. Illinois, 94 U.S. 113 (1877)]

But twenty years later, a new Supreme Court capitulated to the force of complaints about the outpouring of state economic legislation. For nearly 40 years, until the late 1930s, a doctrine known as "substantive due process" reigned in the courts. This doctrine was used to invalidate numerous state and federal laws regulating commercial, industrial, and labor conditions. For example, the Supreme Court struck down a New York law limiting the numbers of hours bakers could work. The law was intended to create healthier conditions for bakers (who were forced to work more than ten hours a day six days a week), but the Court agreed with the argument of the employers that the law arbitrarily interfered with the bakers' "liberty to contract." [Lochner v. New York, 198 U.S. 45 (1905)] As Edwin S. Corwin summarized the theory, "the term 'due process of law,' in short, simply drops out of the (due process) clause, which comes to read 'no person (including corporations) shall be deprived of property,' period." The courts eventually overthrew this substantive or "economic" due process concept in the 1930s, and today it is dead. The states and the federal government are free to regulate economic activity as long as in doing so (1) they do not violate some other provision of the Constitution, and (2) the law is rationally related to the legislature's particular goal.

But a substantive notion of due process has not disappeared. Today it has a political or social, rather than economic, flavor. For instance, the Supreme Court's decisions overturning state laws that prohibit abortion are grounded at least in part on a conception of personal liberty. The Court's position is that the states cannot, consistent with due process, limit a woman's right to abort a fetus within the first trimester. Similarly, the due process clause has been used to vindicate rights of prisoners, mental patients, and students against arbitrary action by government officials.

The due process clause is also the basis for a host of civil rights decisions in which appurtenances of modern life are at stake: the right to a job; to academic tenure; and to various "privileges" granted by government—for example, a driver's license, a tax exemption, and welfare benefits. The courts have held that each of these is an incident of property which the state cannot take from any person unless the state demonstrates at a *hearing* that it has not acted arbitrarily. In the following case, the Supreme Court used the due process clause to invalidate a long-used procedure by which sellers of goods could repossess, without a hearing, the goods from customers who failed to make installment payments.

FUENTES v. SHEVIN
407 U.S. 67 (1972)

MR. JUSTICE STEWART delivered the opinion of the Court.

We here review the decisions of two three-judge federal District Courts that upheld the constitutionality of Florida and Pennsylvania laws authorizing the summary seizure of goods or chattels in a person's possession under a writ of replevin. Both statutes provide for the issuance of writs ordering state agents to seize a person's possessions, simply upon the *ex parte* application of any other person who claims a right to them and posts a security bond. Neither statute provides for notice to be given to the possessor of the property, and neither statute gives the possessor an opportunity to challenge the seizure at any kind of prior hearing. The question is whether these statutory procedures violate the Fourteenth Amendment's guarantee that no State shall deprive any person of property without due process of law.

The appellant in No. 5039, Margarita Fuentes, is a resident of Florida. She purchased a gas stove and service policy from the Firestone Tire and Rubber Co. (Firestone) under a conditional sales contract calling for monthly payments over a period of time. A few months later, she purchased a stereophonic phonograph from the same company under the same sort of contract. The total cost of the stove and stereo was about $500, plus an additional financing charge of over $100. Under the contracts, Firestone retained title to the merchandise, but Mrs. Fuentes was entitled to possession unless and until she should default on her installment payments.

For more than a year, Mrs. Fuentes made her installment payments. But then, with only about $200 remaining to be paid, a dispute developed between her and Firestone over the servicing of the stove. Firestone instituted an action in a small-claims court for repossession of both the stove and the stereo, claiming that Mrs. Fuentes had refused to make her remaining payments. Simultaneously with the filing of that action and before Mrs. Fuentes had even received a summons to answer its complaint, Firestone obtained a writ of replevin ordering a sheriff to seize the disputed goods at once.

In conformance with Florida procedure, Firestone had only to fill in the blanks on the appropriate form documents and submit them to the clerk of the small-claims court. The clerk signed and stamped the documents and issued a writ of replevin. Later the same day, a local deputy sheriff and an agent of Firestone went to Mrs. Fuentes' home and seized the stove and stereo.

Shortly thereafter, Mrs. Fuentes instituted the present action in a federal district court, challenging the constitutionality of the Florida prejudgment replevin procedures under the Due Process Clause of the Fourteenth Amendment. She sought declaratory and injunctive relief against continued enforcement of the procedural provisions of the state statutes that authorize prejudgment replevin.

* * *

For more than a century the central meaning of procedural due process has been clear: "Parties whose rights are to be affected are entitled to be heard; and in order that they may enjoy that right they must first be notified." It is equally fundamental that the right to notice and an opportunity to be heard "must be granted at a meaningful time and in a meaningful manner."

The primary question in the present cases is whether these state statutes are constitutionally defective in failing to provide for hearings "at a meaningful time." The Florida replevin process guarantees an opportunity for a hearing after the seizure of goods, and the Pennsylvania process allows a post-seizure hearing if the aggrieved party shoulders the burden of initiating one. But neither the Florida nor the Pennsylvania statute provides for notice or an opportunity to be heard *before* the seizure. The issue is whether procedural due process in the context of these cases requires an opportunity for a hearing *before* the State authorizes its agents to seize property in the possession of a person upon the application of another.

The constitutional right to be heard is a basic aspect of the duty of government to follow a fair process of decision-making when it acts to deprive a person of his possessions. The purpose of this requirement is not only to ensure abstract fair play to the individual. Its purpose, more particularly, is to protect his use and possession of property from arbitrary encroachment—to minimize substantively unfair or mistaken deprivations of property, a danger that is especially great when the State seizes goods simply upon the application of and for the benefit of a private party. So viewed, the prohibition against the deprivation of property without due process of law reflects the high value, embedded in our constitutional and political history, that we place on a person's right to enjoy what is his, free of governmental interference.

The requirement of notice and an opportunity to be heard raises no impenetrable barrier to the taking of a person's possessions. But the fair process of decision-making that it guarantees works, by itself, to protect against arbitrary deprivation of property. For when a person has an opportunity to speak up in his own defense, and when the State must listen to what he has to say, substantively unfair and simply mistaken deprivations of property interests can be prevented. It has long been recognized that "fairness can rarely be obtained by secret, one-sided determination of facts decisive of rights. . . . [And n]o better instrument has been devised for arriving at truth than to give a person in jeopardy of serious loss notice of the case against him and opportunity to meet it."

If the right to notice and a hearing is to serve its full purpose, then, it is clear that it must be granted at a time when the deprivation can still be prevented. At a later hearing, an individual's possessions can be returned to him if they were unfairly or mistakenly taken in the first place. Damages may even be awarded to him for the wrongful deprivation. But no later hearing and no damage award can undo the fact that the arbitrary taking that was subject to the right of procedural due process has already occurred. "This Court has not . . . embraced the general proposition that a wrong may be done if it can be undone."

* * *

The Florida and Pennsylvania prejudgment replevin statutes fly in the face of this principle. To be sure, the requirements that a party seeking a writ must first post a bond, allege conclusorily that he is entitled to specific goods, and open himself to possible liability in damages if he is wrong, serve to deter wholly unfounded applications for a writ. But those requirements are hardly a substitute for a prior hearing, for they test no more than the strength of the applicant's own belief in his rights. Since his private gain is at stake, the danger is all too great that his confidence in his cause will be misplaced. . . .

The minimal deterrent effect of a bond requirement is, in a practical sense, no substitute for an informed evaluation by a neutral official. More specifically, as a matter of constitutional principle, it is no replacement for the right to a prior hearing that is the only truly effective safeguard against arbitrary deprivation of property. While the existence of these other, less effective, safeguards may be among the considerations that affect the form of hearing demanded by due process, they are far from enough by themselves to obviate the right to a prior hearing of some kind.

* * *

We hold that the Florida and Pennsylvania prejudgment replevin provisions work a deprivation of property without due process of law insofar as they deny the right to a prior opportunity to be heard before chattels are taken from their possessor. Our holding, however, is a narrow one. We do not question the power of a State to seize goods before a final judgment in order to protect the security interests of creditors so long as those creditors have tested their claim to the goods through the process of a fair prior hearing. The nature and form of such prior hearings, moreover, are legitimately open to many potential variations and are a subject, at this point, for legislation—not adjudication. Since the essential reason for the requirement of a prior hearing is to prevent unfair and mistaken deprivations of property, however, it is axiomatic that the hearing must provide a real test. "[D]ue process is afforded only by the kinds of 'notice' and 'hearing' that are aimed at establishing the validity, or at least the probable validity, of the underlying claim against the alleged debtor *before* he can be deprived of his property . . . ."

For the foregoing reasons, the judgments of the District Courts are vacated and these cases are remanded for further proceedings consistent with this opinion.

It is so ordered.

Equal Protection

Closely related to due process is the equal protection clause of the Fourteenth Amendment, quoted on p. 23. In essence, the clause means that the states may not arbitrarily or invidiously classify people in such a way that the different categories of persons will be treated unequally. This clause has had its most obvious use with respect to racial classifications. Beginning with the seminal case of *Brown* v. *Board of Education,* the Supreme Court has made it clear that neither the Fourteenth Amendment nor the due process clause of the Fifth Amendment will tolerate governmental classifications of individuals by race.

BROWN v. BOARD OF EDUCATION
347 U.S. 483 (1954)

MR. CHIEF JUSTICE WARREN delivered the opinion of the Court.

These cases come to us from the States of Kansas, South Carolina, Virginia, and Delaware. . . .

In each of the cases, minors of the Negro race, through their legal representatives, seek the aid of the courts in obtaining admission to the public schools of their community on a nonsegregated basis. In each instance, they had been denied admission to schools attended by white children under laws requiring or permitting segregation according to race. This segregation was alleged to deprive the plaintiffs of the equal protection of the laws under the Fourteenth Amendment. In each of the cases other than the Delaware case, a three-judge federal district court denied relief to the plaintiffs on the so-called "separate but equal" doctrine announced by this Court in *Plessy* v. *Ferguson,* 163 U.S. 537. Under that doctrine, equality of treatment is accorded when the races are provided substantially equal facilities, even though these facilities be separate. In the Delaware case, the Supreme Court of Delaware adhered to that doctrine, but ordered that the plaintiffs be admitted to the white schools because of their superiority to the Negro schools.

The plaintiffs contend that segregated public schools are not "equal" and cannot be made "equal," and that hence they are deprived of the equal protection of the laws.

* * *

In approaching this problem, we cannot turn the clock back to 1868 when the Amendment was adopted, or even to 1896 when *Plessy* v. *Ferguson* was written. We must consider public education in the light of its full development and its present place in American life throughout the Nation. Only in this way can it be determined if segregation in public schools deprives these plaintiffs of the equal protection of the laws.

Today, education is perhaps the most important function of state and local governments. Compulsory school attendance laws and the great expenditures for education both demonstrate our recognition of the importance of education to our democratic society. It is required in the performance of our most basic public responsibilities, even service in the armed forces. It is the very foundation of good citizenship. Today it is a principal instrument in awakening the child to cultural values, in preparing him for later professional training, and in helping him to adjust normally to his environment. In these days, it is doubtful that any child may reasonably be expected to succeed in life if he is denied the opportunity of an education. Such an opportunity, where the state has undertaken to provide it, is a right which must be made available to all on equal terms.

We come then to the question presented: Does segregation of children in public schools solely on the basis of race, even though the physical facilities and other "tangible" factors may be equal, deprive the children of the minority group of equal educational opportunities? We believe that it does.

In *Sweatt* v. *Painter,* in finding that a segregated law school for Negroes could not provide them equal educational opportunities, this Court relied in large part on "those qualities which are incapable of objective measurement but which make for greatness in a law school." In *McLaurin* v. *Oklahoma State Regents,* the Court, in requiring that a Negro admitted to a white graduate school be treated like all other students, again resorted to intangible considerations: ". . . his ability to study, to engage in discussions and exchange views with other students, and, in general, to learn his profession." Such considerations apply with added force to children in grade and high schools. To separate them from others of similar age and qualifications solely because of their race generates a feeling of inferiority as to their status in the community that may affect their hearts and minds in a way unlikely ever to be undone. The effect of this separation on their educational opportunities was well stated by a finding in the Kansas case by a court which nevertheless felt compelled to rule against the Negro plaintiffs:

> Segregation of white and colored children in public schools has a detrimental effect upon the colored children. The impact is greater when it has the sanction of the law; for the policy of separating the races is usually interpreted as denoting the inferiority of the negro group. A sense of inferiority affects the motivation of a child to learn. Segregation with the sanction of law, therefore, has a tendency to [retard] the educational and mental development of negro children and to deprive them of some of the benefits they would receive in a racial[ly] integrated school system.

Whatever may have been the extent of psychological knowledge at the time of *Plessy* v. *Ferguson,* this finding is amply supported by modern authority. Any language in *Plessy* v. *Ferguson* contrary to this finding is rejected.

We conclude that in the field of public education the doctrine of "separate but equal" has no place. [Separate educational facilities are inherently unequal.] Therefore, we hold that the plaintiffs and others similarly situated for whom the actions have been brought are, by reason of the segregation complained of, deprived of the equal protection of the laws guaranteed by the Fourteenth Amendment.

The equal protection clause, as interpreted from 1954 on, has had a profound impact on American society. It has led to reapportionment of state legislatures and fundamental revamping of voting laws throughout the United States. It has prompted a variety of reforms in the legal condition of women, the poor, children, ethnic and linguistic minority groups, and aliens.

Although in recent years the equal protection clause has led the courts to transform American society in many important ways, business has found little solace in its commands. With insignificant exceptions, the courts have refused to strike down economic regulations on equal protection grounds. In general, companies have argued that in prohibiting one kind of economic activity, but allowing largely similar ones to continue, the states have unconstitutionally discriminated against the prohibited activity. For example, a New York City ordinance prohibited trucks from displaying advertisements on their sides unless the advertisements were for the regular business of the truck owners. A nationwide express delivery company, employing a fleet of 1,900 trucks in New York City alone, regularly sold display space to merchants who wished to advertise their products. The company insisted that the ordinance unfairly discriminated against it since the corner laundry truck could advertise its own business with the same distraction to traffic and pedestrians as if the fleet trucks advertised. The company argued further that "the classification which the regulation makes has no relation to the traffic problem since a violation turns not on what kind of advertisements are carried on trucks but on whose trucks they are carried." The Supreme Court rejected the argument:

> The local authorities may well have concluded that those who advertise their own wares on their trucks do not present the same traffic problem in view of the nature or extent of the advertising which they use. It would take a degree of omniscience which we lack to say that such is not the case. . . . And the fact that New York City sees fit to eliminate from traffic this kind of distraction but does not touch what may be even greater ones in a different category, such as the vivid displays on Times Square, is immaterial. It is no requirement of equal protection that all evils of the same genus be eradicated or none at all. [Railway Express Agency v. New York, 326 U.S. 106 (1949)]

In the same way, the Supreme Court has refused to invalidate Sunday closing laws which exempt some businesses from the requirement that they not sell on Sundays and also a New Orleans ordinance that prohibited all pushcart vendors from operating in the French Court except those who had been operating continuously for eight years before 1972. [McGowan

v. Maryland, 366 U.S. 429 (1961); New Orleans v. Dukes, 427 U.S. 297 (1976)]

State Action

With one exception, the Constitution does not apply to private conduct. It limits *government* power. (The exception is the slavery prohibition in the Thirteenth Amendment, applicable to government and private individuals alike.) A state, for example, may not pass a law prohibiting people from speaking out against (or in favor of) nuclear power, but a private company may enforce its own rule against its employees' doing so—at least insofar as the Constitution is concerned. For protection of the right to speak against private prohibitions, employees must look to state and federal statutes. Some states have begun to enact such legislation.

This rule, that the Constitution restricts only government, has equal application to the due process and equal protection clauses. In order for a court to invalidate an act claimed to violate one of these constitutional provisions, there must have been **state action**—that is, some branch of some government must have somehow been involved. In 1883, the Supreme Court struck down a Congressional enactment barring inns, railroads, and theaters from discriminating against patrons on the basis of race. The Fourteenth Amendment gives Congress the power to enforce its provisions, and Congress asserted that the enforcement clause enabled it to legislate against discrimination generally. The Court ruled, however, that since the Fourteenth Amendment does not apply directly to private action, Congress had no such power. [Civil Rights Cases, 109 U.S. 3 (1883)]

By contrast, the state action in segregated public schools was obvious: the schools were public institutions. Likewise, state statutes that demanded segregation in private institutions were examples of state involvement.

State action need not be confined to legislative enactments or administrative acts. In 1948, the Supreme Court wiped out the invidious practice of *racially restrictive covenants* in land deeds. The covenant let a seller prevent any subsequent buyer from later selling his land to a member of a minority group. The Court said that although placing the restriction in the deed was a private act, those who wish to enforce it (when an owner decided to violate the covenant) would not be permitted to seek the aid of a court, since a court ruling in favor of the restrictive covenant would be a government order approving classification by race. [Shelley v. Kraemer, 334 U.S. 1 (1948)] Since judicial enforcement is the only means of enforcing a covenant (nondiscriminatory types of covenants remain lawful) the racially restrictive covenant became, at one blow, a dead letter throughout the country.

But the search for state action has not stopped at the most obvious examples, because the state has become ever more involved in private activities. Thus, a private defense contractor that gets 90 percent of its business from the federal government has been held to be public for purposes of enforcing the constitutional right to free speech (the company had a rule barring its employees from speaking out in public against its corporate position). It has even been argued that public regulation of private activity is sufficient to convert the private into public activity, thus subjecting it to the requirements of due process. But the Supreme Court rejected this extreme view in 1974 when it refused to require private power companies, regulated by the state, to give customers a hearing before cutting off electricity for failure to pay the bill. [Jackson v. Metropolitan Edison Co., 419 U.S. 345 (1974)]

Prohibitions of Local Protectionism

Although the states are generally free to enact economic legislation under their police power to protect the public health, safety, and morals, the courts have discerned one significant constitutional limitation on state commercial regulation. That limitation stems from the Commerce Clause.

We have already seen that when Congress enacts laws regulating interstate commerce, the Supremacy Clause of Article VI preempts any conflicting state laws. Suppose Congress has not spoken. Does the Supremacy Clause grant Congress the *exclusive* power to regulate commerce? In 1851, the Court said no. The states may regulate commerce as long as they are regulating purely "local" matters even if the regulation has an incidental effect on national commerce. [Cooley v. Port of Wardens of the Port of Philadelphia, 12 How. 299 (1851)] For nearly a century, the Court had the difficult task of distinguishing between "local" and "national" subjects of regulation. The dividing line was usually indistinct. Eventually, the Court outgrew these labels and developed a "balancing test," as stated most concisely by Justice Potter Stewart:

> Where the statue regulates evenhandedly to effectuate a legitimate local public interest, and its effects on interstate commerce are only incidental, it will be upheld unless the burden imposed on such commerce is clearly excessive in relation to the putative local benefits. If a legitimate local purpose is found, then the question becomes one of degree. And the extent of the burden that will be tolerated will of course depend on the nature of the local interest involved, and on whether it could be promoted as well with a lesser impact on interstate activities. [Pike v. Bruce Church, Inc., 397 U.S. 137 (1970)]

This understanding of the Commerce Clause means that when a state (usually in alliance with a particular company or local industry) tries to protect its own residents to the detriment of consumers and businesses outside the state, the Court will be vigilant in striking down these laws. On numerous occasions, the Court has invalidated state laws that smacked of local protectionism by burdening out-of-state businesses, hindering access of competitors out of state to local markets, or otherwise discriminating against the national market. In the next case, North Carolina sought to protect its local apple growers from the sale of superior apples from the State of Washington.

HUNT v. WASHINGTON APPLE ADVERTISING COMMISSION
432 U.S. 33 (1977)

MR. CHIEF JUSTICE BURGER delivered the opinion of the Court.

In 1973, North Carolina enacted a statute which required, inter alia, all closed containers of apples sold, offered for sale, or shipped into the State to bear "no grade other than the applicable U.S. grade or standard." . . . Washington State is the Nation's largest producer of apples, its crops accounting for approximately 30% of all apples grown domestically and nearly half of all apples shipped in closed containers in interstate commerce. [Because] of the importance of the apple industry to the State, its legislature has undertaken to protect and enhance the reputation of Washington apples by establishing a stringent, mandatory inspection program [which] requires all apples shipped in interstate commerce to be tested under strict quality standards and graded accordingly. In all cases, the Washington State grades [are] the equivalent of, or superior to, the comparable grades and standards adopted by the [U.S. Dept. of] Agriculture (USDA).

[In] 1972, the North Carolina Board of Agriculture adopted an administrative regulation, unique in the 50 States, which in effect required all closed containers of apples shipped into or sold in the State to display either the applicable USDA grade or a notice indicating no classification. State grades were expressly prohibited. In addition to its obvious consequence—prohibiting the display of Washington State apple grades on containers of apples shipped into North Carolina—the regulation presented the Washington apple industry with a marketing problem of potentially nationwide significance. Washington apple growers annually ship in commerce approximately 40 million closed containers of apples, nearly 500,000 of which eventually find their way into North Carolina, stamped with the applicable Washington State variety and grade. [Compliance] with North Carolina's unique regulation would have required Washington growers to obliterate the printed labels on containers shipped to North Carolina, thus giving their product a damaged appearance. Alternatively, they could have changed their marketing practices to accommodate the needs of the North Carolina market, i.e., repack apples to be shipped to North Carolina in containers bearing only the USDA grade, and/or store the estimated portion of the harvest destined for that market in such special containers. As a last resort, they could discontinue the use of the preprinted containers entirely. None of these costly and less efficient options was very attractive to the industry. Moreover, in the event a number of other States followed North Carolina's lead, the resultant inability to display the Washington grades could force the Washington growers to abandon the State's expensive inspection and grading system which their customers had come to know and rely on over the 60-odd years of its existence. . . .

Unsuccessful in its attempts to secure administrative relief, the Commission instituted this action challenging the constitutionality of the statute. [The] District Court found that the North Carolina statute, while neutral on its face, actually discriminated against Washington State growers and dealers in favor of their local counterparts [and] concluded that this discrimination [was] not justified by the asserted local interest—the elimination of deception and confusion from the marketplace—arguably furthered by the [statute].

. . . [North Carolina] maintains that [the] burdens on the interstate sale of Washington apples were far outweighed by the local benefits flowing from what they contend was a valid exercise of North Carolina's [police powers]. Prior to the statute's enactment, . . . apples from 13 different States were shipped into North Carolina for sale. Seven of those States, including [Washington], had their own grading systems which, while differing in their standards, used similar descriptive labels (e.g., fancy, extra fancy, etc.). This multiplicity of inconsistent state grades [posed] dangers of deception and confusion not only in the North Carolina market, but in the Nation as a whole. The North Carolina statute, appellants claim, was enacted to eliminate this source of deception and confusion. [Moreover], it is contended that North Carolina sought to accomplish this goal of uniformity in an evenhanded manner as evidenced by the fact that its statute applies to all apples sold in closed containers in the State without regard to their point of origin.

[As] the appellants properly point out, not every exercise of state authority imposing some burden on the free flow of commerce is invalid, [especially] when the State acts to protect its citizenry in matters pertaining to the sale of foodstuffs. By the same token, however, a finding that state legislation furthers matters of legitimate local concern, even in the health and consumer protection areas, does not end the inquiry. Rather, when such state legislation comes into conflict with the Commerce Clause's overriding requirement of a national "common market," we are confronted with the task of effecting an accommodation of the competing national and local interests. We turn to that task.

As the District Court correctly found, the challenged statute has the practical effect of not only burdening interstate sales of Washington apples, but also discriminating against them. This discrimination takes various forms. The first, and most obvious, is the statute's consequence of *raising the costs* of doing business in the North Carolina market for Washington apple growers and dealers, while leaving those of their North Carolina counterparts unaffected. [This] disparate effect results from the fact that North Carolina apple producers, unlike their Washington competitors, were not forced to alter their marketing practices in order to comply with the statute. They were still free to market their wares under the USDA grade or none at all as they had done prior to the statute's enactment. Obviously, the increased costs imposed by the statute would tend to shield the local apple industry from the competition of Washington apple growers and dealers who are already at a competitive disadvantage because of their great distance from the North Carolina market. Second, the statute has the effect of *stripping away* from the Washington apple industry the competitive and economic advantages it has earned for itself through its expensive inspection and grading system. The record demonstrates that the Washington apple-grading system has gained nationwide acceptance in the apple trade. [The record] contains numerous affidavits [stating a] preference [for] apples graded under the Washington, as opposed to the USDA, system because of the former's greater consistency, its emphasis on color, and its supporting mandatory inspections. Once again, the statute had no similar impact on the North Carolina apple industry and thus operated to its benefit.

Third, by *prohibiting* Washington growers and dealers from *marketing* apples under their State's grades, the statute has a *leveling effect* which insidiously operates to the advantage of local apple producers. [With] free market forces at work, Washington sellers would normally enjoy a distinct market advantage vis-à-vis local producers in those categories where the Washington grade is superior. However, because of the statute's operation, Washington apples which would otherwise qualify for and be sold under the superior Washington grades will now have to be marketed under their inferior USDA counterparts. Such "downgrading" offers the North Carolina apple industry the very sort of protection against competing out-of-state products that the Commerce Clause was designed to prohibit. At worst, it will have the effect of an embargo against those Washington apples in the superior grades as Washington dealers withhold them from the North Carolina market. At best, it will deprive Washington sellers of the market premium that such apples would otherwise command.

Despite the statute's facial neutrality, the Commission suggests that its discriminatory impact on interstate commerce was not an unintended byproduct, and there are some indications in the record to that effect. The most glaring is the response of the North Carolina Agriculture Commissioner to the Commission's request for an exemption following the statute's passage in which he indicated that before he could support such an exemption, he would "want to have the sentiment from our apple producers *since they were mainly responsible for this legislation being passed.*" [Moreover], we find it somewhat suspect that North Carolina singled out only closed containers of apples, the very means by which apples are transported in commerce, to effectuate the statute's ostensible consumer protection purpose when apples are not generally sold at retail in their shipping containers. However, we need not ascribe an economic protection motive to the North Carolina Legislature to resolve this case; we conclude that the challenged statute cannot stand insofar as it prohibits the display of Washington State grades even if enacted for the declared purpose of protecting consumers from deception and fraud in the marketplace.

When discrimination against commerce of the type we have found is demonstrated, the burden falls on the State to justify it both in terms of the local benefits flowing from the statute and the unavailability of nondiscriminatory alternatives adequate to preserve the local interests at stake. North Carolina has failed to sustain that burden on both scores. [The] States unquestionably possess a substantial interest in protecting their citizens from confusion and deception in the marketing of foodstuffs, but the challenged statute does remarkably little to further that laudable goal at least with respect to Washington apples and grades. The statute [permits] the marketing of closed containers of apples under *no* grades at all. Such a result can hardly be thought to eliminate the problems of deception and confusion created by the multiplicity of differing state grades; indeed, it magnifies them by depriving purchasers of all information concerning the quality of the contents of closed apple containers. Moreover, although the statute is ostensibly a consumer protection measure, it directs its primary efforts, not at the consuming public at large, but at apple wholesalers and brokers who are the principal purchasers of closed containers of apples. And those individuals are presumably the most knowledgeable individuals in this area. Since the statute does nothing at all to purify the flow of information at the retail level, it does little to protect consumers against the problems it was designed to eliminate. Finally, we note that any potential for confusion and deception created by the Washington grades was not of the type that led to the statute's enactment. Since Washington grades are in all cases equal or superior to their USDA counterparts, they could only "deceive" or "confuse" a consumer to his benefit, hardly a harmful result.

In addition, it appears that nondiscriminatory alternatives to the outright ban of Washington State grades are readily available. For example, North Carolina could effectuate its goal by permitting out-of-state growers to utilize state grades only if they also marked their shipments with the applicable USDA label. In that case, the USDA grade would serve as a benchmark against which the consumer could evaluate the quality of the various state grades. . . .

[The court affirmed the lower court's holding that the North Carolina statute was unconstitutional.]

Through the Commerce Clause, the Constitution thus guarantees a truly national market against the splintering effects of local regulation. As Justice Jackson summed up the general rule and the policy that underlies it:

> The Commerce Clause is one of the most prolific sources of national power and an equally prolific source of conflict with legislation of the state. While the Constitution vests in Congress the power to regulate commerce among the states, it does not say what the states may or may not do in the absence of congressional action. . . . Perhaps even more than by interpretation of its written word, this Court has advanced the solidarity and prosperity of this Nation by the meaning it has given to these great silences of the Constitution. . . . This distinction between the power of the State to shelter its people from menaces to their health or safety and from fraud, even when those dangers emanate from interstate commerce, and its lack of power to retard, burden or constrict the flow of such commerce for their economic advantage, is one deeply rooted in

both our history and our law. . . . This Court consistently has rebuffed attempts of states to advance their own commercial interests by curtailing the movement of articles of commerce, either into or out of the state, while generally supporting their right to impose even burdensome regulations in the interest of local health and safety. . . . The principle that our economic unit is the Nation, which alone has the gamut of powers necessary to control of the economy, including the vital power of erecting customs barriers against foreign competition, has as its corollary that the states are not separable economic units. . . . The material success that has come to inhabitants of the states which make up this federal free trade unit has been the most impressive in the history of commerce, but the established interdependence of the states only emphasizes the necessity of protecting interstate movement of goods against local burdens and repressions. We need only consider the consequences if each of the few states that produce copper, lead, high-grade iron ore, timber, cotton, oil or gas should decree that industries located in that state shall have priority. What fantastic rivalries and dislocations and reprisals would ensue if such practices are begun! Or suppose that the field of discrimination and retaliation be industry. May Michigan provide that automobiles cannot be taken out of that State until local dealers' demands are fully met? Would she not have every argument in the favor of such a statute that can be offered in support of New York's limiting sales of milk for out-of-state shipment to protect the economic interests of her competing dealers and local consumers? Could Ohio then pounce upon the rubber-tire industry, on which she has a substantial grip, to retaliate for Michigan's auto monopoly? Our system, fostered by the Commerce Clause, is that every farmer and every craftsman shall be encouraged to produce by the certainty that he will have free access to every market in the Nation, that no home embargoes will withhold his exports, and no foreign state will by customs duties or regulations exclude them. Likewise, every consumer may look to the free competition from every producing area in the Nation to protect him from exploitation by any. Such was the vision of the Founders; such has been the doctrine of this Court which has given it reality. [H.P. Hood & Sons v. Du Mond, 336 U.S. 525 (1949)]

Regulating Businesses: The Constitutional Rights of Business

Freedom of Speech and Press

The First Amendment is the most significant charter of political freedom in America. In forty-five words, the First Amendment succinctly commands the government to let private individuals exercise their essential liberties:

> Congress shall make no law respecting an establishment of religion, or prohibiting the free exercise thereof; or abridging the freedom of speech, or of the press; or the right of the people peaceably to assemble, and to petition the Government for a redress of grievances.

In numerous cases, the Supreme Court (and other courts) have spelled out dozens of principles contained in these few words. Among them are the right to associate with anyone and to say or print whatever you please without first obtaining permission from the government. Freedom of speech and freedom of the press, along with the other rights guaranteed by the First Amendment, are now secure against intrusion not only by the federal government but also by the state governments. (The Court has interpreted the Fourteenth Amendment to mean that First Amendment rights apply also to intrusion by states.)

The First Amendment has been said to contain "preferred freedoms." By that, the Court means that it will take special pains to scrutinize laws that appear to infringe on First Amendment freedoms.

The First Amendment does not mean, however, that you can say whatever you want whenever you want to without fear of subsequent penalty. Libel and slander are actionable. Those who advertise in a false or deceptive manner can be punished. The states may regulate the time and manner of expression: you are not free in most towns to drive along residential streets at midnight blaring political slogans through a microphone. But it has long been held that the expression of political, religious, social, economic, cultural, and other ideas—no matter how obnoxious to others in the community—are protected by the First Amendment.

For many years, the mantle of protection was not thought to surround "commercial speech." Thus the courts have often struck down as unconstitutional ordinances that forbade picketing or the passing out of handbills advocating a political or religious position, but they left untouched similar laws barring the handing out of advertisements for a local retailer. Not until the 1970s did the Supreme Court reverse course and give a significant measure of First Amendment protection to the "purely commercial," as the next case shows.

VIRGINIA STATE BOARD OF PHARMACY v. VIRGINIA CITIZENS CONSUMER COUNCIL, INC. 425 U.S. 748 (1976)

MR. JUSTICE BLACKMUN delivered the opinion of the Court.

The plaintiff-appellees in this case attack, as violative of the First and Fourteenth Amendments, that portion of § 54-524.35 of Va. Code Ann. (1974), which provides that a pharmacist licensed in Virginia is guilty of unprofessional conduct if he "publishes, advertises or promotes, directly or indirectly, in any manner whatsoever, any amount, price, fee, premium, discount, rebate or credit terms . . . for any drugs which may be dispensed only by prescription." The three-judge District Court declared the quoted portion of the statute "void and of no effect," . . . and enjoined the defendant-appellants, the Virginia State Board of Pharmacy and the individual members of that Board, from enforcing it.

* * *

Once licensed, a pharmacist is subject to a civil monetary penalty, or to revocation or suspension of his license, if the [Virginia State] Board [of Pharmacy] finds that he . . . is guilty of "unprofessional conduct." "Unprofessional conduct" [includes] advertising of the price for any prescription drug, and is the subject of this litigation.

Inasmuch as only a licensed pharmacist may dispense prescription drugs in Virginia, advertising or other affirmative dissemination of prescription drug price information is effectively forbidden in the State. Some pharmacies refuse even to quote prescription drug prices over the telephone.

* * *

The present attack on the statute is one made not by one directly subject to its prohibition, that is, a pharmacist, but by prescription drug consumers who claim that they would greatly benefit if the prohibition were lifted and advertising freely allowed. The plaintiffs are an individual Virginia resident who suffers from diseases that require her to take prescription drugs on a daily basis, and two nonprofit organizations. Their claim is that the First Amendment entitles the user of prescription drugs to receive information that pharmacists wish to communicate to them through advertising and other promotional means, concerning the prices of such drugs.

Certainly that information may be of value. Drug prices in Virginia, for both prescription and nonprescription items, strikingly vary from outlet to outlet even within the same locality. It is stipulated, for example, that in Richmond "the cost of 40 Achromycin tablets ranges from $2.59 to $6.00, a difference of 140% [*sic*]," and that in the Newport News-Hampton area the cost of tetracycline ranges from $1.20 to $9.00, a difference of 650%.

* * *

The appellants contend that the advertisement of prescription drug prices is outside the protection of the First Amendment because it is "commercial speech."

* * *

Last Term, in *Bigelow* v. *Virginia,* 421 U.S. 809 (1975), the notion of unprotected "commercial speech" all but passed from the scene. We reversed a conviction for violation of a Virginia statute that made the circulation of any publication to encourage or promote the processing of an abortion in Virginia a misdemeanor. The defendant had published in his newspaper the availability of abortions in New York. The advertisement in question, in addition to announcing that abortions were legal in New York, offered the services of a referral agency in that State. We rejected the contention that the publication was unprotected because it was commercial. . . . We concluded that "the Virginia courts erred in their assumptions that advertising, as such, was entitled to no First Amendment protection," and we observed that the "relationship of speech to the marketplace of products or of services does not make it valueless in the marketplace of ideas."

* * *

Here, in contrast, the question whether there is a First Amendment exception for "commercial speech" is squarely before us. Our pharmacist does not wish to editorialize on any subject, cultural, philosophical, or political. He does not wish to report any particularly newsworthy fact, or to make generalized observations even about commercial matters. The "idea" he wishes to communicate is simply this: "I will sell you the X prescription drug at the Y price." Our question, then, is whether this communication is wholly outside the protection of the First Amendment.

We begin with several propositions that already are settled or beyond serious dispute. It is clear, for example, that speech does not lose its First Amendment protection because money is spent to protect it, as in a paid advertisement of one form or another. Speech likewise is protected even though it is carried in a form that is "sold" for profit, and even though it may involve a solicitation to purchase or otherwise pay or contribute money.

If there is a kind of commercial speech that lacks all First Amendment protection, therefore, it must be distinguished by its content. Yet the speech whose content deprives it of protection cannot simply be speech on a commercial subject. No one would contend that our pharmacist may be prevented from being heard on the subject of whether, in general, pharmaceutical prices should be regulated, or their advertisement forbidden. Nor can it be dispositive that a commercial advertisement is noneditorial, and merely reports a fact. Purely factual matter of public interest may claim protection.

* * *

Focusing first on the individual parties to the transaction that is proposed in the commercial advertisement, we may assume that the advertiser's interest is a purely economic one. That hardly disqualifies him from protection under the First Amendment. The interests of the contestants in a labor dispute are primarily economic, but it has long been settled that both the employee and the employer are protected by the First Amendment when they express themselves on the merits of the dispute in order to influence its outcome. . . .

As to the particular consumer's interest in the free flow of commercial information, that interest may be as keen, if not keener by far, than his interest in the day's most urgent political debate. Appellees' case in this respect is a convincing one. Those whom the suppression of prescription drug price information hits the hardest are the poor, the sick, and particularly the aged. A disproportionate amount of their income tends to be spent on prescription drugs; yet they are the least able to learn, by shopping from pharmacist to pharmacist, where their scarce dollars are best spent. When drug prices vary as strikingly as they do, information as to who is charging what becomes more than a convenience. It could mean the alleviation of physical pain or the enjoyment of basic necessities.

Generalizing, society also may have a strong interest in the free flow of commercial information. Even an individual advertisement, though entirely "commercial," may be of general public interest. . . .

Moreover, there is another consideration that suggests that no line between publicly "interesting" or "important" commercial advertising and the opposite kind could ever be drawn. Advertising, however tasteless and excessive it sometimes may seem, is nonetheless dissemination of information as to who is producing and selling what product, for what reason, and at what price. So long as we preserve a predominantly free enterprise economy, the allocation of our resources in large measure will be made through numerous private economic decisions. It is a matter of public interest that those decisions, in the aggregate, be intelligent and well informed. To this end, the free flow of commercial information is indispensable. . . .

* * *

It appears to be feared that if the pharmacist who wishes to provide low cost, and assertedly low quality, services is permitted to advertise, he will be taken up on his offer by too many unwitting customers. They will choose the low-cost, low-quality service and drive the "professional" pharmacist out of business. . . .

There is, of course, an alternative to this highly paternalistic approach. That alternative is to assume that this information is not in itself harmful, that people will perceive their own best interests if only they are well enough informed, and that the best means to that end is to open the channels of communication rather than to close them. If they are truly open, nothing prevents the "professional" pharmacist from marketing his own assertedly superior product, and contrasting it with that of the low-cost, high-volume prescription drug retailer. But the choice among these alternative approaches is not ours to make or the Virginia General Assembly's. It is precisely this kind of choice, between the dangers of suppressing information, and the dangers of its misuse if it is freely available, that the First Amendment makes for us. Virginia is free to require whatever professional standards it wishes of its pharmacists; it may subsidize them or protect them from competition in other ways. But it may not do so by keeping the public in ignorance of the entirely lawful terms that competing pharmacists are offering. . . .

* * *

The judgment of the District Court is affirmed.

Until relatively recently, few cases had tested the power of the states to limit the right of corporations to spend their own funds to speak the "corporate mind." Most corporate free speech cases concerned advertising, and few states have enacted laws that directly impinge on the freedom of companies to advertise. But some have done so, usually to limit the ability of corporations to sway voters in public referenda. In 1978, the Supreme Court finally confronted the issue head on.

FIRST NATIONAL BANK OF BOSTON v. BELLOTTI
435 U.S. 765 (1978)

MR. JUSTICE POWELL delivered the opinion of the Court.

In sustaining a state criminal statute that forbids certain expenditures by banks and business corporations for the purpose of influencing the vote on referendum proposals, the Massachusetts Supreme Judicial Court held that the First Amendment rights of a corporation are limited to issues that materially affect its business, property, or assets. The court rejected appellants' claim that the statute abridges freedom of speech in violation of the First and Fourteenth Amendments. The issue presented in this context is one of first impression in this Court. We postponed the question of jurisdiction to our consideration of the merits. We now reverse.

The statute at issue, Mass. Gen. Laws Ann., ch. 55, § 8 (West Supp. 1977), prohibits appellants, two national banking associations and three business corporations, from making contributions or expenditures "for the purpose of . . . influencing or affecting the vote on any question submitted to the voters, other than one materially affecting any of the property, business or assets of the corporation." The statute further specifies that "[n]o question submitted to the voters solely concerning the taxation of the income, property or transactions of individuals shall be deemed materially to affect the property, business or assets of the corporation." A corporation that violates § 8 may receive a maximum fine of $50,000; a corporate officer, director, or agent who violates the section may receive a maximum fine of $10,000 or imprisonment for up to one year, or both. Appellants wanted to spend money to publicize their views on a proposed constitutional amendment that was to be submitted to the voters as a ballot question at a general election on November 2, 1976. The amendment would have permitted the legislature to impose a graduated tax on the income of individuals. After appellee, the Attorney General of Massachusetts, informed appellants that he intended to enforce § 8 against them, they brought this action seeking to have the statute declared unconstitutional.

* * *

The court below framed the principal question in this case as whether and to what extent corporations have First Amendment rights. We believe that the court posed the wrong question. The Constitution often protects interests broader than those of the party seeking their vindication. The First Amendment, in particular, serves significant societal interests. The proper question therefore is not whether corporations "have" First Amendment rights and, if so, whether they are coextensive with those of natural persons. Instead, the question must be whether § 8 abridges expression that the First Amendment was meant to protect. We hold that it does.

The speech proposed by appellants is at the heart of the First Amendment's protection.

> The freedom of speech and of the press guaranteed by the Constitution embraces at the least the liberty to discuss publicly and truthfully all matters of public concern without previous restraint or fear of subsequent punishment. . . . Freedom of discussion, if it would fulfill its historic function in this nation, must embrace all issues about which information is needed or appropriate to enable the members of society to cope with the exigencies of their period. *Thornhill v. Alabama,* 310 U.S. 88, 101–102 (1940).

The referendum issue that appellants wish to address falls squarely within this description. In appellants' view, the enactment of a graduated personal income tax, as proposed to be authorized by constitutional amendment, would have a seriously adverse effect on the economy of the State. The importance of the referendum issue to the people and government of Massachusetts is not disputed. Its merits, however, are the subject of sharp disagreement.

* * *

We thus find no support in the First or Fourteenth Amendment, or in the decisions of this Court, for the proposition that speech that otherwise would be within the protection of the First Amendment loses that protection simply because its source is a corporation that cannot prove, to the satisfaction of a court, a material effect on its business or property. The "materially affecting" requirement is not an identification of the boundaries of corporate speech etched by the Constitution itself. Rather, it amounts to an impermissible legislative prohibition of speech based on the identity of the interests that spokesmen may represent in public debate over controversial issues and a requirement that the speaker have a sufficiently great interest in the subject to justify communication.

Section 8 permits a corporation to communicate to the public its views on certain referendum subjects—those materially affecting its business—but not others. It also singles out one kind of ballot question—individual taxation—as a subject about which corporations may never make their ideas public. The legislature has drawn the line between permissible and impermissible speech according to whether there is a sufficient nexus, as defined by the legislature, between the issue presented to the voters and the business interests of the speaker.

In the realm of protected speech, the legislature is constitutionally disqualified from dictating the subjects about which persons may speak and the speakers who may address a public issue. If a legislature may direct business corporations to "stick to business," it also may limit other corporations—religious, charitable, or civic—to their respective "business" when addressing the public. Such power in government to channel the expression of views is unacceptable under the First Amendment. Especially where, as here, the legislature's suppression of speech suggests an attempt to give one side of a debatable public question an advantage in expressing its views to the people, the First Amendment is plainly offended.

* * *

Because that portion of § 8 challenged by appellants prohibits protected speech in a manner unjustified by a compelling state interest, it must be invalidated. The judgment of the Supreme Judicial Court is reversed.

In a series of other rulings, the Supreme Court has broadened free speech rights. It has held, for example, that a state public service commission may not prohibit an electric utility from advertising, even though the commission's purpose was to conserve energy. [Central Hudson Gas v. Public Service Commission, 447 U.S. 557 (1980)] It refused to sanction an ordinance prohibiting home owners from posting "for sale" signs to promote a racially integrated community and to stem "white flight." [Linmark Associates, Inc. v. Willingboro, 431 U.S. 85 (1977)] But in 1986, the Court may have turned about-face in holding that Puerto Rico may ban casinos from gambling advertising designed to reach residents of the island. The Court seemed to be saying that legislatures may ban advertising of any activity that itself could be banned (even if it has not in fact been banned)—such as gambling, the sale of liquor and cigarettes, and other products now legal but considered harmful. [Posadas de Puerto Rico Associates v. Tourism Co. of Puerto Rico, 106 S.Ct. 2968 (1986)]

Other Rights of the Corporation

In 1887, without any discussion, the Supreme Court declared that corporations are "persons" within the meaning of the Fourteenth Amendment. But to say that a corporation is a person does not automatically describe what its rights are, for the courts have not accorded the corporation every right guaranteed a human being. However, the courts have concluded that corporations are entitled to the essential constitutional protections of due process. They are also entitled to Fourth Amendment protection against unreasonable search and seizure; in other words, the police must have a search warrant to enter corporate premises and look through files. The double jeopardy clause applies to criminal prosecutions of corporations; an acquittal cannot be appealed, nor can the case be retried. For purposes of the federal courts' diversity jurisdiction (see pp. 69–70), a corporation is deemed to be a citizen both of the state in which it is incorporated and the state in which it has its principal place of business.

The cases are equally clear, though, that corporations lack certain rights that natural persons possess. For example, corporations do not have a privilege against self-incrimination, guaranteed by the Fifth and Fourteenth Amendments. In any legal proceeding, the courts may force the corporation to turn over incriminating documents, even if they also incriminate officers or employees of the corporation. Corporations are not citizens under the "privileges and immunities" clause of Article IV of the Constitution, so that the states may discriminate between domestic and foreign corporations. And the corporation is not entitled to federal review of state criminal convictions, as are many individuals.

The Right to Property: Eminent Domain and Just Compensation

At common law, the sovereign could take private property for public use as long as the owner was compensated for the loss. The Fifth Amendment incorporated this power of "eminent domain," requiring the federal government to pay "just compensation" for any property it takes. Both a public purpose and a just compensation are constitutionally prerequisite to the taking.

Originally, the Fifth Amendment's command to pay just compensation applied to the federal government only, but with the ratification of the Fourteenth Amendment, the clause came to be applied to the states as well. In 1896 the Court ruled that a state may take property only for a public use, and the next year it held that just compensation is an essential element of any exercise of eminent domain.

What constitutes a public use is largely for the states themselves to say.

The courts are ordinarily unwilling to contradict a state's declaration that the taking is for a public purpose. Thus, in a recent case, the Supreme Court upheld the Hawaii legislature's decision to force the seventy-two private landowners who held nearly half the state's land (almost all the rest was held by the state and federal governments) to sell to their tenants. As long as the owners were compensated, the legislature's determination to correct "the land oligopoly problem" was held to be a rational exercise of eminent domain. The land's transfer to private individuals did not invalidate the *purpose* of the taking, which was to remedy a pressing *public* problem. [Hawaii Housing Authority v. Midkiff, 467 U.S. 229 (1984)] We discuss this case further on p. 642.

The principle of just compensation is simple enough when applied to a physical taking of the property—when the state actually takes over a building or condemns a parcel of land to build a highway. A more difficult problem arises when a state does not take the property outright, but through some economic regulation, interferes with its use. Modern regulations constantly interfere with the ways we use our property; indeed, that is their very purpose. The problem of taking is thus transferred from the confiscation of title to the losses that flow from regulation.

When government regulates an activity clearly injurious to the public, the courts are unlikely to find that the owner has suffered compensable harm. A factory that pollutes the air or waterways will not find the courts receptive to its plea that it be compensated for loss of the opportunity to continue to pollute. But suppose the town council decides it wants to preserve old buildings so that the current owner is hamstrung in how the house or office may be used. Has the property been "taken," in Justice Holmes's arresting phrase, through "the petty larceny of the police power?" Holmes declared that the premise for regulation without compensation was necessity: "Government could hardly go on if to some extent values incident to property could not be diminished without paying for every such change in the general law. As long recognized, some values are enjoyed under an implied limitation and must yield to the police power. But obviously the implied limitation must have its limits." When are losses only incidental to regulation, so that no compensation need be paid? When is the regulation so severe that it amounts to a taking for which just compensation becomes a constitutional requirement?

The answer is that each case turns on its specific facts. The Court has upheld the general principle of zoning, so that a municipality may determine that some property may be used for residences and others only for business, without the municipality having to compensate owners who would rather devote their property to another use. [Euclid v. Ambler Realty Co., 272 U.S. 365 (1926)] Even when the zoning ordinance drastically limits the use of land, the Court will ordinarily uphold the ordinance if the land may be used at all. Thus, in a 1980 case, the Court upheld an ordinance that rezoned suburban land so that a developer could no longer build as many housing units as he had planned; the Court noted that the ordinance did not "prevent the best use" of the land. [Agins v. Tiburon, 447 U.S. 255 (1980); see p. 644.]

But in 1987, the court signaled that it may be moving in a new direction. At issue was a Los Angeles County ordinance designed to cope with serious flooding. Heavy rainstorms had washed away an area previously devastated by fire; the ordinance banned construction in the area. A church that ran a campground for handicapped children was effectively barred from rebuilding its campsite. It sued on an "inverse condemnation" theory, a claim that the county had in effect condemned the land and thus owed the church compensation for the loss of its property. The state courts, following precedent, held that Los Angeles was not obliged to provide compensation for this regulation because at most the deprivation was merely temporary. The theory was that no compensation is due until a court has first ruled that a regulation has "taken" the property. The remedy for this "temporary taking" is the court's declaration that the taking is unconstitutional unless compensated. The jurisdiction that enacted the ordinance may then repeal the ordinance; if it does, no compensation will be due, because the taking was merely temporary. If the ordinance is not repealed, compensation must then be paid only for the time after the ruling that the owner was deprived of the use of his property. Noting that the case had taken six years in the state courts and during that entire time the church was totally barred from using its property, the Supreme Court held that the county would have to compensate the church for the loss of its use from the time the ordinance first went into effect. [First English Evangelical Lutheran Church of Glendale v. Los Angeles, 107 S.Ct. 2378 (1987)]

The Court also ruled in 1987 that a zoning ordinance designed to protect beachfront views could not require, without compensation, beachfront owners (a married couple) to give the public an easement to the ocean across their property in return for permission to rebuild their house. The Court said that an outright denial of a permit would not have been a taking, assuming that the denial "substantially advanced" a legitimate state interest. But the easement had no relationship whatsoever to the rebuilding permit; linking the two was simply a means of extracting an easement from the owners, and the direct imposition of an easement would clearly have been a taking requiring compensation. [Nollan v. California Coastal Commission, 107 S.Ct. 3141 (1987)]

Whether these decisions mean that legislatures everywhere must be far more wary about adopting "police power" regulations that affect the use of property remains to be seen. Such decisions may indicate that the Court will be far tougher in the future about the impact of regulations on the loss of use, or they may simply mean that the Court will look askance at any regulation that either deprives an owner of *all* use or gives physical access to others. "One thing is certain," said Justice Stevens in dissent. "The Court's decision will generate a great deal of litigation."

But even before these decisions, it was clear that the Court would not countenance actual physical invasions of property unless the taking authority paid compensation. For example, a New York ordinance required owners of rental buildings to allow cable television companies to install cables on the buildings without charge. But even though the cables occupied little space (between one-eighth and one-and-one-half cubic feet), the Court said that the cable company had to pay for any "permanent physical occupation." [Loretto v. TelePrompter Manhattan CATV Corp., 458 U.S. 419 (1982)]

The Right to Unimpaired Contracts

Article I of the Constitution prohibits states from passing any "law impairing the obligation of contracts." This clause was aimed at legislation that would absolve debtors of their financial obligations. An important provision at the time of ratification, it became relatively impotent by the mid-nineteenth century, when the Court had ruled that the states' police power (that is, the power to protect the health, safety, good order, comfort, and general welfare of the community) may not be bargained away. If you and I enter a contract for the sale of lottery tickets, the Contract Clause will not prevent the state thereafter from passing a law prohibiting such a transaction. In 1934, in the midst of the Depression, the Supreme Court went so far as to uphold a Minnesota "mortgage moratorium" law, suspending for two years the right of banks to foreclose on defaulted mortgages. The Court noted that the law was temporary and did not repudiate the debts but was limited to changes in the remedy provided in the law for breach of contract. [Home Building & Loan Ass'n v. Blaisdell, 290 U.S. 398 (1934)] The Contract Clause seemed almost dead.

But in 1977 the Court revived it, holding against New Jersey in its attempt to repeal a covenant it had enacted as security for holders of bonds of the Port Authority of New York and New Jersey. The covenant made it difficult for the Port Authority to use bond revenues to subsidize rail operations. The Court held that although courts must generally defer to states when they interfere with private contracts, the courts must scrutinize any state attempts to impair their own contractual obligations, as in this case. [United States Trust Co. v. New Jersey, 431 U.S. 1 (1977)]

In 1978, the Court expanded the reach of the Contract Clause to protect private contracts against state claims of necessity when it struck down a Minnesota law requiring employers with established pension plans to modify retroactively the obligations they assumed toward their employees. [Allied Structural Steel Co. v. Spannaus, 438 U.S. 234 (1978)] But in later cases, the Court has pulled away from the more exacting scrutiny that it seemed to have announced in 1978. Thus, in a 1983 case, the Court upheld a Kansas law that effectively blocked a private supplier of natural gas from taking advantage of a clause in a contract that required a private utility to pay more for gas whenever the federal government increased the price at which suppliers could sell gas. The Court said that when anyone asserts a Contract Clause claim, courts must undertake a three-party inquiry: (1) Was a contractual right substantially impaired? (2) If so, did the state have any significant and legitimate public purpose in regulating? (3) If it did, was the contractual modification reasonably related to the reasons justifying the legislation? Unless the complainant can show that the state had no legitimate purpose in imposing a substantial impairment or that it had failed to adjust the modification of the contract to the law's purpose, the courts must defer to the states. [Energy Reserves Group v. Kansas Power & Light Co., 459 U.S. 400 (1983)] It seems unlikely that many challenges will withstand the rigors of this test, given a Court that in modern times is generally willing to defer to legislative judgments in the economic arena. That does not mean there is no remedy. As the Court said more than a century ago: "For protection against abuses by legislatures the people must resort to the polls."

Chapter Summary

Article I of the U.S. Constitution gives Congress the power to regulate interstate and foreign commerce. The Supreme Court has broadly construed the Commerce Clause. "Commerce" means more than merely buying or selling; it connotes the whole stream of activities, including the manufacture and transportation of commodities and the providing of services. Congress can reach deeply into economic matters within the states, for any activity that "affects" interstate commerce is subject to federal regulation. If Congress has enacted a law under the Commerce Clause any state law or regulation that conflicts with it is invalid.

The states continue to have a large role in business regulation. Under their "police powers," the state may enact all sorts of regulations that reasonably relate to the public health, safety, morals, and welfare. Although the Supreme Court once limited the power of states to act (by declaring certain types of economic regulations invalid under the due process clause), today the courts for the most part have recognized the constitutional validity of economic regulation, as long as the means employed rationally relate to a legitimate state goal. Wholly arbitrary laws, however, will be struck down. Moreover, before taking away property or denying some other valuable right, or permitting private individuals to do so, the state must provide a hearing to those whose property or rights are affected.

Although the equal protection clause of the Fourteenth Amendment, as interpreted in recent years, has provided women, minorities, and other groups with a powerful means of ending legalized discrimination, businesses generally cannot claim its protection. The Supreme Court almost always allows the states to distinguish among different types of economic activities when enacting laws or writing regulations.

Despite the breadth of the police power, the states may not enact regulations over commerce if the effect is to discriminate against out-of-state business or to burden interstate commerce. Local protectionism is a violation of the Commerce Clause. The theory of the Constitution is that a national market without barriers shall exist among the states to ensure the flow of trade.

Corporations enjoy certain rights available to all persons. These include the freedoms of speech and press. The government may not tell business how or what it may truthfully advertise. But companies are not entitled to every right applicable to individuals. For example, corporations do not enjoy the privilege against self-incrimination—corporations must turn over incriminating documents to the courts on demand.

The government may seize private property for a public purpose if it pays just compensation. Any sort of physical invasion or occupation is deemed a taking for payment purposes. But not every interference with the use of property amounts to a taking so that only some economic regulations require payment to those whose use or enjoyment of property is undermined by the regulation.

The Contract Clause says that the states may not impair the obligation of contracts, but for the most part the courts have held that all private contracts are subject to the reasonable exercise of the police power.

Problems

1. A congressional investigation revealed that conditions in a particular mining industry were perilous to the miners. As a result of the investigation, Congress proposed to enact a statute regulating the number of hours that workers could spend in the mines and setting forth a variety of safety measures that the mining companies would have to follow. Critics of the proposed law objected on the ground that the industry was concentrated entirely in one state and that the state for years had refused to regulate it. What source of power for Congress to regulate mining conditions could proponents of the federal law point to? What facts about the industry would have to be assumed for Congress to invoke that power?
2. A student is suspected of smoking marijuana in a local high school. The principal wishes to suspend him. Must the principal give the student a hearing before doing so? Why? A book club decides to terminate a member because she has not paid her bill. Must the club give the member a hearing before doing so? Why? What does your answer depend on? Assuming that there is no law dealing with the book club, what branch(es) of which government(s) could make one?

3. You make a deal with Fred to paint the outside of your house with a special paint that Fred prepares. It is a lead-based paint that will give your house special protection. You give Fred a down payment, but before he can start the job, your town council passes an ordinance banning, for health reasons, the use of lead-based paint on any structure. Fred refuses to use the paint, and you sue him for breach of contract. You assert that your contract with Fred has been impaired by the ordinance and that it is therefore unconstitutional. What result?
4. Your city has a major league baseball franchise. The team threatens to move because it doesn't like the way its fans have been treating it (they boo and throw beer cans onto the infield). The city council passes a bill "seizing" the team's franchise under its power of eminent domain. What arguments could the team make in challenging the seizure? Who would win?
5. The state passes a law requiring all opticians to have a prescription from a medical doctor before selling lenses or frames to any customer. The law even requires that a customer who wants a new frame for her lenses must have a prescription before the optician can fit her current lenses into the new frame. The law exempts sellers of ready-to-wear sunglasses. What constitutional objections can the opticians make to this law? Who will win in a court test of the law?

3

Courts and the Legal Process

In the United States, law and government are interdependent. The Constitution created the basic framework of government and imposes certain limitations on the powers of government. In turn, the various branches of government are intimately involved in the making, enforcing, and interpreting of law. Much of the law today is statutory—emanating from Congress and the state legislatures. But the student of law is concerned with the courts, because it is there that law in its broadest sense is interpreted and understood—it is up to the courts to determine what a law in a particular case actually means.

The Relationship of the State and Federal Court Systems

It is sometimes said that there are two separate court systems in the United States: state and federal. The reality is more complex. In fact there are fifty-two court systems: those of the fifty states, the local court systems in the

District of Columbia, and the federal court system. At the same time, these are not entirely separate. They have several points of contact.

From the states' perspective, there are a number of instances in which the local courts must honor federal law or the laws of other states.

1. State courts are bound to uphold federal law in the face of conflicting state laws under the Supremacy Clause of the Constitution.
2. There are a number of claims arising under federal statutes that may be tried in the state courts. In other words, the jurisdiction of the federal courts to hear cases under federal law is not always *exclusive*.
3. Under the Full Faith and Credit Clause, each state court is obligated to respect the final judgments of courts in other states. Thus, a divorce decree handed down by an Arkansas court cannot be relitigated in North Dakota.
4. State courts frequently must consider the laws of other states in deciding cases involving issues that cut across state lines—two drivers, each from a different state, collide in a third state. A body of law known as "conflicts of laws" dictates, under these circumstances, that courts should look to the law of the state where the accident happened.

As state courts are concerned with federal law, so federal courts often are concerned with proceedings in state courts. Because federal law is supreme, decisions of the state courts sometimes can be appealed to the federal courts. Usually appeal is from the state supreme court to the U.S. Supreme Court. In certain types of cases, a lower federal court can hear an appeal—for example, a *habeas corpus* petition from a prisoner in a state jail complaining that his constitutional rights were violated during his trial. Federal courts also consider state claims when a case involves both state and federal issues. The federal issues permit the federal court to take jurisdiction over the whole case, including the state issues; the federal court is said to exercise "pendent jurisdiction" over the state claims.

There is also a broad category of cases heard in federal courts that concern only state legal issues—namely, cases that arise between citizens of different states. The federal courts are permitted to hear these cases under their so-called **diversity of citizenship** jurisdiction, or diversity jurisdiction. A citizen of New Jersey may sue a citizen of New York over a contract dispute in federal court, whereas if both were citizens of New Jersey, the plaintiff would be limited to the state courts. This diversity jurisdiction was established in the Constitution because it was feared that local courts would be hostile toward people from other states and that they therefore needed politically separate courts. Today, one quarter of all lawsuits filed in federal court are based on diversity of citizenship. Although it is unlikely that the outcome of many cases in state court would be affected by the citizenship of the parties, there can be advantages to pressing a suit in federal court. Federal procedures are often more efficient than state court procedures, federal dockets are often less crowded and hence a case can go forward faster, and many lawyers enjoy the generally higher status that comes in practicing before the federal bench. But in any federal case based on diversity jurisdiction, the court must apply state law, whether legislative enactment or judicial decision. When the law of the state is unclear, the federal courts are not free to substitute their own independent judgment; they must attempt to predict how the state courts would rule on the issue if presented with the same case.

State Court Systems

Most lawsuits in America are brought to state courts. Despite the great variety of court systems that exist from state to state, two types of judicial *functions* are common to all: trials and appeals. A court exercising a **trial** function has *original jurisdiction*—that is, jurisdiction to determine the facts of the case and apply the law to them. A court that hears **appeals** from the trial court is said to have *appellate jurisdiction*—it must accept the facts as determined by the trial court and limit its review to the lower court's theory of the applicable law.

Limited Jurisdiction Courts In most of the large urban states, and in many of the smaller states, there are four and sometimes five levels of courts. The lowest level is that of the **limited jurisdiction** courts. These are usually the county or municipal courts with original jurisdiction to hear minor criminal cases (petty assaults, traffic offenses, breach of peace, and the like) and civil cases involving monetary amounts up to a fixed ceiling (in most states no more than $10,000 and in many states far less). Most disputes in the United States that wind up in court are handled in the 18,000-plus limited jurisdiction courts, which are estimated to hear more than 80 percent of all cases in the states.

A variant of the limited jurisdiction court is the **small claims court**, with jurisdiction to hear civil cases involving claims for amounts ranging between $1,000 and $5,000 in about half the states and in the other states for considerably less ($500 to $1,000). The advantage of the small claims court is that its procedures are informal, it is often located in neighborhoods outside the business districts, it is usually open after business hours, and it is speedy. Lawyers are not necessary to present the case and in some states are not allowed to appear in court.

General Jurisdiction Courts All other civil and criminal cases are heard in the general trial courts, or courts of **general jurisdiction.** These go by a variety of names—often, Superior, Circuit, District, or Common Pleas Court. (New York anomalously calls its general trial court the Supreme Court.) It is to these courts that suitors seek redress for injuries suffered in automobile accidents, for breach of contract, and for the thousands of other calamities that can befall the individual or corporation in the modern world. In these courts also the state prosecutes those accused of murder, rape, robbery, and other serious crimes. Generally at the election of the parties, the fact-finder in the courts of general jurisdiction is not the judge, as in the lower courts, but a jury of citizens.

Although courts of general jurisdiction can hear every type of case, in most states more than half the civil filings involve family matters (divorce, child custody disputes, and the like). A study conducted by the U.S. Department of Justice showed that in a specially selected sample of five general jurisdiction courts, commercial cases made up about one-third of the courts' dockets in the late 1970s. About 12 percent of the dockets were devoted to automobile accident cases and other torts (discussed in Chapter 9).

Many states have specialized courts that hear only a certain class of cases—for example, landlord-tenant disputes or probate of wills.

By and large, cases decided by judges in the courts of limited jurisdiction are concluded at that point. Some of these cases can be retried, if one of the parties is dissatisfied with the outcome, in a court of general jurisdiction. This kind of retrial is known as a trial *de novo*. It is not an appeal, since the case is begun afresh.

Appellate Courts In most states, the losing party in a general jurisdiction court can take an appeal to an **intermediate appellate** court—usually called the Court of Appeals. These courts do not retry the evidence but sit instead to determine whether the trial was conducted in a procedurally proper manner and whether appropriate law was applied properly to the facts. For example, the **appellant** (the losing party who takes the appeal) might complain that the judge wrongly instructed the jury on the meaning of the law, or improperly admitted into evidence the testimony of a particular witness, or misconstrued the law in question. (The party who won in the lower court and is defending that judgment is called the **appellee**.) The appellate court can *affirm* the judgment of the lower court, *modify* it, *reverse* it, or *reverse and remand*—that is, return the case to the lower court for retrial.

The final avenue of appeal within the state court systems is to the state supreme court, which in most states sits in the state capital as a single panel of between five and nine judges. (The intermediate appellate courts usually sit in panels of three judges and are located in various parts of the state.) In a few states the highest court goes by a different name; in New York, for example, it is known as the Court of Appeals. Some types of cases may be appealed at the option of the appellant (appeal *of right*). In many states, however, the supreme court has the discretion to select the cases it wishes to hear. For most litigants, the ruling of the state supreme court is final. In a relatively narrow class of cases—those in which federal constitutional claims are made—appeal to the U.S. Supreme Court remains a possibility.

The Federal Court System

District Courts The federal judicial system is uniform throughout the United States and consists of three levels. The trial courts are known as **district** courts. Every state is divided into federal districts, ranging from one in the less populous states to four in California, Texas, and New York. The federal court with the heaviest commercial docket is the United States District Court for the Southern District of New York (Manhattan). There are 97 district courts, and Congress has authorized 575 U.S. district judges. The district judge conducts all federal trials, criminal and civil.

Courts of Appeals Cases can be appealed to the circuit courts of appeal, of which there are thirteen (Figure 3-1). Each circuit oversees the work of the district courts in several states. For example, the U.S. Court of Appeals for the Second Circuit hears appeals from the district courts in New York, Connecticut, and Vermont. The U.S. Court of Appeals for the Ninth Circuit hears appeals from the district courts in California, Oregon, Nevada, Montana, Washington, Idaho, Arizona, Alaska, Hawaii, and Guam. The U.S. Court of Appeals for the District of Columbia Circuit hears appeals from the district court in Washington, D.C., as well as from numerous federal administrative agencies (see Chapter 5). The U.S. Court of Appeals for the Federal Circuit, also located in Washington, D.C., hears appeals in patent and customs cases. Appeals are heard by panels of three judges. Congress has authorized 168 circuit judges.

There are also several specialized courts in the federal judicial system. These include the U.S. Tax Court and the Court of Claims.

United States Supreme Court Overseeing the circuit courts is the U.S. Supreme Court, which sits in Washington, D.C. It consists of nine justices—the chief justice of the United States and eight associate justices. (This number is not constitutionally required; Congress can establish any number. It has been set at nine since after the Civil War.) The Supreme Court has discretionary control over most of its docket. The cases that by law it must hear represent only a tiny fraction of the cases that pour in. During its 1986–1987 term, of the 4,339 cases the Supreme Court disposed of, it granted *certiorari*—a writ to a lower court to hand over the records in a case for review—in fewer than 250 and disposed of only 277 cases on the merits. The Supreme Court does not sit in panels. All the justices hear and consider each case together. The Supreme Court can also hear appeals from state cases. These usually are appeals from the decisions of state supreme courts, but if there is no other avenue of appeal and constitutional issues are raised, a case can be appealed even from courts of limited jurisdiction.

Unlike state judges, most of whom are elected and sit for a fixed term

Figure 3-1 The Thirteen Federal Judicial Circuits

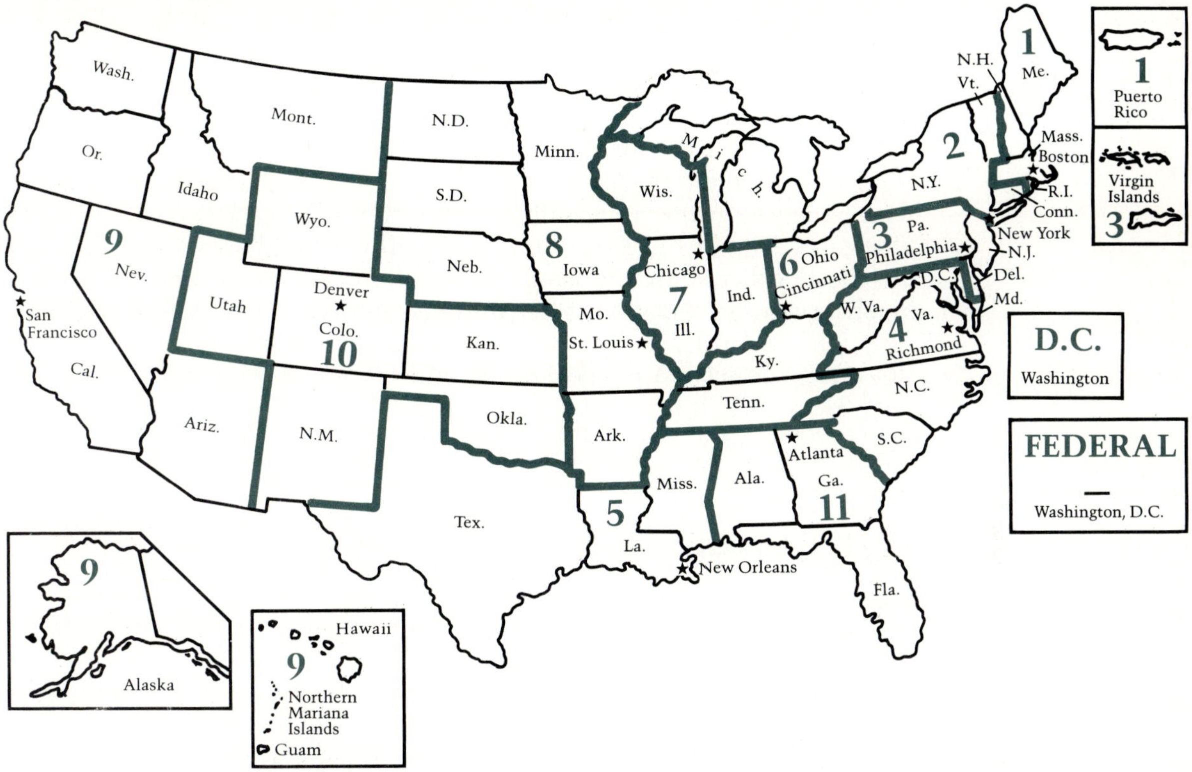

of years, federal judges are nominated by the president and must be confirmed by the Senate. They sit for life, although a law providing for retirement at age seventy at full pay induces most federal judges to retire and become "senior" judges. They may continue to hear cases but need not maintain a full workload. Retired judges are not counted in the totals of authorized judges, so the president may appoint a new judge when a sitting judge "takes senior status."

Federal Jurisdiction The federal judicial system hears few cases relative to the state dockets. Its jurisdiction is spelled out in the Constitution. Congress can limit the jurisdiction of federal courts—for example, until 1875, Congress did not permit the federal district courts to hear cases arising under federal law. But, as Chief Justice Marshall taught in *Marbury* v. *Madison*, Congress may not enlarge federal jurisdiction.

Today, federal courts have jurisdiction virtually coextensive with that laid down as permissible in the Constitution. That includes: (1) cases to which the United States itself is a party; (2) disputes between states, between a state and citizens of another state, between citizens of different states (diversity of citizenship, as discussed on pp. 69–70), between a state or its citizens and a foreign government or its citizens, and disputes affecting foreign ambassadors and other such officials; (3) cases "arising under [the] Constitution, the laws of the United States, and treaties made, or which shall be made, under their authority"; and (4) admiralty and maritime cases. The first and third categories provide the bulk of the cases now in federal court. Cases "arising under" the Constitution and federal law involve claims of violations of civil rights, antitrust, environmental, patent, copyright, securities, and scores of other congressional statutes. For diversity cases, the second category above, the amount in controversy must exceed $10,000; if it is smaller, the dispute must be heard in state court.

Legal Procedure

Adjudication and the Adversary System

Courts are not the only institutions that can resolve disputes. We will examine alternative forums in Chapter 4. For now, let us consider the nature of **adjudication,** the process by which courts make decisions.

Courts do not resolve disputes any which way they please. Judicial decision-making is a distinctive form of dispute resolution. In the first place, courts sit to resolve **disputes,** not problems or generalized grievances—to get the attention of a court, the litigant must make a claim of legal right or entitlement. Second, courts do not reach out for cases. A case must be brought to the court in a particular way that we will explore shortly.

Once at the court, the case will proceed through the **proofs** (submission of evidence) and **arguments** (debate about the meaning of the evidence and the law) of contesting parties. This is the essential characteristic of the **adversary system,** in which those who oppose each other may attack the other's case through proofs and cross-examination. Every person in the United States who wishes to take a case to court is entitled to hire a lawyer. In felony cases—that is, serious crimes—and in many cases involving lesser crimes (misdemeanors) the state must provide a lawyer free to a defendant who cannot afford one. The lawyer works for his client, not the court, and serves him as an advocate. The client wishes to persuade the court of the accuracy and propriety of his position. The lawyer's duty is to shape the evidence and the argument—that is, the line of reasoning about the evidence—to advance his client's cause and persuade the court of its rightness. The lawyer for the opposing **party** (as a litigant is known in court) will be doing the same thing, of course, for her client. From this crossfire of evidence and argument the judge (or, if one is sitting, the jury) must sort out the facts and reach a conclusion.

The method of adjudication has several important characteristics. (1) It places the issues in controversy in sharp focus. Tangential concerns are minimized or excluded altogether. **Relevance** is a key concept in any trial. The judge is required to decide the questions presented at the trial, not to discourse on related matters that a legislature might wish to take up if the matter were before the people's elected representatives. (2) Adjudication requires that the judge's decision be reasoned, which is why judges write opinions explaining their decisions (an opinion may be omitted when the verdict comes from the jury). (3) The judge's decision must not only be reasoned, but also be responsive to the case presented: the judge is not free to say that the case bores him or is unimportant and that he therefore will ignore it. Unlike other branches of government that are free to ignore problems pressing upon them, judges *must* decide cases. By contrast, the legislature need not enact a law, no matter how many people petition it to do so. (4) Moreover, the court must respond in a certain way. The judge must pay attention to the parties' arguments and his decision must be an outgrowth of their proofs and arguments.

Because it must proceed from the parties' proofs and arguments, the judicial decision cannot turn on the whim of the judge. Moreover, there are particular standards for determining which side must prevail, although the standards can be difficult to apply in any given case. These standards are called the **burden of proof.** In all cases, the **plaintiff**—the party making a claim and initiating the lawsuit (in a criminal case the plaintiff is the **prosecution**)—has the burden of proving his case. If he fails to prove it, the **defendant**—the party being sued or prosecuted—will win. Criminal prosecutions carry the most rigorous burden of proof: the government must prove its case against the defendant *beyond a reasonable doubt.* Even if it seems more probable than not that the defendant committed the crime, as long as there remains some reasonable doubt—perhaps she was not clearly identified as the culprit, perhaps she has an alibi that could be legitimate—she must be acquitted. Certain types of civil cases, especially those involving decisions of administrative agencies of the government, call for *clear and convincing* proof. This burden, too, is higher than a more-probable-than-not standard. The burden in ordinary civil cases—those dealing with contracts, personal injuries, and most of the cases in this book—is that of a *preponderance of the evidence,* which simply means that the plaintiff's evidence of his claim that he was wrongfully injured by the defendant must outweigh the defendant's evidence casting doubt on the plaintiff's claim.

The adversary system has been praised and deplored. Its detractors stress that it values winning too highly and demeans the truth and the sensibilities of people who stand in the way of a client's victory. Moreover, an adversary system can impose high costs and long delays on the parties.

When fact-finding is in the hands of the parties themselves, they can employ one artifice or another to stretch out the proceedings in an attempt to cause their opponents to lose heart or pocketbook.

At the same time, the adversary process is a bulwark of liberty in a free society. Without independent counsel, free to contest the claims of a government bent on jailing its political enemies, dissenters can rather easily be imprisoned, though they committed no crimes—as the records of the Soviet Union and of other authoritarian regimes clearly demonstrate. Likewise, without the ability to search relentlessly for facts and to probe the other side, serious wrongs would go unredressed. The law itself might be an empty shell.

Adjudication and the adversary system imply certain other characteristics of courts. (1) Judges must be impartial. Those with a personal interest in a matter before them must refuse to hear it. (2) The ruling of a court, after all appeals are exhausted, is final. This principle is known as *res judicata* (Latin for "the thing is decided"), which means that the parties may not take up their quarrel in another court at another time. (3) Finally, a court must proceed according to a public set of formal procedural rules; a judge cannot make up the rules of the game as he goes along. To these rules we now turn.

How a Case Goes Through Court

Complaint and Summons Beginning a lawsuit is simple and is spelled out in the rules of procedure by which each court system operates. In the federal system, the plaintiff begins a lawsuit by filing a **complaint**—a typed document spelling out in general terms his grounds for suit—with the clerk of the court. The court marshal will then serve the defendant with the complaint and a **summons**, a court document stating the name of the plaintiff and his attorney and directing the defendant to **answer** (respond to) the complaint within a fixed period. Many state court systems use the same rule. Others permit suits to be initiated by serving the defendant directly, either with the summons and complaint or sometimes with just the summons, before going to court. For ease of description, the discussion in this section speaks in terms of actions by plaintiff and defendant; in most cases, the actions will be taken by their lawyers.

The timing of the filing can be important. Virtually every possible legal complaint is governed by a federal or state **statute of limitations**, which requires a lawsuit to be filed within a certain period of time. For example, in many states a lawsuit for injuries resulting from an automobile accident must be filed within two years of the accident or the plaintiff forfeits his right to proceed.

Jurisdiction and Venue The place of filing is equally important. Two considerations govern. The first is **jurisdiction**—the proper type of court. A claim for breach of contract, in which the amount at stake is $1 million, cannot be brought in a local county court with jurisdiction to hear cases involving sums of up to only $1,000. Likewise, a claim for copyright violation cannot be brought in state superior court, since copyright cases are within the exclusive jurisdiction of the federal courts. Jurisdiction of the courts is determined by federal and state statute.

The second consideration is **venue**—that is, the proper geographic location of the court. For example, every county in a state might have a superior court, but the plaintiff is not free to pick any county. Again, a statute will spell out to which court the plaintiff must go—for instance, the county in which he resides or the county in which the defendant resides or maintains an office.

Service of Process The defendant must be **served**—that is, she must receive notice that she has been sued. Usually service can be done by physically presenting the defendant with a copy of the summons and complaint. But sometimes the defendant is difficult to find, or deliberately avoids the marshal or other process server. The rules spell out a variety of ways by which individuals and corporations can be served, including by mail and by service on a designated agent.

One of the most troublesome problems is service on a defendant who is out of state. The jurisdiction of a state court ordinarily reaches only those found within the state. If the plaintiff claims that an out-of-state defendant injured him in some way, must the plaintiff go to the defendant's home state? Unless the defendant had some significant contact with the plaintiff's state, the plaintiff may indeed have to. For instance, suppose a traveler from Maine stopped in at a roadside diner in Montana and ordered a slice of homemade pie that was tainted and caused him to be sick. The traveler may not simply return home and mail the diner a notice that he is suing it in a Maine court. But if out-of-state defendants have some contact with the plaintiff's state of residence, there might be grounds to bring them within the jurisdiction of the plaintiff's state courts. The basic rationale is set forth in the following case.

INTERNATIONAL SHOE CO. v. WASHINGTON
326 U.S. 310 (1945)

MR. CHIEF JUSTICE STONE delivered the opinion of the Court.

The question for decision is whether, within the limitations of the due process clause of the Fourteenth Amendment, appellant, a Delaware corporation, has by its activities in the State of Washington rendered itself amenable to proceedings in the courts of that state to recover unpaid contributions to the state unemployment compensation fund exacted by state statutes. . . .

* * *

The statutes in question set up a comprehensive scheme of unemployment compensation, the costs of which are defrayed by contributions required to be made by employers to a state unemployment compensation fund. The contributions are a specified percentage of the wages payable annually by each employer for his employees' services in the state. The assessment and collection of the contributions and the fund are administered by appellees. Section 14 (c) of the Act . . . authorizes appellee Commissioner to issue an order and notice of assessment of delinquent contributions upon prescribed personal service of the notice upon the employer if found within the state, or, if not so found, by mailing the notice to the employer by registered mail at his last known address. . . .

In this case notice of assessment for the years in question was personally served upon a sales solicitor employed by appellant in the State of Washington, and a copy of the notice was mailed by registered mail to appellant at its address in St. Louis, Missouri. Appellant appeared specially before the office of unemployment and moved to set aside the order and notice of assessment on the ground that the service upon appellant's salesman was not proper service upon appellant; that appellant was not a corporation of the State of Washington and was not doing business within the state; that it had no agent within the state upon whom service could be made; and that appellant is not an employer and does not furnish employment within the meaning of the statute.

The motion was heard on evidence and a stipulation of facts by the appeal tribunal which denied the motion and ruled that appellee Commissioner was entitled to recover the unpaid contributions. That action was affirmed by the Commissioner; both the Superior Court and the Supreme Court affirmed. . . .

The facts as found by the appeal tribunal and accepted by the state Superior Court and Supreme Court, are not in dispute. Appellant is a Delaware corporation, having its principal place of business in St. Louis, Missouri, and is engaged in the manufacture and sale of shoes and other footwear. It maintains places of business in several states, other than Washington, at which its manufacturing is carried on and from which its merchandise is distributed interstate through several sales units or branches located outside the State of Washington.

Appellant has no office in Washington and makes no contracts either for sale or purchase of merchandise there. It maintains no stock of merchandise in that state and makes there no deliveries of goods in intrastate commerce. During the years from 1937 to 1940, now in question, appellant employed eleven to thirteen salesmen under direct supervision and control of sales managers located in St. Louis. These salesmen resided in Washington; their principal activities were confined to that state; and they were compensated by commissions based upon the amount of their sales. The commissions for each year totaled more than $31,000. Appellant supplies its salesmen with a line of samples, each consisting of one shoe of a pair, which they display to prospective purchasers. On occasion they rent permanent sample rooms, for exhibiting samples, in business buildings, or rent rooms in hotels or business buildings temporarily for that purpose. The cost of such rentals is reimbursed by appellant.

The authority of the salesmen is limited to exhibiting their samples and soliciting orders from prospective buyers, at prices and on terms fixed by appellant. The salesmen transmit the orders to appellant's office in St. Louis for acceptance or rejection, and when accepted the merchandise for filling the orders is shipped f.o.b. from points outside Washington to the purchasers within the state. All the merchandise shipped into Washington is invoiced at the place of shipment from which collections are made. No salesman has authority to enter into contracts or to make collections.

* * *

Appellant also insists that its activities within the state were not sufficient to manifest its "presence" there and that in its absence the state courts were without jurisdiction, that consequently it was a denial of due process for the state to subject appellant to suit.

* * *

Historically the jurisdiction of courts to render judgment *in personam* is grounded on their de facto power over the defendant's person. Hence his presence within the territorial jurisdiction of a court was prerequisite to its rendition of a judgment personally binding him. But now . . . , due process requires only that in order to subject a defendant to a judgment *in personam,* if he be not present within the territory of the forum, he have certain minimum contacts with it such that the maintenance of the suit does not offend "traditional notions of fair play and substantial justice." *Milliken* v. *Meyer,* 311 U.S. 457, 463.

Since the corporate personality is a fiction, although a fiction intended to be acted upon as though it were a fact, it is clear that unlike an individual its "presence" without, as well as within, the state of its origin can be manifested only by activities carried on in its behalf by those who are authorized to act for it. To say that the corporation is so far "present" there as to satisfy due process requirements, for purposes of taxation or the maintenance of suits against it in the courts of the state, is to beg the question to be decided. For the terms "present" or "presence" are used merely to symbolize those activities of the corporation's agent within the state which courts will deem to be sufficient to satisfy the demands of due process.

* * *

It is evident that the criteria by which we mark the boundary line between those activities which justify the subjection of a corporation to suit, and those which do not, cannot be simply mechanical or quantitative. The test is not merely, as has sometimes been suggested, whether the activity, which the corporation has seen fit to procure through its agents in another state, is a little more or a little less. Whether due process is satisfied must depend rather upon the quality and nature of the activity in relation to the fair and orderly administration of the laws which it was the purpose of the due process clause to insure. That clause does not contemplate that a state may make binding a judgment *in personam* against an individual or corporate defendant with which the state has no contacts, ties, or relations.

But to the extent that a corporation exercises the privilege of conducting activities within a state, it enjoys the benefits and protection of the laws of that state. The exercise of that privilege may give rise to obligations, and, so far as those obligations arise out of or are connected with the activities within the state, a procedure which requires the corporation to respond to a suit brought to enforce them can, in most instances, hardly be said to be undue.

Applying these standards, the activities carried on in behalf of appellant in the State of Washington were neither irregular nor casual. They were systematic and continuous throughout the years in question. They resulted in a large volume of interstate business, in the course of which appellant received the benefits and protection of the laws of the state, including the right to resort to the courts for the enforcement of its rights. The obligation which is here sued upon arose out of those very activities. It is evident that these operations establish sufficient contacts or ties with the state of the forum to make it reasonable and just, according to our traditional conception of fair play and substantial justice, to permit the state to enforce the obligations which appellant has incurred there. Hence we cannot say that the maintenance of the present suit in the State of Washington involves an unreasonable or undue procedure.

We are likewise unable to conclude that the service of the process within the state upon an agent whose activities establish appellant's "presence" there was not sufficient notice of the suit, or that the suit was so unrelated to those activities as to make the agent an inappropriate vehicle for communicating the notice. It is enough that appellant has established such contacts with the state that the particular form of substituted service adopted there gives reasonable assurance that the notice will be actual. Nor can we say that the mailing of the notice of suit to appellant by registered mail at its home office was not reasonably calculated to apprise appellant of the suit.

* * *

Affirmed.

Decision on the Pleadings The initial papers in a lawsuit are called the **pleadings.** These include the complaint, the answer, and the **countercomplaint**, if there is one, in which the defendant asserts counterclaims against the plaintiff. In effect, the defendant becomes the plaintiff for the claims she has against the original plaintiff. The complaint must state the nature of the plaintiff's claim, the jurisdiction of the court, and the nature of the relief that he seeks (an award of money, an injunction, a declaration of legal rights). In her answer, the defendant might deny the entire complaint, or admit to certain of its allegations and deny others. The pleadings are usually quite general and give little detail.

Cases can be decided on the pleadings alone as follows: (1) If the defendant fails to answer the complaint, the court can enter a **default judgment**, awarding the plaintiff what he seeks. (2) The defendant can move to dismiss the complaint on the grounds that the plaintiff failed to "state a claim on which relief can be granted." The defendant is saying, in effect, that even if all the plaintiff's allegations are true, they do not amount to a legal claim. For example, a claim that the defendant induced a woman to stop dating the plaintiff is not actionable, and the court will dismiss the complaint without any further proceedings. This type of dismissal is often called a **demurrer.** (3) The defendant can admit all the facts in the complaint, and either party can then move for **summary judgment.** By so doing, they are telling the court that there is no factual dispute. Each argues that he is entitled to prevail because his position is the proper one under the law. For example, the parties might stipulate that they made an oral contract for the sale of land and that the defendant-seller refuses to tender the deed. The only question is a legal one: is an oral agreement for the sale of land enforceable? The motion for summary judgment asks the court to make a legal ruling for one party or the other without the necessity of taking any evidence.

Discovery If there is a factual dispute, the case then moves into a pretrial stage at which each party ferrets out information in the possession of the other party. This is known as **discovery.** Until around the 1940s, a lawsuit was frequently a game in which each party took advantage of the rules to surprise the other party in court. Beginning with a change in the Federal Rules of Civil Procedure, adopted by the Supreme Court in 1938 and subsequently followed by many of the states, the parties have been given considerable latitude to learn the facts of the case before trial.

The purpose of all discovery is to help the parties determine what the evidence might be, who the potential witnesses are, and what specific issues are relevant. Discovery can proceed by several methods. A party may serve an **interrogatory** on his adversary. This is written request for answers to specific questions. Or a party may **depose** the other party or a witness. A **deposition** is a live question-and-answer session at which the witness answers questions put to him by one of the parties' lawyers. His answers are recorded verbatim and may be used at trial.

The parties are also entitled to inspect books, documents, and other physical records and tangible things in the possession of the other. This is a sweeping right, since it is not limited to evidence that is admissible at trial. Discovery of physical evidence means that a plaintiff may inspect a company's accounts, customer lists, assets, profit-and-loss statements and balance sheet, engineering and quality-control reports, sales reports, and virtually any other document.

The discovery process is run by the lawyers, not by the court. One party simply makes a written demand on the other, stating the time at which the deposition will take place or the type of documents it wishes to inspect and make copies of. The party on whom the demand is made can apply to the court for a protective order if it can show that the demand is for privileged material (for example, a party's lawyers' records are not open for inspection) or that the demand was made to harass. In complex cases between companies, the discovery of documents can run into tens of millions of pages and can take years. Depositions can consume days or even weeks of an executive's time.

Pretrial Conference At various times during the discovery process, depending on the nature and complexity of the case, the court may hold a pretrial conference to attempt to clarify the issues and establish a timetable for proceeding. The court may also hold a settlement conference for the express purpose of seeing whether the parties can be induced to settle their differences and avoid trial altogether.

Once discovery is completed, the case moves on to trial if it has not been settled. Most cases are in fact settled before this stage; perhaps 85 percent of all civil cases are terminated before trial, and more than 90 percent of criminal prosecutions end with a guilty plea.

Trial At trial the first order of business is to select a jury if there is to be one. The judge and sometimes the lawyers are permitted to question the jurors to be sure that they are unbiased. The questioning is known as the **voir dire.** Most juries consist of twelve regular members and two or three alternates, who will substitute for a regular juror who chances to fall ill and must leave the courtroom. Beginning in the 1970s, a number of states began to experiment with smaller juries in order to save time and money.

After the jury is sworn and seated, the plaintiff's lawyer makes an **opening statement**, laying out the nature of the plaintiff's claim, the facts of the case as the plaintiff sees them, and the evidence that the lawyer will present. The defendant's lawyer may also make an opening statement or may reserve his right to do so at the conclusion of the plaintiff's case.

The plaintiff's lawyer then calls witnesses and presents the physical evidence relevant to her proof. The **direct testimony** at trial is usually far from a smooth narration. The rules of evidence (governing the kinds of testimony and documents that may be introduced at trial) and the question-and-answer format ensure that the presentation of evidence is choppy and sometimes difficult to follow. Anyone who has watched an actual televised trial or a television melodrama featuring a trial scene will appreciate the nature of the trial itself: witnesses are asked questions about a number of issues that may or may not be related, the opposing lawyer will frequently jump up to object to the question or the form in which it is asked, and the jury may be sent from the room while the lawyers wrangle.

After direct testimony of each witness is concluded, the opposing lawyer may conduct **cross-examination.** This is a crucial constitutional right; in criminal cases it is enshrined in the Sixth Amendment to the Constitution, the right to confront one's accusers in open court. The stilted rules of direct testimony are relaxed, and the cross-examiner may probe the witness more informally, asking questions that may not seem immediately relevant, and pounding hard at the witness—all in an attempt to impeach the credibility of the witness, to trip her up and show that the answers she gave are false or not to be trusted. It is the use of cross-examination and the criterion of responsiveness (p. 75) that chiefly distinguish common-law courts from those of authoritarian regimes around the world. Following cross-examination, the plaintiff's lawyer may then question the witness again; this is called **re-direct examination** and is used to rehabilitate the witness by clarifying the answers she gave and to show that the implications suggested by the cross-examiner were unwarranted. The cross-examiner may then engage the witness in **re-cross-examination,** and so on. The process usually stops after cross-examination or re-direct.

During the trial the judge's chief responsibility is to rule on the admissibility of evidence. If he rules a particular question out of order or a given document irrelevant, the lawyer proffering it has the right to appeal the judge's ruling after the trial.

At the conclusion of the plaintiff's case the defendant presents his case, following the same procedure just outlined. Thereafter, the plaintiff is entitled to present **rebuttal** witnesses if necessary to controvert evidence that the defendant has introduced. The defendant in turn may present **surrebuttal** witnesses.

When all testimony has been introduced, either party may ask the judge for a **directed verdict**—a verdict declared by the judge without advice from the jury. This motion should be granted if the plaintiff has failed to introduce evidence legally sufficient to meet her burden of proof or if the defendant has failed to do likewise on issues on which he has the burden of proof. (For example, the plaintiff alleges that the defendant owes her money and introduces a signed promissory note. The defendant cannot show that the note is invalid. The defendant must lose the case unless he can show that the debt has been paid or otherwise discharged.) The defendant can move for a directed verdict at the close of the plaintiff's case, but the judge will usually wait to hear the entire case until deciding whether to do so. Directed verdicts are not usually granted, since it is the jury's province to determine the facts in dispute. Moreover, the parties will rarely take a weak case—one in which the facts are either unclear or unprovable—all the way to trial; they will usually settle the case outside the court.

If the judge refuses to grant a directed verdict, each lawyer will then present a **closing argument** to the jury (or, if there is no jury, to the judge alone if the latter wants to hear it). The closing argument is frequently crucial, for it is by this often dramatic presentation that the lawyer ties up the loose ends, relates the bewildering stream of seemingly unrelated facts into a smooth whole, and shows how the evidence supports his client's case.

Thereafter, the judge will **instruct** the jury. Each lawyer will have prepared in writing a set of instructions that he hopes the judge will give to the jury; these will be tailored to advance his client's case. The purpose of a jury instruction is to explain to the jurors the meaning of the law as it relates to the issues they are considering and to tell the jurors what facts they must determine if they are to give a verdict for one party or the other. Dozens or even hundreds of factual issues can be raised during the course of an even moderately complicated trial; the juror's job is not an easy or enviable one. Instructing the jury in how to go about it is likewise a tricky business. Many a verdict has been upset on appeal because a trial judge has wrongly instructed the jury. As a consequence, most judges use form instructions known as "pattern jury instructions." These are sometimes long, badly worded, and difficult to follow. But they are safe because appellate courts will approve their use if challenged on appeal.

After all instructions are given, the jury will retire to a private room and deliberate for as long as it takes to reach a unanimous verdict. (Some minor cases do not require a unanimous verdict.) If the jury cannot reach a decision (a "hung jury"), the case will have to be retried. When a jury does reach a verdict, it delivers it in open court with the parties and lawyers present, the jury is discharged, and control over the case returns to the judge. If the judge is sitting without a jury, he will usually announce his findings of fact and application of the law to those facts in a written opinion. Juries announce only their verdicts and do not state their reasons for reaching them.

Posttrial Motions The losing party can ask the judge either for a new trial or for a *judgment notwithstanding the verdict* (often called a *judgment n.o.v.*, from the Latin initials for *non obstante veredicto*). A judge who decides that a directed verdict is appropriate usually will wait to see what the jury's verdict will be. If it is favorable to the party the judge thinks should win, he can rely on that verdict. If the verdict is for the other party, he can grant the motion for judgment n.o.v. This is a safer way to proceed because if he is reversed on appeal, there need not be a new trial. The jury's verdict always can be restored, whereas without a jury verdict (as happens when a directed verdict is granted before the case goes to the jury) the entire case must be presented to a new jury.

Appeal If the loser's motion for a new trial or a judgment n.o.v. is denied, his only recourse is to appeal the decision, citing one of several grounds of error to the appellate court—for example, that the judge erroneously admitted evidence, failed to admit proper evidence that he should have, or wrongly instructed the jury. Enforcement of the court's **judgment**—an award of money, an injunction—is usually **stayed** (postponed) until the appellate court has ruled. As noted earlier, the party making the appeal is called the appellant; the party defending the judgment is the appellee (in some courts, they are known as petitioner and respondent).

Appellate and trial processes are different. The appellate court does not hear witnesses or accept evidence. It reviews the *record* of the case—that is, the transcript of the witnesses' testimony and the documents received into evidence at trial—in a search for legal error on a specific request of one or both of the parties. The parties' lawyers prepare **briefs**—written statements containing the facts in the case, the procedural steps taken, and the argument, or discussion of the meaning of the law and its application to the facts. At some time, perhaps months or even years later, the appellate court will hear **oral argument.** Each lawyer is given a short period of time, usually no more than thirty minutes, to present his client's case. The lawyer rarely gets a chance for an extended statement because he is usually interrupted and peppered with questions from the judges. Through this colloquy between judges and lawyers, specific legal positions can be tested and their limits explored.

Depending on its conclusion, the appellate court will *affirm* the lower court's judgment, *modify* it, *reverse* it, or *remand* it to the lower court for retrial or other action directed by the higher court. The appellate court itself does not take specific action in the case; it sits only to rule on contested issues of law. The lower court must issue the final judgment in the case. As we have already seen, there is the possibility of appealing from an intermediate appellate court to the state supreme court in twenty-nine states, and the U.S. Supreme Court from a ruling of a federal circuit court of appeal. In cases raising constitutional issues, there is also the possibility of appeal to the Supreme Court from the state courts.

Precedent Like trial judges, appellate judges are bound by precedent. But not every previous case is a precedent for a given court. Generally speaking, decisions of higher courts must be respected only by lower courts in the same system. Courts in one state are not bound by decisions of courts in other states, nor in general are state courts bound by decisions of federal courts, except on points of federal law emanating from federal courts within the state or federal circuit in which the state court sits. State supreme courts are not bound by case law in other states, although decisions of sister supreme courts may influence the judges' reasoning. Federal district courts are bound by the decisions of the court of appeals in their circuit, but decisions by one circuit court are not precedents for courts in other circuits. Federal courts are also bound by decisions of the state supreme courts within their geographic territory in diversity jurisdiction cases. All courts are bound by decisions of the United States Supreme Court, except the Supreme Court itself.

Not everything a court says in an opinion is a precedent. Strictly speaking, only the exact **holding** is binding on the lower courts. A holding is the theory of the law that applies to the particular circumstances presented in the case. The courts may also discourse, even declare what they believe the law to be, on other points. These declarations are called **dicta** (singular: *dictum*), and the lower courts need not give them the same weight as holdings (with some exceptions; see pp. 33–35).

Judgment and Order

After all appeals are exhausted, the parties will be left with a judgment and order of the trial court. The **order**, directing the specific relief to which the parties are entitled, is usually prepared by the parties' lawyers at the conclusion of the trial. Each party offers the version that he believes best comports with the judgment or verdict, and the judge will accept or modify one and sign it as the order of the court. It is this order that the losing party must abide by.

Sometimes a contested sum of money has been paid to the court pending a decision, or a bond may have been posted. In either event, issuance of a final order will cause the money to be paid over to the winner.

If the loser is recalcitrant, the judgment can be enforced in a variety of ways. If the judgment requires one party to pay money to the other, the marshal or sheriff is authorized, upon application, to seize the loser's property to satisfy it. Subject to specific statutes, a losing party's wages or other income can be **garnished**, and the employer will be legally required to pay the winning party a certain portion of the losing party's wages until the judgment is paid off (see pp. 310–13). If the final judgment is an injunction, failure to abide by it may subject the party against whom it is issued to a **contempt** citation, following which he may be fined or jailed.

Who May Bring a Lawsuit

Whether or not a quarrel is one that a court will hear depends, among other things, on whether it is a **legal dispute.** A legal dispute is one in which the aggrieved party asserts a **legal entitlement**—that is, a right determined by law. Not every aggrieved person has such a right. The citizen has no right to impress her views of economic policy on the Federal Reserve Board. A restaurant patron may have no legal right to prevent another patron from smoking. For a court to entertain a case, the assertion of entitlement must rest on a legal rather than political, moral, or spiritual basis.

Case or Controversy?

Courts do not render "advisory" opinions. For a court to exercise its jurisdiction, there must be a dispute in which the parties are actual antagonists. A sham proceeding in which the supposed parties are not truly opposed but merely want an opinion of a court on the meaning of legislation will not be heard.

With some ingenuity, nearly any question can be converted into a dispute between two sides. For a variety of reasons, people might wish to have a court make an official pronouncement on a question of importance to them (and to others). Suppose, for example, that an organization offers a reward to anyone who comes forward with certain information (Box 3-1). Normally, the law of contracts would bind the organization to carry out its promise if someone supplies the information. But courts will not invariably reach such a conclusion because an inflexible rule to that effect could ultimately place every question of this nature before judges, who have enough cases to handle. In the following case, the Wisconsin Supreme Court squarely faced the question of whether every controversy is in fact a legal "case," concluding that no such generalization is possible.

CUDAHY JUNIOR CHAMBER OF COMMERCE v. QUIRK
41 Wis.2d 698, 165 N.W.2d 116 (1969)

FACTS

In the spring election of 1966, the voters of the city of Cudahy were to decide by referendum whether the community water supply was to be fluoridated. A leading proponent of fluoridation was the Cudahy Junior Chamber of Commerce. A leading foe of fluoridating the water was James Quirk, working as or through The Greater Milwaukee Committee Against Fluoridation.

In the midst of the spirited campaign, Quirk "challenged" the Jaycees, offering to give them $1,000 ". . . if a daily dose of four glasses [of fluoridated water] cannot cause 'dermatologic, gastrointestinal and neurological disorders' " and adding, "If the Jaycees should find that we have misrepresented matters in this paper, we will then also pay the sum of $1,000." The Jaycees did some checking, so found to their satisfaction, demanded payment by Quirk of $1,000. When payment was refused, the Jaycees brought this action, seeking (1) a court finding that Quirk did misrepresent matters in his brochure; (2) a court finding that four glasses of fluoridated water cannot cause the mentioned disorders; (3) a court judgment for $1,000. Trial was had to a jury. The jury found misrepresentation. . . . Defendant Quirk appeals.

* * *

ROBERT W. HANSEN, J.

* * *

What have we here? In the eyes of the law, exactly what is this sort of challenge made in the heat of an election campaign? Was it an offer that, upon acceptance, became a binding contract? Was it a reward, analogous to the sums of money offered for information leading to the arrest and conviction of the perpetrator of a crime? Was it a bet, a wagering of $1,000 against the possibility that one might be wrong?

In 2 Restatement, *Contracts,* pp. 1007, 1008, sec. 520, comment *c,* the following is stated: "A wager may relate to a trial of skill, or to *proof of an actual fact* or even to a certain event that happened in the past." (Emphasis supplied.) . . .

. . . In essence the Quirk challenge was a wa-

Box 3-1 Case or Controversy?

California Judge Rules Holocaust Did Happen

LOS ANGELES, Oct. 9(AP)—A Superior Court judge, acting on a suit filed against a group that contends the Holocaust was a myth, ruled today that "Jews were gassed to death in Auschwitz in Poland in the summer of 1944."

In taking "judicial notice" of the Holocaust, Judge Thomas T. Johnson was ruling on one part of a lawsuit by Mel Mermelstein, 55 years old, a businessman from Long Beach, Calif. Mr. Mermelstein, who survived the Auschwitz concentration camp, is suing the Institute of Historical Review, a right-wing group that contends the Holocaust was fabricated by Jews.

The institute had offered a $50,000 reward to anyone who could prove the contrary, and Mr. Mermelstein contended the group had failed to pay off though it had seen his proof.

The judge did not rule on the question of whether the institute actually had a legal contract with the businessman.

The institute and Mr. Mermelstein had exchanged letters that William Cox, Mr. Mermelstein's attorney, contends constituted a contract.

The suit also asks for a summary judgment and payment to Mr. Mermelstein of $1 million in damages for the psychological suffering.

The institute contends that Mr. Mermelstein did not meet all the criteria for collecting the reward.

Source: *New York Times*, October 10, 1981

ger—"I'll gamble my $1,000 against your efforts to prove me wrong that my statements are correct." It is not close kin to a bet that the Green Bay Packers will best the Chicago Bears in their next gridiron encounter. It is, however, a twin to the bet that Babe Ruth once pitched for the Boston Red Sox. It is the essential nature of a transaction, rather than the label attached to it by the parties, that determines whether it is in truth and fact a wager.

Who won the bet? The jury's finding, which was sustained by the trial court, was that the Jaycees won the wager. This amounted to an acceptance of the credibility of the testimony offered by the Jaycees that Quirk had "misrepresented matters" in his brochure. We do not reach the issue of fact as to who won and who lost the wager. Our holding is that the participants in a wager may not use the court to settle their dispute because gambling debts cannot be established or collected in the courts.

The question of public policy? In addition to the judicial reluctance to hold the stakes or decide the winner in a betting situation, there are sound reasons of public policy for not having court or jury decide whose gloved fist is to be lifted in victory in this dispute. It is clear that, while $1,000 would be a welcome addition to club coffers, the primary concern of the Jaycees is to vindicate the rightness of their position that fluoridation of the Cudahy water supply involves no harmful side effects. It is at least as clear that James Quirk's principal interest is in seeking court confirmation of his contention that fluoridation of a community's drinking water risks harmful consequences. He appeared as his own counsel, and his brief and oral argument dealt only with the rightness of his antifluoridation stance. In fact, in rejecting the demand for payment of the Jaycees, he wrote, with copies to local press, "Top promoters of fluoridation will turn aghast at airing the harm and stupidity of fluoridation in open court. We welcome the opportunity of a court hearing." The time-honored explanation, "It isn't the money. It's the principle of the thing" describes both the intensity of conviction and explains the gap between the points of view of the parties to this action.

If disputants on the issue of the harmful effects of fluoridation can by the process of challenge and acceptance bring their dispute on this issue of public concern to the courts for adjudication, the list of matters in which litigants could seek determinations by the court of questions of public policy would be a long one. Dedicated crusaders for varying points of view, pro and con, by the process of challenge and response, could have courts rule on whether birth control pills have harmful side-effects, whether cigarettes cause cancer, whether sugar substitutes alter chromosomes. If there are ways of bringing such controversies to court, putting up $1,000 to be paid to anyone who can prove you wrong does not make the courts the forum or the referee. Here the true controversy is as to the effects of fluoridation. We have grave doubts as to whether this is a justiciable issue—one appropriate for judicial inquiry.

* * *

It is understandable that the Jaycees, a civic organization of young men with an established record for effective participation in civic enterprises, would want to have its presentation of facts found to be accurate, and that of its principal adversary found to be false, misleading and misrepresented. It is not the role or function of the judicial branch of our government to make that determination. Some may see it as a weakness but it is the heart of the referendum law and the democratic process that, in this situation, the voters, not judge or jury, are to bring in the verdict. We can with propriety commend all individuals and all groups who participate in securing the expressed will of an informed electorate, but it is not for us to determine whose presentation had either the greatest accuracy or greatest persuasiveness. The cases, affirmative and negative, were submitted to the jury at the polls. They were not for a jury in a courtroom to affirm or reverse.

The what, why, when and where of this case require that the judgment be reversed and the case dismissed.

Standing to Sue

A closely related question is that of **standing** to sue. Suppose you see a sixteen-wheel moving van drive across your neighbor's flowerbed, destroying her prize-winning dahlias and chrysanthemums. Since she is on vacation, you file a lawsuit against the company to recover for the economic loss she has suffered. The court will reject your suit. You do not have standing to sue because you were not injured by the moving van. Only a person whose interests are affected has the legal capacity to sue.

The "standing" doctrine is easy to understand in straightforward cases. Litigation is expensive and intrusive. The decision of whether or not to sue should be left in the hands of those who have suffered an injury and stand to gain by court action. Most of us suffer injuries from time to time that are legally redressable but that for a variety of reasons we would not go to the extreme of seeking redress for. We might want to avoid publicity, expense, discomfort; we might hope that an amicable settlement will permit us to continue in an ongoing relationship. If anyone could bring a lawsuit on our behalf, our lives would be to some degree out of our control.

But in recent years, complex disputes have made the standing doctrine a baffling one. Suppose for example, that Congress has enacted a law authorizing and appropriating $1 billion for the purchase of balloons to decorate the hallways of federal buildings. This strikes you as the height of fiscal folly and you are searching for a way to block the expenditure. What might you do? One line of attack is to sue in federal court, alleging that Congress has no constitutional power to make such an appropriation. Do you have standing? You might suppose that the answer is obvious: as a taxpayer, your pocketbook is affected every time Congress votes to spend the public money. In 1923, however, the Supreme Court ruled that a taxpayer has no standing in a case involving appropriation of federal funds to be turned over to the states to provide for maternal health care. To hold otherwise, the Court said, would invite millions of people to sue whenever Congress appropriated any sum of money. [Frothingham v. Mellon, 262 U.S. 447 (1923)] Beginning in 1968 and continuing through the 1970s, the Supreme Court decided a series of cases suggesting that taxpayers may sometimes have standing to bring suits. The principal effect of these cases is to permit, at least on some occasions, private groups to contest governmental actions that affect their members.

Class Actions

Most lawsuits concern a dispute between one individual and another, or between an individual and a company or other organization. But it not infrequently happens that a wrongdoer injures more than one person at the same time. It is purely fortuitous whether a driver who runs a red light hits another car carrying only one person or many more. If several people are injured in the same accident, they each have the right to sue the driver for the damage that he caused them. Could they sue as a group? Ordinarily not, because the extent of the damages would not likely be the same for each person, and different facts would have to be proved at the trial. Moreover, the driver of the car that was struck might have been partially to blame, so the defendant's liability toward him might be different from his liability toward the passengers.

If, however, the potential plaintiffs were all injured in the same manner and their injuries were identical, a single lawsuit might be a far more efficient way of fixing liability and assessing financial responsibility than a host of individual lawsuits. How could such a suit be brought? All the injured parties could hire the same lawyer, who could present their common case. But with a group numbering more than a handful of people, the logistical problems could be insurmountable. How could a million stockholders allegedly defrauded by a corporation, or a million purchasers of a product allegedly overcharged because of an antitrust conspiracy, ever get together?

Consequently, there is a legal procedure that permits one person or a small group of people to serve as stand-ins for all others similarly situated. This is the **class action.** (Note that "action" means "suit," so the phrase "class action lawsuit" frequently seen in the newspapers is redundant.) The class action is provided for in the Federal Rules of Civil Procedure (Rule 23) and in the separate codes of civil procedure in the states. These rules differ and are often complex in detail, but in general, anyone may file a class action in an appropriate case subject to approval of the court. Once the class is "certified," or adjudged to be a legally adequate group complaining of common injuries, the lawyers for the named plaintiffs become in effect the lawyers for the entire class. Usually a person who does not wish to be in the class may opt out. If she does, she will not be included in an eventual judgment or settlement. But a potential plaintiff who is included in the class cannot, after a final judgment is awarded, seek to relitigate the issue if she is dissatisfied with the outcome, even though she did not participate at all in the legal proceeding.

The older rule that prohibited class actions from being used in cases in which damages are not uniform has been at least partially overcome. A case involving numerous plaintiffs presenting an identical question of liability can be tried as a class action, with separate proof of damages thereafter. Such a case may or may not be a class action in the technical sense.

Comparative Review of Legal Systems

The Anglo-American System

Most countries that are today members of the British Commonwealth have adopted the common-law system to their own use. The common-law system also operates in many countries formerly colonized by Great Britain. These include Canada, Australia, India, and many African nations. Unlike England, which to this day does not have a written constitution, most of these nations have adopted a formal written constitution, but their judiciaries are not always fully independent of the executive authority.

Unlike the United States, which has only one class of lawyer, most other common law countries, including Great Britain, have two classes: **solicitors** and **barristers**. Solicitors are "office lawyers"; they see clients in their offices, draw up legal instruments such as wills, and give advice, but they do not represent clients in most courts. Those who actually litigate in court are called barristers. They do not actually serve the parties directly. Barristers are retained by the solicitors, not by the clients, and so they come more directly under the control of courts than do their American counterparts.

The Continental System

In Europe, quite a different legal system developed. In classical times, Roman law spread throughout most of the known world. After the collapse of Rome and the breakup of Europe into dozens of countries and principalities, the unifying force of the Roman law was lost, and each political jurisdiction evolved its own quite different set of laws. Frequently the law within each country was tangled and inconsistent. This was true well into the eighteenth century. Voltaire wrote that in traveling through France one would come across a different set of laws as often as one changed horses. (One type of law did contain common elements from country to country:

the **law merchant**, which was virtually the only functioning type of international law in medieval Europe; many of its elements were imported into the common law during the eighteenth century.)

Finally in the early nineteenth century, under the personal sponsorship of Napoleon, the law was **codified**—that is, rationalized and written down in the form of a code—in France. The spirit of the Napoleonic Code spread to other countries, where further reforms were made. **Continental law**, as European law is generally known, has been largely imported into South America, though each country has made procedural and substantive modifications over the course of time. The continental legal system survives today in vestigial form in Louisiana, which was still under French control while the Napoleonic Code was being drafted. Although the Louisiana private law stems from the continental rather than the common law tradition, the state's legal system has been heavily transformed by American constitutional requirements.

Two principal differences between common law and continental law are worth noting. The continental criminal law system is **inquisitorial** rather an **accusatorial**. The accusatorial system is our own adversary system, in which the public prosecutor accuses the defendant and must then meet a heavy burden of proof in open court. The prosecutor in our system may not question the accused against his wishes, and the accused has the legal right to representation by a lawyer who can help him plan his defense from the first moment he is arrested. In the inquisitorial system, the accused has far fewer rights to consult with a lawyer. The prosecutor has the power to hold the accused incommunicado and to question him at length without counsel present. The defendant has much less power to control the process of fact-gathering or the course of the trial than his American or English counterpart.

The second difference worth noting is that of the power of courts to make law. The continental law codes spell out legal relations and rights in much more detail than is true in the common law countries, where the law resides in judicial precedents. Theoretically, the law is complete and courts need not interpret. They simply look up the law and apply it to the facts of the case. In fact, no law can be completely given and so courts do need to fill in gaps. But their decisions do not serve as precedents the way they do in common law countries. The trial judge is much freer to interpret the law afresh; he is much less bound by the decisions of the higher courts.

Communist Legal Systems

The legal systems and law of Communist nations are alien to the common law tradition in both spirit and substance. Though they contain many Western forms—such as constitutions, courts, and legislatures—in practice these institutions are fundamentally different. There is no separation of powers, for example, despite the language of the constitutions, because all government branches are subject to the will of the Communist party. There is no true adversary system; the lawyer is employed by the state, not the individual, though in some civil proceedings lawyers can be retained and are paid by their clients. The judiciary is not independent, and though the party does not dictate the outcome of most cases—because it has more pressing work to do—it does direct the verdict in criminal cases in which it takes an interest. The norm of responsiveness is thus missing: the judge need pay no attention to the proofs offered and the arguments made. Again, though the constitutions spell out what appear to be individual rights, these are not absolute but are to be granted only as long as they are exercised consistent with the "interests" of the state, as defined by party policy.

There are differences among the legal systems in the Communist world. Cultural traditions of the people continue to influence national institutions. Soviet forms are more Western than Chinese, for example. During the Chinese Great Cultural Revolution of the 1960s, the only law school in China was shut down and lawyers played virtually no role in the affairs of the country. Today, as China once again looks toward the West, law schools have opened, a legal profession is being developed, and codes of law are being drafted. This should not be surprising: commerce requires a common approach to legal problems; without it, trade and business cannot function.

Chapter Summary

This chapter has provided an overview of courts and how they work. Understanding what courts are, how they operate, and what it means to "think legally" is essential to understanding any particular body of law. In the United States, the study of law is complicated by the multiplicity of court systems. There are fifty-two different court systems: the federal court system, and the court systems of each state and the District of Columbia. State and federal trial courts have the authority to conduct hearings to determine the facts and to apply the law to those facts. Litigants dissatisfied with the results in the trial courts may appeal decisions in trial courts to appellate courts, which are empowered to review the lower court's application of the law. Ordinarily state courts hear state claims and federal courts hear claims based on federal law, but in some instances state courts may hear federal claims and vice versa. State supreme court decisions may be appealed on constitutional grounds to the U.S. Supreme Court.

Cases move through courts in a manner laid down by rules of procedure. The general method is known as the adversary system, operating through independent lawyers for each party to the case. Commencing with the original pleadings (complaint and answer), the lawyers for each party develop the facts of a case before going to the courtroom, where rules of evidence and procedure dictate how the facts are presented to the judge and jury. Not every quarrel can land in a courtroom. There must be a genuine controversy between two or more parties based on a claim of legal entitlement.

Lawsuits are not limited to controversies between two individuals. Cases involving dozens, or even thousands, of plaintiffs can be brought against multiple defendants. In a class action, a single plaintiff can represent an entire class of people whose claims are identical to the class representative.

Problems

1. Name some types of cases that can be heard only in federal courts. Name some that can be heard only in state courts.
2. Under what circumstances would a federal court apply state rather than federal law to the case before it? Under what circumstances would a state court apply federal law rather than state law to the case before it? Under what circumstances would a state court apply the law of some other state to the case before it?
3. Dick sued Iris, claiming that he had an I.O.U. from her for $5,000, that she had never paid. Iris said the I.O.U. was a forgery. The jury agreed with Iris. Dick wants to appeal the case, contending that the jury made the wrong decision. May he appeal? What result?
4. Must the U.S. Supreme Court hear every case appealed to it? Why or why not? Where would one find out what types of cases a particular court must hear or may not hear?
5. What is the adversary system and what are its distinguishing characteristics?
6. Define the following terms: *jurisdiction, venue, discovery, complaint, answer, injunction, class action, directed verdict.*
7. What is a "burden of proof"? Name some different standards.
8. The Postal Service decides to issue a commemorative stamp honoring Elvis Presley. The Society for the Preservation of Virtue sues to enjoin it from doing so. What result?

4

Relations with Lawyers and Alternative Dispute Resolution

Introduction

The law should be the possession of every person. At times, legal topics become part of a broad public debate—as, for example, when the ways of interpreting the Constitution were spread out before a television audience during the Senate's 1987 hearings on President Reagan's nomination of Judge Robert Bork to the Supreme Court. Usually, however, the volume and complexity of law make it relatively inaccessible. The legal life of the nation is filtered, therefore, through the legal profession.

Unlike the work of particle physicists or arbitrageurs, the lawyer's job may seem generally familiar. After all, lawyers have been the staple of literature for centuries (Shakespeare and Dickens could not have done without them). For the better part of this century, in the movies America's leading actors have been cast as lawyers, whether heroes or villains. Television audiences for the past two generations have learned their law from Raymond Burr *(Perry Mason),* John Houseman (Prof. Kingsfield in *Paper*

Chase), Veronica Hamel (Joyce Davenport in *Hill Street Blues*), Harry Hamlin (Michael Kuzak in *L.A. Law*), and many others. But with all the Hollywood gloss, the real work of lawyers remains largely unknown.

This chapter looks at the organization of the profession and examines how lawyers go about their work. Understanding how lawyers carry out their tasks is as crucial as understanding the outlines of the law they are interpreting for their clients. It is important also to know that what we so often see portrayed on the screen—a courtroom trial—is not the only way that legal disputes can be resolved. This chapter concludes by looking at a variety of alternatives to litigation.

Relations with Lawyers

Organization of the Legal Profession

The number of U.S. lawyers topped the half-million mark around 1980, and by the end of 1988 had climbed to nearly three-quarters of a million. By the end of the century, it is estimated there will be more than one million lawyers practicing law in the United States. More than 100,000 students are enrolled in the 175 accredited American law schools, and some 30,000 new lawyers graduate each year.

To practice law, a lawyer must be admitted to *the bar* of a state. In some states admission is more or less automatic following graduation from an accredited school in the state. In most states, however, the graduate must take a written examination and be screened by a character committee appointed by the supervising court.

Lawyers are admitted state by state. No general admission to practice exists in the United States. Permission to appear in the federal courts in each state is usually routine following admission to the bar of the state. When a company has a legal problem outside its home state, it will usually retain local lawyers to work with its own lawyers.

Bar associations provide a variety of services. They offer continuing professional education and public education, and work on law reform. The American Bar Association (ABA) is the largest voluntary professional association in the world, with more than 300,000 members. Its hundreds of committees are engaged in innumerable professional projects; it has a complex internal political structure through which its members debate important public issues. Its committees frequently testify on legal matters before Congress and the state legislatures. One of its most important committees is that which screens presidential nominations to the federal courts. There is a separate state bar association in each state, and in the larger states there are dozens of local bar associations. There are also several other specialty associations, such as the Association of Trial Lawyers of America, whose members are largely lawyers who litigate on behalf of plaintiffs in personal-injury and other types of lawsuits.

Unlike in many professions, the major scholarly work of the legal profession is not published in the bar associations' numerous journals. The legal profession is unique in that the academic journals, called law reviews or law journals, are usually edited and run by students in the law schools (for example, the *Harvard Law Review,* the *Yale Law Journal*). The schools publish more than 300 law reviews, some of general and some of specialized interest. Articles by leading academic scholars and others that appear in the twenty or so most prominent journals are frequently cited in judicial opinions.

Lawyers practice law in assorted ways. Perhaps half the practicing lawyers in the country practice by themselves (solo) or with one or two partners. Beginning in the 1960s, law firms, as legal partnerships are known, began to grow as the needs of corporate clients mushroomed. Today, there are hundreds of firms throughout the United States with more than 100 lawyers, and dozens have more than 200 or 300 lawyers. Generally speaking, there are two classes of lawyers in these firms. *Partners* are like corporate officers; they run the show and split the profits. Younger lawyers are salaried and are usually called *associates.* In between the solo practitioner and the giant firm are thousands of law firms of varying sizes. Regardless of size, many firms today employ employees known as *paralegals,* or legal assistants, whose skills lie between those of legal secretaries and those of lawyers.

In addition to the *independent practitioners* (lawyers practicing by themselves or with other lawyers), increasing numbers of lawyers work as employees for government and private corporations. The head of a company's legal department is generally termed *general counsel* or *house counsel.* The *in-house* lawyer is one who is salaried by a company or other organization. During the 1970s, corporations began to build up their in-house legal staffs, sometimes dramatically. Today dozens of companies employ a hundred or more lawyers to work on every conceivable type of corporate problem: litigation, securities, antitrust, real estate, taxation, personnel, and the like.

Professional Responsibility and Ethics

Lawyers serve their clients in a variety of roles. They act as advocates in court and as negotiators, counselors, and lobbyists. As representative for the client, a lawyer is expected to work zealously in his behalf, whatever the personal consequences to the lawyer. But the lawyer is usually careful not to personally endorse the client's position. Lawyers may defend clients whose views they detest. That is the nature of the lawyer's role, and it is a frequently misunderstood one, leading lawyers to be wrongly condemned for representing those whom society despises. It is precisely those who are most despised who most need counsel, and an adversary system will ensure that they have it.

Nevertheless, there are limits to the zeal that a lawyer may bring to the representation of his client's interests. These limits are spelled out in a formal code of ethics, generally known throughout the country as the Code of Professional Responsibility. Commissioned by the American Bar Association, this code is the product of many minds and drafters. The original written code was adopted in Alabama in 1887. The first "model" code of the ABA was published in 1906. It is a model code because the ABA is private and has no authority to promulgate binding rules. The code of ethics draws its legal force by being officially adopted by the state supreme courts. These courts have not adopted the model code in full; there are variations from state to state. The model code that most states have adopted was issued in 1970; a revised version was released in 1983, but few states have yet adopted it.

From the perspective of the business client, two aspects of the ethical rules are paramount: the lawyer is bound to respect the confidences of his clients, and the lawyer may not engage in a conflict of interest.

Confidentiality A lawyer may not ethically reveal what he has learned from his client during the course of his representation. This rule has an analogue in the courtroom. Under the law of evidence, a party is protected by the **lawyer-client privilege**: a client may prevent her lawyer from testifying about facts he has learned from her and from turning over papers that he developed during the course of his representation. This is an important rule. Without it, a client might well hesitate to disclose sensitive information that could be used against her in competitive or other situations.

There is a difficulty, however. A person cannot go to a lawyer for advice about committing "the perfect crime." The rule has always contained an exception for future or continuing crimes. If the client says, "I committed a crime and I need help," the lawyer may work with her and may not disclose what the client has said. This rule has always been interpreted strictly. On the other hand, if the client says, "Help me out with this scheme to defraud the public," the confidentiality rule does not apply and the lawyer need not keep quiet. To the contrary, the lawyer might have to go public.

This latter requirement, if it is one, poses problems for corporate clients. A common example is the preparation of legal papers necessary for registration of a securities offering with the Securities and Exchange Commission. The securities laws (see Chapter 18) require companies to make a number of public disclosures about such things as assets, costs, and expenditures. The regulations are complex, and it is frequently a close question whether or not a particular item of information legally must be disclosed. If the lawyer says, "You must disclose the discovery of this new oil field," and the responsible officer refuses to do so, what should the lawyer do? In a close case, where the line between legality and illegality is difficult to draw, the lawyer is permitted to give his best advice; if the client wishes to take the risk of being brought to court by the government, it is not unethical for the lawyer to keep quiet while the client tests the case in court. To the contrary, it is probably ethically necessary for the lawyer to keep quiet. But if the client clearly steps over the line of illegality, should the lawyer speak out? There are few precedents that resolve this question, but two cases that received considerable publicity during the 1970s suggest that under certain circumstances the lawyer does indeed have a duty to speak out, or at least will not be condemned for doing so. [Securities and Exchange Commission v. National Student Marketing Corp., 457 F.Supp. 682 (D.D.C. 1978); Meyerhofer v. Empire Fire and Marine Insurance Co., 497 F.2d 1190 (2nd Cir. 1974)]

Conflict of Interest The second important ethical consideration for the lawyer in corporate practice is the rule that prohibits any lawyer from engaging in a **conflict of interest.** This generally means that a lawyer may not represent two parties whose interests are adverse—for example, a lawyer may not represent both the plaintiff and the defendant in court.

When the clients are individuals, it is usually easy to determine whether there is a conflict of interest. Having once given legal advice to an employer in connection with a certain matter, a lawyer may not subsequently represent an employee who wishes to sue the employer over that matter. But when the lawyer represents a corporation, who exactly is the client? A corporation, after all, is a "legal fiction" (see Chapter 17); it is a collection of individuals who manage and operate the affairs of the enterprise. Is the client the chief executive officer? the board of directors? the officers as a whole?

The answer is that the client is the corporation itself, and not any of the officers, agents, or employees. Of course, in representing the corporation, the lawyer will necessarily deal with the chief executive, other officers, and to a lesser degree, the board and other employees. But they are not the client. As long as the corporation's interest and that of an individual employee are identical, the lawyer may serve them both. There will be occasions, however, when the interest of the corporation as a whole will be adverse to that of an individual who works for it. It is important to bear in mind that in a showdown, the lawyer must choose the corporation's interest over that of any individual. An officer or other employee who finds himself in such a conflict-of-interest situation will do well to retain his own independent lawyer.

The rule that the corporation or other organization, not the individual, is the client has an important bearing on the rule of confidentiality. A lawyer must respect the confidences of the client, but not those of others. If individual employees are not the client, then presumably the lawyer need not pledge to keep secret what they tell him. But a corporation as an abstract cannot talk—only people can. Does this mean that the corporate lawyer is not bound to respect corporate confidentiality? The answer is that the lawyer must keep confidential any company-related legal matters that he learns from employees. All employees? At one time, the courts employed a "control group" test: anything a lawyer learned from those who controlled the management of the company was subject to the rules regarding confidentiality and the lawyer-client privilege. For many years lower-level employees were thought not to be covered by the rule. In 1981, the Supreme Court ruled for the first time that they were.

UPJOHN CO. v. UNITED STATES 449 U.S. 383 (1981)

JUSTICE REHNQUIST delivered the opinion of the Court.

* * *

Petitioner Upjohn Co. manufactures and sells pharmaceuticals here and abroad. In January 1976 independent accountants conducting an audit of one of Upjohn's foreign subsidiaries discovered that the subsidiary made payments to or for the benefit of foreign government officials in order to secure government business. The accountants so informed petitioner Mr. Gerard Thomas, Upjohn's Vice President, Secretary, and General Counsel. Thomas is a member of the Michigan and New York Bars, and has been Upjohn's General Counsel for 20 years. He consulted with outside counsel and R. T. Parfet, Jr., Upjohn's Chairman of the Board. It was decided that the company would conduct an internal investigation of what were termed "questionable payments." As part of this investigation the attorneys prepared a letter containing a questionnaire which was sent to "All Foreign General and Area Managers" over the Chairman's signature. The letter began by noting recent disclosures that several American companies made "possibly illegal" payments to foreign government officials and emphasized that the management needed full information concerning any such payments made by Upjohn. The letter indicated that the Chairman had asked Thomas, identified as "the company's General Counsel," "to conduct an investigation for the purpose of determining the nature and magnitude of any payments made by the Upjohn Company or any of its subsidiaries to any employee or official of a foreign government." The questionnaire sought detailed information concerning such payments. Managers were instructed to treat the investigation as "highly confidential" and not to discuss it with anyone other than Upjohn employees who might be helpful in providing the requested information. Responses were to be sent directly to Thomas. Thomas and outside counsel also interviewed the recipients of the questionnaire and some 33 other Upjohn officers or employees as part of the investigation.

On March 26, 1976, the company voluntarily submitted a preliminary report to the Securities and Exchange Commission on Form 8-K disclosing certain questionable payments. A copy of the report was simultaneously submitted to the Internal Revenue Service, which immediately began an investigation to determine the tax consequences of the payments. Special agents conducting the investigation were given lists by Upjohn of all those interviewed and all who had responded to the questionnaire. On November 23, 1976, the Service issued a summons pursuant to 26 U. S. C. § 7602 demanding production of:

> All files relative to the investigation conducted under the supervision of Gerard Thomas to identify payments to employees of foreign governments and any political contributions made by the Upjohn Company or any of its affiliates since January 1, 1971 and to determine whether any funds of the Upjohn Company had been improperly accounted for on the corporate books during the same period.
>
> The records should include but not be limited to written questionnaires sent to managers of the Upjohn Company's foreign affiliates, and memorandums or notes of the interviews conducted in the United States and abroad with officers and employees of the Upjohn Company and its subsidiaries.

The company declined to produce the documents specified in the second paragraph on the grounds that they were protected from disclosure by the attorney-client privilege and constituted the work product of attorneys prepared in anticipation of litigation. On August 31, 1977, the United States filed a petition seeking enforcement of the summons . . . in the United States District Court for the Western District of Michigan. That court adopted the recommendation of a Magistrate who concluded that the summons should be enforced. Petitioners appealed to the Court of Appeals for the Sixth Circuit which rejected the Magistrate's finding of a waiver of the attorney-client privilege, but agreed that the privilege did not apply "[t]o the extent that the communications were made by officers and agents not responsible for directing Upjohn's actions in response to legal advice . . . for the simple reason that the communications were not the 'client's.' " The court reasoned that accepting petitioners' claim for a broader application of the privilege would encourage upper-echelon management to ignore unpleasant facts and create too broad a "zone of silence." Noting that Upjohn's counsel had interviewed officials such as the Chairman and President, the Court of Appeals remanded to the District Court so that a determination of who was within the "control group" could be made. . . .

Federal Rule of Evidence 501 provides that "the privilege of a witness . . . shall be governed by the principles of the common law as they may be interpreted by the courts of the United States in light of reason and experience." The attorney-client privilege is the oldest of the privileges for confidential communications known to the common law. Its purpose is to encourage full and frank communication between attorneys and their clients and thereby promote broader public interests in the observance of law and administration of justice. The privilege recognizes that sound legal advice or advocacy serves public ends and that such advice or advocacy depends upon the lawyer's being fully informed by the client.

* * *

In the case of the individual client the provider of information and the person who acts on the lawyer's advice are one and the same. In the corporate context, however, it will frequently be employees beyond the control group as defined by the court below—"officers and agents . . . responsible for directing [the company's] actions in response to legal advice"—who will possess the information needed by the corporation's lawyers. Middle-level—and indeed lower-level—employees can, by actions within the scope of their employment, embroil the corporation in serious legal difficulties, and it is only natural that these employees would have the relevant information needed by corporate counsel if he is adequately to advise the client with respect to such actual or potential difficulties.

* * *

The control group test adopted by the court below thus frustrates the very purpose of the privilege by discouraging the communication of relevant information by employees of the client to attorneys seeking to render legal advice to the client corporation. The attorney's advice will also frequently be more significant to noncontrol group members than to those who officially sanction the advice, and the control group test makes it more difficult to convey full and frank legal advice to the employees who will put into effect the client corporation's policy. . . .

The narrow scope given the attorney-client privilege by the court below not only makes it difficult for corporate attorneys to formulate sound advice when their client is faced with a specific legal problem but also threatens to limit the valuable efforts of corporate counsel to ensure their client's compliance with the law. In light of the vast and complicated array of regulatory legislation confronting the modern corporation, corporations, unlike most individuals, "constantly go to lawyers to find out how to obey the law," particularly since compliance with the law in this area is hardly an instinctive matter. . . .

The communications at issue were made by Upjohn employees to counsel for Upjohn acting as such, at the direction of corporate superiors in order to secure legal advice from counsel. . . . Information, not available from upper-echelon management, was needed to supply a basis for legal advice concerning compliance with securities and tax laws, foreign laws, currency regulations, duties to shareholders, and potential litigation in each of these areas. The communications concerned matters within the scope of the employees' corporate duties, and the employees themselves were sufficiently aware that they were being questioned in order that the corporation could obtain legal advice. . . . Consistent with the underlying purposes of the attorney-client privilege, these communications must be protected against compelled disclosure.

* * *

Accordingly, the judgment of the Court of Appeals is reversed, and the case remanded for further proceedings.

Legal Fees and Legal Costs

Fees Lawyers charge for their services in one of three different ways: flat rate, hourly rate, and contingent fee. The flat rate charge is used usually when the work is relatively routine and the lawyer knows in advance approximately how long it will take to do the job. Drawing a will or doing a real estate closing on a residence are the types of jobs for which lawyers are often paid a flat rate. The rate itself may be based on a percentage of the worth of the matter—1 percent of the selling price of the home, for example.

Lawyers generally charge by the hour for courtroom time and for ongoing representation in commercial matters. Virtually every sizable law firm bills its clients by hourly rates, which in large cities range from a low of perhaps \$50–75 for the time of a junior associate to \$150–300 and more for the time of the senior partner. The rapid climb in hourly rates has led many corporations to expand the size of their legal staffs in order to bring these costs under control. It is obviously cheaper to pay a full-time lawyer a salary than to pay high hourly rates to outside lawyers, because the lawyers' office overhead is built into these rates. Even the largest corporations cannot afford to bring all their legal work in-house, however, because from time to time legal matters crop up that call for the help of specialists who would not be used on a full-time basis. Private law firms can keep such specialists busy because they serve many different clients.

The contingent fee is one that is paid only if the lawyer wins—that is, it is contingent on success. This type of fee arrangement is used most often in personal injury cases (automobile accidents, product liability, and professional malpractice, for example). The desirability of the contingent fee is hotly debated. Trial lawyers justify it by pointing to the high cost of preparing for such lawsuits. A typical automobile accident case can cost several thousand dollars to prepare, and a complicated product liability case can cost tens of thousands of dollars. Few people have that kind of money or would be willing to spend it on the chance that they might win a lawsuit. Corporate and professional defendants complain that the contingent fee gives lawyers a license to go "big game hunting"—to file suits against "deep pocket" (wealthy) defendants in the hopes of forcing them to settle. Trial lawyers respond that the contingent fee arrangement forces them to screen cases and weed out the unmeritorious ones, because it is not worth their time to spend the hundreds of hours necessary on such cases if their chances of winning are slim or nonexistent.

Costs In England and many other countries, the losing party must pay the legal expenses of the winning party, including attorneys' fees. That is not the general rule in the United States. Here, each party must bear most of its own costs, including, especially, the fees of lawyers. Certain relatively minor costs, such as filing fees for various documents required in court, are chargeable to the losing side at the discretion of the judge. This is known as the "American rule," in contrast to the "British rule."

There are two exceptions to the American rule. By statute, Congress and the state legislatures have provided that the winning party in enumerated classes of cases may recover its full legal costs from the loser—for example, the federal antitrust laws so provide and so does the federal Equal Access to Justice Act (see Box 4-1). The other exception applies to litigants who either bring lawsuits in bad faith, with no expectation of winning, or who defend them in bad faith, in order to put the plaintiff to great expense. Under these circumstances, a court has the discretion to award attorneys' fees to the winner. But this rule is not infinitely flexible, and courts do not have *carte blanche* to award attorneys' fees in any cases they happen to think are especially meritorious.

Alternative Means of Resolving Disputes

Disputes need not be settled in court. No law requires parties who have a legal dispute to seek judicial resolution if they can resolve their disagreement privately or through some other public forum. Indeed, lawsuits frequently serve as a spur to private negotiation. Filing a lawsuit may convince one party that the other party is serious. Or the parties may decide that they do not wish to wait the three or four years it can frequently take for a case to move up on the court calendar and will come to terms privately.

Beginning around 1980, a movement toward "alternative dispute resolution" (ADR) has gained force throughout the United States. Corporations, private groups, and the courts themselves have begun to seek quicker and cheaper ways for litigants and potential litigants to settle many different types of quarrels than through the courts. In a number of communities, "neighborhood justice centers" or "dispute resolution centers" have sprung up to help in settling disputes, of both civil and criminal nature, that ought not to consume the time and money of courts or of the parties in lengthy proceedings.

These alternative forums use a variety of techniques, including arbitration and mediation, to bring about rapprochement. The techniques vary, and their differences are worth noting. Calling to mind the nature of the judicial process, there are two significant variables: the power to influence the process, and the power to influence the outcome. The first is the degree to which the parties retain control over the shaping of the issues, the information, and the evidence that will constitute the basis for the decision.

Box 4-1 Recovering Attorney's Fees

U.S. Must Pay Whistle-Blower's Fees

WASHINGTON—Attorneys for A. Ernest Fitzgerald, the Air Force employee who lost his job after blowing the whistle on cost overruns in the C5-A procurement program, will be able to recover their fees from the federal government, U.S. District Judge William M. Bryant has ruled.

The fees probably will be "between $100,000 and $200,000," according to Mr. Fitzgerald's lead attorney, John Bodner Jr. of Washington's Howrey & Simon.

Mr. Fitzgerald sued the Air Force after officials evaded a 1972 Civil Service Commission order directing that he be restored to his old job or an equivalent position. *Fitzgerald* v. *Hampton,* 76-1486. Judge Bryant found last year that the job Mr. Fitzgerald was given was not equivalent to his original position, and a hearing will be held this May to determine whether the Air Force has yet complied with the 1972 CSC order.

On March 30, Judge Bryant ruled that the Equal Access to Justice Act entitles Mr. Fitzgerald's attorneys, who had been handling the case for the American Civil Liberties Union on a pro bono basis, to recover fees from the Air Force.

Air Force conduct in the case was "vexatious and obstructive" and exhibited "bad faith," Judge Bryant ruled.

Mr. Fitzgerald has also sued former President Richard M. Nixon and several of his associates, charging that Mr. Nixon violated his civil rights by ordering his firing. That case, *Nixon* v. *Fitzgerald,* 79-1738, is now before the Supreme Court on the question of presidential immunity.—*David Lauter*

Source: *The National Law Journal,* April 19, 1982

The second is the degree to which one or the other or both parties retain control to determine the outcome of the dispute unilaterally. In a court, the parties retain little control over the decision, much control over the process. In private bargaining, the parties retain total control over both process and decision.

Arbitration

Arbitration is a species of adjudication. The parties use a private decisionmaker, the **arbitrator**, and the rules of procedure are considerably more relaxed than those that apply in the courtroom. The parties may agree to resolve an existing dispute through arbitration, or they may agree in a contract before any dispute arises that all future disputes will be resolved by arbitration. They may spell out the rules of procedure to be used and the method for choosing the arbitrator. For example, they may name the specific person, or delegate the responsibility of choosing to some neutral person, or they may each designate a person and the two designees may jointly pick a third arbitrator.

Some 40,000 arbitrations a year take place under the auspices of the American Arbitration Association (AAA), a private organization headquartered in New York, with regional offices in many other cities. The AAA uses published sets of rules for various types of arbitration (for example, labor arbitration or commercial arbitration); parties who provide in contracts for arbitration through the AAA are agreeing to be bound by the AAA rules.

Arbitration has a twofold advantage over litigation. First, it is usually much quicker, because the arbitrator does not have a backlog of cases and because the procedures are simpler. Second, in complex cases, the quality of the decision may be higher, because the parties can select an arbitrator knowledgeable in the field. Under both federal and state law, arbitration is favored, and a decision rendered by an arbitrator is by law binding and may be enforced by the courts. Judicial review of an arbitrator's decision is limited, as illustrated by the following case.

UNITED PAPERWORKERS INTERN. UNION v. MISCO, INC.
108 S.Ct. 364 (1987)

JUSTICE WHITE delivered the opinion of the Court.

The issue for decision involves several aspects of when a federal court may refuse to enforce an arbitration award rendered under a collective-bargaining agreement.

Misco, Inc., (Misco, or the Company) operates a paper converting plant in Monroe, Louisiana. The Company is a party to a collective-bargaining agreement with the United Paperworkers International Union, AFL-CIO, and its union local (the Union); the agreement covers the production and maintenance employees at the plant. Under the agreement, the Company or the Union may submit to arbitration any grievance that arises from the interpretation or application of its terms, and the arbitrator's decision is final and binding upon the parties. The arbitrator's authority is limited to interpretation and application of the terms contained in the agreement itself. The agreement reserves to management the right to establish, amend, and enforce "rules and regulations regulating the discipline or discharge of employees" and the procedures for imposing discipline. Such rules were to be posted and were to be in effect "until ruled on by grievance and arbitration procedures as to fairness and necessity." For about a decade, the Company's rules had listed as causes for discharge the bringing of intoxicants, narcotics, or controlled substances on to plant property or consuming any of them there, as well as reporting for work under the influence of such substances. At the time of the events involved in this case, the Company was very concerned about the use of drugs at the plant, especially among employees on the night shift.

Isiah Cooper, who worked on the night shift for Misco, was one of the employees covered by the collective-bargaining agreement. He operated a slitter-rewinder machine, which uses sharp blades to cut rolling coils of paper. The arbitrator found that this machine is hazardous and had caused numerous injuries in recent years. Cooper had been reprimanded twice in a few months for deficient performance. On January 21, 1983, one day after the second reprimand, the police searched Cooper's house pursuant to a warrant, and a substantial amount of marijuana was found. Contemporaneously, a police officer was detailed to keep Cooper's car under observation at the Company's parking lot. At about 6:30 p.m., Cooper was seen walking in the parking lot during work hours with two other men. The three men entered Cooper's car momentarily, then walked to another car, a white Cutlass, and entered it. After the other two men later returned to the plant, Cooper was apprehended by police in the backseat of this car with marijuana smoke in the air and a lighted marijuana cigarette in the front-seat ashtray. The police also searched Cooper's car and found a plastic scales case and marijuana gleanings. Cooper was arrested and charged with marijuana possession.

On January 24, Cooper told the Company that he had been arrested for possession of marijuana at his home; the Company did not learn of the marijuana cigarette in the white Cutlass until January 27. It then investigated and on February 7 discharged Cooper, asserting that in the circumstances, his presence in the Cutlass violated the rule against having drugs on the plant premises. Cooper filed a grievance protesting his discharge the same day, and the matter proceeded to arbitration. The Company was not aware until September 21, five days before the hearing before the arbitrator was scheduled, that marijuana had been found in Cooper's car. That fact did not become known to the Union until the hearing began. At the hearing it was stipulated that the issue was whether the Company had "just cause to discharge the Grievant under Rule II.1" and, "[i]f not, what if any should be the remedy."

The arbitrator upheld the grievance and ordered the Company to reinstate Cooper with backpay and full seniority. The arbitrator based his finding that there was not just cause for the discharge on his consideration of seven criteria. In particular, the arbitrator found that the Company failed to prove that the employee had possessed or used marijuana on company property: finding Cooper in the backseat of a car and a burning cigarette in the frontseat ashtray was insufficient proof that Cooper was using or possessed marijuana on company property. The arbitrator refused to accept into evidence the fact that marijuana had been found in Cooper's car on company premises because the Company did not know of this fact when Cooper was discharged and therefore did not rely on it as a basis for the discharge.

The Company filed suit in District Court, seeking to vacate the arbitration award on several grounds, one of which was that ordering reinstatement of Cooper, who had allegedly possessed marijuana on the plant premises, was contrary to public policy. The District Court agreed that the award must be set aside as contrary to public policy because it ran counter to general safety concerns that arise from the operation of dangerous machinery while under the influence of drugs, as well as to state criminal laws against drug possession. The Court of Appeals affirmed, with one judge dissenting. The court ruled that reinstatement would violate the public policy "against the operation of dangerous machinery by persons under the influence of drugs or alcohol." The arbitrator had found that Cooper was apprehended on company premises in an atmosphere of marijuana smoke in another's car and that marijuana was found in his own car on the company lot. These facts established that Cooper had violated the Company's rules and gave the company just cause to discharge him. The arbitrator did not reach this conclusion because of a "narrow focus on Cooper's procedural rights" that led him to ignore what he "knew was in fact true: that Cooper *did* bring marijuana onto his employer's premises." Even if the arbitrator had not known of this fact at the time he entered his award, "it is doubtful that the award should be enforced today in light of what is now known."

Because the Courts of Appeals are divided on the question of when courts may set aside arbitration awards as contravening public policy, we granted the Union's petition for a writ of certiorari, and now reverse the judgment of the Court of Appeals.

* * *

Collective-bargaining agreements commonly provide grievance procedures to settle disputes between union and employer with respect to the interpretation and application of the agreement and require binding arbitration for unsettled grievances. In such cases, and this is such a case, the Court made clear almost 30 years ago that the courts play only a limited role when asked to review the decision of an arbitrator. The courts are not authorized to reconsider the merits of an award even though the parties may allege that the award rests on errors of fact or on misinterpretation of the contract.

* * *

Because the parties have contracted to have disputes settled by an arbitrator chosen by them rather than by a judge, it is the arbitrator's view of the facts and of the meaning of the contract that they have agreed to accept. Courts thus do not sit to hear claims of factual or legal error by an arbitrator as an appellate court does in reviewing decisions of lower courts. To resolve disputes about the application of a collective-bargaining agreement, an arbitrator must find facts and a court may not reject those findings simply because it disagrees with them. The same is true of the arbitrator's interpretation of the contract. The arbitrator may not ignore the plain language of the contract; but the parties having authorized the arbitrator to give meaning to the language of the agreement, a court should not reject an award on the ground that the arbitrator misread the contract. So, too, where it is contemplated that the arbitrator will determine remedies for contract violations that he finds, courts have no authority to disagree with his honest judgment in that respect. If the courts were free to intervene on these grounds, the speedy resolution of grievances by private mechanisms would be greatly undermined. . . . Of course, decisions procured by the parties through fraud or through the arbitrator's dishonesty need not be enforced. But there is nothing of that sort involved in this case.

The Company's position, simply put, is that the arbitrator committed grievous error in finding that the evidence was insufficient to prove that Cooper had possessed or used marijuana on company property. But the Court of Appeals, although it took a distinctly jaundiced view of the arbitrator's decision in this regard, was not free to refuse enforcement because it considered Cooper's presence in the white Cutlass, in the circumstances, to be ample proof that Rule II.1 was violated. No dishonesty is alleged; only improvident, even silly, factfinding is claimed. This is hardly sufficient basis for disregarding what the agent appointed by the parties determined to be the historical facts.

Nor was it open to the Court of Appeals to refuse to enforce the award because the arbitrator, in deciding whether there was just cause to discharge, refused to consider evidence unknown to the Company at the time Cooper was fired. The parties bargained for arbitration to settle disputes and were free to set the procedural rules for arbitrators to follow if they chose. Section VI of the agreement, entitled "Arbitration Procedure," did set some ground rules for the arbitration process. It forbade the arbitrator to consider hearsay evidence, for example, but evidentiary matters were otherwise left to the arbitrator. Here the arbitrator ruled that in determining whether Cooper had violated Rule II.1, he should not consider evidence not relied on by the employer in ordering the discharge, particularly in a case like this where there was no notice to the employee or the Union prior to the hearing that the Company would attempt to rely on after-discovered evidence. This, in effect, was a construction of what the contract required when deciding discharge cases: an arbitrator was to look only at the evidence before the employer at the time of discharge. As the arbitrator noted, this approach was consistent with the practice followed by other arbitrators. . . .

Under the Arbitration Act, the federal courts are empowered to set aside arbitration awards on such grounds only when "the arbitrators were guilty of misconduct . . . in refusing to hear evidence pertinent and material to the controversy." 9 U.S.C. § 10(c). If we apply that same standard here and assume that the arbitrator erred in refusing to consider the disputed evidence, his error was not in bad faith or so gross as to amount to affirmative misconduct. Finally, it is worth noting that putting aside the evidence about the marijuana found in Cooper's car during this arbitration did not forever foreclose the Company from using that evidence as the basis for a discharge.

Even if it were open to the Court of Appeals to have found a violation of Rule II.1 because of the marijuana found in Cooper's car, the question remains whether the court could properly set aside the award because in its view discharge was the correct remedy. Normally, an arbitrator is authorized to disagree with the sanction imposed for employee misconduct. . . .

. . . [The Court of Appeals] held that the evidence of marijuana in Cooper's car required that the award be set aside because to reinstate a person who had brought drugs onto the property was contrary to the public policy "against the operation of dangerous machinery by persons under the influence of drugs or alcohol." We cannot affirm that judgment.

A court's refusal to enforce an arbitrator's award under a collective-bargaining agreement because it is contrary to public policy is a specific application of the more general doctrine, rooted in the common law, that a court may refuse to enforce contracts that violate law or public policy. *W. R. Grace & Co. v. Rubber Workers,* 461 U.S. 757 (1983). That doctrine derives from the basic notion that no court will lend its aid to one who founds a cause of action upon an immoral or illegal act, and is further justified by the observation that the public's interests in confining the scope of private agreements to which it is not a party will go unrepresented unless the judiciary takes account of those interests when it considers whether to enforce such agreements. In the common law of contracts, this doctrine has served as the foundation for occasional exercises of judicial power to abrogate private agreements.

In *W. R. Grace,* we recognized that "a court may not enforce a collective-bargaining agreement that is contrary to public policy," and stated that "the question of public policy is ultimately one for resolution by the courts." We cautioned, however, that a court's refusal to enforce an arbitrator's *interpretation* of such contracts is limited to situations where the contract as interpreted would violate "some explicit public policy" that is "well defined and dominant, and is to be ascertained 'by reference to the laws and legal precedents and not from general considerations of supposed public interests.' " In *W. R. Grace,* we identified two important public policies that were potentially jeopardized by the arbitrator's interpretation of the contract: obedience to judicial orders and voluntary compliance with Title VII. We went on to hold that enforcement of the arbitration award in that case did not compromise either of the two public policies allegedly threatened by the award. Two points follow from our decision in *W. R. Grace*. First, a court may refuse to enforce a collective-bargaining agreement when the specific terms contained in that agreement violate public policy. Second, it is apparent that our decision in that case does not otherwise sanction a broad judicial power to set aside arbitration awards as against public policy. Although we discussed the effect of that award on two broad areas of public policy, our decision turned on our examination of whether the award created any explicit conflict with other "laws and legal precedents" rather than an assessment of "general considerations of supposed public interests." At the very least, an alleged public policy must be properly framed under the approach set out in *W. R. Grace,* and the violation of such a policy must be clearly shown if an award is not to be enforced.

As we see it, the formulation of public policy set out by the Court of Appeals did not comply with the statement that such a policy must be "ascertained 'by reference to the laws and legal precedents and not from general considerations of supposed public interests.' " The Court of Appeals made no attempt to review existing laws and legal precedents in order to demonstrate that they establish a "well defined and dominant" policy against the operation of dangerous machinery while under the influence of drugs. Although certainly such a judgment is firmly roted in common sense, we explicitly held in *W. R. Grace* that a formulation of public policy based only on "general considerations of supposed public interests" is not the sort that permits a court to set aside an arbitration award that was entered in accordance with a valid collective-bargaining agreement.

Even if the Court of Appeals' formulation of public policy is to be accepted, no violation of that policy was clearly shown in this case. In pursuing its public policy inquiry, the Court of Appeals quite properly considered the established fact that traces of marijuana had been found in Cooper's car. Yet the assumed connection between the marijuana gleanings found in Cooper's car and Cooper's actual use of drugs in the workplace is tenuous at best and provides an insufficient basis for holding that his reinstatement would actually violate the public policy identified by the Court of Appeals "against the operation of dangerous machinery by persons under the influence of drugs or alcohol." A refusal to enforce an award must rest on more than speculation or assumption.

In any event, it was inappropriate for the Court of Appeals itself to draw the necessary inference. To conclude from the fact that marijuana had been found in Cooper's car that Cooper had ever been or would be under the influence of marijuana while he was on the job and operating dangerous machinery is an exercise in factfinding about Cooper's use of drugs and his amenability to discipline, a task that exceeds the authority of a court asked to overturn an arbitration award. The parties did not bargain for the facts to be found by a court, but by an arbitrator chosen by them who had more opportunity to observe Cooper and to be familiar with the plant and its problems. . . .

The judgment of the Court of Appeals is reversed.

United Paperworkers is one of several recent decisions in which the Supreme Court has ruled in favor of arbitration. The Court, for instance, has decided that agreements between securities brokers and their clients to arbitrate alleged violations of securities law are enforceable. [Shearson/American Express, Inc. v. McMahon, 107 S. Ct. 2332 (1987)] Also see the discussion of the *Mitsubishi* decision on p. 708.

By and large, both parties must consent to submit to arbitration. But some states have experimented with "court-annexed arbitration," in which certain types of cases (in California, for instance, cases for money damages in the amount of $25,000 or less) are assigned to designated arbitrators in an attempt to save time and expense.

"Rent-a-Judge"

Most states have a statutory procedure that permits litigants to refer a lawsuit to a private judge for resolution. This procedure, dubbed "rent-a-judge" in the 1980s (but known formally as "trial by reference"), has several advantages for corporate litigants who are prepared to pay the judge's fee. The trial can be held at the parties' convenience, in private, and, in many states, without any record being kept. The judge's decision is binding and enforceable; unlike arbitration, the judge is bound to follow the ordinary rules of evidence, and the decision may be appealed to a regular appellate court. Since almost all private judges to whom cases are referred under this procedure are retired judges, the case can be scheduled far more quickly than the civil dockets of most major courts permit, and the judge can render a decision within a period agreed on by both parties. Another advantage of the reference procedure is expertise: the parties can hire a judge who is knowledgeable in the area of the dispute—for example, patents, antitrust, or environmental litigation.

Mediation

Unlike adjudication, mediation gives the mediator no power to impose a decision. Instead, the mediator acts as a go-between who attempts to help the parties negotiate a solution. He can communicate the parties' positions to each other, facilitate the finding of common ground, and suggest outcomes. But the parties have complete control over both process and decision. The outcome need not be responsive to the claims initially raised, nor does it require the application of an articulated, rational standard. The parties may come up with *any* resolution of their dispute that satisfies them.

Mediation, because it is an unstructured and informal process, has no ground rules beyond those the parties themselves agree to follow. Mediation can be exceptionally helpful when (1) the emotional level is high; (2) the parties are at an impasse; (3) the issues are complex; (4) there is no one obvious right answer; (5) many parties are involved; and (6) the need to resolve the issues is urgent. Mediation works because it permits a neutral who has gained the trust of the parties "to learn intimate facts from both sides that they would never have shared with each other in the course of trial preparation. By building on the parties' trust in the mediator, the process thus allows the parties to explore workable options. With the knowledge that he gains, the mediator can learn how far apart the parties are and devise ways of bridging the gap." (Lieberman and Henry, 1986, p. 428)

The Mini-Trial

Perhaps the most celebrated new corporate dispute resolution technique of the 1980s is the "mini-trial." This device is not in fact a trial at all, but a formalized method of settlement negotiation. Box 4-2 describes the invention of the mini-trial in 1977. During the 1980s, a host of well-known companies and even government agencies designed a mini-trial process to resolve expensive, time-consuming lawsuits. The companies included Allied Corp., Amoco, Austin Industries, Borden, Continental Can, Control Data Corp., Gillette, Honeywell, Shell Oil Co., Texaco, TRW, Union Carbide Corp., and Wisconsin Electric Power Co.; among the government agencies were NASA and the Army Corps of Engineers.

No single procedural model of the mini-trial has been universally adopted. The parties are free to design their own process. But, in general, the mini-trial has the following characteristics:

1. Preparation time is short—perhaps six weeks to two months—compared to the years of the pre-trial phase of a lawsuit.
2. The hearing is highly abbreviated—no more than a day or two—compared to the months that a complex antitrust or commercial lawsuit can take in court.
3. The hearing is usually conducted before a third-party neutral known as the "neutral advisor," who has no authority to decide the dispute.
4. There is no judge or jury. The case is presented to representatives of the parties, who have the authority to settle.
5. The lawyers present their "best" case; they do not spend time on side issues.
6. Immediately after the presentations, the parties meet privately to negotiate a settlement.
7. If they fail to settle, the neutral advisor may, if agreed in advance, render an advisory opinion on how he thinks the case would come out if it went to trial. The parties might then meet again.
8. The hearings are confidential; the parties and the neutral advisor commit themselves to refrain from disclosing details of the proceeding to outsiders.

The mini-trial has several advantages: (1) costs are dramatically lower than litigation; (2) the process allows for creative problem-solving; the parties can reach resolutions not possible in court; (3) the parties are free to maintain ongoing relationships; (4) the parties can avail themselves of a knowledgeable neutral, rather than, as in court, a judge chosen at random; (5) the disputants can design whatever process and rules suit them best; (6) the entire proceedings can be kept confidential; and (7) much time can be saved over conventional legal process.

Box 4-2 The First Minitrial

Business Saves Big Money with the 'Minitrial'

When 17 representatives of TRW Inc. and Telecredit Inc. sat down around an oversize table in a small room at the Century Plaza Hotel in Los Angeles in July, 1977, they did not suppose they were plotting a revolution. They were hoping to find a quick means of settling a lawsuit. Their complicated patent squabble had already consumed more than two years of increasingly rancorous pretrial maneuvering and outlays of more than $500,000 each, most of it spent on lawyers.

But the method they devised for resolving their dispute—a method now generally known as "minitrial"—has been adopted in one form or another by several companies and has saved each of them hundreds of thousands of dollars. To make the concept more accessible, the Center for Public Resources (CPR), a nonprofit business-oriented think tank based in New York, this month plans to publish a manual that shows how the snares in many types of lawsuits can be avoided.

Telecredit, a company with 1975 sales of some $8 million, had accused giant TRW of infringing on a number of patents in its computerized credit-card and check-authorization machines. It sought $6 million in damages and an injunction against further infringement. TRW heatedly denied infringement and plunged into its legal defense.

During the next two years, as the companies' lawyers went about collecting each other's documents, emotions ran high. "The feelings between the two companies and even the lawyers were extremely negative," recalls Lee A. Ault III, Telecredit president and chief executive. Each company was convinced its legal position was correct.

DELAYS

TRW repeatedly asked Telecredit to demonstrate how the patents had been infringed. "We wanted a showing," explains Eric D. Green, one of TRW's lawyers and now a professor at Boston University Law School. "We referred to it as a 'dog and pony show,' " he says. The case dragged on, delayed in part by a judge who was unfamiliar with patent law and reluctant to bring it to a conclusion.

After many refusals to step outside the framework of the lawsuit, Telecredit asked TRW whom it would believe. Green responded that the company would accept the finding of a neutral outside expert, but TRW rejected Telecredit's first suggestion—to submit the case to binding arbitration—in part for fear that for technical reasons an arbitrator's award would not be enforceable.

THE ELEMENTS OF A MINITRIAL

Before the "trial":
- Formal court proceedings stayed
- Parties write their own rules
- Fix short deadlines
- Choose neutral expert
- Draw up short statements of case

At the "trial":
- Follow rigid two-day schedule
- Present "best" case to expert adviser
- Top managers must be present

After the "trial":
- Managers immediately discuss settlement
- Adviser issues nonbinding opinion if no settlement is reached quickly

---

TRW lawyers negotiated with Telecredit cofounder (and nonlawyer) Ronald A. Katz, then the company's patent licensing administrator, and gradually they evolved the minitrial strategy. They agreed that each company would present its case to a third-party expert who would act as an adviser, not a judge. The minitrial itself was governed by an eight-page set of rules calling for a two-day secret hearing, in which each side would have four hours to present witnesses and to argue its case not only to the neutral expert but also to top managers from each company. The rest of the time was devoted to rebuttals.

(continues on next page)

Box 4-2, *continued*

Ault represented Telecredit; TRW sent Vice-President Richard A. Campbell. The adviser was James F. Davis, a former U.S. Court of Claims trial judge.

SAVINGS OF $1 MILLION

The tension in the room was palpable, Ault says, but Davis kept the case moving, and the lawyers stuck to the schedule. Immediately after the final rebuttal, Ault and Campbell met privately and within 30 minutes sketched out a compromise: TRW would pay for a license against certain credits, if the Patent Office would issue Telecredit new patents. (It did, this summer.) From the time when the minitrial was first broached to the signing of the settlement, only three months had elapsed, and the saving in lawyers' fees was at least $1 million, Ault estimates.

The minitrial worked, says Telecredit's patent lawyer, Byard G. Nilsson of Los Angeles, because the parties assumed a "negotiating rather than a battle stance." Katz, now an independent consultant, agrees: "We have to remove lawyers from their pugilistic environment and bring in the problem-solving abilities of businessmen."

Observers of the TRW-Telecredit minitrial and the half dozen others conducted since believe that two factors are critical to success: the presence of a neutral adviser, and, after litigation begins, the necessity of arguing the staunchest positions to top management.

The third-party adviser, chosen because he is an expert in the field, avoids what Katz calls the "Russian-roulette" quality of the federal system, in which a company seeking to protect its patent, for example, can draw a judge who always rules patents invalid or a judge who has never had such a case and is frightened or bored by the prospect. Moreover, extra pressure on the parties comes from the expectation that the adviser will write an opinion if they fail to settle. Auditors of a public company handed an adverse opinion might have to disclose its existence, lawyers say, and stockholders could create trouble if a company sought to litigate in the face of an opinion by a neutral expert that the company was in the wrong.

SPEEDY JUSTICE

The neutral adviser, or private judge, need not be reserved for a late stage of bitter litigation. As a dispute between Shell Oil Co. and Intel Corp. shows, the neutral expert can profitably be employed at the outset. Shell filed suit against Intel in January, 1979, charging infringement of patents on a semiconductor memory. Intel denied the charge but agreed that if it had infringed the patent it would owe some $500,000. In April, before any discovery or other activity in the suit could begin, the dispute was submitted to a neutral patent attorney, who spent four hours with the parties considering depositions and other evidence. Three weeks later he sent a summary opinion indicating that Shell would win the lawsuit.

"Our total out-of-pocket expenses were under $10,000," says Roger S. Borovoy, Intel's corporate secretary and counsel. He estimates that had the case been fully litigated, it would have taken four years at trial and on appeal and would have consumed more than $1 million in lawyers' fees for both sides and $300,000 more for the appeal. "The issues aren't worth that," he says.

Despite Intel's loss, Borovoy says company management was "pleased we didn't go the rug bazaar route" and negotiate a split-the-difference settlement, which Shell offered. "Our decision to proceed with the minitrial cost us $250,000," he says, "but management was particularly satisfied nevertheless, because even though we thought we were right, the case was disposed of rationally and in a fair way."

THE COST OF ALOOFNESS

If the neutral expert is, in Katz's phrase, "a congealing force," no less necessary to the success of a minitrial is the requirement that top management be present. "Management doesn't get as involved as it probably should," says Ault. Notes Katz: "It's seldom that a manager in any business

(continues on next page)

Box 4-2, *continued*

would give a subordinate an open checkbook, but in litigation they usually do." That is because the byways of litigation are so highly specialized that the manager is afraid to interfere—and blame for the loss of a case can be pinned on the lawyer. But in remaining aloof, minitrial advocates say, the executive deprives the dispute of his own skill: a problem-solving and negotiating ability.

Bringing management into the picture can ease the lawyer's burden, but at the same time management gains a way of seeing how well-prepared, competent, and strong its advocates are. "It takes a courageous general counsel to expose himself to an appraisal by his clients of how well he does," says Green.

Nevertheless, more and more lawyers are seeking ways of doing just that. "There is an overwhelming desire by corporate general counsel to study ways of reducing costs," says John A. Stichnoth, vice-president and general counsel of Union Carbide Corp. and chairman of the CPR group that has compiled a manual on minitrials and other means of resolving complex business disputes quickly. The CPR plans to market the manual aggressively, he says, so that lawyers "won't have to reinvent procedures and forms" that have been shown to work.

A PRIVATE AFFAIR

Although a majority of the minitrials to date have concerned patents, these private forums have also dealt with antitrust, unfair competition, and contractual claims. Green is currently preparing a minitrial scheduled for November in a "major" products liability case actively litigated for three years. It involves the failure of an electronic component that the end user helped design. Whenever a complex business suit raises "mixed questions of fact and law"—such as the antitrust notion of relevant market or the patent standard of "obviousness"—it is amenable to minitrial procedures, Green says. Only if a case turns on the credibility of witnesses or involves "pure law" is it likely that conventional litigation will be necessary.

So far the minitrial has remained a private affair, tailored by the parties to their own needs. But a federal judge in Hawaii has recently pushed the parties in a patent infringement case to adopt minitrial procedures, and Katz served as a consultant in a case in which one of the parties was a federal agency. Green thinks that an "imaginative, early use" of federal rules of procedure and evidence could lead to widespread adoption. He reports that a survey he has just completed of the views of all federal judges is "extremely encouraging."

Next year, to give the idea even more currency, Katz plans to tape a "mock minitrial" in conjunction with the schools of management and law at the University of California at Los Angeles for showing around the country. The minitrial, he says, "provides a telescopic view of a case under the best of conditions, and this is a point that impresses everyone who sees how they work."

* * *

Source: *Business Week,* October 13, 1980, pp. 170–72

Inquisitorial Approach

Unlike the adjudicator, the decision-maker in an inquisitorial approach has power over both the outcome and the process. A familiar example of the inquisitorial approach is the legislative committee hearing. The legislative committee may listen to whomever it pleases, deny anyone it chooses the right to appear before it, and take any action it chooses (including none), regardless of the arguments made by those who appeared before it. Legislative committees do not ordinarily resolve individual disputes. One version of the inquisitorial model has caught a certain degree of public attention:

the **ombudsman**. The term comes from the Scandinavian administrative system in which a public official has the power to intervene in administrative decisions on behalf of complaining citizens. In effect, the ombudsman is a people's trouble-shooter.

Legislation

If private bargaining is at one end of the dispute-resolution continuum, legislation is at the other. In private bargaining, the parties retain total power over both process and outcome. In legislation, they retain neither. The legislator neither can nor does give a hearing to all those affected by the contemplated action. No hearing at all need be held, no evidence introduced to the decision-makers. Unlike judges, legislators are not bound by any authoritative standard. Legislators may pursue political, economic, and social goals of their own choosing. Their decision need not be "rational," in the sense that the goal must follow necessarily from the means chosen. Obviously, most legislators prefer to be rational, but because they must compromise hotly contested points of view, their decisions often will not be considered rational. Moreover, there rarely are articulated standards by which the rationality of a legislative enactment can be measured, unlike a judicial decision.

Managing and Preventing Disputes

Many corporations have begun to look beyond the particular techniques for resolving disputes and are scrutinizing the ways they respond to business disputes when they first flare up—or even before. They are learning, in other words, to manage and prevent disputes, as well as to resolve them.

Managing Disputes The philosophy of corporate dispute management is that the company law department should be considered a center for the management of investments and that litigation should be managed through tools of cost accounting and business judgment, just as other business functions are managed. Successfully implementing this philosophy requires management to understand litigation and the legal system (one of the reasons that business law courses are important) and lawyers to understand management. During the mid-1970s, the law department of Xerox Corp. began using budgeting and financial planning. The result was that from 1976 to 1982, the company's outside legal expenses fell from $12 million per year to $3 million at a time of sharp inflation, and the number of in-house lawyers dropped from 152 to 70.

Among the management tools available to management-oriented lawyers are litigation budgeting and risk analysis. The lawyer looks at a lawsuit as a marketing executive looks at a product that needs to be sold. The lawyer asks: What will I get for my investment? For instance, lawyers in conventional practice handed a lawsuit might decide to take depositions of dozens of executives, without regard to cost. The manager wants to know what dividends those depositions will pay.

Preventive Law Disputes that do not arise need never be resolved. Companies are learning to head off obvious difficulties by establishing compliance programs to ensure that employees abide by the law. Companies also are beginning to undertake litigation audits to determine, by inspecting existing lawsuits, where such companies are vulnerable and what changes in procedure might reduce their legal exposure.

A commitment to exploring alternatives to lawsuits is a form of prevention that is beginning to gain favor with some companies. When IBM settled a product-piracy suit against Hitachi, for example, the companies agreed on an elaborate arbitration system should the situation ever arise again. Knowing that their companies are bound to follow a particular procedure with tough sanctions might dissuade some executives from engaging in behavior that would invoke the process. (And, as Box 4-3 illustrates, once a company learns that it can solve complex problems outside the courtroom, it will tend to design a dispute-resolution system invoking a variety of alternative processes to settle future disputes.)

Why ADR Might Fail

Alternative dispute resolution is not a panacea. Non-courtroom procedures may fail for a variety of reasons. First, ADR may not work because each party may be reluctant to suggest it, for fear that the opposition will perceive the suggestion as a sign of weakness. A possible solution to this difficulty is the Alternative Dispute Resolution Pledge sponsored by the Center for Public Resources in New York. More than 200 major American corporations have subscribed to this pledge (see Box 4-4). Each signatory undertakes to explore an alternative to litigation if the company with which it has had a dispute has also subscribed to the Policy Statement. Although lawsuits will scarcely fade away—more than 10 million cases are filed every year in the state and federal courts—there are hopeful signs that business realizes that sensible settlement is not a weakness but a strength.

A second reason for the failure of ADR may be the emotional state of the people involved. Even if there are no sound business reasons for hiring lawyers and paying the escalating legal fees, executives can be caught up in the "game." Psychologists refer to this process as "entrapment." People often spend much more of their time and money in resolving a conflict than seems justified. One study (Teger, 1979) indicates two reasons for entrapment: (1) economic reasons—the drive for the very last dollar that can be exacted; and (2) interpersonal relations, such as the desire to save face or to prove that the manager is the best. At the outset the parties might have sound economic motives for pursuing the dispute, but at some point in the litigation process the interpersonal aspects can come to the fore, and

Box 4-3 Many Strategies to Resolving Disputes Out of Court

Neutrals Deployed Several Kinds of ADR to Solve IBM-Fujitsu Copyright Dispute

When IBM and Fujitsu—respectively the world's first and fourth largest computer companies—resolved their four-year fight over software copyright in mid-September, nearly all news media called the highly publicized procedure an arbitration.

But an *Alternatives* analysis of the case documents shows that not only arbitration, but also mediation, an ADR contract clause, neutral expert factfinding, negotiation by executives and attorneys, and preventive-law concepts were all deployed by the two neutrals in their ADR resolution of this complex, high-stakes battle. Moreover, the neutrals will have continuing oversight of the ongoing resolution, thus functioning very much like special masters have in large court cases.

Thus, the lessons of the case are that several kinds of ADR can be profitably employed in a dispute and, perhaps more importantly, that the failure of one ADR strategy does not mean others will be fruitless.

The nub of the dispute was IBM's claim that Fujitsu, which makes IBM-compatible hardware and software, had violated IBM's copyrights in the latter. The controversy arose gradually during the late 1970's and early 1980's, in part because U.S. copyright law was evolving. Before 1980, few thought copyrights were available for computer software. But in that year Congress passed the Computer Software Act, extending such protection to this intellectual property.

GLOBAL CASE

The dispute was a major one in the computer market. These two multinational corporations compete in Asia, Brazil, Europe and the Pacific Rim. Hundreds of millions of dollars were at stake. So significant was the disagreement that senior officials from both companies spent eight months negotiating a settlement after IBM lodged its formal complaint with Fujitsu in October 1982.

Under that 1983 accord, Fujitsu paid substantial sums to IBM for its previous distribution of certain computer programs, and agreed to make semiannual payments for its future marketing of them. In turn, IBM granted immunity to Fujitsu, which admitted no copyright infringement, and waived all past and future claims regarding that software. The companies also set up a system for making available certain software information to each other in the future.

The 1983 agreements, however, were "confusing" and "incomplete," according to Stanford Law Prof. Robert Mnookin and retired railroad executive and computer expert John Jones, the two neutrals who orchestrated the most recent resolution. Under the weight of many disagreements about their meaning, the pacts collapsed not long after their creation. As Messrs. Jones and Mnookin note in their September 15 opinion, the two computer makers then "attempted to negotiate a resolution of disputes through voluminous correspondence and numerous meetings of technical and business personnel." But, they observe, "None of these attempts was successful."

TWO-FOLD SOLUTION

After these vain efforts to revive the 1983 agreements, the parties embarked in June 1985 on the recently concluded ADR initiative. The solution, described in an order issued by the neutrals simultaneously with their September 15 opinion, is an ongoing one, with many details to be worked out. In essence, the solution is two-fold, with the first applying to disputes over existing software and the second to potential disputes over future software.

The first part is Fujitsu's payment of a sum—yet to be determined by the neutrals—for all past and future use of an agreed-upon list of existing software programs. Mr. Jones terms this a "paid-up license" for these programs, for which Fujitsu will get a guarantee of "complete immunity" from IBM.

(continues on next page)

Box 4-3, *continued*

Second is the establishment of a "Secured Facility Regime," under which each company can examine, under elaborate safeguards, certain parts of the software of the other. In return for adequate compensation, the examining company can use the obtained information in developing its own software, and be assured of immunity from claims of copyright violations. Monitored by an independent expert and expected to last for five to ten years as the neutrals may decide, the Secured Facility Regime "will constitute the intellectual property law between these two companies," said Professor Mnookin on September 15.

In detail too profuse to recount here, the neutrals have set out the operation of this two-part decision in their September 15 opinion and award. Interested readers can obtain those documents from the American Arbitration Association, the organization under which the ADR was conducted, at 140 West 51 St., New York, NY 10020. Heard in the AAA Commercial Arbitration Tribunal, the case is titled *International Business Machines Corp. v. Fujitsu Ltd.*, No. 13T-117-0636-85.

For ADR advocates, however, the breadth of ADR devices deployed in the case may be its most interesting aspect. The following is a selected schematic of the variety of ADR strategies used in the resolution of the dispute.

ADR CONTRACT CLAUSE

While neutrals Mnookin and Jones had little good to say about the collapsed 1983 agreements between IBM and Fujitsu, it was in fact the ADR clause in that accord that started the ball rolling toward the September 15 resolution of the case.

The clause mandated a two-part ADR procedure: negotiation and arbitration. First, "(T)he parties agreed to submit any dispute with respect to the agreements to a meeting of responsible executives of both parties," the neutrals note in their opinion. Second, they continue, the two computer makers "agreed to submit any dispute which remained unresolved after sixty days to binding arbitration under the auspices of the AAA."

ARBITRATION

Two types of arbitration were used in the case. At first, the parties each chose an arbitrator, Mr. Jones for IBM and Professor Mnookin for Fujitsu. Those two party-arbitrators appointed a third, neutral arbitrator, Donald A. Macdonald.

But at the first meeting of this panel with the parties in December 1985, "the parties and the Arbitrators agreed that all Arbitrators would serve as neutrals, that the AAA rules and ethical standards would apply, and that there would be no ex parte communications with the parties except as authorized by the Panel," neutrals Jones and Mnookin note in their opinion. Neutral Macdonald resigned in May 1987, leaving the other two to handle the case from there on.

'MINI-TRIAL'

The neutrals began their handling of the case in conventional arbitration fashion, hearing and deciding in February 1986 various procedural issues relating to the 1983 agreements.

But at that time the neutrals also drew on another ADR principle, the involvement of business executives, in their attempts to resolve the dispute. Messrs. Jones, Macdonald and Mnookin required that "responsible executives of both parties meet, under the guidance of the Panel, with respect to [Fujitsu's] software development process," and that "each party brief and argue, to the Panel and responsible executives, whether, and to what extent, such [Fujitsu] procedures violated IBM's rights under the 1983 agreements."

ADR advocates know that this process, the briefing and arguing of the issues before neutrals and settlement-empowered executives, followed by negotiations, is the hallmark of the mini-trial, an increasingly popular settlement procedure. (*Alternatives*, September 1986.)

MEDIATION

The "mini-trial" process, conducted through June and July 1986, failed. Though some ancillary issues were settled, "The fundamental dispute could not be resolved through negotiation by

(continues on next page)

responsible executives," the neutrals say in their opinion. Next, the neutrals used another device favored by advocates of expedited dispute resolution: summary judgment.

And simultaneously with their rulings on the summary-judgment motions, the neutrals made the apparently crucial decision to engage the parties in yet another ADR procedure, mediation. With Messrs. Jones and Mnookin acting as mediators, the parties worked through the winter of 1986–'87.

Unlike the "mini-trial," this ADR strategy worked. "The Arbitrators' mediation efforts were successful, resulting in the execution of new agreements between the parties," the neutrals report in their opinion.

The fruits of the mediation were memorialized in two documents. In the first, the "1986 Agreement," the parties "settled all of IBM's intellectual property claims with respect to hundreds of [Fujitsu] programs," the neutrals recount. "The 1986 Agreement thereby successfully resolved almost all of the parties' disputes with respect to [Fujitsu's] past use of IBM programming material." The second accord, the "Washington Agreement," provided "a framework for the resolution of all issues remaining in dispute and the foundation for the Order," they add.

PREVENTIVE PRACTICES

The resolution of this major software dispute, reached through a host of ADR techniques, incorporates in its Secured Facility provisions yet another ADR tactic: preventive law. Professor Mnookin explained these notions in full on September 15, and his description is a good summary of the advantages of the preventive approach:

"The Secured Facility regime provides a unique advantage as a means of settling complicated issues in evolving technological and legal fields. In the past, IBM could never know exactly how Fujitsu was using IBM programming material. In order to determine if some violation of its rights may have occurred, IBM had to wait until after the public release of a Fujitsu program and then conduct an elaborate technical examination of the program. Then, if it chose to pursue a claim, it was extremely expensive and time-consuming.

"Meanwhile, of course, the Fujitsu program at issue was already in the markeplace. Even the threat that IBM might at some point pursue a claim would create a potential problem for both Fujitsu and for the Fujitsu customers using a new Fujitsu program.

"The Secured Facility exposes and resolves disagreements *before* public release of software. The determination made in the facility as to what goes on the survey sheet is the final word on what material of one company can be used by the other company. Once that sheet leaves the facility, the issue is settled. IBM can be assured that only the material allowed by the instructions is being shared. Fujitsu can be assured that IBM will not make a claim with respect to the use of that material at some date in the future. And customers who license Fujitsu operating system software can be assured that no future controversy will disrupt their use of these programs."

The neutrals found use for still other ADR tools in this high-stakes, high-tech case. For example, the Secured Facility supervisor, described at length in the neutrals' award, will function as an expert factfinder of sorts under their direction. The supervisor "shall be an experienced, unbiased, and qualified person or firm . . . with relevant systems programming experience," the neutrals order. And the neutrals themselves, who will supervise this ongoing resolution and handle any disputes that the parties alone cannot resolve, thus function as monitors or special masters.

The breadth of ADR devices used in the case should please ADR advocates. So should the simple fact that this case of global implications, involving hundreds of millions of dollars, high emotions and cultural differences, was susceptible of ADR resolution.

Source: *Alternatives to the High Cost of Litigation,* Nov. 1987, pp. 187–90

Box 4-4 Resolving to Try a Simpler Way

THE ALTERNATIVE DISPUTE RESOLUTION PLEDGE

We recognize that for many business disputes there is a less expensive, more effective method of resolution than the traditional lawsuit. Alternative dispute resolution (ADR) techniques involve collaborative techniques which often can spare businesses the high cost and wear and tear of litigation.

In recognition of the foregoing, we subscribe to the following statement of principle. In the event of a business dispute between our corporation and another corporation which has made or will then make a similar statement, we are prepared to explore, with that other party, resolution of the dispute through negotiation or ADR techniques, before resorting to full-scale litigation. If either party believes that the dispute is not suitable for ADR techniques, or if such techniques do not produce results satisfactory to the disputants, either party may proceed with litigation.

X CORPORATION

____

Chief Executive Officer

____

Chief Legal Officer

____

Date

at this point a rational ADR approach will give way to the emotions of the lawsuit.

A third reason ADR might not lead away from the courtroom is that a company, for reasons of *business strategy,* might prefer litigation. Among the strategic reasons for preferring lawsuits:

- Managers attempt to avoid personal responsibility for losses by shifting responsibility to the law department or a court.
- By litigating a particular case, the company can *signal* outsiders that it is adopting an aggressive posture in certain matters. For example, some accounting firms blame increases in liability insurance rates on the willingness of other firms to settle cases rather than litigate. (*Wall Street Journal,* Nov. 8, 1984, p. 4)
- Some companies use litigation as part of their competitive strategy to hinder start-up ventures or (if they have substantial resources) to wear down or frighten off an opponent. When Computerland posted a $283 million cash bond to appeal a judgment worth over $500 million awarded a group of investors known as Micro/Vest, Computerland's president noted: "I can only say it is going to be a lot more than Micro/Vest and its speculators can afford. This ups their ante considerably." (The losing party on appeal must pay the cost of the bond—an estimated $14 million.) The Micro/Vest attorney responded: "What they're really saying is we're going to cost you a lot more money and we'll see if you can withstand the monetary gap." (*San Francisco Chronicle,* May 9, 1985, p. 33)

- A party saddled with a poor case might prefer to litigate to defer the payment of damages. In some types of cases, interest is also deferred until the court renders a judgment. For example, Federal District Judge Miles Lord accused A. H. Robins Co. of stalling Dalkon Shield litigation because ". . . the interest you earn in the interim covers the cost of the cases." (*Wall Street Journal,* Aug. 23, 1985, p. 6.) An individual manager might also have financial reasons for preferring litigation—for example, to delay posting a loss on the balance sheet until he moves on to a new position.
- A company might feel, entirely as a matter of principle, that the case is more important than its cost. According to William Langston, corporate counsel, "An executive may tell counsel, 'So and so owes us $10 million. He's a thief. Sue him. And don't tell me about the cost; this is a matter of principle.' " (*Wall Street Journal,* Dec. 13, 1982, p. 22)
- Through discovery (pp. 80–81) in litigation, a company can obtain valuable information—for instance, it might learn about a competitor's advertising strategies, market-share trends, and product failures.
- Litigation is the only appropriate approach when a company wishes to establish a new legal theory as precedent for future cases.
- Publicity is an important part of corporate strategy—either in defending one's own reputation or besmirching a competitor's. When Maryland banned the sale of certain Gerber food products after state officials received complaints about glass in the company's jars, Gerber responded by suing the state for $150 million on the grounds that the state action was not justified. (*Ann Arbor News,* March 9, 1986, p. 37)
- Finally, litigation is often preferred when the issue—for example, the validity of a key patent—is vital to the success of a company.

But even if litigation is preferred for strategic reasons, the astute manager will not simply turn the matter over to the lawyer and wash her hands of any involvement in the litigation strategy. Like any other business activity, litigation is most sensibly pursued as an opportunity that makes sense only if cost effective. During the 1980s, smart managers and lawyers began to apply decision analysis to the realm of litigation.

Decision Analysis

Alternatives to litigation require greater management involvement than in the past. Decision tree analysis is an especially useful technique that allows management to play a more active role in legal decision-making. **Decision analysis,** a term first coined in 1963, is a discipline devoted to the systematic analysis of important decisions. **Decision tree analysis** refers to a particular technique for dealing with the uncertainty that is present in most difficult decisions. Decision tree analysis has been used for many years to analyze business decisions, and, in recent years, corporate attorneys have

Figure 4-1 A Decision Tree

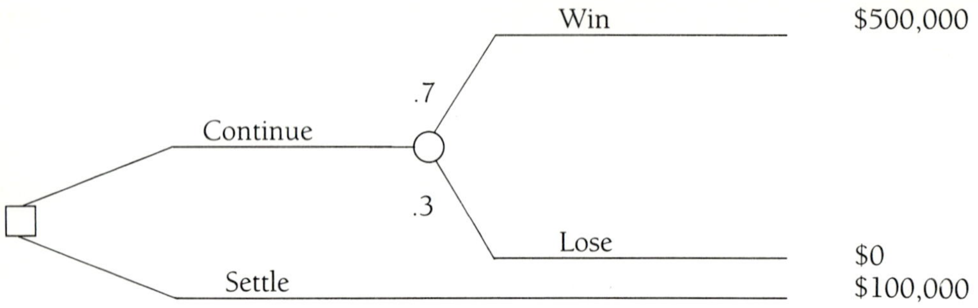

recognized its value in making settlement decisions. The use of decision tree analysis is especially attractive because it facilitates communication between attorneys and executives who often find it difficult to deal with the uncertainty and complexity inherent in litigation.

When used in legal decision-making, decision tree analysis requires the creation of a model of the decision, called a decision tree, that represents the value of uncertain events. A simplified decision tree depicting a $500,000 case in which the plaintiff has received a $100,000 settlement offer is presented in Figure 4-1. The plaintiff's attorney has estimated the probability of winning to be 70%. Squares are used to represent decisions (here the decision whether to settle or continue the litigation), while circles represent uncontrollable events (in this case, the court's decision). A more elaborate decision tree would include each specific issue necessary to determine whether the plaintiff is likely to win the case, along with probabilities for a range of possible recoveries.

Once created, the model can be used to calculate the value of refusing the settlement offer and continuing with the litigation, the overall probability of success, and discovery costs. As indicated in Box 4-5, law firms are now using software to perform these calculations.

Chapter Summary

No one in business can afford to be ignorant of the way lawyers practice law. With nearly 750,000 lawyers, the American legal profession is the means by which people resolve or prevent most significant legal disputes.

About half the lawyers in the United States practice on their own or with one or two partners; the other half practice in firms varying in size from a few to more than 300 partners. Increasingly, these firms perform highly specialized services.

Box 4-5 A New Method Takes Root

Decision Trees

More lawyers are learning to apply decision-tree analysis to litigation problems, says its master teacher, lawyer Marc Victor of Menlo Park, Calif.

"It's really catching on in the legal community," Victor said. About 600 lawyers are learning what he calls "litigation-risk analysis"—double the number enrolled when Victor began teaching it in 1980.

"Litigation-risk analysis is a discipline for lawyers to get their thinking straight," Victor said. "It's most useful in cases where a lawyer does not have a wealth of previous experience to go on."

To do the analysis, lawyers must express probabilities in numbers rather than words. When trying to decide whether to try a case or settle, for example, a lawyer avoids ambiguity by telling a client the probability of winning is 70 percent rather than "very likely." Otherwise, "one lawyer may mean 40 percent when he says 'good possibility,' while another could mean 70 percent," Victor said.

Building a decision tree enables lawyers to assess the risks of pursuing various strategies and to put a percentage on the probability of recovery of various types of claims. "Trying to build such a picture ensures that counsel think carefully not only about the most important uncertainties in the case, but also about the interrelationships among all the important factors," Victor said.

Victor especially recommends use of decision trees in complex litigation in which "keeping track of all the factors in one's head would quickly become impossible."

In fact, plaintiffs' attorneys alleging multibillion-dollar cost overruns and construction delays in the massive South Texas nuclear project used Victor and his litigation-risk analysis to help get a tentative $750 million settlement. Defendants were Brown & Root Inc.—the architect, engineer and contractor—and its corporate parent, Dallas-based Halliburton Co.

"Lawyers are now taking decision-analysis courses at business schools, but it ought to be taught in law schools," Victor said. "Legal problems have as much uncertainty and complexity as business problems."

To help with complex legal problems, Texas Instruments has developed a decision-tree software product called Arborist. "The software can perform the decision-tree calculations," Victor said. "The computer is great for questions like: 'What if we could improve one area of research by 10 percent?' It then tells you that the value of the case would improve by X dollars. It helps you figure out whether the benefits outweigh the cost." But he cautioned that lawyers must understand decision-tree techniques before applying computer software to them.

"Software doesn't have all the answers," he said. "It can do the last 10 percent of the work, but the first 90 percent of the job for the lawyer is building the tree."

One highly automated law firm whose lawyers are using decision-tree software products is Wilmer Cutler & Pickering in Washington.

Source: *The American Bar Association Journal,* 33 (1986)

Lawyers serve clients in a variety of roles—as advocates, negotiators, counselors, and lobbyists. The position of the client should not be imputed to the lawyer who often works for interests that she might personally dislike. But the lawyer may not do anything the client wishes; the lawyer is constrained by a formal code of ethics. One of the key provisions is that of confidentiality (unless the client seeks assistance to plan a future crime). Another key ethical provision is that a lawyer may not work for two clients whose interests conflict.

In the corporate setting, determining who is the client can be a problem. Ordinarily, the lawyer represents the corporation as a whole, not the individual officers or employees. When the corporation's interests conflict with those of the employee, the employee should retain his own lawyer. But for purposes of confidentiality, the lawyer is bound to protect the confidences not just of the abstract corporate entity, but of any employees who speak to the lawyer about a specific company legal problem within the scope of their particular responsibiltities.

Lawyers charge their clients in different ways, depending on the type of problem—an hourly fee, a flat rate for services rendered, or a contingent fee. In the United States, the winning party is not automatically entitled to recover legal costs (including fees paid to the lawyer) from the losing party. "Fee shifting" is permissible only if a statute specifically authorizes it (as, for example, in antitrust cases).

Litigation in court is not the only method of resolving legal disputes. Other techniques include arbitration, "rent-a-judge," mediation, and newer forms of alternative dispute resolution (ADR), such as the mini-trial. The mini-trial is a highly structured settlement negotiation in which lawyers present the case to executives of the disputing companies. Although some forms of ADR are quite ancient (arbitration has been practiced throughout the history of the United States), beginning in the 1980s business has increasingly turned to newer methods to avoid the costs and pitfalls of litigation.

Business is also learning to manage and prevent disputes at the outset. One type of preventive law is the litigation audit.

ADR is not a panacea. Alternative processes might fail because each party may fear being perceived as weak (although many companies have publicly signed a pledge to invoke ADR). Another reason for failure is that emotions get in the way of business sense. Finally, companies may avoid ADR and pursue litigation for reasons of business strategy: to wear down an opponent, minimize interest costs, obtain information, or establish a precedent.

Problems

1. The Internal Revenue Service begins a tax audit of Acme Company's 1987 tax returns. In preparing the company's defense, Acme's lawyer talks to Jeremy, a vice president. Jeremy confesses to the lawyer that he has been padding his expense account. What obligations does the lawyer have to respect Jeremy's confidences and keep the information secret from the government? From the company? What difficulty might Jeremy have in relying on the company lawyer? What should Jeremy do under the circumstances?
2. Tom has a contract to buy all his scrap iron from Leslie. The contract says that the two parties must take any disputes arising out of the

contract to arbitration. Leslie discovers that Tom has bought some scrap iron from someone else and threatens to take him to court. Must Tom go to court? Suppose that Leslie and Tom have their dispute arbitrated and Leslie is dissatisfied with the result. May she appeal to a court? Why or why not?

3. Frank and Joyce are neighbors. For several years, Frank's dog has been barking early in the morning, to Joyce's great annoyance. Several times she has called Frank to complain, but he has always slammed down the phone. Last week she called the police, and Frank retaliated by dumping his garbage over her fence. Joyce has now contacted a lawyer and wants to sue. The lawyer has suggested a mediator. How could the mediator help resolve this dispute? What kind of resolution would you suggest if you were the mediator?
4. For its new CAW (Computer Assisted Widget) Mobile, Ace Widgets has used Luster-Ware's new Widget-Chip, a microchip on which Luster holds a patent. Ace has paid no royalties, and Luster sues, asserting an infringement of its patent. Ace cites an agreement signed a year earlier, under which, according to Ace's interpretation, Ace could use the chip for "publicity purposes" without paying royalties. Describe the different ways Ace and Luster could resolve this dispute. What other facts might you need to know to determine which method would be most likely to succeed?
5. Alice sues her employer, Macho Products, charging the company with sex discrimination for promoting a less qualified employee—a man—to the position of sales manager. Macho's executive vice president, Sam, calls the law firm the company has used for the past fifty years. Van, the law firm's senior partner, tells Sam: "Leave it to me." Is this a good or bad idea? Why? If you think it's a bad idea, what should Sam do?

5

Administrative Law

From the 1930s on, administrative agencies, law, and procedures have virtually remade our government and much of private life. Business must deal daily with rules and decisions of administrative agencies, federal and state. Substantive administrative law is voluminous: thousands of new regulations pour forth each year. Many of the subsequent chapters in this text take up subject by subject the substance of administratively generated law.

To the lawyer, administrative law means something different: it is the study of the way in which administrative agencies work and of the means by which both the agencies and their laws can be judicially reviewed. In this chapter we consider the nature of administrative agencies and their impact on the operations of the business enterprise.

Administrative Agencies: Their Structure and Powers

Congress created the first federal agency, the Interstate Commerce Commission (ICC), in 1887, and delegated it power to enforce federal laws against railroad rate discrimination and other unfair pricing practices. Although the ICC assumed that it had the power to fix rates, the Supreme Court ruled in 1897 that it did not. During the twentieth century, that would change.

Beginning with the Federal Trade Commission (FTC) in 1914, Congress has created numerous other agencies, many of them familiar actors in American government. Today more than eighty-five federal agencies have jurisdiction to regulate some form of private activity. Most were created since 1930, more than a third since 1960.

They are generally classified into two broad groups: independent agencies and executive branch agencies. In addition to the ICC and FTC, the major independent agencies are the Federal Communications Commission (1934), Securities and Exchange Commission (1934), National Labor Relations Board (1935), and Environmental Protection Agency (1970). Dozens of other agencies—the executive branch agencies—are components of the major federal departments. The Food and Drug Administration is a part of the Department of Health and Human Resources; the Nuclear Regulatory Agency (formerly the Atomic Energy Commission) and the Federal Energy Regulation Agency (formerly the Federal Power Commission), of the Department of Energy; the Occupational Safety and Health Administration, of the Department of Labor. The Department of Agriculture has broad supervisory powers over farm practices and pricing. The Internal Revenue Service, a part of the Treasury Department, plays a major role in the financial life of virtually everyone in the country.

The primary distinction between independent and executive branch agencies is in the terms of office of their members. Commissioners of the independent agencies serve for fixed statutory terms, and the president may not remove them. To some degree like the courts, therefore, they are independent of the political process. By contrast, members of executive branch agencies serve at the pleasure of the president and are therefore far more amenable to political control. One consequence of this distinction is that the rules that independent agencies promulgate may not be reviewed by the president or his staff—only Congress may directly overrule them—whereas the White House or higher authority in the various cabinet departments may oversee the work of the agencies contained within them.

Agencies have a variety of powers. Many of the original statutes that created them, like the Federal Communications Act, gave them licensing power. No party can enter into the productive activity covered by the act without prior license from the agency—for example, no utility can start up a nuclear power plant unless first approved by the Nuclear Regulatory Agency. In recent years, the move toward deregulation of the economy has led to diminution of some licensing power. Many agencies also have the authority to set the rates charged by companies that are subject to the agency's jurisdiction. Finally, the agencies can regulate business practices. The Federal Trade Commission has general jurisdiction over all business in interstate commerce to monitor and root out "unfair acts" and "deceptive practices." The Securities and Exchange Commission oversees the issuance of corporate securities and other investments and monitors the practices of the stock exchanges. The Interstate Commerce Commission continues to have broad regulatory power over railroad practices, as well as over those of truckers and interstate water carriers.

A similar growth has occurred at the state level. Most states now have dozens of regulatory agencies, many of them overlapping in function with the federal bodies.

Unlike courts, administrative agencies are charged with the responsibility of carrying out a specific assignment or reaching a goal or set of goals. They are not to remain neutral on the various issues of the day; they must act. They have been given legislative powers because in a society growing ever more complex, Congress does not know how to legislate with the kind of detail that is necessary, nor would it have the time to approach all the sectors of society even if it tried. Precisely because they are to do what general legislative bodies cannot do, agencies are specialized bodies. Through years of experience in dealing with similar problems they accumulate a body of knowledge that they can apply to accomplish their statutory duties.

All administrative agencies have two different sorts of personnel. The heads, whether a single administrator or a collegial body of commissioners, are political appointees and serve for relatively limited terms. Below them is a more or less permanent staff—the bureaucracy. Much policy-making occurs at the staff level, because these employees are in essential control of gathering facts and presenting data and argument to the commissioners, who wield the ultimate power of the agencies.

Controlling Administrative Agencies

Not surprisingly, during the course of the past fifty years a substantial debate has been conducted, often in shrill terms, about the legitimacy of administrative law-making. One criticism is that agencies are "captured" by the industry they are directed to regulate. Another is that they overregulate, stifling individual initiative and the ability to compete. During the 1960s and 1970s, a massive outpouring of federal law created many new agencies and greatly strengthened the hands of existing ones. Beginning in the late 1970s during the Carter administration and even more so under the Reagan administration, Congress has been pressed to deregulate American society.

Administrative agencies are the focal point of controversy because they are policy-making bodies, incorporating facets of legislative, executive, and judicial power in a hybrid form that fits uneasily at best in the framework of American government. They are necessarily at the center of tugging and hauling by legislature, executive, and courts, each of which has different means of exercising control over them.

Legislative Control

Congress can always pass a law repealing a regulation that an agency promulgates. Because this is a time-consuming process that runs counter to the reason for creating administrative bodies, it happens rarely. Another approach to controlling agencies is to limit their life expectancies when creating them. A **sunset law** is one that sets a term of years, after which operations terminate and the agency ceases to exist unless Congress has first renewed it. It is hoped that agencies will be more responsive to the will of Congress, and thus ultimately to that of the people, if they must justify their existence every so many years. One difficulty already being experienced, however, is that the task of deciding whether to renew the agency's franchise is time-consuming and burdensome and could deflect Congress from other equally or more pressing concerns.

Executive Control

The president (or governor) can exercise considerable control over agencies that are part of his cabinet departments and that are not statutorily defined as independent. Federal agencies, moreover, are subject to the fiscal scrutiny of the Office of Management and Budget (OMB), subject to the direct control of the president. Agencies are not permitted to go directly to Congress for increases in budget; these requests must be submitted through OMB, giving the president indirect leverage over the continuation of administrators' programs and policies.

Judicial Control

Administrative agencies are creatures of law and like everyone else must obey the law. The courts have jurisdiction to hear claims that the agencies have overstepped their legal authority or have acted in some unlawful manner.

The statutory delegation of power to administrative agencies raises an initial constitutional question. Legislative power is vested in Congress, and it may not give away all of its power nor delegate power to legislate in the complete absence of standards. In 1935, in *Schechter Poultry Corp.* v. *United States* [295 U.S. 495 (1935)], the Supreme Court upset the National Industrial Recovery Act on the ground that the congressional delegation of power was too broad. Under the law, industry trade groups were granted the authority to devise a code of fair competition for the entire industry, and these codes became law if approved by the president. No administrative body was created to scrutinize the arguments for a particular code, to develop evidence, or to test one version of a code against another.

During the fifty years since the *Schechter* decision, Congress has enacted scores of laws directing agencies to carry out vaguely worded goals. The

Supreme Court has never since seen fit to overturn a grant of legislative power on the ground that Congress placed too much discretion in the hands of the administrators. The reasons vary. Courts have become cautious in overturning broad economic legislation of Congress. Neither before nor since has Congress delegated power so broadly as it had in the statute that the 1935 Court upset. Finally, courts confronted with what appear to be excessively vague standards will try to save them by construing them narrowly to accord with past administrative practices and judicial precedents. Nevertheless, many administrative standards remain loose to the point of vanishing. The touchstone for officials of the Federal Communications Commission, for instance, is "public convenience, interest, or necessity."

Despite the generally cautious approach of courts, in 1986, the Supreme Court struck down the Gramm-Rudman-Hollings Act, intended to eliminate deficit spending, on the grounds that Congress had delegated to the wrong official *executive power* to determine where cuts in the federal budget must be made if Congress and the president spent more than certain target amounts. Congress gave final authority to dictate the cuts to the Comptroller General of the United States. The Comptroller General is an agent of Congress, the legislative branch of government. Since the power to make cuts was executive power, the Court said, it could be delegated only to an executive branch official. [Bowsher v. Synar, 106 S.Ct. 3181 (1986)]

Beyond the constitutional question, courts in reviewing administrative action have a variety of tools by which to control the administrative process. They can look to the statute empowering the agency to act to see whether it has exceeded its authority. They can ask whether the agency has followed its own rules and, if not, set aside the agency's action. And they can look to the Administrative Procedure Act, the general law that governs the procedures that all federal administrative agencies must follow.

The Administrative Procedure Act

In 1946, Congress enacted the Administrative Procedure Act (APA). This fundamental statute detailed for all federal administrative agencies how they must function when they are deciding cases or issuing regulations, the two basic tasks of administration. At the state level, the Model State Administrative Procedure Act, issued in 1946 and revised in 1961, has been adopted in about twenty states, and some twenty-five other states have statutes that resemble it to some degree.

Trial-type Hearings

Deciding cases is a major task of many agencies. Thus the FTC is empowered to charge a company with having violated the Federal Trade Commission Act—perhaps a seller is accused of making deceptive claims in its advertising. Proceeding in a manner similar to a court, staff counsel will prepare a case against the company, which can defend itself through its lawyers. The case is tried before an **administrative law judge** (ALJ), formerly known as an administrative hearing examiner. The change in nomenclature was made in 1972 to enhance ALJs' prestige and more accurately reflect their duties. Although not appointed for life as federal judges are, the ALJ must be free of assignments inconsistent with the judicial function and is not subject to supervision by anyone in the agency who carries on an investigative or prosecutorial function.

The accused parties are entitled to receive notice of the issues to be raised, to present evidence, to argue, to cross-examine, and to appear with their lawyers. *Ex parte* communications—contacts between the ALJ and outsiders or one party when both parties are not present—are prohibited. However, the usual burden-of-proof standard followed in a civil proceeding in court does not apply: the ALJ is not bound to decide in favor of that party producing the more persuasive evidence. The rule in most administrative proceedings is "substantial evidence"—not flimsy or weak evidence, but not necessarily overwhelming evidence either. The ALJ in most cases will write an opinion. That opinion is not the decision of the agency, which can be made only by the commissioners or agency head. In effect, the ALJ's opinion is appealed to the commission itself.

Certain types of agency actions that have a direct impact on individuals need not be filtered through a full-scale hearing. Safety and quality inspections (grading of food, inspection of airplanes) can be made on the spot by skilled inspectors. Certain licenses can be administered through tests without a hearing (a test for a driver's license), and some decisions can be made by election of those affected (labor union elections).

Rule-making

Trial-type hearings generally impose on particular parties liabilities based on past or present facts. Because these cases will serve as precedents, they are a partial guide to future conduct by others. But they do not directly apply to nonparties, who may argue in a subsequent case that their conduct does not fit within the holding announced in the case. Agencies can affect future conduct far more directly by announcing rules that apply to all who come within the agency's jurisdiction.

The acts creating most of the major federal agencies expressly grant them authority to engage in rule-making—in essence, to legislate. The outpouring of federal regulations has been immense. As Professor Bernard Schwartz has noted:

> From its establishment in 1935, the Federal Register [see below] has in size vastly exceeded the Statutes at Large. The sheer mass of agency regulations is appalling. The Federal Register for 1974 contained 45,420 pages. But, to check all the federal regulations, one had to search the Code of Federal Regulations,

> with its 127 volumes, containing 65,249 pages. The C.F.R. now contains over 50 million words—seventy times as many as in the Bible and sixty times as many as in a complete Shakespeare. (Schwartz, 1976, p. 148)

The APA directs agencies about to engage in rule-making to give notice in the *Federal Register* of their intent to do so. The *Federal Register* is published daily, Monday through Friday, in Washington and contains notice of various actions, including announcements of proposed rule-making and regulations as adopted. The notice must be specific enough to identify the time, place, and nature of the rule-making and offer a description of the proposed rule or the issues involved. Any interested person or organization is entitled to participate by submitting written "data, views or arguments." Agencies are not legally required to air debate over proposed rules, though they often do so.

The procedure just described is known as "informal" rule-making. A different procedure is required for "formal" rule-making, defined as those instances in which the enabling legislation directs an agency to make rules "on the record after opportunity for an agency hearing." The Supreme Court has interpreted that language to require agencies to hold an adversary hearing when engaging in formal rule-making.

Administrative regulations are not legally binding unless they are published. Agencies must publish in the *Federal Register* the text of final regulations, which ordinarily do not become effective until thirty days later. Every year the annual output of regulations is collected and reprinted in the *Code of Federal Regulations (CFR),* a multivolume paperback series containing all federal rules and regulations keyed to the fifty titles of the United States Code (the compilation of all federal statutes enacted by Congress and grouped according to subject).

Administrative Burdens on Business Operations

The administrative process is not frictionless. The interplay between government agency and private enterprise can burden business operations in a number of ways. Several of these are noted in this section.

The Paperwork Burden

Deciding whether and how to act is not a decision that government agencies reach "out of the blue." They rely heavily on information garnered from business itself. Dozens of federal agencies require corporations to keep hundreds of types of records and to file numerous periodic reports. The Commission on Federal Paperwork, established during the Ford administration to consider ways of reducing the paperwork burden, estimated in its final report in 1977 that the total annual cost of federal paperwork amounted to $50 billion and that the 10,000 largest business enterprises spent $10 billion annually on paperwork alone. The paperwork involved in licensing a single nuclear power plant, the commission said, costs upwards of $15 million.

Not surprisingly, therefore, businesses have sought ways of avoiding requests for data. Since the 1940s, the FTC has collected economic data on corporate performance from individual companies for statistical purposes. As long as each company engages in a single line of business, data are comparable. When the era of conglomerates began in the 1970s, with widely divergent types of businesses brought together under the roof of a single corporate parent, the data became useless for purposes of examining the competitive behavior of different industries. So the FTC ordered dozens of large companies to break out their economic information according to each line of business that they carried on. The companies resisted, and the U.S. District Court for the District of Columbia granted summary judgment to the FTC. Many companies appealed to the U.S. Court of Appeals for the District of Columbia Circuit, where much of the litigation over federal administrative action is decided. But that court directed the companies to comply with the commission's order, holding that the Federal Trade Commission Act clearly permits the agency to collect information for investigatory purposes. [In Re: FTC Line of Business Report Litigation, 595 F.2d 685 (D.C.Cir. 1978)]

Inspections

No one likes surprise inspections. A section of the Occupational Safety and Health Act of 1970 empowers agents of OSHA to search work areas for safety hazards and for violations of OSHA regulations. The act does not specify whether inspectors are required to obtain search warrants, required under the Fourth Amendment in criminal cases. For many years the government insisted that surprise inspections are not unreasonable and that the time required to obtain a warrant would defeat the surprise element. The Supreme Court finally ruled squarely on the issue in 1978.

MARSHALL v. BARLOW'S, INC.
436 U.S. 307 (1978)

MR. JUSTICE WHITE delivered the opinion of the Court.

Section 8(a) of the Occupational Safety and Health Act of 1970 (OSHA or Act) empowers agents of the Secretary of Labor (Secretary) to search the work area of any employment facility within the Act's jurisdiction. The purpose of the search is to inspect for safety hazards and violations of OSHA regulations. No search warrant or other process is expressly required under the Act.

On the morning of September 11, 1975, an OSHA inspector entered the customer service area of Barlow's, Inc., an electrical and plumbing installation business located in Pocatello, Idaho. The president and general manager, Ferrol G. "Bill" Barlow, was on hand; and the OSHA inspector, after showing his credentials, informed Mr. Barlow that he wished to conduct a search of the working areas of the business. Mr. Barlow inquired whether any complaint had been received about his company. The inspector answered no, but that Barlow's, Inc., had simply turned up in the agency's selection process. The inspector again asked to enter the nonpublic area of the business; Mr. Barlow's response was to inquire whether the inspector had a search warrant. The inspector had none. Thereupon, Mr. Barlow refused the inspector admission to the employee area of his business. He said he was relying on his rights as guaranteed by the Fourth Amendment of the United States Constitution.

Three months later, the Secretary petitioned the United States District Court for the District of Idaho to issue an order compelling Mr. Barlow to admit the inspector. The requested order was issued on December 30, 1975, and was presented to Mr. Barlow on January 5, 1976. Mr. Barlow again refused admission, and he sought his own injunctive relief against the warrantless searches assertedly permitted by OSHA. . . .

The Warrant Clause of the Fourth Amendment protects commercial buildings as well as private homes. To hold otherwise would belie the origin of that Amendment, and the American colonial experience. An important forerunner of the first 10 Amendments to the United States Constitution, the Virginia Bill of Rights, specifically opposed "general warrants, whereby an officer or messenger may be commanded to search suspected places without evidence of a fact committed." The general warrant was a recurring point of contention in the Colonies immediately preceding the Revolution. The particular offensiveness it engendered was acutely felt by the merchants and businessmen whose premises and products were inspected for compliance with the several parliamentary revenue measures that most irritated the colonists. . . .

* * *

This Court has already held that warrantless searches are generally unreasonable, and that this rule applies to commercial premises as well as homes. In *Camara* v. *Municipal Court,* we held:

> [E]xcept in certain carefully defined classes of cases, a search of private property without proper consent is 'unreasonable' unless it has been authorized by a valid search warrant.

On the same day, we also ruled:

> As we explained in *Camara,* a search of private houses is presumptively unreasonable if conducted without a warrant. The businessman, like the occupant of a residence, has a constitutional right to go about his business free from unreasonable official entries upon his private commercial property. The businessman, too, has that right placed in jeopardy if the decision to enter and inspect for violation of regulatory laws can be made and enforced by the inspector in the field without official authority evidenced by a warrant.

These same cases also held that the Fourth Amendment prohibition against unreasonable searches protects against warrantless intrusions during civil as well as criminal investigations. The reason is found in the "basic purpose of this Amendment . . . [which] is to safeguard the privacy and security of individuals against arbitrary invasions by governmental officials." If the government intrudes on a person's property, the privacy interest suffers whether the government's motivation is to investigate violations of criminal laws or breaches of other statutory or regulatory standards. . . .

[A]n exception from the search warrant requirement has been recognized for "pervasively regulated business[es]," *United States* v. *Biswell,* 406 U.S. 311, 316 (1972), and for "closely regulated" industries "long subject to close supervision and inspection." *Colonnade Catering Corp.* v. *United States,* 397 U.S. 72, 74, 77 (1970). These cases are indeed exceptions, but they represent responses to relatively unique circumstances. Certain industries have such a history of government oversight that no reasonable expectation of privacy could exist for a proprietor over the stock of such an enterprise. Liquor *(Colonnade)* and firearms *(Biswell)* are industries of this type; when an entrepreneur embarks upon such a business, he has voluntarily chosen to subject himself to a full arsenal of governmental regulation.

* * *

The clear import of our cases is that the closely regulated industry of the type involved in *Colonnade* and *Biswell* is the exception. The Secretary would make it the rule. Invoking the Walsh-Healey Act of

1936, 41 U.S.C. § 35 *et seq.*, the Secretary attempts to support a conclusion that all businesses involved in interstate commerce have long been subjected to close supervision of employee safety and health conditions. But . . . [i]t is quite unconvincing to argue that the imposition of minimum wages and maximum hours on employers who contracted with the Government under the Walsh-Healey Act prepared the entirety of American interstate commerce for regulation of working conditions to the minutest detail. Nor can any but the most fictional sense of voluntary consent to later searches be found in the single fact that one conducts a business affecting interstate commerce; under current practice and law, few businesses can be conducted without having some effect on interstate commerce.

* * *

The critical fact in this case is that entry over Mr. Barlow's objection is being sought by a Government agent. Employees are not being prohibited from reporting OSHA violations. What they observe in their daily functions is undoubtedly beyond the employer's reasonable expectation of privacy. The Government inspector, however, is not an employee. Without a warrant he stands in no better position than a member of the public. What is observable by the public is observable, without a warrant, by the Government inspector as well. The owner of a business has not, by the necessary utilization of employees in his operation, thrown open the areas where employees alone are permitted to the warrantless scrutiny of Government agents. That an employee is free to report, and the Government is free to use, any evidence of noncompliance with OSHA that the employee observes furnishes no justification for federal agents to enter a place of business from which the public is restricted and to conduct their own warrantless search.

* * *

We hold that Barlow was entitled to a declaratory judgment that the Act is unconstitutional insofar as it purports to authorize inspections without warrant or its equivalent and to an injunction enjoining the Act's enforcement to that extent. The judgment of the District Court is therefore affirmed.

Access to Business Information in Government Files

In 1966, Congress enacted the Freedom of Information Act (FOIA), opening up to the citizenry many of the files of the government. (The act was amended in 1974 and again in 1976 to overcome a tendency of many agencies to stall or refuse access to their files.) Under the FOIA, any person has a legally enforceable right of access to all government documents, with nine specific exceptions, such as classified military intelligence, medical files, and trade secrets and commercial or financial information if "obtained from a person and privileged or confidential." Without the trade-secret and financial-information exemption, business competitors could, merely by requesting it, obtain highly sensitive competitive information sitting in government files. Indeed, though proponents thought that the press and broadcast media would be the primary seekers of information under the act, in fact business corporations have sought access to government records far more often, usually to obtain competitive business data.

Many agencies have rejected requests for such information, and the issue has come up frequently in court. In a significant 1974 case, the National Park Service refused the request of the National Parks and Conservation Association, a private organization, for detailed financial information submitted by private individuals and companies operating food and other concessions in national parks. The question the court had to address was the meaning of the word "confidential." What makes information sufficiently confidential that a government agency is legally entitled to refuse access to it?

NATIONAL PARKS AND CONSERVATION ASSOCIATION v. MORTON
498 F.2d 765 (D.C.Cir. 1974)

TAMM, CIRCUIT JUDGE:

Appellant brought this action under the Freedom of Information Act, 5 U.S.C. § 552 (1970), seeking to enjoin officials of the Department of the Interior from refusing to permit inspection and copying of certain agency records concerning concessions operated in the national parks. The district court granted summary judgment for the defendant on the ground that the information sought is exempt from disclosure under section 552(b)(4) of the Act which states:

> (b) This section does not apply to matters that are—
>
> *　　*　　*
>
> (4) trade secrets and commercial or financial information obtained from a person and privileged or confidential. . . .

In order to bring a matter (other than a trade secret) within this exemption, it must be shown that the information is (a) commercial or financial, (b) obtained from a person, and (c) privileged or confidential. Since the parties agree that the matter in question is financial information obtained from a person and that it is not privileged, the only issue on appeal is whether the information is "confidential" within the meaning of the exemption.

Unfortunately, the statute contains no definition of the word "confidential." In the past, our decisions concerning this exemption have been guided by the following passage from the Senate Report, particularly the italicized portion:

> This exception is necessary to protect the confidentiality of information which is obtained by the Government through questionnaires or other inquiries, *but which would customarily not be released to the public by the person from whom it was obtained.*

*　　*　　*

Whether particular information would customarily be disclosed to the public by the person from whom it was obtained is not the only relevant inquiry. . . . A court must also be satisfied that nondisclosure is justified by the legislative purpose which underlies the exemption.

*　　*　　*

The "financial information" exemption recognizes the need of government policymakers to have access to commercial and financial data. Unless persons having necessary information can be assured that it will remain confidential, they may decline to cooperate with officials and the ability of the Government to make intelligent, well informed decisions will be impaired. This concern finds expression in the legislative history as well as the case law. During debate on a predecessor to the bill which was ultimately enacted, Senator Humphrey pointed out that sources of information relied upon by the Bureau of Labor Statistics would be "seriously jeopardized" unless the information collected by the Bureau was exempt from disclosure. He was assured that such information was fully protected. . . . As the Senate Report explains:

> This exception is necessary to protect the confidentiality of information which is obtained by the Government through *questionnaires or other inquiries.* . . .

The House Report states with respect to section 552(b)(4):

> It would also include information which is given to an agency in confidence, since a citizen must be able to confide in his Government. Moreover, where the Government has obligated itself in good faith not to disclose documents or information which it receives, it should be able to honor such obligations.

This court has formulated a similar definition of the governmental interest protected by the exemption:

> This exemption is intended to encourage individuals to provide certain kinds of confidential information to the Government, and it must be read narrowly in accordance with that purpose.

Apart from encouraging cooperation with the Government by persons having information useful to officials, section 552(b)(4) serves another distinct but equally important purpose. It protects persons who submit financial or commercial data to government agencies from the competitive disadvantages which would result from its publication.

* * *

To summarize, commercial or financial matter is "confidential" for purposes of the exemption if disclosure of the information is likely to have either of the following effects: (1) to impair the Government's ability to obtain necessary information in the future; or (2) to cause substantial harm to the competitive position of the person from whom the information was obtained.

The financial information sought by appellant consists of audits conducted upon the books of companies operating concessions in national parks, annual financial statements filed by the concessioners with the National Park Service and other financial information. The district court concluded that this information was of the kind "that would not generally be made available for public perusal." While we discern no error in this finding, we do not think that, by itself, it supports application of the financial information exemption. The district court must also inquire into the possibility that disclosure will harm legitimate private or governmental interests in secrecy.

* * *

[Case remanded to the district court.]

Despite rulings in cases such as *National Parks* that agencies may withhold information "likely to cause substantial harm to the competitive position" of the business that submitted it, the business itself has no legal standing to intervene in the suit to object. When delivering data to the government, most companies specify those portions that they consider confidential, and most agencies notify a company whose data they are about to disclose. But these practices are not legally required.

The Scope of Judicial Review

Neither an administrative adjudication nor issuance of a regulation is necessarily final. Many administrative actions can be appealed to the courts. Most federal agency decisions are appealable to the federal circuit courts. To get to court, the appellant must overcome numerous complex hurdles. He must have standing—that is, be in some sense directly affected by the decision or regulation. The case must be ripe for review; administrative remedies such as further appeal within the agency must have been exhausted.

Once these obstacles are cleared, the court may look at one of a series of claims. The appellant might assert that the agency's action was *ultra vires*—beyond the scope of its authority as set down in the statute. This attack is rarely successful. A somewhat more successful claim is that the agency did not abide by its own procedures or those imposed upon it by the Administrative Procedure Act.

The appellant also might insist that the agency lacked substantial evidence for the determination that it made. If there is virtually no evidence to support the agency's findings, the court may reverse. But findings of fact are not often upset. Courts have a much freer hand when the question is whether the agency's interpretation of the law was correct.

These conclusions apply also to an agency's rule-making. There has long been a presumption that when an agency issues a regulation it has the authority to do so: those opposing the regulation must bear a heavy burden in court to upset it. This is not a surprising rule, for otherwise courts, not administrators, would be the authors of regulations. Nevertheless, regulations cannot exceed the scope of the authority conferred by Congress on the agency. In an important 1981 case before the Supreme Court, the issue was whether the Secretary of Labor, acting through OSHA, could lawfully issue a standard limiting exposure to cotton dust in the workplace without first undertaking a cost-benefit analysis. A dozen cotton textile manufacturers and the American Textile Manufacturers Institute, representing 175 companies, asserted that the cotton dust standard was unlawful because it did not rationally relate the benefits to be derived from the standard to the costs that the standard would impose. The Supreme Court tackled the issue head on.

AMERICAN TEXTILE MANUFACTURERS INSTITUTE v. DONOVAN
452 U.S. 490 (1981)

JUSTICE BRENNAN delivered the opinion of the Court.

Congress enacted the Occupational Safety and Health Act of 1970 (Act) "to assure so far as possible every working man and woman in the Nation safe and healthful working conditions. . . ." The Act authorizes the Secretary of Labor to establish, after notice and opportunity to comment, mandatory nationwide standards governing health and safety in the workplace. In 1978, the Secretary, acting through the Occupational Safety and Health Administration (OSHA), promulgated a standard limiting occupational exposure to cotton dust, an airborne particle byproduct of the preparation and manufacture of cotton products, exposure to which induces a "constellation of respiratory effects" known as "byssinosis." This disease was one of the expressly recognized health hazards that led to passage of the Act.

Petitioners in these consolidated cases, representing the interests of the cotton industry, challenged the validity of the "Cotton Dust Standard" in the Court of Appeals for the District of Columbia Circuit pursuant to § 6 (f) of the Act, 29 U.S.C. § 655 (f). They contend in this Court, as they did below, that the Act requires OSHA to demonstrate that its Standard reflects a reasonable relationship between the costs and benefits associated with the Standard. Respondents, the Secretary of Labor and two labor organizations, counter that Congress balanced the costs and benefits in the Act itself, and that the Act should therefore be construed not to require OSHA to do so. They interpret the Act as mandating that OSHA enact the most protective standard possible to eliminate a significant risk of material health impairment, subject to the constraints of economic and technological feasibility. The Court of Appeals held that the Act did not require OSHA to compare costs and benefits. We granted certiorari, 449 U.S. 817 (1980), to resolve this important question, which was presented but not decided in last Term's *Industrial Union Dept.* v. *American Petroleum Institute,* 448 U.S. 607 (1980), and to decide other issues related to the Cotton Dust Standard.

* * *

The starting point of our analysis is the language of the statute itself. Section 6(b)(5) of the Act, 29 U.S.C. § 655(b)(5) (emphasis added), provides:

> The Secretary, in promulgating standards dealing with toxic materials or harmful physical agents under this subsection, shall set the standard which most adequately assures, *to the extent feasible,* on the basis of the best available evidence, that no employee will suffer material impairment of health or functional capacity even if such employee has regular exposure to the hazard dealt with by such standard for the period of his working life.

Although their interpretations differ, all parties agree that the phrase "to the extent feasible" contains the critical language in § 6(b)(5) for purposes of these cases.

The plain meaning of the word "feasible" supports respondents' interpretation of the statute. According to Webster's Third New International Dictionary of the English Language 831 (1976), "feasible" means "capable of being done, executed, or effected." Accord, the Oxford English Dictionary 116 (1933) ("Capable of being done, accomplished or carried out"); Funk & Wagnalls New "Standard" Dictionary of the English Language 903 (1957) ("That may be done, performed or effected"). Thus, § 6(b)(5) directs the Secretary to issue the standard that "most adequately assures . . . that no employee will suffer material impairment of health," limited only by the extent to which this is "capable of being done." In effect then, as the Court of Appeals held, Congress itself defined the basic relationship between costs and benefits, by placing the "benefit" of worker health above all other considerations save those making attainment of this "benefit" unachievable. Any standard based on a balancing of costs and benefits by the Secretary that strikes a different balance than that struck by Congress would be inconsistent with the command set forth in § 6(b)(5). Thus, cost-benefit analysis by OSHA is not required by the statute because feasibility analysis is.

When Congress has intended that an agency engage in cost-benefit analysis, it has clearly indicated such intent on the face of the statute. One early example is the Flood Control Act of 1936, 33 U.S.C. § 701:

> [T]he Federal Government should improve or participate in the improvement of navigable waters or their tributaries, including watersheds thereof, for flood-control purposes if the *benefits to whomsoever they may accrue are in excess of the estimated costs,* and if the lives and social security of people are otherwise adversely affected. (Emphasis added.)

A more recent example is the Outer Continental Shelf Lands Act Amendments of 1978, providing that offshore drilling operations shall use

> the best available and safest technologies which the Secretary determines to be economically *feasible,* wherever failure of equipment would have a significant effect on safety, health, or the environment, except where the Secretary determines that the *incremental benefits are clearly insufficient to justify the incremental costs of using such technologies.*

These and other statutes demonstrate that Congress uses specific language when intending that an agency engage in cost-benefit analysis. Certainly in light of its ordinary meaning, the word "feasible" cannot be construed to articulate such congressional intent. We therefore reject the argument that Congress required cost-benefit analysis in § 6(b)(5).

Suing the Government

In the modern administrative state, the range of government activity is immense, and administrative agencies frequently get in the way of business enterprise. Often bureaucratic involvement is wholly legitimate, compelled by law; sometimes, however, agencies or government officials may overstep their bounds, in a fit of zeal or spite. What recourse does the private individual or company have?

Mainly for historical reasons, it has always been more difficult to sue the government than to haul private individuals into court. For one thing, the government has long had recourse to the doctrine of *sovereign immunity* (p. 244) as a shield against lawsuits. In 1976, Congress amended the Administrative Procedure Act to waive any federal claim to sovereign immunity in cases of injunctive or other non-monetary relief. In 1946 in the Federal Tort Claims Act, Congress waived sovereign immunity of the federal government for most tort claims for money damages, although the act contains several exceptions for specific agencies. (For example, one cannot sue for injuries resulting from fiscal operations of the Treasury Department, or for injuries stemming from activities of the military in wartime.) The act also contains a major exception for claims "based upon [an official's] exercise or performance or the failure to exercise or perform a discretionary function or duty." This exception prevents suits against parole boards for paroling dangerous criminals who then kill or maim in the course of another crime and against officials whose decision to ship explosive materials by public carrier leads to mass deaths and injuries following an explosion en route. [Dalehite v. United States, 346 U.S. 15 (1953)]

In recent years, the Supreme Court has been stripping away the traditional immunity enjoyed by many government officials against personal suits. Some government employees—judges, prosecutors, legislators, and the president, for example—have absolute immunity against suit for official actions. But many public administrators and government employees have at best a qualified immunity. Under a provision of the Civil Rights Act of 1871 (so-called Section 1983 actions), *state* officials can be sued in federal court for money damages whenever "under color of any state law" they deprive anyone of his rights under the Constitution or federal law. In *Bivens* v. *Six Unknown Federal Narcotics Agents,* 403 U.S. 388 (1971), the Supreme Court held that *federal* agents may be sued for violating the plaintiff's Fourth Amendment rights against an unlawful search of his home. Subsequent cases have followed this logic to permit suits for violations of other constitutional provisions. This area of the law is in a state of flux, and it is likely to continue to evolve.

Chapter Summary

Administrative rules and regulations constitute the largest body of laws that directly affect business. These regulations are issued by dozens of federal and state agencies that regulate virtually every aspect of modern business life, including the natural environment, corporate finance, transportation, telecommunications, energy, labor relations, and trade practices. The administrative agencies derive their power to promulgate regulations from statutes passed by Congress or state legislatures.

The agencies have a variety of powers. They can license companies to carry on certain activities or prohibit them from doing so, lay down codes of conduct, set rates that companies may charge for their services, and supervise various aspects of business.

At the federal level, administrative agencies are governed by the Administrative Procedure Act, which separates judicial functions within agencies from their rule-making functions. Many agency decisions may be appealed to the courts, which are, however, forbidden from substituting their own judgment about the worth of the regulations. The courts' role is limited to ascertaining whether the administrative regulations exceed the legislative authority delegated to the agency and whether it had sufficient evidence to make the ruling it did in a particular case.

Problems

1. Assume that the Federal Trade Commission issued a regulation stating that henceforth all used-car dealers would have to tell prospective customers how many miles the car had been driven and which parts of the car were used and how old they were. To what branch or branches of government could the used-car lobby turn to eliminate the regulation? What action could other branches of the government take to eliminate the regulation?
2. Suppose the State Commerce Commission, which regulates trucking, were to adopt a rule permitting any trucker who might be affected by a tariff decision to have ninety days to object after the tariff is published. Constant Truckers, Inc., objects to a tariff that sets a price of five dollars per mile maximum for hauling certain types of goods between the capital and any city in the state. When published, the tariff says it will take effect in thirty days. On the forty-fifth day, Constant objects and charges a customer ten dollars a mile. The customer complains, and the agency commences a disciplinary action against Constant to see whether the trucker's license should be suspended. What is Constant's defense?
3. The Equal Employment Opportunity Commission seeks data about the racial composition of Terrific Textiles's labor force. Terrific refuses on the grounds that inadvertent disclosure of the numbers might cause certain "elements" to picket its factories. The EEOC takes Terrific to court to get the data. What result?

4. In order to police the profession, the state legislature has just passed a law permitting the State Plumbers' Association the power to hold hearings to determine whether a particular plumber has violated the plumbing code of ethics, written by the Association. Sam, a plumber, objects to the convening of a hearing when he is accused by Roger, a fellow plumber, of acting unethically by soliciting business from Roger's customers. Sam goes to court, seeking to enjoin the Association's Disciplinary Committee from holding the hearing. What result? How would you argue Sam's case? The Association's case?

6

Business Ethics and Social Responsibility

In Chapter 1 (pp. 6–7) we noted the relationship between ethical principles and the law. Here we explore this relationship in greater detail and examine how it affects management decision making.

The dictionaries define ethics as a system of moral conduct, but establishing an ethical standard in specific cases is difficult because our pluralistic society has many different moral codes. To be sure, some kinds of conduct are condemned by all moral codes and thus from time immemorial have been incorporated into legal codes: murder, rape, theft, and fraud are obvious examples. Regarding other types of conduct, society is far more equivocal.

Abortion, for example, is widely condemned as murder and widely justified as the free choice of a woman over her body. Although as individuals we can debate this issue long into the night, as a society we rarely have the luxury of embracing, or avoiding, both standards. Specific cases almost always require yes or no answers. Should the law permit women freely to seek abortions or prohibit them from doing so? When the Supreme Court considered the issue in *Roe* v. *Wade,* 410 U.S. 113 (1973), Justice Blackmun noted "briefly the wide divergence of thinking on this most sensitive and difficult question":

> There has always been strong support of the view that life does not begin until live birth. This was the belief of the Stoics. It appears to be the predominant, though not the unanimous, attitude of the Jewish faith. It may be taken to represent also the position of a large segment of the Protestant community. . . . The Aristotelian theory of "mediate animation," that held sway throughout the Middle Ages and the Renaissance in Europe, continued to be official Roman Catholic dogma until the 19th century, despite opposition to this "ensoulment" theory from those in the Church who would recognize the existence of life from the moment of conception. The latter is now, of course, the official belief of the Catholic Church. As one brief *amicus* discloses, this is a view strongly held by many non-Catholics as well, and by many physicians.

In resolving this issue, the Court put the law onto a path that coincides with certain moral systems only because so many different approaches exist. The 7–2 majority held that secular courts cannot definitively determine when life begins and that legally the fetus has never been regarded as a whole person. Given a woman's constitutional right to control her body, the Court's answer was to recognize women's freedom to choose abortions during the first trimester of pregnancy and to permit the states to regulate the procedures of abortion thereafter and even to prohibit abortion, to preserve the potential life of the fetus in the third trimester. This is a *legal* resolution of the abortion controversy, but not an *ethical* one—a woman may have an abortion but is obviously not required to have one.

Ethical conundrums exist in the business community as well. Suppose your boss says you are doing fine work but at the moment the company cannot afford to give you a formal raise. Instead, she suggests that the company "won't look too closely at your expense accounts for a while." Is it ethical to pad your expense account on the ground that the boss has implicitly given you a raise through a different route? As we will see, the business community is split to some extent on whether this is appropriate behavior (p. 156).

Even when there is a consensus on an ethical standard, law and morality are not necessarily the same. In some cases, legal principles may mesh closely with ethical standards, even though the ethical standards are not attainable by the average person. In a famous British case, *Regina* v. *Dudley and Stephens,* 14 Q.B.D. 273 (1884), two sailors were prosecuted for murder in killing and actually eating the body of the cabin boy after nine days in a shipwreck on the high seas. The courts upheld the murder conviction, even while acknowledging that the sailors would have died had they done anything different. Recognizing that the sailors acted from an instinct for survival, the queen commuted their sentence to six months' imprisonment. In other cases, the law may diverge from the ethical rule—as noted earlier, the law generally imposes no duty on a bystander to help someone in distress (p. 6).

In the discussion that follows, we will first examine situations in which law and business ethics converge. We will then examine two situations in which they diverge—that is, when conduct is illegal but ethical, and when it is legal but unethical. In the following diagram, boxes 1 and 4 represent the convergent situations, and boxes 2 and 3 the divergent settings.

	Legal	Illegal
Ethical	1	2
Unethical	3	4

Convergence of the Law and Business Ethics

Behavior is often both legal and ethical or, conversely, illegal and unethical. Within the business community, many examples illustrate this convergence.

Contracts

Contract law imposes a duty to act in good faith. This duty is found in both the Restatement (Second) of Contracts, Section 205, and the Uniform Commercial Code, Section 1–203. When this duty is breached, the aggrieved party may obtain remedies beyond those normally provided for in contract law if the contracting parties had a special relationship (such as that between an insurer and insured) and, in some states, even in the absence of a special relationship, as the next case demonstrates.

SEAMAN'S DIRECT BUYING SERVICE, INC. v. STANDARD OIL CO. OF CAL.
36 Cal.3d 752, 686 P.2d 1158 (1984)

[The plaintiff, Seaman's Direct Buying Service, Inc., a dealer in ship supplies, sued Standard Oil Company of California for breaching a marine dealership contract that Seaman's needed in order to lease marine space from the City of Eureka, California. When conditions in the oil industry changed and a federal allocation program went into effect, Standard told Seaman's that federal regulations prevented performance of the contract.]

In telephone calls and personal meetings with Seaman's, Standard indicated that the new federal regulations were the *only* barrier to the contract. "[I]f it wasn't for the [federal agency], . . . [Standard] would be willing to go ahead with the contract. . . ." "If [Seaman's could] get the federal government to change that order so that Standard could supply [Seaman's] with fuel [Standard] would be very happy. . . ." Standard even supplied Seaman's with the forms necessary to seek a supply authorization from the federal agency and helped fill them out.

As a result of these efforts, a supply order was issued on February 4, 1974. Standard responded by changing its position. The company contended now that no binding agreement with Seaman's had ever been reached. Therefore, Standard decided to appeal the order "[b]ecause [it] did not want to take on any new business." When Seaman's learned of the appeal, it twice wrote to Standard requesting an explanation. None was forthcoming. Standard's federal appeal was successful. Internal memoranda reveal Standard's reaction to this result: "[g]reat!!" "We are recommending to other div[isions] that they follow your example."

Seaman's then appealed and this decision was, in turn, reversed. The new decision provided that an order "direct[ing] [Standard] to fulfill supply obligations to Seaman's" would be issued upon the filing of a copy of a court decree that a valid contract existed between the parties under state law.

Seaman's asked Standard to stipulate to the existence of a contract, explaining that it could not continue in operation throughout the time that a trial would take. In reply, Standard's representative laughed and said, "See you in court." Seaman's testified that if Standard had cooperated, Seaman's would have borrowed funds to remain in business until 1976 when the new marina opened.

Seaman's discontinued operations in early 1975. Soon thereafter, the company filed suit against Standard, charging Standard with breach of contract, fraud, breach of the implied covenant of good faith and fair dealing, and interference with Seaman's contractual relationship with the City. The case was tried before a jury which returned a verdict for Seaman's on all but the fraud cause of action. For breach of contract, the jury awarded compensatory damages of $397,050. For tortious breach of the implied covenant of good faith and fair dealing, they awarded $397,050 in compensatory damages and $11,058,810 in punitive damages. Finally, for intentional interference with an advantageous business relationship, the jury set compensatory damages at $1,588,200 and punitive damages at $11,058,810.

Standard moved for a new trial, charging, inter alia, that the damages were excessive as a matter of law. The trial court conditionally granted the motion unless Seaman's consented to a reduction of punitive damages on the interference count to $6 million and on the good faith count to $1 million. Seaman's consented to the reduction, and judgment was entered accordingly. Standard appeals from the judgment. Seaman's has filed a cross-appeal.

* * *

The principal issue raised by this appeal is whether, and under what circumstances, a breach of the implied covenant of good faith and fair dealing in a commercial contract may give rise to an action in tort. Standard contends that a tort action for breach of the implied covenant has always been, and should continue to be, limited to cases where the underlying contract is one of insurance. Seaman's, pointing to several recent cases decided by this court and the Courts of Appeal, challenges this contention. A brief review of the development of the tort is in order.

It is well settled that, in California, the law implies in *every* contract a covenant of good faith and fair dealing. . . . Broadly stated, that covenant requires that neither party do anything which will deprive the other of the benefits of the agreement.

* * *

While the proposition that the law implies a covenant of good faith and fair dealing in all contracts is well established, the proposition advanced by Seaman's—that breach of the covenant always gives rise to an action in tort—is not so clear. In holding that a tort action is available for breach of the covenant in an insurance contract, we have emphasized the "special relationship" between insurer and insured, characterized by elements of public interest, adhesion, and fiduciary responsibility. (*Egan* v. *Mutual of Omaha Ins. Co.,* 24 Cal.3d at p. 820, 169 Cal.Rptr. 691, 620 P.2d 141.) No doubt there are other relationships with similar characteristics and deserving of similar legal treatment.

When we move from such special relationships to consideration of the tort remedy in the context of the ordinary commercial contract, we move into largely uncharted and potentially dangerous waters. Here, parties of roughly equal bargaining power are free to shape the contours of their agreement and to include provisions for attorney fees and liquidated damages in the event of breach. They may not be permitted to disclaim the covenant of good faith but they are free, within reasonable limits at least, to agree upon the standards by which application of the covenant is to be measured. In such contracts, it may be difficult to distinguish between breach of the covenant and breach of contract, and there is the risk that interjecting tort remedies will intrude upon the expectations of the parties. This is not to say that tort remedies have no place in such a commercial context, but that it is wise to proceed with caution in determining their scope and application.

For the purposes of this case it is unnecessary to decide the broad question which Seaman's poses. Indeed, it is not even necessary to predicate liability on a breach of the implied covenant. It is sufficient to recognize that a party to a contract may incur tort remedies when, in addition to breaching the contract, it seeks to shield itself from liability by denying, in bad faith and without probable cause, that the contract exists.

It has been held that a party to a contract may be subject to tort liability, including punitive damages, if he coerces the other party to pay more than is due under the contract terms through the threat of a lawsuit, made " 'without probable cause and with no belief in the existence of the cause of action.' " (*Crater Well Drilling, Inc.* (1976) 276 Or. 789, 556 P.2d 679, 681.) There is little difference, in principle, between a contracting party obtaining excess payment in such manner, and a contracting party seeking to avoid all liability on a meritorious contract claim by adopting a "stonewall" position ("see you in court") without probable cause and with no belief in the existence of a defense. Such conduct goes beyond the mere breach of contract. It offends accepted notions of business ethics. Acceptance of tort remedies in such a situation is not likely to intrude upon the bargaining relationship or upset reasonable expectations of the contracting parties.

* * *

[The court reversed the judgment for Seaman's and remanded for further proceedings on the grounds that the trial judge gave erroneous instructions to the jury.]

A person making a contract has another ethical duty enshrined in law: the duty to avoid acting unconscionably. We examine later (p. 315) how courts have sought to give content to this rather amorphous term, but whatever it might mean, and however its meaning might shift from case to case, the duty is solidly rooted in law. The Uniform Commercial Code (described in Chapter 8, p. 196) empowers the courts to ignore any term of a contract that is unconscionable when made, or even to refuse to enforce the contract altogether.

Agency Law

Ethical concepts also affect the relationship between principal and agent (discussed at greater length in Chapter 13). An agent (employee) legally owes the principal (employer) a *fiduciary duty*, a duty of the highest trust and loyalty (see p. 363). Principals are also not free to act as they please; they too owe duties to agents. Quite recently, for example, some courts and legislatures have begun to recognize exceptions to the ancient "employment-at-will" doctrine (see p. 446) that gives employers the absolute legal right to fire employees whenever they like, with or without reason. For example, a public policy exception that has developed in several states bars employers from discharging "whistleblowers"—employees who tell public authorities about illegal activities in which employers are engaged. Still, the principal is generally less legally constrained than the agent (see, for example, the *Pierce* case, p. 150).

Corporate Officers and Directors

Officers and directors of corporations owe a general fiduciary duty to shareholders and to their corporation as a separate entity. This duty arises at common law, and since the 1930s it has been embedded in federal securities laws. For example, the Securities Exchange Act of 1934 bars insider trading and requires those with inside information to disclose it to the general public before they can trade in the stock (see Chapter 18). However, this duty does not apply to everyone: There is no duty to disclose, the Supreme Court has said, in cases where the person who traded on inside information "was not [the corporation's] agent, . . . was not a fiduciary, [or] was not a person in whom the sellers [of securities] had placed their trust and confidence." [Chiarella v. United States, 445 U.S. 222 (1980)] The law thus imposes legal duties only on those who, under broad community standards, would also have an ethical duty to disclose.

Trade Regulation

With the passage of the Federal Trade Commission Act of 1914 (see Chapter 21), Congress created a federal agency, the Federal Trade Commission, to curb "unfair methods of competition" and "unfair or deceptive acts or practices." Though not defined in the legislation, it is clear that the law aims at precisely those kinds of acts that are commonly understood to be "unfair" in the moral sense. One example is the "bait and switch" advertisement, which brags of sale merchandise to lure customers into the store, only to discover that the item advertised is unavailable, and that some other, perhaps inferior, certainly more expensive, merchandise is waiting.

Divergence of the Law and Business Ethics

When law and ethics are congruent, few have reason to complain about legal sanctions. But when they diverge, managers face a dilemma. On the one hand, managers who make decisions solely on the basis of what they perceive to be ethical conduct run the risk that their actions will be in violation of the law. On the other hand, managers who choose to adopt legal rules as the sole guide to their decision making ignore the fact that the law often embraces only minimal standards of ethical behavior. As Alexander Solzhenitsyn pointed out in his celebrated Harvard graduation address in 1978:

> I have spent all my life under a Communist regime, and I will tell you that a society without any objective legal scale is a terrible one indeed. But a society with no other scale but the legal one is not quite worthy of man either. The letter of the law is too cold and formal to have a beneficial influence on society. Whenever the tissue of life is woven of legalistic relations, there is an atmosphere of moral mediocrity, paralyzing man's noblest impulses.

Illegal but Ethical Conduct

Under various circumstances, conduct that may be considered ethical on the basis of an individual's personal or professional standards violates a principle of law. For example, under the formal canons of professional ethics of many engineering societies, members may not solicit clients from other engineers. This ethical standard is justified in part as a means to ensure that engineers do not do unsafe work because they have underbid to get a job. Unfortunately, this ethical standard violates the federal antitrust laws, as the *National Society of Professional Engineers* case shows (p. 534).

Similarly, a personal standard can run afoul of the law. Assume that the majority shareholder of a business corporation decides that the corporation (1) should donate a substantial amount of money to her alma mater, and (2) should be run for humanitarian purposes. Could minority shareholders challenge these ethical decisions on legal grounds? As is so often the case in legal analysis, the answer is yes and no. As the following case demonstrates, corporations may engage in humanitarian activities to a limited degree.

A.P. SMITH MFG. CO. v. BARLOW
26 N.J.Super 106, 97 A.2d 186 (1953)

* * *

Stripped to its simplest form, the question calling for decision is whether a New Jersey corporation, organized in 1896 to engage in industry for purposes of profit, may lawfully in 1951 donate from its funds for the general maintenance of an educational institution like Princeton University; private in nature, in the sense that it is privately supported, it being an institution where learning is advanced by the teaching of learned languages, the liberal arts and sciences, architecture, engineering, and political science. The plaintiff company, speaking through its directors, answers this question affirmatively. . . .

* * *

. . . .The facts are not in dispute. The only evidence before the court is that adduced by the plaintiff. The defendants offered no proof. Thus the process of arriving at a decision is here considerably eased. Many of the facts testified to in this case by leaders of American industry and by front-line educators are matters of such common, almost universal, familiarity that the court might well have taken judicial notice of them. It needs no proof that the universities and colleges of the land are eleemosynary institutions. . . . At Princeton, as at most American universities and colleges, the tuition paid for instruction meets only fractionally the per capita cost of the education furnished. Not only that, but a large segment of the student body is assisted by scholarships and by direct financial aid from the school's treasury. So widespread has been for many years this policy of aid to the needy student that it cannot in truth be said that any deserving youth of ambition and promise cannot obtain at some American university or college that aid, in whole or in part, necessary to put him through an undergraduate career and even a post-graduate course. Unlike the system of higher education in other countries, the tremendous growth and expansion over the years of the American universities and colleges have created and furnished to the youth of the land the broadest of opportunity for instruction and development in the area of advanced learning in arts and pure and applied science and in the field of economics and government. It is from the millions of young men and women who are the products of higher American education that industry has picked, and will have need to pick, its scientists and its business executives. It is the youth of today which also furnishes tomorrow's leaders in economics and in government, thereby erecting a strong breastwork against any onslaught from hostile forces which would change our way of life either in respect of private enterprise or democratic self-government. The proofs before me are abundant that Princeton emphasizes by precept and indoctrination the principles which are very vital to the preservation of our own democratic system of business and government, particularly vital at this time when alien ideologies seek to impose themselves upon our habits and our dreams for the future. I cannot conceive of any greater benefit to corporations in this country than to build, and continue to build, respect for and adherence to a system of free enterprise and democratic government, the serious impairment of either of which may well spell the destruction of all corporate enterprise. Nothing that aids or promotes the growth and service of the American university or college in respect of the matters here discussed can possibly be anything short of direct benefit to every corporation in the land. The college-trained men and women are a ready reservoir from which industry may draw to satisfy its need for scientific or executive talent. It is no answer to say that a company is not so benefited unless such need is immediate. A long-range view must be taken of the matter. A small company today might be under no imperative requirement to engage the services of a research chemist or other scientist, but its growth in a few years may be such that it must have available an ample pool from which it may obtain the needed service. It must also be remembered that industry cannot function efficiently or enjoy development and expansion unless it has at all times the advantage of enlightened leadership and direction. The value of that kind of service depends in great measure upon the training, ideologies and character of the personnel available. All of these considerations must lead the reflecting mind to the conclusion that nothing conducive to public welfare, other than perhaps public safety, is more important than the preservation of the privately supported institutions of learning which embrace in their enrollment about half the college-attending youth of the country. Even public safety depends heavily upon the educated mind; witness what scientific research at Princeton and elsewhere was able to accomplish in discovering and making of practical utilization what had since the beginning of time been the mystery of the atom. Princeton is preeminent in its encouragement of the searching mind both in science and in public affairs. Its preservation is indeed of first importance to the welfare of the State.

The court was furnished with proofs that Princeton, like most other privately supported institutions of higher education, is presently facing a serious threat, if not to its very existence then certainly to the extent of its public usefulness. High taxation against individual incomes and inflationary living costs have dried up the sources which heretofore nourished and sustained the school's activities. The school's budgetary deficits are mounting and are assuming threatening proportions. To turn to the State for help carries with it a certain decided disadvantage. The award of state funds is a matter of political administration. Such grants certainly present the hazard of political interference or control. The experience of the University of Louisiana, a state university, can hardly be forgotten. That school for a time became a political football, a condition hardly to be courted. I am strongly persuaded by the evidence that the only hope for the survival of the privately supported American college and university lies in the willingness of corporate wealth to furnish in moderation some support to institutions which are so essential to public welfare and therefore, of necessity, to corporate welfare. What promotes the general good inescapably advances the corporate weal. I hold that corporate contributions to Princeton and institutions rendering the like public service are, if held within reasonable limitations, a matter of direct benefit to the giving corporations, and this without regard to the extent or sweep of the donors' business. The benefits derived from such contributions are nation-wide and promote the welfare of everyone anywhere in the land.

* * *

[The court concluded that the contributions were within the powers of the corporation.]

Barlow's conclusion is now incorporated into most modern corporation statutes. But to run a business corporation entirely for humanitarian purposes, though it might be ethical by the standards of the managers, would be contrary to the law.

In a famous case, *Dodge* v. *Ford Motor Co.*, 170 N.W. 668 (Mich. 1919), the Dodge brothers sued the Ford Motor Company to enjoin the company from building a new plant and to force the directors to declare a dividend. During the trial, Henry Ford testified that he wanted to plow money that could otherwise be paid as dividends back into the company because he was against "awful profits." Ford's ambition, in his words, was "to employ still more men, to spread the benefits of this industrial system to the greatest possible number, to help them build up their lives and their homes. To do this we are putting the greatest share of our profits back in the business." The result: the court ordered the company to pay the dividends, since a corporation is run for its shareholders, not for humanity. (The court, however, refused to halt the corporate expansion because "judges are not business experts.")

Beyond the legal result in the *Ford* case, there is room to disagree over whether Ford was acting ethically. Father R. L. Bruckberger, a French priest, thought he was. Commenting on Ford's stance, Father Bruckberger suggested that "in all the world's universities all young people seeking some knowledge of political economy should be required to learn [Ford's philosophy] . . . by heart. It is as important in economics as the Declaration of Independence is in politics. . . . [It] should be looked upon as the businessman's Hippocratic Oath." (Lewis, 1976, pp. 101–102) But Milton Friedman, the well-known University of Chicago economist, demurs: ". . . [T]here is one and only one social responsibility of business—to use its resources and engage in activities designed to increase its profits so long as it stays within the rules of the game, which is to say, engages in open and free competition, without deception or fraud." (Friedman, 1962, p. 133)

Legal but Unethical Conduct

There is a vast range of instances in which the law has allowed conduct that many consider unethical—from the publication of pornographic literature to investment in South Africa. Individuals face special problems when confronted with this conduct because it is sanctioned by the law. For example, suppose a real estate developer hires a woman to buy homes from elderly, poor homeowners in a deteriorating neighborhood. The developer instructs her to act on his behalf as a secret agent; that is, not to disclose to any of the sellers that she is working for the developer. The woman knows that if she fully discloses the facts, property values will double. Her feeling that this activity is unethical finds no support in the law, which upholds contracts made by secret agents (Chapter 14). Consequently, she must resolve her dilemma on the basis of her personal standards. If she chooses to follow the dictates of her conscience, rather than the letter of the law, she will not—unlike Henry Ford—have violated the law. However, as the following case notes, she may still face extralegal sanctions, such as the loss of her job.

PIERCE v. ORTHO PHARMACEUTICAL CORP.
84 N.J. 58, 417 A.2d 505 (1980)

POLLOCK, J.

This case presents the question whether an employee at will has a cause of action against her employer to recover damages for the termination of her employment following her refusal to continue a project she viewed as medically unethical. Resolution of this question involves an examination of the common law doctrine of at will employment to determine whether we should adopt an exception to the rule allowing an employer to discharge an at will employee without cause.

Plaintiff, Dr. Grace Pierce, sued for damages after termination of her employment with defendant, Ortho Pharmaceutical Corporation. The trial judge granted defendant's motion for summary judgment. The Appellate Division reversed and remanded for a full trial. We granted defendant's petition for certification. We now reverse the Appellate Division and reinstate the summary judgment granted by the Law Division.

* * *

Ortho specializes in the development and manufacture of therapeutic and reproductive drugs. Dr. Pierce is a medical doctor who was first employed by Ortho in 1971 as an Associate Director of Medical Research. She signed no contract except a secrecy agreement, and her employment was not for a fixed term. She was an employee at will. In 1973, she became the Director of Medical Research/Therapeutics, one of three major sections of the Medical Research Department. Her primary responsibilities were to oversee development of therapeutic drugs and to establish procedures for testing those drugs for safety, effectiveness, and marketability. Her immediate supervisor was Dr. Samuel Pasquale, Executive Medical Director.

In the spring of 1975, Dr. Pierce was the only medical doctor on a project team developing loperamide, a liquid drug for treatment of diarrhea in infants, children, and elderly persons. The proposed formulation contained saccharin. Although the concentration was consistent with the formula for loperamide marketed in Europe, the project team agreed that the formula was unsuitable for use in the United States. An alternative formulation containing less saccharin might have been developed within approximately three months.

By March 28, however, the project team, except for Dr. Pierce, decided to continue with the development of loperamide. That decision was made apparently in response to a directive from the Marketing Division of Ortho. This decision meant that Ortho would file an investigational new drug application (IND) with the Federal Food and Drug Administration (FDA), continuing laboratory studies on loperamide, and begin work on a formulation. FDA approval is required before any new drug is tested clinically on humans. Therefore, loperamide would be tested on patients only if the FDA approved the saccharin formulation.

Dr. Pierce knew that the IND would have to be filed with and approved by the FDA before clinical testing could begin. Nonetheless, she continued to oppose the work being done on loperamide at Ortho. On April 21, 1975, she sent a memorandum to the project team expressing her disagreement with its decision to proceed with the development of the drug. In her opinion, there was no justification for seeking FDA permission to use the drug in light of medical controversy over the safety of saccharin.

Dr. Pierce met with Dr. Pasquale on May 9 and informed him that she disagreed with the decision to file an IND with the FDA. She felt that by continuing to work on loperamide she would violate her interpretation of the Hippocratic oath. She concluded that the risk that saccharin might be harmful should preclude testing the formula on children or elderly persons, especially when an alternative formulation might soon be available.

Dr. Pierce recognized that she was joined in a difference of "viewpoints" or "opinion" with Dr. Pasquale and others at Ortho concerning the use of a formula containing saccharin. In her opinion, the safety of saccharin in loperamide pediatric drops was medically debatable. She acknowledged that Dr. Pasquale was entitled to his opinion to proceed with the IND. On depositions, she testified concerning the reason for her difference of opinion about the safety of using saccharin in loperamide pediatric drops:

> Q That was because in your medical opinion that was an unsafe thing to do. Is that so?
> A No. I didn't know. The question of saccharin was one of potential harm. It was controversial. Even though the rulings presently look even less favorable for saccharin it is still a controversial issue.

After their meeting on May 9, Dr. Pasquale informed Dr. Pierce that she would no longer be assigned to the loperamide project. On May 14, Dr. Pasquale asked Dr. Pierce to choose other projects. After Dr. Pierce returned from vacation in Finland, she met on June 16 with Dr. Pasquale to discuss other projects, but she did not choose a project at that meeting. She felt she was being demoted, even though her salary would not be decreased. Dr. Pierce summarized her impression of that meeting in her letter of resignation submitted to Dr. Pasquale the following day. In that letter, she stated:

> Upon learning in our meeting June 16, 1975, that you believe I have not 'acted as a Director', have displayed inadequacies as to my competence, responsibility, productivity, inability to relate to the Marketing Personnel, that you, and reportedly Dr. George Braun and Mr. Verne Willaman consider me to be non-promotable and that I am now or soon will be demoted, I find it impossible to continue my employment at Ortho.

The letter made no specific mention of her difference of opinion with Dr. Pasquale over continuing the work on loperamide. Nonetheless, viewing the matter most favorably to Dr. Pierce, we assume the sole reason for the termination of her employment was the dispute over the loperamide project. Dr. Pasquale accepted her resignation.

* * *

There was a fact question whether Ortho induced Dr. Pierce to resign. Consequently, the trial judge properly denied summary judgment on the alternative ground that her resignation barred this action. That determination is not challenged on this appeal. Therefore, we do not reach the question whether resignation bars an action for wrongful discharge.

* * *

Under the common law, in the absence of an employment contract, employers or employees have been free to terminate the employment relationship with or without cause.

* * *

In the last century, the common law developed in a laissez-faire climate that encouraged industrial growth and approved the right of an employer to control his own business, including the right to fire without cause an employee at will. The twentieth century has witnessed significant changes in socioeconomic values that have led to reassessment of the common law rule. Businesses have evolved from small and medium size firms to gigantic corporations in which ownership is separate from management. Formerly there was a clear delineation between employers, who frequently were owners of their own businesses, and employees. The employer in the old sense has been replaced by a superior in the corporate hierarchy who is himself an employer. We are a nation of employees. Growth in the number of employees has been accompanied by increasing recognition of the need for stability in labor relations.

Commentators have questioned the compatibility of the traditional at will doctrine with the realities of modern economics and employment practices. The common law rule has been modified by the enactment of labor relations legislation. The National Labor Relations Act and other labor legislation illustrate the governmental policy of preventing employers from using the right of discharge as a means of oppression. Consistent with this policy, many states have recognized the need to protect employees who are not parties to a collective bargaining agreement or other contract from abusive practices by the employer.

Recently those states have recognized a common law cause of action for employees at will who were discharged for reasons that were in some way "wrongful." The courts in those jurisdictions have taken varied approaches, some recognizing the action in tort, some in contract. Nearly all jurisdictions link the success of the wrongful discharged employee's action to proof that the discharge violated public policy.

* * *

We hold that an employee has a cause of action for wrongful discharge when the discharge is contrary to a clear mandate of public policy. The sources of public policy include legislation; administrative rules, regulations or decisions; and judicial decisions. In certain instances, a professional code of ethics may contain an expression of public policy. However, not all such sources express a clear mandate of public policy. For example, a code of ethics designed to serve only the interests of a profession or an administrative regulation concerned with technical matters probably would not be sufficient. Absent legislation, the judiciary must define the cause of action in case-by-case determinations. An employer's right to discharge an employee at will carries a correlative duty not to discharge an employee who declines to perform an act that would require a violation of a clear mandate of public policy. However, unless an employee at will identifies a specific expression of public policy, he may be discharged with or without cause.

* * *

Viewing the matter most favorably to Dr. Pierce, the controversy at Ortho involved a difference in medical opinions. Dr. Pierce acknowledged that Dr. Pasquale was entitled to his opinion that the oath did not forbid work on loperamide. Nonetheless, implicit in Dr. Pierce's position is the contention that Dr. Pasquale and Ortho were obliged to accept her opinion. Dr. Pierce contends, in effect, that Ortho should have stopped research on loperamide because of her opinion about the controversial nature of the drug.

Dr. Pierce espouses a doctrine that would lead to disorder in drug research. Under her theory, a professional employee could redetermine the propriety of a research project even if the research did not involve a violation of a clear mandate of public policy. Chaos would result if a single doctor engaged in research were allowed to determine, according to his or her individual conscience, whether a project should continue. An employee does not have a right to continued employment when he or she refuses to conduct research simply because it would contravene his or her personal morals. An employee at will who refuses to work for an employer in answer to a call of conscience should recognize that older employees and their employer might heed a different call. However, nothing in this opinion should be construed to restrict the right of an employee at will to refuse to work on a project that he or she believes is unethical. In sum, an employer may discharge an employee who refuses to work unless the refusal is based on a clear mandate of public policy.

As stated above, the thrust of Dr. Pierce's complaint is not that saccharin is dangerous, but that it is controversial. At oral argument, Dr. Pierce's attorney conceded that she did not intend to submit the question of the safety of saccharin to the jury. That is, plaintiff did not intend to adduce expert testimony demonstrating the dangers of the formulation of loperamide containing the proposed level of saccharin. As a matter of law, there is no public policy against conducting research on drugs that may be controversial, but potentially beneficial to mankind, particularly where continuation of the research is subject to approval by the FDA. Consequently, although we recognize an employee may maintain an action for wrongful discharge, we hold there are no issues of material fact to be resolved at trial.

Under these circumstances, we conclude that the Hippocratic oath does not contain a clear mandate of public policy that prevented Dr. Pierce from continuing her research on loperamide. To hold otherwise would seriously impair the ability of drug manufacturers to develop new drugs according to their best judgment.

* * *

Accordingly, we reverse the judgment of the Appellate Division and remand the cause to the trial court for entry of judgment for defendant.

The Law and Social Change

Neither law nor ethics is static. Legal and ethical standards often develop separately and move closer to (or farther from) each other in ways difficult to predict. For example, as we saw on pp. 6–7, under common-law rule, one person has no legal duty to help another person in trouble, although the bystander may feel a moral duty to aid the victim. As noted in Box 1-1 (p. 7), this traditional rule is now being changed by legislatures in some states: a 1983 Rhode Island law provides a penalty of up to a year in jail for any witness (other than the victim) who fails to report a rape to the police. As the following case shows, courts also are free to move in the same direction: toward a recognition that the law must enforce the moral principle that "each member of a community has a right that each other member treat him with the minimal respect due a fellow human being." (Dworkin, 1978, p. 98)

SOLDANO v. O'DANIELS
141 Cal.App.3d 443, 190 Cal.Rptr. 310 (Ct.App. 1983)

ANDREEN, ASSOCIATE JUSTICE.

Does a business establishment incur liability for wrongful death if it denies use of its telephone to a good samaritan who explains an emergency situation occurring without and wishes to call the police?

This appeal follows a judgment of dismissal of the second cause of action of a complaint for wrongful death upon a motion for summary judgment. The motion was supported only by a declaration of defense counsel. Both briefs on appeal adopt the defense averments:

> "This action arises out of a shooting death occurring on August 9, 1977. Plaintiff's father [Darrell Soldano] was shot and killed by one Rudolph Villanueva on that date at defendant's Happy Jack's Saloon. This defendant owns and operates the Circle Inn which is an eating establishment located across the street from Happy Jack's. Plaintiff's second cause of action against this defendant is one for negligence.
>
> "Plaintiff alleges that on the date of the shooting, a patron of Happy Jack's Saloon came into the Circle Inn and informed a Circle Inn employee that a man had been threatened at Happy Jack's. He requested the employee either call the police or allow him to use the Circle Inn phone to call the police. That employee allegedly refused to call the police and allegedly refused to allow the patron to use the phone to make his own call. Plaintiff alleges that the actions of the Circle Inn employee were a breach of the legal duty that the Circle Inn owed to the decedent."

We were advised at oral argument that the employee was the defendant's bartender. The state of the record is unsatisfactory in that it does not disclose the physical location of the telephone—whether on the bar, in a private office behind a closed door or elsewhere. The only factual matter before the trial court was a verified statement of the defense attorney which set forth those acts quoted above. Following normal rules applicable to motions for summary judgment, we strictly construe the defense affidavit. Accordingly, we assume the telephone was not in a private office but in a position where it could be used by a patron without inconvenience to the defendant or his guests. We also assume the call was a local one and would not result in expense to defendant.

* * *

Defendant argues that the request that its employee call the police is a request that it *do* something. He points to the established rule that one who has not created a peril ordinarily does not have a duty to take affirmative action to assist an imperiled person. It is urged that the alternative request of the patron from Happy Jack's Saloon that he be allowed to use defendant's telephone so that he personally could make the call is again a request that the defendant do something—assist another to give aid. Defendant points out that the Restatement sections which impose liability for negligent interference with a third person giving aid to another do not impose the additional duty to *aid* the good samaritan.

The refusal of the law to recognize the moral obligation of one to aid another when he is in peril and when such aid may be given without danger and at little cost in effort has been roundly criticized. Prosser describes the case law sanctioning such inaction as a "refus[al] to recognize the moral obligation of common decency and common humanity" and characterizes some of these decisions as "shocking in the extreme. . . .

Such decisions are revolting to any moral sense. They have been denounced with vigor by legal writers." A similar rule has been termed "morally questionable" by our Supreme Court.

* * *

The consequences to the community of imposing a duty is termed "the administrative factor" by Professor Green in his analysis of determining whether a duty exists in a given case. The administrative factor is simply the pragmatic concern of fashioning a workable rule and the impact of such a rule on the judicial machinery. It is the policy of major concern in this case.

* * *

Many citizens simply "don't want to get involved." No rule should be adopted which would require a citizen to open up his or her house to a stranger so that the latter may use the telephone call for emergency assistance. As Mrs. Alexander in Anthony Burgess' A Clockwork Orange learned to her horror, such an action may be fraught with danger. It does not follow, however, that use of a telephone in a public portion of a business should be refused for a legitimate emergency call. Imposing liability for such a refusal would not subject innocent citizens to possible attack by the "good samaritan," for it would be limited to an establishment open to the public during times when it is open to business, and to places within the establishment ordinarily accessible to the public. Nor would a stranger's mere assertion that an "emergency" situation is occurring create the duty to utilize an accessible telephone because the duty would arise if and only if it were clearly conveyed that there exists an imminent danger of physical harm.

Such a holding would not involve difficulties in proof, overburden the courts or unduly hamper self-determination or enterprise.

A business establishment such as the Circle Inn is open for profit. The owner encourages the public to enter, for his earnings depend on it. A telephone is a necessary adjunct to such a place. It is not unusual in such circumstances for patrons to use the telephone to call a taxicab or family member.

We acknowledge that defendant contracted for the use of his telephone, and its use is a species of property. But if it exists in a public place as defined above, there is no privacy or ownership interest in it such that the owner should be permitted to interfere with a good faith attempt to use it by a third person to come to the aid of another.

* * *

We conclude that the bartender owed a duty to the plaintiff's decedent to permit the patron from Happy Jack's to place a call to the police or to place the call himself.

It bears emphasizing that the duty in this case does not require that one must go to the aid of another. That is not the issue here. The employee was not the good samaritan intent on aiding another. The patron was.

It would not be appropriate to await legislative action in this area. The rule was fashioned in the common law tradition, as were the exceptions to the rule. To the extent this opinion expands the reach of section 327 of the Restatement, it represents logical and needed growth, the hallmark of the common law. It does not involve the sacrifice of other respectable interests.

The courts have a special responsibility to reshape, refine and guide legal doctrine they have created. As our Supreme Court summarized in *People* v. *Pierce* (1964) 61 Cal.2d 879, 882, 40 Cal.Rptr. 845, 395 P.2d 893, in response to an argument that any departure from common law precedent should be left to legislative action, "In effect the contention is a request that courts abdicate their responsibility for the upkeep of the common law. That upkeep it needs continuously, as this case demonstrates."

* * *

We conclude there are sufficient justiciable issues to permit the case to go to trial and therefore reverse.

Corporate Social Responsibility

For several years, those concerned with business mores have debated a code of business ethics. The debate became especially heated in the 1970s in the wake of Watergate and Securities & Exchange Commission corporate bribery disclosures. Spurred by enactment of the Foreign Corrupt Practices Act in 1977 (see pp. 495–97), dozens of companies began to draft codes of corporate conduct. In a 1980 survey of corporate codes of conduct, more than three-quarters of the 700 responding companies had written codes, and the larger the company the more likely that it had issued one. (White, 1980, pp. 381ff)

The bulk of most of the codes simply restate maxims to which lip service, if not actual adherence, has long been given—for example, proscriptions against conflicts of interest (75 percent of the codes in the survey contained such provisions), misuse of corporate assets (50 percent), and price-fixing (40 percent). Surprisingly, only 17 percent of the codes referred to the Foreign Corrupt Practices Act, although 63 percent of the codes do deal with payments to government officials and political parties. But some of their provisions are new, and include structures to ensure that they will be better policed than before—for example, a requirement that a majority of the board of directors not be in management positions in the company.

No general rule has emerged from the welter of codes. Perhaps the one to which most companies would assent was wryly put in 1976 by Arjay Miller, then dean of Stanford's Graduate School of Business: "Do that which you would feel comfortable explaining on television." (Morgenthaler & Calame, 1976, p. 1)

In Europe, many companies have gone far beyond their American counterparts in issuing "social balance sheets." Thus the Swiss food manufacturer Migros-Genossenschafts-Bund issued an eighty-nine-page printed report in the late 1970s that declared that it paid its women less than men, that many of its jobs were "extremely boring," and that it had emitted two percent more nitrous dioxide, a noxious pollutant, over the previous four years. (*Business Week,* Nov. 6, 1978, p. 175) This European trend developed in large part as a means of defusing criticism that might lead to restraining legislation.

It is perhaps still too early to say what the long-term outlook will be for the flurry of concern about business ethics in the 1970s and 1980s. There is some evidence that many executives expect more of their employees than the general public (Box 6-1). On the other hand, even when a company is

Box 6-1 Varying Perceptions of Business Ethics

Executives Apply Stiffer Standards Than Public to Ethical Dilemmas

BY ROGER RICKLEFS

It's the sort of dilemma companies encounter all the time.

An employer finds that the candidate who is by far the best qualified for a job really earned only $18,000 a year in his last job, and not the $28,000 he claimed. Should the employer hire the candidate anyway, or should he choose someone else even though that person will be considerably less qualified?

In a Gallup Organization poll conducted for The Wall Street Journal, general citizens overwhelmingly back the lenient approach: Some 63% surveyed recommend hiring the able but errant applicant, and only 27% say the employer should choose somebody else. But among the executives polled, 52% would choose somebody else, and only 47% would hire the applicant with a false claim.

As part of its poll on ethics in America, Gallup posed several dilemmas like this to find out how Americans would actually handle specific situations involving ethical issues. It found that general citizens are considerably more inclined than executives to condone wrongdoing if there are mitigating circumstances.

Sometimes Gallup threw in complications. For instance, in the case of the candidate who lied about his previous salary, it asked half the members of its sample what they would do if the real salary were *$25,000,* only $3,000 less than the amount claimed. (In all other respects, the question was phrased the same for both subsamples.)

The general public reacts about the same as when the real salary was $18,000. Some 68% would hire the candidate and 22% wouldn't. But to executives, the amount involved matters. When the discrepancy between claimed salary and real salary was only $3,000 a year, 60% of the executives would hire the candidate and only 38% wouldn't.

To obtain this data, Gallup this summer polled a representative national general-public sample of 1,558 adults and a sample of 396 middle-level big-company executives. It interviewed the general citizens in person and mailed confidential questionnaires to the executives. The polling organization figures there is a sampling error of up to 3% in the general-public poll and up to 5% in the smaller executive poll.

Here is how the people Gallup surveyed say they would handle the dilemmas:

FAMILY VS. ETHICS

Jim, a 56-year-old middle manager with children in college, discovers that the owners of his company are cheating the government out of several thousand dollars a year in taxes. Jim is the only employee who would be in a position to know this. Should Jim report the owners to the Internal Revenue Service at the risk of endangering his own livelihood, or disregard the discovery in order to protect his family's livelihood?

More often than not, both executives and general citizens say family responsibilities should take precedence. Roughly half—49% of the public and 52% of the executives—think Jim should disregard his discovery in order to protect his family. About 34% of both the executives and the public think he should report the owners.

The money involved "isn't worth the loss of a job," says a manufacturing executive in his 50s. "Hundreds of thousands could make a difference." A company controller urges disregarding the cheating and adds: "The IRS has auditors to catch this kind of thing."

A financial executive says that to disregard the cheating "is not my real answer, but the chances of a 56-year-old 'whistleblower' finding employment in this society might be difficult." Some executives suggest options that weren't offered in the question: resign or look for another job.

THE ROUNDABOUT RAISE

When Joe asks for a raise, his boss praises his work but says the company's rigid budget won't allow any further merit raises for the time being. Instead, the boss suggests that the company "won't look too closely at your expense accounts for a while." Should Joe take this as authorization to pad his expense account on grounds that he is simply getting the same money he deserves through a different route, or not take this roundabout "raise"?

Though the public took a permissive approach to some of the other dilemmas, it decisively rejected the roundabout raise—and the executives rejected it even more overwhelmingly. Some 65% of the general citizens and 91% of the executives say Joe should turn down the circuitous raise. Only 25% of the public and 7% of the executives think he should "take this as authorization to pad his expense account."

THE FAKED DEGREE

Bill has done a sound job for over a year. Bill's boss learns that he got the job by claiming to have a college degree, although he actually never graduated. Should his boss dismiss him for submitting a fraudulent resume or overlook the false claim since Bill has otherwise proven to be conscientious and honorable, and making an issue of the degree might ruin Bill's career?

More executives recommend dismissing Bill (50%) than suggest overlooking the claim (43%). The general public decisively recommends (66% to 22%) overlooking the false claim rather than dismissing Bill.

Within the general public, however, 33% of those with professional occupations recommend dismissal. Gallup points out that academic credentials might be particularly important to people in these occupations.

In an otherwise identical question asked of a subsample, Bill didn't merely fail to graduate—he never attended college at all. But the distinction didn't seem to matter. Both subsamples gave similar answers to the question.

SNEAKING PHONE CALLS

Helen discovers that a fellow employee regularly makes about $100 a month worth of personal long-distance telephone calls from an office telephone. Should Helen report the employee to the company or disregard the calls on the grounds that many people make personal calls at the office.

In an otherwise identical question asked of part of the sample, Gallup has the employee making only $10 a month worth of personal long-distance calls instead of $100.

The difference matters, especially to executives. When the employee is sneaking $100 a month worth of calls, 64% of the public and 76% of the executives think that Helen should report him. Some 26% of the public and 19% of the managers favor disregarding the calls.

But when the amount involved is $10 a month, only 47% of the public and 48% of the executives favor reporting the employee. About 38% of the public and 47% of the executives favor disregarding the calls.

Put another way, when $100 a month is involved, the executives are tougher than the public. But when the figure is only $10 a month, the executives are more inclined than the public to disregard the calls.

COVER-UP TEMPTATION

Bill discovers that the chemical plant he manages is creating slightly more water pollution in a nearby lake than is legally permitted. Revealing the problem will bring considerable unfavorable publicity to the plant, hurt the lakeside town's resort business and create a scare in the community. Solving the problem will cost the company well over $100,000. It is unlikely that outsiders will discover the problem. The violation poses no danger whatever to people. At most, it will endanger a small number of fish. Should Bill reveal the problem despite the cost to his company, or consider the problem as little more than a technicality and disregard it?

The respondent can find all sorts of rationales for letting Bill disregard the pollution problem. Yet general citizens and executives alike took a tough line. Some 63% of the general pubic and 70% of the executives say Bill should reveal the problem and spend the money. Only 25% of the general citizens and 24% of the executives think he should disregard it as a technicality.

This is the only ethical-dilemma question in which young people are "significantly more likely to take the stricter ethical option" than their

(continues on next page)

Box 6-1, *continued*

elders, observes Andrew Kohut, president of the Gallup Organization. "There are great environmental concerns among the young," he adds.

Those who worry about the ethics of young America may find at least a little welcome news in the reaction to this question. For all the permissiveness the young reveal throughout the survey, they appear quite capable of developing a stricter ethical standard on some issues than their elders. "Ethics follow values," Mr. Kohut observes.

Source: *Wall Street Journal,* November 3, 1983

concerned with ethical conduct, individuals often go astray (Box 6-2). And many executives have indicated privately that it is unlikely their companies will invariably abide by such laws as the Foreign Corrupt Practices Act when it is demonstrably necessary in certain countries to make payments to foreign officials to compete with foreign companies legally free to secure contracts in such a way.

The implicit, gloomy conclusion—that ethical conduct is harmful to profitability—is not compelling. It often results simply from laziness or incompetence. Attention to behavior that is morally appropriate can reap financial dividends. Consider, for example, DuPont's great concern with the safety of its employees. The first item on the agenda of DuPont's weekly top management meeting is safety. According to a 1982 study, DuPont's accident rate is only 4.3 percent of the American industry average, saving the company an estimated $26 million (nearly 4 percent of net profit) that it would otherwise have spent on additional compensation and other accident-related costs. (Main, 1982, p. 68) It surely is no coincidence that a moral concern for employee safety has financial benefits.

Chapter Summary

In a pluralistic society such as the United States, there is no consensus on a single ethical code that can be concretely applied in all circumstances. The closest we come to such a guide is the law itself. But the law and some widely-held ethical precepts can diverge. The law in most states, for example, does not require bystanders to rescue people in trouble, whereas most moral codes do.

In some important instances relevant to business, the law and ethical standards converge. Examples include the contract duty to act in good faith and to avoid unconscionable terms, agents' fiduciary duty to their principals, corporate officers' and directors' fiduciary duty to their corporations, and merchants' and marketers' obligations to avoid deceptive and unfair commercial acts or practices.

Box 6-2 Corporate Ethics: A Case Study

GE's Image Makes Conviction More Jarring Fraud Case Illustrates Difficulty of Enforcing Standards

BY DOUGLAS R. SEASE

For years, General Electric Co. has been regarded as one of the nation's exemplary companies, a tough but fair competitor, a breeding ground for manager's excellence and a good corporate citizen.

Along the way, it also acquired a less enviable record. Three times in the past 25 years, GE has been convicted of crimes: price fixing, bribery and fraud. The latest came in April, when GE pleaded guilty to charges of defrauding the government on missile-warhead contracts. That defense-contract investigation continues, promising to yield still more embarrassing headlines for the company.

GE wasn't the only company singled out for misconduct in any of these cases. But its carefully burnished public persona made GE's crimes particularly jarring. That they occurred at all—and how the company's top management responded—suggest how easily ethical standards can become blurred within big organizations.

EFFORT TO COMBAT CRIME

As the GE story shows, profit and time pressures can lead otherwise honest people to violate their principles—and the law. And the larger and more complex a company is, the more difficult enforcement of ethical standards becomes. Though GE years ago initiated an unusually aggressive effort to combat crime within its ranks, its size—330,000 employees making a wide variety of products in hundreds of plants—increases the likelihood of occasional lapses.

GE chairman Jack Welch concedes as much. "I am not naive enough or presumptuous enough or self-righteous enough," he says, "to think that despite our best efforts we won't have isolated incidents."

To a surprising degree, however, the public doesn't seem to care much. "In the short run, people are aware of misconduct in a corporation, but in the long run there isn't any moral outrage," says Diane Vaughan, a Boston College sociology professor who studies organizational ethics. "There is a great forgiveness rule that applies to executives and corporations."

There seems little doubt that GE means business when it comes to heading off employee crime. Ever since the 1960 price fixing case, GE lawyers have annually briefed managers to stress that sharing competitive information with rivals is a crime. Up-and-coming GE managers attending executive training sessions at GE's retreat in Croton-on-Hudson, N.Y., get a heavy dose of ethics along with other management lessons. And over the years, GE has drawn up one of corporate America's most comprehensive policies on business ethics.

MORE STRINGENT MEASURES

The recent Defense Department fraud conviction has inspired still more stringent measures. Mr. Welch has appointed a corporate ombudsman authorized to investigate any allegations of wrongdoing within the company. GE's thick policy manual has been expanded to ensure that strict accounting procedures are followed in government contracts and to forbid GE employees from providing gifts—including lunches—to government officials. Employee time cards now bear the warning that falsifying time charges is a crime. In the Pentagon case, GE tried to minimize cost overruns by transferring charges from one contract to another.

Workers at the Philadelphia missile-warhead plant where the fraud occurred confirm that GE is tightening accounting procedures and checking time-card charges to prevent falsifications. But they stress that plant employees were fully aware of correct procedures long before the fraud occurred.

Lest anyone doubt the seriousness of GE's intent, Mr. Welch issues a stern warning in a videotape being shown to employees. Pressure to meet corporate goals won't excuse misbehavior, he says, adding that such pressures are intensifying as GE battles competitors around the globe. He also urges employees to come forward with

(continues on next page)

Box 6-2, *continued*

their suspicions of wrongdoing. "Whistle blowing, speaking out, telling it like it is, is part of what we're after," he says. "I can assure anybody who wants to talk about abuses of integrity in this company that they will be welcomed."

But rules and lectures are ineffective against an excess of loyalty to an employer. Unlike former LTV Corp. Chairman Paul Thayer or Tennessee banker Jake Butcher, both of whom recently drew prison sentences for illegally using their positions to enrich themselves, the GE managers who have violated laws did so to bolster the company's fortunes, not their own.

HOYT STEELE CASE

A case in point is Hoyt P. Steele, who, as GE's vice president for international sales, was charged in 1973 with authorizing a $1 million bribe to a Puerto Rican official to secure a $93 million power plant contract for GE. Mr. Steele had little to gain personally by winning the contract. At 64, he was approaching GE's then-mandatory retirement age. Nor, with an annual salary of $185,000, was he desperate for money.

But for GE the contract was crucial. An earlier bid to build a power plant of similar design in Mexico had failed, and the company wanted a prototype to help it sell the plants to other developing nations around the world.

Mr. Steele won't discuss the case today, but his testimony at his 1981 trial shows how he rationalized the scheme. He initially rejected subordinates' suggestions that a bribe might be necessary to win the contract. But after the bids were opened and GE's archrival, Westinghouse Corp., seemed to have a chance of winning the contract, Mr. Steele authorized a $300,000 payment to a Water Resources Board official who subordinates said had asked for money to ensure that GE won the contract. After the Puerto Rican official rejected that offer as insultingly low, Mr. Steele upped the ante to $1 million. He later refused a request for another $250,000.

Mr. Steele testified that he knew the payment violated GE policy. But he contended that it wasn't a crime because GE hadn't initiated the offer. "I authorized a payment, yes; not a bribe," he said. The objective "was to avoid being cheated out of an order that belonged to us." Both GE and Mr. Steele were convicted of mail fraud, wire fraud, conspiracy and interstate or foreign travel in aid of racketeering. The convictions were reversed on appeal, and three counts were ordered retried. Prosecutors settled for a no contest plea from GE to a fraud charge and dropped charges against Mr. Steele.

Source: *Wall Street Journal,* July 5, 1985

In some situations, ethical standards held by certain groups (such as professional societies) diverge from legal requirements (embodied in antitrust laws, for instance). In these instances, the law will necessarily prevail. For example, the law imposes limits on the degree to which a company can devote its resources to projects that will not ultimately benefit its shareholders. The law may also permit conduct that falls short of personal ethical standards. A person who refuses to engage in such conduct risks extralegal sanctions, such as losing a job.

Because law and ethics are never static, these two general codes of conduct are a continuing influence on one another and on the society out of which they grew.

Problems

1. Velma is the secretary to the chief executive of a manufacturer of fine paper products. Her company has just acquired a huge tract of uncut timber in a remote forest. Although no law bars the company from cutting the trees, there is sentiment in the legislature for a forest preservation law that would drastically reduce the number of logs it could harvest. The company sets out to cut the trees quickly and secretly. As a member of the National Save the Tree League, Velma is outraged and leaks the plan to the local newspaper, which publishes the story. When Velma's boss learns that she has leaked the story, he fires her. Meanwhile, the legislature hurriedly debates a bill to stop the company from cutting the trees. The company rushes to put its plan into effect. The bill is enacted, and takes effect in thirty days. Figuring that by working twenty-four-hour shifts during the next month it can cut most of the lumber it needs, the company begins to saw away. Was Velma legally in the right to leak her company's plan? Morally? Was the company right (legally or ethically) in firing her? Was the company right (legally or ethically) in cutting timber, knowing the law was due to take effect in thirty days?
2. MuchdoGood Enterprises, Inc., manufacturer of quality turpets, decides to declare no dividends, although it has had an extremely profitable year. Instead, it intends to plow its profits back into the company to permit it to build a fire station for the community, not only to appear a good "corporate citizen," but also to ensure modern equipment for the extra fire hazards the town faces as a result of the chemicals it maintains at its factory. In a suit brought by enraged stockholders to force it to declare dividends, who will win and why?
3. NICOTINE (National Institute to Combat Old Tobacco Inhalers' Narcotic Enormities), a public-interest group opposed to all forms of tobacco manufacture and sale, calls on *The Bugle,* a local newspaper, to refrain from accepting cigarette advertising. *The Bugle* has frequently inveighed against the sins of smoking, but it desperately needs the considerable revenue it takes in from the tobacco companies for their ads. Asserting that the advertisements contribute to adolescent smoking, and thus eventually to many diseases, NICOTINE threatens to sue the paper to enjoin it from taking the ads. What result? Why? What should *The Bugle* do?

7

Criminal Law

The Nature of Criminal Law

Criminal law is the most ancient branch of the law. The number of commentators who have attempted to define and explain it is legion, and the explanations themselves include some of the most subtle and metaphysical passages in the literature of the law. We need not be concerned with much of the criminal jurisprudence, however. Our purpose is to have a working knowledge of basic principles. We omit entirely discussion of many crimes that make up the traditional criminal law course—for example, kidnapping, rape, breach of peace—and ignore the many perplexities of criminal intent and responsibility. Similarly, though we consider certain of the constitutional rights accorded the accused, the student should note that the subject is vast and complex; space limitations alone prevent our considering more than its most basic aspects.

Criminal law is designed to deter socially harmful conduct. Crime has been defined simply as "any social harm defined and made punishable by law" (Perkins, 1969, p. 9). "Harm to society" is a matter of definition and is not necessarily intrinsic to the act itself. For example, in a minor quarrel in the privacy of one's home that results in a fistfight, the crimes of assault and battery have been committed, even though no one else knows about the fight and the people involved later make up. By contrast, when a major corporation publicly announces that it will not honor a contractual commitment, and many thousands of people must nervously contemplate whether their own contracts will be enforced, no crime has been committed. The effects on society may be much greater in the second example than in the first, but the former is the crime and not the latter according to the law.

Crimes are generally defined by statute. For constitutional reasons, courts are limited in their ability to create crimes as they have created the civil side of the common law: it would violate due process to prosecute someone for conduct that is not clearly spelled out beforehand as criminal. Of course, most people do not read statutes, and it is a commonplace that "ignorance is no excuse." Nevertheless, the legislature must set out the nature of the conduct it wishes to outlaw in order for the government to punish a person for breaking the law.

The statutes themselves must be clear. The courts have overturned many legislative criminal enactments because they have been vague and unclear. For example, vagrancy was long held to be a crime, but recently many courts have begun to overturn vagrancy and "suspicious person" statutes on the grounds that they are too vague for people to know what it is they are being asked to refrain from doing.

However, not every constitutional statute defining a crime is necessarily clear the way a lay person would define clarity, and an understanding of common law and its history remains critical. Many statutes use terminology developed by the common-law courts. For example, a California statute defines murder as "the unlawful killing of a human being, with malice aforethought." If no history backed up these words, they would be unconstitutionally vague. But there is a rich history, sufficient to provide a meaning for much of the arcane language strewn about in the statute books.

Because a crime is an act that the legislature has defined as socially harmful, the parties involved cannot agree among themselves to forget a particular incident, such as a barroom brawl, if the authorities decide to prosecute. This is one of the critical distinctions between criminal and civil law. An assault is both a crime and a tort. The person who was assaulted may choose to forgive his assailant and not to sue him for damages. But he cannot force the prosecutor to refrain from prosecuting the assailant for the crime of assault. It frequently happens, though, that because of the fearfully crowded criminal court dockets that cause interminable delays, the victim may decline to "press charges" (make an official complaint). In the absence of a victim who willingly will testify, busy prosecutors usually will refrain from filing charges on their own.

A crime consists of an **act** and an **intent**. A person who has a burning desire to kill, but who does not act on his desire, is guilty of no crime. A person who is forced to pull a trigger against his will is not guilty of the resulting death.

Methods of Classifying

Most classifications of crime turn on the seriousness of the act. In general, seriousness is defined by the nature or duration of the punishment set out in the statute. **Felonies** are crimes punishable (usually) by imprisonment of more than one year or by death. Crimes punishable by death are sometimes known as capital crimes; they are increasingly rare in the United States. The major felonies include murder, rape, kidnapping, armed robbery, embezzlement, and the like. All other crimes are usually known as **misdemeanors** or **petty offenses**. Under federal law, a petty offense is one punishable by six months' imprisonment or less or by a fine of $500 or less.

Another way of viewing crimes is by the type of social harm the statute is intended to prevent or deter. This is the classification we will employ in the following discussion.

Types of Crimes

Offenses Against the Person

Homicide Homicide is the killing of one person by another. Not every killing is criminal. When the law permits one to kill another—for example, a soldier killing an enemy on the battlefield during war, or a killing in self-defense—the death is said to be a **justifiable homicide**. An **excusable homicide** is one in which death results from an accident in which the killer is not at fault.

All other homicides are criminal. The most severely punished form is **murder**, defined as homicide committed with **malice aforethought**. This is a term with an ancient lineage. It means, in essence, an intent to kill. A killing need not be premeditated, in the sense that it is planned out well in advance. A killing is murder if it is committed an instant after the intention to do so occurs. A homicide sometimes can be murder even if there is no intent to kill; an intent to inflict great bodily harm or a dangerous action that is undertaken with wanton disregard for human life can be murder if the result is the death of another person.

A killing that takes place while a felony such as armed robbery is being committed is also murder, whether or not the killer intended any harm. This is the so-called **felony murder rule**. Examples are the accidental discharge of a gun that kills an innocent bystander or the asphyxiation death of a firefighter from smoke resulting from a fire set by an arsonist. The felony murder rule is more significant than it sounds, because it also applies to the accomplices of one who does the killing. Thus, the driver of a getaway car stationed a block away from the scene of the robbery can be convicted of murder if a gun accidentally fires during the robbery and someone is killed.

Manslaughter is an act of killing that does not amount to murder. **Voluntary manslaughter** is an intentional killing but one carried out in the "sudden heat of passion" as the result of some provocation. An example is a fight that gets out of hand. **Involuntary manslaughter** entails a lesser degree of willfulness; it usually occurs when someone has taken a reckless action that results in death—for example, a death resulting from a traffic accident in which one driver wantonly runs a red light.

Assault and Battery In common parlance, we say that a person who has struck another has assaulted him. Technically, that is a **battery**—the unlawful application of force to another person. The force need not be violent. Indeed, a man who kisses a woman is guilty of a battery if he does it against her will. The other person may consent to the force. That is one reason why surgeons require patients to sign "consent forms" giving the doctor permission to operate. In the absence of such a consent, an operation is a battery. That is also why defensive tackles in football games are not constantly being charged with battery. Those who agree to play football agree to submit to the rules of the game, which of course include the right to tackle. But the consent does not apply to all acts of physical force: a hockey player who hits an opponent over the head with a hockey stick can be prosecuted for the crime of battery.

Criminal **assault** is an *attempt* to commit a battery or the deliberate placing of another in fear of receiving an immediate battery. If you throw a rock at a friend, but she manages to dodge it, you have committed an assault. Some states limit an assault to an attempt to commit a battery by one who has a "present ability" to do so. Pointing an unloaded gun and threatening to shoot would not be an assault—nor, of course, could it be a battery. The modern tendency, however, is to define an assault as an attempt to commit a battery by one with an *apparent* ability to do so.

Assault and battery may be excused. One form of excuse is consent by the victim. Excuse may also be provided by law; for example, a bar owner may use reasonable force to remove an unruly patron.

Offenses against Property

Theft: Larceny, Robbery, Embezzlement, False Pretenses The concept of theft is familiar enough. Less familiar is the way the law has treated various aspects of the act of stealing. Criminal law distinguishes among many different crimes that are popularly known as theft. Many technical words have entered the language—burglary, larceny, robbery—but are used loosely and often inaccurately. What follows is a brief definition of the more common terms.

The basic crime of stealing personal property is **larceny**. By its technical definition, larceny is the wrongful "taking and carrying away of the personal property of another with intent to steal the same." Its various components gave no end of trouble under the common law. A common example is the theft of fruit. If someone walking through an orchard plucks a peach from a tree and eats it, she is not guilty of larceny because she has not taken away *personal* property—the peach is part of the land, being connected to the tree. But if she picks up a peach lying on the ground, she is guilty of larceny.

The crime of larceny is not committed unless something capable of being carried away is taken. Thus, sneaking into a movie theater without paying is not an act of larceny (though in most states it is a criminal act). Stealing electricity by tapping into the power lines of an electric utility baffled judges late in the nineteenth century, because it was not clear whether electricity is a "something" that can be taken. Modern statutes have tended to make clear that electricity can be the object of larceny.

The taking must be with an intent to steal, that is, to deprive the owner of property permanently. If you borrow your friend's car without his permission in order to go to the grocery store, intending to return it within a few minutes, and do return it, you have not committed larceny.

A particular form of larceny is **robbery**, which is defined as larceny from a person by means of violence or intimidation.

Larceny involves the taking of property from the possession of another. Suppose that a person legitimately comes to possess the property of another and wrongfully appropriates it—for example, an automobile mechanic entrusted with your car refuses to return it, or a bank teller who is entitled to temporary possession of cash in his drawer takes it home with him. The common law had trouble with such cases because the thief in these cases already had possession; his crime was in assuming ownership. Today, such wrongful conversion, known as **embezzlement**, has been made a statutory offense in all states.

Statutes against larceny and embezzlement did not cover all the gaps in the law. A conceptual problem arises in the case of one who is tricked into giving up title to property. In larceny and embezzlement, the thief gains possession or ownership without any consent of the owner or custodian of the property. Suppose, however, that an automobile dealer agrees to take his customer's present car as a trade-in. The customer says that she has full title to the car. In fact, the customer is still paying off an installment loan and the finance company has an interest in the old car. If the finance company repossesses the car, the customer—who got a new car at a discount because of her false representation—cannot be said to have taken the new car by larceny or embezzlement. Nevertheless, she tricked the dealer into selling, and the dealer will have lost the value of the repossessed car. Obviously, the customer is guilty of a criminal act; the statutes outlawing it refer to this trickery as the crime of **false pretenses**—defined as obtaining ownership of the property of another by making untrue representations of fact with intent to defraud.

A number of problems have arisen in the judicial interpretation of false pretense statutes. One concerns whether the taking is permanent or only temporary. The following case shows the subtle questions that can be presented and the dangers inherent in committing "a little fraud."

STATE v. MILLS
96 Ariz. 377, 396 P.2d 5 (1964)

LOCKWOOD, VICE CHIEF JUSTICE:

Defendants appeal from a conviction on two counts of obtaining money by false pretenses in violation of A.R.S. §§ 13-661.A.3. and 13-663.A.1.

The material facts, viewed ". . . in the light most favorable to sustaining the conviction," State v. Evans, 88 Ariz. 364, 366, 356 P.2d 1106, 1107 (1960) are as follows: Defendant William Mills was a builder and owned approximately 150 homes in Tucson in December, 1960. Mills conducted his business in his home. In 1960 defendant Winifred Mills, his wife, participated in the business generally by answering the telephone, typing, and receiving clients who came to the office.

In December 1960, Mills showed the complainant, Nathan Pivowar, a house at 1155 Knox Drive and another at 1210 Easy Street, and asked Pivowar if he would loan money on the Knox Drive house. Pivowar did not indicate at that time whether he would agree to such a transaction. Later in the same month Nathan Pivowar told the defendants that he and his brother, Joe Pivowar, would loan $5,000 and $4,000 on the two houses. Three or four days later Mrs. Mills, at Pivowar's request, showed him these homes again.

Mills had prepared two typed mortgages for Pivowar. Pivowar objected to the wording, so in Mills' office Mrs. Mills retyped the mortgages under Pivowar's dictation. After the mortgages had been recorded on December 31, 1960, Pivowar gave Mills a bank check for $5,791.87, some cash, and a second mortgage formerly obtained from Mills in the approximate sum of $3,000. In exchange Mills gave Pivowar two personal notes in the sums of $5,250.00 and $4,200.00 and the two mortgages as security for the loan.

Although the due date for Mills' personal notes passed without payment being made, the complainant did not present the notes for payment, did not demand that they be paid, and did not sue upon them. In 1962 the complainant learned that the mortgages which he had taken as security in the transaction were not first mortgages on the Knox Drive and Easy Street properties. These mortgages actually covered two vacant lots on which there were outstanding senior mortgages. On learning this, Pivowar signed a complaint charging the defendants with the crime of theft by false pretenses.

On appeal defendants contend that the trial court erred in denying their motion to dismiss the information. They urge that a permanent taking of property must be proved in order to establish the crime of theft by false pretenses. Since the complainant had the right to sue on the defendants' notes, the defendants assert that complainant cannot be said to have been deprived of his property permanently.

Defendants misconceive the elements of the crime of theft by false pretenses. Stated in a different form, their argument is that although the complainant has parted with his cash, a bank check, and a second mortgage, the defendants intend to repay the loan.

Defendants admit that the proposition of law which they assert is a novel one in this jurisdiction. Respectable authority in other states persuades us that their contention is without merit. A creditor has a right to determine for himself whether he wishes to be a secured or an unsecured creditor. In the former case, he has a right to know about the security. If he extends credit in reliance upon security which is falsely represented to be adequate, he has been defrauded even if the debtor intends to repay the debt. His position is now that of an unsecured creditor; at the very least, an unreasonable risk of loss has been forced upon him by reason of the deceit. This risk which he did not intend to assume has been imposed upon him by the intentional act of the debtor, and such action constitutes an intent to defraud.

* * *

The cases cited by defendants in support of their contention are distinguishable from the instant case in that they involved theft by larceny. Since the crime of larceny is designed to protect a person's possessory interest in property whereas the crime of false pretenses protects one's title interest, the requirement of a permanent deprivation is appropriate to the former. Accordingly, we hold that an intent to repay a loan obtained on the basis of a false representation of the security for the loan is no defense.

* * *

Affirmed in part, reversed in part, and remanded for resentencing.

In the *Mills* case, the claim was that a mortgage instrument dealing with one parcel of land was used instead for another. This is a false representation of fact. Suppose, by contrast, that a person misrepresents his state of mind: "I will pay you back tomorrow," he says, knowing full well that he does not intend to. Can such a misrepresentation amount to false pretenses punishable as a criminal offense? In most jurisdictions it cannot. A false pretense violation relates to a past event or existing fact, not to a statement of intention. If it were otherwise, a person who failed to pay a debt might find himself facing criminal prosecution, and business would be less prone to take risks.

Not all states follow this rule. The California Supreme Court has specifically rejected it.

The problem of proving intent is especially difficult when a person has availed himself of the services of another without paying. A common example is absconding from a hotel or restaurant without paying for the room or meal. In most states, this is specifically defined in the statutes as **theft of services**.

Receiving Stolen Property One who receives stolen property with knowledge that it is stolen is guilty of a felony or misdemeanor, depending on the value of the property. The receipt need not be personal; if the property is delivered to a place under the control of the receiver, then he is deemed to have received it. "Knowledge" is construed broadly: not merely actual knowledge, but (correct) belief and suspicion (strong enough not to investigate for fear that the property will turn out to have been stolen) are sufficient for conviction.

Forgery Forgery is false writing of a document with legal significance (or apparent legal significance) with intent to defraud. It includes the making up of a false document or the alteration of an existing one. The writing need not be done by hand but can be by any means—typing, printing, and so forth. Documents commonly the subject of forgery are negotiable instruments (checks, money orders, and the like), deeds, receipts, contracts, and bills of lading. The forged instrument must itself be false, not merely contain a falsehood. If you fake your neighbor's signature on one of her checks made out to cash, you have committed forgery. But if you sign a check of your own that is made out to cash, knowing that there is no money in your checking account, the instrument is not forged, though the act may be criminal if done with the intent to defraud.

The mere making of a forged instrument is unlawful. So is the **uttering**—presentation—of such an instrument, whether or not the one uttering it actually forged it.

The usual example of a false signature is by no means the only way to commit forgery. If done with intent to defraud, the backdating of a document, the modification of a corporate name, or the filling in of lines left blank on a form can all constitute forgery.

Extortion Under common law, extortion could only be committed by a government official, who corruptly collected an unlawful fee under color of office. A common example is a salaried building inspector who refuses to issue a permit unless the permittee pays him. Under modern statutes, the crime of extortion has been broadened to include the wrongful collection of money or something else of value by anyone by means of a threat (short of a threat of immediate physical violence, for such a threat would make the demand an act of robbery). This kind of extortion is usually called **blackmail**. The blackmail threat commonly is to expose some fact of the victim's private life or to make a false accusation about him.

Offenses against Habitation

Burglary Burglary is not a crime against property. It is defined as "the breaking and entering of the dwelling of another in the nighttime with intent to commit a felony." The intent need not be to steal; a man who sneaks into a woman's home intent on raping her has committed a burglary, even if he does not carry out the act. The astute student will note that the definition provides plenty of room for argument. What is "breaking"? (The courts do not require actual destruction; the mere opening of a closed door, even if unlocked, is enough.) What is entry? When does night begin? What kind of intent? Whose dwelling? Can a landlord burglarize the dwelling of his tenant? Yes. Can a person burglarize her own home? No.

Arson Under common law, arson was the malicious burning of the dwelling of another. Burning one's own house for purposes of collecting insurance was not an act of arson under common law. The statutes today make it a felony intentionally to set fire to any building, whether or not it is a dwelling and whether or not the purpose is to collect insurance.

Other Offenses

Bribery Bribery is a corrupt payment (or receipt of such a payment) for official action. The payment can be in cash or in the form of any goods, intangibles, or services that the recipient would find valuable. Under common law, only a public official could be bribed. In most states, "public official" has been given an expansive meaning, so that one performing a public function, though not an employee of the government, may be capable of being bribed.

In many states, bribery is no longer limited to payments to public officials. Purchasing agents and other agents of private enterprise can also be bribed by sellers and others. The statutes have been broadened to encompass commissions, gifts, or gratuities or promises to pay them to agents and employees in order to influence any action related to the business of their principal or employer.

Perjury Perjury is the crime of giving a false oath, either orally or in writing, in a judicial or other official proceeding. Lies made in proceedings other than courts are sometimes termed "false swearing." To be perjurious, the oath must have been made corruptly—that is, with knowledge that it was false or without sincere belief that it was true. An innocent mistake is not perjury. A statement, though true, is perjury if the maker of it believes it to be false. Statements such as "I don't remember" or "to the best of my knowledge" are not sufficient to protect a person who is lying from conviction for perjury. To support a charge of perjury, however, the false statement must be **material**—that is, related to the matter in controversy.

White-collar Crime

The term "white-collar crime," as distinguished from "street crime," refers generally to fraud-related acts carried out in a nonviolent way, usually connected with business. Armed robbery is not a white-collar crime; embezzlement by a teller from a bank is. Many white-collar crimes are included within the statutory definitions of embezzlement and false pretenses. Most are violations of state law. Depending on how they are carried out, many of these same crimes are violations also of federal law. Federal statutes outlaw mail, wire, and securities fraud, for instance. Any act of fraud in which the U.S. Postal System is used or which involves interstate telephone calls is a violation of federal law. Likewise, a host of acts concerned with buying and selling of securities can run afoul of federal securities laws and give rise to criminal liability. Other white-collar crimes include tax fraud, price-fixing, violations of food, drug, and environmental laws, corporate bribery of foreign companies, and—the newest form—computer fraud. Some of these are discussed below; others are covered in later chapters.

White-collar crime is not limited to occasional acts of errant bank tellers, nor are corporations always the victims of such crime. Sometimes they are the criminals. A *Fortune* magazine study (December 1, 1980, pp. 57ff.) of major federal cases against big corporations between 1970 and 1980 showed that of the 1,043 companies prosecuted (among them were 800 of the largest corporations in America), 117 were convicted of (or otherwise settled) criminal charges, including illegal political contributions, price-fixing, and tax evasion. Among the companies were some of the most well-known industrial names in the country, including American Airlines, Bethlehem Steel, Boise Cascade, Carnation, E. I. duPont de Nemours & Co., Gulf Oil, Gulf & Western, Litton Industries, PepsiCo, R.J. Reynolds, Rockwell International, Singer, and United Brands.

Mail and Wire Fraud Federal law prohibits the use of the mails or any interstate electronic communications medium for the purpose of furthering a "scheme or artifice to defraud." In 1987, the Supreme Court ruled that the law protects intangible as well as tangible property. As a result, the law has become a major weapon in insider trading cases in which defendants are charged with taking confidential business information. [Winans v. United States, 56 U.S.L.W. 4007 (1987)]

Violations of Antitrust Law In Chapters 19–20, we consider the fundamentals of antitrust law, which for the most part affects the business enterprise civilly. But violations of Section 1 of the Sherman Act, which condemns activities in "restraint of trade," including price-fixing, are also crimes. Beginning in the late 1970s, the U.S. Department of Justice stepped up its criminal enforcement of the Sherman Act. At the same time, Congress increased the penalties. The maximum fine for individual violators has been increased to $100,000 from $50,000, the maximum prison term to three years from one year, and corporate defendants can now be fined a maximum of $1 million.

Violations of the Food and Drug Act The federal Food, Drug and Cosmetic Act prohibits any person or corporation from sending into interstate commerce any adulterated or misbranded food, drug, cosmetics, or related device. Unlike in most criminal statutes, willfulness or deliberate misconduct is not an element of the Food and Drug Act. As the *Park* case (pp. 181–83) shows, an executive can be held criminally liable even though he had no personal knowledge of the violation.

Environmental Crimes Many federal environmental statutes (discussed in Chapter 23) have criminal provisions. These include the Federal Water Pollution Control Act (commonly called the Clean Water Act), the Rivers and Harbors Act of 1899 (the Refuse Act), the Clean Air Act, the Federal Insecticide, Fungicide and Rodenticide Act (FIFRA), the Toxic Substances Control Act (TSCA), and the Resource Conservation and Recovery Act (RCRA). Under the Clean Water Act, for example, wrongful discharge of pollutants into navigable waters carries a fine ranging from $2,500 to $25,000 per day and imprisonment for up to one year. "Responsible corporate officers" are specifically included as potential defendants in criminal prosecutions under the act.

Violations of the Foreign Corrupt Practices Act byproduct of Watergate, federal officials at the Securities and Exchange Commission and the Internal Revenue Service uncovered numerous instances of bribes paid by major corporations to officials of foreign governments to secure contracts to do business with their countries. Congress responded in 1977 with the Foreign Corrupt Practices Act, which imposed a stringent requirement that the disposition of assets be accurately and fairly accounted for in a company's books and records. The act also made illegal the payment of bribes to foreign officials or to anyone who will transmit the money to a foreign official to assist the payor in getting business. The act is discussed in greater detail on pp. 495–97.

Violations of the Racketeer Influenced and Corrupt Organizations Act 1970 Congress enacted the Racketeer Influenced and Corrupt Organizations Act (RICO), aimed at ending organized crime's infiltration into legitimate business. The act tells courts to construe its language broadly "to effectuate its remedial purpose," and many who do not fall into the organized crime classification have been successfully prosecuted under the act.

RICO bans from interstate commerce anyone engaged in a "pattern of racketeering." A pattern of racketeering is broadly defined as the commission of at least two acts within ten years of any of a variety of already-existing crimes, including mail, wire, and securities fraud. Businesses that have committed (and not necessarily been convicted of) such crimes violate RICO if any proceeds from the crimes are used to enable the company to participate in interstate commerce or to acquire an interest in an enterprise engaged in interstate commerce. The act thus makes many types of fraud subject to more severe penalties than provided for by state law. In addition to imposing fines and jail sentences, the courts may order violators to forfeit any assets acquired through a violation of the act.

Criminal penalties do not exhaust RICO's potency. Congress built in a consequence more far reaching than criminal prosecution: under RICO, anyone "injured in his business or property by reason of" a pattern of racketeering may file a civil suit. A successful plaintiff can collect triple damages and recover attorney fees. During the 1980s, these provisions have provided strong incentive to add RICO complaints in many commercial lawsuits, including disputes over breach of contract, wrongful discharge, lease violations, and product liability. A Justice Department survey in 1985 found that companies had filed more than 500 civil RICO suits; most were based on claims that the defendants had engaged in securities or mail fraud. Many civil RICO suits have been extremely imaginative: the state of Illinois, for example, prevailed in one such case against a company that failed to hand over sales taxes; the state's theory was that by neglecting to pay the taxes, the company had engaged in fraud, entitling it to collect triple the tax that was owed. Because the potential liability is so large, many companies have been lobbying for changes to RICO, but so far Congress has been unwilling to budge.

Computer Crime No specific provision of federal law deals explicitly with computer crime, but some forty different statutes may be brought into play when computer crime has been committed. "Computer crime generally falls into four categories: (1) theft of money, financial instruments, or property; (2) misappropriation of computer time; (3) theft of programs; and (4) illegal acquisition of information. The possibilities appear to be limited only by the bounds of the perpetrator's imagination" (*Amer. Crim. L. Rev.*, 1980, p. 371). In one notorious case, a Los Angeles bank's computer consultant secretly telephoned the bank's computer to transfer $10.2 million to an account in a New York bank. He then flew to Switzerland to buy diamonds and was caught only because one of his associates gave him away to the FBI.

The Nature of a Criminal Act

To be guilty of a crime, you must have acted. Mental desire or intent to do so is insufficient. But what constitutes an act? This question becomes important when someone begins to commit a crime, or does so in association with others, or intends to do one thing but winds up doing something else.

Attempt

It is not necessary to commit the intended crime to be found guilty of a criminal offense. An *attempt* to commit the crime is punishable as well, though usually not as severely. For example, Bluebeard points a gun at Agatha, intending to shoot her dead. He pulls the trigger but his aim is off, and he misses her heart by four feet. He is guilty of an attempt to murder. Suppose, however, that earlier in the day, when he was preparing to shoot Agatha, Bluebeard had been overheard in his apartment muttering to himself of his intention, and that a neighbor called the police. When they arrived, he was just snapping his gun into his shoulder holster. At that point, courts in most states would not consider him guilty of an attempt because he had not passed beyond the stage of *preparation*. After having buttoned his jacket he might have reconsidered and put the gun away. Determining when the accused has passed beyond mere preparation and taken an actual step toward *perpetrating* the crime is often difficult and is usually for the jury to decide.

Impossibility

If the defendant intends to do something that was not criminal, no act in furtherance of his intention can be an attempt. Suppose Bluebeard purchases a television set from a man on a street corner late one evening, believing the television to be stolen. In fact it was not stolen. Bluebeard cannot be convicted of an attempt to receive stolen property. Thus the following rule: "An accused cannot be convicted of an attempt to commit a crime unless he could have been convicted of the crime itself if his attempt had been successful. Where the act, if accomplished, would not constitute the crime intended, there is no indictable attempt." [Nemecek v. State, 114 P.2d 492 (Okla. 1941)]

Whether an accomplished act will result in a crime depends on the circumstances. In the following case, Hall stole electrical wire from a factory and was arrested while in possession of the wire. The police interrogated him and discovered he was intending to sell it to others. He agreed to cooperate with the police and called his prospective customers, saying he had stolen the wire and would leave the truck for them as arranged. Following their arrest for receiving stolen property, they argued that since the property was no longer stolen (because it had been recovered by the police), they could not be convicted of receiving it.

PEOPLE v. ROJAS
55 Cal.2d 252, 358 P.2d 921 (1961)

SCHAUER, JUSTICE.

In a trial by the court, after proper waiver of jury, defendants Rojas and Hidalgo were found guilty of a charge of receiving stolen property. Defendants' motions for new trial were denied. Rojas was granted probation without imposition of sentence and Hidalgo was sentenced to state prison. They appeal, respectively, from the order granting probation, the judgment, and the orders denying the motions for new trial.

Defendants urge that they were guilty of no crime (or, at most, of an attempt to receive stolen property) because when they received the property it had been recovered by the police and was no longer in a stolen condition. The attorney general argues that because the thief stole the property pursuant to prearrangement with defendants he took it as their agent, and the crime of receiving stolen property was complete when the thief began its asportation toward defendants and before the police intercepted him and recovered the property. We have concluded that defendants are guilty of attempting to receive stolen goods.

* * *

The offense with which defendants were charged and of which they were convicted was receiving "property which has been *stolen . . . , knowing the same to be so stolen.*" Pen. Code, §496, subd. 1; italics added. Defendants urge that they neither received stolen goods nor criminally attempted to do so because the conduit, when defendants received it, was not in a stolen condition but had been recovered by the police. In the Jaffe case the stolen property was recovered by the owner while it was en route to the would-be receiver and, by arrangement with the police, was delivered to such receiver as a decoy, not as property in a stolen condition. The New York Court of Appeals held that there was no attempt to receive stolen goods "because neither [defendant] nor anyone else in the world could know that the property was stolen property inasmuch as it was not in fact stolen property. . . . If all which an accused person intends to do would if done constitute no crime it cannot be a crime to attempt to do with the same purpose a part of the thing intended."

* * *

In the case at bench the criminality of the attempt is not destroyed by the fact that the goods, having been recovered by the commendably alert and efficient action of the Los Angles police, had, unknown to defendants, lost their "stolen" status, any more than the criminality of the attempt in the case of In re Magidson (1917), 32 Cal.App. 566, 568, 163 P. 689, was destroyed by impossibility caused by the fact that the police had recovered the goods and taken them from the place where the would-be receiver went to get them. In our opinion the consequences of intent and acts such as those of defendants here should be more serious than pleased amazement that because of the timeliness of the police the projected criminality was not merely detected but also wiped out.

* * *

The orders denying defendants' motions for new trial are affirmed. The trial court's finding that defendants are guilty as charged is modified to find them guilty of the offense of attempting to receive stolen property.

Conspiracy

Under both federal and state laws, it is a separate offense to work with others toward the commission of a crime. When two or more people combine to carry out an unlawful purpose, they are engaged in a **conspiracy.** The law of conspiracy is quite broad, especially when it is used by prosecutors in connection with white-collar crimes. Many people can be swept up in the net of conspiracy, because it is unnecessary to show that the actions they took were sufficient to constitute either the crime or an attempt. Under the usual rule, an agreement and a single overt act are sufficient to constitute the offense. Thus, if three people agreed to rob a bank, and one of them goes to a store to purchase a gun to be used in the holdup, the three can be convicted of conspiracy to commit robbery. Even the purchase of an automobile to be used as the getaway car could support such a conviction. Moreover, the act of any one of the conspirators is imputed to the other members of the conspiracy. It does not matter, for instance, that only one of the bank robbers fired the gun that killed a guard. All can be convicted of murder. That is so even if one of the conspirators was stationed as a lookout several blocks away and even if he specifically told the others that his agreement to cooperate would end "just as soon as there is shooting."

Nevertheless, as the next case shows, there are limits to the connection between individuals for purposes of assessing criminal liability.

UNITED STATES v. FALCONE
109 F.2d 579 (2d Cir. 1940)

L. HAND, CIRCUIT JUDGE.

These appeals are from convictions for a conspiracy to operate illicit stills.

* * *

The case against Joseph Falcone was that during the year 1937 he sold sugar to a number of grocers in Utica, who in turn sold to the distillers. He was a jobber in Utica, and bought his supply from a New York firm of sugar brokers; between March first and September 14, 1937, he bought 8,600 bags of sugar of 100 pounds each, which he disposed of to three customers: Frank Bonomo & Company, Pauline Aiello, and Alberico and Funicello, all wholesale grocers in Utica. Some of the bags in which this sugar was delivered were later found at the stills, when these were raided by the officials; and Falcone was seen on one occasion assisting in delivering the sugar at Bonomo's warehouse, when a truckload arrived. His business in sugar was far greater while the stills were active than either before they were set up, or after they were seized, and we shall assume that the evidence was enough to charge him with notice that his customers were supplying the distillers.

* * *

In the light of all this, it is apparent that the first question is whether the seller of goods, in themselves innocent, becomes a conspirator with—or, what is in substance the same thing, an abettor of—the buyer because he knows that the buyer means to use the goods to commit a crime. That came up a number of times in circuit courts of appeal while the Eighteenth Amendment was in force, and the answer was not entirely uniform.

* * *

. . . We are ourselves committed to the view of the Fifth Circuit. United States v. Peoni, 2 Cir., 100 F.2d 401. In that case we tried to trace down the doctrine as to abetting and conspiracy, as it exists in our criminal law, and concluded that the seller's knowledge was not alone enough. Civilly, a man's liability extends to any injuries which he should have apprehended to be likely to follow from his acts. If they do, he must excuse his conduct by showing that the interest which he was promoting outweighed the dangers which its protection imposed upon others; but in civil cases there has been a loss, and the only question is whether the law shall transfer it from the sufferer to another. There are indeed instances of criminal liability of the same kind, where the law imposes punishment merely because the accused did not forbear to do that from which the wrong was likely to follow; but in prosecutions for conspiracy or abetting, his attitude towards the forbidden undertaking must be more positive. It is not enough that he does not forego a normally lawful activity, of the fruits of which he knows that others will make an unlawful use; he must in some sense promote their venture himself, make it his own, have a stake in its outcome. The distinction is especially important today when so many prosecutors seek to sweep within the drag-net of conspiracy all those who have been associated in any degree whatever with the main offenders. That there are opportunities of great oppression in such a doctrine is very plain, and it is only by circumscribing the scope of such all comprehensive indictments that they can be avoided. We may agree that morally the defendants at bar should have refused to sell to illicit distillers; but, both morally and legally, to do so was toto coelo different from joining with them in running the stills.

For these reasons the prosecution did not make out a case against either of the Falcones, Alberico, or John Nole; and this is especially true of Salvatore

Falcone. As to Nicholas Nole the question is closer, for when he began to do business as the "Acme Yeast Company," he hid behind the name of a cousin, whom he caused to swear falsely that the affiant was to do the business. Yet it seems to us that this was as likely to have come from a belief that it was a crime to sell the yeast and the cans to distillers as from being in fact any further involved in their business. It showed a desire to escape detection, and that was evidence of a consciousness of guilt, but the consciousness may have as well arisen from a mistake of law as from a purpose to do what the law in fact forbade. We think therefore that even as to him no case was made out.

* * *

[Convictions reversed.]

Agency and Corporations

A person can be guilty of a crime if he acts through another. As we have just noted, the usual reason for imputing the guilt of the actor to another is that both were engaged in a conspiracy. But imputation of guilt is not limited to a conspiracy. The agent may be innocent even though he participates. A corporate officer directs a junior employee to take a certain bag and deliver it to the officer's home. The employee reasonably believes that the officer is entitled to the bag. Unbeknownst to the employee, the bag contains money that belongs to the company, and the officer wishes to keep it. This is not a conspiracy. The employee is not guilty of larceny, the officer is—the agent's act is imputed to him.

Ordinarily, the imputation of crime does not work in reverse. Since intent is a necessary component of crime, an agent's intent cannot be imputed to his principal if the principal did not share the intent. The company president tells her sales manager: "Go make sure our biggest customer renews his contract for next year"—by which she meant, "Don't ignore our biggest customer." Standing before the customer's purchasing agent, the sales manager threatens to tell the purchasing agent's boss that the purchasing agent has been cheating on his expense account, unless he signs a new contract. The sales manager could be convicted of blackmail, but the company president could not.

Can a corporation be guilty of a crime? The law is clear that for many types of crimes, the guilt of individual employees may be imputed to the corporation. Thus, the antitrust statutes explicitly state that the corporation may be convicted and fined for violations by employees. That is true even though the shareholders are the ones who ultimately must pay the price—and who may have had nothing to do with the crime nor power to stop it. The law of corporate criminal responsibility has been changing in recent years. The tendency is to hold the corporation criminally liable if the criminal act, such as larceny or murder, has been directed by a responsible officer or group within the corporation (the president or board of directors).

Responsibility

In General

For an accused to be held responsible for a criminal act, he must have a "criminal intent," often referred to as *mens rea,* Latin for "guilty mind." What the state of mind must be depends on the nature of the crime and all the circumstance surrounding the act. In general, though, the requirement means that the accused must in some way have intended the criminal consequences of his act. Suppose, for example, that Bluebeard gives Agatha a poison capsule to swallow. That is the act. If Agatha dies, is Bluebeard guilty of murder? The answer depends on what his state of mind was. Obviously, if he gave it to her intending to kill her, the act was murder. What if he gave it to her knowing that the capsule was poison but believing that it would only make her mildly ill? The act is still murder, because one is liable for the consequences of a willful act in which lurks danger to others. However, if Agatha had asked Bluebeard for aspirin, and he handed her two pills that he reasonably believed to be aspirin (they came from the aspirin bottle and looked like aspirin) but that turned out to be poison, the act would not be murder, because he had neither intent nor a state of knowledge from which intent could be inferred.

Not every criminal law requires criminal intent as an ingredient of the crime. Many regulatory codes dealing with the public health and safety impose strict requirements. Failure to adhere is a violation, whether or not the violator had *mens rea*. The next two cases, both decisions of the U.S. Supreme Court, show the different considerations involved.

MORISSETTE v. UNITED STATES
342 U.S. 246 (1952)

MR. JUSTICE JACKSON delivered the opinion of the Court.

*   *   *

On a large tract of uninhabited and untilled land in a wooded and sparsely populated area of Michigan, the government established a practice bombing range over which the Air Force dropped simulated bombs at ground targets. These bombs consisted of a metal cylinder about forty inches long and eight inches across, filled with sand and enough black powder to cause a smoke puff by which the strike could be located. At various places about the range signs read "Danger—Keep Out—Bombing Range." Nevertheless, the range was known as good deer country and was extensively hunted.

Spent bomb casings were cleared from the targets and thrown into piles "so that they will be out of the way." They were not stacked or piled in any order but were dumped in heaps, some of which had been accumulating for four years or upwards, were exposed to the weather and rusting away.

Morissette, in December of 1948, went hunting in this area but did not get a deer. He thought to meet expenses of the trip by salvaging some of these casings. He loaded three tons of them on his truck and took them to a nearby farm, where they were flattened by driving a tractor over them. After expending this labor and trucking them to market in Flint, he realized $84.

*   *   *

The loading, crushing and transporting of these casings were all in broad daylight, in full view of passers-by, without the slightest effort at concealment. When an investigation was started, Morissette voluntarily, promptly and candidly told the whole story to the authorities, saying that he had no intention of stealing but thought the property was abandoned, unwanted and considered of no value to the Government. He was indicted, however, on the charge that he "did unlawfully, wilfully and knowingly steal and convert" property of the United States of the value of $84, in violation of 18 U.S.C. §641, which provides that "whoever embezzles, steals, purloins, or knowingly converts" government property is punishable by fine and imprisonment. Morissette was convicted and sentenced to imprisonment for two months or to pay a fine of $200. The Court of Appeals affirmed, one judge dissenting.

On his trial, Morissette, as he had at all times told investigating officers, testified that from appearance he believed the casings were cast-off and abandoned, that he did not intend to steal the property, and took it with no wrongful or criminal intent. The trial court, however, was unimpressed, and ruled: ". . . I don't think anybody can have the defense they thought the property was abandoned on another man's piece of property." . . . The court refused to submit or to allow counsel to argue to the jury whether Morissette acted with innocent intention.

* * *

The contention that an injury can amount to a crime only when inflicted by intention is no provincial or transient notion. It is as universal and persistent in mature systems of law as belief in freedom of the human will and a consequent ability and duty of the normal individual to choose between good and evil. A relation between some mental element and punishment for a harmful act is almost as instinctive as the child's familiar exculpatory "But I didn't mean to."

* * *

Crime, as a compound concept, generally constituted only from concurrence of an evil-meaning mind with an evil-doing hand, was congenial to an intense individualism and took deep and early root in American soil. As the states codified the common law of crimes, even if their enactments were silent on the subject, their courts assumed that the omission did not signify disapproval of the principle but merely recognized that intent was so inherent in the idea of the offense that it required no statutory affirmation. . . . Courts of various jurisdictions, and for the purposes of different offenses, have devised working formulae, if not scientific ones, for the instruction of juries around such terms as "felonious intent," "criminal intent," "malice aforethought," "guilty knowledge," "fraudulent intent," "wilfulness," "*scienter*," to denote guilty knowledge, or "*mens rea*," to signify an evil purpose or mental culpability. By the use or combination of these various tokens, they have sought to protect those who were not blameworthy in mind from conviction of infamous common-law crimes.

However, [certain other] offenses belong to a category of another character, with very different antecedents and origins. The crimes there involved depend on no mental element but consist only of forbidden acts or omissions. . . . The industrial revolution multiplied the number of workmen exposed to injury from increasingly powerful and complex mechanisms, driven by freshly discovered sources of energy, requiring higher precautions by employers. Traffic of velocities, volumes and varieties unheard of came to subject the wayfarer to intolerable casualty risks if owners and drivers were not to observe new cares and uniformities of conduct. Congestion of cities and crowding of quarters called for health and welfare regulations undreamed of in simpler times. Wide distribution of goods became an instrument of wide distribution of harm when those who dispersed food, drink, drugs, and even securities, did not comply with reasonable standards of quality, integrity, disclosure and care. Such dangers have engendered increasingly numerous and detailed regulations which heighten the duties of those in control of particular industries, trades, properties or activities that affect public health, safety or welfare.

While many of these duties are sanctioned by a more strict civil liability, lawmakers, whether wisely or not, have sought to make such regulations more effective by invoking criminal sanctions to be applied by the familiar technique of criminal prosecutions and convictions. This has confronted the courts with a multitude of prosecutions, based on statutes or administrative regulations, for what have been aptly called "public welfare offenses." . . . The accused, if he does not will the violations, usually is in a position to prevent it with no more care than society might reasonably exact from one who assumed his responsibilities. Also, penalties commonly are relatively small, and conviction does no grave damage to an offender's reputation. Under such considerations, courts have turned to construing statutes and regulations which make no mention of intent as dispensing with it and holding that the guilty act alone makes out the crime. This has not, however, been without expressions of misgiving.

* * *

Stealing, larceny, and its variants and equivalents, were among the earliest offenses known to the law that existed before legislation; they are invasions of rights of property which stir a sense of insecurity in the whole community . . . State courts of last resort, on whom fall the heaviest burden of interpreting criminal law in this country, have consistently retained the requirement of intent in larceny-type offenses. If any state has deviated, the exception has neither been called to our attention nor disclosed by our research.

* * *

The Government asks us by a feat of construction radically to change the weights and balances in the scales of justice. The purpose and obvious effect of doing away with the requirement of a guilty intent is to ease the prosecution's path to conviction, to strip the defendant of such benefit as he derived at common law from innocence of evil purpose, and to circumscribe the freedom heretofore allowed juries. Such a manifest impairment of the immunities of the individual should not be extended to common-law crimes on judicial initiative.

* * *

We hold that mere omission from §641 of any mention of intent will not be construed as eliminating that element from the crimes denounced.

* * *

Congress, by the language of this section, has been at pains to incriminate only "knowing" conversions. . . . Knowing conversion requires more than knowledge that defendant was taking the property into his possession. He must have had knowledge of the facts, though not necessarily the law, that made the taking a conversion. In the case before us, whether the mental element that Congress required be spoken of as knowledge or as intent, would not seem to alter its bearing on guilt. For it is not apparent how Morissette could have knowingly or intentionally converted property that he did not know could be converted, as would be the case if it was in fact abandoned or if he truly believed it to be abandoned and unwanted property. . . .

Of course, the jury, considering Morissette's awareness that these casings were on government property, his failure to seek any permission for their removal and his self-interest as a witness, might have disbelieved his profession of innocent intent and concluded that his assertion of a belief that the casings were abandoned was an afterthought. Had the jury convicted on proper instructions it would be the end of the matter. But juries are not bound by what seems inescapable logic to judges. They might have concluded that the heaps of spent casings left in the hinterland to rust away presented an appearance of unwanted and abandoned junk, and that lack of any conscious deprivation of property or intentional injury was indicated by Morissette's good character, the openness of the taking, crushing and transporting of the casings, and the candor with which it was all admitted. They might have refused to brand Morissette as a thief. Had they done so, that too would have been the end of the matter.

* * *

Reversed.

UNITED STATES v. PARK
421 U.S. 658 (1975)

MR. CHIEF JUSTICE BURGER delivered the opinion of the Court.

We granted certiorari to consider whether the jury instructions in the prosecution of a corporate officer under §301 (k) of the Federal Food, Drug, and Cosmetic Act, 52 Stat. 1042, as amended, 21 U.S.C. §331 (k), were appropriate under *United States* v. *Dotterweich,* 320 U.S. 277 (1943).

Acme Markets, Inc., is a national retail food chain with approximately 36,000 employees, 874 retail outlets, 12 general warehouses, and four special warehouses. Its headquarters, including the office of the president, respondent Park, who is chief executive officer of the corporation, are located in Philadelphia, Pa. In a five-count information filed in the United States District Court for the District of Maryland, the Government charged Acme and respondent with violations of the Federal Food, Drug, and Cosmetic Act. Each count of the information alleged that the defendants had received food that had been shipped in interstate commerce and that, while the food was being held for sale in Acme's Baltimore warehouse following shipment in interstate commerce, they caused it to be held in a building accessible to rodents and to be exposed to contamination by rodents. These acts were alleged to have resulted in the food's being adulterated within the meaning of 21 U.S.C. §§342 (a)(3) and (4), in violation of 21 U.S.C. §331 (k).

Acme pleaded guilty to each count of the information. Respondent pleaded not guilty. The evidence at trial demonstrated that in April 1970 the Food and Drug Administration (FDA) advised respondent by letter of the insanitary conditions in Acme's Philadelphia warehouse. In 1971 the FDA found that similar conditions existed in the firm's Baltimore warehouse. An FDA consumer safety officer testified concerning evidence of rodent infestation and other insanitary conditions discovered during a 12-day inspection of the Baltimore warehouse in November and December 1971. He also related that a second inspection of the warehouse had been conducted in March 1972. On that occasion the inspectors found that there had been improvement in the sanitary conditions, but that "there was still evidence of rodent activity in the building and in the warehouses and we found some rodent-contaminated lots of food items."

The Government also presented testimony by the Chief of Compliance of the FDA's Baltimore office, who informed respondent by letter of the conditions at the Baltimore warehouse after the first inspection. There was testimony by Acme's Baltimore division vice president, who had responded to the letter on behalf of Acme and respondent and who described the steps taken to remedy the insanitary conditions discovered by both inspections. The Government's final witness, Acme's vice president for legal affairs and assistant secretary, identified respondent as the president and chief executive officer of the company and read a bylaw prescribing the duties of the chief executive officer. He testified that respondent functioned by delegating "normal operating duties," including sanitation, but that he retained "certain things, which are the big, broad, principles of the operation of the company," and had "the responsibility of seeing that they all work together."

At the close of the Government's case in chief, respondent moved for a judgment of acquittal on the ground that "the evidence in chief has shown that Mr. Park is not personally concerned in this Food and Drug violation." The trial judge denied the motion, stating that *United States* v. *Dotterweich,* 320 U.S. 277 (1943), was controlling.

Respondent was the only defense witness. He testified that, although all of Acme's employees were in a sense under his general direction, the company had an "organizational structure for responsibilities for certain functions" according to which different phases of its operation were "assigned to individuals who, in turn, have staff and departments under them." He identified those individuals responsible for sanitation, and related that upon receipt of the January 1972 FDA letter, he had conferred with the vice president for legal affairs, who informed him that the Baltimore division vice president "was investigating the situation immediately and would be taking corrective action and would be preparing a summary of the corrective action to reply to the letter." Respondent stated that he did not "believe there was anything [he] could have done more constructively than what [he] found was being done."

On cross-examination, respondent conceded that providing sanitary conditions for food offered for sale to the public was something that he was "responsible for in the entire operation of the company," and he stated that it was one of many phases of the company that he assigned to "dependable subordinates." Respondent was asked about and, over the objections of his counsel, admitted receiving, the April 1970 letter addressed to him from the FDA regarding insanitary conditions at Acme's Philadelphia warehouse. He acknowledged that, with the exception of the division vice president, the same individuals had responsibility for sanitation in both Baltimore and Philadelphia. Finally, in response to questions concerning the Philadelphia and Baltimore incidents, respondent admitted that the Baltimore problem indicated the system for handling sanitation "wasn't working perfectly" and that as Acme's chief executive officer he was responsible for "any result which occurs in our company." . . . The jury found respondent guilty on all counts of the information, and he was subsequently sentenced to pay a fine of $50 on each count.

The Court of Appeals reversed the conviction and remanded for a new trial.

* * *

The question presented by the Government's petition for certiorari in *United States* v. *Dotterweich, supra,* and the focus of this Court's opinion, was whether "the manager of a corporation, as well as the corporation itself, may be prosecuted under the Federal Food, Drug, and Cosmetic Act of 1938 for the introduction of misbranded and adulterated articles into interstate commerce." In *Dotterweich,* a jury had disagreed as to the corporation, a jobber purchasing drugs from manufacturers and shipping them in interstate commerce under its own label, but had convicted Dotterweich, the corporation's president and general manager. The Court of Appeals reversed the conviction on the ground that only the drug dealer, whether corporation or individual, was subject to the criminal provisions of the Act, and that where the dealer was a corporation, an individual connected therewith might be held personally only if he was operating the corporation "as his 'alter ego.' "

In reversing the judgment of the Court of Appeals and reinstating Dotterweich's conviction, this Court looked to the purposes of the Act and noted that they "touch phases of the lives and health of people which, in the circumstances of modern industrialism, are largely beyond self-protection." It observed that the Act is of "a now familiar type" which "dispenses with the conventional requirement for criminal conduct—awareness of some wrongdoing. In the interest of the larger good it puts the burden of acting at hazard upon a person otherwise innocent but standing in responsible relation to a public danger."

Central to the Court's conclusion that individuals other than proprietors are subject to the criminal provisions of the Act was the reality that "the only way in which a corporation can act is through the individuals who act on its behalf."

* * *

Thus *Dotterweich* and the cases which have followed reveal that in providing sanctions which reach and touch the individuals who execute the corporate mission—and this is by no means necessarily confined to a single corporate agent or employee—the Act imposes not only a positive duty to seek out and remedy violations when they occur but also, and primarily, a duty to implement measures that will insure that violations will not occur. The requirements of foresight and vigilance imposed on responsible corporate agents are beyond question demanding, and perhaps onerous, but they are no more stringent than the public has a right to expect of those who voluntarily assume positions of authority in business enterprises whose services and products affect the health and well-being of the public that supports them.

* * *

Reading the entire charge satisfies us that the jury's attention was adequately focused on the issue of respondent's authority with respect to the conditions that formed the basis of the alleged violations. Viewed as a whole, the charge did not permit the jury to find guilt solely on the basis of respondent's position in the corporation; rather, it fairly advised the jury that to find guilt it must find respondent "had a responsible relation to the situation," and "by virture of his position . . . had . . . authority and responsibility" to deal with the situation. The situation referred to could only be "food . . . held in unsanitary conditions in a warehouse with the result that it consisted, in part, of filth or . . . may have been contaminated with filth."

* * *

Our conclusion that the Court of Appeals erred in its reading of the jury charge suggests as well our disagreement with that court concerning the admissibility of evidence demonstrating that respondent was advised by the FDA in 1970 of insanitary conditions in Acme's Philadelphia warehouse. We are satisfied that the Act imposes the highest standard of care and permits conviction of responsible corporate officials who, in light of this standard of care, have the power to prevent or correct violations of its provisions.

* * *

Reversed.

Excuses That Limit or Overcome Responsibility

Mistake of Fact and Mistake of Law Ordinarily, ignorance of the law is not an excuse. If you believe that it is permissible to turn right on a red light but the city ordinance prohibits it, your belief, even if reasonable, does not excuse your violation of the law. Under certain circumstances, however, ignorance of law will be excused. If a statute imposes criminal penalties for an action taken without a license, and the government official responsible for issuing the license formally tells you that you do not need one (though in fact you do), a conviction for violating the statute cannot stand. In rare cases, a lawyer's advice, contrary to the statute, will be held to excuse the client, but usually the client is responsible for his attorney's mistakes. Otherwise, as it is said, the lawyer would be superior to the law.

Ignorance or mistake of *fact* more frequently will serve as an excuse. If you take a coat from a restaurant, believing it to be yours, you cannot be convicted of larceny if it is not. Your honest mistake of fact negates the requisite intent. In general, the rule is that a mistaken belief of fact will excuse criminal responsibility if (1) the belief is honestly held; (2) it is reasonable to hold it; and (3) the act would not have been criminal if the facts were as they were supposed to have been.

Entrapment One common technique of criminal investigation is the use of an undercover agent or decoy—the policeman who poses as a buyer of drugs from a street dealer or the elaborate "sting" operations in which ostensibly stolen goods are "sold" to underworld "fences." Sometimes these methods are the only way by which certain kinds of crime can be rooted out and convictions secured.

But a rule against *entrapment* limits the legal ability of the police to play the role of criminals. The police are permitted to use such techniques to detect criminal activity; they are not permitted to do so to instigate crime. The distinction is usually made between a person who intends to commit a crime and one who does not. If the police provide the former with an opportunity to commit a criminal act—the sale of drugs to an undercover agent, for example—there is no defense of entrapment. But if the police knock on the door of one not known to be a drug user, and persist in a demand that he purchase drugs from them, finally overcoming his will to resist, a conviction for purchase and possession of drugs can be overturned on the ground of entrapment.

Other Excuses A number of other circumstances can limit or excuse criminal liability. These include compulsion (a gun pointed at one's head by a masked man who apparently is unafraid to use the weapon and who demands that you help him rob a store), honest consent of the "victim" (the quarterback who is tackled), adherence to the requirements of legitimate public authority lawfully exercised (a policeman directs a towing company to remove a car parked in a tow-away zone), the proper exercise of domestic authority (a parent may spank a child, within limits), and defense of self, others, property, and habitation. Each of these excuses is a complex subject in itself.

Lack of Capacity A further defense to criminal prosecution is the lack of mental capacity to commit the crime. Infants and children are considered incapable of committing a crime; under common law any child under the age of seven could not be prosecuted for any act. Today the age is governed by statutes that vary in each state. Likewise, insanity or mental disease or defect can be a complete defense. Intoxication can be a defense to certain crimes, but the mere fact of drunkenness is not ordinarily sufficient.

Procedure

The procedure followed in criminal prosecutions is complex and varies in particulars from state to state. Space here permits only the most abbreviated summary.

A criminal case begins either with an **arrest**—if the defendant is caught in the act or fleeing from the scene—or with a **warrant** for arrest. The warrant is issued by a judge or appropriate magistrate upon receiving a **complaint** detailing the charge of a specific crime against the accused. It is not enough for a police officer to go before a judge and say, "I'd like you to arrest Bluebeard because I think he's just murdered Agatha." The police officer must supply enough information to satisfy the magistrate that there is **probable cause** (reasonable grounds) to believe that the accused committed the crime. The warrant will be issued to the police or other appropriate public officer, who may then arrest the accused.

The accused will be brought before the magistrate for a **preliminary hearing** to determine whether there is sufficient reason to hold the accused for trial. If so, the accused can be sent to jail or be permitted to make **bail.**

Bail is a sum of money paid to the court to secure the accused's attendance at trial. If he fails to appear, he forfeits the money. Constitutionally, bail can be withheld only if there is reason to believe that the accused will flee the jurisdiction. Although there is much pressure to permit bail to be denied if the accused presents a danger to the community, that is not now the constitutional rule.

Once the arrest is made, the case is in the hands of the **prosecutor.** In the states, prosecution is a function of the district attorney's office. These offices are usually organized on a county-by-county basis. In the federal system, criminal prosecution is handled by the office of the United States Attorney, one of whom is appointed for every federal district. Lawyers working for the district attorney or the U.S. Attorney are known as assistant district attorneys or assistant U.S. attorneys.

Following the preliminary hearing, the prosecutor must either file an **information** (a document stating the crime of which the person being held is accused) or ask the *grand jury* for an *indictment.* In many states, an information may be substituted for an indictment only for lesser crimes. The **grand jury** consists of twenty-three people who sit to determine whether there is sufficient evidence to warrant a prosecution. It does not sit to determine guilt or innocence. The **indictment** is the grand jury's formal declaration of charges on which the accused will be tried. If indicted, the accused formally becomes a **defendant.**

The defendant will then be **arraigned**—that is, brought before a judge to answer the accusation in the information or indictment. The defendant may plead guilty or not guilty. If he pleads not guilty, the case will be tried before a jury—sometimes referred to as a *petit jury*. The case will proceed more or less as outlined in the discussion on pp. 81–83 dealing with civil trials. One significant difference is that the jury cannot convict unless it finds the defendant guilty "beyond a reasonable doubt."

The defendant might have pleaded guilty to the offense or to a lesser charge, often referred to as a "lesser included offense." (Simple larceny, for example, is a lesser included offense of robbery because the defendant may not have used violence but nevertheless stole from the victim.) Such a plea is usually arranged through **plea bargaining** with the prosecution. In return for the plea, the prosecutor promises to recommend to the judge that the sentence be limited.

The defendant is also permitted to file a plea of *nolo contendere* (no contest) in prosecutions for certain crimes. In so doing, he neither affirms nor denies his guilt. He may be sentenced as though he had pleaded guilty, although usually a nolo plea is the result of a plea bargain. Why plead nolo? In some offenses, such as violations of the antitrust laws, the statutes provide that private plaintiffs may use a conviction or a guilty plea as proof that the defendant violated the law and short-circuit a civil trial for damages. All that they need prove is the extent of their damages, not the liability of the defendant. The nolo plea permits the defendant to avoid this difficulty.

Following a guilty plea or a verdict of guilt, the judge will impose a sentence after presentencing reports are written by various court officials, often probation officers. Permissible sentences are spelled out in statutes, though these frequently give the judge a range within which to work (for example, "twenty years to life"). The judge may sentence the defendant to imprisonment, a fine, or both, or may decide to *suspend* sentence—that is, the defendant will not have to serve the sentence as long as he stays out of trouble.

Sentencing usually precedes appeal. As in civil cases, the defendant, now convicted, has the right to take at least one appeal, and frequently two or three, to higher courts, where issues of procedure and constitutional rights may be debated.

Constitutional Rights of the Accused

The rights of those accused of a crime are spelled out in four of the ten constitutional amendments that make up the Bill of Rights (Amendments Four, Five, Six, and Eight). For the most part, these amendments have been held to apply to both the federal and state governments.

Search and Seizure

The Fourth Amendment says in part that "the right of the people to be secure in their persons, houses, papers, and effects, against unreasonable searches and seizures, shall not be violated." Although there are numerous and tricky exceptions to the general rule, ordinarily the police may not break into a person's house or confiscate papers or make an arrest unless they have a warrant to do so. This means, for instance, that a police officer cannot simply stop you on a street corner and ask to see what is in your pockets (a power the police enjoy in many other countries), nor can your home be raided without probable cause to believe that you have committed a crime. What if the police do search or seize unreasonably? The courts have devised a remedy for the use at trial of the "fruits" of an unlawful search or seizure. Evidence that is unconstitutionally seized is excluded from the trial. This is the so-called **exclusionary rule**, first made applicable in federal cases in 1914, and brought home to the states in 1961. The exclusionary rule is highly controversial and there are numerous exceptions to it. But it remains generally true that the prosecutor may not use evidence willfully taken by the police in the absence of a legitimate warrant.

Double Jeopardy

The Fifth Amendment prohibits the government from prosecuting a person twice for the same offense; the amendment says that no person shall be "subject for the same offence to be twice put in jeopardy of life or limb." If a defendant is acquitted, the government may not appeal. Although state and federal laws may overlap, it is not double jeopardy for both the state and federal government to prosecute a defendant for acts that violate similar federal and state statutes.

Self-incrimination

Another hotly debated right is the Fifth Amendment's right against self-incrimination (no person "shall be compelled in any criminal case to be a witness against himself"). The debate over the limits of this right has given rise to an immense literature, which cannot be summarized here. In broadest outline, the right against self-incrimination means that the prosecutor may not call a defendant to the witness stand during trial and may not comment to the jury on the defendant's failure to take the stand. Moreover, a defendant's confession must be excluded from evidence if it was not voluntarily made (if, for example, the police beat the person into giving a confession). In *Miranda* v. *Arizona* [384 U.S. 436 (1966)], the Supreme Court ruled that no confession is admissible if the police have not first advised a suspect of his constitutional rights, including the right to have a lawyer present to advise him during the questioning. These so-called *Miranda warnings* have prompted scores of follow-up cases that have made this branch of jurisprudence especially complex.

Speedy Trial

The Sixth Amendment tells the government that it must try defendants speedily. How long a delay is too long depends on the circumstances in each case. In 1975, Congress enacted the Speedy Trial Act to give priority to criminal cases in federal courts. It requires all criminal prosecutions to go to trial within seventy-five days, although the law lists many permissible reasons for delay.

Right to Cross-examine

The Sixth Amendment also states that the defendant shall have the right to confront witnesses against him. No testimony is permitted to be shown to the jury unless the person making it is present and subject to cross-examination by the defendant's counsel.

Assistance of Counsel

The Sixth Amendment guarantees criminal defendants the right to have the assistance of defense counsel. During the eighteenth century and before, the British courts frequently refused to permit defendants to have lawyers in the courtroom during trial. The right to counsel is much broader in this country, as the result of Supreme Court decisions that require the state to pay for a lawyer for indigent defendants in most criminal cases.

Cruel and Unusual Punishment

Punishment under the common law was frequently horrifying. Death was common punishment for relatively minor crimes. The unlucky defendant who found himself convicted could face brutal torture before death. The Eighth Amendment banned these actions with the words that "cruel and unusual punishments" shall not be inflicted. Virtually all such punishments either never were enacted or have been eliminated from the statute books in the United States. Nevertheless, this provision has become controversial with the Supreme Court's rulings during the 1970s that the death penalty, as haphazardly applied in various states, amounted to cruel and unusual punishment. The death penalty as such, however, has not been held to be unconstitutional.

Chapter Summary

Criminal law is that branch of law governing offenses against society. Most criminal law requires a specific intent to commit the prohibited act, although a very few economic acts, made criminal by modern legislation, dispense with the requirement of intent. In this way, criminal law is different from much of civil law—for example, from the tort of negligence, in which carelessness, rather than intent, can result in liability.

Major crimes are known as felonies; minor ones, misdemeanors. Most people have a general notion about familiar crimes—murder, theft, and the like. But conventional knowledge does not suffice for understanding technical distinctions among related crimes such as larceny, robbery, and false pretenses. These distinctions can be important because an individual can be found guilty not merely for committing one of the acts defined in the criminal law but also for attempting or conspiring to commit such an act. It is usually easier to convict someone of an attempt or conspiracy than of the main crime, and a person involved in a conspiracy to commit a felony may find that very little is required to put him into serious trouble. Ignorance of the law is rarely an excuse, although under proper circumstances ignorance of certain facts may excuse a person who would otherwise be guilty of a crime.

Of major concern to the business executive is white-collar crime, which encompasses a host of offenses, including bribery, embezzlement, fraud, restraints of trade, and computer crime.

Persons accused of crime should know that they always have the right to consult a lawyer and should always do so.

Problems

1. Edward is accused of stealing some food from a grocery store. When the police arrested him on the street five minutes after the grocery store clerk phoned for help, he had none of the stolen goods on his person. He said he was on his way home from a movie and protested that he knew nothing about the crime. The clerk, the only witness, testified at the trial that he "thought Edward was the robber, but I can't be sure because it was dark." Should this case go to the jury? Why or why not?
2. Bill is the chief executive of a small computer manufacturing company that desperately needs funds to continue operating. One day a stranger comes to Bill to induce him to take part in a cocaine smuggling deal that would net Bill millions of dollars. Unbeknownst to Bill, the stranger is an undercover police officer. Bill tells the stranger to go away. The stranger persists, and after five months of arguing and cajoling, the stranger wears down Bill's will to resist. Bill agrees to take delivery of the cocaine and hands over a "down payment" of $10,000 to the undercover agent, who promptly arrests him for conspiracy to violate the narcotics laws. What defenses does Bill have?
3. You are the manager of a bookstore. A customer becomes irritated at having to stand in line and begins to shout at the salesclerk for refusing to wait on him. You come out of your office and ask the customer to calm down. He shouts at you. You tell him to leave. He refuses. So you and the salesclerk pick him up and shove him bodily out the door. He calls the police to have you arrested for battery. Should the police arrest you? Assuming that they do, how would you defend yourself in court?
4. Under what circumstances can a corporation be held guilty of a crime?
5. Marilyn is arrested for arson against a nuclear utility, a crime under both state and federal law. She is convicted in state court and sentenced to five years in jail. Then the federal government decides to prosecute her for the same offense. Does she have a double-jeopardy defense against the federal prosecution?

PART TWO

FOUNDATIONS OF BUSINESS

8

Contracts

In this chapter and the next we examine the two fundamental concepts considered the twin cornerstones of business relationships: contract and tort. These concepts surface periodically throughout the book. In Chapter 10, for instance, we discuss the contract and tort theories asserted in the typical product liability case.

Although both contract and tort involve the concept of duty, creation of the duty differs in a manner that is important to business. The parties create *contract* duties through a bargaining process. The key element in the process is control; an individual is in control of a situation because she has the freedom to decide whether to enter into a contractual relationship. *Tort* duties, in contrast, are obligations the law imposes. Despite the obvious difficulty in controlling tort liability, an understanding of tort theory is important because it is a critical factor in strategic planning and risk management.

General Perspectives on Contracts

The Role of Contract in Society

Contract is probably the most familiar legal concept in our society because it is so central to a deeply held conviction about the essence of our political, economic, and social life. In common parlance, the term is used interchangeably with agreement, bargain, undertaking, or deal; but whatever the word, it embodies our notion of freedom to pursue our own lives together with others. Contract is central because it is the means by which a free society orders what would otherwise be a jostling, frenetic anarchy.

So commonplace is the concept of contract—and our freedom to make contracts with each other—that it is difficult to imagine a time when contracts were rare, an age when people's everyday associations with one another were not freely determined. Yet in historical terms, it was not so long ago that contracts were rare, entered into if at all by very few. In "primitive" societies and in the medieval Europe from which our institutions sprang, the relationships among people were largely fixed; traditions spelled out duties that each person owed to family, tribe, or manor. Though he may have oversimplified, Sir Henry Maine, a nineteenth-century historian, sketched the development of society in his classic book *Ancient Law*. As he put it:

> [F]rom a condition of society in which all the relations of Persons are summed up in the relations of Family, we seem to have steadily moved towards a phase of social order in which all these relations arise from the free agreement of Individuals. . . . Thus the status of the Slave has disappeared—it has been superseded by the contractual relation of the servant to his master. . . . The status of the Female under Tutelage . . . has also ceased to exist. . . . So too the status of the Son under Power has no true place in the law of modern European societies. If any civil obligation binds together the Parent and the child of full age, it is one to which only contract gives its legal validity. . . . If then we employ Status, agreeably with the usage of the best writers, to signify these personal conditions [arising from ancient legal privileges of the Family] only, we may say that the movement of the progressive societies has hitherto been a movement *from Status to Contract*. ([1869] 1930, pp. 180–182)

This movement was not accidental. It went hand-in-glove with the emerging industrial order; from the fifteenth to the nineteenth centuries, as England, especially, evolved into a booming mercantile economy with all that that implies—flourishing trade, growing cities, an expanding monetary system, commercialization of agriculture, mushrooming manufacturing—contract law was created of necessity.

Contract law did not develop, however, according to a conscious, farseeing plan. It was a response to changing conditions, and the judges who created it frequently resisted, preferring the quieter, imagined pastoral life of their forefathers. Not until the nineteenth century, in both the United States and England, did a full-fledged law of contracts arise together with and help create modern capitalism.

Contract Defined

As usual in the law, the legal definition of "**contract**" is formalistic. The Restatement says: "A contract is a promise or a set of promises for the breach of which the law gives a remedy, or the performance of which the law in some way recognizes as a duty." (*Restatement (Second) of Contracts,* Section 1) Similarly, the Uniform Commercial Code says: " 'Contract' means the total legal obligation which results from the parties' agreement as affected by this Act and any other applicable rules of law." (Section 1-201(11))

A Cross-cultural View of Contract

Because contracts are so familiar to us, it is tempting to believe that their function, and the legal rules that govern them, are universal. However, in Communist societies, contract plays a very different role. In the Soviet Union, for example, the contract does not determine the nature of an economic transaction. That transaction is first set forth by the state's planning authorities; only thereafter are the predetermined provisions set down in a written contract. This fundamental difference gives rise to a state of affairs quite difficult to imagine in the United States—litigation over what *should* be written into the contract, rather than, as in this country, over what *is* written in the contract. Such disputes arise because one of the parties—a factory perhaps—may balk at a particular term (for example, delivery date of raw materials) already dictated by the authorities and may refuse to embody it in the contract. In a capitalist economy, such a refusal would mean that there would be no contract and hence no legal rights and obligations. In a fully planned economy, the contract as such is a formality that the parties can be forced to enter into. Moreover, under such a regime, performance of most contracts can be strictly required, since most contracts are not private but imposed by the state.

Economic View of Contract Law

In *An Economic Analysis of Law* (1973), Judge Richard A. Posner (a former University of Chicago law professor) suggests that contract law performs three significant economic functions. First, it helps maintain incentives to individuals to exchange goods and services efficiently. Second, it reduces the costs of economic transactions because its very existence means that the parties need not go to the trouble of negotiating a variety of rules and terms already spelled out. Third, the law of contracts alerts the parties to trouble spots that have arisen in the past, thus making it easier to plan the transactions more intelligently and avoid potential pitfalls.

Sources of Contract Law

There are four basic sources of contract law: the Constitution, federal and state statutes, federal and state case law, and administrative law. For our purposes, the most important of these, and the ones that we will examine at some length, are case law and statutes.

Case Law

Because contract law was forged in the common-law courtroom, hammered out case by case on the anvil of individual judges, it grew in the course of time to formidable proportions. By the early twentieth century, tens of thousands of contract disputes had been submitted to the courts for resolution, and the published opinions, if collected in one place, would have filled dozens of bookshelves. Clearly this mass of material was too unwieldy for efficient use. A similar problem had developed in the other leading branches of the common law. Disturbed by the profusion of cases and the resulting uncertainty of the law, a group of prominent American judges, lawyers, and teachers founded the American Law Institute in 1923 to attempt to clarify, simplify, and improve the law. One of its first projects, and ultimately one of its most successful, was the drafting of the *Restatement of the Law of Contracts,* completed in 1932. A revision—the *Restatement (Second) of Contracts*—was undertaken in 1946 and finally completed in 1979.

The Restatements (others exist in the fields of torts, agency, conflicts of laws, judgments, property, restitution, security, and trusts) are detailed analyses of the decided cases in the field. These analyses are made with an eye to discerning the various principles that have emerged from the courts, and to the maximum extent possible, the Restatements declare the law as the courts have determined it to be. The Restatements, guided by a Reporter (the director of the project) and a staff of legal scholars, go through several so-called "tentative" drafts—sometimes as many as fifteen or twenty—and are screened by various committees within the American Law Institute before they are eventually published as final documents.

The *Restatement of Contracts* won prompt respect in the courts and has been cited in innumerable cases. The Restatements are not authoritative, in the sense that they are not actual judicial precedents, but they are nevertheless weighty interpretive texts, and judges frequently look to them for guidance. They are as close to "black letter" rules of law as exist anywhere in the American legal system.

Statutory Law: The Uniform Commercial Code

Common law contract principles are still important for many types of contract disputes. But in one area they have been superseded by an important statute: the Uniform Commercial Code (UCC), especially Article 2, which deals with the sale of goods.

A Brief History The UCC is a model law developed by the American Law Institute and the National Conference of Commissioners on Uniform State Laws; it has been adopted in one form or another in all fifty states, the

District of Columbia, and the American territories. It is the only "national" law not enacted by Congress.

Before the UCC was written, commercial law varied, sometimes greatly, from state to state. This first proved a nuisance and then a serious impediment to business as the American economy became nationwide during the twentieth century. Although there had been some uniform laws concerned with commercial deals—including the Uniform Sales Act, first published in 1906—few were widely adopted and none nationally. As a result, the law governing sales of goods, negotiable instruments, warehouse receipts, securities, and other matters crucial to doing business in an industrial, market economy was a crazy quilt of untidy provisions that did not mesh well from state to state.

Initial drafting of the UCC began in 1942 and was ten years in the making, involving the efforts of hundreds of practicing lawyers, law teachers, and judges. A final draft, promulgated by the Institute and the Conference, was endorsed by the American Bar Association and published in 1951.

Pennsylvania enacted the code in its entirety in 1953. It was the only state to enact the original version, because the Law Revision Commission of the New York State legislature began to examine it line by line and had serious objections. Three years later, in 1956, a revised code was issued. This version, known as the 1957 Official Text, was enacted in Massachusetts and Kentucky. In 1958, the Conference and the Institute amended the Code further and again reissued it, this time as the 1958 Official Text. Sixteen states, including Pennsylvania, adopted this version.

But in so doing, many of these states changed particular provisions. As a consequence, the Uniform Commercial Code was no longer so uniform. Responding to this development, the American Law Institute established a permanent editorial board to oversee future revisions of the code. Various subcommittees went to work redrafting, and a 1962 Official Text was eventually published. Twelve more states adopted the code, eleven of them the 1962 text. By 1966, only three states and two territories had failed to enact any version: Arizona, Idaho, Louisiana, Guam, and Puerto Rico.

Meanwhile, non-uniform provisions continued to be enacted in various states, particularly in Article 9, to which 337 such amendments had been made. In 1971, a redraft of that article was readied and the 1972 Official Text was published. By that time, Louisiana was the only holdout. Two years later, in 1974, Louisiana made the UCC a truly national law when it enacted some but not all of the 1972 text (significantly, Louisiana has not adopted Article 2). One more major change was made, a revision of Article 8, necessitated by the electronics revolution that led to new ways of transferring investment securities from seller to purchaser. This change was incorporated in the 1978 Official Text, the version that remains current.

From this brief history, it is clear that the UCC is now a basic law of relevance to every business and business lawyer in the United States, even though it is not entirely uniform because different states have adopted it at various stages of its evolution—an evolution that continues still.

The Basic Framework of the UCC The UCC embraces the law of "commercial transactions," a term of some ambiguity. A commercial transaction may seem to be a series of separate transactions; it may include, for example, the making of a contract for the sale of goods, the signing of a check, the endorsement of the check, the shipment of goods under a bill of lading, and so on. However, the UCC presupposes that each of these transactions is a facet of one single transaction: the sale of and payment for goods. The code deals with phases of this transaction from start to finish. These phases are organized according to the following "articles":

- *Sales* (Article 2)
- *Commercial Paper* (Article 3)
- *Bank Deposits and Collections* (Article 4)
- *Letters of Credit* (Article 5)
- *Bulk Transfers* (Article 6)
- *Warehouse Receipts, Bills of Lading, and Other Documents of Title* (Article 7)
- *Investment Securities* (Article 8)
- *Secured Transactions; Sales of Accounts and Chattel Paper* (Article 9)

We now turn our attention to the sale—the first facet, and the cornerstone, of the commercial transaction. Sales law is a special type of contract law in that Article 2 applies only to the sale of goods, defined (Section 2-105) in part as "all things . . . which are movable at the time of identification to the contract for sale other than the money in which the price is to be paid. . . ." The only contracts and agreements covered by Article 2 are those relating to the present or future sale of goods.

In certain cases, the courts have difficulty in determining the nature of the object of a sales contract. The problem: How can goods and services be separated in contracts calling for the seller to deliver a combination of goods and services? This difficulty frequently arises in product liability cases in which the buyer sues the seller for breach of one of the UCC warranties to be discussed in Chapter 10. For example, you go to the hairdresser for a permanent and the shampoo gives you a severe scalp rash. May you recover damages on the grounds that either the hairdresser or the manufacturer breached an implied warranty in the sale of goods?

When the goods used are incidental to the service, the courts are split on whether the plaintiff should win. Compare *Epstein* v. *Giannattasio,* 197 A.2d 342 (Conn. 1963), in which the court held that no sale of goods had been made because the plaintiff received a treatment in which the cosmetics were only incidentally used, with *Newmark* v. *Gimbel's Inc.,* 258 A.2d 697 (N.J. 1969), in which the court said "[i]f the permanent wave lotion were sold . . . for home consumption . . . unquestionably an implied warranty of fitness for that purpose would have been an integral incident of the sale." The New Jersey court rejected the defendant's argument that by actually applying the lotion to the patron's head the salon lessened the liability it otherwise would have had if it had simply sold her the lotion.

Another area in which the issue of goods vs. services frequently arises today is liability for the sale of computer programs, as the following case illustrates.

RRX INDUSTRIES, INC. v. LAB-CON, INC.
772 F.2d 543 (9th Cir. 1985)

EUGENE A. WRIGHT, CIRCUIT JUDGE.

Thomas E. Kelly and Associates (TEKA), Lab-Con, Inc., and Thomas E. Kelly (Kelly) appeal from the district court's judgment awarding RRX Industries, Inc. general and consequential damages for breach of contract. Appellants challenge the district court's fact findings on liability and contend that the award of consequential damages was improper. We affirm.

This action arises out of a computer software contract negotiated between RRX and TEKA. TEKA agreed to supply RRX with a software system for use in its medical laboratories. The contract obligated TEKA to correct any malfunctions or "bugs" that arose in the system, but limited TEKA's liability to the contract price.

TEKA began installing the software system in January 1981 and completed it in June 1981. Bugs appeared in them soon after installation. TEKA attempted to repair the bugs by telephone patching. Subsequently, TEKA upgraded the system to make it compatible with more sophisticated hardware. The system, however, remained unreliable because defects continued to exist.

After contracting with RRX, Kelly formed Lab-Con, Inc. in order to market TEKA's software system. Lab-Con was a successor corporation to TEKA. TEKA assigned the RRX software contract to Lab-Con.

In September 1982, RRX instituted this diversity action against TEKA, Lab-Con, Kelly, and other defendants alleging breach of contract and fraud. Following a bench trial, the district court concluded that TEKA had materially breached the software contract. It found Lab-Con and Kelly individually liable and awarded RRX the amount paid under the contract, plus consequential damages. TEKA, Lab-Con, and Kelly (collectively appellants) timely appeal the judgment and award of damages.

* * *

The district court relied on the California Commercial Code to award RRX consequential damages. Such reliance was proper only if the computer software system may be characterized as a "good" rather than a service.

The California Commercial Code defines a good as "all things (including specially manufactured goods) which are movable at the time of identification to the contract for sale other than the money in which the price is to be paid, investment securities (Division 8) and things in action. . . ." Cal. Com.Code § 2105 (West 1964).

In determining whether a contract is one of sale or to provide services we look to the essence of the agreement. When a sale predominates, incidental services provided do not alter the basic transaction. Because software packages vary depending on the needs of the individual consumer, we apply a case-by-case analysis.

Here, the sales aspect of the transaction predominates. The employee training, repair services, and system upgrading were incidental to sale of the software package and did not defeat characterization of the system as a good. [Affirmed.]

In two areas, state legislatures have taken the goods vs. services issue out of the courts' hands and resolved the issue through legislation. One area involves restaurant cases, in which typically the plaintiff charges that he became ill because of tainted food. UCC Section 2-314(1) states that any seller who is regularly a merchant of the goods sold impliedly warrants their merchantability in a contract for their sale. This section explicitly declares that serving food or drink is a sale, whether they are to be consumed on or off the premises.

The second type of case involves blood transfusions, which can give a patient hepatitis, a serious and sometimes fatal disease. Hospitals and blood banks obviously face large potential liability under the UCC provision just referred to on implied warranty of merchantability. Because medical techniques cannot detect the hepatitis virus in any form of blood used, hospitals and blood banks would be in constant jeopardy, without being able to take effective action to minimize the danger. More than forty states have enacted legislation specifically providing that blood supplies to be used in transfusions are a service, not goods, thus relieving the suppliers and hospitals of an onerous burden.

Three Basic Contract Types: Sources of Law

With this brief description of the UCC, it should now be clear that the primary sources of law for the three basic types of contracts are

- Real estate: common law
- Services: common law
- Sale of goods: UCC (as interpreted by the courts)

Common law and UCC rules are often similar. For example, both require good faith in the performance of a contract. However, there are two general differences worth noting between the common law of contracts and the UCC's rules governing the sales of goods. First, the UCC is more liberal than the common law in upholding the existence of a contract. For example, in a sales contract (covered by the UCC), "open" terms—that is, those the parties have not agreed upon—do not require a court to rule that no contract was made. However, open terms in a *nonsales* contract will frequently result in a ruling that there is no contract. Second, although the common law of contracts applies to every person equally, under the UCC "merchants" occasionally receive special treatment. By "merchants" the UCC means persons who have special knowledge or skill who deal in the goods involved in the transaction.

The Convention on Contracts for the International Sale of Goods

A Convention on Contracts for the International Sale of Goods was approved in 1980 at a diplomatic conference in Vienna. (A convention is a preliminary agreement that serves as the basis for a formal treaty.) The Convention has been adopted by several countries, including the United States.

The Convention is significant for three reasons. First, the Convention is a uniform law governing the sale of goods—in effect, an international Uniform Commercial Code. The major goal of the drafters was to produce a uniform law acceptable to countries with different legal, social and economic systems. Second, although provisions in the Convention are generally consistent with the UCC, there are significant differences. For instance, under the Convention, consideration (see p. 207) is not required to form a contract and there is no Statute of Frauds (see p. 213). Finally, the Convention represents the first attempt by the Senate to reform the private law of business through its treaty powers, for the Convention preempts the UCC.

Basic Contract Taxonomy

Contracts are not all cut from the same die. Some are written, some oral; some are explicit, some not. Because contracts can be formed, expressed, and enforced in a variety of ways, a taxonomy of contracts has developed that is useful in lumping together like legal consequences. In general, contracts are classified along these dimensions: explicitness, mutuality, enforceability, and degree of completion. **Explicitness** is concerned with the degree to which the agreement is manifest to those not party to it. **Mutuality** takes into account whether promises are exchanged by two parties or only one. **Enforceability** is the degree to which a given contract is binding. **Completion** considers whether the contract is yet to be performed or the obligations have been fully discharged by one or both parties. We will examine each of these concepts in turn.

Explicitness

Express Contract An **express contract** is one in which the terms are spelled out directly; the parties to an express contract, whether written or oral, are conscious that they are making an enforceable agreement. For example, an agreement to purchase your neighbor's car for $500 and to take title next Monday is an express contract.

Implied Contract An **implied contract** is one that is inferred from the actions of the parties. Although no discussion of terms took place, an implied contract exists if it is clear from the conduct of both parties that they intended there be one. A delicatessen patron who asks for a "turkey sandwich to go" has made a contract and is obligated to pay when the sandwich is made. By ordering the food, the patron is implicitly agreeing to the price, whether posted or not.

Contract Implied in Law: Quasi-contract Both express and implied contracts embody an actual agreement of the parties. A **quasi-contract**, by contrast, is an obligation said to be "imposed by law" in order to avoid unjust enrichment of one person at the expense of another. In fact, a quasi-contract is not a contract at all; it is a fiction that the courts created to prevent injustice. Suppose, for example, that a carpenter mistakenly believes you have hired him to repair your porch; in fact, it is your neighbor who has hired him. One Saturday morning he arrives at your doorstep and begins to work. Rather than stop him, you let him proceed, pleased at the prospect of having your porch fixed for free (since you have never talked to the carpenter, you figure you need not pay his bill). Although it is true there is no contract, the law implies a contract for the value of the work.

Mutuality

The garden-variety contract is one in which the parties make mutual promises. Each is both promisor and promisee; that is, each pledges to do something and each is the recipient of such a pledge. This type of contract is called a **bilateral contract**. But mutual promises are not necessary to constitute a contract. **Unilateral contracts**, in which only one party makes a promise, are equally valid but depend upon performance of the promise to be binding. If Charles says to Fran, "I will pay you five dollars if you wash my car," Charles is contractually bound to pay once Fran washes the car. Fran never makes a promise, but by actually performing she makes Charles liable to pay.

Enforceability

Not every agreement between two people is a binding contract. An agreement that is lacking one of the legal elements of a contract is said to be **void**—that is, not a contract at all. An agreement that is illegal—for example, a promise to commit a crime in return for a money payment—is void. Neither party to a void "contract" may enforce it.

By contrast, a **voidable** contract is one that is unenforceable by one party but enforceable by the other. For example, a minor (any person under eighteen, in most states) may "avoid" a contract with an adult; the adult may not enforce the contract against the minor, if the minor refuses to carry out the bargain. But the adult has no choice if the minor wishes the contract to be performed. (A contract may be voidable by both parties if both are minors.) Ordinarily, the parties to a voidable contract are entitled to be restored to their original condition. Suppose you agree to buy your seventeen-year-old neighbor's car. He delivers it to you in exchange for your agreement to pay him next week. He has the legal right to terminate the deal and recover the car, in which case you will of course have no obligation to pay him. If you have already paid him, he still may legally demand a return to the *status quo ante* (previous state of affairs). You must return the car to him; he must return the cash to you.

A voidable contract remains a valid contract until it is voided. Thus, a contract with a minor remains in force unless the minor decides he does not wish to be bound by it. When the minor reaches his majority, he may "ratify" the contract—that is, agree to be bound by it—in which case the contract will no longer be voidable and will thereafter be fully enforceable.

An **unenforceable** contract is one which some rule of law bars a court from enforcing. For example, Tom owes Pete money, but Pete has waited too long to collect it and the statute of limitations (see p. 76) has run out. The contract for repayment is unenforceable and Pete is out of luck, unless Tom makes a new promise to pay or actually pays part of the debt. (However, if Pete is holding collateral as security for the debt, he is entitled to keep it; not all rights are extinguished because a contract is unenforceable.)

Degree of Completion

In medieval England, contract—defined as set of promises—was not an intuitive concept. The courts gave relief to one who wanted to collect a debt, for in such a case the creditor presumably had already given the debtor something of value, and the failure of the debtor to pay up was seen as manifestly unjust. But the issue was less clear when neither promise had yet been fulfilled. Suppose John agrees to sell Humphrey a quantity of wheat in one month. On the appointed day, Humphrey refuses to take the wheat or to pay. The modern law of contracts holds that a valid contract exists and that Humphrey is required to pay John.

An agreement consisting of a set of promises is called an **executory** contract before either promise is carried out. Most executory contracts are enforceable. If one promise or set of terms has been fulfilled—if, for example, John had delivered the wheat to Humphrey—the contract is called **partially executed**. A contract that has been carried out fully by both parties is called an **executed** contract.

Contract Formation

Although it has countless wrinkles and nuances, contract law asks two principal questions: did the parties create a valid, enforceable contract? What remedies are available when one party breaks the contract? The answer to the first question is not always obvious; the range of factors that must be taken into account can be large and their relationship subtle. Since people in business frequently conduct contract negotiations without the assistance of a lawyer, it is important to attend to the nuances to avoid legal trouble at the outset. Whether a valid enforceable contract has been formed depends in turn on whether:

1. The parties reached an agreement;
2. Consideration was present;
3. The agreement was legal;
4. The parties entered into the contract with capacity to make a contract; and
5. The agreement is in the proper form.

The Agreement

The core of a legal contract is the agreement between the parties. This is not a necessary ingredient; in Communist nations, contracts are routinely negotiated between parties who have had the terms imposed on them. But in the West, and especially in the United States, agreement is of the essence. That is not merely a matter of convenience; it is at the heart of our received philosophical and psychological beliefs. As the great student of contract law, Samuel Williston, put it:

> It was a consequence of the emphasis laid on the ego and the individual will that the formation of a contract should seem impossible unless the wills of the parties concurred. Accordingly we find at the end of the eighteenth century, and the beginning of the nineteenth century, the prevalent idea that there must be a "meeting of the minds" (a new phrase) in order to form a contract. (1921, p. 365)

Although agreements may take any form, including unspoken conduct between the parties (UCC Section 2-204(1)), they are usually structured in terms of an offer and an acceptance. Note, however, that not every agreement, in the broadest sense of the word, need consist of an offer and acceptance, and it is entirely possible, therefore, for two persons to reach agreement without forming a contract. For example, people may agree that the weather is pleasant or that it would be preferable to go out for Chinese food rather than seeing a foreign film; in neither case has a contract been formed. One of the major functions of the law of contracts is to sort out those agreements that are legally binding—those that are contracts—from those that are not.

In interpreting agreements, courts generally apply an objective standard. The *Restatement (Second) of Contracts* defines agreement as a "*manifestation* of mutual assent by two or more persons to one another." (Section 3) The UCC defines agreement as "the bargain of the parties in fact as found in their language or by implication from other circumstances including course of dealing or usage of trade or course of performance." (Section 1-201(3)) The critical question is what the parties said or did, not what they thought they said or did.

The distinction between objective and subjective standards crops up occasionally when one person claims he spoke in jest. The vice president of a manufacturer of punchboards, used in gambling, testified to the Washington State Game Commission that he would pay $100,000 to anyone who found a "crooked board." Barnes, a bartender, who had purchased two that were crooked some time before, brought one to the company office, and demanded payment. The company refused, claiming that the statement was made in jest (the audience before the commission had laughed when the offer was made). The court disagreed, holding that it was reasonable to interpret the pledge of $100,000 as a means of promoting punchboards:

> [I]f the jest is not apparent and a reasonable hearer would believe that an offer was being made, then the speaker risks the formation of a contract which was not intended. It is the objective manifestations of the offeror that count and not secret, unexpressed intentions. If a party's words or acts, judged by a reasonable standard, manifest an intention to agree in regard to the matter in question, that agreement is established, and it is immaterial what may be the real but unexpressed state of the party's mind on the subject. [Barnes v. Treece, 549 P.2d 1152 (Wash. App. 1976)]

As the following case illustrates, a party's real state of mind must be expressed to the other party, rather than in an aside to one's spouse.

LUCY v. ZEHMER
196 Va. 493, 84 S.E.2d 516 (1954)

BUCHANAN, JUSTICE. This suit was instituted by W. O. Lucy and J. C. Lucy, complainants, against A. H. Zehmer and Ida S. Zehmer, his wife, defendants, to have specific performance of a contract by which it was alleged the Zehmers had sold to W. O. Lucy a tract of land owned by A. H. Zehmer in Dinwiddie county containing 471.6 acres, more or less, known as the Ferguson farm, for $50,000. J. C. Lucy, the other complainant, is a brother of W. O. Lucy, to whom W. O. Lucy transferred a half interest in his alleged purchase.

The instrument sought to be enforced was written by A. H. Zehmer on December 20, 1952, in these words: "We hereby agree to sell to W. O. Lucy the Ferguson Farm complete for $50,000.00, title satisfactory to buyer," and signed by the defendants, A. H. Zehmer and Ida S. Zehmer.

The answer of A. H. Zehmer admitted that at the time mentioned W. O. Lucy offered him $50,000 cash for the farm, but that he, Zehmer, considered that the offer was made in jest; that so thinking, and both he and Lucy having had several drinks, he wrote out "the memorandum" quoted above and induced his wife to sign it; that he did not deliver the memorandum to Lucy, but that Lucy picked it up, read it, put it in his pocket, attempted to offer Zehmer $5 to bind the bargain, which Zehmer refused to accept, and realizing for the first time that Lucy was serious, Zehmer assured him that he had no intention of selling the farm and that the whole matter was a joke. Lucy left the premises insisting that he had purchased the farm.

* * *

In his testimony Zehmer claimed that he "was high as a Georgia pine," and that the transaction "was just a bunch of two doggoned drunks bluffing to see who could talk the biggest and say the most." That claim is inconsistent with his attempt to testify in great detail as to what was said and what was done. It is contradicted by other evidence as to the condition of both parties, and rendered of no weight by the testimony of his wife that when Lucy left the restaurant she suggested that Zehmer drive him home. The record is convincing that Zehmer was not intoxicated to the extent of being unable to comprehend the nature and consequences of the instrument he executed, and hence that instrument is not to be invalidated on that ground. It was in fact conceded by defendants' counsel in oral argument that under the evidence Zehmer was not too drunk to make a valid contract.

* * *

The appearance of the contract, the fact that it was under discussion for forty minutes or more before it was signed; Lucy's objection to the first draft because it was written in the singular, and he wanted Mrs. Zehmer to sign it also; the rewriting to meet that objection and the signing by Mrs. Zehmer; the discussion of what was to be included in the sale, the provision of the examination of the title, the completeness of the instrument that was executed, the taking possession of it by Lucy with no request or suggestion by either of the defendants that he give it back, are facts which furnish persuasive evidence that the execution of the contract was a serious business transaction rather than a casual, jesting matter as defendants now contend.

* * *

If it be assumed, contrary to what we think the evidence shows, that Zehmer was jesting about selling his farm to Lucy and that the transaction was intended by him to be a joke, nevertheless the evidence shows that Lucy did not so understand it but considered it to be a serious business transaction and the contract to be binding on the Zehmers as well as on himself. The very next day he arranged with his brother to put up half the money and take a half interest in the land. The day after that he employed an attorney to examine the title. The next night, Tuesday, he was back at Zehmer's place and there Zehmer told him for the first time, Lucy said, that he wasn't going to sell and he told Zehmer, "You know you sold that place fair and square." After receiving the report from his attorney that the title was good he wrote to Zehmer that he was ready to close the deal.

Not only did Lucy actually believe, but the evidence shows he was warranted in believing, that the contract represented a serious business transaction and a good faith sale and purchase of the farm.

In the field of contracts, as generally elsewhere, "We must look to the outward expression of a person as manifesting his intention rather than to his secret and unexpressed intention. 'The law imputes to a person an intention corresponding to the reasonable meaning of his words and acts.' "

At no time prior to the execution of the contract had Zehmer indicated to Lucy by word or act that he was not in earnest about selling the farm. They had argued about it and discussed its terms, as Zehmer admitted, for a long time. Lucy testified that if there was any jesting it was about paying $50,000 that night. The contract and the evidence show that he was not expected to pay the money that night. Zehmer said that after the writing was signed he laid it down on the counter in front of Lucy. Lucy said Zehmer handed it to him. In any event there had been what appeared to be a good faith offer and a good faith acceptance, followed by the execution and apparent delivery of a written contract. Both said that Lucy put the writing in his pocket and then offered Zehmer $5 to seal the bargain. Not until then, even under the defendants' evidence, was anything said or done to indicate that the matter was a joke. Both of the Zehmers testified that when Zehmer asked his wife to sign he whispered that it was a joke so Lucy wouldn't hear and that it was not intended that he should hear.

The mental assent of the parties is not requisite for the formation of a contract. If the words or other acts of one of the parties have but one reasonable meaning, his undisclosed intention is immaterial except when an unreasonable meaning which he attaches to his manifestations is known to the other party.

. . . The law, therefore, judges of an agreement between two persons exclusively from those expressions of their intentions which are communicated between them. . . . Clark on Contracts, 4 ed., § 3, p. 4.

An agreement or mutual assent is of course essential to a valid contract but the law imputes to a person an intention corresponding to the reasonable meaning of his words and acts. If his words and acts, judged by a reasonable standard, manifest an intention to agree, it is immaterial what may be the real but unexpressed state of his mind.

So a person cannot set up that he was merely jesting when his conduct and words would warrant a reasonable person in believing that he intended a real agreement.

Whether the writing signed by the defendants and now sought to be enforced by the complainants was the result of a serious offer by Lucy and a serious acceptance by the defendants, or was a serious offer by Lucy and an acceptance in secret jest by the defendants, in either event it constituted a binding contract of sale between the parties.

* * *

The complainants are entitled to have specific performance of the contract sued on. The decree appealed from is therefore reversed and the cause is remanded for the entry of a proper decree requiring the defendants to perform the contract in accordance with the prayer of the bill.

Reversed and remanded.

An offer is a manifestation of willingness to enter into a bargain such that it would be reasonable for another individual to conclude that assent to the offer would complete the bargain. Offers must be communicated and must be definite; that is, they must spell out terms to which the offeree can assent. However, as Box 8-1 indicates, definiteness is not a universal requirement; the Japanese seem to lack the need for it.

To constitute an agreement, an offer must be accepted. The offeree must manifest his assent to the terms of the offer in a manner invited or required by the offer. Complications arise when an offer is accepted indirectly through correspondence. Although offers and revocations of offers are not effective until received, an acceptance is deemed accepted when sent if the offeree accepts in the manner specified by the offeror.

If the offeror specifies no particular mode, then acceptance is effective when transmitted as long as the offeree uses a reasonable method of acceptance. It is implied that the offeree can use the same means used by the offeror or a means of communication customary to the industry. For example, the use of the postal service is so customary today that acceptances are considered effective when mailed, regardless of the method used to transmit the offer. Indeed, the so-called **mailbox rule** has an ancient lineage, tracing back more than 150 years to the English courts. [Adams v. Lindsell, 1 Barnewall & Alderson 681 (K.B. 1818)]

Consideration

Consideration, is the quid pro quo between the contracting parties in the absence of which the law will not enforce the promise or promises made. Consider the following three "contracts":

Box 8-1 Want Fewer Lawyers? Use Fewer Contracts.

Managing Without Lawyers
By Thomas Lifson

Fed up with suits and countersuits, tedious contracts, procedural delays and mounting legal costs, many American managers wish they could do business with fewer lawyers.

The Japanese have shown it can be done. In all of Japan, with a population of over one hundred million, there are only 15,000 lawyers, fewer than in the state of Ohio. On a per capita basis, that's one twenty-fifth the number in the United States.

This paucity of lawyers is not simply the result of management practice. The Japanese government regulates more by administrative discretion than by explicit statutes and guidelines. Compared to Americans, Japanese interest groups go less often to courts to seek redress.

But Japanese managers also use fewer lawyers in their dealings with other companies. In particular, they do not attach as much importance to contracts in their dealings with suppliers, partners and customers.

In America, the written word of a contract is the chief guarantee that both sides of a business relationship agree on their mutual responsibilities. Therefore, high pressure bargaining occurs at contract writing time. Every contingency imaginable must be addressed and fought over. The stakes are high, for in the face of an uncertain future both sides are locked into the terms written down.

This process requires the services of legal specialists who agree on the precise meanings of words. Once the contract is in place, the specialists are still needed to assure that each party's rights are respected. Thus, while managers are clearly responsible for the substance of a contract, they must delegate procedural issues to lawyers who follow their own logic.

In Japan, by contrast, agreement between firms is not focused on a document. Price, quantity, delivery and other such details are seldom spelled out definitely in advance. Agreement is instead based on a vague and unspecific mutual belief in the long-run benefits of doing business together. Lacking the safeguard of a contract, Japanese managers must learn as much as possible about the other party and its likely behavior under a range of circumstances. At every level of the hierarchy, each organization must feel confident it understands and can rely on the other. . . .

The principal advantage of Japanese agreement is that the two sides are not locked into specific terms. For example, if a supplier is faced with an unexpected rise in costs beyond its control, it can often persuade its customer to accept a rise in price, on the understanding that the supplier will return a similar favor later.

In the United States, unless a provision of the contract specifically anticipated the change in costs, the supplier might have to honor its contractual obligations or risk irksome litigation. . . .

Source: *Wall Street Journal,* September 24, 1979

1. Betty offers to give a book to Lou. Lou accepts.
2. Betty offers Lou the book in exchange for Lou's promise to pay $15. Lou accepts.
3. Betty offers to give Lou the book if Lou promises to pick it up at Betty's house. Lou accepts.

The question is which, if any, is a binding contract? In American law, only situation 2 is a binding contract, because only that contract contains a set of mutual promises in which each party pledges to give up something to the benefit of the other.

The question of what constitutes a binding contract has been answered differently throughout history and in other cultures. For example, under Roman law, any contract that was reduced to writing was binding, whether or not there was consideration in our sense. Moreover, in later Roman times, certain promises of gifts were made binding, whether written or oral, these would not be binding in the United States. And in the Anglo-American tradition, the presence of a seal was once sufficient to make a contract binding without any other consideration. In most states, the seal is no longer a substitute for consideration, although in some states it creates a presumption of consideration; in forty-nine states, the Uniform Commercial Code has abolished the seal on contracts for the sale of goods (Louisiana has not adopted UCC Article 2).

The existence of consideration is determined by examining whether the person against whom a promise is to be enforced (the **promisor**) received something in return from the person to whom he made the promise (the **promisee**). That may seem a simple enough question. But as with much in the law, the complicating situations are never very far away. The "something" that is promised or delivered cannot just be anything: a feeling of pride, warmth, amusement, friendship; it must be something known as a **legal detriment**—an act, a forebearance, or a promise of such from the promisee. The detriment need not be an actual detriment; it may in fact be a benefit to the promisee, or at least not a loss. At the same time, the "detriment" to the promisee need not confer a tangible benefit on the promisor; the promisee can agree to forego something without that something being given to the promisor. Whether consideration is legally sufficient has nothing to do with whether it is morally or economically adequate to make the bargain a fair one. Moreover, legal consideration need not even be certain; it can be a promise contingent on an event that may never happen. Consideration is a *legal* concept, and it centers on the giving up of a *legal* right or benefit.

Consideration has two elements. The first, as just outlined, is whether the promisee has incurred a legal detriment. (Some courts—although a minority—take the view that a bargained-for legal benefit to the promisor is sufficient consideration.) The second is whether the legal detriment was bargained for: did the promisor specifically intend the act, forbearance, or promise in return for his promise? Applying this two-pronged test to the three examples given at the outset of the chapter, we can easily see why only in the second is there legally sufficient consideration. In the first, Lou incurred no legal detriment; he made no pledge to act or to forbear from acting, nor did he in fact act or forbear from acting. In the third example, what might appear to be such a promise is not really so. Betty made a promise on a condition that Lou come to her house; the intent clearly is to make a gift. Betty was not seeking to induce Lou to come to her house by promising the book.

When the only consideration offered the promisor is an act or promise to act to carry out a preexisting duty, there is no valid contract. As the following case makes clear, the promisee suffers no legal detriment in promising to undertake that which he is already obligated to do.

DENNEY v. REPPERT
432 S.W.2d 647 (Ky. 1968)

R. L. MYRE, SR., SPECIAL COMMISSIONER. The sole question presented in this case is which of several claimants is entitled to an award for information leading to the apprehension and conviction of certain bank robbers.

Since the learned circuit judge of the Pulaski Circuit Court correctly set out the facts and the law in this case in a written opinion, we are affirming the judgment entered in accordance thereto and are adopting, in substance, the written opinion of the circuit judge as the opinion of this court.

On June 12th or 13th, 1963, three armed men entered the First State Bank, Eubank, Kentucky, and with a display of arms and threats robbed the bank of over $30,000. Later in the day they were apprehended by State Policemen Garret Godby, Johnny Simms and Tilford Reppert, placed under arrest, and the entire loot was recovered. Later all of the prisoners were convicted and Garret Godby, Johnny Simms and Tilford Reppert appeared as witnesses at the trial.

The First State Bank of Eubank was a member of the Kentucky Bankers Association which provided and advertised a reward of $500.00 for the arrest and conviction of each bank robber. Hence the outstanding reward for the three bank robbers was $1,500.00. Many became claimants for the reward and the Kentucky State Bankers Association being unable to determine the merits of the claims for the reward asked the circuit court to determine the merits of the various claims and to adjudge who was entitled to receive the reward or share in it. All of the claimants were made defendants in the action.

At the time of the robbery the claimants Murrell Denney, Joyce Buis, Rebecca McCollum and Jewell Snyder were employees of the First State Bank of Eubank and came out of the grueling situation with great credit and glory. Each one of them deserves approbation and an accolade. They were vigilant in disclosing to the public and the peace officers the details of the crime, and in describing the culprits, and giving all the information that they possessed that would be useful in capturing the robbers. Undoubtedly, they performed a great service. It is in the evidence that the claimant Murrell Denney was conspicuous and energetic in his efforts to make known the robbery, to acquaint the officers as to the personal appearance of the criminals, and to give other pertinent facts.

The first question for determination is whether the employees of the robbed bank are eligible to receive or share in the reward? The great weight of authority answers in the negative. In Re Waggoner, 47 S.D. 401, 199 N.W. 244, 245 (1924) states the rule thusly:

> To the general rule that, when a reward is offered to the general public for the performance of some specified act, such reward may be claimed by any person who performs such act, is the exception of agents, employees and public officials who are acting within the scope of their employment or official duties.

* * *

At the time of the robbery the claimants Murrell Denney, Joyce Buis, Rebecca McCollum, and Jewell Snyder were employees of the First State Bank of Eubank. They were under duty to protect and conserve the resources and moneys of the bank, and safeguard every interest of the institution furnishing them employment. Each of these employees exhibited great courage, and cool bravery, in a time of stress and danger. The community and the county have recompensed them in commendation, admiration and high praise, and the world looks on them as heroes. But in making known the robbery and assisting in acquainting the public and the officers with details of the crime and with identification of the robbers, they performed a duty to the bank and the public, for which they cannot claim a reward.

The claims of Corbin Reynolds, Julia Reynolds, Alvie Reynolds and Gene Reynolds also must fail. According to their statements they gave valuable information to the arresting officers. However, they did not follow the procedure as set forth in the offer of reward in that they never filed a claim with the Kentucky Bankers Association. It is well established that a claimant of a reward must comply with the terms and conditions of the offer of reward.

State Policemen Garret Godby, Johnny Simms and Tilford Reppert made the arrest of the bank robbers and captured the stolen money. All participated in the prosecution. At the time of the arrest, it was the duty of the state policemen to apprehend the criminals. Under the law they cannot claim or share in the reward and they are interposing no claim to it.

This leaves the defendant, Tilford Reppert the sole eligible claimant. The record shows that at the time of the arrest he was a deputy sheriff in Rockcastle County, but the arrest and recovery of the stolen money took place in Pulaski County. He was out of his jurisdiction, and was thus under no legal duty to make the arrest, and is thus eligible to claim and receive the reward. In Kentucky Bankers Ass'n et al. v. Cassady, 264 Ky. 351, 94 S.W.2d 622, 624, it was said:

> It is . . . well established that a public officer with the authority of the law to make an arrest may accept an offer of reward or compensation for acts or services performed outside of his bailiwick or not within the scope of his official duties. . . .

The claimant Tilford Reppert was present with Garret Godby and Johnny Simms at the time of the arrest and all cooperated in its consummation. The claimant Tilford Reppert personally recovered the stolen money. He recovered $2,000.00 more than the bank records show was stolen. This record does not reveal what became of the $2,000.00 excess.

It is manifest from the record that Tilford Reppert is the only claimant qualified and eligible to receive the reward. Therefore, it is the judgment of the circuit court that he is entitled to receive payment of the $1,500.00 reward now deposited with the Clerk of this Court.

The judgment is affirmed.

In cases of promissory estoppel, the courts will enforce promises without consideration. Simply stated, **promissory estoppel** means that the courts will stop the promisor from claiming that there was no consideration. The doctrine of promissory estoppel is invoked in the interests of justice when three conditions are met: (1) the promise is one that the promisor should reasonably expect to induce the promisee to take action or forbear from taking action of a definite and substantial character; (2) the action or forbearance is taken; and (3) injustice can be avoided only by enforcing the promise.

Timko serves on the board of trustees of a school. He recommends that the school purchase a building for a substantial sum of money, and to induce the trustees to vote for the purchase, he promises to help with the purchase and to pay at the end of five years the purchase price less the down payment. At the end of four years, Timko dies. The school sues his estate, which defends on the ground that there was no consideration for the promise. Timko was promised or given nothing in return, and the purchase of the building was of no direct benefit to him (which would have made the promise enforceable as a unilateral contract). The court ruled that under the three-pronged promissory estoppel test, Timko's estate was liable. [Estate of Timko v. Oral Roberts Evangelistic Assn., 215 N.W.2d 750 (Mich. App. 1974)]

Illegality

In general, illegal contracts are unenforceable. The courts must grapple with two types of illegalities: (1) statutory violations, and (2) violations of public policy not expressly declared unlawful by statute. Examples of the former may be found in Chapter 11 on Consumer Credit Transactions. An example of the latter would be a contract provision that exempts one party from tort liability (see Chapter 9) for harm caused intentionally.

Capacity

A contract is a meeting of minds. If someone lacks mental **capacity** to understand what he is assenting to—or that he is assenting to anything—it is unreasonable to hold him to the consequences of his act.

The general rule is that persons younger than eighteen can avoid their contracts. Although the age of majority was lowered in most states during the 1970s to correspond to the Twenty-sixth Amendment (ratified in 1971, guaranteeing the right to vote at eighteen), some states still put the age of majority at twenty-one. Legal rights for those under twenty-one remain ambiguous, however. Although eighteen-year-olds may assent to binding contracts, not all creditors and landlords believe it, and they may require parents to cosign. For those under twenty-one, there are also legal impediments to holding certain kinds of jobs, signing certain kinds of contracts, marrying, leaving home, and drinking alcohol. There is as yet no uniform set of rules.

The exact day on which the disability of minority vanishes also varies. The old common law rule put it on the day before the twenty-first birthday. Many states have changed this rule so that majority commences on the day of the eighteenth (or twenty-first) birthday.

A minor's contract is voidable, not void. A child wishing to avoid the contract need do nothing positive to disaffirm; the defense of minority to a lawsuit is sufficient. Although the adult cannot enforce the contract, the child can (which is why it is said to be voidable, not void).

When the minor becomes an adult, he has two choices: he may **ratify** the contract or **disaffirm** it. He may ratify explicitly; no further consideration is necessary. He may also do so by implication—for instance, by continuing to make payments or retaining goods for an unreasonable period of time. (In some states, a court may ratify the contract before the child becomes an adult. In California, for example, a state statute permits a movie producer to seek court approval of a contract with a child actor in order to prevent the child from disaffirming it upon reaching majority and suing for additional wages. As quid pro quo, the court can order the producer to pay a percentage of the wages into a trust fund that the child's parents or guardians cannot invade.) If the child has not disaffirmed the contract while still a minor, he may do so within a reasonable time after reaching majority.

In most cases of disavowal, the only obligation is to return the goods (if he still has them) or repay the consideration (unless it has been dissipated). However, in two situations, a minor might incur greater liability: contracts for necessities and misrepresentation of age.

Contract for Necessities At common law, a "necessity" was defined as an essential need of a human being: food, medicine, clothing, and shelter. In recent years, however, the courts have expanded the concept, so that in many states today necessities include property and services that will enable the minor to earn a living and to provide for those dependent on him. If the contract is executory, the minor can simply disaffirm. If the contract has been executed, however, the minor must face more onerous consequences. Although he will not be required to perform under the contract, he will be liable under a theory of "quasi-contract" (see p. 202) for the reasonable value of the necessity.

Misrepresentation of Age In most states, a minor may misrepresent his age and disaffirm in accordance with the general rule. That the adult reasonably believed the minor was also an adult is of no consequence in a contract suit. But some states have enacted statutes that make the minor liable in certain situations. A Michigan statute, for instance, prohibits a minor from disaffirming if he has signed a "separate instrument containing only the statement of age, date of signing and the signature." And some states "estop" him from claiming to be a minor if he falsely represented himself as an adult in making the contract. "Estoppel" is a refusal by the courts on equitable grounds to listen to an otherwise valid defense; unless the minor can return the consideration, the contract will be enforced.

Form

As a general rule, a contract need not be in writing to be enforceable (see Box 8-2). An oral agreement to pay a high-fashion model $1 million to pose for a photograph is as binding as if the language of the deal were printed on vellum and signed in the presence of twenty bishops. For three centuries, however, a large exception grew up around the Statute of Frauds, first enacted in England in 1677 under the formal name "An Act for the Prevention of Frauds and Perjuries." The two sections dealing with contracts read as follows:

> [Sect. 4] . . . no action shall be brought whereby to charge any executor or administrator upon any special promise, to answer damages out of his own

Box 8-2 Are Oral Contracts Enforceable?

The Tripple Ripple Ice Cream Case

By Jill Andresky

In the autumn of 1970 McDonald's Corp. founder and Chairman Ray Kroc came up with what he thought was one great idea. Along with Big Macs and fries, he wanted to sell combinations of vanilla, chocolate and strawberry ice cream in special, slow-dripping cones. No such cone existed at the time, so Kroc contacted Tom Cummings, the son of an old friend, whose Central Ice Cream Co. produced ice cream pops for Chicago's zoo and hospitals, and asked him to design one.

Since no contract was ever written and signed, what happened next has been debated for over 15 years. According to Cummings, Kroc promised him that if Central's "Tripple Ripple" cone passed McDonald's taste test, the fast-food chain would carry it exclusively for 20 years. McDonald's claims there was no exclusive long-term agreement, and, accordingly, the chain phased out Tripple Ripple after it bombed with customers after several years on the menu. Central Ice Cream Co., which had borrowed heavily to upgrade for the production of the cones, headed into Chapter 11. Cummings sued, and after a decade and a half of dispute, Central Ice Cream finally won and now stands to collect $15.5 million in damages for breach of contract and fraud.

Central Ice Cream won because Kroc and McDonald's lost sight of a basic legal principle that can cost businessmen dearly if ignored: Many business contracts do not have to be written down to be enforceable. In much the same way that Texaco was found last year to have induced Getty Oil to break an oral agreement to merge with Pennzoil, and thus wound up being hit with $10.5 billion in trial court damages, McDonald's was found to have induced Central Ice Cream to invest in reliance on a promise that McDonald's disavowed.

"Often these kinds of disputes boil down to whether you believe Sam or Joe," says Klaus Eppler, a senior partner at Proskauer Rose Goetz & Mendelsohn and an authority on contract law. "But in each case there's always the issue of whether the type of oral contract involved is as enforceable as a written one would have been, and that differs from state to state."

Generally, oral or written short-term contracts worth only small sums of money are equally binding. Lawyers have to prove either that both parties agreed to the contract or that one party made an offer and the other party acted in reliance on it. But when contracts are worth more than $500, the Uniform Commercial Code, used in every state with minor variations, requires that agreements be in writing unless both parties admit that an oral contract existed. Moreover, the UCC holds that once a written agreement does exist, its terms supersede any past or future oral understandings on the matter.

In the Tripple Ripple case, it was up to Theodore Becker, Central Ice Cream's attorney, to prove that McDonald's admitted an oral contract existed. A Cook County, Ill. jury bought his argument. What swayed them? The fact that the two companies had been doing business for three years. "The law is full of a lot of mumbo jumbo about when your oral agreement qualifies as a contract," Becker says. "But in my experience, juries make their decisions based on whether they think bad faith was involved in the agreement." Stunned by a $52 million trial court award, McDonald's offered to settle for $15.5 million, which has been accepted.

* * *

When it comes to oral contracts at least, the lesson should be clear: Think before you speak. Better yet, commit your agreement to paper.

Source: *Forbes,* August 25, 1986

estate; (2) or whereby to charge the defendant upon any special promise to answer for the debt, default or miscarriages of another person; (3) or to charge any person upon any agreement made upon consideration of marriage; (4) or upon any contract or sale of lands, tenements or hereditaments, or any interest in or concerning them; (5) or upon any agreement that is not to be performed within the space of one year from the making thereof; (6) unless the agreement upon which such action shall be brought, or some memorandum or note thereof, shall be in writing, and signed by the party to be charged therewith, or some other person thereunto by him lawfully authorized.

[Sect. 17] . . . no contract for the sale of any goods, wares and merchandizes, for the price of ten pounds sterling or upwards, shall be allowed to be good, except the buyer shall accept part of the goods so sold, and actually receive the same, or give something in earnest to bind the bargain, or in part of payment, or that some note or memorandum in writing of the said bargain be made and signed by the parties to be charged by such contract, or their agents thereunto lawfully authorized.

As may be evident from the title of the act and its language, the general purpose of the law is to provide evidence, in areas of some complexity and importance, that a contract was actually made. To a lesser degree, the law serves to caution those about to enter a contract and "to create a climate in which parties often regard their agreements as tentative until there is a signed writing." (*Restatement (Second) of Contracts* Chapter 5, statutory note)

The Statute of Frauds has been enacted in form similar to the seventeenth-century act in every state but Maryland and New Mexico, where judicial decisions have given it legal effect, and in Louisiana. With minor exceptions in Minnesota, Wisconsin, North Carolina, and Pennsylvania, the laws all embrace the same categories of contracts that are required to be in writing. Early in the century, Section 17 was replaced by a section of the Uniform Sales Act, and this in turn has now been replaced by provisions in the Uniform Commercial Code. The UCC requires contracts for the sale of goods for $500 or more and for the sale of securities to be in writing.

Today the Statute of Frauds is used as a technical defense in many contract actions, often with unfair results. Consequently, courts interpret the law strictly and over the years have enunciated a host of exceptions—making what appears to be simple quite complex, as illustrated by the following case.

WILSON FLOORS CO. v. SCIOTA PARK, LTD.
54 Ohio St.2d 451, 377 N.E.2d 514 (1978)

In December of 1971, Wilson Floors Company (hereinafter "Wilson") entered into a contract with Unit, Inc. (hereinafter "Unit"), a Texas corporation, to furnish and install flooring materials for "The Cliffs" project, a development consisting of new apartments and an office building to be located in Columbus, Ohio. Sciota Park, Ltd., a Texas limited partnership, was the owner of the project. Unit, the general partner of Sciota Park, Ltd., was the general contractor for the project. The Pittsburgh National Bank (hereinafter the bank), as the construction lender for the project, held mortgages on The Cliffs property as security for construction loans which the bank had made to Sciota.

As the work progressed on the project Unit fell behind in making payments to Wilson for its completed work in the spring of 1973. At that time, the project was approximately two-thirds completed, the first mortgage money of seven million dollars having been fully dispersed by the bank to Sciota. Appellant thereupon stopped work in May of 1973 and informed Unit that it would not continue until payments were forthcoming. On May 15, 1973, the bank conducted a meeting with the subcontractors in The Cliffs project, including Wilson.

At the meeting, the bank sought to determine whether it would be beneficial at that stage of the project to lend more money to Sciota, foreclose on the mortgage and hire a new contractor to complete the work, or do nothing. Subcontractors were requested to furnish the bank an itemized account of what Unit owed them, and a cost estimate of future services necessary to complete their job contracts. Having reviewed the alternatives, the bank determined that it would be in its best interest to provide additional financing for the project. The bank reasoned that to foreclose on the mortgage and hire a new contractor at this stage of construction would result in higher costs.

There is conflicting testimony in regard to whether the bank made assurances to Wilson at this meeting that it would be paid for all work to be rendered on the project. However, after the May meeting, Wilson, along with the other subcontractors, did return to work.

Payments from Unit again were not forthcoming, resulting in a second work stoppage. The bank then arranged another meeting to be conducted on June 28, 1973.

At this second meeting, there is conflicting testimony concerning the import of the statements made by the bank representative to the subcontractors. The bank representative who spoke at the meeting testified at trial that he had merely advised the subcontractors that adequate funds would be available to complete the job. However, two representatives of Wilson, also in attendance at the meeting, testified that the bank representative had assured Wilson that if it returned to work, it would be paid.

After the meeting, Wilson returned to work and continued to submit its progress billings to Unit for payment. Upon completion of its portion of The Cliffs project, Wilson submitted its final invoice of $15,584.50 to Unit. This amount was adjusted downward to $15,443.06 upon agreement of Unit and Wilson. However, Wilson was not paid this amount.

As a result of nonpayment, Wilson filed suit in the Court of Common Pleas of Franklin County against Unit, Sciota Park, Ltd., and the bank to recover the $15,443.06. On September 26, 1975, Wilson, Unit, and Sciota stipulated that judgment for the sum of $15,365.84, plus interest, be entered against Unit and Sciota. When Unit and Sciota failed to satisfy the judgment, appellant proceeded with its action against the bank.

The Court of Common Pleas, finding that at the June meeting the bank had guaranteed to the subcontractors that they would be paid by Unit, and that such guarantee was a "direct undertaking" by the bank for its own benefit, held in effect that the statute of frauds did not bar Wilson from enforcing the bank's oral promise to pay the debts of Unit. The court awarded Wilson the sum of $15,443.06.

On appeal, the Court of Appeals, although upholding the finding of the trial court that the bank had guaranteed payment of the obligation of Unit to Wilson ". . . regardless of whether or not the additional construction loan was sufficient to pay the costs to complete the project," reversed the judgment, holding that the oral promise made by the bank to Wilson was unenforceable, since the bank, as a result of the promise, did not become primarily liable for payment of the costs of construction, but only secondarily liable.

The cause is now before this court pursuant to allowance of a motion to certify the record.

The central issue in this cause is whether the bank's oral promise to Wilson that payments would be forthcoming upon a resumption of work at The Cliffs project constituted an enforceable oral contract.

R. C. 1335.05 provides:

> No action shall be brought whereby to charge the defendant, upon a special promise, to answer

> for the debt, default, or miscarriage of another person . . . unless the agreement upon which such action is brought, or some memorandum or note thereof, is in writing and signed by the party to be charged therewith or some other person thereunto by him or her lawfully authorized.

In paragraph one of the syllabus in *Crawford* v. *Edison* (1887), 45 Ohio St. 239, however, this court stated:

> When the leading object of the promisor is, not to answer for another, but to subserve some pecuniary or business purpose of his own, involving a benefit to himself, or damage to the other contracting party, his promise is not within the statute of frauds, although it may be in form a promise to pay the debt of another and its performance may incidentally have the effect of extinguishing that liability.

* * *

Because it is unquestioned that the bank in the instant cause did not become primarily liable when it guaranteed the subcontractors that they would be paid, the court must apply the second test set forth in *Crawford* to determine the enforceability of the verbal agreement.

Under the second test, it is of no consequence that when such promise is made, the original obligor remains primarily liable or that the third party continues to look to the original obligor for payment. So long as the promisor undertakes to pay the subcontractor whatever his services are worth irrespective of what he may owe the general contractor, and so long as the main purpose of the promisor is to further his own business or pecuniary interest, the promise is enforceable. See 3 Williston on Contracts (3 Ed. 1960), 466–467, Section 481. Thus, under this test it is not required to show as a condition precedent for enforceability of the oral contract that the original debt is extinguished.

The facts in the instant cause reflect that the bank made its guarantee to Wilson to subserve its own business interest of reducing costs to complete the project. Clearly, the bank induced Wilson to remain on the job and rely on its credit for future payments. To apply the statute of frauds and hold that the bank had no contractual duty to Wilson despite its oral guarantees would not prevent the wrong which the statute's enactment was to prevent, but would in reality effectuate a wrong.

Therefore, this court affirms the finding of the Court of Common Pleas that the verbal agreement made by the bank is enforceable by Wilson, and reverses the judgment of the Court of Appeals.

Remedies

Monetary awards (called "damages"), specific performance, and restitution are the three principal remedies. In view of the importance given to the intention of the parties in forming and interpreting contracts, it may seem surprising that the remedy for every breach is not a judicial order that the obligor carry out his undertakings. But it is not. Of course, some duties cannot be performed after a breach: time and circumstances will have altered their purpose and rendered many worthless. Still, there are numerous occasions on which it would be theoretically possible for courts to order the parties to carry out their contracts, yet the courts will not do it. In 1897, Justice Oliver Wendell Holmes, Jr., declared in a famous line that "the duty to keep a contract at common law means a prediction that you must pay damages if you do not keep it." By that he meant simply that the common law looks more toward compensating the promisee for his loss than toward compelling the promisor to perform. Indeed, the law of remedies often provides the parties with an incentive to break the contract. In short, the promisor has a choice: to perform or pay.

Compensatory Damages

One party has the right to damages (a money award) whenever the other party has breached the contract unless, of course, the contract itself or other circumstances suspend or discharge that right. If the breach caused no loss, the plaintiff is nevertheless entitled to a minor sum, perhaps one dollar, called **nominal damages.** When, for example, a buyer could purchase the same commodity at the same price as that contracted for, without spending any extra time or money, there can be no real damages in the event of breach.

A basic principle of contract law is that a person injured by breach of contract is not entitled to compensation unless the breaching party, at the time the contract was made, had reason to foresee the loss as a probable result of the breach. The leading case, perhaps the most studied case in all the common law, is *Hadley* v. *Baxendale,* decided in England in 1854. Joseph and Jonah Hadley were proprietors of a flour mill in Gloucester. In May 1853, the shaft of the milling engine broke, stopping all milling. An employee went to Pickford and Company, a common carrier, and asked that the shaft be sent as quickly as possible to a Greenwich foundry that would use the shaft as a model to construct a new one. The carrier's agent promised delivery within two days. But through an error the shaft was shipped by canal rather than by rail and did not arrive in Greenwich for seven days. The Hadleys sued Joseph Baxendale, managing director of Pickford, for the profits they lost because of the delay. In ordering a new trial, the Court of Exchequer ruled that Baxendale was not liable because he had had no notice that the mill was stopped:

> Where two parties have made a contract which one of them has broken, the damages which the other party ought to receive in respect of such breach of contract should be such as may fairly and reasonably be considered either arising naturally, i.e., according to the usual course of things, from such breach of contract itself, or such as may reasonably be supposed to have been in the contemplation of both parties, at the time they made the contract, as the probable result of the breach of it. [Hadley v. Baxendale, 9 Ex. 341, 354, 156 Eng.Rep. 145, 151 (1854)]

This rule, it has been argued, was a subtle change from the earlier rule that permitted damages for any consequences as long as the breach caused the injury and the plaintiff did not exacerbate it. But the change was evidently rationalized, at least in part, by the observation that in the "usual course of things," a mill would have on hand a spare shaft, so that its operations would not cease (Danzig, 1975, p. 249).

In the following opinion, Judge Posner discusses the similarities between the rule of *Hadley* v. *Baxendale* and tort law. The *Palsgraf* case noted in the opinion is reprinted on pp. 239–41.

EVRA CORP v. SWISS BANK CORP.
673 F.2d 951 (7th Cir. 1982)

[Plaintiff Hyman-Michaels Company (which later became Evra Corp.), a Chicago scrap dealer, chartered a ship (the *Pandora*) for two years. Hyman-Michaels Company (HMC) was late in making a charter payment because the defendant, Swiss Bank, failed to comply with a telex order to deposit the payment in the shipowner's account. As a result, the owner cancelled the charter and HMC was forced to recharter the *Pandora* at the prevailing market rate, which was $2 million higher than the original agreement. Hyman-Michaels sued Swiss Bank for damages. The trial court concluded that the bank was negligent and liable to Hyman-Michaels for the additional charter payments.]

* * *

Hadley v. *Baxendale,* 9 Ex. 341, 156 Eng.Rep. 145 (1854), is the leading common law case on liability for consequential damages caused by failure or delay in carrying out a commercial undertaking. The engine shaft in plaintiffs' corn mill had broken and they hired the defendants, a common carrier, to transport the shaft to the manufacturer, who was to make a new one using the broken shaft as a model. The carrier failed to deliver the shaft within the time promised. With the engine shaft out of service the mill was shut down. The plaintiffs sued the defendants for the lost profits of the mill during the additional period that it was shut down because of the defendants' breach of their promise. The court held that the lost profits were not a proper item of damages, because "in the great multitude of cases of millers sending off broken shafts to third persons by a carrier under ordinary circumstances, such consequences [the stoppage of the mill and resulting loss of profits] would not, in all probability, have occurred; and these special circumstances were here never communicated by the plaintiffs to the defendants." 9 Ex. at 356, 156 Eng.Rep. at 151.

The rule of *Hadley* v. *Baxendale*—that consequential damages will not be awarded unless the defendant was put on notice of the special circumstances giving rise to them—has been applied in many Illinois cases, and *Hadley* cited approvingly. In *Siegel,* the plaintiff had delivered $200 to Western Union with instructions to transmit it to a friend of the plaintiff's. The money was to be bet (legally) on a horse, but this was not disclosed in the instructions. Western Union misdirected the money order and it did not reach the friend until several hours after the race had taken place. The horse that the plaintiff had intended to bet on won and would have paid $1650 on the plaintiff's $200 bet if the bet had been placed. He sued Western Union for his $1450 lost profit, but the court held that under the rule of *Hadley* v. *Baxendale* Western Union was not liable, because it "had no notice or knowledge of the purpose for which the money was being transmitted." 312 Ill.App. at 93, 37 N.E.2d at 871.

The present case is similar, though Swiss Bank knew more than Western Union knew in *Siegel;* it knew or should have known that Hyman-Michaels was paying the Pandora Shipping Company for the hire of a motor vessel named *Pandora.* But it did not know when payment was due, what the terms of the charter were, or that they had turned out to be extremely favorable to Hyman-Michaels. And it did not know that Hyman-Michaels knew the *Pandora*'s owner would try to cancel the charter, and probably would succeed, if Hyman-Michaels was ever again late in making payment, or that despite this peril Hyman-Michaels would not try to pay until the last possible moment and in the event of a delay in transmission would not do everything in its power to minimize the consequences of the delay. Electronic funds transfers are not so unusual as to automatically place a bank on notice of extraordinary consequences if such a transfer goes awry. Swiss Bank did not have enough information to infer that if it lost a $27,000 payment order it would face a liability in excess of $2 million.

It is true that in both *Hadley* and *Siegel* there was a contract between the parties and here there was none. We cannot be certain that the Illinois courts would apply the principles of those cases outside of the contract area. As so often in diversity cases, there is an irreducible amount of speculation involved in attempting to predict the reaction of a state's courts to a new issue. The best we can do is to assume that the Illinois courts would look to the policies underlying cases such as *Hadley* and *Siegel* and, to the extent they found them pertinent, would apply those cases here.

* * *

Siegel, we conclude, is authority for holding that Swiss Bank is not liable for the consequences of negligently failing to transfer Hyman-Michaels' funds to Banque de Paris; reason for such a holding is found in the animating principle of *Hadley* v. *Baxendale,* which is that the costs of the untoward consequence of a course of dealings should be borne by that party who was able to avert the consequence at least cost and failed to do so. In *Hadley* the untoward consequence was the shutting down of the mill. The carrier could have avoided it by delivering the engine shaft on time. But the mill owners, as the court noted, could have avoided it simply by having a spare shaft. 9 Ex. at 355–56, 156 Eng.Rep. at 151. Prudence required that they have a spare shaft anyway, since a replacement could not be obtained at once even if there was no undue delay in carting the broken shaft to and the replacement shaft from the manufacturer. The court refused to imply a duty on the part of the carrier to guarantee the mill owners against the consequences of their own lack of prudence, though of course if the parties had stipulated for such a guarantee the court would have enforced it. The notice requirement of *Hadley* v. *Baxendale* is designed to assure that such an improbable guarantee really is intended.

This case is much the same, though it arises in a tort rather than a contract setting. Hyman-Michaels showed a lack of prudence throughout.

* * *

We are not the first to remark the affinity between the rule of *Hadley* v. *Baxendale* and the doctrine, which is one of tort as well as contract law and is a settled part of the common law of Illinois, of avoidable consequences.

* * *

The rule of *Hadley* v. *Baxendale* links up with tort concepts in another way. The rule is sometimes stated in the form that only foreseeable damages are recoverable in a breach of contract action. E.g., Restatement (Second) of Contracts § 351 (1979). So expressed, it corresponds to the tort principle that limits liability to the foreseeable consequence of the defendant's carelessness. The amount of care that a person ought to take is a function of the probability and magnitude of the harm that may occur if he does not take care. If he does not know what that probability and magnitude are, he cannot determine how much care to take. That would be Swiss Bank's dilemma if it were liable for consequential damages from failing to carry out payment orders in timely fashion. To estimate the extent of its probable liability in order to know how many and how elaborate fail-safe features to install in its telex rooms or how much insurance to buy against the inevitable failures, Swiss Bank would have to collect reams of information about firms that are not even its regular customers. It had no banking relationship with Hyman-Michaels. It did not know or have reason to know how at once precious and fragile Hyman-Michaels' contract with the *Pandora*'s owner was. These were circumstances too remote from Swiss Bank's practical range of knowledge to have affected its decisions as to who should man the telex machines in the foreign department or whether it should have more intelligent machines or should install more machines in the cable department, any more than the falling of a platform scale because a conductor jostled a passenger who was carrying fireworks was a prospect that could have influenced the amount of care taken by the Long Island Railroad.

In short, Swiss Bank was not required in the absence of a contractual undertaking to take precautions or insure against a harm that it could not measure but that was known with precision to Hyman-Michaels, which could by the exercise of common prudence have averted it completely. As Chief Judge Cardozo (the author of *Palsgraf*) remarked in discussing the application of *Hadley* v.

Baxendale to the liability of telegraph companies for errors in transmission, "The sender can protect himself by insurance in one form or another if the risk of nondelivery or error appears to be too great. . . . The company, if it takes out insurance for itself, can do no more than guess at the loss to be avoided." *Kerr S.S. Co.* v. *Radio Corp. of America,* 245 N.Y. 284, 291–92, 157 N.E. 140, 142 (1927).

* * *

We could remand for new findings based on the proper legal standard, but it is unnecessary to do so. The undisputed facts, recited in this opinion, show as a matter of law that Hyman-Michaels is not entitled to recover consequential damages from Swiss Bank.

* * *

Punitive Damages

Punitive damages are those awarded for the purpose of punishing a defendant in a civil action, in which criminal sanctions are of course unavailable. They are proper in cases in which the defendant has acted willfully and maliciously and are thought to deter others from acting similarly. Since the purpose of contract law is compensation, not punishment, punitive damages have not traditionally been awarded, with one exception: when the breach of contract is also a tort for which punitive damages may be recovered. Punitive damages are permitted in the law of torts (in all but four states) when the behavior is malicious or willful (reckless conduct causing physical harm, deliberate defamation of one's character, a knowingly unlawful taking of someone's property), and some kinds of contract breach are also tortious—for example, when a creditor holding collateral as security under a contract for a loan sells the collateral to a good-faith purchaser for value even though the debtor was not in default, he has breached the contract and committed the tort of **conversion.** Punitive damages may be awarded, assuming the behavior was willful and not merely mistaken.

Punitive damages are not fixed by law. The judge or jury may award at its discretion whatever sum is believed necessary to redress the wrong or deter like conduct in the future. This means that a richer person may be slapped with much heavier punitive damages than a poorer one in the appropriate case. But the judge in all cases may **remit** (lower) some or all of a punitive damage award if he or she considers it excessive.

In recent years, punitive damage claims increasingly have been made in cases dealing with the refusal by insurance companies to honor their contracts. Many of these cases involve disability payments, and among the elements are charges of tortious conduct by the company's agents or employees. California has been the leader among the state courts in their growing willingness to uphold punitive damage awards that are climbing into the millions of dollars—against insurer complaints that the concept of punitive damages is but a device to permit plaintiffs to extort settlements from hapless companies. Courts have also awarded punitive damages against other types of companies for breach of contract (see pp. 143–45).

Specific Performance

Specific performance is a judicial order to the promisor that he undertake the performance to which he obligated himself in a contract. Specific performance is an alternative remedy to damages and may be issued at the discretion of the court, subject to a number of exceptions. (When the promisee is seeking enforcement of a contractual provision for forbearance—a promise that the promisor will refrain from doing something—an **injunction**, a judicial order not to act in a specified manner, may be the appropriate remedy.) Emily signs a contract to sell Charlotte a gold samovar, a Russian antique of great sentimental value because it once belonged to Charlotte's mother. Emily then repudiates the contract while still executory. A court may properly grant Charlotte an order of specific performance against Emily.

Restitution

As the word implies, **restitution** is a restoring to one party of what he gave to the other. Therefore, only to the extent that the injured party conferred a benefit on the other party may the injured party be awarded restitution.

If the claimant has given the other party a sum of money, there can be no dispute over the amount of the restitution interest. Tom gives Tim $100 to chop his tree into firewood. Tim repudiates. Tom's restitution interest is $100. But serious difficulties can arise when the benefit conferred was performance. The courts have considerable discretion to award either the cost of hiring someone else to do the work that the injured party performed (generally, the market price of the service) or the value that was added to the property of the party in breach by virtue of the claimant's performance. Mellors, a gardener, agrees to construct ten fences around Lady Chatterley's flower gardens at the market price of $2,500. After erecting three, Mellors has performed services that would cost $750, market value. Assume that he has increased the value of the Lady's grounds by $800. If the contract is repudiated, there are two measures of Mellors's restitution interest: $800, the value by which the property was enhanced; or $750, the amount it would have cost Lady Chatterley to hire someone else to do the work. Which measure to use depends on who repudiated the contract and for what reason.

Tort vs. Contract Remedies

Frequently a contract breach may also amount to tortious conduct, which is covered in the following chapter. A physician warrants her treatment as perfectly safe but performs the operation negligently, scarring the patient for life. The patient could sue for malpractice (tort) or for breach of warranty (contract). The choice involves at least four considerations:

1. *Statute of limitations.* Most statutes of limitations prescribe longer periods for contract than for tort actions.
2. *Allowable damages.* Punitive damages are more often permitted in tort actions, and certain kinds of injuries are compensable in tort but not in contract suits—for example, pain and suffering.
3. *Expert testimony.* In most cases, the use of experts would be the same in either tort or contract suits, but in certain contract cases, the expert witness could be dispensed with, as, for example, in a contract case charging that the physician abandoned the patient.
4. *Insurance coverage.* Most policies do not cover intentional torts, so a contract theory that avoids the element of willfulness would provide the plaintiff with a surer chance of recovering money damages.

Chapter Summary

In this chapter we have seen that two fundamental sources of contract law are the common law as developed in the state courts and as summarized in the *Restatement (Second) of Contracts,* and the Uniform Commercial Code for the sale of goods.

Sales law is a special type of contract law, governed by Article 2 of the UCC, adopted in every state but Louisiana. Article 2 governs the sale of goods only, defined as things movable at the time of identification to the contract for sale. When the goods are "sold" incidental to a service, the courts do not agree on whether Article 2 applies. For two categories of goods, legislation specifically answers the question: foodstuffs served by a restaurant are goods; blood supplied for transfusions is not.

Types of contracts can be distinguished along these axes: (1) express and implied, including quasi-contracts implied by law; (2) bilateral and unilateral; (3) enforceable and unenforceable; and (4) completed (executed) and uncompleted (executory). To understand contract law, it is necessary to master these distinctions and their nuances.

In order to determine whether a valid, enforceable contract exists, the following questions must be answered: (1) Did the parties reach an agreement? (2) Was consideration present? (3) Was the agreement legal? (4) Did the parties have capacity to make a contract? (5) Was the agreement in the proper form?

Remedies available against someone who breaches a contract include damages, specific performance, and restitution. Frequently the party who is not in breach must choose between tort and contract remedies.

Problems

1. A letter from Bridge Builders, Inc., to the Allied Steel Company states the following:

   > We offer to purchase 10,000 tons of No. 4 steel pipe at today's quoted price for delivery two months from today. Your acceptance must be received in five days.

   Does Bridge Builders intend to create a bilateral or a unilateral contract? Why?
2. When Roscoe visited his barber for a haircut, the barber persuaded him to try a new hair cream called Kid's Stuff. Roscoe tried the product and, upon waking the next morning, discovered that all of his hair had fallen out overnight. Upon investigation he discovered that the loss of hair was due to an improper chemical compound in Kid's Stuff. If Roscoe filed a breach-of-contract action against the barber, would the case be governed by the Uniform Commercial Code? Why?
3. Rachel entered into a contract to purchase a 1954 Rambler from Hanna, who lived in the neighboring apartment. When a dispute arose over the terms of the contract, Hanna argued that, because neither she nor Rachel was a merchant, the dispute should be decided under general principles of common law. Rachel, on the other hand, argued that Hanna was legally considered to be a merchant because she sold the car for profit and that, consequently, the sale was governed by the Uniform Commercial Code. Who is correct? Why?
4. On November 26, Joe wrote to Kate offering to purchase a farm that she owned. Upon receiving the letter on November 28, Kate immediately sent Joe a letter of acceptance. However, shortly after mailing the letter, Kate had second thoughts and called Joe to advise him that she was rejecting his offer. The call was made before Joe received the letter of acceptance. Has a contract been formed? Why?
5. Phil offers George $100 if George will promise to quit smoking marijuana for one year. George promises to quit. Is Phil's promise binding? Why?
6. Cicero purchased a parcel of real estate that was landlocked. Cicero called his neighbor, Plato, and asked if he could use an abandoned drive on Plato's property to travel to his (Cicero's) property from the highway. Plato said: "Sure, anytime." Later Plato and Cierco became engaged in a dispute and Plato blockaded the drive. May Cicerco enforce Plato's promise that he could use the drive "anytime"? Why?
7. Terry leased an apartment from Larry. Despite Terry's numerous complaints, Larry provided no heat or hot water, failed to repair a leaking roof, did not replace burned-out light bulbs in the hallways, and failed to replace damaged mailboxes. Finally Terry sued Larry for breach of contract and asked for $1,000 in punitive damages. Larry's defense

was that punitive damages are not allowed in breach-of-contract actions. Is this a good defense? Why?

8. Dr. Casey was scheduled to perform two operations one morning. He was to perform a gallbladder operation on Millie and a breast biopsy on Tillie. The patients' charts were negligently switched, and the doctor started to perform the gallbladder operation on Tillie. He stopped the operation immediately upon discovering that the patient had a healthy gall bladder. Tillie sued the doctor, claiming $7,500 in actual damages and $75,000 in punitive damages. Should she be allowed to collect punitive damages? Why?

9

Torts

Purpose of Tort Law

Unlike criminal law, which is designed to regulate and deter conduct harmful to society and to punish those who violate its norms, tort law is concerned with the private relations among individuals. "Tort" derives from the Latin *tortus,* meaning "twisted," and came into English through the French *torquere,* meaning "wrong." At one time it was used in everyday speech; today it is used mainly by lawyers.

A **tort** is usually defined as a wrong for which the law will provide redress, most often in the form of money damages but sometimes in the form of an injunction. The definition is circular. It gives no clue to the underlying principles that divide wrongs in the legal sphere from those in the moral sphere. Hurting someone's feelings may be far more devastating than saying something mildly untrue about him behind his back, yet the law will probably redress the latter but not the former.

Although the word is not popularly used, tort suits are the stuff of everyday headlines. Increasing numbers of people injured by exposure to a variety of risks seek redress. Headlines boast of multimillion-dollar lawsuits against doctors who bungled operations, against newspapers that libeled subjects of stories, and against companies that manufacture dangerous substances like asbestos, diethylstilbestrol (DES), and Agent Orange (a herbicide used in the Vietnam War). All are examples of tort suits. Tort law concepts will be discussed in several chapters—including Chapter 10 on product liability and Chapter 23 on the tort liability of a landowner.

The law of torts developed almost entirely in the common-law courts and largely remains in their custody today. Through thousands of cases, the courts have fashioned a series of rules that govern the conduct of individuals in their noncontractual dealings with each other. Through contracts, individuals can shape their own rules. In the absence of agreement, tort law provides the means by which individuals can be held legally accountable for the consequences of their actions and by which those who have suffered losses at the hands of others can be compensated.

Although many acts, like homicide, are both criminal and tortious, torts and crimes are different, and the difference is worth noting. A crime is an act against the people as a whole. Society punishes the murderer; it does not usually compensate the family of the victim. Some states are beginning to adopt victim compensation programs, but the compensation is undertaken through an administrative proceeding unrelated to the criminal prosecution. Tort law, on the other hand, views the death as a private wrong for which damages are owed. The tort victim or his family, not the state, brings the action. The judgment against a defendant in a civil tort suit is, with one exception (see p. 228), not a penalty but a means of making the victim whole, or as nearly whole as possible.

Dimensions of Tort Liability

Fault Tort principles can be viewed along different dimensions. One is the **fault** dimension. Like criminal law, tort law requires an act for there to be liability. Unlike criminal law, however, there need not be a specific intent. Since tort law focuses on injury to the plaintiff, it is less concerned than criminal law about the reasons for the defendant's actions. An innocent act or a relatively innocent one may still provide the basis for liability. Nevertheless, tort law for the most part relies on standards of fault, or blameworthiness.

The most obvious standard is willful conduct. If the defendant, often called the **tortfeasor** (the one committing the tort), intentionally injures another, there is little argument about tort liability. Thus all crimes resulting in injury to a person or property (murder, assault, arson, and so on) are also torts, and the plaintiff may bring a separate lawsuit to recover damages for injuries to his person, family, or property.

Tort suits usually do not rely on *intentional* fault. They are based, rather, on **negligence**—conduct that under the circumstances is careless or poses unreasonable risks of causing damage. Most automobile accident and medical malpractice suits are examples of negligence suits.

The fault dimension is a continuum. At one end is the deliberate desire to do injury. The middle ground is occupied by careless conduct. At the other end is conduct that most would consider entirely blameless, in the moral sense. The defendant may have observed all possible precautions and yet still be held liable. This is called **strict liability.** An example is that incurred by the manufacturer of a defective product that is placed on the market despite all possible precautions, including quality-control inspection. In many states, if the product causes injury, the manufacturer will be held liable.

Nature of Injury Another way of viewing tort liability is by the type of injury caused. The most obvious type is physical harm to the person or property—wrongful death, battery, trespass, arson, accidents caused by the defendant's negligence. Mental suffering can be redressed if it is a result of physical injury—for example, shock and depression following an automobile accident. A few states now permit recovery for mental distress alone, such as a mother's shock at seeing her child injured by a car while both were crossing the street.

Other protected interests include a person's reputation (injured by defamatory statements or writings), privacy (injured by those who divulge secrets of her personal life), and economic interests (misrepresentation to secure an economic advantage, certain forms of unfair competition).

Excuses A third element in the law of torts is the excuse for committing an apparent wrong. The law does not condemn every act that ultimately results in injury. One common rule of exculpation is **assumption of risk.** A baseball fan who sits above third base assumes the risk that a foul ball will fly toward him and strike him. He will not be permitted to complain in court that the batter should have been more careful or that the third baseman should have caught the line drive. Another excuse is negligence of the plaintiff. If two drivers are careless and hit each other on the highway, some states will refuse to permit either to recover from the other. Still another excuse is **consent:** two boxers in the ring consent to the beating that each will administer.

Damages

Since the purpose of tort law is to compensate the victim for harm actually done, damages are usually measured by the extent of the injury. Expressed in money terms, these include replacement of property destroyed, compensation for lost wages, reimbursement for medical expenses, and dollars that are supposed to approximate the pain that is suffered. Damages for these injuries are called **compensatory damages.** Because compensatory damages are intended to make the tort victim whole, they are not taxable. The plaintiff injured in a car crash who recovers $1 million in compensatory damages need pay no income tax on the award.

In certain instances, the courts will permit an award of **punitive damages.** These are meted out as punishment for the defendant's actions. Because a punitive award, sometimes called *exemplary* damages, cuts against the general purpose of tort law, it is allowable only in aggravated situations. The law in most states permits recovery of punitive damages only when the defendant has deliberately committed a wrong with an evil intent or has otherwise done something outrageous. Punitive damages are rarely allowed in negligence cases for that reason. But if someone sets out maliciously to defame another person, punitive damages may well be appropriate. Punitive damages are intended not only to punish the wrongdoer, by exacting an additional and sometimes heavy payment (the exact amount is left to the discretion of jury and judge), but also to deter others from similar conduct. The punitive damage award has been awarded against manufacturers. One fear is that huge damage awards on behalf of a multitude of victims could swiftly bankrupt the defendant (see Box 9-1). Unlike compensatory damages, punitive damages are sometimes taxable.

Intentional Torts

The analysis of most intentional torts is straightforward and parallels the substantive crimes already discussed in Chapter 7. When physical injury or damage to property is caused, there is rarely debate over liability if the plaintiff deliberately undertook to produce the harm. Certain other intentional torts are worth noting for their relevance to business.

False Imprisonment

The tort of false imprisonment originally implied a locking up, as in a prison, but today it can occur if a person is restrained in a room or a car or even if his movements are restricted while walking down the street. People have a right to be free to go as they please, and one who without cause deprives another of personal freedom has committed a tort. Damages are allowed for time lost, discomfort and resulting ill health, mental suffering, humiliation, loss of reputation or business, and expenses such as attorneys' fees incurred as a result of the restraint (such as a false arrest). But as the following case shows, the defendant must be shown to have restrained the plaintiff in order for damages to be allowed.

LESTER v. ALBERS SUPER MARKETS, INC.
94 Ohio App. 313, 114 N.E.2d 529 (1952)

[The plaintiff, carrying a bag of rolls purchased at another store, entered the defendant's grocery store to buy some canned fruit. Seeing her bus outside, she stepped out of line and put the can on the counter. The store manager intercepted her and repeatedly demanded that she submit the bag to be searched. Finally she acquiesced, he looked inside, and said she could go. She testified that several people witnessed the scene, which lasted about 15 minutes, and that she was humiliated. The jury

Box 9-1 Growing Punitive Damages?

More Punitive Damage Awards

When she was four years old, Lee Ann Gryc leaned across an electric stove to turn off a kitchen buzzer. Her cotton pajamas accidentally brushed a lit burner, and she was instantly engulfed in flames. Within 12 seconds her mother rushed to her side to smother them, but by then it was too late: The child suffered severe second- and third-degree burns over 20% of her arms, chest, stomach, back, neck, and chin. Despite numerous skin grafts, Lee Ann, now 15, will be scarred for life. Cruelly, her Minnesota schoolmates refer to her as "Kentucky Fried Chicken," and not surprisingly she has great difficulties coping with her emotional problems.

Last May the Minnesota Supreme Court affirmed a $1.8 million award against Riegel Textile Corp., manufacturer of the pajamas. Such a figure would not ordinarily excite much comment. But in this case, $1 million of the amount was for punitive damages, and the court upheld the jury's verdict even though Riegel showed that it had complied with federal standards. In late October the U.S. Supreme Court declined to review the case, which now looms as an important precedent in the increasing number of product suits in which plaintiffs seek punitive damage judgments against U.S. businesses.

NO HISTORY

In legal theory, punitive damages are used to punish a defendant who intentionally or recklessly causes injury. Executives have long worried that the power to award punitive damages gives lay juries an incentive to levy outsized judgments against a corporation whenever a plaintiff is gruesomely injured. Until recently, however, the fears were largely unwarranted. A 1976 study of product liability awards by the Insurance Services Office, an industry group, declared that no conclusion could be drawn concerning punitive damage trends because there were too few cases from which to make a judgment.

That paucity of cases seems to have changed. "There is no question that since 1976 punitive damages are more commonly awarded by juries," says Malcolm E. Wheeler, a partner in the Los Angeles office of the New York-based law firm Hughes Hubbard & Reed. Wheeler, who successfully helped defend Ford Motor Co. in Indiana last year against criminal charges of reckless homicide arising out of a Pinto car crash, says that the punitive damages that the attorneys for plaintiffs ask for today are "astronomical" compared with the figures sought only five years ago.

And juries are responding. Earlier this year, for example, a Florida jury awarded a Royal Business Machines Inc. dealer $5 million, of which $3.3 million represented punitive damages, for injuries resulting from defects in one of Royal's plain-paper copiers.

NEW KIND OF EVIDENCE

The upsurge of punitive damage claims and awards is due to a change in "the nature of evidence"

---

awarded her $800. She also testified that no one laid a hand on her nor made a move to restrain her from leaving by any one of numerous exits.]

* * *

MATTHEWS, JUDGE. As we view the record, it raises the fundamental question of what is imprisonment. Before any need for a determination of illegality arises there must be proof of imprisonment.

In 35 C.J.S., False Imprisonment, § 11, pages 512, 513, it is said: "Submission to the mere verbal direction of another, unaccompanied by force or by threats of any character, cannot constitute a false imprisonment, and there is no false imprisonment where an employer interviewing an employee declines to terminate the interview if no force or threat of force is used and false imprisonment may not be predicated on a person's unfounded belief that he was restrained."

Many cases are cited in support of the text.

* * *

and not in the standard of proof, says Victor E. Schwartz, former chairman of the Commerce Dept.'s Task Force on Product Liability and now a professor at American University Law School and counsel to the Washington law firm of Crowell & Moring. Plaintiffs must still convince jurors that a manufacturer acted wantonly, but a company can be put in the dock for choosing between cost and safety in complex engineering matters. Ordinarily, the tradeoff may not be the basis for a punitive damage award, since at worst the choice will have been negligent. But there are exceptions, as the Gryc case shows.

Riegel made the pajamas from flannelette, a cotton material that is light, durable, inexpensive, and also, unfortunately, highly flammable. It had not been treated with flame retardant. Resolving against Riegel issues such as the practicability of the treatment and the desirability of warning consumers of flannelette's flammability would warrant a finding only that the pajamas were defective, and an award of compensatory, but not punitive, damages.

However, additional evidence showed that Riegel was aware that the standards established by the Flammable Fabrics Act were invalid and allowed unreasonably dangerous fabrics to pass the test. It was shown at trial that six lawsuits for burn accidents between 1960 and 1967 had put Riegel on notice of the potential hazard.

Minnesota is not alone in allowing punitive damages in product cases. The Wisconsin Supreme Court ruled last June that a punitive claim in the case of an allegedly defective Mustang could proceed against Ford.

OUT OF COURT

So far, few such awards have actually been paid. Since they are taxable to the plaintiff and not recoverable from a defendant's insurer, each party has strong incentives to compromise and settle before an appeal, according to Stuart M. Speiser, a leading New York plaintiffs trial lawyer.

Nevertheless, many corporate lawyers are apprehensive that the new trend may result in repeated, huge assessments when injuries are caused by a product that is mass marketed. "There could be 10,000 suits arising out of a single drug mishap," Schwartz says. One protection for manufacturers would be to let the jury decide on liability and let the judge determine the amount. Such a change in procedure would require legislative action.

Judicially decreed damages would not eliminate all objections, Wheeler says. Although assessed in a civil case, punitive damages are akin to punishment, which is usually surrounded by such constitutional safeguards as grand jury indictment and the right against self-incrimination. So far, the argument has not been pressed. But, says Wheeler, "I'm just waiting for the right case."

Source: Reprinted from *Business Week*, January 12, 1981

In Fenn v. Kroger Grocery & Baking Co., Mo. Sup., 209 S.W. 885, 887, the court said:

> A case was not made out for false arrest. The plaintiff said she was intercepted as she started to leave the store; that Mr. Krause stood where she could not pass him in going out. She does not say that he made any attempt to intercept her. She says he escorted her back to the desk, that he asked her to let him see the change. . . . She does not say that she went unwillingly. . . . Evidence is wholly lacking to show that she was detained by force or threats. It was probably a disagreeable experience, a humiliating one to her, but she came out victorious and was allowed to go when she desired with the assurance of Mr. Krause that it was all right. The demurrer to the evidence on both counts was properly sustained.

The result of the cases is epitomized in 22 Am. Jr. 368, as follows:

> A customer or patron who apparently has not paid for what he has received may be detained for

a reasonable time to investigate the circumstances, but upon payment of the demand, he has the unqualified right to leave the premises without restraint, so far as the proprietor is concerned, and it is false imprisonment for a private individual to detain one for an unreasonable time, or under unreasonable circumstances, for the purpose of investigating a dispute over the payment of a bill alleged to be owed by the person detained for cash services.

* * *

For these reasons, the judgment is reversed and final judgment entered for the defendant-appellant.

Intentional Infliction of Emotional Distress

Until recently, common law ruled that there could be no recovery for acts, even though intentionally undertaken, that caused purely mental or emotional distress. For a case to go to the jury, the courts required that the mental distress result from some physical injury. In recent years, as explained in the following case, many courts have overthrown the older rule and now recognize the so-called "new tort."

ECKENRODE v. LIFE OF AMERICA INSURANCE CO.
470 F.2d 1 (7th Cir. 1972)

KILEY, CIRCUIT JUDGE. Plaintiff, a resident of Pennsylvania, filed this three count diversity complaint to recover damages for severe emotional injury suffered as a result of the deliberate refusal of Life of America Insurance Company (Insurer), of Chicago, to pay her the proceeds of Insurer's policy covering the life of her husband. The district court dismissed the suit. Plaintiff has appealed. We reverse.

* * *

Taking the allegations, properly pleaded in Counts II and III, as true, the following facts are stated: Defendant's life insurance policy covering plaintiff's husband issued September 22, 1967. Under the policy Insurer agreed to pay plaintiff $5,000 immediately upon due proof of death from "accidental causes." On December 17, 1967, insured was an accidental victim of a homicide. Plaintiff met all conditions of the policy and repeatedly demanded payment, but Insurer refused to pay. Decedent left plaintiff with several children, but no property of value. She had no money, none even for the funeral expenses. Denied payment by Insurer, she was required to borrow money to support her family, while her financial condition worsened. The family was required to live with, and accept charity from, relatives.

Further: . . . Insurer, knowing full well that plaintiff needed the proceeds of the policy to provide necessaries for her children, applied "economic coercion" in refusing to make payment on the policy, and in "inviting" plaintiff to "compromise" her claim by implying it (Insurer) had a valid defense to the claim.

The issue before us with respect to Counts II and III is whether plaintiff—beneficiary of her husband's life insurance policy—may on the foregoing "facts" recover damages for severe mental distress allegedly suffered as a result of Insurer's conduct. Illinois law controls our decision, and, in anticipation that the Illinois Supreme Court would hold as we do, we decide the issue in favor of plaintiff.

We have no doubt, in view of Knierim v. Izzo, 22 Ill.2d 73, 174 N.E.2d 157 (1961), that the Illinois Supreme Court would sustain plaintiff's complaint against Insurer's motion to dismiss.

In *Knierim,* plaintiff filed a wrongful death action alleging, inter alia, that defendant Izzo threatened her with the murder of her husband, carried out the threat, and thereby proximately caused her severe emotional distress. The trial court dismissed her complaint, but the Illinois Supreme Court reversed and held that plaintiff had stated a cause of action for an intentional causing of severe emotional distress by Izzo's "outrageous conduct."

The court recognized the "new tort" of intentional infliction of severe emotional distress, following similar recognition by an "increasing number of courts," and cited several state decisions. The court rejected reasons given by other courts not recognizing the "new tort." As to the reason that mental disturbance is incapable of financial measurement, the court pointed out that "pain and suffering" and "mental suffering" are elements of damage, respectively, in personal injury and malicious prosecution cases.

As to the reason that mental consequences are too evanescent for the law to deal with, the court noted that psychosomatic medicine had learned much in the past "thirty years" about the bodily effects of man's emotions, and that symptoms produced by "stronger emotions" are now visible to the professional eye. As to the reason that recognizing the "new tort" would lead to frivolous claims, the court observed that triers of fact from their own experiences would be able to draw a line between "slight hurts" and "outrageous conduct."

*   *   *

In *Knierim* the court, inter alia, relied upon State Rubbish Collectors Association v. Siliznoff, 38 Cal.2d 330, 240 P.2d 282 (1952), and Restatement, Torts § 46 (1948 Supp.). In *Siliznoff* the California Supreme Court, in an opinion by Justice Roger Traynor, recognized the "new tort" for the first time and held that Siliznoff could recover from the cross-defendant Rubbish Collectors Association for mental distress caused by the Association's severe threats to beat him up, destroy his truck and put him out of business unless Siliznoff offered to pay over certain proceeds to the Association. . . .

We think that the California court in *Fletcher* . . . set out correctly the elements of a prima facie case for the tort of "intentional infliction of severe emotional distress":

(1) Outrageous conduct by the defendant;
(2) The defendant's intention of causing, or reckless disregard of the probability of causing emotional distress;
(3) The plaintiff's suffering severe or extreme emotional distress; and
(4) Actual and proximate causation of the emotional distress by the defendant's outrageous conduct.

*   *   *

Here Insurer's alleged bad faith refusal to make payment on the policy, coupled with its deliberate use of "economic coercion" (*i.e.*, by delaying and refusing payment it increased plaintiff's financial distress thereby coercing her to compromise and settle) to force a settlement, clearly rises to the level of "outrageous conduct" to a person of "ordinary sensibilities."

Furthermore, it is common knowledge that one of the most frequent considerations in procuring life insurance is to ensure the continued economic and mental welfare of the beneficiaries upon the death of the insured. The very risks insured against presuppose that upon the death of the insured the beneficiary might be in difficult circumstances and thus particularly susceptible and vulnerable to high pressure tactics by an economically powerful entity. In the case before us Insurer's alleged high pressure methods (economic coercion) were aimed at the very thing insured against, and we think that the insurance company was on notice that plaintiff would be particularly vulnerable to mental distress by reason of her financial plight.

*   *   *

Reversed.

Negligence

Physical harm need not be intentially caused. A pedestrian knocked over by an automobile does not hurt less because the driver intended no wrong but was merely careless. The law imposes a **duty of care** on all of us in our everyday lives. Accidents caused by **negligence** are actionable.

Determining negligence is not always easy. If a driver runs a red light, we can say that she is negligent because a driver must always be careful to ascertain whether the light is red and be able to stop if it is. Suppose that the driver was carrying a badly injured person to a nearby hospital, and after slowing down at an intersection, proceeded through a red light blowing her horn, whereupon a driver to her right, seeing her, drove into the intersection anyway and crashed into her. Must one always stop at a red light? Is proof that the light was red always proof of negligence? Usually, but not always: negligence is an abstract concept that must always be applied to concrete and often widely varying sets of circumstances. Whether someone was or was not negligent is almost always a question of fact for a jury to decide. Rarely is it a legal question that a judge can settle.

Elements of Negligence

The tort of negligence has four elements: (1) standard of care, (2) duty of care, (3) connection between cause and injury, and (4) actual damage or loss. Even if a plaintiff can prove each of these aspects, the defendant may be able to show that the law excuses the conduct that is the basis for the tort claim. We examine each of these factors below.

Standard of Care Not every unintentional act that causes injury is negligent. If you brake to a stop when you see a child dart out in front of your car, and the noise from your tires gives someone in a nearby house a heart attack, you have not acted negligently toward the person in the house. The purpose of the negligence standard is to protect others against the risk of injury that foreseeably would ensue from unreasonably dangerous conduct.

Given the infinite variety of human circumstances and conduct, no general statement of a reasonable standard of care is possible. Nevertheless, the law has tried to encapsulate it in the form of the famous standard of **"the reasonable man."** This fictitious person "of ordinary prudence" is the model that juries are instructed to compare in assessing whether defendants in cases before them have acted negligently. Analysis of this mythical personage has baffled several generations of commentators. How much knowledge must he have of events in the community, of technology, of cause and effect? With what physical attributes, courage, wisdom is this non-existent person supposedly endowed? If the defendant is a person with specialized knowledge, like a doctor or automobile designer, must the jury also treat the "reasonable man" as having this knowledge, even though the average person in the community will not? (Answer: in most cases, yes.)

Despite the many difficulties, the concept of the reasonable man is one on which most negligence cases ultimately turn. If a defendant has acted "unreasonably under the circumstances" and his conduct posed an unreasonable risk of injury, then he is liable for injury caused by his conduct. Perhaps in most instances, it is not difficult to divine what the reasonable man would do. The reasonable man stops for traffic lights and always drives at reasonable speeds, does not throw baseballs through windows, performs surgical operations according to the average standards of the medical profession, ensures that the floors of his grocery store are kept free of fluids that would cause a patron to slip and fall, takes proper precautions to avoid spillage of oil from his supertanker, and so on. But it may sometimes happen that the reasonable man would do something that no one at all in the real world has done because, in the view of courts, the circumstances make it unreasonable for anyone to fail to do so. This situation is presented in the following often-quoted opinion by the renowned jurist, Judge Learned Hand (1872–1961).

THE T. J. HOOPER
60 F.2d 737 (2d Cir. 1932)

L. HAND, CIRCUIT JUDGE.

The barges No. 17 and No. 30, belonging to the Northern Barge Company, had lifted cargoes of coal at Norfolk, Virginia, for New York in March, 1928. They were towed by two tugs of the petitioner, the "Montrose" and the "Hooper," and were lost off the Jersey Coast on March tenth, in an easterly gale. The cargo owners sued the barges under the contracts of carriage; the owner of the barges sued the tugs under the towing contract, both for its own loss and as bailee of the cargoes; the owner of the tug filed a petition to limit its liability. All the suits were joined and heard together, and the judge found that all the vessels were unseaworthy; the tugs, because they did not carry radio receiving sets by which they could have seasonably got warnings of a change in the weather which should have caused them to seek shelter in the Delaware Breakwater en route. He therefore entered an interlocutory decree holding each tug and barge jointly liable to each cargo owner, and each tug for half damages for the loss of its barge. The petitioner appealed, and the barge owner appealed and filed assignments of error.

Each tug had three ocean going coal barges in tow, the lost barge being at the end. The "Montrose," which had the No. 17, took an outside course; the "Hooper" with the No. 30, inside. The weather was fair without ominous symptoms, as the tows passed the Delaware Breakwater about midnight of March eighth, and the barges did not get into serious trouble until they were about opposite Atlantic City some sixty or seventy miles to the north. The wind began to freshen in the morning of the ninth and rose to a gale before noon; by afternoon the second barge of the Hooper's tow was out of hand and signalled the tug, which found that not only this barge needed help, but that the No. 30 was aleak. Both barges anchored and the crew of the No. 30 rode out the storm until the afternoon of the tenth, when she sank, her crew having been meanwhile taken off. The No. 17 sprang a leak about the same time; she too anchored at the Montrose's command and sank on the next morning after her crew also had been rescued. The cargoes and the tugs maintain that the barges were not fit for their service; the cargoes and the barges that the tugs should have gone into the Delaware Breakwater, and besides, did not handle their tows properly.

* * *

[The court summarized extensive evidence that the barges were unseaworthy and that had the tugs used radios to receive weather broadcasts, they would not have put to sea.] To be sure the barges would, as we have said, probably have withstood the gale, had they been well found; but a master is not justified in putting his tow to every test which she will survive, if she be fit. There is a zone in which proper caution will avoid putting her capacity to the proof; a coefficient of prudence that he should not disregard. Taking the situation as a whole, it seems to us that these masters would have taken undue chances, had they got the broadcasts.

They did not, because their private radio receiving sets, which were on board, were not in working order. These belonged to them personally, and were partly a toy, partly a part of the equipment, but neither furnished by the owner, nor supervised by it. It is not fair to say that there was a general custom among coastwise carriers so to equip their tugs. One line alone did it; as for the rest, they relied upon their crews, so far as they can be said to have relied at all. An adequate receiving set suitable for a coastwise tug can now be got at small cost and is reasonably reliable if kept up; obviously it is a source of great protection to their tows. Twice every day they can receive these predictions, based upon the widest possible information, available to every vessel within two or three hundred miles and more. Such a set is the ears of the tug to catch the spoken word, just as the master's binoculars are her eyes to see a storm signal ashore. Whatever may be said as to other vessels, tugs towing heavy coal laden barges, strung out for half a mile, have little power to manœuvre, and do not, as this case proves, expose themselves to weather which would not turn back stauncher craft. They can have at hand protection against dangers of which they can learn in no other way.

Is it then a final answer that the business had not yet generally adopted receiving sets? There are, no doubt, cases where courts seem to make the general practice of the calling the standard of proper diligence. . . . Indeed in most cases reasonable prudence is in fact common prudence; but strictly it is never its measure; a whole calling may have unduly lagged in the adoption of new and available devices. It never may set its own tests, however persuasive be its usages. Courts must in the end say what is required; there are precautions so imperative that even their universal disregard will not excuse their omission. But here there was no custom at all as to receiving sets; some had them, some did not; the most that can be urged is that they had not yet become general. Certainly in such a case we need not pause; when some have thought a device necessary, at least we may say that they were right, and the others too slack. . . . We hold the tugs liable therefore because, had they been properly equipped, they would have got the Arlington reports. The injury was a direct consequence of this unseaworthiness.

Decree affirmed.

Duty of Care The law does not impose on us a duty to care for every person. If the rule were otherwise, we would all, in this interdependent world, be our brothers' keepers, constantly unsure whether any action we took might subject us to liability for its effect on someone else. The law copes with this difficulty by limiting the number of people toward whom we owe a duty to be careful.

In general, the law imposes no obligation to act in a situation to which we are strangers. We may pass the drowning child without risking a lawsuit. (See p. 6. However, several foreign countries impose a duty to rescue strangers. And in the United States, there may be a duty to strangers in certain circumstances. See p. 153.) But if we do act, then the law requires us to act carefully.

The law of negligence requires us to behave with due regard for the foreseeable consequences of our actions in order to avoid unreasonable risks of injury. During the course of the twentieth century, the courts have constantly expanded the notion of "**foreseeability**," so that today many more people are held to be within the zone of injury than was once the case. For example, it was once believed that a manufacturer or supplier owed a duty of care only to immediate purchasers, not to others who might use the product or to whom the product might be resold. This limitation was known as the rule of "privity." End users who were not immediate purchasers were said not to be "in privity" with the supplier or manufacturer. In 1916, Judge Benjamin N. Cardozo, then on the New York Court of Appeals, penned an opinion in a celebrated case that exploded the theory of privity, though it would take half a century before the last state (Mississippi in 1966) would fall in line.

MACPHERSON v. BUICK MOTOR CO.
217 N.Y. 382, 111 N.E. 1050 (1916)

CARDOZO, J. The defendant is a manufacturer of automobiles. It sold an automobile to a retail dealer. The retail dealer resold to the plaintiff. While the plaintiff was in the car it suddenly collapsed. He was thrown out and injured. One of the wheels was made of defective wood, and its spokes crumbled into fragments. The wheel was not made by the defendant; it was bought from another manufacturer. There is evidence, however, that its defects could have been discovered by reasonable inspection, and that inspection was omitted. There is no claim that the defendant knew of the defect and willfully concealed it. . . . The charge is one, not of fraud, but of negligence. The question to be determined is whether the defendant owed a duty of care and vigilance to any one but the immediate purchaser.

The foundations of this branch of the law, at least in this state, were laid in Thomas v. Winchester, 6 N.Y. 397, 57 Am. Dec. 455. A poison was falsely labeled. The sale was made to a druggist, who in turn sold to a customer. The customer recovered damages from the seller who affixed the label. "The defendant's negligence," it was said, "put human life in imminent danger." A poison, falsely labeled, is likely to injure any one who gets it. Because the danger is to be foreseen, there is a duty to avoid the injury.

* * *

We hold, then, that the principle of Thomas v. Winchester is not limited to poisons, explosives, and things of like nature, to things which in their normal operation are implements of destruction. If the nature of a thing is such that it is reasonably certain to place life and limb in peril when negligently made, it is then a thing of danger. Its nature gives warning of the consequences to be expected. If to the element of danger there is added knowledge that the thing will be used by persons other than the purchaser, and used without new tests, then, irrespective of contract, the manufacturer of this thing of danger is under a duty to make it carefully.

* * *

. . . In such circumstances, the presence of a known danger, attendant upon a known use, makes vigilance a duty. We have put aside the notion that the duty to safeguard life and limb, when the consequences of negligence may be foreseen, grows out of contract and nothing else. We have put the source of the obligation where it ought to be. We have put its source in the law.

From this survey of the decisions, there thus emerges a definition of the duty of a manufacturer which enables us to measure this defendant's liability. Beyond all question, the nature of an automobile gives warning of probable danger if its construction is defective. This automobile was designed to go 50 miles an hour. Unless its wheels were sound and strong, injury was almost certain. It was as much a thing of danger as a defective engine for a railroad. The defendant knew the danger. It knew also that the car would be used by persons other than the buyer. This was apparent from its size; there were seats for three persons. It was apparent also from the fact that the buyer was a dealer in cars, who bought to resell. The maker of this car supplied it for the use of purchasers from the dealer just as plainly as the contractor in Devlin v. Smith supplied the scaffold for use by the servants of the owner. The dealer was indeed the one person of whom it might be said with some approach to certainty that by him the car would not be used. Yet the defendant would have us say that he was the one person whom it was under a legal duty to protect. The law does not lead us to so inconsequent a conclusion. Precedents drawn from the days of travel by stagecoach do not fit the conditions of travel to-day. The principle that the danger must be imminent does not change, but the things subject to the principle do change. They are whatever the needs of life in a developing civilization require them to be.

* * *

We think the defendant was not absolved from a duty of inspection because it bought the wheels from a reputable manufacturer. It was not merely a dealer in automobiles. It was a manufacturer of automobiles. It was responsible for the finished product. It was not at liberty to put the finished product on the market without subjecting the component parts to ordinary and simple tests. Under the charge of the trial judge nothing more was required of it. The obligation to inspect must vary with the nature of the thing to be inspected. The more probable the danger the greater the need of caution.

* * *

The judgment should be affirmed, with costs.

Determining to whom a duty of care is owed is a vexing problem. Physicians, for example, are bound by principles of medical ethics to respect the confidences of their patients. Suppose a patient tells a psychiatrist that he intends to kill his girlfriend. Does the physician then have a higher legal duty to warn the prospective victim? The California Supreme Court has said yes. [Tarasoff v. Regents of University of California, 551 P.2d 334 (Cal. 1976)] Hotel security cases present another difficult duty-of-care issue. Is a hotel obligated to keep its guests free from physical attack by intruders? In the well-publicized case involving singer Connie Francis (see Box 9-2), the answer again was yes.

Causation "For want of a nail, the kingdom was lost," as the old saying has it. Virtually any cause of an injury can be traced to some preceding cause. The problem for the law is to know when to draw the line between causes that are immediate and causes too remote for liability reasonably to be assigned to them. In tort theory, the legal phrase for the connection between the act complained of and the resulting injury is **proximate cause.** Like many legal phrases, proximate cause is virtually empty of content; it means nothing more than the boundary beyond which a person will not be held legally liable for the remote consequences of his actions. Nevertheless, proximate cause has been the subject of earnest analysis in probably thousands of cases. One generally useful rule is the *sine qua non* or "but for" test: if an event would not have occurred but for the defendant's conduct, then the defendant is the cause of the event. This rule holds even though there are contributing causes. The person who is the substantial cause of harm cannot avoid liability by showing that other causes contributed to either the fact or the extent of the injury.

Suppose that the person who was injured was not one whom the reasonable man could have expected to be harmed. Such a situation was presented in one of the most famous American tort cases, which was, like the *MacPherson* case, also decided by Judge Cardozo. Although Judge Cardozo persuaded four of his seven brethren to side with his position, the closeness of the case demonstrates the difficulty that unforeseeable consequences and unforeseeable plaintiffs present. The usual solution is for judges to keep hands off and put the matter in the laps of juries.

PALSGRAF v. LONG ISLAND R.R.
248 N.Y. 339, 162 N.E. 99 (1928)

CARDOZO, C. J. Plaintiff was standing on a platform of defendant's railroad after buying a ticket to go to Rockaway Beach. A train stopped at the station, bound for another place. Two men ran forward to catch it. One of the men reached the platform of the car without mishap, though the train was already moving. The other man, carrying a package, jumped aboard the car, but seemed unsteady as if about to fall. A guard on the car, who had held the door open, reached forward to help him in, and another guard on the platform pushed him from behind. In this act, the package was dislodged, and fell upon the rails. It was a package of small size, about fifteen inches long, and was covered by a newspaper. In fact it contained fireworks, but there was nothing in its appearance to give notice of its contents. The fireworks when they fell exploded. The shock of the explosion threw down some scales at the other end of the platform many feet away. The scales struck the plaintiff, causing injuries for which she sues.

The conduct of the defendant's guard, if a wrong in its relation to the holder of the package, was not a wrong in its relation to the plaintiff, standing far away. Relatively to her it was not negligence at all. Nothing in the situation gave notice that the falling package had in it the potency of peril to persons thus removed. Negligence is not actionable unless it involves the invasion of a legally protected interest, the violation of a right. "Proof of negligence in the air, so to speak, will not do." . . . If no hazard was apparent to the eye of ordinary vigilance, an act innocent and harmless, at least to outward seeming, with reference to her, did not take to itself the quality of a tort because it happened to be a wrong, though apparently not one involving the risk of bodily insecurity, with reference to some one else. . . . The plaintiff sues in her own right for a wrong personal to her, and not as the vicarious beneficiary of a breach of duty to another.

A different conclusion will involve us, and swiftly too, in a maze of contradictions. A guard stumbles over a package which has been left upon a platform. It seems to be a bundle of newspapers. It turns out to be a can of dynamite. To the eye of ordinary vigilance, the bundle is abandoned waste, which may be kicked or trod on with impunity. Is a passenger at the other end of the platform protected by the law against the unsuspected hazard concealed beneath the waste? If not, is the result to be any different, so far as the distant passenger is concerned, when the guard stumbles over a valise which a truckman or a porter had left upon the walk? . . . The orbit of the danger as disclosed to the eye of reasonable vigilance would be the orbit of the duty. One who jostles one's neighbor in a crowd does not invade the rights of others standing at the outer fringe when the unintended contact casts a bomb upon the ground. The wrongdoer as to them is the man who carries the bomb, not the one who explodes it without suspicion of the danger. Life will have to be made over, and human nature transformed, before prevision so extravagant can be accepted as the norm of conduct, the customary standard to which behavior must conform.

The argument for the plaintiff is built upon the shifting meanings of such words as "wrong" and "wrongful," and shares their instability. What the plaintiff must show is "a wrong" to herself; i.e., a

Box 9-2 Duty to Protect Others?

Jury Awards Connie Francis $2.5 Million in Westbury Rape
By Max H. Seigel

A jury of six men awarded the singer Connie Francis $2.5 million yesterday as compensation for her rape in a Howard Johnson Motel in Westbury, L.I., on Nov. 8, 1974. Local court experts described it as one of the largest awards ever made in a rape case.

Miss Francis had contended during a month-long trial in Federal Court in Brooklyn that Howard Johnson Motor Lodges Inc. was responsible for the attack on her because it had failed to provide "a safe and secure room."

The jury also awarded Miss Francis's husband, Joseph Garzilli, $150,000 for the loss of his wife's services.

When the jury verdict was announced in court, Miss Francis, who was sitting beside her husband holding hands, burst into tears.

LETTERS RECEIVED

"What [we] went through here," Miss Francis declared a few moments later, "was not easy. But if what we did here could save one girl, it was worth it."

Miss Francis said she had received letters from other women who had suffered assaults in motels all over the country.

Judge Thomas C. Platt, who presided over the trial, brought it more than normal publicity during its first week by barring both the press and public from the courtroom at the request of lawyers for both sides. But two of the reporters covering the trial sued, and the United States Court of Appeals for the Second Circuit overturned the judge's decision.

Miss Francis, who served as the major witness in her own behalf, testified for six days. She told how, when she was asleep in her motel room, at 4 A.M. she was assaulted by a man with a knife.

Following the attack, Miss Francis was hospitalized for four days. And she told the court, she relived the experience in recurring nightmares.

The intruder gained entry into her room, Miss Francis said, through a faulty sliding door. A police officer, who testified at the trial, said that when the sliding doors were in a locked position, they could be opened from the outside simply by a little jiggling. The officer also testified that in 1974 there had been four burglaries through sliding glass doors leading from a patio.

While not conceding that the locks had been faulty, the management of the motel had testified that it had ordered new and better locks, but that their arrival had been delayed by a United Parcel strike.

Miss Francis said yesterday that she had no plans to take up that part of her career that would

violation of her own right, and not merely a wrong to someone else, nor conduct "wrongful" because unsocial, but not "a wrong" to any one. We are told that one who drives at reckless speed through a crowded city street is guilty of a negligent act and therefore of a wrongful one, irrespective of the consequences. Negligent the act is, and wrongful in the sense that it is unsocial, but wrongful and unsocial in relation to other travelers, only because the eye of vigilance perceives the risk of damage. If the same act were to be committed on a speedway or a race course, it would lose its wrongful quality. The risk reasonably to be perceived defines the duty to be obeyed, and risk imports relation; it is risk to another or to others within the range of apprehension. This does not mean, of course, that one who launches a destructive force is always relieved of liability, if the force, though known to be destructive, pursues an unexpected path. . . . Some acts, such as shooting are so imminently dangerous to any one who may come within reach of the missile however unexpectedly, as to impose a duty of preplace her before crowds or cause her to sleep in motels or hotels. She added that she might do some work making records.

She said: "I never received so much as a note from Mr. Howard B. Johnson saying 'We're sorry it happened.' After being shocked, I was very angry. Today, I am pleased."

Thomas S. Kirk, the lawyer representing the motel, moved to have the verdict set aside as excessive. Judge Platt said he would reserve decision pending the receipt of written briefs. He asked that these be submitted by July 12.

Judge Upholds Award by Jury to Connie Francis in L.I. Rape

A Federal judge in Brooklyn upheld yesterday a jury award of $2.5 million to Connie Francis, the singer, to compensate for her rape in a Long Island motel on Nov. 8, 1974.

But the judge, Thomas C. Platt, ruled that the $150,000 awarded Joseph Garzilli, Miss Francis's husband, was excessive and that his compensation should be cut to $25,000.

The damages were awarded the singer and her husband after Miss Francis was raped in Howard Johnson's Motel Lodge in Westbury by an intruder who was said to have easily gained access to her room through an improperly locked sliding glass door.

Following the assault, the 37-year-old singer testified, she was afraid to resume her lucrative career, which had brought her earnings of $325,000 in 1969 and $287,000 in 1970.

Thomas Kirk, lawyer for Howard Johnson's Motor Lodge, said he would appeal the judge's ruling.

Connie Francis, the entertainer, who last July was awarded a $2.5 million jury verdict as compensation after she was raped in a Howard Johnson motel in Westbury, L.I. on Nov. 8, 1974, has settled out of court with the motel chain for $1,475,000. Richard Frank, an attorney for Miss Francis, said that the verdict had been on appeal to the Federal Court of Appeals and that he and Miss Francis had been concerned that it would be set aside. The settlement, believed to be one of the highest ever made in a rape case, is considered "compensation for an injury" under the law—not income—and is therefore not subject to taxation. Miss Francis's original suit charged that the motel had failed to provide her with a safe and secure room.

Source: *New York Times*, July 2, 1976; September 21, 1976; February 23, 1977

vision not far from that of an insurer. Even to-day, and much oftener in earlier stages of the law, one acts sometimes at one's peril. . . . These cases aside, wrong is defined in terms of the natural or probable, at least when unintentional. . . .

Negligence, like risk, is thus a term of relation. Negligence in the abstract, apart from things related, is surely not a tort, if indeed it is understandable at all. . . . One who seeks redress at law does not make out a cause of action by showing without more that there has been damage to his person. If the harm was not willful, he must show that the act as to him had possibilities of danger so many and apparent as to entitle him to be protected against the doing of it though the harm was unintended.

* * *

The judgment of the Appellate Division and that of the Trial Term should be reversed, and the complaint dismissed, with costs in all courts.

Damages For a plaintiff to win a tort case, he must allege and prove that he was injured. The fear that he might be injured in the future is not a sufficient basis for a suit. This rule has proved troublesome in medical malpractice and industrial disease cases. A doctor's negligent act or a company's negligent exposure of a worker to some form of contamination might not become manifest in the body for years. In the meantime, the tort statute of limitations might have run out, barring the victim from suing at all. An increasing number of courts have eased the plaintiff's predicament by ruling that the statute of limitations does not begin to run until the victim discovers that he has been injured or contracted a disease.

The law allows an exception to the general rule that damages must be shown when the plaintiff stands in danger of immediate injury from a hazardous activity. If you discover your neighbor experimenting with explosives in his basement, you could bring suit to enjoin him from further experimentation, even though he has not yet blown up his house—and yours.

Problems of Proof

The plaintiff in a tort suit, as in any other, has the burden of proving his allegations. He must show that the defendant took the actions complained of as negligent, demonstrate the circumstances that make the actions negligent, and prove the occurrence and extent of injury. Factual issues are for the jury to resolve. Since it is frequently difficult to make out the requisite proof, the law allows certain presumptions and rules of evidence that ease the plaintiff's task, on the ground that without them substantial injustice would be done.

One important rule goes by the Latin phrase *res ipsa loquitur,* meaning "the thing speaks for itself." The best evidence is always the most direct evidence: an eyewitness account of the acts in question. But eyewitnesses are often unavailable, and in any event they frequently cannot testify directly to the reasonableness of someone's conduct, which inevitably can only be inferred from the circumstances. In many cases, therefore, **circumstantial evidence** (evidence that is indirect) will be the only evidence or will constitute the bulk of the evidence. Circumstantial evidence can often be quite telling: though no one saw anyone leave the building, muddy footprints tracing a path along the sidewalk are fairly conclusive. *Res ipsa loquitur* is a rule of circumstantial evidence that permits the jury to draw an inference of negligence. A common statement of the rule is the following:

> There must be reasonable evidence of negligence; but where the thing is shown to be under the management of the defendant or his servants, and the accident is such as in the ordinary course of things does not happen if those who have the management use proper care, it affords reasonable evidence, in the absence of explanation by the defendants, that the accident arose from want of care.

[Scott v. London & St. Katherine Docks Co., 3 H. & C. 596, 159 Eng.Rep. 665 (Q.B. 1865)]

If a barrel of flour rolls out of a factory window and hits someone, or a soda bottle explodes, or an airplane crashes, courts in every state permit juries to conclude, in the absence of contrary explanations by the defendants, that there was negligence. The plaintiff is not put to the impossible task of explaining precisely how the accident occurred. A defendant can always offer evidence that he acted reasonably—for example, that the flour barrel was securely fastened and that a bolt of lightning, for which he was not responsible, broke its bands, causing it to roll out the window. But testimony by the factory employees that they secured the barrel, in the absence of any further explanation, will not usually serve to rebut the inference.

Excuses

That the defendant was negligent does not conclude the inquiry or automatically entitle the plaintiff to a judgment. Tort law provides the defendant with several excuses, some of which are discussed briefly in this section.

Contributory and Comparative Negligence Under an old common law rule, it was a complete defense to show that the plaintiff in a negligence suit was himself negligent. Even if the plaintiff was only mildly negligent, most of the fault being chargeable to the defendant, the court would dismiss the suit if the plaintiff's conduct contributed to his injury. In some states today, this rule of **contributory negligence** continues to hold. Although referred to as negligence, the rule encompasses a narrower form than that with which the defendant is charged, because the plaintiff's only error in such cases is in being less careful of himself than he might have been, whereas the defendant is charged with conduct careless toward others. This rule was so manifestly unjust in many cases that most states, either by statute or judicial decision, have substituted for it the rule of **comparative negligence.** Under the rule of comparative negligence, damages are apportioned according to defendant's degree of culpability. If the plaintiff has sustained a $10,000 injury and is 20 percent responsible, the defendant will be liable for $8,000 in damages.

Assumption of Risk Assumption of risk is to defendants what *res ipsa loquitur* is to plaintiffs—a doctrine making it easier to win a case given the difficulties of proving states of mind and facts peculiarly within the knowledge of one person. Risk of injury pervades the modern world, and plaintiffs should not win a lawsuit simply because they took a risk and lost. The law provides, therefore, that when a person knowingly takes a risk he must suffer the consequences.

The **assumption of risk** doctrine comes up in three ways. The plaintiff may have formally agreed with the defendant before entering a risky situation that he will relieve the defendant of liability should injury occur. ("You can borrow my car if you agree not to sue me if the brakes fail; they're worn and I haven't had a chance to replace them.") Or the plaintiff may have entered into a relationship with the defendant knowing that the defendant is not in a position to protect him from known risks (the fan who is hit by a line drive in a ball park). Or the plaintiff may act in the face of a risky situation known in advance to have been created by the defendant's negligence (failure to leave, while there was an opportunity to do so, an automobile when the driver is known to be drunk).

The difficulty in many cases is to determine the dividing line between subjectivity and objectivity. If the plaintiff had no actual knowledge of the risk, he cannot be held to have assumed it. On the other hand, it is easy to claim that you did not appreciate the danger, and the courts will apply an objective standard of community knowledge (a "but you should have known" test) in many situations. When the plaintiff has no real alternative, however, assumption of risk fails as a defense (for example, a landlord who negligently fails to light the exit to the street cannot claim that his tenants assumed the risk of using it).

At the turn of the century, courts applied assumption of risk in industrial cases to bar relief to workers injured on the job. They were said to assume the risk of dangerous conditions or equipment. This rule has been abolished by workers' compensation statutes in most states.

Sovereign Immunity It is a peculiarity of American common law that the government is held to be immune from suit on the ground that the "sovereign," the source of law, cannot be sued without its consent. If this theory made metaphorical sense in England, which for centuries suffered a monarch who did make law, it never made sense in the United States. Nevertheless, the doctrine was imported. As we saw in Chapter 1, many states have abolished sovereign immunity either by statute or by judicial decision. In the Federal Tort Claims Act, Congress has waived sovereign immunity for many classes of torts committed by federal agents.

Act of God Technically, the rule that one is not responsible for an "act of God," or *force majeure,* as it is sometimes called, is not an excuse but a defense premised on a lack of causation. If a force of nature caused the harm, then the defendant was not negligent in the first place. A marina, obligated to look after boats moored at its dock, is not liable if a sudden and fierce storm against which no precaution was possible destroys someone's vessel. However, if it is foreseeable that harm will flow from a negligent condition triggered by a natural event, then there is liability. For example, a work crew failed to remove residue explosive gas from an oil barge. Lightning hit the barge, exploded the gas, and injured several workmen. The plaintiff recovered damages against the company because the negligence consisted in the failure to guard against any one of a number of chance occurrences that could ignite the gas. [Johnson v. Kosmos Portland Cement Co., 64 F.2d 193 (6th Cir. 1933)]

Imputed Negligence

Liability for negligent acts does not always end with the one who was negligent. Under certain circumstances, the liability is imputed to others. For example, an employer is responsible for the negligence of his employees if they were acting in the scope of employment. This rule of **vicarious liability** is often called *respondeat superior,* meaning that the higher authority must respond to claims brought against one of its agents. *Respondeat superior* is not limited to the employment relationship but extends to a number of other agency relationships as well.

Legislatures in many states have enacted laws that make people vicariously liable for acts of certain people with whom they have a relationship, though not necessarily one of agency. It is common, for example, for the owner of an automobile to be liable for the negligence of one to whom the owner lends the car. So-called "dram shop" statutes place liability on bar and tavern owners and others who serve too much alcohol to one who in an intoxicated state later causes injury to others. In these situations, although the injurious act of the drinker stemmed from negligence, the one whom the law holds vicariously liable (the bartender) is not himself necessarily negligent—the law is holding him *strictly liable,* and to this concept we now turn.

Strict Liability

To this point we have considered principles of liability that in some sense depend upon the "fault" of the tortfeasor. This fault is not synonymous with moral blame. Aside from acts intended to harm, the fault lies in a failure to live up to a standard of reasonableness or due care. But this is not the only basis for tort liability. Innocent mistakes can be a sufficient basis. One who unknowingly trespasses on another's property, for example, is liable for the damage that he does, even if he has a reasonable belief that the land is his. And it has long been held that one who engages in "ultrahazardous" (or sometimes just "hazardous") activities is liable for damage that he causes, even though he has taken every possible precaution to avoid harm to someone else. Likewise, the owner of animals that escape from their homes and do mischief elsewhere is often liable, even if the reason for their escape was beyond the power of the owner to stop (for example, a fire started by lightning that burns open a barn door). In such cases, the courts invoke the principle of **strict liability** or, as it is sometimes called, liability without fault. The reason for the rule is explained in the following case.

SPANO v. PERINI CORP.
25 N.Y.2d 11, 250 N.E.2d 31 (1969)

CHIEF JUDGE FULD. The principal question posed on this appeal is whether a person who has sustained property damage caused by blasting on nearby property can maintain an action for damages without a showing that the blaster was negligent. Since 1893, it has been the law of this State that proof of negligence was required unless the blast was accompanied by an actual physical invasion of the damaged property—for example, by rocks or other material being cast upon the premises. We are now asked to reconsider that rule.

The plaintiff Spano is the owner of a garage in Brooklyn which was wrecked by a blast occurring on November 27, 1962. There was then in that garage, for repairs, an automobile owned by the plaintiff Davis which he also claims was damaged by the blasting. Each of the plaintiffs brought suit against the two defendants who, as joint venturers, were engaged in constructing a tunnel in the vicinity pursuant to a contract with the City of New York. The two cases were tried together, without a jury, in the Civil Court of the City of New York, New York County, and judgments were rendered in favor of the plaintiffs. The judgments were reversed by the Appellate Term and the Appellate Division affirmed that order, granting leave to appeal to this court.

It is undisputed that, on the day in question (November 27, 1962), the defendants had set off a total of 194 sticks of dynamite at a construction site which was only 125 feet away from the damaged premises. Although both plaintiffs alleged negligence in their complaints, no attempt was made to show that the defendants had failed to exercise reasonable care or to take necessary precautions when they were blasting. Instead, they chose to rely, upon the trial, solely on the principle of absolute liability either on a tort theory or on the basis of their being third-party beneficiaries of the defendants' contract with the city. At the close of the plaintiff Spano's case, when defendants' attorney moved to dismiss the action on the ground, among others, that no negligence had been proved, the trial judge expressed the view that the defendants could be held liable even though they were not shown to have been careless. The case then proceeded, with evidence being introduced solely on the question of damages and proximate cause. Following the trial, the court awarded damages of some $4,400 to Spano and of $329 to Davis.

On appeal, a divided Appellate Term reversed that judgment, declaring that it deemed itself concluded by the established rule in this State requiring proof of negligence. . . .

The Appellate Division affirmed; it called attention to a decision in the Third Department in which the court observed that "[i]f [the established rule] is to be overruled, 'the announcement thereof should come from the authoritative source and not in the form of interpretation or prediction by an intermediate appellate court.' "

In our view, the time has come for this court to make that "announcement" and declare that one who engages in blasting must assume responsibility, and be liable without fault, for any injury he causes to neighboring property.

The concept of absolute liability in blasting cases is hardly a novel one. The overwhelming majority of American jurisdictions have adopted such a rule. . . .

We need not rely solely, however, upon out-of-state decisions in order to attain our result. Not only has the rationale of the [established rule] been overwhelmingly rejected elsewhere but it appears to be fundamentally inconsistent with earlier cases in our own court which had held . . . that a party was absolutely liable for damages to neighboring property caused by explosions.

* * *

. . . [I]t is clear that the court, in the earlier cases, was not concerned with the particular manner by which the damage was caused but by the simple fact that any explosion in a built-up area was likely to cause damage.

* * *

Such reasoning should, we venture, have led to the conclusion that the *intentional* setting off of explosives—that is, blasting—in an area in which it was likely to cause harm to neighboring property similarly results in absolute liability. However, the court [later] rejected such an extension of the rule for the reason that "[t]o exclude the defendant from blasting to adapt its lot to the contemplated uses, at the instance of the plaintiff, would not be a compromise between conflicting rights, but an extinguishment of the right of the one for the benefit of the other." The court expanded on this by stating, "This sacrifice, we think, the law does not exact. Public policy is promoted by the building up of towns and cities and the improvement of property. Any unnecessary restraint on freedom of action of a property owner hinders this."

This rationale cannot withstand analysis. . . . The question, in other words, was not *whether* it was lawful or proper to engage in blasting but *who* should bear the cost of any resulting damage—the person who engaged in the dangerous activity or the innocent neighbor injured thereby. Viewed in such a light, it clearly appears that [the 1893 case] was wrongly decided and should be forthrightly overruled.

* * *

The order appealed from should be reversed, with costs, and the matter remitted to the Appellate Division for further proceedings in accordance with this opinion.

For the student of business law, the principle of strict liability has had the greatest impact in the area of product liability—that is, the liability of manufacturers and suppliers for harm caused by defective products. The law of product liability has been changing rapidly. As recently as the early 1960s, liability was based largely on negligence. Today in most states strict liability has made deep inroads. Because of its signal importance to business, we will explore it separately in some detail (Chapter 10).

Note on Absolute Liability

Some courts and commentators use the terms "strict liability" and "absolute liability" interchangeably. This is unfortunate, because there is a distinction that the terms can usefully be made to serve. In most cases of strict liability, as the term has been used here, the defendant can be seen to have some responsibility for the harm that occurred, at least in the sense that something originally under his control went awry. By contrast, there are many kinds of injury that are truly accidental, or result from the plaintiff's negligence, or are acts of God. For example, some people are allergic to pure aspirin. To hold the manufacturer liable for the pains and costs of those who are allergic would be to impose a standard of *absolute* liability. Absolute liability is rare. Two significant examples are no-fault automobile insurance and the workers' compensation system (Chapter 13). In the latter, an employer typically pays into a compensation fund (or buys insurance) in order to insure his workers against injury on the job. Any work-related injury entitles the employee to compensation benefits from the fund. In return for this more or less automatic compensation (payments are made after papers are submitted to an administrative board; lawsuits need not be filed), workers are barred from suing their employers, even if the accident happened because of the employer's negligence.

Injury to Economic Interests

Tort law is not confined to tangible physical harm to person or property. It also governs interference with and injury to various intangible interests. In this section, and the two that follow, we consider such torts.

Unfair Competition

The freedom to compete is the touchstone of the American economic system. Although a myriad of public regulations, discussed at some length in this book, restrict or prohibit some types of economic decisions (for example, use of processes that pollute, statements made or not made in selling securities) ordinarily one business has no private right to prevent another from coming into its territory and competing head on. Centuries ago in England, it was a tort for a retailer to "steal" another retailer's customers; today in America, competition is open and wide.

Despite this general rule, not every form of competition is legally acceptable. In particular, a cluster of related acts known as "unfair competition" has led to a sizable body of tort law governing the use of deception in promoting one's products. The two main forms are **passing off** and **misappropriation.**

Passing Off The tort of passing off, sometimes known as "palming off," occurs when the seller falsely represents that his product is that of someone else. In a modern economy, passing off is typically accomplished by imitating someone else's trademark (p. 662), though it is sufficient for the tort to occur if a customer asks for goods supplied by one manufacturer and the seller secretly substitutes the goods of another, even if the goods are identical (for example, if you ask for Brand X aspirin and are given Brand Y aspirin).

The central feature of passing off is confusion of the customer. As long as the customer is not misled about the origin of a product, then it cannot be said to have been passed off (although the seller may have separately violated the trademark laws). Much of the common law of unfair competition has been absorbed by federal trademark law (Chapter 24), and so the rules governing passing off and the use of similar product names and marks has taken on a national character, at least for goods that circulate across state lines.

Misappropriation Related to passing off, misappropriation is the imitation of an idea, design, or product, without claiming that it in fact comes from someone else. For example, suppose a baker achieved great success with a chocolate-chip cookie imaginatively shaped like a plate of spaghetti. May another baker, using her own name, sell a similar cookie? Does an actor who has a famous gesture have a right to prevent another actor from using the same gesture on camera? Does a publisher who produces a list of baseball pitchers, together with their statistics, arranged in a certain way, have a case against another publisher who appropriates the same arrangement? The answers are not easy to give, because the common law of misappropriation runs into the federal law governing copyrights and patents (Chapter 24). Because federal law preempts state law in the event of a conflict, the Supreme Court has held that when a particular product design is not copyrighted or patented, another manufacturer is free to imitate it, as long as the second user does not try to pass it off as her own. [Sears, Roebuck & Co. v. Stiffel Co., 376 U.S. 225 (1964)] Modern decisions have tended to weaken the older common law of misappropriation, leaving wide (though not unfettered) scope to the use and circulation of ideas, designs, and styles that are not otherwise protected.

Interference with Contractual Relations

Since a contract confers benefits on the parties, it is looked upon as a property right. One who interferes with that right by inducing one of the parties to break the contract has committed a tort.

By and large, the courts insist that the defendant must have intended to interfere with the contract. This tort is not based on strict liability or even, generally, on negligence. Thus, a manufacturer who contracts with a shipper to carry her goods cannot maintain a suit against a third party who negligently sinks the barge on which the goods were to be carried.

Not every act that results in a breach of contract is necessarily tortious. The courts have concluded that to protect your own legitimate interests you might have to take actions that lead to a breach of someone else's contract—for example, that of a fellow employee. Thus an employee might point out to her corporate employer the dangers in continuing the employ of another worker who is frequently drunk on the job. But the courts are leery of such justifications when uttered by competitors. Suppose someone you wish to hire is under contract to a competitor. May you hire her away? Since most employment contracts are terminable "at will," the courts generally hold that inducing someone to leave her employment for that of a competitor is not a tort. The original employer has only an expectancy that his employee will continue to work for him. Suppose the employee is also under contract not to reveal her employer's trade secrets. As a competitor, you offer to pay the employee for those secrets. You would then be liable for inducing the employee to breach her contract.

Interfering with contractual relations is not the only type of economic harm for which the law of torts provides a remedy. Numerous other acts that interfere with economic advantage can lead to damage awards. These include disparaging the quality of a plaintiff's goods or title to property, intentionally lying about a plaintiff (stating, for example, that she has gone out of business when in fact she has not), and maliciously exhorting customers to cease patronage of a competitor.

Unjustifiable Litigation

Lawsuits, whether civil or criminal, are easy to initiate, and they can be used by the unscrupulous to cause considerable annoyance, financial cost, and even loss of freedom. **Malicious prosecution** is the tort of causing someone to be prosecuted for a criminal act, knowing that there was no probable cause to believe that the plaintiff committed the crime. The plaintiff must show that the defendant acted with malice or with some purpose other than bringing the guilty to justice. A mere complaint to the authorities is insufficient to establish the tort, but any official proceeding will support the claim—for example, a warrant for the plaintiff's arrest. The criminal proceeding must terminate in the plaintiff's favor in order for his suit to be sustained.

A majority of American courts, though by no means all, permit a suit for wrongful civil proceedings. Civil litigation is usually costly and burdensome, and one who forces another to defend himself against baseless accusations should not be permitted to saddle the one he sues with the costs of defense. However, because, as a matter of public policy, litigation is favored as the means by which legal rights can be vindicated—indeed, the Supreme Court has even ruled that individuals have a constitutional right to litigate—the plaintiff must meet a heavy burden in proving his case. The mere dismissal of the original lawsuit against the plaintiff is not sufficient proof that the suit was unwarranted. The plaintiff in a suit for wrongful civil proceedings must show that the defendant (who was the plaintiff in the original suit) filed the action for an improper purpose and had no reasonable belief that his cause was legally or factually well grounded.

Libel and Slander

Defamation is injury to a person's good name or reputation. In general, if the harm is done through the spoken word—one person to another, by telephone, by radio or television—it is called **slander.** If the defamatory statement is published in written form, it is called **libel.**

Elements

The *Restatement (Second) of Torts* defines a defamatory communication as one that "so tends to harm the reputation of another as to lower him in the estimation of the community or to deter third persons from associating or dealing with him" (1976, Section 559).

A statement is not defamatory unless it is false. Truth is an absolute defense to a charge of libel or slander. Moreover, the statement must be "published"—that is, communicated to a third person. You cannot be libeled by one who sends you a letter full of false accusations and scurrilous statements about you, unless a third person opens it first (your secretary, perhaps). Any living person is capable of being defamed, but the dead are not. Corporations, partnerships, and other forms of associations can also be defamed, if the statements tend to injure their ability to do business or to garner contributions.

The statement must have reference to a particular person, but he need not be identified by name. A statement that "the company president is a crook" is defamatory, as is a statement that "the major network weathermen are imposters." The company president and the network weathermen could show that the words were aimed at them. But statements about large groups will not support an action for defamation (for example, "all doctors are butchers" is not defamatory of any particular doctor).

The law of defamation is largely built on strict liability. That a person did not intend to defame is ordinarily no excuse; a typographical error that converts a true statement into a false one in a newspaper, magazine, or corporate brochure can be sufficient to make out a case of libel. Even the exercise of due care is usually no excuse if the statement is in fact communicated. Repeating a libel is itself a libel; a libel cannot be justified by showing that you were quoting someone else.

Though a plaintiff may be able to prove that a statement was defamatory, he is not necessarily entitled to an award of damages. That is because the law contains a number of privileges that excuse the defamation.

Common Law Privileges

Absolute Privilege Statements made during the course of judicial proceedings are absolutely privileged, meaning that they cannot serve as the basis for a defamation suit. Accurate accounts of judicial or other proceedings are absolutely privileged; a newspaper, for example, may pass on the slanderous utterings of a judge in court. "Judicial" is broadly construed to include most proceedings of administrative bodies of the government. The Constitution exempts members of Congress from suits for libel or slander for any statements made in connection with legislative business. The courts have constructed a similar privilege for many executive branch officials.

Qualified Privilege Absolute privileges pertain to those in the public sector. A narrower privilege exists for private citizens. In general, a statement that would otherwise be actionable is held to be justified if made "in a reasonable manner and for a proper purpose" (Prosser, 1971, p. 786). Thus you may warn a friend to beware of dealing with a third person, and if you had reason to believe that what you said was true, you are privileged to issue the warning, even though false. Likewise, an employee may warn an employer about the conduct or character of a fellow or prospective employee, and a parent may complain to a school board about the competence or conduct of a child's teacher. There is a line to be drawn, however, and a defendant with nothing but an idle interest in the matter (an "officious intermeddler") must take the risk that his information is wrong.

Constitutional Privileges

In 1964, the Supreme Court handed down its historic decision in *New York Times* v. *Sullivan* [376 U.S. 254 (1964)], holding that under the First Amendment a libel judgment brought by a public official against a newspaper cannot stand unless the plaintiff has shown "actual malice," which in turn was defined as "knowledge that [the statement] was false or with a reckless disregard of whether it was false or not." In subsequent cases, the Court extended the constitutional doctrine further, applying it not merely to government officials but to **"public figures"**—people who voluntarily place themselves in the public eye or who involuntarily find themselves the objects of public scrutiny. Whether a private person is or is not a public figure is a difficult question that has so far eluded rigorous definition and has been answered only from case to case. A chief executive officer of a private corporation ordinarily will be considered a private figure, unless he puts himself in the public eye—for example, by starring in the company's TV commercials.

Invasion of Privacy

The right of privacy—the right "to be let alone"—did not receive judicial recognition until the twentieth century, and its legal formulation is still evolving. In fact there is no single right of privacy. Courts and commentators have discerned at least four different types of interests: (1) the right to control the appropriation of your name and picture for commercial purposes; (2) the right to be free of intrusion on your "personal space" or seclusion; (3) freedom from public disclosure of embarrassing and intimate facts of your personal life; and (4) the right not to be presented in a "false light."

Appropriation

The earliest privacy interest to gain judicial recognition was appropriation of name or likeness: placing your photograph on a billboard or cereal box as a model, or using your name as endorsing a product or in the product name. A New York statute makes it a misdemeanor to use the name, portrait, or picture of any person for advertising purposes or for the purposes of trade (business) without first obtaining written consent. The law also permits the aggrieved person to sue for an injunction against continued use and to recover damages, including punitive damages. Because the publishing and advertising industries are concentrated heavily in New York, the statute plays an important part in advertising decisions made throughout the country. Deciding what "commercial" or "trade" purposes are is not always easy. Thus, a newsmagazine may use a baseball player's picture on its cover without first obtaining written permission, but a chocolate manufacturer could not put the player's picture on a candy wrapper without consent.

Intrusion

One form of intrusion upon a person's solitude—trespass—has long been actionable under common law. Physical invasion of home or other property is not a new tort. But in recent years, the notion of intrusion has been broadened considerably, to embrace such disparate acts as electronic eavesdropping or photographing in a private space without consent. (Photographing someone on a city street is not tortious, though subsequent use of the photograph could be.) The next case, involving attempts by the General Motors Corporation to investigate the life of one of its persistent critics, Ralph Nader, shows the direction in which the tort of intrusion on privacy is moving.

NADER v. GENERAL MOTORS CORP.
25 N.Y.2d 560, 255 N.E.2d 765 (1970)

CHIEF JUDGE FULD. On this appeal, taken by permission of the Appellate Division on a certified question, we are called upon to determine the reach of the tort of invasion of privacy as it exists under the law of the District of Columbia.

The complaint, in this action by Ralph Nader, pleads four causes of action against the appellant, General Motors Corporation, and three other defendants allegedly acting as its agents. The first two causes of action charge an invasion of privacy. . . . This appeal concerns only the legal sufficiency of the first two causes of action, which were upheld in the courts below as against the appellant's motion to dismiss.

The plaintiff, an author and lecturer on automotive safety, has, for some years, been an articulate and severe critic of General Motors' products from the standpoint of safety and design. According to the complaint—which, for present purposes, we must assume to be true—the appellant, having learned of the imminent publication of the plaintiff's book "Unsafe at Any Speed," decided to conduct a campaign of intimidation against him in order to "suppress plaintiff's criticism of and prevent his disclosure of information" about its products. To that end, the appellant authorized and directed the other defendants to engage in a series of activities which, the plaintiff claims in his first two causes of action, violated his right to privacy.

Specifically, the plaintiff alleges that the appellant's agents (1) conducted a series of interviews with acquaintances of the plaintiff, "questioning them about, and casting aspersions upon [his] political, social . . . racial and religious views . . . ; his integrity; his sexual proclivities and inclinations; and his personal habits"; (2) kept him under surveillance in public places for an unreasonable length of time; (3) caused him to be accosted by girls for the purpose of entrapping him into illicit relationships; (4) made threatening, harassing and obnoxious telephone calls to him; (5) tapped his telephone and eavesdropped, by means of mechanical and electronic equipment, on his private conversations with others; and (6) conducted a "continuing" and harassing investigation of him. . . .

* * *

The District of Columbia . . . courts have not only recognized a common-law action for invasion of privacy but have broadened the scope of that tort beyond its traditional limits. Thus, in the most recent of its cases on the subject, *Pearson* v. *Dodd* (410 F.2d 710), the Federal Court of Appeals for the District of Columbia declared (p. 704):

> We approve the extension of the tort of invasion of privacy to instances of *intrusion,* whether by physical trespass or not, into spheres from which an ordinary man in a plaintiff's position could reasonably expect that the particular defendant should be excluded. (Italics supplied.)

* * *

Quite obviously, some intrusions into one's private sphere are inevitable concomitants of life in an industrial and densely populated society, which the law does not seek to proscribe even if it were possible to do so. "The law does not provide a remedy for every annoyance that occurs in everyday life."

* * *

It should be emphasized that the mere gathering of information about a particular individual does not give rise to a cause of action under this theory. Privacy is invaded only if the information sought is of a confidential nature and the defendant's conduct was unreasonably intrusive. . . . In order to sustain a cause of action for invasion of privacy, therefore, the plaintiff must show that the appellant's conduct was truly "intrusive" and that it was designed to elicit information which would not be available through normal inquiry or observation.

* * *

Turning, then, to the particular acts charged in the complaint, we cannot find any basis for a claim of invasion of privacy, under District of Columbia law, in the allegations that the appellant, through its agents or employees, interviewed many persons who knew the plaintiff, asking questions about him and casting aspersions on his character. Although those inquiries may have uncovered information of a personal nature, it is difficult to see how they may be said to have invaded the plaintiff's privacy. Information about the plaintiff which was already known to others could hardly be regarded as private to the plaintiff. Presumably, the plaintiff had previously revealed the information to such other persons, and he would necessarily assume the risk that a friend or acquaintance in whom he had confided might breach the confidence. If, as alleged, the questions tended to disparage the plaintiff's character, his remedy would seem to be by way of an action for defamation, not for breach of his right to privacy.

Nor can we find any actionable invasion of privacy in the allegations that the appellant caused the plaintiff to be accosted by girls with illicit proposals, or that it was responsible for the making of a large number of threatening and harassing telephone calls to the plaintiff's home at odd hours. Neither of these activities, howsoever offensive and disturbing, involved intrusion for the purpose of gathering information of a private and confidential nature.

As already indicated, it is manifestly neither practical nor desirable for the law to provide a remedy against any and all activity which an individual might find annoying. On the other hand, where severe mental pain or anguish is inflicted through a deliberate and malicious campaign of harassment or intimidation, a remedy is available in the form of an action for the intentional infliction of emotional distress—the theory underlying the plaintiff's third cause of action. . . .

Apart, however, from the foregoing allegations which we find inadequate to spell out a cause of action for invasion of privacy under District of Columbia law, the complaint contains allegations concerning other activities by the appellant or its agents which do satisfy the requirements for such a cause of action. The one which most clearly meets those requirements is the charge that the appellant and its codefendants engaged in unauthorized wiretapping and eavesdropping by mechanical and electronic means. The Court of Appeals in the *Pearson* case expressly recognized that such conduct constitutes a tortious intrusion and other jurisdictions have reached a similar conclusion. In point of fact, the appellant does not dispute this, acknowledging that, to the extent the two challenged counts charge it with wiretapping and eavesdropping, an actionable invasion of privacy has been stated.

There are additional allegations that the appellant hired people to shadow the plaintiff and keep him under surveillance. In particular, he claims that, on one occasion, one of its agents followed him into a bank, getting sufficiently close to him to see the denomination of the bills he was withdrawing from his account. From what we have already said, it is manifest that the mere observation of the plaintiff in a public place does not amount to invasion of his privacy. But, under certain circumstances, surveillance may be so "overzealous" as to render it actionable. Whether or not the surveillance in the present case falls into this latter category will depend on the nature of the proof. A person does not automatically make public everything he does merely by being in a public place, and the mere fact that Nader was in a bank did not give anyone the right to try to discover the amount of money he was withdrawing. On the other hand, if the plaintiff acted in such a way as to reveal that fact to any casual observer, then, it may not be said that the appellant intruded into his private sphere. In any event, though, it is enough for present purposes to say that the surveillance allegation is not insufficient as a matter of law.

Since, then, the first two causes of action do contain allegations which are adequate to state a cause of action for invasion of privacy under District of Columbia law, the courts below properly denied the appellant's motion to dismiss those causes of action.

* * *

Public Disclosure of Embarrassing Facts

Circulation of false statements that do injury to a person are actionable under the laws of defamation. What about true statements that might be every bit as damaging—for example, disclosure of someone's income tax return, revealing how much he earned? The general rule is that if the facts are truly private and of no "legitimate" concern to the public, then their disclosure is a violation of the right to privacy. There is a constitutional dimension to this tort, as there is to defamation. A person who is in the public eye cannot claim the same protection.

False Light

A final type of privacy invasion is that which paints a false picture. Though false, it might not be libelous, since the publication need contain nothing injurious to reputation. Indeed, the publication might even glorify the plaintiff, making him seem more heroic than he actually is. Subject to the First Amendment requirement that the plaintiff must show intent or extreme recklessness, statements that put a person in a "false light," like a fictionalized biography, are actionable.

The Right of Publicity

Although most states now recognize a right to prevent someone from capitalizing on a person's likeness, traditionally this right did not descend to a person's heirs at death. Like the rule governing defamation, the right was considered personal, not property, and expired when a person died. Thus a federal court has held that Elvis Presley's heirs could not prevent his likeness from being exploited after he died. [Memphis Development Foundation v. Factors, Etc., Inc., 616 F.2d 956 (6th Cir. 1980)] This limitation on the right of privacy gave advertisers considerable freedom to suggest that famous people endorsed their products, as anyone familiar with television commercials can attest. But in recent years, states have begun to enact statutes granting property rights in the likenesses of the deceased, as discussed in Box 9-3.

Tort Reform

During the past decade, the number of tort suits has climbed dramatically, especially against doctors in medical malpractice cases and against manufacturers in product liability suits (Chapter 10). As a result, lobbying groups have mounted a strong push for statutory changes in tort law in most states. Many state legislatures have enacted caps on damage awards. In Missouri, for example, no more than $350,000 may be paid out for punitive damages and pain and suffering. Legislators have also been considering a change in the rule governing "joint-and-several liability." The rule states that when two or more defendants are responsible for causing an injury, the plaintiff may recover the entire amount of damages from any one of the defendants, even if that defendant was only minimally at fault. Many so-called "deep pocket" defendants—those with large treasuries, like corporations and governmental units—are seeking to change the rule so that they could be forced to pay only that percentage of damages corresponding to their degree of fault.

Chapter Summary

The principles of tort law pervade modern society because they spell out the duties of care that we owe each other in our private lives. Tort law has had a significant impact on business because modern technology poses

Box 9-3 Property Rights and the Deceased

The Rights of Dead Celebrities

By Pamela G. Hollie

To advertisers, certain personalities, such as John Wayne, Elvis Presley and W. C. Fields, are as bankable now as when they were alive. In some ways they are even more attractive.

Chances are that such celebrities never did commercials when they were alive and might have objected to being associated with certain endorsements. Until recently, what they would have wished could be ignored. Courts tended to rule that the commercial rights to a person's likeness and name ended with death. Manufacturers, promoters and advertisers were free to use a dead celebrity's name or likeness without penalty or payment.

But things are changing. Several states, including California, have adopted legislation that gives the heirs of celebrities more power over the use of the names and images of their dead relatives. According to new laws in Kentucky and Tennessee, the identity and name of a celebrity are considered property, like a house or a bank account, and can be willed or sold.

Large advertising agencies have routinely sought permission from estates to insure that clients are not embarrassed by a lawsuit. "We have always been careful," said Richard Pollett, vice president and assistant general counsel for the J. Walter Thompson Company. "But we are more careful than ever."

* * *

However, the practice of using ghost stars is still popular. For example, Republic Airlines Inc. featured the silent film star Rudolph Valentino in a mailing to 24,000 travel agents. "We were trying to portray a thought in a few seconds," said Mary Speagh, account supervisor of Kolesar & Hartwell Inc. in Minneapolis, which handles Republic's trade services. "People know him as a lover and a charmer and a romantic. There are some parallels with what we wanted to say, and what we wanted them to feel about Republic."

Likewise, Coca-Cola U.S.A. is using the baseball great Babe Ruth, the "Sultan of Swat" who died 37 years ago, in its advertisements for Coke Classic, the revived original-formula Coke. The advertisements are intended to link Classic Coke with the classic heroes and images of the past.

The SmithKline Beckman Corporation, on the other hand, wanted to inject some humor into its mailings to doctors. It decided to substitute the heads of the Marx Brothers for those of the four Presidents on Mount Rushmore. The theme of the mailing is: "There is no substitute for the real thing."

And, the International Business Machines Corporation saw a connection between its products and Charlie Chaplin, whose "Modern Times" is a classic film about work and mechanization. In 1981, I.B.M. chose Chaplin's "Little Tramp" character to bring humor and familiarity to the promotion of a new personal computer.

In these cases, the companies asked the permission of the celebrities' estates before using the characters. I.B.M. received a license from Bubbles Inc. in Paris before beginning its campaign. Republic paid a stock photography house for the one-time use of a Valentino photograph. "We are very careful about getting permission," Mrs. Speagh said.

* * *

The new state laws are built on years of litigation. "Ten years ago, I felt that something had to be done," said Larry Harmon, who went to court in 1976 to protect his exclusive right to portray Stan Laurel, half of the comedy team of Stan Laurel and Oliver Hardy. Mr. Harmon had purchased the rights to the character from Mr. Laurel, who died in 1965. Mr. Hardy died in 1957. Mr. Harmon won his case against Hal Roach Studios, the film company where most of the Laurel and Hardy pictures were made, in a

(continues on next page)

Box 9-3, *continued*

New York court. "It was an expensive fight," he said. "It cost me $500,000."

The rights to a famous personality can also be costly—sometimes more than $10,000 for one use in a 60-second television commercial. And, the licensing process has become increasingly complicated and restrictive. "The use of a personality is very specific," said Mark Roesler, president of the Curtis Licensing Corporation, a division of the Curtis Publishing Company and the agent for the estates of seven celebrities including Buddy Holly, James Dean and Abbott and Costello.

But perhaps the most-sought-after of the Curtis line is Elvis Presley. "We have 100 different agreements for Elvis," Mr. Roesler said adding that the Presley estate is involved in one lawsuit charging infringement. The Abbott and Costello estates have two such lawsuits pending.

"The most important thing to the families is quality control," Mr. Roesler said. "The Babe Ruth name is controlled by his two daughters and the Babe Ruth Baseball League. They agree that any use of his name be in very good taste. For example, it is not to be used on tobacco or alcohol or be in any way associated with pornography."

Source: *The New York Times*, August 9, 1985, p. D14.

significant dangers and the modern market is so efficient at distributing goods to a wide class of consumers.

Unlike criminal law, tort law does not require the tortfeasor to have a specific intent to commit the act for which he will be held liable to pay damages. Negligence—that is, carelessness—is a major factor in tort liability. In some instances, especially in cases involving injuries caused by products, a no-fault standard called strict liability is applied.

What constitutes a legal injury depends very much on the circumstances. A person can assume a risk or consent to the particular action, thus relieving the person doing the injury from tort liability. To be liable, the tortfeasor must be the proximate cause of the injury, not a remote cause. On the other hand, certain people are held to answer for the torts of another—for example, an employer is usually liable for the torts of his employees, and a bartender might be liable for injuries caused by someone to whom he sold too many drinks. Two types of statutes—workers' compensation and no-fault automobile insurance—have eliminated tort liability for certain kinds of accidents and replaced it with an immediate insurance payment plan.

Among the torts of particular importance to the business community are wrongful death and personal injury caused by products or acts of employees, defamation, unfair competition and interference with contractual relations.

Problems

1. What is the difference between the objectives of tort law and criminal law?
2. A woman fell ill in a store. An employee put the woman in an infirmary but provided no medical care for six hours, and she died. The woman's family sued the store for wrongful death. What arguments could the store make that it was not liable? What arguments could the family make? Which seem the stronger arguments? Why?
3. The signals on a railroad crossing are defective. Although the railroad company was notified of the problem a month earlier, the railroad inspector has failed to order them repaired. Seeing the all-clear signal, a car drives up and stalls on the tracks as a train rounds the bend. For the past two weeks the car had been stalling, and the driver kept putting off taking the car to the shop for a tune-up. As the train rounds the bend the engineer is distracted by a conductor and does not see the car until it is too late to stop. Who is negligent? Who must bear the liability for the damage to the car and to the train?
4. Jake's Bar has been renting the ground floor of Bud's building for ten years. At the time the lease is to be renewed, Bud tells Jake that he has an offer from Mac to pay $12,000 a year for the space, double what Jake is currently paying. Afraid of risking a move, Jake signs a ten-year lease at $12,000. A year later he discovers that Mac had never made any offer at all. Jakes sues Bud. Does Jake have a case? What is his claim? What is Bud's defense? Who should win?
5. SuperGroceryMart, a grocery chain, had been buying its milk from several dairy farmers throughout the state, who had contracts with Ace Truckers to deliver the milk to Super's various stores. A new regional manager at Super decided that it would be more profitable to send its own trucks for the milk. So she sent a letter to all the farmers indicating that she would no longer buy their milk unless they permitted her to pick it up. Since they could not afford to lose their primary buyer, the farmers cancelled their trucking contracts with Ace. Ace sues Super. What result? What additional facts might be helpful to Ace in the lawsuit? To Super?
6. A credit reporting agency received a report from an electronics supplier that Adam's Radios, Inc., had failed to pay for $10,000 worth of merchandise, that it had declared bankruptcy, and that Adam himself had been engaged in "unethical business practices." In fact, all these allegations were untrue. The credit agency put this report in a file, and a few weeks later released it to a finance company from whom Adam was seeking a business loan. The finance company refused the loan and told Adam why. Adam wrote the credit reporting company, demonstrating that the facts were untrue. A manager phoned Adam to say

that the report would be changed, but he forgot to instruct the report clerk to destroy the old report. When Adam then sought a loan from a different finance company, it got the same old report and likewise refused Adam a loan. By the time Adam straightened the matter out, interest rates had soared and Adam was stuck having to pay six percentage points more. Adam sued the credit reporting company for having issued the report to the first finance company and to the second. What is his theory? What result? What additional facts, if any, are needed to determine liability?

7. Mississippi has a law against printing the name of a rape victim in a newspaper or broadcasting it over the air. A local radio station obtained the name of a rape victim from a police log and broadcast it. The woman sued the radio station. What is her legal theory? What result?

PART THREE

THE CONSUMER

10

Product Liability

In this chapter we focus on remedies available when a defective product causes personal injury or other damages. **Product liability** describes a type of claim, not a separate theory of liability. Product liability has strong emotional overtones—ranging from the pro-litigation position of consumer advocates to the conservative perspective of the manufacturers.

Consumer advocates recite the concededly distressing facts about the rate at which products cause injury. Consider this brief recital of some of the dangers that lurk in common products:

> One can hardly escape the news of the latest grisly consumer tragedy. Babies guzzling Drano or strangling in the rungs of their cribs. Children stabbing themselves blind with the sharpened sticks hidden inside their dolls. Housewives getting their sleeves too close to the burner and arriving in the emergency wards with skin seared like grilled steak. Husbands losing feet inside the savage rotors of the family lawnmower. Workers crushing their hands in unguarded machinery. Or unwitting hospital patients getting their brains bored out by defective cranial drills. (Maslow 1975, p. 27)

Product liability can also be a life-or-death matter from the manufacturer's perspective. For example, in 1974, Havir Manufacturing Company of St. Paul, Minnesota, was engulfed in a wave of lawsuits brought by operators who had lost fingers and hands in the punch presses it made. Its product liability insurance premiums, which were only $2,000 in 1970, doubled by 1974, and rose to $10,000 the next year, when its insurance company canceled the policy. To replace the insurance would have cost $200,000, or 10 percent of the company's total sales. The company liquidated (Wysocki, 1976, p. 1).

Nor are small companies the only ones affected by the surge in litigation. In the 1980s, the most prominent class of product liability cases are those that concern diseases resulting from the manufacture and installation of asbestos. In 1982, the nation's largest asbestos producer, the Manville Corporation, one of America's largest industrial companies, filed for bankruptcy to try to shake off more than 16,000 suits (and an anticipated 32,000 more) seeking $2 *billion* in damages (Feder, 1982, p. 1). More than 250 companies have been sued in connection with asbestos-related deaths and diseases, and the total sought is in the billions of dollars. One study predicted that employers of asbestos workers and their insurers may pay out between $38.2 billion to $92 billion in asbestos claims during the next three decades (Joseph, 1982, p. 40).

Although the debate has been heated and at times simplistic, in fact the problem of product liability is complex and most of us must regard it with a high degree of ambivalence. We are all consumers, after all, who profit greatly from living in an industrial society. Perhaps nothing illustrates this ambivalence more than the 1978 case in which a product liability defense attorney, a man who spent his professional life fighting plaintiffs who brought product liability suits against his corporate clients, sued Remington Arms Company, for paralysis resulting from an accident involving a Remington rifle during a hunting trip; the parties settled for $6.8 million, said at the time to be the largest lump-sum payment in a single personal injury case in our history (Geisel, 1978, p. 12).

In this chapter, we will examine in detail the legal theories that underlie product liability cases. In the typical product liability case, three legal theories are asserted—a contract theory and two tort theories. The contract theory is **warranty**, and the two tort theories are **strict liability** and **negligence.** We cover them in turn in the sections that follow.

Warranties

The Uniform Commercial Code (UCC) governs *express warranties* and various *implied warranties,* and until relatively recently it was the only statutory control on the use and meaning of warranties. In 1975, after years of debate, Congress passed and President Ford signed into law a federal statute, the Magnuson-Moss Act, which imposes certain requirements on manufacturers and others who warrant their goods. Our discussion of warranties will examine both the UCC and the Magnuson-Moss Act.

Express Warranty

An **express warranty** is created whenever the seller affirms that the product will have certain characteristics or will perform in a certain manner. Formal words such as "warrant" or "guarantee" are not necessary to create an express warranty. A seller may create an express warranty as part of the basis for the bargain of sale by means of (1) an affirmation of a fact or promise relating to the goods, (2) a description of the goods, or (3) a sample or model. Any of these will create an express warranty that the goods will conform to the fact, promise, description, sample, or model. Thus, a seller who stated "that the use of rustproof linings in the cans would prevent discoloration and adulteration of the Perform solution" has given an express warranty, whether he realized it or not. [Rhodes Pharmacal Co. v. Continental Can Co., 219 N.E.2d 726 (Ill. 1976)]

Nevertheless, the courts will not hold a manufacturer to every statement that could conceivably be interpreted as an express warranty. Manufacturers and sellers constantly "puff" their products, and the law is content to let them inhabit that fuzzy land without having to make good on every claim. Section 2-313(2) says that "an affirmation merely of the value of the goods or a statement purporting to be merely the seller's opinion or commendation of the goods does not create a warranty."

It is not always easy, however, to determine the line between an express warranty and a piece of puffery. A salesperson who says that a strawberry huller is "great" has probably puffed, not warranted, when it turns out that strawberries run through the huller look like victims of a massacre. But consider the classic cases of the defective used car and the faulty bull. In the former, the salesperson said the car was in "A-1 shape" and "mechanically perfect." In the latter, the seller said not only that the bull calf would "put the buyer on the map" but that "his father was the greatest living dairy bull." The car, carrying the buyer's seven-month-old child, broke down while the buyer was en route to visit her husband in the army during World War II. The court said that the salesperson had made an express warranty. [Wat Henry Pontiac Co. v. Bradley, 210 P.2d 348 (Okla. 1949)] The bull calf turned out to be sterile, putting the farmer on the judicial rather than the dairy map. The court said that the seller's spiel was trade talk, not a warranty that the bull would impregnate cows. [Frederickson v. Hackney, 198 N.W. 806 (Minn. 1924)] Is there any qualitative difference between these decisions, other than the quarter century that separates them and the different courts that rendered them? Perhaps the most that can be said is that the more specific and measurable the statement's standards, the more likely it is that a court will hold the seller to a warranty; and that a written statement is easier to construe as a warranty than an oral one. It is also possible that courts look, if only subliminally, at how reasonable the buyer was in relying on the statement, although this ought not be the strict test. A buyer may be unreasonable in expecting a car to get 100 miles to the gallon, but if that is what the seller promised, that ought to be an enforceable warranty.

Implied Warranty

Express warranties are those over which the parties "dickered." They go to the essence of the bargain. An **implied warranty**, by contrast, is one that circumstances alone, not specific language, compel reading into the sale. In short, an implied warranty is one created by law, acting from an impulse of common sense.

Merchantability Section 2-314 lays down the fundamental rule that goods carry an implied warranty of **merchantability** if sold by a merchant seller. What is merchantability? Section 2-314(2) says that merchantable goods are those that conform at least to the following six characteristics:

1. The trade or industry must not object to the goods being described in public as they are in the contract. Thus a microcomputer would not be merchantable under this provision if it were called a mainframe computer in the contract.
2. The goods must, if fungible, be of average quality for the type described.
3. They must be fit for ordinary purposes for which such goods are used. A steel kitchen knife that broke while being used to cut bread would not be merchantable.
4. Goods within a unit and among all units must be "of even kind, quality, and quantity," that is, must not vary too much in kind, quality, and quantity when sold in bulk.
5. They must be adequately contained, packaged, and labeled as the agreement may require.
6. They must conform to whatever factual statements are made on the container or label.

For purposes of Section 2-314 (2)(c), selling and serving food or drink for consumption on or off the premises is a sale subject to the implied warranty of merchantability—the food must be "fit for the ordinary purposes" to which it is put. The problem is common: you bite into a cherry pit in the cherry-vanilla ice cream and break a tooth, or you choke on the clam shells in the chowder. Is such food fit for the ordinary purposes to which it is put? There are two schools of thought. One asks whether the food was natural as prepared. This view adopts the seller's perspective. The other asks what the consumer's reasonable expectation was.

The first test is sometimes said to be the "natural-foreign" test. If the substance in the soup is natural to the substance—as bones are to fish—then the food is fit for consumption. The second test, relying on reasonable expectations, is illustrated in the following case, involving the unfortunate drinker who found an unpitted olive in his martini.

HOCHBERG v. O'DONNELL'S RESTAURANT, INC.
272 A.2d 846 (D.C. Ct. App. 1971)

GALLAGHER, ASSOCIATE JUDGE. This is an appeal from a directed verdict in favor of the defendant at the conclusion of the plaintiff's case in an action for damage to a tooth caused in chewing an olive which had been in a martini cocktail purchased in defendant's restaurant. The complaint alleged a cause of action against O'Donnell's Restaurant for negligence and breach of implied warranty. The restaurant brought a third-party action against Hale Friedenberg, t/a My-Own Food Products, from whom the restaurant had purchased the olive. The latter in turn filed a fourth-party action for indemnity against Vita-Food Products, Inc., from whom the third-party defendant had purchased the olive.

The facts are undisputed, being contained in an approved "Agreed Statement on Appeal" filed under Rule 25 of this court. Appellant went to trial on the theories of negligence and breach of implied warranty. It there developed that appellant ordered a vodka martini at appellee's restaurant, located in Bethesda, Maryland, and during the course of drinking it took the olive from the drink with his fingers, *saw a hole cut in the end of the olive,* and placed it in his mouth. He then bit down, uttered an exclamation, and explained to his dinner partners that he had broken a tooth on an olive pit. The restaurant manager was called to the table and shown part of the tooth and the olive pit. After testimony concerning treatment of the broken tooth and damages incurred, appellant rested and argument was heard on appellee's motion for a directed verdict on the negligence count, which was granted. Appellee next moved for a directed verdict on the implied warranty count on the ground that appellant failed to establish a prima facie case of breach of implied warranty as he failed to establish a necessary element, namely, that the food served was "unwholesome or contained foreign matter" as required by Cushing v. Rodman, 65 App.D.C. 258, 82 F.2d 864 (1936). The restaurant further contended that recovery should be denied where a food dish contains an object that is "naturally a part of or associated with the type of food in which it is found." The court granted a directed verdict on the implied warranty count. No further evidence was heard and judgments were later entered in favor of Friedenberg on the third-party action and to Vita-Food Products, Inc., on the fourth-party action. Appellant later filed a motion for Reconsideration and New Trial, which was denied.

Appellant contends that under local law the trial court erred in directing a verdict for the defendant-appellee at the close of the plaintiff's case. It is apparent that we have before us the question of what test should be applied under the doctrine of implied warranty where an injury is incurred by a patron from an object in food served him in a restaurant. Under the "Uniform Commercial Code—Sales" (effective January 1, 1965), D.C.Code 1967, § 28:2-101 *et seq.*, there is an implied warranty that food sold and consumed on a premises or elsewhere is "fit for the ordinary purposes for which such goods are used." D.C.Code 1967, § 28:2-314. Even prior to this statute, this jurisdiction invoked the implied warranty doctrine where there was an injury as the result of food or drink consumed in a restaurant. In so doing, the test has been whether the food was wholesome and fit for human consumption, and contained no foreign or deleterious substance.

Both parties agree there is a split in the authorities throughout the country as to what test should be applied where an injury is suffered from an object in food or drink consumed in a restaurant. Some courts hold there is no breach of implied warranty on the part of a restaurant if the object in the food causing the injury was "natural" to the food served. On the other hand, if the object was "foreign" to the food there may be a recovery. This has come to be known as the "foreign-natural" test.

On the other side are authorities which hold that under modern conditions the test is—what should reasonably be expected by the consumer to be in the food served to him. This is known as the "reasonable expectation" test.

Appellee asserts that under local law appellant failed to prove a necessary element, namely, that the food he was served was unwholesome or contained foreign matter; and that the sole issue before the trial court was whether a pit in an olive renders the olive unwholesome and unfit for human consumption. Appellant, on the other hand, casts the issue differently. He asserts it as being "whether the jury should have been allowed to decide the reasonableness of his action in assuming the apparently-pitted olive was fit for human consumption."

We are not aware of any appellate decision in this jurisdiction, and counsel cite none, which involved an injury caused by food served in a restaurant containing an object which was natural to it, such as a chicken bone in a chicken sandwich or in chicken chow mein. Consequently, we consider the question before us as one of first impression.

We think the better view in cases involving injury from an object in food served in a restaurant is to apply the reasonable expectation test rather than restrict it, as the trial court did, to whether the food is wholesome (untainted) or contained a foreign substance.

* * *

In our view it is unrealistic to deny recovery *as a matter of law* if, for example, a person is injured from a chicken bone while eating a sliced chicken sandwich in a restaurant, simply because the bone is natural to chicken. The exposure to injury is not much different than if a sliver of glass were there. "Naturalness of the substance to any ingredients in the food served is important only in determining whether the consumer may reasonably expect to find such substance in the particular type of dish or style of food served." Betehia v. Cape Cod Corp., 10 Wis.2d at 328, 103 N.W.2d at 67. Because a substance is natural to a product in one state of preparation does not mean necessarily that it will be reasonably anticipated by the consumer in the final product served. It is a different matter if one is injured by a bone while eating a chicken leg or a steak or a whole baked fish. There, it may well be held as a matter of law that the consumer should reasonably expect to find a bone.

Turning to the facts of this case, it appears the crucial consideration for the purpose of this review is that appellant saw the hole in one end of an olive and therefore assumed it had been pitted, chewed the olive and injured his tooth on the pit. He concedes that if he had not seen the hole in the olive his case would be "extremely tenuous." This narrows the problem to whether on these facts he was reasonably justified in expecting there was no pit in the olive and could chew without care. "What is to be reasonably expected by the consumer is a jury question in most cases. . . ." Betehia v. Cape Code Corp., 10 Wis.2d at 332, 103 N.W.2d at 69. Appellant admits that a fact finder might conclude that he should have exercised greater care in chewing the olive. But he argues he was entitled to have the jury resolve the issue.

We think the question of what appellant was reasonably justified in expecting was properly a jury question here. In so holding, we do not mean to "imply that appellant will necessarily prevail at trial." Brennan v. Shepherd Park Pharmacy, Inc., D.C.Mun.App., 138 A.2d 494, 496 (1958). We simply hold that, viewing appellant's evidence in its strongest light and giving it the benefit of all reasonable inferences, as we must, the question should have been submitted to the jury. Upon retrial, the fundamental question to be resolved by the fact finder on liability under implied warranty is whether, under the circumstances presented, appellant acted in a reasonable fashion in chewing the olive with the expectation that it contained no pit.

Reversed and remanded for a new trial.

Fitness for a Particular Purpose Section 2-315 creates another implied warranty. Whenever a seller, at the time he contracts to make a sale, knows or has reason to know that the buyer is relying on the seller's skill or judgment to select a product that is suitable for the particular purpose the buyer has in mind for the goods to be sold, there is an implied warranty that the goods are fit for that purpose. You go to a hardware store and tell the salesclerk that you need a paint that will dry overnight because you are painting your front door and a thunderstorm is predicted for the next day. The clerk gives you an extremely sluggish oil-based paint that takes a week to dry. The store has breached an implied warranty of fitness.

Note the distinction between "particular" and "ordinary" purposes. Paint is made to color and when dry to protect a surface. That is its ordinary purpose, and had you said only that you wished to buy paint, no implied warranty of fitness would have been breached. It is only because you had a particular application in mind that the implied warranty arose. Suppose you had found a can of paint in a general store and told the same tale, but the proprietor had said, "I don't know anything about paint; help yourself." Not every seller has the requisite degree of skill or knowledge about every product he sells to give rise to an implied warranty. Ultimately, each case turns on its particular circumstances.

Problems with Warranty Theory

It may seem that a consumer asserting a claim for breach of warranty will have a high chance of success under an express warranty or implied warranty theory of merchantability or fitness. In practice, however, consumers in many cases are denied recovery. For instance, the consumer must prove that there was a sale and that the sale was of goods rather than real estate or services. Moreover, the action must be brought within the time allowed by the four-year statute of limitations under UCC Article 2. And under Section 2-607(3)(a), the consumer who fails to give notice of breach within a reasonable time of acceptance will see his suit dismissed, and few consumers know enough to do so, except when making a complaint about a purchase of spoiled milk or about paint that wouldn't dry. In addition to these general problems, the consumer faces additional difficulties stemming directly from the warranty theory. We trace these difficulties immediately below.

Exclusion or Modification of Warranties

The UCC permits sellers to exclude or disclaim warranties in whole or in part.

Express Warranties The simplest way for the seller to exclude express warranties is not to give them. To be sure, Section 2-316(1) forbids courts from giving operation to words in the fine print that negate or limit express warranties if doing so would unreasonably conflict with express warranties stated in the main body of the contract—as, for example, would a blanket statement that "this contract excludes all warranties, express or implied." The purpose of this Code provision is to prevent consumers from being surprised by unbargained-for language.

Implied Warranties Generally Implied warranties can be excluded easily enough also, by describing the product with language such as "as is" or "with all faults." Nor is exclusion simply a function of what the seller says. The buyer who has either examined or refused to examine the goods before entering the contract may not assert an implied warranty with regard to defects that the inspection would have revealed.

Implied Warranty of Merchantability Section 2-316(2) permits the seller to disclaim or modify the implied warranty of merchantability, as long as the statement actually mentions merchantability and, if it is written, is "conspicuous." Note that the disclaimer need not be in writing.

Implied Warranty of Fitness Section 2-316(2) permits the seller also to disclaim or modify an implied warranty of fitness. This disclaimer or modification must be in writing, however, and be conspicuous. It need not explicitly mention fitness; general language will do. The following sentence, for example, is sufficient to exclude all implied warranties of fitness: "There are no warranties which extend beyond the description on the face of this contract."

Here is a standard disclaimer clause found in a Dow Chemical Company agreement:

> Seller warrants that the goods supplied hereunder shall conform to the description stated on the front side hereof, that it will convey good title thereto and that such goods shall be delivered free from any lawful security interest or lien or encumbrance. SELLER MAKES NO WARRANTY OF MERCHANTABILITY OR FITNESS FOR A PARTICULAR USE. NOR IS THERE ANY OTHER EXPRESS OR IMPLIED WARRANTY.

Cumulation and Conflict Express and implied warranties and their exclusion or limitation can often conflict. Section 2-317 provides certain rules for deciding which should prevail. In general, all warranties are to be construed as consistent with each other and as cumulative. When that assumption is unreasonable, the parties' intention governs the interpretation, according to the following rules: (a) exact or technical specifications outweigh inconsistent samples or general descriptive language; (b) a sample from an existing supply of the goods outweighs inconsistent general descriptive language; and (c) express warranties displace inconsistent implied warranties, with one exception. The exception is for an implied warranty of fitness for a particular purpose. Any inconsistency among warranties must always be resolved in favor of the implied warranty of fitness. This does not mean that the implied warranty of fitness cannot be limited or excluded altogether. The parties may do so. But in cases of doubt whether it or some other language applies, the implied warranty of fitness will have a superior claim.

The Magnuson-Moss Act and Phantom Warranties

Generally After years of debate over extending federal law to regulate warranties, Congress enacted the Magnuson-Moss Federal Trade Commission Improvement Act, and President Ford signed it into law on January 4, 1975. Its purposes were set forth by Senator Warren Magnuson in introducing the measure:

> [W]arranties have for many years confused, misled, and frequently angered American consumers. . . . Consumer anger is expected when purchasers of consumer products discover that their warranty may cover a 25-cent part but not the $100 labor charge or that there is full coverage on a piano so long as it is shipped at the purchaser's expense to the factory. . . .
>
> [T]he bill is designed to promote understanding. Far too frequently, there is a paucity of information supplied to the consumer about what in fact is offered him in that piece of paper proudly labeled "warranty." Many of the most important questions concerning the warranty are usually unanswered when there is some sort of product failure. Who should the consumer notify if his product stops working during the warranty period? What are his responsibilities after notification? How soon can he expect a fair replacement? Will repair or replacement cost him anything? There is a growing need to generate consumer understanding by clearly and conspicuously disclosing the terms and conditions of the warranty and by telling the consumer what to do if his guaranteed product becomes defective or malfunctions.

To meet these concerns, the Magnuson-Moss Act contains a variety of provisions regulating the content of warranties and the means of disclosing those contents. The act gives the Federal Trade Commission the authority to promulgate detailed regulations to interpret and enforce it.

Contents The act does not require sellers to give express warranties. The decision to offer a warranty is solely within the discretion of the seller, motivated by competitive factors. But if a seller does offer a written warranty to a consumer covering a "consumer product," the warranty must clearly and conspicuously disclose certain items. Before looking at those items, note that the act applies only to "consumers," not to every potential buyer. A consumer is defined as a buyer of a consumer product who does not use it for resale or in the ordinary course of his business, or a person to whom the buyer transferred the product (for example, to a member of his family). "Consumer product" means any tangible personal property distributed in commerce and normally used for personal, family, or household purposes. Products purchased solely for commercial or industrial use are excluded.

The FTC regulations require that any written warranty for a product actually costing a consumer more than $10 must disclose in a single document and, in readily understood language, the following nine items of information:

1. the identity of the people to whom the warranty is extended, if the warrantor intends to limit the warranty to the original purchaser or fewer than all who might come to own the product during the warranty period;
2. a clear description of products, parts, characteristics, components, or properties covered and, where necessary for clarity, a description of what is excluded;
3. a statement of what the warrantor will do in the event of a defect or a failure to conform to the warranty, including items or services the warrantor will pay for and, if necessary for clarity, those which he will not pay for;
4. a statement of when the warranty period begins and how long it runs;
5. a step-by-step explanation of what the consumer must do to get satisfaction under the warranty, including names and addresses of those to whom the consumer must bring the product;
6. instructions to the consumer on how he can avail himself of any informal dispute settlement mechanism established by the warrantor;
7. any limitations on the duration of implied warranties—since some states do not permit such limitations, the warranty must contain a statement that says that any limitation given may not apply to the particular consumer;
8. any limitations or exclusions on relief, such as consequential damages—as above, the warranty must contain a statement explaining that some states do not permit such limitations;
9. the following statement: "This warranty gives you specific legal rights, and you may also have other rights which vary from state to state."

In addition to these requirements, the act requires that the warranty be labeled either *full* or *limited*. A "**full**" warranty means that (1) the defective product or part will be fixed or replaced free, including removal and reinstallation if necessary, (2) it will be fixed within a reasonable time after the consumer complains, (3) the consumer need do nothing unreasonable (like shipping a piano to the factory) to get warranty service, (4) the warranty is good for anyone who owns the product during the warranty period, and (5) the consumer gets his money back or a new product if the defective product cannot be fixed within a reasonable number of attempts. Despite this seeming all-inclusiveness, a full warranty need not cover the whole product; a full warranty may cover only the picture tube in the television set, for example. Of course, it must state what parts are included and excluded. A "**limited**" warranty is less inclusive. It may cover the cost of only parts, not labor; it may require the consumer to bring the product in to the store for service; it may impose a charge for handling; it may cover only the first purchaser. Both full and limited warranties may exclude consequential damages.

Disclosure The FTC regulations require the warrantor to make the provisions of the warranty available prior to sale; this can be done in various ways. The text of the written warranty can be attached to the product or placed "in close conjunction" to it. It can be maintained in a binder kept in each department or otherwise easily accessible to the consumer. The binders must either be in plain sight or signs must be posted to call the prospective buyer's attention to them. A notice containing the text of the warranty can be posted. Or the warranty itself can be printed on the product's package or container.

Phantom Warranties As we have seen, the UCC permits the seller to disclaim implied warranties. This authority often led sellers to give what were called "phantom warranties," that is, limited express warranties that contained disclaimers of implied warranties, thus leaving the consumer with fewer rights than if no express warranty had been given at all. In the words of the legislative report on the Magnuson-Moss Act, "The bold print giveth and the fine print taketh away." The act abolished these phantom warranties by providing that if the seller gives a written warranty, whether full or limited, he cannot disclaim or modify implied warranties. However, if the warranty is limited, the *duration* of the implied warranty may be modified in a reasonable manner.

A seller's ability to disclaim implied warranties is also limited by state law in two ways. First, a few states prohibit disclaimers whenever consumer products are sold. Second, in all states a disclaimer that is unconscionable is not allowed. (Unconscionability is discussed in Chapter 11 and in the *Henningsen* case, pp. 276–79.)

Privity

If one of the problems with warranty law is the degree to which sellers can disclaim or modify, another equally serious difficulty is the doctrine of **privity.** Privity is the legal term for the direct connection between the seller and buyer, the two contracting parties. For decades, the doctrine of privity has held that one party can have legal recourse against another only if they are in privity. But in a modern industrial economy, the product is transported through a much larger chain:

Manufacturer
↓
Wholesaler
↓
Retailer
↓
Buyer
↓
Family, Friends

Two questions arise: (1) Is the manufacturer or wholesaler liable to the buyer under warranty theory? (2) May the buyer's family or friends assert warranty rights?

Liability to Buyer As just noted, the traditional rule is that remote parties are not liable; the lack of privity is a defense to a suit by a remote buyer or transferee against a remote seller. The buyer may recover damages from the retailer but not from the original manufacturer, who after all made the product and who may be much more able financially to honor the warranty. Over the past few years, however, the judicial trend has been to abolish the privity requirement. Some courts had made exceptions to the privity rule for defective foodstuffs and cosmetics that caused injury. But the fundamental shift toward abolishing the privity requirement in cases involving all products began in 1958, when the Michigan Supreme Court overturned the old theory in an opinion by Justice John D. Voelker (who also wrote the novel *Anatomy of a Murder,* under the pen name Robert Traver). [Spence v. Three Rivers Builders & Masonry Supply, Inc., 90 N.W.2d 873 (Mich. 1958)]

Despite the clear trend toward the abolition of the privity rule in warranty cases involving personal injury, privity remains a problem for the plaintiff. For example, if a purchaser suffers an economic loss (that is, lost profits as opposed to a claim based on personal injury or property damage) and sues a remote seller on an implied warranty theory, most courts hold that privity remains a defense.

Suppose the buyer, anticipating these difficulties, chooses to sue only the immediate seller. What recourse does the retailer, say, have against the manufacturer? Under Section 2-607(5)(a), any buyer whose seller is answerable to him for a breach of warranty (as the selling manufacturer would be answerable for breach of an implied warranty to a buying retailer) can send a notice of the suit to the seller and request that he join in the defense. This is known as "vouching in" the manufacturer or other prior seller.

Another way that retailers can be indemnified in the event that they are sued is by requiring manufacturers whose products the stores carry to sign a "vendor's broad form." This is an indemnification agreement that obligates the manufacturer to reimburse the retailer for any damages the retailer suffers in a product liability lawsuit over the manufacturer's product, as long as the store did not physically damage or alter the product.

Liability Beyond the Buyer May the buyer's family or friends, who have not contracted with the sellers, assert warranty rights? In one of its rare instances of non-uniformity, the UCC does not dictate the result, but gives the states three choices, labeled in Section 2-318 as Alternatives A, B, and C.

Alternative A says that a seller's warranty extends "to any natural person who is in the family or household of his buyer or who is a guest in his home." The only limitations on the seller's liability under Alternative A are these: (1) it must be reasonable to expect the person injured to use, consume, or be affected by the goods, and (2) the warranty extends only to personal injury.

Alternative B "extends to any natural person who may reasonably be expected to use, consume, or be affected by the goods, and who is injured in person by breach of the warranty." It is less restrictive than the first alternative in that it extends protection to people beyond those in the buyer's home. It does not extend protection to organizations; "natural person" refers to individuals.

Alternative C is identical to Alternative B, except that it applies not merely to any "natural person" but "to any person who is injured by breach of the warranty." This is the most liberal alternative, because it provides redress for damage to *property* as well as for *personal* injury and it extends protection to corporations and other institutional buyers.

We now turn to the case that prompted what Dean Prosser has called "the most rapid and altogether spectacular overturn of an established rule in the entire history of the law of torts" (Prosser, 1971, p. 654)—the *Henningsen* case in 1960. At issue in this case were both the right to disclaim an implied warranty and the privity doctrine. In holding that a manufacturer's warranty extended to the ultimate purchaser regardless of lack of privity, and that the warranty could not be disclaimed, the New Jersey Supreme Court prompted a flood of other court decisions, so that today most other states recognize the right of a consumer to recover under an implied warranty for injuries caused by the product. The case was important also because it prompted the courts to go even further: once it is recognized that an implied warranty can be the basis for recovery, it is not a great leap toward doing without a contract theory at all. *Henningsen* thus helped pave the way for the strict liability revolution.

HENNINGSEN v. BLOOMFIELD MOTORS, INC.
32 N.J. 358, 161 A.2d 69 (1960)

FRANCIS, J. Plaintiff Claus H. Henningsen purchased a Plymouth automobile, manufactured by defendant Chrysler Corporation, from defendant Bloomfield Motors, Inc. His wife, plaintiff Helen Henningsen, was injured while driving it and instituted suit against both defendants to recover damages on account of her injuries. Her husband joined in the action seeking compensation for his consequential losses. The complaint was predicated upon breach of express and implied warranties and upon negligence. At the trial the negligence counts were dismissed by the court and the cause was submitted to the jury for determination solely on the issues of implied warranty of merchantability. Verdicts were returned against both defendants and in favor of the plaintiffs. Defendants appealed and plaintiffs cross-appealed from the dismissal of their negligence claim. The matter was certified by this court prior to consideration in the Appellate Division.

The facts are not complicated, but a general outline of them is necessary to an understanding of the case.

On May 7, 1955 Mr. and Mrs. Henningsen visited the place of business of Bloomfield Motors, Inc., an authorized De Soto and Plymouth dealer, to look at a Plymouth. They wanted to buy a car and were considering a Ford or a Chevrolet as well as a Plymouth. They were shown a Plymouth which appealed to them and the purchase followed. The record indicates that Mr. Henningsen intended the car as a Mother's Day gift to his wife. He said the intention was communicated to the dealer. When the purchase order or contract was prepared and presented, the husband executed it alone. His wife did not join as a party.

The purchase order was a printed form of one page. On the front it contained blanks to be filled in with a description of the automobile to be sold, the various accessories to be included, and the details of the financing. The particular car selected was described as a 1955 Plymouth, Plaza "6", Club Sedan. The type used in the printed parts of the form became smaller in size, different in style, and less readable toward the bottom where the line for the purchaser's signature was placed. The smallest type on the page appears in the two paragraphs, one of two and one-quarter lines and the second of one and one-half lines, on which great stress is laid by the defense in the case. These two paragraphs are the least legible and the most difficult to read in the instrument, but they are most important in the evaluation of the rights of the contesting parties. They do not attract attention and there is nothing about the format which would draw the reader's eye to them. In fact, a studied and concentrated effort would have to be made to read them. Deemphasis seems the motive rather than emphasis. More particularly, most of the printing in the body of the order appears to be 12 point block type, and easy to read. In the short paragraphs under discussion, however, the type appears to be six point script and the print is solid, that is, the lines are very close together.

The two paragraphs are:

> The front and back of this Order comprise the entire agreement affecting this purchase and no other agreement or understanding of any nature concerning same has been made or entered into, or will be recognized. I hereby certify that no credit has been extended to me for the purchase of the motor vehicle except as appears in writing on the face of this agreement.
>
> I have read the matter printed on the back hereof and agree to it as a part of this order the same as if it were printed above my signature. I certify that I am 21 years of age, or older, and hereby acknowledge receipt of a copy of this order.

* * *

The reverse side of the contract contains 8½ inches of fine print.

* * *

In the seventh paragraph, about two-thirds of the way down the page, the warranty, which is the focal point of the case, is set forth. It is as follows:

> 7. It is expressly agreed that there are no warranties, express or implied, *made* by either the dealer or the manufacturer on the motor vehicle, chassis, or parts furnished hereunder except as follows.
>
> "The manufacturer warrants each new motor vehicle (including original equipment placed thereon

by the manufacturer except tires), chassis or parts manufactured by it to be free from defects in material or workmanship under normal use and service. Its obligation under this warranty being limited to making good at its factory any part or parts thereof which shall, within ninety (90) days after delivery of such vehicle *to the original purchaser* or before such vehicle has been driven 4,000 miles, whichever event shall first occur, be returned to it with transportation charges prepaid and which its examination shall disclose to its satisfaction to have been thus defective; *this warranty being expressly in lieu of all other warranties expressed or implied, and all other obligations or liabilities on its part,* and it neither assumes nor authorizes any other person to assume for it any other liability in connection with the sale of its vehicles." (Emphasis ours.)

* * *

The new Plymouth was turned over to the Henningsens on May 9, 1955.

* * *

It had no servicing and no mishaps of any kind before the event of May 19. That day, Mrs. Henningsen drove to Asbury Park. On the way down and in returning the car performed in normal fashion until the accident occurred. She was proceeding north on Route 36 in Highlands, New Jersey, at 20–22 miles per hour. The highway was paved and smooth, and contained two lanes for northbound travel. She was riding in the right-hand lane. Suddenly she heard a loud noise "from the bottom, by the hood." It "felt as if something cracked." The steering wheel spun in her hands; the car veered sharply to the right and crashed into a highway sign and a brick wall. No other vehicle was in any way involved. A bus operator driving in the left-hand lane testified that he observed plaintiffs' car approaching in normal fashion in the opposite direction; "all of sudden [it] veered at 90 degrees . . . and right into this wall." As a result of the impact, the front of the car was so badly damaged that it was impossible to determine if any of the parts of the steering wheel mechanism or workmanship or assembly were defective or improper prior to the accident. The condition was such that the collision insurance carrier, after inspection, declared the vehicle a total loss. It had 468 miles on the speedometer at the time.

* * *

THE CLAIM OF IMPLIED WARRANTY AGAINST THE MANUFACTURER.

* * *

Chrysler points out that an implied warranty of merchantability is an incident of a contract of sale. It concedes, of course, the making of the original sale to Bloomfield Motors, Inc., but maintains that this transaction marked the terminal point of its contractual connection with the car. Then Chrysler urges that since it was not a party to the sale by the dealer to Henningsen, there is no privity of contract between it and the plaintiffs, and the absence of this privity eliminates any such implied warranty.

* * *

With the advent of mass marketing, the manufacturer became remote from the purchaser, sales were accomplished through intermediaries, and the demand for the product was created by advertising media. In such an economy it became obvious that the consumer was the person being cultivated. Manifestly, the connotation of "consumer" was broader than that of "buyer." He signified such a person who, in the reasonable contemplation of the parties to the sale, might be expected to use the product. Thus, where the commodities sold are such that if defectively manufactured they will be dangerous to life or limb, then society's interests can only be protected by eliminating the requirement of privity between the maker and his dealers and the reasonably expected ultimate consumer. In that way the burden of losses consequent upon use of defective articles is borne by those who are in a position to either control the danger or make an equitable distribution of the losses when they do occur.

* * *

Under modern conditions the ordinary layman, on responding to the importuning of colorful advertising, has neither the opportunity nor the capacity to inspect or to determine the fitness of an automobile for use; he must rely on the manufacturer who has control of its construction, and to some degree on the dealer who, to the limited extent called for by the manufacturer's instructions, inspects and services it before delivery. In such a marketing milieu his remedies and those of persons who properly claim through him should not depend "upon the intricacies of the law of sales. The obligation of the manufacturer should not be based alone on privity of contract. It should rest, as was once said, upon 'the demands of social justice.' " Mazetti v. Armour & Co., 75 Wash. 622, 135 P. 633, 635, 48 L.R.A.,N.S., 213 (Sup.Ct.1913). "If privity of contract is required," then, under the circumstances of modern merchandising, "privity of contract exists in the consciousness and understanding of all right-thinking persons." Madouros v. Kansas City Coca-Cola Bottling Co., 90 S.W.2d at page 450.

Accordingly, we hold that under modern marketing conditions, when a manufacturer puts a new automobile in the stream of trade and promotes its purchase by the public, an implied warranty that it is reasonably suitable for use as such accompanies it into the hands of the ultimate purchaser. Absence of agency between the manufacturer and the dealer who makes the ultimate sale is immaterial.

THE EFFECT OF THE DISCLAIMER AND LIMITATION OF LIABILITY CLAUSES ON THE IMPLIED WARRANTY OF MERCHANTABILITY.

* * *

The warranty before us is a standardized form designed for mass use. It is imposed upon the automobile consumer. He takes it or leaves it, and he must take it to buy an automobile. No bargaining is engaged in with respect to it. In fact, the dealer through whom it comes to the buyer is without authority to alter it; his function is ministerial—simply to deliver it.

* * *

The gross inequality of bargaining position occupied by the consumer in the automobile industry is thus apparent. There is no competition among the car makers in the area of the express warranty. Where can the buyer go to negotiate for better protection? Such control and limitation of his remedies are inimical to the public welfare and, at the very least, call for great care by the courts to avoid injustice through application of strict common law principles of freedom of contract. Because there is no competition among the motor vehicle manufacturers with respect to the scope of protection guaranteed to the buyer, there is no incentive on their part to stimulate good will in that field of public relations. Thus, there is lacking a factor existing in more competitive fields, one which tends to guarantee the safe construction of the article sold. Since all competitors operate in the same way, the urge to be careful is not so pressing.

* * *

In the framework of this case, illuminated as it is by the facts and the many decisions noted, we are of the opinion that Chrysler's attempted disclaimer of an implied warranty of merchantability and of the obligations arising therefrom is so inimical to the public good as to compel an adjudication of its invalidity.

* * *

THE DEALER'S IMPLIED WARRANTY.

* * *

For the reasons set forth [above] . . . , we conclude that the disclaimer of an implied warranty of merchantability by the dealer, as well as the attempted elimination of all obligations other than replacement of defective parts, are violative of public policy and void.

* * *

Both defendants contend that since there was no privity of contract between them and Mrs. Henningsen, she cannot recover for breach of any warranty made by either of them. On the facts, as they were developed, we agree that she was not a party to the purchase agreement. Her right to maintain the action, therefore, depends upon whether she occupies such legal status thereunder as to permit her to take advantage of a breach of defendants' implied warranties.

* * *

It is important to express the right of Mrs. Henningsen to maintain her action in terms of a general principle. To what extent may lack of privity be disregarded in suits on such warranties? . . . It is our opinion that an implied warranty of merchantability chargeable to either an automobile manufacturer or a dealer extends to the purchaser of the car, members of his family, and to other persons occupying or using it with his consent. It would be wholly opposed to reality to say that use by such persons is not within the anticipation of parties to such a warranty of reasonable suitability of an automobile for ordinary highway operation. Those persons must be considered within the distributive chain.

* * *

Under all of the circumstances outlined above, the judgments in favor of the plaintiffs and against the defendants are affirmed.

Contributory Negligence, Comparative Negligence, and Assumption of Risk

Three common-law concepts remain as possible impediments to the contract-based warranty theories: *assumption of risk, contributory negligence,* and *comparative negligence*. These are discussed in Chapter 9.

Courts uniformly hold that assumption of risk is a defense for sellers against a claim of breach of warranty, while there is a split of authority over whether comparative and contributory negligence are defenses. However, the courts' use of this terminology is often conflicting and confusing. The ultimate question is really one of causation: Was the seller's breach of the warranty the cause of the plaintiff's injuries?

The UCC is not markedly helpful in clearing away the cobwebs strewn about over the years in discussions of assumption of risk and contributory negligence. Section 2-715(2)(b) says that among the forms of consequential damage for which recovery can be sought is "injury to person or property *proximately* resulting from any breach of warranty" (emphasis added). But "proximately" is a troublesome word. Indeed, ultimately it is a circular word, for it means nothing more than that the defendant must have been a direct enough cause of the injury that the courts will impose liability. Comment 5 to this section says that

> [w]here the injury involved follows the use of goods without discovery of the defect causing the damage, the question of "proximate" cause turns on whether it was reasonable for the buyer to use the goods without such inspection as would have revealed the defects. If it was not reasonable for him to do so, or if he did in fact discover the defect prior to his use, the injury would not proximately result from the breach of warranty.

Obviously if a sky diver buys a parachute and then discovers a few holes in it, his family would not likely prevail in court when they sued to recover for his death because the parachute failed to function after he jumped at 5,000 feet. But the general notion that it must have been reasonable for a buyer to use goods without inspection can make a warranty case difficult to prove.

Strict Liability in Tort

The warranties grounded in the UCC often are ineffective in assuring recoveries for a plaintiff's injuries. The notice requirement and the ability of a seller to disclaim remain especially bothersome problems, as does the privity requirement in those states that continue to adhere to it. To overcome the obstacles, judges have gone beyond the commercial statutes. They have fashioned a tort theory of product liability based on the principle of **strict liability**.

Defined

The formulation of strict liability that most courts use is Section 402A of the *Restatement of Torts, Second,* set out in full as follows:

> (1) One who sells any product in a defective condition unreasonably dangerous to the user or consumer or to his property is subject to liability for physical harm thereby caused to the ultimate user or consumer, or to his property, if
> (a) the seller is engaged in the business of selling such a product, and
> (b) it is expected to and does reach the user or consumer without substantial change in the condition in which it is sold.
> (2) The rule stated in Subsection (1) applies although
> (a) the seller has exercised all possible care in the preparation and sale of his product, and
> (b) the user or consumer has not bought the product from or entered into any contractual relation with the seller.

Restatement Section 402A avoids the warranty booby traps. It states a rule of law not governed by the UCC, and so limitations and exclusions in warranties will not apply to a suit based on the Restatement theory. Nor is privity a requirement; Section 402A is not limited to buyer and seller. And the consumer is under no obligation to give notice to the seller within a reasonable time of any injuries.

Note that the *Restatement of Torts, Second,* is not a statute like the UCC. It is a private, model code of law, a statement of what the American Law Institute, a private body of lawyers and judges, thinks the law should be. Although courts in most states have adopted the concept of strict liability embodied in Section 402A, many courts depart from some of its specific elements, to a consideration of which we now turn.

Section 402A Elements

"One Who Sells Any Product in a Defective Condition" As under the UCC, sales of goods are covered but not sales of services. Furthermore, the plaintiff will not prevail if the product was safe for normal handling and consumption when sold. A glass soda bottle that is properly capped is not in a defective condition merely because it can be broken if the consumer should happen to drop it, making the jagged glass dangerous. Chocolate candy bars are not defective merely because you can become quite ill by eating too many of them at once. On the other hand, a seller would be liable for a product defectively packaged, so that it could explode or deteriorate and change its chemical composition. A product can also be in a defective condition if there is danger that could come from an anticipated wrongful use, such as a drug safe only when taken in limited doses. Under those circumstances, failure to place an adequate dosage warning on the container makes the product defective.

The plaintiff bears the burden of proving that the product is in a defective condition, and this burden can be difficult to meet. Many products are the result of complex feats of engineering. Expert witnesses are necessary to prove that the products were defectively manufactured, and these are not always easy to come by. This difficulty of proof is one reason why many cases raise the failure to warn as the dispositive issue, since in the right case that issue is far easier to prove.

As the following case demonstrates, the plaintiff cannot prevail under the theory of strict liability simply because he was injured. It is not the fact of injury that is determinative but the defective condition of the product.

ANDERSON v. ASSOCIATED GROCERS, INC.
11 Wash.App. 74, 525 P.2d 284 (1974)

GREEN, CHIEF JUDGE. Plaintiff appeals from an order granting summary judgment of dismissal in favor of the defendant, Associated Grocers, Inc. The propriety of this order presents the sole question on appeal.

Shortly after 8 a.m. on July 23, 1970, Associated Grocers delivered a pallet of produce to the back room of the Thriftway Market in Pasco. On top of the stack of produce was one cardboard box of Chiquita brand bananas. The bananas were unwrapped and the box contained breather holes. Later that morning, Tom Anderson, the produce manager, removed the box of bananas from the top of the stack. When he reached for a lug of radishes that had been under the bananas, a spider, identified as Heteropoda Venatoria, commonly called a banana spider, 6 inches in diameter, leaped from some wet burlap onto his left hand and bit him. Nine months later, April 24, 1971, Tom Anderson died of heart failure.

His wife, Johnnie Anderson, as administratrix of her husband's estate, brought this action to recover damages for the alleged wrongful death of her husband. The action is grounded upon three theories: (1) strict liability for a defect in product under Restatement (Second) of Torts § 402A (1965); (2) breach of implied warranty of merchantability and fitness based upon RCW 62A.2-314; and (3) negligence. In granting summary judgment for Associated Grocers, the trial court rejected the first two theories and found no evidence to support an issue of fact as to negligence.

On appeal, error is assigned to the granting of summary judgment in favor of defendant rather than plaintiff on the first two theories. No error having been assigned to the granting of summary judgment on the negligence theory, it is not before us.

With respect to the other two theories, plaintiff contends that the bananas delivered to the Pasco Thriftway and handled by her deceased husband were defective and thereby unfit for the ordinary purpose for which the bananas were to be used. The trial court rejected this contention because there was no showing that the bananas were in any way defective or unfit for the purpose intended. The court noted that the spider was not in the bananas nor the container, and ruled that although the container may have transported the spider, the product was not defective or unfit. We affirm.

Section 402A of the Restatement of Torts, as well as RCW 62A.2-314, and the cases cited to us by plaintiff, involve defects in the product itself. None involve transient insects or spiders. In the instant case, the spider was not in the bananas, but was on a piece of wet burlap on top of a box of radishes. There was nothing wrong with the bananas; they were edible and saleable. In these circumstances, neither the doctrine of strict liability nor breach of implied warranty of fitness applies.

Affirmed.

"Unreasonably Dangerous" The requirement that the product be "unreasonably dangerous" has been especially troublesome. The product must be not merely dangerous, but *unreasonably* dangerous. Most products have characteristics that make them dangerous in certain circumstances. As the Restatement commentators note, sugar is not inherently dangerous but is deadly to diabetics, and all food and drugs pose some danger, if only from overconsumption. Under Section 402A, "the article sold must be dangerous to an extent beyond that which would be contemplated by the ordinary consumer who purchases it, with the ordinary knowledge common to the community as to its characteristics." This definition is, of course, slippery. The commentator argues that "good tobacco is not unreasonably dangerous merely because the effects of smoking may be harmful," but perhaps some day, when the evidence matures on the causal connection to cancer, it will be held to be unreasonably dangerous.

Even high risks of danger are not necessarily unreasonable. Some products are unavoidably unsafe, as for example rabies vaccine, which can cause dreadful side effects. But the disease itself, almost always fatal, is worse. A product is unavoidably unsafe when it cannot be made safe for its intended purpose given the present state of human knowledge. Because important benefits may flow from the product's use, its producer or seller ought not be held liable for its danger.

However, the failure to *warn* a potential user of potential hazards can make a product defective under Section 402A, whether unreasonably dangerous or even unavoidably unsafe. The dairy farmer need not warn those with common allergies to eggs, because it will be presumed that the person with an allergic reaction to common foodstuffs will be aware of them. But when the product contains an ingredient that could cause toxic effects in a substantial number of people and its danger is not widely known (or if known, is not an ingredient that would commonly be supposed to be in the product), the lack of a warning could make the product unreasonably dangerous within the meaning of Section 402A. Many of the suits brought by asbestos workers charge exactly this point: "The utility of an insulation product containing asbestos may outweigh the known or foreseeable risk to the insulation workers and thus justify its marketing. The product could still be unreasonably dangerous, however, if unaccompanied by adequate warnings. An insulation worker, no less than any other product user, has a right to decide whether to expose himself to the risk." [Circuit Judge John Minor Wisdom, in Borel v. Fibreboard Paper Products Corp., 493 F.2d 1076 (5th Cir. 1973).] This rule of law has lately come to haunt the Manville Corporation and other producers of asbestos.

"Engaged in the Business of Selling" Section 402A(1)(a) limits liability to sellers "engaged in the business of selling such a product." The rule is intended to apply to people and entities engaged in *business,* not to casual one-time sellers. The business need not be solely in the defective product; a movie theater that sells popcorn with a razor blade inside is no less liable than a grocery store that does so. But strict liability under this rule does not attach to a private individual who sells his own automobile. In this sense, Section 402A is analogous to the UCC's limitation of the warranty of merchantability to the merchant.

The requirement that the defendant be in the business of selling stems in part from a public policy that the courts often articulate: Businesses should shoulder the cost of injuries because they are in the best position to spread the risk and distribute the expense among the public. A dramatic example of how judgments are ultimately assessed against the buying public came in the wake of a $5.3 million judgment against Riddell, Inc., the leading manufacturer of football helmets, in a suit brought by a high school football player who charged that a defective Riddell helmet left him paralyzed when a blow to the back of his neck severed his spinal cord. Riddell's annual product liability insurance premiums had been $40,000; three years after Riddell lost the case, its premiums had shot up to $1.5 million, or about 10 percent of its annual sales of $15 million. The premiums were said to add about $7 to the price of a $35 helmet. This same policy has been the rationale for holding bailors and lessors liable for defective equipment just as if they had been sellers, as the *Martin* v. *Ryder Rental, Inc.* case (pp. 284–86) illustrates.

Reaches the User Without Change in Condition Section 402A(1)(b) limits strict liability to those defective products that are expected to and do reach the user or consumer without substantial change in the condition in which sold. A product safe when delivered cannot subject the seller to liability if it is subsequently mishandled or changed. The seller, however, must anticipate in appropriate cases that the product will be stored; faulty packaging or sterilization may be the grounds for liability if the product deteriorates before being used.

Liability Despite Exercise of All Due Care Strict liability applies under the Restatement rule even though "the seller has exercised all possible care in the preparation and sale of his product." This is the crux of "strict liability" and distinguishes it from the conventional theory of negligence. It does not matter how reasonably the seller acted or how exemplary is a manufacturer's quality control system—what matters is whether the product was defective and the user injured as a result. Suppose an automated bottle factory manufactures 1,000 bottles an hour under exacting standards, with a rigorous and costly quality-control program designed to weed out any bottles showing even an infinitesimal amount of stress. The plant is "state of the art," and its computerized quality-control operation is the best in the world. It regularly detects the one out of every 10,000 bottles that analysis has shown will be defective. Despite this intense effort, it proves impossible to weed out every defective bottle; one out of one million, say, will still escape detection. Assume that that bottle, filled with soda, finds its way into a consumer's home, explodes when handled, sends glass shards into his eye, and blinds him. Under strict liability, the bottler will be liable to the consumer.

Liability Without Contractual Relation Under Section 402A(2)(b), strict liability applies even though the user has not bought the product from the seller nor entered into any contractual relation with him. In short, privity is abolished and the injured user may use the theory of strict liability against manufacturers and wholesalers as well as retailers. Here, however, the courts have announced certain limitations to the abolition of privity. For example, in some states the rule of privity still applies to bystanders. Suppose the brakes in a car are defective, and they fail while the owner is driving the car downtown. He hits a pedestrian, who sues the automobile manufacturer. Some state courts will not hold the manufacturer liable on the grounds of strict liability; the pedestrian will have to show that the manufacturer was negligent, that is, was careless in installing the brake system. The Restatement explicitly leaves open the question of the bystander's right to recover under strict liability.

The following case shows how one court tackled this question and approved the application of strict liability against a bailor truck-rental agency when a bystander was injured because of faulty brakes.

MARTIN v. RYDER TRUCK RENTAL, INC.
353 A.2d 581 (Del. 1976)

HERRMANN, CHIEF JUSTICE. We hold today that a bailment-lease of a motor vehicle, entered into in the regular course of a truck rental business, is subject to application of the doctrine of strict tort liability in favor of an injured bystander.

According to the plaintiffs in this case:

A truck was leased by the defendant, Ryder Truck Rental, Inc., to Gagliardi Brothers, Inc., in the regular course of Ryder's truck rental business. The truck, operated by a Gagliardi employee, was involved in an intersectional collision. Due to a failure of its braking system, the truck did not stop for a traffic light and struck the rear of an automobile which had stopped for the signal, causing that automobile to collide with the vehicle driven by the plaintiff, Dorothy Martin. As a result, she was injured, her car was damaged, and this suit was brought by her and her husband against Ryder.

The plaintiffs base their cause of action solely upon the doctrine of strict tort liability, *i.e.,* tort liability without proof of negligence. The Superior Court granted summary judgment in favor of Ryder, holding that the doctrine is not applicable to the factual situation here presented. We disagree.

* * *

The development of the doctrine of strict tort liability in the law of products liability has evolved rapidly during the past decade, until it has become the prevailing remedy throughout the country. It is now the rule in approximately two-thirds of the states, including Pennsylvania and New Jersey.

Strict tort liability in the field of products liability has developed in a "step by step" process out of the law of contract warranty into the law of tort, for the purpose of the greater protection of the user and the public against defective goods by eliminating the "luggage" and "undesirable complications" of the contract-warranty remedy in direct sales transactions, such as the requirement of a sale and notice, and the provision for limitation and disclaimer, generally prescribed by the Uniform Sales Act and the UCC.

At the forefront of this development was the landmark case of *Henningsen* v. *Bloomfield Motors, Inc.*, 32 N.J. 358, 161 A.2d 69 (1960), which brought a "breakthrough" in extending strict warranty liability to products other than food and drink.

The first significant application of the strict tort liability concept in a products liability case was the landmark decision of *Greenman* v. *Yuba Power Products, Inc.*, 59 Cal.2d 57, 27 Cal. Rptr. 697, 377 P.2d 897 (1963), termed "certainly the most important decision since *Henningsen* and perhaps the most important since *MacPherson* v. *Buick* [217 N.Y. 382, 111 N.E. 1050 (1916)]." 2 Frumer & Friedman § 16A[1], at 3-238. The defendant remote-manufacturer there sought to avoid liability for breach of warranty on a defective power tool on the ground that reasonable notice of the breach had not been given under the notice requirements of the California Sales Act governing contract warranties. The Court held otherwise, stating:

> A manufacturer is strictly liable in tort when an article he places on the market, knowing that it is to be used without inspection for defects, proves to have a defect that causes injury to a human being. . . .
>
> Although . . . strict liability has usually been based on the theory of an express or implied warranty running from the manufacturer to the plaintiff, . . . the liability is not one governed by the law of contract warranties but by the law of strict liability in tort. Accordingly, rules defining and governing warranties that were developed to meet the needs of commercial transactions cannot properly be invoked to govern the manufacturer's liability to those injured by their defective products unless those rules also serve the purposes for which such liability is imposed.
>
> . . . The purpose of such liability is to insure that the costs of injuries resulting from defective products are borne by the manufacturers that put such products on the market rather than by the injured persons who are powerless to protect themselves. Sales warranties serve this purpose fitfully at best. . . . Implicit in the machine's presence on the market . . . was a representation that it would safely do the jobs for which it was built. . . . To establish the manufacturer's liability it was sufficient that plaintiff proved that he was injured while using the [product] in a way it was intended to be used as a result of a defect in design and manufacture of which plaintiff was not aware that made the [product] unsafe for its intended use. 377 P.2d at 900, 901.

Influenced, as were other courts, by *Yuba's* reasoning, the Supreme Court of New Jersey in 1965 abandoned the warranty terminology of *Henningsen* and embraced strict tort liability in *Santor* v. *A. and M. Karagheusian, Inc.* 44 N.J. 52, 207 A.2d 305 (1965).

* * *

Since *Yuba* and *Santor,* the doctrine of strict tort liability has met with widespread acceptance throughout the country. Consequently, in the past decade, the protection afforded to a person injured by a defective product has been greatly enhanced by the steady and consistent expansion of the concept. The doctrine was developed at the outset for application against remote manufacturers for the protection of users and consumers. It has been in a constant state of refinement and extension, however. One of the extensions of the doctrine has been to bailors and lessors; another has been to injured bystanders. Once again, the leading decisions emanate from California and New Jersey.

In *Cintrone* v. *Hertz Truck Leasing, etc.*, 45 N.J. 434, 212 A.2d 769 (1969), the New Jersey Supreme Court applied strict liability in tort to a motor vehicle bailment situation because "[a] bailor for hire, such as a person in the U-drive-it business, puts motor vehicles in the stream of commerce in a fashion not unlike a manufacturer or retailer"; subjects such a leased vehicle "to more sustained use on the highways than most ordinary car purchasers"; and by the very nature of his business, exposes "the bailee, his employees, passengers and the traveling public . . . to a greater *quantum* of potential danger of harm from defective vehicles than usually arises out of sales by the manufacturer." 212 A.2d at 777.

* * *

The extension of the doctrine of strict tort liability to bailors-lessors has been limited, however, to leases made in the regular course of a rental business, the doctrine being applicable only in a commercial setting by its very nature.

* * *

The remaining question is whether the doctrine is applicable to the case of an injured bystander.

The doctrine of strict liability in tort has been extended to injured bystanders. We endorse the rationale of *Elmore* v. *American Motors Corporation,* 70 Cal.2d 578, 75 Cal.Rptr. 652, 451 P.2d 84 (1969):

> If anything, bystanders should be entitled to greater protection than the consumer or user where injury to bystanders from the defect is reasonably foreseeable. Consumers and users, at least, have the opportunity to inspect for defects, . . . whereas the bystander ordinarily has no such opportunities. In short, the bystander is in greater need of protection from defective products which are dangerous, and if any distinction should be made between bystanders and users, it should be made . . . to extend greater liability in favor of the bystanders. 75 Cal.Rptr. at 657, 451 P.2d at 89.

Bystander recovery is the prevailing rule in the application of the doctrine of strict tort liability by the overwhelming weight of authority. Fairness and logic, as well as the philosophy underlying the doctrine, require that an injured bystander be covered in its application. We so hold.

It is noteworthy that under the UCC § 2-318 an injured bystander may be protected as one "affected by" a defective product in a direct sale situation covered by an implied warranty. Thus, the conclusion reached here is in accord with the public policy underlying § 2-318.

* * *

The judgment below is reversed and the cause remanded for further proceedings consistent herewith.

Broadening the Circle of Liability

Although the abolition of the privity defense allows the plaintiff to recover from a wholesaler or manufacturer with whom he did not contract, the plaintiff still is required to prove that the defendant sold the product in a defective condition. However, in 1980, the California Supreme Court delighted the personal injury bar and dismayed the corporate defense bar with what has been characterized as a "revolutionary" ruling in *Sindell* v. *Abbott Laboratories,* 607 P.2d 924 (Cal. 1980), that an *entire industry* can be held responsible for injury caused by a defective drug if the plaintiff could not prove which company had manufactured it.

The drug in question was diethylstilbestrol (DES), prescribed between 1945 and 1971 to prevent miscarriages in millions of pregnant women. Unfortunately, DES proved to have extremely toxic effects on daughters born to these mothers. Ten to twenty years later, between one and four women per 1,000 whose mothers had taken DES developed adenocarcinoma, a fast-spreading, extremely virulent form of vaginal cancer. A much larger number of daughters, between 30 and 90 percent, developed adenosis, precancerous vaginal and cervical growths which can spread to other parts of the body. But it was difficult even getting to court to prove that the manufacturer had put a defective drug on the market because it was necessary first to find and sue the particular manufacturer whose product a plaintiff's mother used. The drugs, manufactured by more than 200 pharmaceutical companies, were sold generically, so that even if records were available from two decades or more earlier, it was impossible to show who had made the particular drug taken.

Judith Sindell, twenty-six when her cancer struck in 1976, argued in her lawsuit against the five largest manufacturers of DES that they were all responsible because they had followed a mutually agreed upon formula, had collaborated in marketing and promoting the drug, and had relied on the results of each other's tests. The California Supreme Court agreed that it would be unfair to bar her suit simply because she could not identify the particular manufacturer. Instead, it said, the burden of proof would shift to the defendants to show that they could not have been the manufacturers. In overturning a lower court dismissal of the suit and allowing the plaintiff to proceed to trial, the court allowed the big five to bring other manufacturers into the suit. Under the court's "market-share liability" theory, "each defendant will be held liable for the proportion of the judgment represented by its share of that market unless it demonstrates that it could not have made the product."

Negligence

Negligence is the third theory raised in the typical product liability case. Like strict liability, it is a tort theory. We considered negligence in detail in Chapter 9. The principles discussed in that chapter apply equally in a product liability case. One question, however, should be addressed here: Why should plaintiffs bother with the negligence theory when they can use strict liability, where sellers are liable even though they have taken all possible care? The answer lies in two types of cases: those in which plaintiffs charge that the *design* of a product is defective, and those in which they charge inadequate *warnings*.

Design Cases

Manufacturers can be, and often are, held liable for injuries caused by products that were defectively designed. Although these cases are sometimes taken to be illustrations of strict liability theory, in fact most ultimately turn on the question of whether the designer used reasonable care in designing a product reasonably safe for its foreseeable use. The concern over reasonableness and standards of care are elements of negligence theory.

Design cases can pose severe problems for manufacturing and safety engineers, as the case outlined in Box 10-1 suggests. More safety means more cost, and the altered design may impair the functioning of the product. At what point safety and performance come into reasonable balance is impossible to forecast accurately, though some factors can be taken into account. The cheaper a safety device is the more likely its absence will be taken as unreasonable. If other manufacturers are marketing comparable products whose designs are intrinsically safer, the less-safe products are likely to lose a test of reasonableness in court.

Warning Cases

We noted above that a product may be defective if the manufacturer fails adequately to warn the user of potential dangers. Whether a warning should have been affixed is often a question of what is reasonably foreseeable, and the failure to affix a warning will be treated as negligent. The manufacturer of a weed killer with poisonous ingredients is certainly acting negligently when it fails to warn the consumer that the contents are potentially lethal.

The law governing the necessity to warn and the adequacy of the warnings is complex. What is reasonable turns on the degree to which a product is likely to be misused and, as the following case illustrates, whether the hazard is obvious.

LAAPERI v. SEARS, ROEBUCK & CO., INC.
787 F.2d 726 (1st Cir. 1986)

LEVIN CAMPBELL, (C.J.) In March 1976, plaintiff Albin Laaperi purchased a smoke detector from Sears. The detector, manufactured by the Pittway Corporation, was designed to be powered by AC (electrical) current. Laaperi installed the detector himself in one of the two upstairs bedrooms in his home.

Early in the morning of December 27, 1976, a fire broke out in the Laaperi home. The three boys in one of the upstairs bedrooms were killed in the blaze. Laaperi's 13-year-old daughter Janet, who was sleeping in the other upstairs bedroom, received burns over 12 percent of her body and was hospitalized for three weeks.

The uncontroverted testimony at trial was that the smoke detector did not sound an alarm on the night of the fire. The cause of the fire was later found to be a short circuit in an electrical cord that was located in a cedar closet in the boys' bedroom. The Laaperi home had two separate electrical circuits in the upstairs bedrooms: one which provided electricity to the outlets and one which powered the lighting fixtures. The smoke detector had been connected to the outlet circuit, which was the circuit that shorted and cut off. Because the circuit was shorted, the AC-operated smoke detector received no power on the night of the fire. Therefore, although the detector itself was in no sense defective (indeed, after the fire the charred detector was tested and found to be operable), no alarm sounded.

Laaperi brought this diversity action against defendants Sears and Pittway, asserting negligent de-

Box 10-1 What Happens When Design Standards Conflict?

A policeman was severely injured in a Chrysler-built patrol car in New Jersey. It slammed into a steel pole and crushed him against the windshield. At the trial, his expert witnesses demonstrated that the pole pushed through the automobile in a seventeen-inch gap in its noncontinuous frame. An alternative design was possible and was known to the industry; it is a continuous frame, which, according to the expert witnesses, would have prevented the accident. The experts conceded on cross-examination, however, that the continuous frame would have cost some $300 more per car and added an additional 250 pounds. The alternative design would be more expensive and less efficient—and it would subject riders to a greater risk that they would be injured in a different kind of accident (the more rigid body would transmit the shock of collisions to persons inside, whereas a noncontinuous frame would absorb and mute the force of a collision). The vehicle conformed to federal motor vehicle safety standards. But the National Traffic and Motor Vehicle Safety Act explicitly provides that such compliance does not exempt manufacturers from common law liability. Therefore, ruled the United States Court of Appeals in Philadelphia in 1980, the jury's finding that the noncontinuous frame construction was faulty and its $2 million verdict must stand, even though it would be entirely possible for a different jury to hold the alternative continuous-frame design defective in another case. Only Congress can effect the cure for this Catch-22 situation, the court said. Dawson v. Chrysler Corp., 49 L. W. 2200 (3rd. Cir. 1980).

Source: Jethro K. Lieberman, *The Litigious Society,* 1981, p. 46

sign, negligent manufacture, breach of warranty, and negligent failure to warn of inherent dangers. The parties agreed that the applicable law is that of Massachusetts. Before the claims went to the jury, verdicts were directed in favor of defendants on all theories of liability other than failure to warn.

Laaperi's claim under the failure to warn theory was that he was unaware of the danger that the very short circuit which might ignite a fire in his home could, at the same time, incapacitate the smoke detector. He contended that had he been warned of this danger, he would have purchased a battery-powered smoke detector as a backup or taken some other precaution, such as wiring the detector to a circuit of its own, in order better to protect his family in the event of an electrical fire.

The jury returned verdicts in favor of Laaperi in all four actions on the failure to warn claim. The jury assessed damages in the amount of $350,000 in each of the three actions brought on behalf of the deceased sons, and $750,000 in the action brought on behalf of Janet Laaperi. The defendants' motions for directed verdict and judgment notwithstanding the verdict were denied, and defendants appealed.

* * *

Defendants ask us to declare that the risk that an electrical fire could incapacitate an AC-powered smoke detector is so obvious that the average consumer would not benefit from a warning. This is not a trivial argument; in earlier—some might say sounder—days, we might have accepted it. Our sense of the current state of the tort law in Massachusetts and most other jurisdictions, however, leads us to conclude that, today, the matter before us poses a jury question; that "obviousness" in a situation such as this would be treated by the Massachusetts courts as presenting a question of fact, not of law. To be sure, it would be obvious to anyone that an electrical outage would cause this smoke detector to fail. But the average purchaser might not comprehend the specific danger that a fire-causing electrical problem can simultaneously knock out the circuit into which a smoke detector is wired, causing the detector to fail at the very moment it is needed. Thus, while the failure of a detector to function as the result of an electrical malfunction due, say, to a broken power line or a neighborhood power outage would, we think, be obvious as a matter of law, the failure that occurred here, being associated with the very risk—fire—for which the device was purchased, was not, or so a jury could find.

* * *

Finally, defendants contend that the award of $750,000 in damages to Janet Laaperi was excessive, and should have been overturned by the district court.

* * *

The jury undoubtedly, and understandably, felt a great deal of sympathy for a young girl who, at the age of 13, lost three brothers in a tragic fire. But by law the jury was only permitted to compensate her for those damages associated with her own injuries. Her injuries included fright and pain at the time of and after the fire, a three-week hospital stay, some minor discomfort for several weeks after discharge, and a permanent scar on her lower back.

* * *

The judgments in favor of Albin Laaperi in his capacity as administrator of the estates of his three sons are affirmed. In the action on behalf of Janet Laaperi, the verdict of the jury is set aside, the judgment of the district court vacated, and the cause remanded to that court for a new trial limited to the issue of damages.

Product Liability Law Reform

We began this chapter by noting some of the more dramatic illustrations of the impact that product liability law can have—and has had—on business. A scholarly survey of the impact of this branch of law on manufacturers in California in the late 1970s confirmed what others had reported anecdotally. Insurance premiums had climbed markedly, as had deductible limits; most complainants charged manufacturers with defective design, and most suits were filed by consumers, although suits against small manufacturers were filed in equal numbers by injured workers; the dollar amount of verdicts and settlements had risen over the five-year period of the survey; twenty percent of the respondents said that they dropped product lines for fear of lawsuits, and increasing numbers of manufacturers, through their trade associations, were looking to the state legislatures to modify court-made product liability law (McInturff, 1981, 359–60).

State Reforms

The last conclusion is especially significant. As we have seen, in developing strict liability theory, courts have gone well beyond the warranty theory embodied in legislation. Prodded by astute lobbying by manufacturing and other business trade associations, state legislatures in the late 1970s began to respond to the audible cry of manufacturers about the hardships that the judicial transformation of the product liability lawsuit ostensibly worked on them. By the early 1980s, more than half the state legislatures had enacted at least one of some three dozen "reform" proposals being pressed on them. Some of these measures do little more than affirm and clarify case law. Among the most important to pass in several states are the following:

Statutes of Repose Perhaps nothing so frightens the manufacturer as the occasional reports of cases involving products, like punch presses, that were fifty or sixty or more years old at the time they injured the plaintiff. More than a third of the states have addressed this problem by enacting the so-called *statute of repose*. This statute establishes a time period, generally ranging from six to twelve years; the manufacturer is not liable for injuries caused by the product after this time has passed.

State of the Art Defense Several states have enacted laws that prevent advances in technology from being held against the manufacturer. The fear is that a plaintiff will convince a jury a product was defective because it did not use technology that was later available. Manufacturers have often failed to adopt new advances in technology for fear that the change will be held against them in a product liability suit. These new statutes declare that a manufacturer has a valid defense if it would have been technologically impossible to have used the new and safer technology at the time the product was manufactured.

Failure to Warn Since it is often easier to prove that an injury resulted because the manufacturer failed to warn against a certain use than that it was caused by a defective design, manufacturers are subjected to a considerable degree of hindsight. Some of the state statutes limit the degree to which the failure to warn can be used to connect the product and the injury—for example, the manufacturer has a valid defense if it would have been impossible to foresee that the consumer might misuse the product in a certain way.

Comparative Fault for Consumer Misuse Contributory negligence is generally not a defense in a strict liability action, while assumption of risk is. In states that have enacted so-called "comparative fault" statutes, the user's damages are pegged to the percentage of responsibility for the injury that the defendant bears. Thus, if the consumer's misuse of the product is assessed as having been 20 percent responsible for the accident (or for the extent of the injuries), the consumer is entitled to only 80 percent of damages, the amount for which the defendant manufacturer is responsible.

Federal Reform

Piecemeal reform of product liability law in each state has contributed to the basic lack of uniformity from state to state, giving it a crazy-quilt effect. In the last century, this might have made little difference, but today most manufacturers sell in the national market, and are subjected to the varying requirements of the law in every state. For several years there has been talk in and out of Congress of enacting a federal product liability law that would include reforms adopted in many states, as discussed above. The U.S. Department of Commerce first proposed a draft federal bill in 1979. Since then, several other bills have been introduced in Congress, so far without success.

Congressional tort legislation is not the only possible federal action to cope with product-related injuries. In 1972, Congress created the Consumer Product Safety Commission (CPSC), and gave it broad power to act to *prevent* unsafe consumer products. The CPSC can issue mandatory safety standards governing design, construction, contents, performance, packaging, and labeling of more than 10,000 consumer products. It can recall unsafe products, recover costs on behalf of injured consumers, prosecute those who violate standards, and require manufacturers to issue warnings on hazardous products. It also regulates four federal laws previously administered by other departments: the Flammable Fabrics Act, the Hazardous Substances Act, the Poison Prevention Packaging Act, and the Refrigerator Door Safety Act. In its early years, the Commission issued standards for bicycles, power mowers, television sets, architectural glass, extension cords, book matches, pool slides, and space heaters. But the list of products is long and the Commission's record is mixed: it has come under fire for being short on regulation and for taking too long to promulgate the relatively few safety standards it has issued in a decade.

European Reform

In 1985, the Council of Ministers of the European Economic Community adopted a directive that creates new product liability risks for companies that export products to Europe. The directive embraces the concept of strict liability by allowing consumers to collect for injuries from defective products even when the manufacturer is not negligent. However, the rights of the consumer expire ten years after the product is put into circulation. The directive includes a "state of the art" defense but allows member countries to eliminate the defense. The directive further provides that a manufacturer's liability may be reduced when a consumer's negligence contributes to the injury.

Chapter Summary

Product liability describes a type of claim—for injury caused by a defective product—and not a separate theory of liability. In the typical case, three legal doctrines may be asserted: (1) warranty, (2) strict liability, and (3) negligence.

If a seller asserts that a product will perform in a certain manner, or has certain characteristics, he has given an express warranty, and he will be held liable for damages if the warranty is breached—that is, if the goods do not live up to the warranty. Not every conceivable claim is an express warranty; the courts permit a certain degree of "puffing."

An implied warranty is one created by law. Goods sold by a merchant seller carry an implied warranty of merchantability, meaning that they must possess certain characteristics, such as being of average quality for the type described and being fit for the ordinary purposes for which they are intended.

An implied warranty of fitness for a particular purpose is created whenever a seller knows or has reason to know that the buyer is relying on the seller's knowledge and skill to select a product for the buyer's particular purposes.

Article 2 permits sellers to exclude or disclaim warranties in whole or in part. Thus a seller may exclude express warranties. He may also disclaim many implied warranties—for example, by noting that the sale is "as is." The Magnuson-Moss Act sets out certain types of information that must be included in any written warranty. The act requires the manufacturer or seller to label the warranty either as "full" or "limited" depending on what types of defects are covered and what the customer must do to obtain repair or replacement. The act also abolishes "phantom warranties."

Privity once stood as a bar to recovery in suits brought by those one or more steps removed in the distribution chain from the party who breached a warranty. But the nearly universal trend in the state courts has been to abolish privity as a defense.

Because various impediments stand in the way of warranty suits, most courts have adopted a tort theory of strict liability, under which a seller is liable for injuries resulting from the sale of any product in a defective condition if it is unreasonably dangerous to the user or consumer. Typical issues in strict liability cases are these: Is the defendant a seller engaged in the business of selling? Was the product sold in a defective condition? Was it unreasonably dangerous, either on its face or because of a failure to warn? Did the product reach the consumer in an unchanged condition? Strict liability applies regardless of how careful the seller was and regardless of his lack of contractual relation with the consumer or user.

Manufacturers can also be held liable for negligence—most often for faulty design of products and inadequate warnings about the hazards of using the product.

The product liability revolution has prompted many state legislatures to enact certain laws limiting to some degree the manufacturer's responsibility for defective products. These laws include statutes of repose and provide a number of other defenses.

Problems

1. Ralph's Hardware decided to automate its accounting system and agreed to purchase a computer system from a manufacturer, Bits and Bytes (BB). During contract negotiations, BB's sales representative promised that the system was "A-1" and "perfect." However, the written contract which the parties later signed disclaimed all warranties, express and implied. After installation the computer produced only random numbers and letters, rather than the desired accounting information. Is BB liable for breaching an express warranty? Why?
2. Kate owned a small grocery store. One day John purchased a can of chip dip from the store which, unknown to Kate or John, was adulterated. John became seriously ill after eating the dip and sued Kate for damages on the grounds that she breached an implied warranty of merchantability. Is Kate liable? Why?
3. Carrie visited a neighborhood store to purchase some ham, which a salesperson cut by machine in the store. The next day she made a ham sandwich. In eating the sandwich, Carrie bit into a piece of cartilage in the ham and, as a result, lost a tooth, had to undergo root canal treatments, and must wear a full coverage crown to replace the tooth. Is the store liable for the damage? Why?
4. Clarence, a business executive, decided to hold a garage sale. At the sale, his neighbor Betty mentioned to Clarence that she was the catcher on her city-league baseball team and was having trouble catching knuckleball pitches, which required a special catcher's mitt. Clarence pulled an old mitt from a pile of items which were on sale and said, "Here, try this." Betty purchased the mitt but discovered during her next game that it didn't work. Has Clarence breached an express or implied warranty? Why?
5. Sarah purchased several elegant picture frames to hang in her dorm room. She also purchased a package of self-sticking hangers. Late one evening, while Sarah was studying business law in the library, the hangers came loose and her frames came crashing to the floor. After Sarah returned to her room and discovered the rubble, she examined the box in which the hangers were packaged and found the following language: "There are no warranties except for the description on this package and specifically there is NO IMPLIED WARRANTY OF MERCHANTABILITY." Assuming the hangers are not of fair, average, ordinary quality, would the hanger company be liable for breaching an implied warranty of merchantability? Why?
6. A thirteen-year-old boy received a "Golfing Gizmo"—a device for training novice golfers—as a gift from his mother. The label expressly states that the Gizmo is safe, but the boy is injured while using it. Should the fact that plaintiff is not in privity with the manufacturer bar his warranty claims? Why?

7. A bank repossessed a boat and sold it to Donald. During the negotiations with Donald, Donald stated that he wanted to use the boat for charter service in Florida. The bank officers handling the sale made no representations concerning the boat during negotiations. Donald later discovered that the boat was defective and sued the bank for breach of warranty. Is the bank liable? Why?
8. A whiskey company manufactured a high-grade blend called Exxxtra Plus. A company employee, who had been sampling the company's product during work, carelessly poured fuel oil into one bottle. The bottle was purchased by Frank who, after three drinks, became seriously ill. Another bottle, which was not tainted with fuel oil, was purchased by Elmo, an alcoholic, who drank the bottle in one sitting and became just as ill as Frank. Both Frank and Elmo sue the company on a strict liability theory. Will they win? Why?

11

Consumer Credit Transactions

Consumer debt—the amount Americans owe to banks and mortgage lenders, stores, automobile dealers, and other merchants who sell on credit—stands at an all-time high: in the 1980s, Americans owed more than $1 *trillion*. To pay this debt, the average family spends 23 cents of every take-home (after-tax) dollar it earns. The availability of credit is thus an important factor in the American economy, and not surprisingly a number of statutes have been enacted in recent years to protect the consumer both before and after signing credit agreements.

The statutes tend to fall within three broad categories. First, several statutes are especially important when a consumer enters into a credit transaction. These include laws that regulate credit costs, the credit application, and the applicant's right to check a credit record. Second, after a consumer has contracted for credit, certain statutes give a consumer the right to cancel the contract and correct billing mistakes. Third, if the consumer fails to pay a debt, the creditor has several traditional debt collection remedies that today are tightly regulated by the government.

Entering Into a Credit Transaction

The Cost of Credit

Lenders, whether banks or retailers, are not free to charge whatever they wish for credit. Usury laws establish a maximum rate of lawful interest. The penalties for violating usury laws vary from state to state. The heaviest penalties are loss of both principal and interest, or loss of a multiple of the interest the creditor charged. The courts often interpret these laws stringently, so that even if the impetus for a usurious loan comes from the borrower, the contract can be avoided, as the next case shows.

MATTER OF THE ESTATE OF DANE
55 A.D.2d 224, 390 N.Y.S.2d 249 (1976)

MAHONEY, JUSTICE. On December 17, 1968, after repeated requests by decedent that appellant loan him $10,500, the latter drew a demand note in that amount and with decedent's consent fixed the interest rate at 7½% per annum, the then maximum annual interest permitted being 7¼% (3 NYCRR 4.1). Decedent executed the note and appellant gave him the full amount of the note in cash. After letters of co-administration with the will annexed were issued to respondents on January 21, 1975, they moved for summary judgment voiding the note on the ground that it was a usurious loan. . . . The Surrogate granted the motion, voided the note and enjoined any prosecution on it thereafter. Appellant's cross motion to enforce the claim was denied.

New York's usury laws are harsh, and courts have been reluctant to extend them beyond cases that fall squarely under the statutes. Subdivision 1 of section 5-511 of the General Obligations Law makes any note for which more than the legal rate of interest is "reserved or taken" or "agreed to be reserved or taken" void. Subdivision 2 of section 5-511 commands cancellation of a note in violation of subdivision 1 of section 5-511. Here, since both sides concede that the note evidences the complete agreement between the parties, we cannot aid appellant by reliance upon the presumption that he did not make the loan at a usurious rate. The terms of the loan are not in dispute. Thus, the note itself establishes, on its face, clear evidence of usury. There is no requirement of a specific intent to violate the usury statute. A general intent to charge more than the legal rate as evidenced by the note, is all that is needed. If the lender intends to take and receive a rate in excess of the legal percentage at the time the note is made, the statute condemns the act and mandates its cancellation. The showing, as here, that the note reserves to the lender an illegal rate of interest satisfies respondents' burden of proving a usurious loan.

Next, where the rate of interest on the face of a note is in excess of the legal rate, it cannot be argued that such a loan may be saved because the borrower promoted the loan or even set the rate. The usury statutes are for the protection of the borrower and the purpose of section 5-511 of the General Obligations Law would be thwarted if the lender could avoid its consequences by asking the borrower to set the rate. Since the respondents herein asserted the defense of usury, it cannot be said that the decedent waived the defense by setting or agreeing to the 7½% rate of interest.

Finally, equitable considerations cannot be indulged when, as here, a statute specifically condemns an act. The statute fixes the law, and it must be followed.

The order should be affirmed, without costs.

Order affirmed, without costs.

Several states have eliminated interest rate limits. In other states, usury law is riddled with exceptions, making the interpretation of the statutes extremely complex. In some states, the exceptions have almost eaten up the general rule. Here are some of the more common exceptions:

- *Loans to businesses* In many states, any interest rate may be charged, although some states limit this exception to incorporated businesses.
- *Mortgage loans* Mortgage loans are often subject to special usury laws. The allowable interest rates vary, depending on whether a first mortgage or a subordinate mortgage is given.
- *Installment loans* In most states, still another set of usury laws (retail installment sales acts) governs the extension of credit by retailers and others for payment of goods purchased in fixed installments.
- *Credit card and "overdraft" checking* These common and increasingly easy forms of credit are also frequently governed by a special rate.
- *Time-price differential* Retailers may collect from buyers a so-called **time-price differential,** or sales finance charge, which means that the price of goods sold on time (credit) may be higher than those sold for cash, and the difference in most states may exceed the "normal" usury rate. The reason is that a seller who extends credit is not thought to be granting a loan, in the absence of which the usury laws do not apply.

Certain charges are not considered interest, such as fees to record documents in a public office and charges for services such as title examinations, deed preparation, credit reports, appraisals, and loan processing. But a creditor may not use these devices to cloak what is in fact a usurious bargain; it is not the form but the substance of the agreement that controls (a principle taken more or less seriously in the United States but winked at, often for sound financial reasons, in countries with cultures that reject the charging of any interest; see Box 11-1). Sam sells to Mary for $1,000 a painting worth $1,500 and gets an option to repurchase it six months later for $1,250. This is not a true sale but in effect a means of lending money at a high rate of interest (12.5 percent for six months, or 25 percent per annum). Why? If Sam does not buy it back, Mary has a painting worth 50 percent more than she bought it for; Sam will lose more by leaving it with Mary than by buying it back, which is why the deal was structured this way.

Disclosure of Credit Costs

Until 1969, lenders were generally free to disclose the true cost of money loaned or credit extended in any way they saw fit—and so they did. Financing and credit terms varied widely, and it was difficult and sometimes impossible to understand what the true cost was of a particular loan, much less to "comparison shop." After years of failure, consumer interests finally persuaded Congress to pass a national law requiring disclosure of credit

Box 11-1 Another Approach: Sharia Law

Islam's Revival Spreads Use of the Sharia Law, a Flexible Legal Setup
By Ray Vicker

RIYADH, Saudi Arabia—The defendant and the plaintiff sit side by side on a bench in a plain, plaster-walled courtroom here. The only decoration is an Arabic inscription on the wall behind the white-robed qadi, or judge. It says, "Justice should be applied equally among all people."

The qadi, sitting at a table about 10 feet before the defendant and the plaintiff, is a bearded man of gentle manner who looks more like a holy man than a judge. That isn't surprising. Most of his early life was spent in religious schools, and all qadis here need degrees from religious universities.

Now, he is deciding a young Yemeni man's fate under Sharia law. Sharia (pronounced Shah-REE-ah) means "path to follow." It is a code introduced by the Prophet Mohammed 1,400 years ago. It sets the religious duties for nearly 800 million Moslems, telling them when and how to pray, to fast, to make a pilgrimage to Mecca and to pay religious taxes. Sharia also provides a legal system that some Islamic nations—Saudi Arabia, for example—follow strictly. It condemns thievery, protects private property, lays down inheritance procedures and generally defines the rights and obligations of individuals.

Islam's revival is moving more and more Moslem nations away from Western-type legal systems and closer to Sharia. Disillusionment with Western systems is strong in Iran, Pakistan, Libya and Abu Dhabi. Sudan, Kuwait and Nigeria are considering changing their statutes to conform to Sharia. Sharia's spread means more Westerners may come into contact with a legal system that most don't understand.

Westerners generally know only that Sharia can prescribe gory punishments for certain crimes. Indeed, lashing is a standard sentence, and the 1975 beheading of the Saudi prince who killed King Faisal got world-wide attention. But such punishments as beheading for murderers, stoning for adulterers and cutting off a thief's hand aren't invoked lightly in Saudi Arabia.

* * *

Sharia is flexible because it draws its precepts from several sources. Chief among them are the Koran, which Moslems regard as God's word given to Mohammed, and the Sunna, or pattern of life of the Prophet. Many books describe how Mohammed lived, what he considered to be right and wrong, and how he judged various cases presented to him.

* * *

Analogy also applies. Mohammed didn't envision highway speed limits, but the Koran preaches moderation in all things. So it is easy to see by analogy that traffic laws conform to the Koran.

Then there is the law of necessity. It teaches that if something is necessary for the survival of the community, it is worthwhile. And when all else fails, hiyal can enter. Hiyal is the name for legal devices used to circumvent Sharia. For example, Sharia prohibits the collecting of interest on loans. Banks in Moslem lands get around the problem by assessing a "service charge."

* * *

Sharia courts don't handle all litigation in Saudi Arabia; administrative tribunals are established in several fields. The Committee for the Settlement of Commercial Disputes is a court that handles many business matters. Of course, business law must conform to Sharia law, and in cases of conflict Sharia takes precedence.

For Western businessmen, this can sometimes present a problem. In the Yemen Arab Republic (North Yemen) capital of Sanaa, for example, foreign banks, including Citibank have been competing hard for business. Only after they had pushed out substantial loan volume did they begin to realize that the country's Sharia law system, with its non-recognition of interest, didn't provide any protection for the banks against slow

(continues on next page)

Box 11-1, *continued*

payers. Banks assess "service charges" instead of interest. But if the loan is in default, the banks can only ask the Sharia court for repayment of principal, not interest.

"In North Yemen, the law is so vague that the lender hasn't any way to press the borrower even for the principal," says one banker in Sanaa.

* * *

Source: *Wall Street Journal*, May 11, 1979, p. 1

costs. Officially called the Consumer Credit Protection Act, Part I of the law that took effect on July 1, 1969, is more popularly known as the **Truth-in-Lending Act.**

The act provides what its name implies: that lenders must *inform* borrowers about significant terms of the credit transaction. Truth-in-Lending does not establish maximum interest rates; these continue to be governed by state law. The two key terms that must be disclosed are the finance charge and the annual percentage rate. To see why, consider two simple loans of $1,000, each carrying interest of 10 percent, one payable at the end of twelve months and the other in twelve equal installments. Although the actual charge in each is the same—$100—the interest rate is not. Why? Because with the first loan you will have the use of the full $1,000 for the entire year; with the second, for much less than the year because you must begin repaying part of the principal within a month. In fact, with the second loan you will have use of only about half the money for the entire year, and so the actual rate of interest is closer to 15 percent. Things become much more complex when interest is compounded and stated as a monthly figure, when different rates apply to various portions of the loan, and when processing charges and other fees are stated separately.

By requiring that the finance charge and the annual percentage rate be disclosed on a uniform basis, the Truth-in-Lending law makes understanding and comparison of loans much easier. The **finance charge** is the total of all money paid for credit; it includes the interest paid over the life of the loan and all processing charges. The **annual percentage rate** is the true rate of interest for money or credit actually available to the borrower. The annual percentage rate must be calculated using the total finance charge (including all extra fees). See Box 11-2 for an example of a disclosure form used by creditors.

Creditors who violate the Truth-in-Lending Act are subject to both criminal and civil sanctions. Of these, the most important are the civil remedies open to consumers. If a creditor fails to disclose the required information, a customer may sue to recover twice the finance charge, plus court costs and reasonable attorney's fees (but not less than $100 or more than $1,000).

The federal Truth-in-Lending Act is not the only statute dealing with credit disclosures. A uniform state act, the Uniform Consumer Credit Code

Box 11-2 Sample Disclosure Form

Big Wheel Auto Alice Green

ANNUAL PERCENTAGE RATE The cost of your credit as a yearly rate	**FINANCE CHARGE** The dollar amount the credit will cost you	Amount Financed The amount of credit provided to you or on your behalf	Total of Payments The amount you will have paid after you have made all payments as scheduled	Total Sale Price The total cost of your purchase on credit, including your downpayment of $ 1500—
14.84 %	$1496.80	$ 6107.50	$ 7604.30	$ 9104.30

You have the right to receive at this time an itemization of the Amount Financed
☐ I want an itemization ☒ I do not want an itemization

Your payment schedule will be:

Number of Payments	Amount of Payments	When Payments Are Due
36	$211.23	Monthly beginning 6-1-85

Insurance
Credit life insurance and credit disability insurance are not required to obtain credit, and will not be provided unless you sign and agree to pay the additional cost

Type	Premium	Signature	
Credit Life	$120—	I want credit life insurance	Alice Green Signature
Credit Disability		I want credit disability insurance	Signature
Credit Life and Disability		I want credit life and disability insurance	Signature

Security: You are giving a security interest in:
☒ the goods being purchased.
☐ ____________

Filing fees $ 12.50 Non-filing insurance $ ________

Late Charge: If a payment is late, you will be charged $10.

Prepayment: If you pay off early, you
☐ may ☐ will not have to pay a penalty.
☒ may ☐ will not be entitled to a refund of part of the the finance charge.

See your contract documents for any additional information about nonpayment, default, any required repayment in full before the scheduled date, and prepayment refunds and penalties.

I have received a copy of this statement.

Alice Green 5-1-85
Signature Date

e means an estimate

(UCCC), is now on the books in several states. Unlike the federal law, which does not control the amount or rate a creditor can charge, the UCCC sets maximums (36 percent per year when the principal is $300 or less, 21 percent for sums up to $1,000). It also outlaws certain types of agreements—for example, multiple sales agreements on single purchases (if a merchant could break down a higher-priced item into smaller components, the interest charge could be greater); so-called "balloon" payments (a charge, usually at the time the final payment is due, that is significantly higher than the average payments); and wage assignments as security for credit. Like the federal law, though, the UCCC requires a number of identical or similar disclosures, including disclosure of the annual percentage rate and other charges. (Note: Although several states are considering adopting the UCCC, it lacks uniformity among the states that have adopted it so far.)

Applying for Credit

Through the 1960s, banks and other lending and credit-granting institutions regularly discriminated against women. Banks told single women to find a cosigner for loans. Divorced women discovered that they could not open store charge accounts because they lacked a prior credit history, even though they had contributed to the family income on which previous accounts had been based. Married couples found that the wife's earnings were not counted when they sought credit; indeed, families planning to buy homes were occasionally even told that the bank would grant a mortgage if the wife would submit to a hysterectomy. In all these cases, the premise of the refusal to treat women equally was the unstated—and usually false—belief that women would quit work to have children or simply to stay home.

By the 1970s, as women became a major factor in the labor force, Congress reacted to the manifest unfairness of the discrimination by enacting (as part of the Consumer Credit Protection Act) the **Equal Credit Opportunity Act** of 1974. The act prohibits any creditor from discriminating "against any applicant on the basis of sex or marital status with respect to any aspect of a credit transaction." In 1976, Congress broadened the law to bar discrimination (1) on the basis of race, color, religion, national origin, and age; (2) because all or a part of the applicant's income is from a public assistance program; and (3) because the applicant has exercised his or her rights under the Consumer Credit Protection Act.

Under the Equal Credit Opportunity Act, a creditor may not ask a credit applicant to state sex, race, national origin, or religion. And unless the applicant is seeking a joint loan or account or lives in a community property state, the creditor may not ask for a statement of marital status or, if you have voluntarily disclosed that you are married, for information about your spouse. All questions concerning plans for children are improper. In assessing the creditworthiness of an applicant, the creditor must consider all sources of income, including regularly received alimony and child support payments. And if credit is refused, the creditor must, on demand, tell you the specific reasons for rejection.

The wording of the law is plain and has few complications. As lenders learned early in the act's history, it means, as the following case demonstrates, exactly what it says.

MARKHAM v. COLONIAL MORTGAGE SERVICE CO., ASSOCIATES 605 F.2d 566 (D.C. Cir. 1979)

SWYGERT, CIRCUIT JUDGE. The Equal Credit Opportunity Act, 15 U.S.C. §§ 1691, *et seq.,* prohibits creditors from discriminating against applicants on the basis of sex or marital status. We are asked to decide whether this prohibition prevents creditors from refusing to aggregate the incomes of two unmarried joint mortgage applicants when determining their creditworthiness in a situation where the incomes of two similarly situated married joint applicants would have been aggregated. The plaintiffs in this action, Jerry and Marcia Markham, appeal the judgment of the district court granting defendant Illinois Federal Service Savings and Loan Association's motion for summary judgment. We reverse.

* * *

In November 1976, plaintiffs Marcia J. Harris and Jerry Markham announced their engagement and began looking for a residence in the Capitol Hill section of Washington, D.C. One of the real estate firms which they contacted, defendant B. W. Real Estate, Inc., found suitable property for them, and in December 1976, Markham and Harris signed a contract of sale for the property.

* * *

Plaintiffs and B. W. Real Estate had decided that February 4, 1977 would be an appropriate closing date for the purchase of the Capitol Hill residence. Accordingly, plaintiffs arranged to terminate their current leases, change mailing addresses, and begin utility service at the new property. On February 1, the loan committee of Illinois Federal rejected the plaintiffs' application. On February 3, the eve of the settlement date, plaintiffs were informed through a B. W. Real Estate agent that their loan application had been denied because they were not married. They were advised that their application would be resubmitted to the "investor"—who was not identified—on February 8, but that approval would be contingent upon the submission of a marriage certificate.

On February 8, the Illinois Federal loan committee reconsidered the plaintiffs' application, but again denied it. A letter was sent that date from Illinois Federal, which letter stated that the application had been rejected with the statement: "Separate income not sufficient for loan and job tenure."

* * *

We turn to a consideration of whether the Equal Credit Opportunity Act's prohibition of discrimination on the basis of sex or marital status makes illegal Illinois Federal's refusal to aggregate plaintiffs' income when determining their creditworthiness. Illinois Federal contends that neither the purpose nor the language of the Act requires it to combine the incomes of unmarried joint applicants when making that determination.

We start, as we must, with the language of the statute itself. 15 U.S.C. § 1691(a) provides:

> It shall be unlawful for any creditor to discriminate against any applicant, with respect to any aspect of a credit transaction—
> (1) on the basis of . . . sex or marital status. . . .

* * *

This language is simple, and its meaning is not difficult to comprehend. Illinois Federal itself has correctly phrased the standard in its brief: The Act forbids discrimination "on the basis of a person's marital status, that is, to treat persons differently, all other facts being the same, because of their marital status. . . ." Brief for Defendant Illinois Federal at 18. Illinois Federal does not contend that they would not have aggregated plaintiffs' income had they been married at the time. Indeed, Illinois Federal concedes that the law would have required it to do so. Thus, it is plain that Illinois Federal treated plaintiffs differently—that is, refused to aggregate their incomes—solely because of their marital status, which is precisely the sort of discrimination prohibited by section 169(a)(1) on its face.

Despite the section's clarity of language, Illinois Federal seeks to avoid a finding of prohibited discrimination by arguing that it was not the Congressional purpose to require such an aggregation of the incomes of non-married applicants. It can be assumed, *arguendo,* that one, perhaps even the main, purpose of the act was to eradicate credit discrimination waged against women, especially married women whom creditors traditionally refused to consider apart from their husbands as individually worthy of credit. But granting such an assumption does not negate the clear language of the Act itself that discrimination against *any* applicant, with respect to *any* aspect of a credit transaction, which is based on marital status is outlawed. When the plain meaning of a statute appears on its face, we need not concern ourselves with legislative history, especially when evidence of the legislation's history as has been presented to us does not argue persuasively for a narrower meaning than that which is apparent from the statutory language. We believe that the meaning of the words chosen by Congress is readily apparent.

Illinois Federal expresses the fear that a holding such as we reach today will require it to aggregate the incomes of all persons who apply for credit as a group. Lest it be misinterpreted, we note that our holding is not itself that far-reaching. It does no more than require Illinois Federal to treat plaintiffs—a couple jointly applying for credit—the same as they would be treated if married. We have not been asked to decide what the effect of the Act would have been had plaintiffs not applied for credit jointly. Nor do we have before us a question of whether the Act's marital status provision in any way applies to a situation where more than two people jointly request credit. We hold only that, under the Act Illinois Federal should have treated plaintiffs—an unmarried couple applying for credit jointly—the same as it would have treated them had they been married at the time.

* * *

Checking the Credit Record

Because credit is such a big business, a number of support industries have grown up around it. One of the most important is the "credit reporting" industry. Certain companies—"credit bureaus"—collect information about borrowers, holders of credit cards, store accounts, and installment purchasers. For a fee this information—currently held on tens of millions of Americans—is sold to companies anxious to know whether applicants are creditworthy. If the information is inaccurate, it can lead to rejection of a credit application that should be approved and wind up in other files where it can live to do more damage. In 1970, Congress enacted, as part of the Consumer Credit Protection Act, the **Fair Credit Reporting Act** (FCRA) to give consumers access to their credit files in order to correct errors.

Under this statute, an applicant denied credit has the right to be told the name and address of the credit bureau (called "consumer reporting agency" in the act) that prepared the report on which the denial was based. (The law covers reports used to screen insurance and job applicants as well as to determine creditworthiness.) The agency must list the nature and substance of the information (except medical information) and its sources (unless they contributed to an investigative-type report). A credit report lists such information as name, address, employer, salary history, loans outstanding, and the like; see Box 11-3. An investigative report is one that results from personal interviews and may contain nonfinancial information, like drinking and other personal habits, character, or participation in dangerous sports. Since the investigators rely on talks with neighbors and co-workers, their reports are usually subjective and can often be misleading and inaccurate.

The agency must furnish the consumer the information free if requested within thirty days of rejection and must also specify the name and address of anyone who has received the report within the preceding six months (two years if furnished for employment purposes).

If the information turns out to be inaccurate, the agency must correct its records; if investigative material cannot be verified, it must be removed from the file. Those to whom it was distributed must be notified of the changes. When the agency and the consumer disagree about the validity of the information, the consumer's version must be placed in the file and included in future distributions of the report. After seven years, any adverse information must be removed (ten years in the case of bankruptcy).

Under the FCRA, any person who obtains information from a credit agency under false pretenses is subject to criminal penalties. The statute does not say whether a person injured by one who wrongly obtains information can sue for damages. Such a case arose under unlikely circumstances, when George Hansen, the 1974 Republican candidate for Congress in Idaho, defeated the incumbent Congressman, Orval Hansen, in the primary. A credit report on George Hansen was supplied to a Congressional committee investigating improper campaign financing procedures; Orval Hansen happened to be a committee member. George Hansen, who subsequently won the election but then pleaded guilty to violating the Federal Election Campaign Act, sued.

HANSEN v. MORGAN
582 F.2d 1214 (9th Cir. 1978)

JAMES M. CARTER, CIRCUIT JUDGE. This case grew out of a strenuous campaign for the 1974 Republican candidacy for the United States Congress in the Second District of Idaho. Orval Hansen, the incumbent congressman, was defeated in the Republican primary election by appellant George Hansen. Thereafter two Idaho citizens filed complaints with the clerk of the United States House of Representatives alleging improper campaign financing procedures by George Hansen. This caused an investigation of George Hansen by the House Administration Committee, of which incumbent Orval Hansen was a member until his term as Congressman expired.

Judith Austin, who had filed one of the above complaints, was a friend of Orval Hansen. She had a conversation with Orval Hansen in which it was discussed that a credit report on George Hansen could be interesting for what it might disclose about

Box 11-3 A Credit Report

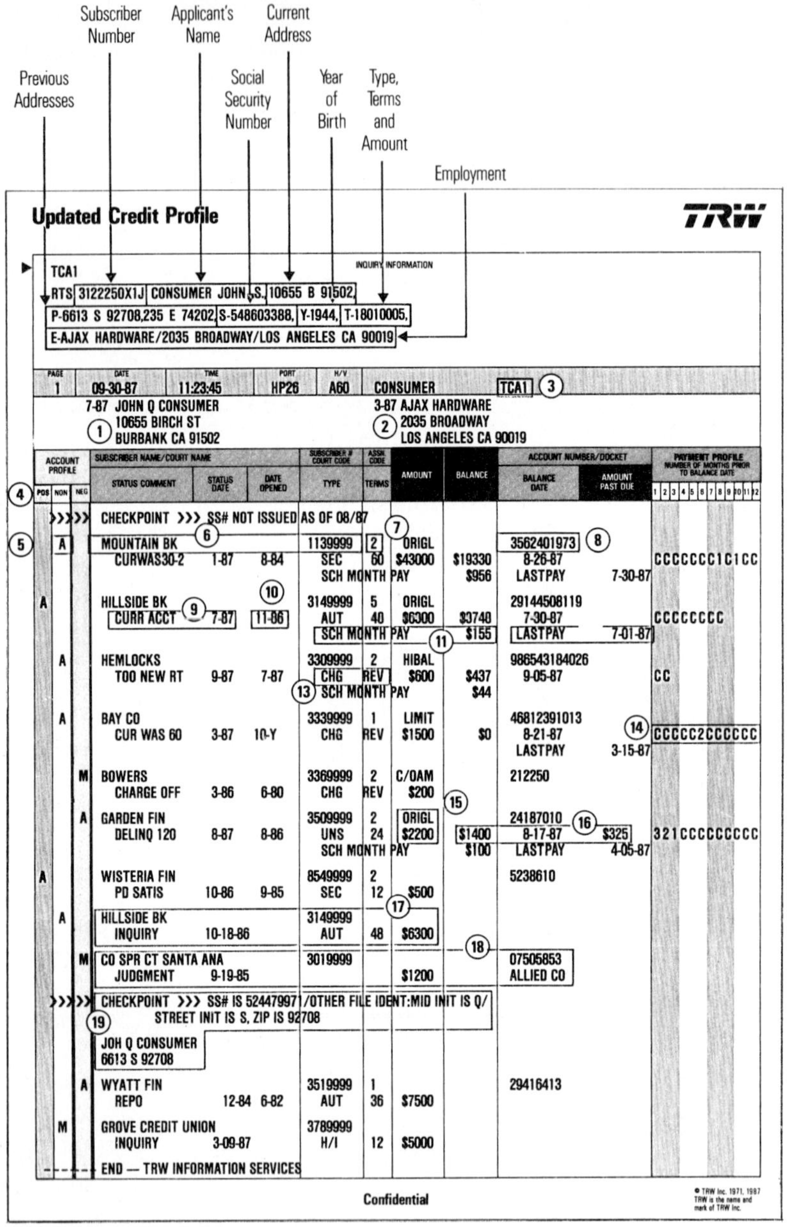

1. Name and address as recorded on automated subscriber tapes, including date of most recent update.
2. Employment name and address as reported by a subscriber through an inquiry on the date shown.
3. A code designating the TRW or Credit Bureau office nearest the consumer's current address, for your use in consumer referrals.
4. Three columns indicating positive, nonevaluated, and negative status comments.
5. A (Automated) and M (Instant Update or Manual Form) indicate the method by which the credit grantor reports information to TRW.
6. Name and number of reporting subscriber.
7. Association code describing the legal relationship to the account.
8. Account or docket number.
9. Status comment reflecting the payment condition of the account as of the status date.
10. Date the account was opened.
11. Scheduled monthly payment amount.
12. Date last payment was made.
13. Type and terms of the account.
14. The applicant's payment history during the past 12 months. The code reflects the status of the account for each month, displayed for balance reporting subscribers only.

C	—	Current
1	—	30 days past due
2	—	60 days past due
3	—	90 days past due
4	—	120 days past due
5	—	150 days past due
6	—	180 days past due
— (Dash)	—	No history reported for that month.
Blank	—	No history maintained; see status comment.

15. The original loan amount (ORIGL), credit limit (LIMIT), historical high balance (HIBAL), or original amount charged to loss (C/OAM), represented in dollar amounts.
16. Balance owing, balance date, and amount past due, if applicable.
17. Inquiries indicate a request for the applicant's credit information—inquiring subscriber; date of inquiry; and type, terms and amount, if available.
18. Public Record: Court name, court code, docket number, type of public record, filing date, amount, and judgment creditor. This information may include bankruptcies, liens and/or judgments against the applicant.
19. Profile report messages alert the subscriber about a credit applicant's social security number, name, address, generation, or year of birth. See back page for further explanation.

his campaign financing. Therefore Austin later telephoned one Rose Bowman. The substance of Austin's conversation with Bowman is in part disputed, but it is agreed that a credit report on George Hansen was discussed and that Melvin Morgan was considered as someone who might be able to obtain such a report.

Appellee Melvin Morgan is the principal stockholder and chief executive of appellee Nate Morgan Jewelers of Pocatello, a corporation. The corporation is a member of the Pocatello Credit Bureau, entitled to receive credit reports from the Bureau. On about August 10, 1974, Melvin Morgan received a telephone call from Rose Bowman which he construed to be a request for a credit report on George Hansen. Morgan contends he agreed to obtain the report upon the belief that it was desired by Orval Hansen to assist the House Administration Committee's investigation of George Hansen. Upon Melvin Morgan's request the credit report was provided without question by the Pocatello Credit Bureau. The report was issued in the names of both George V. Hansen and his wife, Connie. It contained no information adverse to either of them.

When he received the report, Morgan delivered it personally to Orval Hansen's office in Washington D.C. Eventually the report reached the House Administration Committee.

Upon learning of the existence of the credit report, George and Connie Hansen filed suit against the Morgans and various other parties involved in the obtaining of the report. After extensive discovery, the Hansens dropped their complaint against all parties except the Morgans. Their amended complaint alleged that the Morgans, by willfully or negligently failing to comply with the requirements of § 1681b and § 1681e(a) "and other related Sections" of the FCRA, unlawfully violated the Hansens' right to privacy. Damages were sought under §§ 1681n and 1681*o* which authorize civil causes of action for noncompliance with the requirements of the act.

The Morgans moved for summary judgment contending as a matter of law that their conduct violated no provision of the FCRA, leaving no basis from which a civil suit based on the FCRA could be launched. In an opinion which reviewed the requirements imposed by each of the noncriminal provisions of the FCRA, the district judge agreed with the Morgans and granted their motion for summary judgment. The Hansens appeal.

* * *

[Sections 1681n and 1681*o*] create civil liability for willful (§ 1681n) or negligent (§1681*o*) noncompliance by a consumer reporting agency or user of information who fails to comply with "any requirement imposed under this subchapter with respect to any consumer. . . ." If the Morgans have negligently or willfully failed to comply with any "requirement" imposed by the FCRA on users of credit information, they can be held liable by the Hansens.

The crucial issue is what constitutes "any requirement imposed under this subchapter" for purposes of § 1681n and § 1681*o*. The district court apparently concluded only the noncriminal provisions of the FCRA state "requirements" for purposes of civil liability under the act. The opinion below reviewed each of the noncriminal provisions of the act which regulate conduct, concluding that no provision which applies to users of credit information, as opposed to consumer reporting agencies, had been violated by the Morgans. No mention was made of the criminal provision—§ 1681q.

However, we conclude § 1681q does state a "requirement imposed under this subchapter". 15 U.S.C. § 1681q provides:

> "Any person who knowingly and willfully obtains information on a consumer from a consumer reporting agency under false pretenses shall be fined not more than $5,000 or imprisoned not more than one year, or both."

This section requires that users of consumer information refrain from obtaining such information from credit reporting agencies under false pretenses. Its violation therefore, forms a basis of civil liability under either § 1681n or § 1681*o*.

The standard for determining when a consumer report has been obtained under false pretenses will usually be defined in relation to the permissible purposes of consumer reports which are enumerated in 15 U.S.C. § 1681b. This is because a consumer reporting agency can legally issue a report only for the purposes listed in § 1681b. If the agency is complying with the statute, then a user cannot utilize an account with a consumer reporting agency to obtain consumer information for a purpose not permitted by § 1681b without using a false pretense.

We hold that obtaining a consumer report in violation of the terms of the statute without disclosing the impermissible purpose for which the report is desired can constitute obtaining consumer information under false pretenses, and that the facts in this case demonstrate that the consumer report was so obtained.

This construction of the FCRA is not only consistent with the intent of Congress as revealed by the explicit language of § 1681n, the legislative history, and the stated purpose of the Act, but also comports with Supreme Court precedent relating to civil liability based on criminal provisions of federal statutes in general. When introducing the Fair Credit Reporting Bill in the Senate, Senator Proxmire stated that the bill would require:

> ". . . that credit bureaus have in effect procedures for guaranteeing the confidentiality of the information they collect and that no such information be released to noncreditors such as governmental investigative agencies without the express consent of the person involved."

As explained, § 1681q extends to users of information the requirement that they refrain from obtaining consumer information for such impermissible purposes.

The declared purpose of the FCRA is to assure that "consumer credit, personnel, insurance and other information" is collected, disseminated and used in a manner which will protect the interest of the consumer in "confidentiality, accuracy, relevancy, and proper utilization of such information. . . ." 15 U.S.C. § 1681(b). The principle mechanism for accomplishing this goal is the regulation of reporting of consumer information by consumer reporting agencies. But requirements were also placed on users of credit information. This was necessary because the objectives of the act could be defeated if users could obtain information from consumer reporting agencies under false pretenses with impunity. Even consumer reporting agencies acting in complete good faith cannot prohibit illicit use of consumer information if users are not bound to obtain consumer reports only for permissible purposes. Section 1681q is a response to this concern.

*   *   *

The judgment of the district court is reversed and remanded for a trial.

Consumer Rights After a Credit Transaction

Cancellation Rights

Ordinarily, a contract is binding when signed. But many of the newer consumer-protection laws provide an escape valve. For example, a Federal Trade Commission regulation gives consumers three days to cancel contracts made with door-to-door salespersons. Under this **cooling-off provision**, the cancellation is effective if made by midnight of the third business day after the date of the purchase agreement. The salesperson must notify consumers of this right and supply them with two copies of a cancellation form, and the sales agreement must contain a statement explaining the right. The purchaser cancels by returning one copy of the cancellation form to the seller, who is obligated either to pick up the goods or to pay shipping costs. The three-day cancellation privilege applies only to sales of $25 or more made either in the home or away from the seller's place of business; it does not apply to sales made by mail or telephone or to emergency repair, certain other home repair, and real estate, insurance, or securities sales.

The Truth-in-Lending Act protects consumers in a similar way. For certain "big ticket" purchases (such as installations made in the course of major home improvements), sellers sometimes require a mortgage (which is subordinate to any preexisting mortgages) on the home. The law gives such customers three days to rescind the contract. Many states have laws similar to the FTC's three-day cooling-off period, and these may apply to transactions not covered by the federal rule (for example, to purchases of less than $25 and even to certain contracts made at the seller's place of business).

Correcting Billing Mistakes

In 1975, Congress enacted the **Fair Credit Billing Act** as an amendment to the Consumer Credit Protection Act. It was intended to put to an end the phenomenon, by then a standard part of any comedian's repertoire, of the many ways a computer could insist that you pay a bill, despite errors and despite letters you might have written to complain. The act, which applies only to open-end credit and not to installment sales, sets out a procedure that creditors and customers must follow to rectify claimed errors. The customer has sixty days to notify the creditor of the nature of the error and the amount. Errors can include charges not incurred or billed with the wrong description or for goods never delivered, accounting or arithmetic errors, failure to credit payments or returns, and even billings for which you simply request additional information, including proof of sale. During the time the creditor is replying, you need not pay the questioned item or any finance charge on the disputed amount.

The creditor has thirty days to respond and ninety days to correct your account or explain why your belief that an error has been committed is incorrect. If you do turn out to be wrong, the creditor is entitled to all back finance charges and to prompt payment of the disputed amount. If you persist in disagreeing and notifying the creditor within ten days, it is obligated to tell all credit bureaus to whom it sends notices of delinquency that the bill continues to be disputed and to tell you to whom such reports have been sent; when the dispute has been settled, the creditor must notify the credit bureaus of this fact. Failure of the creditor to follow the rules, an explanation of which must be provided to each customer every six months and when a dispute arises, bars it from collecting the first $50 in dispute, plus finance charges, even if the creditor turns out to be correct.

While disputes over the quality of goods are not "billing errors," the act does apply to unsatisfactory goods or services purchased by credit card (except for store credit cards); the customer may assert against the credit card company any claims or defenses he or she may have against the seller. This means that under certain circumstances the customer may withhold payments without incurring additional finance charges. However, this right is limited to goods or services in excess of $50 that were purchased either in the home state or within 100 miles of the customer's current mailing address.

Debt-collection Practices

Banks, financial institutions, and retailers have different incentives for extending credit—for some, a loan is simply a means of making money, for others, it is an inducement to buyers. But in either case, credit is a risk because the consumer may default; the creditor needs a means of collecting when the customer fails to pay. Open-end credit is usually given without collateral. The creditor can, of course, sue, but if the consumer has no assets, collection can be troublesome. Historically, three different means of recovering the debt have evolved: garnishment, wage assignment, and confession of judgment.

Garnishment

This is a legal process by which a creditor obtains a court order directing the debtor's employer (or any party who owes money to the debtor) to pay directly to the creditor a certain portion of the employee's wages until the debt is paid. Until 1970, garnishment was regulated by state law, and its effects could be devastating—in some cases even leading to suicide (see Box 11-4). In 1970, Title III of the Consumer Credit Protection Act asserted federal control over garnishment proceedings for the first time. The federal wage garnishment law limits the amount of employee earnings that may be withheld in any one pay period—the lesser of 25 percent of disposable (after-tax) earnings or the amount by which disposable weekly earnings exceed thirty times the highest current federal minimum wage. The federal law covers everyone who receives personal earnings, including wages, salary, commission, bonus, and retirement income (though not tips), but it allows courts to garnish above the federal maximum in support cases (for example, alimony), in personal bankruptcy cases, and in cases of state or federal tax levies.

The federal wage garnishment law also prohibits an employer from firing any worker solely because the worker's pay has been garnished for one debt (multiple garnishments may be grounds for discharge). The penalty for violating this provision is a $1,000 fine, one year imprisonment, or both. But the law does not say that an employee fired for having one debt garnished may sue the employer for damages. In a 1980 case, the Fifth Circuit denied an employee the right to sue, holding that the statute places enforcement exclusively in the hands of the Secretary of Labor. [Smith v. Cotton Brothers Baking Co., Inc., 609 F.2d 738 (5th Cir. 1980)]

The 1970 statute is not the only limitation on the garnishment process. There is an important constitutional limitation as well. Many states permitted a creditor to garnish the employee's wages even before the case came to court; a simple form from the clerk of the court was enough to freeze a debtor's wages, often before the debtor knew a suit had been brought. In

Box 11-4 The Impact of Garnishment

Unions, Firms, Lawyers Seek to Curb Garnishing As Its Incidence Rises

BY JAMES P. GANNON

CHICAGO—One payday in January, auto worker Carl W. Clark discovered his entire week's take-home pay of $112.39 had been turned over to the state of Indiana for delinquent state income taxes. Beset by debts, he asked officials at Ford Motor Co.'s plant in suburban Chicago Heights, Ill., for his accrued vacation pay to tide him over.

Next payday, he learned Indiana—the state where he used to live—had received $208.84 out of his $363.93 in wages and vacation pay. The 24-year-old father of a young boy, not knowing how much he owed Indiana tax collectors, (the two deductions actually satisfied the claim) became despondent over the pay loss. Two days later, Carl Clark placed a .22 calibre rifle under his chin and shot a bullet into his brain.

This suicide has spurred anew wide-ranging inquiries into the consequences of consumer debt problems. Under special scrutiny is the rising number of wage garnishments and other forms of pay seizure by creditors, including state and Federal tax collectors. The spotlight on pay attachment also has illuminated a misery-multiplying debtor's course that runs from garnishment and loss of job to bankruptcy and going on relief.

* * *

Because the wage garnishments are issued by thousands of local courts, there aren't any national statistics on their volume. But checks of big courts in some metropolitan areas indicate more and more workers are finding part of their wages confiscated to pay overdue debts.

In Chicago, the Cook County Circuit Court issued 84,513 garnishments last year, 15% more than in 1964 and 72% more than in 1961. The marshal of the municipal courts of Los Angeles County served 114,972 wage garnishments in the fiscal year ended last June 30, up 6% from the prior year, and garnishments there this year are running at an annual rate of 122,000. Court officials in New York, Cleveland and other big cities also cite rising garnishment totals.

The figures don't disclose the full extent of pay impounding. They don't include the huge volume of wage "assignments," which are legally distinct but similar in effect to garnishments. Under a wage assignment, a debtor pledges his future wages to repay the debt if he defaults; execution of the wage assignment doesn't normally require a court judgment, as a garnishment usually does. The garnishment figures also don't include tax levies, such as that in the Carl Clark case.

* * *

Garnishment often causes workers to lose their jobs. Many employers fire employees whose debt problems lead to excessive wage attachments, arguing that company handling of garnishment paperwork and court appearances by employees are costly and time-consuming. The Cook County Credit Bureau in Chicago surveyed 1,100 employers in 1964 and found that processing a single garnishment costs a company from $15 to $35; the estimated costs of garnishments to the surveyed employers totaled $12 million annually.

Few companies will discuss the firing of workers for garnishments. A personnel official at one General Motors Corp. plant near Chicago confirms union reports that 45 men were discharged at the plant for that reason last year. Another Chicago manufacturer admits firing "25 or 30" men for garnishments.

Union officials liken the practice of firing debt-burdened workers to the medieval custom of locking debtors in prison. "Under both practices, the debtor has a harder time paying his bills," says one. Most companies say they try to keep a man as long as he is making sincere efforts to straighten out his debts.

* * *

Source: *Wall Street Journal,* April 16, 1966.

1969, the U.S. Supreme Court held that this prejudgment garnishment procedure was unconstitutional.

SNIADACH v. FAMILY FINANCE CORP. OF BAY VIEW
395 U.S. 337 (1969)

MR. JUSTICE DOUGLAS delivered the opinion of the Court.

Respondents instituted a garnishment action against petitioner as defendant and Miller Harris Instrument Co., her employer, as garnishee. The complaint alleged a claim of $420 on a promissory note. The garnishee filed its answer stating it had wages of $63.18 under its control earned by petitioner and unpaid, and that it would pay one-half to petitioner as a subsistence allowance and hold the other half subject to the order of the court.

Petitioner moved that the garnishment proceedings be dismissed for failure to satisfy the due process requirements of the Fourteenth Amendment. The Wisconsin Supreme Court sustained the lower state court in approving the procedure. The case is here on a petition for a writ of certiorari. 393 U.S. 1078.

The Wisconsin statute gives a plaintiff 10 days in which to serve the summons and complaint on the defendant after service on the garnishee. In this case petitioner was served the same day as the garnishee. She nonetheless claims that the Wisconsin garnishment procedure violates that due process required by the Fourteenth Amendment, in that notice and an opportunity to be heard are not given before the *in rem* seizure of the wages. What happened in Wisconsin is that the clerk of the court issues the summons at the request of the creditor's lawyer; and it is the latter who by serving the garnishee sets in motion the machinery whereby the wages are frozen. They may, it is true, be unfrozen if the trial of the main suit is ever had and the wage earner wins on the merits. But in the interim the wage earner is deprived of his enjoyment of earned wages without any opportunity to be heard and to tender any defense he may have, whether it be fraud or otherwise.

Such summary procedure may well meet the requirements of due process in extraordinary situations. But in the present case no situation requiring special protection to a state or creditor interest is presented by the facts; nor is the Wisconsin statute narrowly drawn to meet any such unusual condition. Petitioner was a resident of this Wisconsin community and *in personam* jurisdiction was readily obtainable.

The question is not whether the Wisconsin law is a wise law or unwise law. Our concern is not what philosophy Wisconsin should or should not embrace. We do not sit as a super-legislative body. In this case the sole question is whether there has been a taking of property without that procedural due process that is required by the Fourteenth Amendment. We have dealt over and over again with the question of what constitutes "the right to be heard" (*Schroeder* v. *New York*, 371 U.S. 208, 212) within the meaning of procedural due process. See *Mullane* v. *Central Hanover Trust Co.*, 339 U.S. 306, 314. In the latter case we said that the right to be heard "has little reality or worth unless one is informed that the matter is pending and can choose for himself whether to appear or default, acquiesce or contest." 339 U.S., at 314. In the context of this case the question is whether the interim freezing of the wages without a chance to be heard violates procedural due process.

A procedural rule that may satisfy due process for attachments in general, see *McKay* v. *McInnes*, 279 U.S. 820, does not necessarily satisfy procedural due process in every case. The fact that a procedure would pass muster under a feudal regime does not mean it gives necessary protection to all property in its modern forms. We deal here with wages—a specialized type of property presenting distinct problems in our economic system. We turn then to the nature of that property and problems of procedural due process.

A prejudgment garnishment of the Wisconsin type is a taking which may impose tremendous hardship on wage earners with families to support. Until a recent Act of Congress, § 304 of which forbids discharge of employees on the ground that their wages have been garnished, garnishment often meant the loss of a job. Over and beyond that was the great drain on family income. As stated by Congressman Reuss:

> The idea of wage garnishment in advance of judgment, of trustee process, of wage attachment, or whatever it is called is a most inhuman doctrine. It compels the wage earner, trying to keep his family together, to be driven below the poverty level.

Recent investigations of the problem have disclosed the grave injustices made possible by prejudgment garnishment whereby the sole opportunity to be heard comes after the taking. Congressman Sullivan, Chairman of the House Subcommittee on Consumer Affairs who held extensive hearings on this and related problems stated:

> What we know from our study of this problem is that in a vast number of cases the debt is a fraudulent one, saddled on a poor ignorant person who is trapped in an easy credit nightmare, in which he is charged double for something he could not pay for even if the proper price was called for, and then hounded into giving up his pound of flesh, and being fired besides.

The leverage of the creditor on the wage earner is enormous. The creditor tenders not only the original debt but the "collection fees" incurred by his attorneys in the garnishment proceedings:

> The debtor whose wages are tied up by a writ of garnishment, and who is usually in need of money, is in no position to resist demands for collection fees. If the debt is small, the debtor will be under considerable pressure to pay the debt and collection charges in order to get his wages back. If the debt is large, he will often sign a new contract or 'payment schedule' which incorporates these additional charges.

Apart from those collateral consequences, it appears that in Wisconsin the statutory exemption granted the wage earner is "generally insufficient to support the debtor for any one week."

The result is that a prejudgment garnishment of the Wisconsin type may as a practical matter drive a wage-earning family to the wall. Where the taking of one's property is so obvious, it needs no extended argument to conclude that absent notice and a prior hearing (cf. *Coe* v. *Armour Fertilizer Works,* 237 U.S. 413, 423) this prejudgment garnishment procedure violates the fundamental principles of due process.

Reversed.

Wage Assignment

A **wage assignment** is an agreement by an employee that a creditor may take future wages as security for a loan or to pay an existing debt. With a wage assignment, the creditor can collect directly from the employer. However, in some states wage assignments are unlawful and an employer need not honor the agreement (indeed, would be liable to the employee if it did). Other states regulate wage assignments in various ways—for example, by requiring that the assignment be a separate instrument, not part of the loan agreement, and by specifying that no wage assignment is valid beyond a certain period of time (two or three years).

Confession of Judgment

Because suing is at best nettlesome, many creditors have developed forms that allow them to sidestep the courthouse when debtors have defaulted. As part of the original credit agreement, the consumer or borrower waives his right to defend himself in court by signing a **confession of judgment.** This written instrument recites the debtor's agreement that a court order be automatically entered against him in the event of default. The creditor's lawyer simply takes the confession of judgment to the clerk of the court, who enters it in the judgment book of the court without ever consulting a judge. Entry of the judgment entitles the creditor to attach the debtor's assets to satisfy the debt. Like prejudgment garnishment, a confession of judgment gives the consumer no right to be heard, and it has been banned by statute or court decisions in many states.

Fair Debt Collection Practices Act

Many stores, hospitals, and other organizations attempt on their own to collect unpaid bills, but thousands of merchants, professionals, and small businesses rely on collection agencies to recover accounts receivable. More than 5,000 such agencies go after debt in excess of $5 billion annually. For decades, some of these collectors used harassing tactics: posing as government agents or attorneys, calling at the debtor's workplace, threatening physical harm or loss of property or imprisonment, using abusive language, publishing a "deadbeats" list, misrepresenting the size of the debt, and telling friends and neighbors about the debt. To provide a remedy for these abuses, Congress enacted, as part of the Consumer Credit Protection Act, the Fair Debt Collection Practices Act in 1977.

This law regulates the manner by which collection agencies may conduct their business. The law covers collection of all personal, family, and household debts by collection agencies. (It does not deal with collection by creditors like stores or banks themselves.) The collector may contact the debtor only during reasonable hours and not at work if the employer prohibits it. The debtor may write the collector to cease contact, in which case the agency is prohibited from further contact (except to confirm that there will be no further contact). In talking to others to trace the debtor's whereabouts, collectors may not tell them that the inquiry concerns a debt, and if the debtor has an attorney, only the attorney may be contacted. A denial that money is owed stops the bill collector for thirty days, and he can resume again only after the debtor is sent proof of the debt. Collectors may no longer file suit in remote places hoping for default judgments; any suit must be filed in a court where the debtor lives or where the underlying contract was signed. The use of harassing and abusive tactics, including false and misleading representations to the debtor and others, is prohibited. The federal statute gives debtors the right to sue the collector for damages (a right extended in few of the thirty-seven states with collection laws) for violating the statute and for causing such injuries as job loss or harm to reputation.

FTC Credit Practices Rule

In 1984, the Federal Trade Commission adopted a rule, effective March 1, 1985, prohibiting confessions of judgment and wage assignments in consumer credit contracts used by lenders and retail installment sellers. The purpose of the rule is to protect consumers from unfair or deceptive collection practices.

Unconscionability

In addition to federal regulation, state law governing unconscionable contracts also plays an important role in shaping creditor practices. The relevant law is found in Section 2-302(1) of the Uniform Commercial Code (UCC), which allows courts to tinker with a contract if they determine that it is particularly unfair. The provision reads as follows:

> If the court as a matter of law finds the contract or any clause of the contract to have been unconscionable at the time it was made the court may refuse to enforce the contract, or it may enforce the remainder of the contract without the unconscionable clause, or it may so limit the application of any unconscionable clause as to avoid any unconscionable result.

The court thus has considerable flexibility. It may refuse to enforce the entire contract, or strike a particular clause or set of clauses, or limit the application of a particular clause or set of clauses.

But what does "unconscionable" mean? The UCC provides little guidance on this crucial question. According to comment 1 to Section 2-302, the "basic test is: whether, in the light of the general commercial background and the commercial needs of the particular trade or case, the clauses involved are so one-sided as to be unconscionable under the circumstances existing at the time of the making of the contract. . . . The principle is one of the prevention of oppression and unfair surprise and not of disturbance of allocation of risks because of superior bargaining power." It should be apparent that the definition is somewhat circular. For the most part, judges have had to develop the concept with little help from the statutory language. Unconscionability is much like U.S. Supreme Court Justice Potter Stewart's famous statement about obscenity: "I can't define it, but I know it when I see it."

In the following leading case, Judge J. Skelly Wright attempted to develop a framework for analysis. He refined the meaning of unconscionability by focusing on "absence of meaningful choice" (often referred to as "procedural unconscionability") and on terms that are "unreasonably favorable" (commonly referred to as "substantive unconscionability"). An example of procedural unconscionability is the salesperson who says: "Don't worry about all that little type on the back of this form." Substantive unconscionability is the harsh term—the provision that permits the taking of a pound of flesh if the contract is not honored. (Although the UCC was not yet law in the District of Columbia when the case arose, Congress had enacted it by the time the case reached court. The Court of Appeals relied on the congressional policy to declare that the common law mirrored the statute.)

WILLIAMS v. WALKER-THOMAS FURNITURE COMPANY
350 F.2d 445 (D.C. Cir. 1965)

J. SKELLY WRIGHT, CIRCUIT JUDGE. Appellee, Walker-Thomas Furniture Company, operates a retail furniture store in the District of Columbia. During the period from 1957 to 1962 each appellant in these cases purchased a number of household items from Walker-Thomas, for which payment was to be made in installments. The terms of each purchase were contained in a printed form contract which set forth the value of the purchased item and purported to lease the item to appellant for a stipulated monthly rent payment. The contract then provided, in substance, that title would remain in Walker-Thomas until the total of all the monthly payments made equaled the stated value of the item, at which time appellants could take title. In the event of a default in the payment of any monthly installment, Walker-Thomas could repossess the item.

The contract further provided that

> the amount of each periodical installment payment to be made by [purchaser] to the Company under this present lease shall be inclusive of and not in addition to the amount of each installment payment to be made by [purchaser] under such prior leases, bills or accounts; *and all payments now and hereafter made by [purchaser] shall be credited pro rata on all outstanding leases, bills and accounts* due the Company by [purchaser] at the time each such payment is made. [Emphasis added.]

The effect of this rather obscure provision was to keep a balance due on every item purchased until the balance due on all items, whenever purchased, was liquidated. As a result, the debt incurred at the time of purchase of each item was secured by the right to repossess all the items previously purchased by the same purchaser, and each new item purchased automatically became subject to a security interest arising out of the previous dealings.

On May 12, 1962, appellant Thorne purchased an item described as a Daveno, three tables, and two lamps, having total stated value of $391.10. Shortly thereafter, he defaulted on his monthly payments and appellee sought to replevy all the items purchased since the first transaction in 1958. Similarly, on April 17, 1962, appellant Williams bought a stereo set of stated value of $514.95. She too defaulted shortly thereafter, and appellee sought to replevy all the items purchased since December, 1957. The Court of General Sessions granted judgment for appellee. The District of Columbia Court of Appeals affirmed, and we granted appellants' motion for leave to appeal to this court.

* * *

We do not agree that the court lacked the power to refuse enforcement to contracts found to be unconscionable. In other jurisdictions, it has been held as a matter of common law that unconscionable contracts are not enforceable. While no decision of this court so holding has been found, the notion that an unconscionable bargain should not be given full enforcement is by no means novel. In Scott v. United States, 79 U.S. (12 Wall.) 443, 445, 20 L.Ed. 438 (1870), the Supreme Court stated:

> . . . If a contract be unreasonable and unconscionable, but not void for fraud, a court of law will give to the party who sues for its breach damages, not according to its letter, but only such as he is equitably entitled to. . . .

Since we have never adopted or rejected such a rule, the question here presented is actually one of first impression.

* * *

Unconscionability has generally been recognized to include an absence of meaningful choice on the part of one of the parties together with contract terms which are unreasonably favorable to the other party. Whether a meaningful choice is present in a particular case can only be determined by consideration of all the circumstances surrounding the transaction. In many cases the meaningfulness of the choice is negated by a gross inequality of bargaining power. The manner in which the contract was entered is also relevant to this consideration. Did each party to the contract, considering his obvious education or lack of it, have a reasonable opportunity to understand the terms of the contract, or were the important terms hidden in a maze of fine print and minimized by deceptive sales practices? Ordinarily, one who signs an agreement without full knowledge of its terms might be held to assume the risk that he has entered a one-sided bargain. But when a party of little bargaining power, and hence little real choice, signs a commercially unreasonable contract with little or no knowledge of its terms, it is hardly likely that his consent, or even an objective manifestation of his consent, was ever given to all the terms. In such a case the usual rule that the terms of the agreement are not to be questioned should be abandoned and the court should consider whether the terms of the contract are so unfair that enforcement should be withheld.

In determining unreasonableness or fairness, the primary concern must be with the terms of the contract considered in light of the circumstances existing when the contract was made. The test is not simple, nor can it be mechanically applied. The terms are to be considered "in light of the general commercial background and the commercial needs of the particular trade or case." Corbin suggests the test as being whether the terms are "so extreme as to appear unconscionable according to the mores and business practices of the time and place." We think this formulation correctly states the test to be applied in those cases where no meaningful choice was exercised upon entering the contract.

Because the trial court and the appellate court did not feel that enforcement could be refused, no findings were made on the possible unconscionability of the contracts in these cases. Since the record is not sufficient for our deciding the issue as a matter of law, the cases must be remanded to the trial court for further proceedings.

So ordered.

Despite its fuzziness, the concept of unconscionability has had a dramatic impact in American law. In many cases, in fact, the traditional notion of *caveat emptor* has changed to *caveat venditor* ("let the seller beware"). So important is this provision that the courts have even applied the doctrine in cases not governed by the UCC.

Chapter Summary

The rise in consumer debt in recent years has been matched by an increase in federal regulation of consumer credit transactions. Consumers granted credit receive protection through usury laws (that establish a maximum interest rate), the Truth-in-Lending Act (requiring disclosure of credit terms), the Equal Credit Opportunity Act (prohibiting certain types of discrimination), and the Fair Credit Reporting Act (giving consumers access to their credit files).

After entering into a credit transaction, a consumer has certain cancellation rights and may use a procedure prescribed by the Fair Credit Billing Act to correct billing errors. Traditional debt collection practices—garnishment, wage assignments and confession of judgment clauses—are now subject to federal regulation, as are the practices of collection agencies under the Fair Debt Collection Practices Act. State law also plays an important role in consumer credit transactions, notably in the form of the unconscionability section of the Uniform Commercial Code.

Problems

1. Chauncey borrowed $10,000 from Victor and gave Victor a note for $13,000, which was due one year after the loan was made. Chauncey was to use the loan to run his business, which was producing dental floss. The maximum rate of interest in the state was 10 percent. Is the loan usurious? Why?
2. Sara used a credit card to make a number of purchases. She was charged the maximum interest rate allowed by law and, in addition, she paid an annual membership fee. Does the fee violate the usury law? Why?
3. Bill took his car to a mechanic after hearing a noise in the power steering. The mechanic, Roger, overhauled the steering and Bill, using his credit card, paid Roger $250. Later the same day the noise returned. When Bill immediately took the car to another mechanic, he learned that the overhaul was unnecessary because the problem was a fluid leak in the steering, which cost $200 to repair. Discuss Bill's rights against his credit card company.
4. Zeke, a welfare recipient, was convicted of welfare fraud. A county representative visited Zeke and convinced him to sign a confession of judgment, dated December 26, 1984, for an alleged overpayment of welfare benefits. Is the confession of judgment valid? Why?
5. Would the conclusion and reason in problem 4 be different if Zeke had signed the confession of judgment on December 26, 1985? Why?
6. A debt collector who had not yet decided to bring suit sent a debtor a letter that included the following language: "We are not representing either directly or by implication that legal action has been or is being taken against you at this time." Discuss the legality of this language.
7. In *Williams* v. *Walker-Thomas Furniture Company* (p. 401), Judge Wright remanded the case for further proceedings. If you were the trial judge, how would you decided the case on remand? Why?
8. A major utility company purchased a $10,000,000 generator from Westinghouse. When the generator broke down, Westinghouse relied on a clause in the contract limiting its liability. The utility argued that the clause was unconscionable. Is this a proper case for application of the rule of unconscionability? Why?

12

Bankruptcy

Bankruptcy law governs the rights of creditors and insolvent debtors who cannot pay their debts. In broadest terms, bankruptcy deals with the seizure of the debtor's assets and their distribution to the debtor's various creditors. The term derives from the Renaissance custom of Italian traders, who did their trading from benches in town marketplaces. Creditors literally "broke the bench" of a merchant who failed to pay his debts. The term *banca rotta* (broken bench) thus came to apply to business failures.

In the Victorian era, many people in both England and the United States viewed someone who became bankrupt as a wicked person. In part this attitude was prompted by the law itself, which to a greater degree in England and to a lesser degree in the United States treated the insolvent debtor as a sort of felon. Until the second half of the nineteenth century, British insolvents could be imprisoned; jail for insolvent debtors was abolished earlier in the United States. And the entire administration of bankruptcy law favored the creditor, who could with a mere filing throw the financial affairs of the alleged insolvent into complete disarray.

Today a more enlightened attitude prevails. Bankruptcy is understood as an aspect of financing, a system that permits creditors to receive an equitable distribution of the bankrupt's assets and promises new hope to debtors facing impossible financial burdens. Without such a law, we may reasonably suppose that the level of economic activity would be far less than it is, for few would be willing to risk being personally burdened forever by crushing debt.

Alternatives to Bankruptcy

Assignment for Benefit of Creditors

Under a common law **assignment for the benefit of creditors**, the debtor transfers some or all of his assets to a trustee—usually someone appointed by the adjustment bureau of a local credit managers' association—who sells the assets and apportions the proceeds in some agreed manner, usually pro rata, to the creditors. Of course, not every creditor need agree with such a distribution. Strictly speaking, the common law assignment does not discharge the balance of the debt. Many state statutes attempt to address this problem either by prohibiting creditors who accept a partial payment of debt under an assignment from claiming the balance, or by permitting debtors to demand a release from creditors who accept partial payment.

Composition

A **composition** is simply an agreement by creditors to accept less than the full amount of the debt and to discharge the debtor from further liability. As a contract, composition requires consideration; the mutual agreement among creditors to accept a pro rata share of the proceeds is held to be sufficient consideration to support the discharge. The essential difference between assignment and composition lies in the creditors' agreement: an assignment implies no agreement among the creditors, whereas a composition does. Not all creditors of the particular debtor need agree to the composition for it to be valid. A creditor who does not agree to the composition remains free to attempt to collect the full sum owed; in particular, a creditor not inclined to compose the debt could attach the debtor's assets while other creditors were bargaining over the details of the composition agreement.

Receivership

A creditor may petition the court to appoint a receiver; this is a long-established procedure in equity whereby the receiver takes over the debtor's property under instructions from the court. The receiver may liquidate the property, continue to operate the business, or preserve the assets without operating the business until the court finally determines how to dispose of the debtor's property.

The difficulty with most of the alternatives to bankruptcy lies in their voluntary character: A creditor who refuses to go along with an agreement to discharge the debtor can usually manage to thwart the debtor and his fellow creditors. The only final protection, therefore, is to be found in the bankruptcy law.

The Bankruptcy Reform Act

History of the Bankruptcy System

Constitutional Basis The Constitution prohibits the states from impairing the "obligation of a contract." This means that no state can directly provide a means for discharging a debtor unless the debt has been entirely paid. But the Constitution in Article I, Paragraph 8, does give the federal government such a power by providing that Congress may enact a uniform bankruptcy law.

Bankruptcy Statutes Congress passed bankruptcy laws in 1800, 1841, and 1867. These lasted only a few years each. In 1898, Congress enacted the Bankruptcy Act, which together with the Chandler Act amendments in 1938, lasted until 1978. In 1978, Congress passed the Bankruptcy Reform Act, superseding all the prior laws. The Bankruptcy Reform Act was adopted to eliminate a number of undesirable practices, including inefficient administration of businesses undergoing bankruptcy proceedings, costly procedures generated by adversary procedures even when no true adversaries were present, and inequities from one court to another. The act was an outgrowth of a special commission that Congress established in 1970, prompted by a 1,000 percent increase in the annual volume of cases of consumer bankruptcies since 1950. The commission proposed a law in 1973, but it took five years of lobbying and compromising before President Carter could sign the new act into law. This law, as amended in 1984, is the subject of our chapter.

Consequences of the Bankruptcy Reform Act

At the beginning of the century, bankruptcies averaged fewer than 20,000 per year. Even in 1935, at the height of the Great Depression, bankruptcy filings in federal court climbed only to 69,000. At the end of World War II in 1945 they stood at 13,000. From 1950 on, the statistics show a steep increase. During the decade before the Bankruptcy Reform Act was passed, bankruptcy filings in court averaged 181,000 a year—reaching a high of 254,000 in 1975. In 1978, the year the act was passed, they totaled 203,000. Thereafter the numbers soared. Many commentators have suggested that the upsurge was at least partly due to the Bankruptcy Reform Act, which expanded the list and dollar value of assets—equity in homes and cars, personal property such as clothing, jewelry, and tools of one's trade—that the consumer debtor may retain after declaring bankruptcy, and which made it easier for a bankrupt business to keep its own management in charge while the company is being reorganized.

Bankruptcy Courts and Judges

As originally enacted, the Bankruptcy Reform Act provided for a new bankruptcy court system effective in 1984. Each federal judicial district was to have a U.S. Bankruptcy Court, whose judges were to be appointed by the president to fourteen-year terms. The bankruptcy court was to have all the traditional powers of the courts except that it could not punish a contempt of court committed outside the judge's presence, nor could it send anyone to jail. The scope of the bankruptcy jurisdiction was broad. The courts could hear bankruptcy matters, and "all civil proceedings arising . . . in or related to cases" under the Bankruptcy Reform Act.

However, in *Northern Pipeline Construction Company* v. *Marathon Pipe Line Company,* 458 U.S. 50 (1982), the Supreme Court decided that these powers violated Article III of the Constitution, which requires that such powers be vested in courts where judges have life tenure. Following this decision, Congress amended the act in 1984 to provide that, unless both sides agree otherwise, bankruptcy judges are to hear only bankruptcy matters (called "core proceedings"). The 1984 amendments also call for the appointment of bankruptcy judges by U.S. Courts of Appeals.

Overview of Key Provisions

The Bankruptcy Reform Act provided for four different types of bankruptcy proceedings. Each is covered by its own chapter in the act and is usually referred to by its chapter number.

- Liquidation (Chapter 7)
- Adjustment of debts of a municipality (Chapter 9)
- Reorganization (Chapter 11)
- Adjustment of debts of an individual with regular income (Chapter 13)

A **liquidation** is a "straight" bankruptcy proceeding. It entails selling the debtor's nonexempt assets for cash and distributing the cash to the creditors, thereby discharging the insolvent person or business from any further liability for the debt. With New York City and other municipalities on the verge of bankruptcy during the 1970s, serious questions arose over the capacity of the old bankruptcy law to deal with municipal insolvency. Chapter 9 of the Bankruptcy Reform Act provides a mechanism to **adjust the debts of a municipality.** (The law does not suppose that a town, city, or county will go out of existence in the wake of insolvency.) **Reorganization** is the means by which a financially troubled company can continue to operate while its financial affairs are put on a sounder basis. A business might liquidate following reorganization, but will probably take on new life after negotiations with creditors on how the old debt is to be paid off. A company may voluntarily decide to seek Chapter 11 protection in court, or it may be forced involuntarily into a Chapter 11 proceeding. Like the business, an individual may wish to negotiate a limit to his indebtedness. Chapter 13 permits an **individual with regular income** to establish a repayment plan, usually either a composition (see p. 320) or an extension (a stretch-out of the time for paying the entire debt).

Before 1986, many family farmers could not qualify for reorganization under Chapter 13 because of the low debt ceiling (see p. 340) and, under Chapter 11, the proceeding was often complicated and expensive. As a result, in 1986, Congress created Chapter 12 entitled "Adjustment of Debts of a Family Farmer with Regular Annual Income." Chapter 12 applies only to farmers whose total debts do not exceed $1,500,000.

The Bankruptcy Reform Act includes three chapters that set forth the procedures to be applied to the various proceedings. Chapter 1, "General Provisions," establishes who is eligible for relief under the act. Chapter 3, "Case Administration," spells out the powers of the various officials involved in the bankruptcy proceedings and establishes the methods for instituting bankruptcy cases. Chapter 5, "Creditors, the Debtor, and the Estate," deals with the debtor's "estate"—his assets. It lays down ground rules for determining which property is to be included in the estate, sets out the powers of the bankruptcy trustee to "avoid" (invalidate) transactions by which the debtor sought to remove property from the estate, orders the distribution of property to creditors, and sets forth the duties and benefits that accrue the debtor under the act.

To illustrate how these procedural chapters (especially Chapters 3 and 5) apply, we focus on the most common proceeding: liquidation (Chapter 7). Most of the principles of bankruptcy law discussed in connection with liquidation apply to the other types of proceedings as well. However, some principles vary, and we conclude the chapter by noting special features of two other important proceedings—Chapters 13 and 11.

Liquidation

Recall that the purpose of liquidation is to convert the debtor's assets—except those exempt under the law—into cash for distribution to the creditors and thereafter to discharge the debtor from further liability. With certain exceptions any person may voluntarily file a petition to liquidate under Chapter 7. A person is defined as any individual, partnership, or corporation. The exceptions are for railroads and insurance companies, banks, savings and loan associations, credit unions, and the like.

Case Administration

For a Chapter 7 liquidation proceeding, as for bankruptcy proceedings in general, the various aspects of case administration are covered by Chapter 3. These include the rules governing commencement of the proceedings, the effect of the petition in bankruptcy, the first meeting of the creditors, and the duties and powers of trustees.

Commencement: Voluntary and Involuntary Petition The persons noted above may file a voluntary petition in bankruptcy. To prevent "substantial abuse" of the law, the court may prohibit an individual having primarily consumer debts from using Chapter 7, as the following case illustrates.

In re BRYANT
47 B.R. 21 (W.D. No. Car. 1984)

MARVIN R. WOOTEN, Bankruptcy Judge.

The Debtor, Mitchell W. Bryant, on October 24, 1984 filed a Voluntary Petition with this Court under Chapter 7 of the Bankruptcy Code.

* * *

At hearing the Debtor ignored his secured obligations and reasserted he owed only six debts. He further testified that three of these (to Custom Printers, Ford Motor Credit Company, and Namaco; totaling $40,248.00) were personally guaranteed business debts. He argued that inasmuch as these were not "primarily consumer debts" as contemplated by § 707(b) with respect to *amount,* the Court could not dismiss his case under § 707(b).

The Court at hearing, however, determined the Debtor's home mortgages to be consumer obligations and included them with his other consumer debts. These are as follows:

Cameron-Brown Company (First Mortgage on Residence)	$32,260.00
AVCO (Second Mortgage on Residence)	12,000.00
Berry, Hogewood, Edwards & Freeman, P.A.	512.82
First Citizens Bank & Trust (MasterCard Div.)	1,038.10
First Citizens Bank & Trust (VISA Division)	1,034.05
Total Listed Consumer Debts	$46,844.97

Additionally, the Debtor's testimony acknowledged that he had intentionally omitted in his petition a credit line with Wachovia Bank and balances he owed on at least seven to eight credit cards which he possessed at the time of filing. The Court found these to be consumer debts of substantial amount but the Debtor was unable, or at least unwilling, to identify these or give their amounts. It is therefore impossible to determine with any precision what amounts were owed on these unlisted debts and to whom.

The Court found the Debtor to have non-consumer debts in the following amounts:

Custom Printers & Design Graphix, Inc.	$10,000.00
Ford Motor Credit Company	9,248.00
Namaco Industries	21,000.00
Total Listed Non-Consumer Debts	$40,248.00

Debtor's Statement of Monthly Expenses estimated the average future monthly expenses for his family of four as follows:

Rent/Mortgage payments	671.00
Utilities	245.00
Food	500.00
Credit card payments	400.00
Car Payments (1984 Buick)	381.00
Transportation	250.00
Clothing	500.00
Medical/Drug Expenses	200.00

Laundry	100.00
Recreation	100.00
Cable Television	65.00
Car Rental	50.00
Automobile Insurance	50.00
Newspapers	25.00
Total Estimated Monthly Expenses	$3,537.00

The record discloses that the Debtor and his wife own a home located in Mathews, North Carolina with an estimated fair market value of $52,500.00. The property is encumbered by the secured claims of Cameron-Brown Company and AVCO. There is some $8,000.00 of equity in the property, which would be totally offset by the Debtor and his wife's exemptions under N.C. law. The Debtor is employed by Mathews Home Furnishings, Inc; a closely-held business which is owned by his wife. His testimony indicates his family's annual income exceeds $38,000.00; his petition disclosed a monthly income of $3,420.00 or $41,400.00 annually.

Under § 707(b) of the Code, Bankruptcy Judges are authorized to dismiss, sua sponte, cases filed by individual debtors having "primarily consumer debts", where the Court finds that to allow the case to proceed would be a "substantial abuse" of the provisions of Chapter 7. The Bankruptcy Amendments and Federal Judgeship Act (of which 707(b) is a part) failed to define the phrases "primarily consumer debts" and "substantial abuse". The section is of such recent vintage that no published cases have construed the terms.

The Debtor has not suggested that the words "substantial abuse" should be given anything other than their ordinary, plain meaning and the court so construes them. By this definition, it is readily apparent that this case is one in which allowing the Debtor relief would constitute a substantial abuse of Chapter 7.

It was the philosophy of the constitutional authors and the intent of Congress in establishing the Bankruptcy Code, that this relief was to provide a fresh start for financially troubled persons. Bankruptcy was not intended to provide a means for the unscrupulous to avoid their creditors, but was designed to provide a second chance for persons who for reasons of calamity, sickness, unemployment, and the like were unable to meet their obligations. The case before the Court is not such a case.

First, this case was brought, not because of the Debtor's unemployment or an inability to pay on his part, but because he simply desired to shuck a couple of his debts. His testimony was that he had previously guaranteed a number of business debts and he filed this bankruptcy in order to "get rid" of the same. The Debtor claims he intended to pay his non-business-related debts; however, he seeks relief which would discharge *both* these guaranteed debts *and* his personal obligations.

Secondly, the Court finds on the part of the Debtor an utter disregard of his duties under the § 522 of the Code to truthfully list all of his obligations, his monthly expenses, and to disclose his general financial position to the Court.

* * *

Third, it is the opinion of the court that the Debtor's Statement of Monthly Expenses filed with his petition was done in bad faith and that these amounts were greatly overstated with the intention of misrepresenting his financial picture. For example, he avers that his average monthly expenses for feeding himself, his wife, and his two children exceeds $500.00, (excluding dining out for which he allocates another $100.00). The Debtor submits that maintaining his wife's 1984 Buick and his personal use of a "company" car costs better than $250.00 per month, discounting car payments ($381.00), rent ($50.00) and auto insurance ($50.00). Likewise, the Debtor informs the Court that while his family has no recurrent medical expenses (apart from one set of braces), his monthly medical bills exceed $200.00. Even his most diminutive bills take on gargantuan proportions—he claims to spend $100.00 per month for laundry costs although the family owns a washing machine.

* * *

In like measure, the Debtor claims expenses of $100.00 per month for dining out and for going to movies. He claims another $65.00 per month for cable television. Even if these amounts are accurate, the Court has serious questions about their appropriateness for a Debtor in Chapter 7. While Congress intended to give the Debtors relief in such cases, it was not the design of the Bankruptcy laws to allow the Debtor to lead the life of Riley while his creditors suffer on his behalf.

Therefore, in light of the Debtor's purpose in filing this petition; his fraudulent and misleading omissions in his petition; his attempts to pad his expenses statement in order to misrepresent his financial position; and the relatively exorbitant lifestyle which he seeks to maintain while taking shelter from his creditors under the Bankruptcy provisions, the Court concludes that to allow this petition would be a substantial abuse of the provisions of Chapter 7. The Bankruptcy Courts have their foundations in the Courts of Equity, and here the clean hands maxim applies: To receive equity, one must do equity. This the Debtor has not done.

In considering dismissal under 707(b) the Court must, in addition to finding "substantial abuse" determine that the Debtor's obligations were also "primarily consumer debts". As with substantial abuse, what constitutes "primarily consumer debts" was not defined in the Code and has yet to be determined by case law.

* * *

This certainly is a case involving primarily consumer debts. The Court has found the Debtor's consumer obligations to include his home mortgages and to total $46,844.97. (To this should be added his unlisted credit card debts which are of uncertain amount.) On the other hand, his nonconsumer debts total only $40,248.00. The Debtor's consumer debts outweigh his nonconsumer debts by more than seven thousand dollars and dispel the Debtor's notion that these are by amount nonconsumer debts. Similarly, with regard to number, at least twelve of the Debtor's fifteen or sixteen obligations are consumer debts, and in this respect, also, his case is one involving primarily consumer debts.

The case at hand involves acts of a Debtor in conscious disregard of the Bankruptcy provisions, his fraudulent attempts to hide his debts and distort his financial circumstances; and his bad faith effort to avoid paying his creditors. These obligations are, to the extent ascertainable, primarily consumer debts with respect to number and amount. The Court is therefore of the opinion that this is a case of substantial abuse of Chapter 7 and hereby dismisses the same under § 707(b) of the Code

It is so ordered.

Involuntary bankruptcy is also possible and may be started against any person except a farmer or a charitable enterprise. To put anyone into bankruptcy involuntarily, the petitioning creditors must meet three conditions: (1) they must have claims for unsecured debt amounting to at least $5,000; (2) three creditors must join in the petition whenever twelve or more creditors have claims against the particular debtor—otherwise one creditor may file an involuntary petition, as long as his claim is for at least $5,000; and (3) they must have particular grounds for relief.

The Bankruptcy Reform Act specifies two grounds for relief: (1) the debtor is generally not paying his debts as they become due; (2) within 120 days of the filing, the debtor made a general assignment for the benefit of creditors. These grounds are far clearer than the "acts of bankruptcy" called for under the older bankruptcy acts.

Effect of the Petition The petition operates as a **stay** against suits or other actions against the debtor to recover claims, enforce judgments, or create liens. In other words, once the petition is filed, the debtor is freed from worry over other proceedings affecting his finances or property. Anyone with a claim, secured or unsecured, must seek relief in the bankruptcy court. This provision in the act can have dramatic consequences. Beset by tens of thousands of product liability suits for damages caused by asbestos, UNR Industries and Manville Corporation, the nation's largest asbestos producers, filed (separate) voluntary bankruptcy petitions in 1982; those filings automatically stayed all pending lawsuits.

First Meeting of Creditors Once a petition is filed, the court issues an "order of relief." In a voluntary case the petition operates as an order for relief. In an involuntary case, the order may be issued only (1) if the debtor does not contest the petition, or (2) the court determines that one or the other grounds for relief exists. If the debtor does contest the order and no grounds for relief exist, the court must dismiss the petition.

Assuming that the order has been properly issued, the creditors must meet within a reasonable time. The debtor is obligated to appear at the meeting and submit to examination under oath. The judge does not preside and, indeed, is not even entitled to attend the meeting.

When the judge issues an order for relief, he appoints an **interim trustee,** one who is authorized initially to take control of the debtor's assets. The trustee is required to collect the property, liquidate the debtor's estate, and distribute the proceeds to the creditors. The trustee may sue and be sued in the name of the estate. Under every chapter except Chapter 7, the court has sole discretion to name the trustee. Under Chapter 7, however, the creditors may select their own trustee, as long as they do so at the first meeting and follow certain voting provisions laid down in the act.

Trustee's Powers and Duties The Bankruptcy Reform Act empowers the trustee to use, sell, or lease the debtor's property in the ordinary course of business or, after notice and a hearing, to do so even if not in the ordinary course of business. In all cases, the trustee must protect any security interests in the property. As long as the court has authorized the debtor's business to continue, the trustee may also obtain credit in the ordinary course of business. He may invest money in the estate to yield the maximum but reasonably safe return. Subject to the court's approval, he may employ various professionals, such as attorneys, accountants, and appraisers, and may, with some exceptions, assume or reject executory contracts and unexpired leases that the debtor has made. The trustee also has the authority to avoid many pre-bankruptcy transactions in order to recover property of the debtor to be included in the liquidation.

Creditors

We now turn to the three major matters covered in Chapter 5 of the Bankruptcy Reform Act: *creditors' claims, debtors' exemptions and discharge,* and the *property to be included in the estate.* We begin with the rules governing proof of claims by creditors and the priority of their claims.

Claims and Creditors A **claim** is defined as a right to payment, whether or not it is reduced to judgment, liquidated, unliquidated, fixed, contingent, matured, unmatured, disputed, undisputed, legal, equitable, secured, or unsecured. A **creditor** is defined as any person or entity with a claim that arose no later than when the court issues the order for relief. These are very broad definitions; they are intended to give the debtor the broadest possible relief when finally discharged.

Proof of Claims Before the trustee can distribute proceeds of the estate, creditors must file a **proof of claim,** prima facie evidence that they are owed some amount of money. Only unsecured creditors must file proof of claim, and they must do so within six months after the first date set for the first meeting of creditors. A creditor who fails to file on time will have his claim disallowed, even though the claim is valid. A party in interest, such as the trustee or creditor, may object to a proof of claim, in which case the court must determine whether to allow it. In the absence of objections, the claim is "deemed allowed." The court will not allow some claims. These include unenforceable claims, claims for unmatured interest, claims that may be offset by debts the creditor owes the debtor, and unreasonable charges by an insider or attorney.

Claims with Priority The Bankruptcy Reform Act sets out categories of claimants and establishes priorities among them. The law is complex because it sets up different orders of priorities. In simple terms, the following rules apply. First, secured creditors are entitled to receive their security interests before anyone else is satisfied, because the security interest is not part of the property that the trustee is entitled to bring into the estate. To the extent that secured creditors have claims in excess of their collateral, they are considered to be unsecured or general creditors and are lumped in with general creditors of the appropriate class.

Second, of the six classes of claimants (see p. 339), the first is known as that of "priority" claims. It is subdivided into seven categories ranked in order of priority. The highest priority class within the general class of priority claims must be paid off in full before the next class can share in a distribution from the estate, and so on. Only if all seven subcategories of the priority class are satisfied can the remaining five classes receive a share of the estate. The seven priority classes, in the order of priorities from highest to lowest, are as follows:

- *Administration expenses* This category includes all expenses necessary to preserve and administer the estate, such as the trustee's expenses, witness fees, expenses and fees of accountants, attorneys, appraisers, and the like.
- *"Gap" creditor claims* After an involuntary petition has been filed, but

before a trustee is appointed or an order of relief is issued, certain creditors may have extended credit to the debtor in the ordinary course of the debtor's business. These claims, known as "gap" creditor claims, are entitled to second priority.

- *Employees' wages, salaries, and commissions* To prevent undue hardship to employees, third priority goes to employees with unsecured claims for up to $2,000 in wages, salaries, or commissions, earned within ninety days of the filing of the petition or cessation of the business.
- *Contributions to employee benefit plans* Fourth priority goes to unsecured claims for contributions to employee benefit plans. The act limits these claims by time (they must have been incurred within 180 days of filing or cessation) and by amount ($2,000 times the number of employees less amounts paid for wage claims).
- *Grain producers and U.S. fishermen* These creditors have fifth priority for unsecured claims (up to $2,000 for each individual) against debtors who own or operate grain or fish storage facilities.
- *Consumer creditor claims* Next in line are consumer creditors with claims of up to $900 per creditor for deposits of money for undelivered goods or unperformed services or rental of property, as long as the deposits were for goods, services, or property for nonbusiness use.
- *Taxes* The final priority category consists of claims for federal, state, and local income, property, employment, and excise taxes.

The Debtor's Exemptions and Discharge

Exemptions The Bankruptcy Reform Act exempts certain property from the estate of an *individual* debtor, so that she will not be impoverished upon discharge. Exactly what is exempt may depend on state law, since the federal act permits the states to establish their own list of exemptions. (The liberal exemptions available in Texas are discussed in Box 12-1). If a state opts out of the federal exemptions, then the debtor in the state must look to the state list and to certain federal exemptions contained in federal laws other than the Bankruptcy Reform Act. If the state has not rejected the federal list, then the debtor has the choice of the federal or state list. By the mid-1980s, over thirty states had opted out.

The federal exemptions include the following:

1. up to $7,500 in equity in a residence;
2. up to $1,200 equity in one motor vehicle;
3. up to $200 for each item of ordinary household furnishings and clothing (including household goods, books, animals, musical instruments and the like), but the total value cannot exceed $4,000;
4. up to $500 in jewelry;
5. up to $750 in books and tools used in the debtor's trade;

Box 12-1 Exemptions—Texas Style

Home Free
BY LAURA JERESKI

The Arena I is 21 stories of black glass perched over the Southwest Freeway, with a 360-degree view of Houston. When Melvin Lane Powers, the Houston real estate developer, filed for reorganization in 1983, he called the duplex penthouse home. In fact, he went to court and called the whole building home.

Welcome to Texas, where a man's castle is his home or, to be more precise, his homestead. The Homestead Act grants every Texan a homestead, exempt from creditors' claims, up to 200 acres of rural land or up to an acre of urban land and all its improvements. Hence Powers' assertion: The office building, valued at $67.5 million in 1983, fits in an acre, and darned if he hasn't improved the lot.

When the smoke cleared and Powers emerged from Chapter 11 in May 1985, debts forgiven, he had indeed succeeded in claiming Arena I, with its rooftop pool, as his homestead.

(Unfortunately, Powers then foolishly followed the advice of counsel and traded his exemption away in order to make a deal with Bank of America, holder of a $49 million first lien on Arena I. Poor Powers. He was unable to live up to the terms of the deal, and the bank foreclosed in May 1986. Equipped with new counsel, Powers then contended the foreclosure infringed on his constitutional homestead rights, but it was too late. This time the court refused to go along.)

Texans find Powers' kind of homesteading bold but not at all unreasonable. After all, the state was founded by debtors fleeing claims in the South and Northeast, where debtors could keep nothing. The first exemptions date to Texas independence in 1836, and the Homestead Act is enshrined in the Texas Constitution of 1876.

How much, then, can you get away with? As Texas bankruptcy lawyers like to say, "If you can fit the Taj Mahal on an acre in downtown Houston, it's yours." Besides buildings of any dollar value—say $67.5 million—the Homestead Act is replete with other exemptions. The law alternatively allows a business homestead; moreover, it further allows a "buggy" (it can be an automobile, of course); a second vehicle; two firearms; athletic equipment, a horse, say Seattle Slew; and wearing apparel, including jewelry. But there are limits. Powers claimed a 165-foot yacht—the largest registered under the U.S. flag—was essential to his reorganization. The judge didn't bite.

But there's nothing to say the "buggy" couldn't be the working Bugatti Royale collector's car that was recently auctioned for $6.5 million. The law also allows another vehicle, say a truck or bus

6. up to $400, plus up to $3,750 not used in (1) above, in any property owned by the debtor;
7. any unmatured life insurance contract owned by the debtor other than a credit life insurance contract;
8. up to $4,000 cash surrender or loan value of an unmatured life insurance contract owned by the debtor and on the debtor's life;
9. alimony and child support payments;
10. certain rights in pension and profit-sharing plans, and other annuity plans, including Social Security and veterans and disability benefits; and
11. up to $7,500 in payments from an award in a personal injury lawsuit.

(one debtor spent $250,000 refurbishing a Greyhound bus). And two firearms—one could easily spend $25,000 each. Plus athletic equipment: Powers spent $15,000 on his gym; obviously he was a piker. True, there's a $30,000 net worth ceiling on all personal property. However, debtors can skirt that by taking out, say, a big car loan before filing, Moreover, since personal property is valued at firesale prices, any friendly appraiser ought to be able to certify Picassos as "wall hangings, $250" or Louis XV chairs at a functional replacement value of $50, and leave creditors to prove otherwise. So a resourceful and creative Texas debtor like Powers could conceivably come away with $70 million, free and clear. The only drawback: Texans can't take out home equity loans, the only type of loans where interest is deductible under the new tax laws.

The homestead exemption has been successfully challenged only once. In 1979 a bankrupt Lubbock businessman named Hugh Reed tried to cheat his creditors. He had bought a share in a shell corporation, Triple BS Corp. (the significance of the initials is not elucidated in the record), and converted a pile of nonexempt cash into an exempt homestead on the eve of his filing. The court, unable to disallow his homestead claim, countered by denying him the discharge of his debts. These days, Texas lawyers wink knowingly at news reports that troubled real estate syndicator Craig Hall paid down a $1.5 million mortgage, giving him a homestead free and clear. One wonders if the Hunt brothers are looking to trade up from their relatively modest homes near Dallas. . . .

Few other states had exemptions until the Federal Bankruptcy Code was revised in 1978, and none are as generous as those of Texas. The state of Florida does allow up to 160 rural acres and half an urban acre. That's enough for Charles Agee Atkins. When he was riding high, managing a group of partnerships set up to take advantage of tax laws, he lived at posh One Sutton Place in New York. Now a debtor, he lives on an Amelia Island, Fla. estate valued at $455,000.

But most other states put a dollar cap on the exemption: $60,000 or $200 a month in rent in Massachusetts; $45,000 in California; $20,000 in Colorado. What will $20,000 buy even in Denver these days? Which is why, as Hugh Ray, a managing partner with the Houston firm of Andrews & Kurth, says "People would move here from out of state, buy up as much land as they could, then go bankrupt. It's a deadbeat's paradise."

Source: *Forbes,* October 27, 1986

Secured Property As already noted, secured creditors generally have priority, even above the priority claims. For this reason banks and other lending institutions have shifted their loan portfolios markedly from unsecured loans to secured lending. But despite the general rule, the debtor can avoid certain types of security interests. For example, the debtor can avoid a lien on property that would otherwise have been exempt if the lien is a nonpossessory, nonpurchase-money security interest in any household furnishings, goods, and the like "held primarily for the personal, family, or household use of the debtor or a dependent of the debtor." As the next case shows, this rule is limited to exempt property, and the debtor will be unsuccessful in asserting that just because collateral happens to be lying around his house it is therefore "personal" and thus not subject to repossession by the secured party. Although this is a Chapter 13 case, the same principle applies to liquidations.

MATTER OF NOGGLE
30 B.R. 303 (E.D. Mich. 1983)

George Brody, Bankruptcy Judge. The question presented is whether a Winchester rifle is a household good within the meaning of section 522(d)(3) and 522 (f)(2)(A) of the Code.

Robert Noggle (debtor) filed a voluntary petition in bankruptcy pursuant to chapter 13 of the Bankruptcy Code. The debtor claimed exemptions pursuant to section 522(d)(3). This section provides that a debtor may claim as exempt certain basic property interests. Specifically, a debtor may claim as exempt his interest in

> household furnishings, household goods, wearing apparel, appliances, books, animals, crops, or musical instruments, that are held primarily for the personal, family, or household use of the debtor or a dependent of the debtor [with a value not exceeding $200].

Prior to the filing of the petition, the debtor borrowed $1,005.72 from Beneficial Finance Company. To obtain the loan, the debtor gave Beneficial a security interest in certain designated household goods, cameras, appliances, and a Winchester rifle. Beneficial filed a financing statement to perfect its security interest in the described property. The debtor, during the administration of the case, filed a complaint to avoid Beneficial's nonpossessory, nonpurchase-money security interest in the collateral by virtue of section 522 (f)(2) of the Code.

Section 522(f)(2)(A) provides:

> (f) Notwithstanding any waiver of exemptions, the debtor may avoid the fixing of a lien on an interest of the debtor in property to the extent that such lien impairs an exemption to which the debtor would have been entitled under subsection (b) of this section, if such a lien is—
>
> * * *
>
> (2) a nonpossessory, nonpurchase-money security interest in any—
>
> (A) household furnishings, household goods, wearing apparel, appliances, books, animals, crops, musical instruments, or jewelry that are held primarily for the personal, family, or household use of the debtor or a dependent of the debtor;

Section 522(f) applies in a chapter 13 proceeding. Beneficial concedes that the lien was invalid as to all the property involved except for the lien on the Winchester .88 rifle. It is the position of Beneficial that the rifle is not encompassed by the term household goods in section 522(d)(3) or 522(f)(2)(A).

* * *

It is necessary, therefore, to decide whether the term household goods as employed in section 522(f) covers the rifle. Section 522(f) permits a debtor to avoid a nonpossessory, nonpurchase-money security interest in designated property that a debtor claims as exempt pursuant to section 522(d)(3). Section 522(d)(3) separately identifies many items of property that a debtor may claim as exempt. Household goods are merely one of the items set forth. If Congress had intended to permit a debtor to avoid a lien on all items kept in a household, there would have been no need to separately list property such as appliances, books, musical instruments or jewelry. Separately listing such items evidences an intent that not all property kept in the household is encompassed by the term household goods.

Additionally, "[a] fundamental canon of statutory construction is that, unless otherwise defined, words will be interpreted as taking their ordinary, contemporary, common meaning." *Perrin v. United States,* 444 U.S. 37, 42, 100 S.Ct. 311, 314, 62 L.Ed.2d 199 (1979). A rifle is generally not understood to be a household good. The mere fact that it is kept in the household does not make it so within the meaning of section 522(d)(3) or 522(f)(2)(A). The common understanding that a rifle is not a household good is reflected in the provisions of many state exemption provisions. State legislatures, when they confer the right to claim weapons as exempt, generally do so explicitly. If it was generally understood that a rifle or any other weapon was covered by the term "household goods", there would have been no necessity to provide a separate exemption for this class of property.

The term "household goods" appears in both section[s] 522(d)(2) and 522(f)(2)(A). To determine whether a rifle is a household good within the meaning of those sections, the background leading to the enactment of section 522(f) cannot be ignored. Prior to the adoption of the Code, financing companies would take a security interest in property essential to the debtor's survival, not because of the intrinsic value of the collateral, but because of the leverage it gave them in a bankruptcy proceeding. When the debtor filed a petition in bankruptcy, the secured creditor used "the threat of repossession, rarely carried out, to extract more than he would be able to if he did foreclose or repossess." H.R.Rep. No. 595, 95th Cong., 1st Sess. 127 (1977), *reprinted in* 1978 U.S.Code Cong. & Ad.News 5787, 5963, 6088. Section 522(f)(2)(A) was enacted to prevent a creditor from exerting this pressure with respect to the limited property enumerated in that section. It was designed to protect "the debtor's essential needs and to enable him to have a fresh start economically." *United States v. Security Industrial Bank,* —— U.S.——, 103 S.Ct. 407, 415, 74 L.Ed.2d 235 (1982) (Blackmun, J., concurring). To include a rifle within the term household goods would not serve that purpose. "[S]ince Section 522 (f) does materially affect the rights of secured creditors, its application should not be extended beyond the evil it attempted to reach." *Credithrift of America, Inc. v. Meyers (In re Meyers),* 2 B.R. 603, 606 (Bkrtcy.E.D.Mich.1980).

An appropriate order to be submitted.

Discharge Once discharged, the debtor is no longer legally liable to pay any remaining unpaid debts (except nondischargeable debts) that arose before the court issued the order of relief. The discharge operates to void any money judgments already rendered against the debtor and to bar the judgment creditor from seeking to recover the judgment.

Some debts are not dischargeable in bankruptcy. These include

1. certain taxes and customs duties;
2. debts not listed with the court, unless the creditor had actual notice of the bankruptcy proceeding;
3. liability for the fraudulent obtaining of money while acting in a fiduciary capacity, for embezzlement, or for larceny;
4. liability for willfully and deliberately injuring another's person or property (this exclusion does not apply to liability for negligent acts);
5. fines, penalties, and forfeitures payable to a governmental entity for the benefit of the entity;
6. alimony and child support;
7. debts that could have been or actually were listed in a previous bankruptcy in which the debtor waived or was denied discharge; and
8. educational loans that first became due within five years of the filing of the bankruptcy petition if they were "made, insured, or guaranteed by a governmental unit, or made under any program funded in whole or in part by a governmental unit or a nonprofit institution," unless

preventing the debt from being discharged would work an "undue hardship" on the debtor or his family.

Furthermore, 1984 amendments to the Bankruptcy Reform Act provide that a debt of over $500 incurred to purchase luxury items within forty days before filing, or debts resulting from certain cash advances of more than $1,000 within twenty days before filing are presumed to be nondischargeable. These provisions are designed to prevent debtors from "loading up" on luxury goods in anticipation of bankruptcy.

The 1984 amendments also provide that a discharge is denied for debts resulting from the debtor's drunk driving. Before this amendment, courts had to address the question of whether such debts fall within the "willful injury" category, as the following case illustrates.

MATTER OF WOOTEN
30 B.R. 357 (N.D. Ala. 1983)

Stephen B. Coleman, Bankruptcy Judge. This case arises out of a serious injury to Plaintiffs resulting from the drunken driving of Defendant provoking an accident that occurred on the evening of July 25, 1981. Jill Prosch, while walking single file behind her husband, Kevin Prosch, was hit by a careening automobile driven by the Debtor/Defendant, William Craig Wooten. The Prosches were pushing their bicycles on the left-hand sidewalk up the rather steep incline of Pawnee Avenue on the Southside of Birmingham. The Defendant was coming down Pawnee Avenue from the Eastwood Mall area when the crash occurred. The time was approximately 10:00 o'clock, P.M. The testimony revealed a chance meeting in a bar and drinking, and a hurried dash across town.

William Wooten testified that his lady passenger was interfering with his driving by putting her hands all over him. While trying to push her away with one arm, Mr. Wooten stated that an oncoming car veered slightly into his lane of traffic causing him to swerve. Not being able to control his car properly, he ran up onto the sidewalk, hitting the pregnant Mrs. Prosch and finally coming to rest against a tree. Since it all happened so suddenly, Plaintiffs could offer no testimony as to how the accident occurred.

Jill Prosch was hospitalized with extensive injuries, but fortunately, her baby was born at a later date with no complications.

Plaintiffs' suit asked for a judgment based on damages sustained in the wreck, but it was agreed by the parties before trial that only dischargeability should be determined by the Bankruptcy Judge, leaving the issue of damages to be determined by a jury in an appropriate Court.

Issue

Plaintiffs base their Complaint on Section 523(a)(6), and argue that Defendant's actions were willful and malicious in that Mr. Wooten "was grossly intoxicated and had totally lost control of his faculties and was unable to operate the vehicle which he was driving; further, the said Defendant voluntarily had consumed alcoholic beverages and/or substances defined under the Alabama Uniform Controlled Substances Act."

The Court listened to the testimony, and determined therefrom that Mr. Wooten was "drunk" when the accident occurred, and as a result, was unable to maintain proper control over his car. The issue thus becomes, was Debtor guilty of willful and malicious conduct on this occasion?

At least three times since the Code of 1978 went into effect has this Court wrestled with the term "willful and malicious." While these cases are different in many respects, each one recognizes the proposition that personal ill will towards the injured party is not a requirement of Section 523(a)(6).

* * *

While citing several cases that hold drunken driving is not per se willful and malicious conduct, the *In Re Brown* opinion is to the effect that "The circumstances must show a defendant's driving to be of such a gross nature as to imply malice." It is Mr. Wooten's gross misconduct in this case that sets it apart. Jill and Kevin Prosch were not the object of specific malice, only the victims of Mr. Wooten's intentional misconduct. His willfulness and maliciousness lay in the fact that he *intentionally* intoxicated himself and then *intentionally* drove a "lethal weapon" through the streets of Birmingham, with utter disregard of the consequences.

Defendant has cited cases holding that debts arising from an accident involving drunk driving are dischargeable. His argument is that although he may be guilty of gross negligence, the legislative history of Section 523(a)(6) demands a softer standard in determining dischargeability. The Court in *In re Greenwell,* 21 B.R. 419 (Dist.Ct.Ohio 1982), did apply a harsher standard, yet found no error in the Bankruptcy Court's interpretation and review of Section 523(a)(6) and its legislative history, specifically, the Historical and Revision Note following Section 523 that provides:

> Under this paragraph (6) "willful" means deliberate or intentional. To the extent that *Tinker v. Colwell,* 139 [193] U.S. 473 (1902) [24 S.Ct. 505,48 L.Ed. 754] held that a less strict standard is intended, and to the extent that other cases have relied on *Tinker* to apply a "reckless disregard" standard, they are overruled.

Greenwell held, and this Court agrees with their stance, that:

> What is to be gleaned from this review is that Congress intended that it not be sufficient to classify an act as willful and malicious that it be one done for reckless disregard for consequences. An intentional act is required. It is not, however, necessary to find that personal ill will existed in order for there to be a finding of willful and malicious injury. In the case before us now, we hold that the voluntary drinking by defendant constituted an intentional act sufficient to support the conclusion that the injury caused by defendant was willful and malicious. That is, while the legislature meant to circumscribe the scope of the *Tinker* case, its holding that "willful and malicious" under the statute is satisfied where there is an intentional injury remains valid. Defendant's intentional drinking unleashed the unbroken causative chain which led to the injury to plaintiff's vehicle. It will not avail defendant in his effort to avoid this result to argue that he did not know plaintiff prior to the accident and therefore the injury could not have been intentionally caused. One is responsible under the law for the natural outcome of his actions.

In re Rice involved a situation where an innocent bystander was shot by a pistol-wielding participant in a barroom brawl. Malice was not directed at the victim, but was implied nevertheless, because of the inherently dangerous nature of the defendant's actions. A quote borrowed and adopted from page 566 of *In re Rice* provides an appropriate conclusion:

> Miscreants who choose to engage in gun battles in public places, endangering the lives of innocent people, should not find a haven for their wrong doing in the Bankruptcy Court.

That Congress has under consideration legislation with which this Opinion is *in line* is illustrated by the quote from *Congressional Record—Senate,* April 27, 1983, S5326, in which Senator DeConcini stated on the floor of the Senate:

> . . . What disturbs me more than anything else, Mr. President, quite frankly, is that I have an amendment that would change the standard and would not permit discharge in bankruptcy of obligations arising from the infliction of willful, wanton, or reckless injury.
>
> Today there exists in the bankruptcy statute an unconscionable loophole which makes it possible for drunk drivers or others who have acted with willful, wanton, or reckless conduct and who have injured, killed, or caused property damage to others to escape civil liability for their actions by having their judgment debt discharged in Federal bankruptcy court. This loophole affords opportunity for scandalous abuse. . . .
>
> . . . Bankruptcy was never meant to be a shield behind which drunk drivers, and others who have acted in a reckless manner, can absolve themselves of liability. The concept of the fresh start for a debtor must defer to the possibility of a fresh start of the innocent victim. . . .

. . . The term reckless generally is understood to mean that the perpetrator of the injury knew of the risk and went ahead with his action anyway. He adverted to the harm. Surely, we do not want to insulate from liability people that conduct themselves in a willful, wanton, or reckless manner as these words are generally understood. It may even be questionable whether we want to discharge a negligent tort-feasor, but my amendment does not address that. . . .

The Court determines that the debt and obligation due Plaintiffs is *not* dischargeable in bankruptcy and accordingly so orders, and this case shall be set for determination of damages in a proper hearing.

Reaffirmation A bankrupt may reaffirm a debt that was discharged. The Bankruptcy Reform Act provides important protection to the debtor intent on doing so. No reaffirmation is binding unless four conditions are satisfied: (1) the reaffirmation must have been made prior to the granting of the discharge; (2) the debtor must be given sixty days after the agreement is filed with the court to rescind the agreement; (3) if the debtor is an individual, the court must hold a discharge hearing at which the debtor is told about the legal consequences of reaffirmation; (4) court approval is required for reaffirmation of a debt, except for consumer debts secured by the debtor's real property, if an individual debtor is not represented by an attorney.

Property Included in the Estate

When a bankruptcy petition is filed, an estate is created consisting of all the debtor's then-existing property interests, whether legal or equitable. In addition, the estate includes any bequests, inheritances, and certain other distributions of property that the debtor receives within the next 180 days. It also includes property recovered by the trustee under certain powers granted by the Bankruptcy Reform Act.

Trustee's Avoiding Powers The Bankruptcy Reform Act confers on the trustee certain powers to recover property for the estate that the debtor transferred before bankruptcy. One such power is to act as a **hypothetical lien creditor.** This power is best explained by an example. Suppose J. R. Ewing purchases equipment on credit from Naive Supply Company. Naive fails to perfect its security interest and a few weeks later J. R. files a bankruptcy petition. By virtue of a section conferring on the trustee the status of a hypothetical lien creditor, the trustee can act as though he had a lien on the equipment, with priority over Naive's unperfected security interest. Thus the trustee can avoid Naive's security interest, with the result that Naive would be treated as an unsecured creditor.

Another power is to avoid transactions known as **voidable preferences**—transactions highly favorable to particular creditors. A transfer of property is voidable if it was made (1) to a creditor or for his benefit, (2) on account of a debt owed before the transfer was made, (3) while the debtor was insolvent, (4) on or within ninety days before the filing of the petition, and (5) to enable a creditor to receive more than he would have under Chapter 7. If the creditor was an "insider"—one who had a special relationship with the debtor, for example, a relative or general partner of the debtor or a corporation which the debtor controls or serves as director or officer—then the trustee may void the transaction if it was made within one year of the filing of the petition, assuming that the debtor was insolvent at the time the transaction was made.

Some transfers that seem to fall within these provisions do not. The most important exceptions are (1) transfers made for new value (the debtor buys a refrigerator for cash one week before filing a petition; this is an exchange for new value and the trustee may not void it); (2) a transfer that creates a purchase money security interest securing new value if the secured party perfects within ten days after the debtor receives the goods; (3) payment of a debt incurred in the ordinary course of business, on ordinary business terms; and (4) transfers totalling less than $600 by an individual whose debts are primarily consumer debts.

The following case demonstrates the application of the voidable preference rules.

In re MERITT
7 B.R. 876 (W.D. Mo. 1980)

FRANK P. BARKER, Jr., Bankruptcy Judge. This is an action to set aside a preferential transfer under Section 547 of the Bankruptcy Code. The matter was tried before me in Jefferson City, Missouri on November 6, 1980, all parties being represented in person and by counsel.

At the outset of trial, the Trustee dismissed paragraph 18 of his complaint, stating that he had no interest or claim to the $7,000 allegedly paid the bank by the debtors.

The relevant facts are as follows: The debtors in this case decided to purchase thirty (30) stainless steel farrowing crates for their hog farm operation. On June 4, 1979 the defendant, The Callaway Bank, loaned the debtors $10,000 (see Defendant's Ex. # 1–Promissory Note) and took a security agreement describing these farrowing crates from the debtors. Eunice Meritt testified that shortly thereafter the debtors purchased the crates with this money.

James Curtis Yancey, Vice President of The Callaway Bank, testified that the note was to be paid from the sale of wheat in 60 days, but that this did not occur. The note was subsequently extended for numerous 60-day periods.

A U. C. C. financing statement was signed June 4, 1979 but was not filed with the Callaway County Recorder of Deeds' office until March 6, 1980. No evidence was presented as to filing with the Secretary of State's office. The financing statement's description of collateral was "machinery and equipment". Bankruptcy was filed by the debtors on May 5, 1980 and thus, the financing statement was filed within 90 days of the filing of bankruptcy.

Sale of these crates was first attempted at a close-out sale held by the debtors. The highest bid received however, was $195.00 and the crates were left in the debtor's barn unsold. Eunice Meritt testified that the reason the crates were not sold was that the bank had set a lowest bid limit of $200.00 each on the crates, however, she was not present when the bank set the limit. Mr. Yancey testified that an upset price was discussed and the Meritts' wanted $250.00 each crate. The bank later sold 15 of the crates for $200.00 each and the remaining 15 for

$130.00 each, with sales expenses of $195.00 for total proceeds of $4,755.00

The Trustee argues that based on the facts, the filing of the financing statement by the bank within 90 days prior to bankruptcy, changed its creditor status from a secured to a perfected secured party, and as such is a preferential transfer under Bankruptcy Code § 547.

* * *

Based on the above facts and statutory language, we find that the transfer was "made" on March 6, 1980, and that a determination of whether all the voidable preference elements are present must be done using this date.

* * *

From the proof and the entire record the Court finds all five elements of a preference. (1) This transfer was certainly a benefit to the bank as their status changed from a secured to a perfected secured party. (2) This transfer was on account of an antecedent debt. The only consideration received by the debtor was at the time of his actual execution of the transfer—no other consideration was received between that time and the time the transfer was "made". (3) § 547(f) presumes insolvency within the 90 days preceding the filing of the petition, and the transferee has failed to rebut this presumption. (4) The date the transfer was "made" was March 6, 1980 and well within 90 days before the petition in bankruptcy was filed May 5, 1980. (5) Finally, a change in the bank's status from a secured to a perfected secured party would enable the creditor to receive more than he would if he were forced to share the value of the farrowing crates with other unperfected secured creditors. Even though the trustee, pursuant to the Code can otherwise avoid a claim as preferential, the Code incorporates a number of exceptions in § 547(c) to this avoidance power. Thus, the bank would be protected to the extent it qualifies under any one of the exceptions. The bank argues that exception § 547(c)(1) is appropriate in this case. § 547(c)(1) states:

> (c) The trustee may not avoid under this section a transfer—
> (1) to the extent that such transfer was—
> (A) intended by the debtor and the creditor to or for whose benefit such transfer was made to be a contemporaneous exchange for new value given to the debtor; and
> (B) in fact a substantially contemporaneous exchange;

* * *

This Court not only finds that the Congress did not intend that this exception apply to our factual situation, but that because of the substantial time between the transfer (when the security interest was perfected) and the making of the debt (over eight (8) months), this Court finds that the exchange was not in fact substantially contemporaneous.

* * *

This Court thus determines this transaction to be a voidable preference under § 547 and that the trustee is entitled to the proceeds of the sale of the crates in the amount of $4,755.00 and that the expenses of sale by the bank of $195.00 were reasonable. It is ordered that defendant turn over to the trustee the sum of $4,560.00.

The trustee may also avoid **fraudulent transfers** made within one year before the date that the bankruptcy petition was filed. This provision contemplates various types of fraud. For example, while insolvent the debtor might transfer property to a relative for less than it was worth, intending to recover it after discharge. This situation should be distinguished from the voidable preference discussed above, in which the debtor pays a favored creditor what he actually owes, but in so doing cannot then pay other creditors.

Liquidation of the Estate

Except as noted, the above provisions apply to each of the five types of bankruptcy proceedings. The following discussion is limited to certain provisions under Chapter 7.

Trustee's Duties In addition to the duties already noted (p. 327), the trustee has other duties under Chapter 7. He must sell the property for money, close up the estate "as expeditiously as is compatible with the best interests of parties in interest," investigate the debtor's financial affairs, examine proofs of claims, reject improper ones, oppose the discharge of the debtor where doing so is advisable in the trustee's opinion, furnish a creditor with information about the estate and his administration (unless the court orders otherwise), file tax reports if the business continues to be operated, and make a final report and file it with the court.

Distribution of the Estate After payment of claims with priority, the trustee must distribute the estate to the following persons in the order given:

1. unsecured creditors who filed their claims on time
2. unsecured creditors who were tardy in filing claims
3. persons claiming fines, penalties, forfeitures, or exemplary or punitive damages to the extent that the claims are not for actual pecuniary loss suffered by the claimant
4. all creditors, who are entitled to interest at the legal rate
5. the debtor, who receives anything remaining.

Discharge Once the estate is distributed, the court will order the debtor discharged, unless one of the following exceptions applies:

1. the debtor is not an individual
2. the debtor has concealed or destroyed property with intent to defraud, hinder, or delay within twelve months preceding filing of the petition
3. the debtor has concealed, destroyed, or falsified books and records
4. the debtor has lied under oath, knowingly given a false account, presented or used a false claim, or given or received bribes
5. the debtor has failed to explain satisfactorily any loss of assets
6. the debtor has refused to obey any lawful order of the court or answer any material question approved by the court during the proceeding
7. the debtor has committed any one of the preceding acts within one year of the filing of the petition in connection with another case concerning an insider
8. another court has granted the debtor a discharge in another case commenced within the last six years
9. the court has approved a written waiver of discharge executed by the debtor after the order for relief was issued.

The Bankruptcy Reform Act prohibits governmental units from discriminating against a person who has gone through bankruptcy. Debtors are also protected from discrimination by private employers; for example, a private employer may not fire a debtor because of the bankruptcy.

Adjustments of Debts of an Individual with Regular Income—Chapter 13

Anyone with a steady income who is having difficulty paying off accumulated debts may seek the protection of a bankruptcy court in a Chapter 13 proceeding. Under this chapter, the individual debtor presents a payment plan to creditors and the court appoints a trustee. If the creditors wind up with more under the plan presented than they would receive in a Chapter 7 proceeding, then the court is likely to approve it. In general, a Chapter 13 repayment plan extends the time to pay the debt and may reduce it so that the debtor need not pay it all. Typically, the debtor will pay a fixed sum monthly to the trustee, who will distribute it to the creditors. The provisions of Chapters 3 and 5 discussed above apply also to this chapter; therefore, the discussion that follows focuses on some unique features of Chapter 13.

Eligibility

Chapter 13 is voluntary only. Anyone who has a regular income, unsecured debts of less than $100,000 and secured debts of less than $350,000 is eligible to seek its protection. The debts must be unpaid and owing at the time the debtor applies for relief.

The Plan

Plans are typically extensions or compositions (p. 320). Chapter 13 limits the stretch-out period to three years, unless the court approves a longer period of up to five years. The plan must provide for payments of all future income or a sufficient portion of it to the trustee. Priority creditors are entitled to be paid in full, although they may be paid later than required under the original indebtedness. As long as the plan is being carried out, the debtor may enjoin any creditors from suing to collect the original debt.

Confirmation

The court must approve the plan if it meets certain requirements. These include (1) distribution of property to unsecured creditors whose claims are allowed in an amount no less than that which they would have received had the estate been liquidated under Chapter 7; (2) acceptance by secured creditors, with some exceptions, such as when the debtor surrenders the secured property to the creditor; and (3) proposal of the plan "in good faith." Under the 1984 amendments, however, if the trustee or an unsecured creditor objects to confirmation, the plan must meet additional tests. For example, a plan will be approved if all of the debtor's disposable income over a three-year period will be used to make payments under the plan.

The good faith requirement, which has triggered more litigation than any other provision, is discussed in the following case.

In re WALDRON
785 F.2d 936 (11th Cir. 1986)

* * *

On June 24, 1983 Edward J. Waldron and his wife Elizabeth filed a joint voluntary petition under Chapter 13 of the Bankruptcy Code, 11 U.S.C. §§ 1301–1330 (1982 & Supp. II 1984). The Chapter 13 petition listed one creditor, Shell Oil Company, but the Waldrons, in fact, owe no debts. The Waldrons are completely solvent, own a home in Coral Gables, Florida, valued at $125,000.00 and an impressive portfolio of stocks. The Waldrons also own, subject to an option agreement, a parcel of land located at 2727 West Flagler Street in Miami, Florida.

On January 15, 1964 the Waldrons had granted Shell Oil the option to purchase this parcel of land. The option agreement provided that Shell Oil would have the right to exercise the option at a price of $40,000.00 "at any time after January 1, 1984" through December 31, 1993. The Waldrons granted Shell Oil this option as part of a single transaction in which Shell Oil purchased for $100,000 an adjacent parcel of land from Mr. Waldron's father and an easement in front of the parcel located at 2727 West Flagler Street. Shell had desired to purchase both parcels of land in 1964 to construct a full facility service station but agreed to the two step procedure to accommodate the Waldrons. The option agreement recited a consideration of $10.00 and Mr. Waldron later stipulated that he actually received the money. The option agreement, the easement granted to Shell Oil and the warranty deed for the adjacent parcel were recorded simultaneously in the Official Records of Dade County, Florida.

In their Chapter 13 petition, the Waldrons sought to reject the option agreement pursuant to 11 U.S.C. § 365(a) (1982). Mr. Waldron, an attorney specializing in bankruptcy law, admitted that he "filed this Chapter 13 for the sole purpose of rejecting [the] option agreement." Financially secure and without any debts, the Waldrons thus set out to use the bankruptcy process in attempting to reject a contract which they felt might not be as profitable as it could be. In essence, the Waldrons wanted to breach the option agreement and prevent Shell Oil from seeking specific performance in state court.

Initially, the bankruptcy court questioned the Waldrons' preposterous scheme. The court recognized that the Waldrons were not financially distressed and had no real need to invoke the protections of the bankruptcy laws. Nevertheless, the bankruptcy court concluded that the bankruptcy laws were intended to be widely available and thus even a "trouble-free debtor" must not be "precluded from utilizing Chapter 13 solely to reject the option contract." *In re Waldron,* 36 Bankr. 633, 636 (Bankr.S.D.Fla.1984). The district court upheld the bankruptcy court's order. This appeal promptly followed.

The Bankruptcy Code expressly provides that a bankruptcy court may not confirm a Chapter 13 plan unless "the plan has been proposed in good faith and not by any means forbidden by law." 11 U.S.C. § 1325(a)(3) (1982). Indeed, "the 'good faith' requirement of § 1325(a) is the only safety valve available through which plans attempting to twist the law to malevolent ends may be cast out. The good faith test should be used accordingly." *In re Leal,* 7 Bankr. 245, 248 (Bankr.D.Colo.1980). In this case, the bankruptcy court should have used the good faith test to cast out the Waldrons' malevolent scheme.

* * *

In this case, the Waldrons admittedly filed their Chapter 13 petition for the sole purpose of rejecting the option agreement with Shell Oil. The Waldrons were not financially distressed and had no real need for the bankruptcy process. The Waldrons' only motive was to enhance their financial coffers by manipulating and abusing the bankruptcy process. Their Chapter 13 petition should not have been confirmed.

"The bankruptcy laws are intended as a shield, not as a sword." *In re Penn Central Transportation Co.,* 458 F.Supp. 1346, 1356 (E.D.Pa.1978). Congress could not have intended that the debt-free, financially secure Waldrons be permitted to engage the bankruptcy machinery solely to avoid an enforceable option contract. From all that appears, the contract was negotiated at arms length; if the Waldrons now feel that it is less attractive than it should be, the difference is attributable to changes in the economic climate not to the Waldrons' financial situation. . . . The bankruptcy laws were simply not intended to be used as a sword by the rapacious.

Nevertheless, the bankruptcy court permitted the Waldrons to reject the option contract because "it is clear that [the Waldrons] could readily refile their bankruptcy petition under Chapter 11." *In re Waldron,* 36 B.R. at 635. Apparently, the bankruptcy court relied on cases which hold "that it is not an abuse of the bankruptcy process to file a petition under Chapter 7 or 11 solely to reject an executory contract." . . . The bankruptcy court, however, failed to recognize the true import of these decisions. In each case, rejection of the executory contract served a useful purpose for a debtor who was indeed financially troubled. In each case, rejection was permitted to serve the intended purpose of Chapter 11—to facilitate the adjustment of debts through reorganization.

For example, in *In re Marina Enterprises,* a Chapter 11 debtor-in-possession, whose sole asset was an undeveloped parcel of land subject to a lease, applied for rejection of the lease. The bankruptcy court permitted rejection, finding that "there can be no realistic anticipation of successful reorganization or rehabilitation without rejection of the lease." 14 B.R. at 333. The bankruptcy court also recognized that "the rent [the debtor-in-possession was to receive under the lease] will probably not cover debt service, much less give a realistic return on investment," *id.* at n. 4, and noted that the debtor-in-possession "was unable to obtain construction financing" because of the improvident lease. *Id.* at 333. Indeed, rejection was necessary to successfully reorganize the debtor-in-possession's business and allow the financially troubled debtor a "fresh start."

* * *

We hold that with section 1325(a)(3) Congress intended to provide bankruptcy courts with a discretionary means to preserve the bankruptcy process for its intended purpose. Accordingly, whenever a Chapter 13 petition appears to be tainted with a questionable purpose, it is incumbent upon the bankruptcy courts to examine and question the debtor's motives. If the court discovers unmistakable manifestations of bad faith, as we do here, confirmation must be denied.

Unmistakable manifestations of bad faith need not be based upon a finding of actual fraud, requiring proof of malice, scienter or an intent to defraud. We simply require that the bankruptcy courts preserve the integrity of the bankruptcy process by refusing to condone its abuse.

The cornerstone of the bankruptcy courts has always been the doing of equity. The protections and forgiveness inherent in the bankruptcy laws surely require conduct consistent with the concepts of basic honesty. Good faith or basic honesty is the very antithesis of attempting to circumvent a legal obligation through a technicality of the law. The Waldrons, it seems clear to us, sought to abuse the process through a technicality to serve their own malevolent and selfish aims. This abuse should not have been permitted. We therefore reverse the decision of the district court and remand with instructions to dismiss the Waldrons' petition.

Reversed and remanded.

Discharge

Once a debtor has made all payments called for in the plan, the court will discharge him from all debts except certain long-term debts and obligations to pay alimony, maintenance, and support. Indeed, Chapter 13 is so broad that it permits the court to discharge the debtor from many debts considered nondischargeable under Chapter 7 and to discharge him even if he has not made all the payments, assuming that (1) the failure to pay stemmed from circumstances for which he should not be held accountable, (2) the creditors received no less than what they would have received under Chapter 7, and (3) the plan would be impractical to modify.

Reorganization—Chapter 11

Chapter 11 provides a means by which corporations, partnerships, and other businesses, including sole proprietorships, can rehabilitate themselves and continue to operate free from the burden of debts that they cannot pay.

It is simple enough to apply for the protection of the court in a Chapter 11 proceeding, and in recent years, more and more large, financially ailing companies have sought shelter in Chapter 11. An increasing number of corporations have turned to Chapter 11 even though, by conventional terms, they were solvent. Doing so enables them to negotiate with creditors to reduce debt. It also may even permit courts to snuff out lawsuits that have not yet been filed.

As before, Chapters 3 and 5 discussed above under "liquidation" apply to Chapter 11 proceedings also. Our discussion, therefore, is limited to special features of Chapter 11.

Eligibility

Any person eligible for discharge in a Chapter 7 proceeding is eligible for a Chapter 11 proceeding, except stockbrokers and commodity brokers. Railroad corporations are also eligible for Chapter 11 protection. A company may voluntarily enter Chapter 11 or may be put there involuntarily by creditors. However, as Box 12-2 indicates, Chapter 11 reorganizations may provide little protection outside the United States.

Operation of Business

Unless a trustee is appointed, the debtor will retain possession of the business and may continue to operate with its own management. The court may appoint a trustee on request of any party in interest after notice and a

Box 12-2 Chapter 11 and International Trade

There's No Word for Chapter 11 in Dutch
BY TODD VOGEL

Malcom P. McLean thought his 27-ship fleet could keep cruising the oceans while his company, U.S. Lines Inc., reworked its $1.3 billion debt in bankruptcy court. "There's no question about it. I can pull this out," claimed the president of parent company McLean Industries Inc. after the filing a year ago.

But since then, Japanese trade unions seeking back wages stormed the company's offices and held a manager hostage. Creditors in Hong Kong and Singapore ignored a U.S. court order, seized four of McLean's massive container ships, and sold the $46 million vessels at close to scrap value. And creditors in nine other nations have attached company assets around the globe. "We were just picked off in country after country," says John G. Gellene, a lawyer at Milbank, Tweed, Hadley & McCloy, which represents U.S. Lines. While proceedings wind through courts in seven countries, the company's shipping business is being liquidated, not reorganized. "I'm too blue to talk about it," McLean says.

The shipping tycoon isn't alone in struggling to fend off creditors abroad. U.S. bankruptcy laws simply don't offer much of a shield. And foreign courts typically don't recognize the idea of bankruptcy reorganization, which gives debtors time to attempt a fresh start in business. "Only the U.S. has this strange Chapter 11 legislation," says one lawyer in Geneva.

OUT THE BACK DOOR

In most nations, bankruptcy means only one thing: liquidation. As a result, foreign creditors seeking to cut their losses grab any available assets. But their actions can rip apart reorganization plans and raise thorny legal conflicts around the globe. "In almost every case of any size these days, you have the problem," says John D. Honsberger, a Toronto legal expert on international bankruptcy.

The biggest such case is Texaco Inc., which placed some U.S. operations under Chapter 11 protection last April. Fearing that foreigners would try to snatch assets, Texaco dispatched nearly 60 employees around the globe to allay the fears of creditors. "It took a while to stabilize them," says Harvey R. Miller, Texaco's lead bankruptcy lawyer at Weil, Gotshal & Manges in New York.

LTV Corp.'s Chapter 11 filing in July, 1986, nearly cost it a pending sale of $190 million worth of missiles to the Netherlands. On hearing the news, the Dutch immediately called off negotiations. But Howard M. Fish, vice-president of LTV Aerospace & Defense Co., went to work lobbying Dutch officials. He stationed an LTV employee in the Netherlands, and after three months of assurances, LTV got the contract.

A prime reason for the hardline policy is the worry by foreigners that cash and property will disappear before they're paid off. And because no law indisputably sets the rules for global bankruptcy, nearly any move is fair game. Take the case of Storage Technology Corp. in Louisville,

hearing. The appointment may be made for cause—such as dishonesty, incompetence, or gross mismanagement—or if it is otherwise in the best interests of the creditors. In the following case the court states the reasons for appointing a trustee and discusses the philosophy of Chapter 11.

Colo. On the day it filed for Chapter 11 protection in 1984, the company's local bankers barged into one foreign office to grab $2 million in cash. A top company official says employees dashed out the back door and drove around the city for three days with the cash in the trunk. Then they split it into smaller chunks and deposited the money in other banks to evade the lenders.

Even related companies that aren't involved in Chapter 11 can be thrown into disarray. When the Hunt brothers placed Placid Oil Co. into bankruptcy reorganization, a separate U.S. subsidiary, Placid International Oil Ltd., was drilling for natural gas in the Dutch North Sea. The Netherlands' Economic Affairs Minister threatened to revoke gas licenses for the subsidiary, endangering $100 million worth of yearly revenues. Only hours before the deadline, Placid's international unit struck an agreement to insulate the Dutch government from the U.S. proceedings. "An ad hoc bankruptcy is essentially what happened," says Henry W. Simon Jr., Placid's lawyer.

Besides hiding cash, Storage Technology came up with a more traditional way to avoid asset seizure. The company's envoys showed creditors in Europe, Saudi Arabia, and the Far East how little they'd get if they forced a liquidation. "We basically threw the keys on the table," says one official. "As soon as they thought we were deadly serious, they were very accommodating. . . . I call it enlightened self-interest." The fast action worked. Storage Technology emerged from bankruptcy in July.

U.S. Lines learned the hard way that foreigners play by a different set of rules. The four freighters were seized in Hong Kong and Singapore by creditors, led by GAC Marine Fuels Ltd. A $5,000-a-day fine from the U.S. court didn't faze the creditors, and a frustrated U.S. judge accused them of "contemptuous conduct." But U.S. Lines was unable to halt the auction, which brought only a total of $16 million for the ships that cost $184 million to build. Ironically, the buyers were a group of U.S. Lines' American bankers, headed by Bank of America and Citibank, that had lent the company money to build the ships. Shipping competitors fear that the banks will quickly sell the ships, aggravating a worldwide containership glut.

LITTLE AGREEMENT

The prospect of treaties addressing the problem looks bleak. The Scandinavian Convention, which covers five countries, and the Bustamente Code of Private International Law, which links 15 Latin American countries, provide blueprints for bankruptcy negotiations. But even the European Community has bickered since 1980 over a bankruptcy pact. And the U.S. has failed to reach a treaty with Canada.

Texaco lawyer Miller predicts that a string of global business failures spawned by the current strains in financial markets would focus attention on the problem. That, of course, would be a drastic solution. In the meantime, ingenuity and blind luck will rule.

Source: *Business Week,* November 30, 1987

In re DEENA PACKAGING INDUSTRIES, INC. 29 B.R. 705 (S.D. N.Y. 1983)

EDWARD J. RYAN, BANKRUPTCY JUDGE. On July 6, 1978, Deena Packaging Industries, Inc. (Deena) filed a voluntary petition in bankruptcy under Chapter XI, section 322 of the Bankruptcy Act. At that time, Flushing Savings Bank (Flushing), as a major creditor of Deena, held a mortgage on Deena's manufacturing plant. The 200,000 square foot plant was Deena's major asset. This court confirmed a plan whereby the mortgage was extended and Deena was to pay certain sums in repayment each month to Flushing. After Deena defaulted on its August 1981 payment, Flushing obtained a foreclosure judgment against Deena in New York State Supreme Court in the amount of $1,724,141. On the eve of the foreclosure sale initiated by Flushing, however, an involuntary petition in bankruptcy was filed against Deena pursuant to section 303 of the Bankruptcy Code. Consequently the foreclosure sale was stayed.

On August 16, 1982 Deena entered into a written lease with a third party for the rental of the fourth floor of the mortgaged premises. On October 6, 1982, Deena filed a voluntary Chapter 11 petition. The above mentioned lease was not included in that petition. In November 1982 Deena executed a second lease whereby another portion of the mortgaged premises was rented. The annual rental proceeds were approximately $100,000.

Deena incurred brokerage fee liabilities in connection with these leases. The arrangement between Deena and the broker who secured the tenants was that the broker's fee would be due and owing only when rental income was received by Deena. As rental income is earned, therefore, Deena becomes liable for brokerage fees on that amount. The total broker's fees payable on these two leases is not to exceed $45,000. When Deena amended its voluntary petition on December 17, 1982, by filing additional schedules and a statement of financial affairs, it disclosed neither the leases nor the brokerage liability.

Previously, Flushing had moved to have a trustee appointed to protect its rights as a secured creditor. A trial took place on the issue of appointment on the 17th day of December 1982 and was continued through January 25, 1983. This court concludes that the appointment of a trustee is entirely appropriate in these circumstances.

The appointment of a trustee in bankruptcy is governed by 11 U.S.C. § 1104 (1978 Supp.). The court may appoint a trustee for cause, or, under section 1104(a)(2), to protect the interests of creditors. Appointing a trustee for cause is not a discretionary function and necessarily includes a showing of "fraud, dishonesty, incompetence, or gross mismanagement of the affairs of the debtor by current management, either before or after the commencement of the case." Appointing a trustee to protect the interests of creditors, however, entails equitable considerations through which the court may exercise its discretionary powers.

The appointment of a trustee in Chapter 11 cases has been held by some courts to be extraordinary relief. This is consistent with the presumption that a Chapter 11 debtor should remain in possession and continue to manage its own affairs. Indeed, no trustee need be appointed in instances of slight mismanagement or where there are no discrepancies uncovered in the accounting records of a debtor. Section 1104, however, specifically proscribes certain conduct by debtors in possession; dishonesty is one such enumerated, prohibited act.

Although the grounds for cause were not specified in Flushing's papers, the trial record reveals that Deena's failure to include relevant financial data on their original and amended schedules raises questions of dishonest conduct. Under Bankruptcy Rules 108 and 10-108, the debtor is required to list *all* its assets and liabilities with the court.

The *In re Horn & Hardart* case, 22 B.R. 668, 7 C.B.C.2d 65 (Bkrtcy.E.D.Pa.1982), illustrates grounds for finding cause under section 1104(a)(1). Although the specific allegation therein was gross mismanagement, the court viewed the debtor's failure to file several operating statements mandated by the bankruptcy rules as an important consideration when determining whether or not cause existed for the appointment of a trustee. The court wrote in support of its view "that the debtor has poorly fulfilled the responsibilities imposed by the Bankruptcy Code and Rules." That situation, coupled with continuing operating losses, led the court to appoint a trustee for cause.

In another recent decision, the Bankruptcy Court for the Eastern District of Pennsylvania appointed a trustee in a Chapter 11 proceeding for cause and to protect the interests of the creditors. The debtor corporation in *In re Philadelphia Athletic Club, Inc.*, 15 B.R. 60 (Bkrtcy.S.D.N.Y.1981) was found to be grossly mismanaged; the debtor could not overcome allegations of mismanagement because it had failed to keep adequate books and records. The court reasoned that full disclosure of the debtor's financial position is necessary to determine whether the debtor can operate profitably or should be liquidated.

The respective debtors' failure to file relevant post-petition financial information in the *Horn &*

Hardart and the *Philadelphia Athletic Club* cases contributed to the courts' appointment of trustees. In the case at hand, Deena omitted the rental income and brokerage liability from the original and amended petitions. The debtor's omissions violate the disclosure requirements of Bankruptcy Rules 108 and 10-108. Since the debtor has proffered no justification whatsoever for the nondisclosure of the leases in the petitions, this court concludes that these omissions be characterized as dishonest conduct for the purposes of section 1104(a)(1). Consequently, the cause requirement under section 1104(a)(1) has been met.

Even if Flushing had been unable to demonstrate sufficient cause, this court is empowered under section 1104(a)(2) to appoint a trustee to protect Flushing's rights as a creditor. The ability of the debtor to profitably operate its business is a substantial concern of the creditors. Deena conceded in its post trial memorandum that the operation of the building, its only income producing activity, is "almost self-sustaining, although not yet profitable." Such a concession raises doubts as to whether Deena should continue to act as a debtor in possession or whether its assets should be liquidated and its creditors paid off.

Accurate information as to the debtor's viability must reach the court and the creditors. Because Deena has failed to provide a full and truthful statement of its financial condition, it is necessary to appoint a trustee so that the court and Deena's creditors are fully informed.

Accordingly, the United States Trustee is directed to appoint a disinterested person to serve as trustee in accordance with Code Section 1104(c).

Settle an appropriate order.

Creditors' Committee

The court must appoint a committee of unsecured creditors as soon as practicable after issuing the order for relief. The committee must consist of creditors willing to serve who have the seven largest claims, unless the court decides to continue a committee formed before the filing, if the committee was fairly chosen and adequately represents the various claims. The committee has several duties, including: (1) to investigate the debtor's financial affairs; (2) to determine whether to seek appointment of a trustee or to let the business continue to operate; and (3) to consult with the debtor or trustee throughout the case.

The Reorganization Plan

The debtor may always file its own plan, whether in a voluntary or involuntary case. If the court leaves the debtor in possession without appointing a trustee, the debtor has the exclusive right to file a reorganization plan during the first 120 days. If it does file, it will then have another 60 days to obtain the creditors' acceptances. Although its exclusivity expires at the end of 180 days, the court may lengthen or shorten the period for good cause. At the end of the exclusive period, the creditors' committee, a single creditor, or a holder of equity in the debtor's property may file a plan. If the court does appoint a trustee, any party in interest may file a plan at any time.

The Bankruptcy Reform Act specifies certain features of the plan and permits others to be included. Among other things, the plan must (1) designate classes of claims and ownership interests; (2) specify which classes or interests are *impaired*—a claim or ownership interest is impaired if the creditor's legal, equitable, or contractual rights are altered under the plan; (3) specify the treatment of any class of claims or interests that is impaired under the plan; (4) provide the same treatment for each claim or interest of a particular class, unless the holder of a particular claim or interest agrees to a less favorable treatment; and (5) provide adequate means for carrying out the plan.

Acceptance of Plan

The act requires the plan to be accepted by certain proportions of each impaired class of claims and interests. A class of claims accepts a plan if creditors representing at least two-thirds of the dollar amount of claims and more than one-half the number of allowed claims vote in favor. A class of property interests accepts the plan if creditors representing two-thirds of the dollar amount of the allowed ownership interests vote in favor. Unimpaired classes of claims and interests are deemed to have accepted the plan; it is unnecessary to solicit their acceptance.

Confirmation of Plan

The final act necessary under Chapter 11 is **confirmation** by the court. Once the court confirms the plan, the plan is binding on all creditors. The rules governing confirmation are complex, but in essence, they include the following requirements:

1. The plan must have been proposed in good faith. Companies must also make a good faith attempt to negotiate modifications in their collective bargaining agreements; see p. 425.
2. All provisions of the Bankruptcy Reform Act must have been complied with.
3. The court must have determined that the reorganized business will be likely to succeed and be unlikely to require further financial reorganization in the foreseeable future.
4. Impaired classes of claims and interests must have accepted the plan, unless the plan treats the impaired class in a "fair and equitable" manner, in which case consent is not required. This is sometimes referred to as the *cram-down* provision.
5. All members of every class must have received no less value than they would have in a Chapter 7 liquidation.

Chapter Summary

The federal bankruptcy law governs the rights of creditors and insolvent debtors who cannot pay their debts. Alternatives to bankruptcy are assignment for benefit of creditors, composition (agreement by creditors to accept less than the face amount of the debt), and receivership. Since these are voluntary procedures, they are often ineffective when all parties fail to agree to them.

The Constitution lodges in Congress the power to legislate on bankruptcy. The current law is the Bankruptcy Reform Act of 1978, which provides for five types of proceedings: (1) liquidation (Chapter 7), (2) adjustment of debts of a municipality (Chapter 9), (3) reorganization (Chapter 11), (4) adjustment of debts of a family farmer with regular income, (Chapter 12), and (5) adjustment of debts of an individual with regular income (Chapter 13).

With some exceptions, any individual, partnership, or corporation seeking liquidation may file a voluntary petition in bankruptcy. An involuntary petition may be filed against any person except a farmer or charitable enterprise. Petitioning creditors in an involuntary bankruptcy must have claims for unsecured debt amounting to at least $5,000. Three creditors must join in the petition if there are twelve or more creditors, and must have particular grounds for relief.

A petition operates as a stay against suits against the debtor to recover claims or enforce judgments or liens. The judge will issue an order of relief and appoint a trustee, who takes over the debtor's property and preserves security interests. To recover monies owed, creditors must file proof of claims. The trustee has certain powers to recover property for the estate that the debtor transferred before bankruptcy. These include the power to act as a hypothetical lien creditor and to avoid fraudulent transfers and transactions known as voidable preferences.

The Bankruptcy Reform Act sets out categories of claimants and establishes priorities among them. The highest priority groups are (1) administration expenses, (2) gap creditor claims, (3) employees' wages, salaries, and commissions, (4) contributions to employee benefit plans, (5) grain producers and U.S. fishermen, (6) consumer creditor claims, and (7) taxes. After payment of these priority claims, the trustee must distribute the estate in the following order: unsecured creditors who filed claims on time, tardy unsecured creditors, persons claiming fines and the like, all other creditors, and finally the debtor.

Certain property is exempted from the estate of an individual debtor. States may opt out of a federal list of exemptions and substitute their own. Over half of the states have opted out.

Once discharged, the debtor is no longer legally liable for most debts.

However, some categories of debts are not dischargeable. Under certain conditions, a debtor may reaffirm a discharged debt.

Anyone with regular income who has difficulty paying off accumulated debts may voluntarily seek the protection of a bankruptcy court in a Chapter 13 proceeding. The individual presents a payment plan to creditors and the court appoints a trustee. The plan extends the time to pay and may reduce the size of the debt. If the creditors wind up with more in this proceeding than they would have in a Chapter 7 proceeding, the court is likely to approve the plan. The court may approve a stretch-out of five years. Chapter 13 is limited to those with regular income who have unsecured debts of less than $100,000 and secured debts of less than $350,000.

In a reorganization under Chapter 11, the debtor retains possession of the business and may continue to operate with its own management unless the court appoints a trustee. The court may do so either for cause or if it is in the best interests of the creditors. Any person eligible for discharge in Chapter 7 is eligible for Chapter 11, except stockbrokers and commodity brokers. The court must appoint a committee of unsecured creditors, who remain active throughout the proceeding. The debtor may file its own reorganization plan, and has the exclusive right to do so within 120 days if it remains in possession. The plan must be accepted by certain proportions of each impaired class of claims and interests. It is binding on all creditors and the debtor is discharged from all debts once the court confirms the plan.

Problems

1. David has debts of $9,000 and few assets. He decides to file for bankruptcy but, because he has debts of less than $10,000, prefers to use the state court system rather than the federal system. Describe the procedure David should follow to file for bankruptcy at the state level.
2. In problem 1, assume that David has developed a plan for paying off his creditors. What type of bankruptcy proceeding should David use—Chapter 7, 11, or 13? Why?
3. Assume in problem 1 that David does not want to file for bankruptcy. He has two creditors and owes each of them $4,500. May one of the creditors force David into bankruptcy? Why?
4. Assume in problem 1 that one of David's creditors is the federal government, which has a claim for $3,000 in unpaid federal taxes. David also owes the attorney who handled his bankruptcy $750. If David has only $750 in nonexempt assets, who is entitled to them—the government or the attorney? Why?
5. Assume that David owns the following unsecured property: a $2,000 oboe, a $2,000 piano, a $500 diamond ring, a $1,000 car, and a life insurance policy with a cash surrender value of $3,500. How much of

this property is available for distribution to his creditors in bankruptcy? Why?

6. If David owes his ex-wife alimony and child support, and is obligated to pay $3,000 for an educational loan, what effect will his discharge in bankruptcy have on these obligations? Why?
7. Assume that David owns a corporation which he wants to liquidate under Chapter 7. After the corporate assets are distributed to creditors, what major obstacle does David face in obtaining a court order discharging the corporation? Why?
8. Instead of using Chapter 7 (see problem 7), David decides to develop a reorganization plan for his company. What chapter of the Bankruptcy Reform Act should he use? Must all of the company's creditors approve the plan? Why?

PART FOUR

THE EMPLOYEE

13

Relationships Between Principal and Agent

Let every eye negotiate for itself,
And trust no agent.
—SHAKESPEARE

Introduction

An **agent** is a person who acts in the name of another, having been given or assumed some degree of authority to do so. Most organized human activity—and virtually all commercial activity—is carried on through agency. No corporation would be possible, even in theory, without such a concept. Likewise, partnerships and other business organizations rely extensively on agents to conduct their business. Indeed, it is not an exaggeration to say that agency is the cornerstone of enterprise organization. In a partnership each partner is a general agent, while under corporation law the officers and all employees are agents of the corporation.

The existence of agents does not, however, require a whole new law of torts or contracts. A tort is no less harmful for being committed by an agent; a contract is no less meant to be binding for having been negotiated by an agent. What does need to be taken into account, though, is the manner in which an agent acts on behalf of his principal and toward a third party.

Consider John Alden, one of the most famous agents in American literature. His task, celebrated in Henry Wadsworth Longfellow's "The Courtship of Miles Standish," was to woo Priscilla, "the loveliest maiden of Plymouth," on behalf of Captain Miles Standish, a valiant soldier who grew weak at the thought of proposing marriage. Standish turned to John Alden, his young and eloquent protégé, and beseeched him to speak on his behalf, not knowing that Alden himself was madly in love with Priscilla. Alden accepted his Captain's assignment, despite the knowledge that he would thus lose Priscilla for himself, and sought the lady out. But Alden was so tongue-tied that his vaunted eloquence fell short, turned Priscilla cold toward the object of Alden's mission, and eventually led her to turn the tables in one of the most famous lines in American poetry: "Why don't you speak for yourself, John?"

Let us analyze this sequence of events in legal terms—recognizing, of course, that this example is an analogy and that the law, even today, would not impose consequences on Alden for his failure to carry out Captain Standish's wishes. Alden was the captain's agent: he was specifically authorized to speak in his name, in a manner agreed on, toward a specified end, and he accepted the assignment in consideration of the captain's friendship. He had, however, a conflict of interest. He attempted to carry out the assignment, but he did not perform according to expectations. Eventually, he wound up with the prize himself. Here are some questions to consider, the same questions that will recur throughout the discussion of agency:

1. How extensive was John's authority? Could he have made promises to Priscilla on the captain's behalf—for example, that Standish would have built her a fine house?
2. Could he have, through a tortious action, imposed liability on his principal? Suppose, for example, that he had ridden at breakneck speed to reach Priscilla's side and while en route ran into and injured a pedestrian on the road. Could the pedestrian have sued Standish?
3. Suppose Alden had injured himself on the journey. Would Standish be liable to Alden?
4. Is Alden liable to Standish for stealing the heart of Priscilla—that is, for taking the "profits" of the enterprise for himself?

As these questions suggest, agency law often involves three parties—the principal, the agent, and a third party. It therefore deals with three different relationships: between principal and agent, between principal and the third party, and between agent and third party. These relationships can be summed up in a simple diagram:

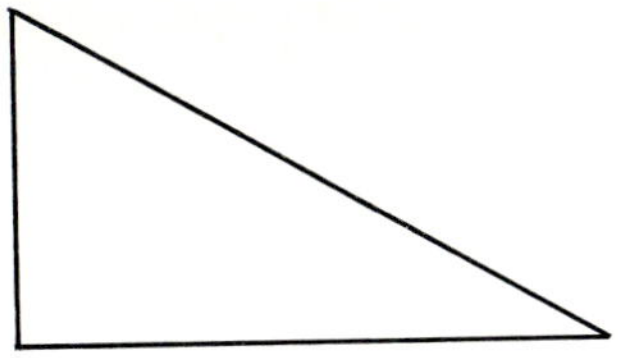

In this chapter, we will consider the principal–agent side of the triangle. In the next chapter we will turn to relationships involving third parties.

Types of Agents

General Agent

The **general agent** possesses the authority to carry out a broad range of transactions in the name and on behalf of the principal. The general agent may be the manager of a business or he may have a more limited but nevertheless ongoing role—as a purchasing agent, for example, or a life insurance agent authorized to sign up customers for the home office. In either case, the general agent has authority to alter the principal's legal relationships with third parties. One who is designated a general agent has the authority to act in any way required by the principal's business. To restrict the general agent's authority, the principal must spell out the limitations explicitly, and even so the principal may be liable for any of the agent's acts in excess of his authority (see "apparent" authority, p. 384).

Normally, the general agent is a business agent, but there are circumstances under which an individual may appoint a general agent for personal purposes. One common form of a personal general agent is the person who holds another's **power of attorney**. This is a delegation of authority to another to act in his stead; it can be accomplished by executing a simple form (see the Minnesota general form, Box 13-1). Ordinarily, the power of attorney is used for a special purpose; for example, to sell real estate or securities in the absence of the owner. But a person facing a lengthy operation and recuperation in a hospital might give a general power of attorney to a trusted family member or friend.

Special Agent

The **special agent** is one who has authority to act only in a specifically designated instance or in a specifically designated set of transactions. For example, a real estate broker is usually a special agent hired to find a buyer for the principal's land. Suppose Sam, the seller, appoints an agent Al to

Box 13-1 Power of Attorney

General Form of Power of Attorney

Know All Men by These Presents, that ________ of the County of ________ and State of ________, do __ by these presents hereby make, constitute and appoint ________ of the County of ________ and State of ________, ________ true and lawful Attorney in Fact for ________ and in ________ name, place and stead, to ________________ granting and giving unto said Attorney in Fact full authority and power to do and perform any and all other acts necessary or incident to the performance and execution of the powers herein expressly granted, with power to do and perform all acts authorized hereby, as fully to all intents and purposes as the grantor might or could do if personally present, with full power of substitution.

In Testimony Whereof, ________ ha __ hereunto set ________ hand __ this ________ day of ________, 19____.

In presence of ____________

____________ ____________

____________ ____________

____

[*Acknowledgment*]

Source: Minnesota Statutes Annotated § 6792

find a buyer for his property. Al's commission depends on the selling price, which, Sam states in a letter to Al, "in any event may be no less than $50,000." If Al locates a buyer, Bob, who agrees to purchase the property for $60,000, Al's signature on the contract of sale will not bind Sam. As a special agent, Al only had authority to find a buyer; he had no authority to sign the contract.

Agency Coupled with an Interest

An agent whose reimbursement depends upon his continuing to have the authority to act as an agent is said to have an "**agency coupled with an interest**" if he has a property interest in the business. A literary or author's agent, for example, customarily agrees to sell a literary work to a publisher in return for a percentage of all monies the author earns from the sale of the work. The literary agent also acts as a collection agent to ensure that his commission will be paid. By agreeing with the principal that the agency is coupled with an interest, the agent can prevent his own rights in a particular literary work from being terminated to his detriment.

Subagent

To carry out his duties, an agent will often need to appoint his own agents. These appointments may or may not be authorized by the principal. An insurance company, for example, might name a general agent to open offices in cities throughout a certain state. The agent will necessarily conduct his business through agents of his own choosing. These agents are "**subagents**" of the principal if the general agent had the express or implied authority of the principal to hire them. For legal purposes, they are agents of both the principal and the principal's general agent and both are liable for the subagent's conduct, although normally the general agent agrees to be primarily liable.

Servant

A final category of agent is the servant or, in modern parlance, employee. The *Restatement (Second) of Agency,* Section 2, defines a servant as "an agent employed by a master [employer] to perform service in his affairs whose physical conduct in the performance of the service is controlled or is subject to the right to control by the master." A common image of the servant is the household employee with which we identify the word "servant" today; others include the factory worker, the truck driver, the farmhand. This image of the servant as unskilled or semi-skilled laborer is no longer adequate, however. In a modern economy, most of us are servants in the eyes of the law. Even the managers of the largest companies are servants, because they are employees of the corporations which they serve.

Independent Contractors

Not every contract for services necessarily creates a master-servant relationship. There is an important distinction made between the status of a servant and that of the **independent contractor.** According to the *Restatement (Second) of Agency,* Section 2, "an independent contractor is a person who contracts with another to do something for him but who is not controlled by the other nor subject to the other's right to control with respect to his physical conduct in the performance of the undertaking." As the name implies, the independent contractor is legally autonomous from the other contracting party. A plumber salaried to a building contractor is an employee and agent of the contractor. But a plumber who hires himself out to repair pipes in people's homes is an independent contractor.

This distinction has important legal consequences bearing on taxation, workers' compensation, and liability insurance. For example, employers are required to withhold income taxes from the paychecks of their employees. But payment to an independent contractor, such as the plumber for hire, does not require such withholding. Deciding who is an independent contractor is not always easy; there is no single factor or mechanical answer. In *Robinson* v. *New York Commodities Corp.,* 396 N.Y.S.2d 725 (App.Div. 1977), an injured salesman sought workers' compensation benefits, claiming to be an employee of the New York Commodities Corporation. But the state workmen's compensation board ruled against him, citing a variety of factors. The claimant sold canned meats, making rounds in his car from his home. The company did not establish hours for him, did not control his movements in any way, nor did it reimburse him for mileage or any other expenses or withhold taxes from its straight commission payments to him. He reported his taxes on a form for the self-employed and hired an accountant to prepare it for him. The Appellate Division of the New York Supreme Court agreed with the compensation board that these facts established the salesman's status as an independent contractor.

It is important to bear in mind that the factual situation in each case determines whether a worker is an employee or an independent contractor. Neither the company nor the worker can establish the worker's status by agreement. As the North Dakota Workmen's Compensation Bureau put it in a bulletin to real estate brokers: "It has come to the Bureau's attention that many employers are requiring that those who work for them sign 'independent contractor' forms so that the employer does not have to pay workmen's compensation premiums for his employees. Such forms are meaningless if the worker is in fact an employee."

In addition to determining a worker's status for tax and compensation insurance purposes, it is also sometimes critical to decisions involving personal liability insurance policies, which usually exclude from coverage accidents involving employees of the insureds, as the following case will show.

GENERAL ACCIDENT FIRE & LIFE ASSUR. CORP. v. PRO GOLF ASSN. 40 Ill.App.3d 592, 352 N.E.2d 441 (1976)

KARNS, PRESIDING JUSTICE

* * *

The insurance policy in question provides certain coverage to members of the Professional Golfers Association. Gerald Hall, a professional golfer employed by the defendant-appellee Taylorville Community Pleasure Driveway District (hereinafter District), a municipal corporation, is an insured member afforded coverage under the policy. The issue presented for review concerns the applicability of a policy exclusion as to "bodily injury to any employee of the insured arising out of and in the course of his employment by the insured." The lower court determined this exclusion inapplicable, and the issue presented for review is whether the judgment of the lower court is against the manifest weight of the evidence. Also assigned as error are certain rulings of the trial court on the admission of evidence.

On June 15, 1973, Bradley Martin, age 13, was present at the golf course owned by the District to participate in junior golf league play. Gerald Hall, the golf professional employed by the District, asked a group of boys including Martin if one of them wished to retrieve or "shag" golf balls to be hit during a golf lesson Hall was to give. Martin agreed to do so. There was no conversation regarding compensation at the time. Hall testified that Martin would be compensated in some manner, "either through golf instructions or money or hot dogs or whatever." During the course of the lesson, a golf ball struck by Hall hit Martin in the eye. Martin instituted an action for damages for the injury to his eye, naming as defendants Hall and the District.

It is General Accident's position that Martin was an employee of Hall at the time of the accident and that the employee exclusion of its policy is applicable to the occurrence. The defendants argue that Martin was either an independent contractor or volunteer, and was not an employee within the meaning of the policy of insurance.

The exclusion in question is commonly referred to as the workmen's compensation exclusion. It is a standard provision of liability policies. Its purpose is to distinguish an employer's liability to his employees from liability to the general public, since the extent of the employer's liability to his employees is as provided by workmen's compensation statutes. It would be costly and redundant to insure against liability to employees under general liability policies of insurance.

We are directed to cases involving an application of the Workmen's Compensation Act to determine whether Martin was an employee of Hall at the time of occurrence. In *O'Brien* v. *Industrial Commission,* 48 Ill.2d 304, 269 N.E.2d 471 (1971), the court observed that the determination of a person's status as an employee or independent contractor "is one of the most vexatious and difficult to determine in the law of compensation." The court reviewed the customary tests of master-servant, that is, right to control the manner of doing the work; manner of payment of compensation; right to discharge; and furnishing of material, equipment or tools. Applying these tests to the instant facts, appellant argues that Martin was an employee of Hall and the contrary decision below was against the manifest weight of the evidence. Specifically, support can be found in the record that Hall had the right to control the manner in which Martin was to pick up the golf balls as the ball that struck Martin was intended as a signal to position him farther back on the practice range; that equipment, a bag and golf cart, was furnished Martin by Hall; that Martin was to be compensated in some manner as he had been compensated in the past for doing the same work, which required little skill or judgment; and that the record, while silent, supports the clear inference that Hall had the right to discharge Martin.

Appellees argue that the facts, which are not in substantial dispute, support with greater force the trial court's finding that Martin was not an employee. There was no evidence of any agreement as to compensation. Hall sometimes gave instruction or food to the boys who "shagged" golf balls, but there was no express understanding as to compensation. While the chore was a simple one, Martin was not instructed or directed in the manner of performing the task, and he was hired to produce a result, viz., to pick up the golf balls; no control was exercised over him, and the ball that struck him was not directing him in the manner of performing the work but was simply a signal for him to back up since balls were to be driven farther down range. No equipment other than a bag in which to place balls as picked up was required to perform the task.

* * *

We believe the evidence is susceptible of different inferences. The question is one of fact for the court's determination, and we cannot say that the decision of the trial court is against the manifest weight of the evidence.

* * *

Creation of Agency

The agency relationship can be created in two ways: by contract or by operation of law.

By Contract

The general rules of contract law govern the law of agency, but two contract principles are especially important: the first is the requirement for a writing and the second concerns contractual capacity.

Most oral agency contracts are legally binding; the law does not require that they be reduced to writing. In practice, many agency contracts are written out to avoid problems of proof. But there are three circumstances pertinent to agency in which the Statute of Frauds does require the contract to be in writing: (1) if the agreed upon purpose of the agency cannot be fulfilled within one year or if the agency relationship is to last more than one year; (2) in many states, an agreement to pay a commission to a real estate broker; and (3) in many states, authority given to an agent to sell real estate.

Even when the agency contract is not required to be in writing, contracts that agents make with third parties often must be in writing. Thus Section 2-201 of the UCC specifically requires contracts for the sale of goods for the price of $500 or more to be in writing and "signed by the party against whom enforcement is sought *or by his authorized agent*. . . ."

A contract is void or voidable when one of the parties lacks capacity to make one. If both principal and agent lack capacity—for example, a minor appoints another minor to negotiate or sign an agreement—there can be no question of the contract's voidability. But suppose only one or the other lacks capacity. Generally, the law focuses on the principal. If the principal is a minor or otherwise lacks capacity, the contract can be avoided, even if the agent is fully competent. There are, however, a few situations in which the capacity of the agent is important. Thus, a mentally incompetent agent cannot bind a principal.

By Operation of Law

Most agencies spring into being contractually. But in areas of social need, courts have declared an agency to exist in the absence of an agreement. The agency relationship then is said to have been created "by operation of law." Children in most states and wives in many may purchase necessary items—food or medical services—on the father's or husband's account. Longstanding social policy deems it desirable for the head of a family to support his dependents and the courts will put the expense on the father (or the mother, if she is the family head) in order to provide for their welfare. The courts achieve this result by supposing the dependent to be the family head's agent, thus allowing creditors to sue the family head for the debt. Not every expense is a necessary, of course, and where the father is already supplying the need, the mother may not incur additional expense chargeable to the father on the ground that she prefers a different doctor or has a different conception of an adequate diet. In recent years, concern with equal rights has caused some courts to hold that wives are liable for necessaries purchased by their husbands, or that neither spouse should be liable for necessaries purchased by the other.

Agent's Duties to Principal

Fiduciary Duty

In a nonagency contractual situation, the parties' responsibilities terminate at the border of the contract. There is no relationship beyond the agreement. This literalist approach is justified by the more general principle that we ought each be free to act unless we commit ourselves to a particular course.

But the agency relationship is more than a contractual one, and the agent's responsibilities go beyond the border of the contract. Agency imposes a higher duty than that simply to abide by the contract terms. It imposes a **fiduciary duty.** The law infiltrates the contract creating the agency relationship and reverses the general principle that the parties are free to act in the absence of agreement. As a fiduciary of the principal, the agent stands in a position of special trust. His responsibility is to subordinate his self-interest to that of his principal. The fiduciary responsibility is imposed by law. The absence of any clause in the contract detailing the agent's fiduciary duty does not relieve him of it.

The agent thus has two types of duties to his principal. One is contractual and flows from the agreement actually entered into. The other springs from the laws of torts and trusts, which define the nature and limits of fiduciary responsibility.

Duty to Avoid Self-Dealing A fiduciary may not lawfully profit from a conflict between his personal interest in a transaction and his principal's interest in that same transaction. A broker hired as a purchasing agent, for instance, may not sell to his principal through a company in which he or his family has a financial interest. The penalty for breach of fiduciary duty is loss of compensation and profit and possible damages for breach of trust, as the Frito-Lay suit in Box 13-2 makes clear. On January 3, 1979, the *Wall Street Journal* reported that the Frito-Lay suit had been settled. Although the settlement terms were not disclosed, Frito-Lay reportedly was given control of American Business Management Corporation and also received $5 million in damages.

Duty to Preserve Confidential Information To further his objectives, a principal will usually need to reveal a number of secrets to his agent—how much he is willing to sell or pay for property, marketing strategies, and the like. Such information could easily be turned to the disadvantage of the principal if the agent were to compete with the principal or were to sell it to those who do. The law therefore prohibits an agent from using for his own purposes or in ways that would injure the interests of the principal information confidentially given or acquired. This prohibition extends to

Box 13-2 A Breach of Fiduciary Duty

Tortilla Flap
By Bill Abrams

DALLAS—Authors of self-improvement success manuals usually warn you that you'll never get rich working on salary for a giant corporation. It's time they heard about James H. Stafford, who not long ago was fired by the Frito-Lay Inc. subsidiary of PepsiCo Inc., the $4 billion-a-year soft-drink and snack-food conglomerate.

Mr. Stafford is a millionaire several times over. There seems no dispute that the six-foot-four, former high-school vocational agriculture teacher, now in his late 50s, made his money during his 24 years on the Frito-Lay payroll. For the last 19 years he has been the company's commodity purchasing manager.

It takes millions of pounds of corn, vegetable oil, salt and spices to turn out all the Fritos, Doritos, Tostitos and other snacks that Frito-Lay sells; Mr. Stafford's shopping list amounted to more than $150 million a year, making him one of the nation's largest commodity buyers.

The catch was, according to the company, that Mr. Stafford secretly owned a major interest in a West Texas company, American Business Management Corp., that was Frito-Lay's largest corn supplier; he also was receiving thousands of dollars every year in consulting fees from Lacy-Logan Co., a Dallas vegetable-oils broker that handled much of Frito-Lay's oil purchases, Frito-Lay alleges.

Frito-Lay said it didn't find out about Mr. Stafford's outside interests until this year, and when it did, it promptly fired him on Aug. 21. The following day it filed suit in Dallas County state district court against him, Grain Handling Corp. (which had acquired American Business Management), and other principals of that closely held corporation for more than $18 million in damages. The defendants have denied any wrongdoing. . . .

One ironic aspect of the case is that Frito-Lay has yet to show what harm it has suffered as a result of Mr. Stafford's handling of commodities purchases. Frito-Lay has always been one of PepsiCo's most profitable subsidiaries. And Mr. Stafford was widely viewed by commodities sellers as one of Frito-Lay's key assets; they say he was a hard bargainer with an uncanny feel for the edible-oils market.

"He's the finest oil trader this country has ever had," says one vegetable-oil refiner. "He was rough. When you did business with Jim Stafford, you knew you'd been through a fight." Mr. Stafford, himself, claims in court papers that in the past five years he bought vegetable oil for Frito-Lay at prices "approximately $100 million less than the market price." . . .

The main ingredient in corn chips is, of course, corn. Until the mid-1960s, Frito-Lay had purchased its corn directly from farmers, some as far away as California, and had cleaned, stored and delivered the grain itself. Then the company decided to get out of the corn-handling business.

Frito-Lay says that Mr. Stafford was given the task of finding an outside corn supplier. He turned in 1968 to KornKo Inc., a company founded by Melvin N. Tekell, a Texas corn broker; Mr. Tekell's wife, and James T. Hair, an accountant. Mr. Hair also happens to be Mr. Stafford's son-in-law, the husband of the former Sherry Lynne Stafford. There was, Frito-Lay alleges, another partner in KornKo, albeit a silent one: James H. Stafford, himself. . . .

. . . Within five years, KornKo, then known

information gleaned from the principal though unrelated to the agent's assignment. "[A]n agent who is told by the principal of his plans, or who secretly examines books or memoranda of the employer, is not privileged to use such information at his principal's expense." (*Restatement (Second) of Agency*, Section 395) Nor may the agent use confidential information after as American Business Management Corp., had become Frito-Lay's single largest corn supplier, contracting to sell at least 250 million pounds in 1973 for roughly $15 million. . . .

Mr. Stafford, as an American Business Management shareholder, received nearly $19,000 in dividends between 1973 and 1976. Frito-Lay also contends that Mr. Stafford's 2,000-acre ranch, Rockbrook Farms, received "management fees" of more than $50,000 annually from the corn concern. . . .

It was Mr. Stafford's job to buy the edible oils—peanut, corn, soy or cotton oil—that were used to fry corn chips. Like most big buyers, Frito-Lay bought most of its oils through brokers who could provide up-to-date market information and conceal a buyer's identity from the marketplace.

Among oils sellers, it was common knowledge that one Dallas broker—Lacy-Logan—had, as one broker describes it, "a lock on Frito-Lay's business." . . .

Mr. Stafford became a consultant to Lacy-Logan. His fee was about $15 per carload of oil bought by Frito-Lay, according to a former Lacy-Logan employee familiar with the arrangement. This came to roughly $40,000 a year; court records show that between 1968 and 1976 Lacy-Logan paid Mr. Stafford $388,159.

In 1975 Mr. Lacy sold the company to American Business Management. One acquaintance says the reason was that Mr. Lacy "was terrified of getting caught" and upset by demands from Mr. Stafford for more money.

In 1976, American Business Management itself was sold to Quality Grain Processors Inc., later to be known as Grain Handling Corp., for $36 million in cash and notes. . . .

Mr. Stafford's immediate cash windfall as a result of the sale came to $6 million. . . .

At the time of the windfall, Mr. Stafford's salary at Frito-Lay was probably between $40,000 and $45,000, according to his former associates. Court records in the current case indicate that he may have received perhaps another $100,000 a year from kickbacks, dividends and other payments from Frito-Lay's corn and oil suppliers.

Frito-Lay is now trying to recover those monies. The company claims Mr. Stafford "placed himself in a position of conflict of interest, breached his duty of loyalty and trust and/or his fiduciary duty to Frito-Lay." . . .

Why didn't PepsiCo's internal auditors or Arthur Young & Co., PepsiCo's outside auditor since 1965, uncover the irregularities? William A. McNamara, the Arthur Young partner who coordinates PepsiCo audits, says, "This was the kind of thing that I don't think is possible to catch in a normal audit."

Mr. McNamara says Arthur Young and PepsiCo, since the Stafford affair, have been trying to come up with new controls that would prevent it from happening again. "We can't really come up with much. It was an isolated situation that happened in a subsidiary."

Since 1976, PepsiCo executives have been subject to an elaborate printed "Code of Conduct," which, among other things, bars company employees and members of their families from "any significant interest in enterprises which conduct or seek to conduct business with PepsiCo" without first obtaining a statement of clearance from the company's legal department indicating that the employee's decisions won't be influenced by his ownership of the outside interest.

Source: *Wall Street Journal,* November 14, 1978

resigning his agency. Though he is free, in the absence of contract, to compete with his former principal, he may not use information learned in the course of his agency, such as trade secrets and—as shown by the following case—customer lists.

ARNOLD'S ICE CREAM CO. v. CARLSON
330 F.Supp. 1185 (E.D.N.Y. 1971)

JUDD, DISTRICT JUDGE.

* * *

THE FACTS

In the fall of 1969, Borden's Milk Co. closed down its ice cream facilities in the Nassau-Suffolk market and plaintiff established an outlet there employing four drivers and three salesmen to promote its product. Prior to that time, Borden's was servicing more than 1,500 customers. Plaintiff's efforts to cultivate part of this market were apparently successful, since in its 1970 fiscal year it had sales of approximately $300,000 and delivered its product to about 190 customers, most of whom were formerly served by Borden's.

The defendants Mesloh and Carlson were formerly employed by Borden's as truck drivers delivering ice cream in the Nassau-Suffolk County area. When Borden's ceased doing business in the market in October 3, 1969, the defendants were hired by plaintiff; defendant Stevens was an alternate driver for plaintiff. Their duties for plaintiff included delivering orders previously phoned in and making route sales as the individual customers required. In order to carry out their employment, defendants were supplied with pricing and product information as well as customer names.

On March 31, 1971, at the end of the day, the individual defendants submitted their resignations to plaintiff, effective immediately. Prior to that time, in February 1971, the East End Ice Cream Co. and the West End Ice Cream Co. were incorporated by the wives of two of the defendants. During early March 1971, the defendant corporations acquired trucks which were subsequently used to deliver ice cream products. Affidavits from customers and employees of plaintiff indicate that before March 31, 1971 the individual defendants approached plaintiff's customers and solicited sales on behalf of the corporate defendants. The individual defendants also attempted to convince some of plaintiff's other employees to join them in a proposed competing business prior to submitting their resignations. During the last 10 days of March 1971, the combined sales of Mesloh and Carlson dropped 25% to 30% from sales in the beginning of March, thus creating an unfilled need for April orders. The defendants had also used up all their vacation time in the three months preceding their resignation.

Since defendants began their separate business, in less than one month about 45 customers ceased to buy from plaintiff, and 85 others have either been solicited by the defendants or sold some of their products. A number of these are customers with substantial volume. The total sales in jeopardy as a result of defendants' activity amount to approximately $100,000 per year.

The defendants did not testify at the hearing. While most of the accounts solicited were former Borden's customers, it does not appear how many of the defendants' customers were known to the individual defendants through their work at Borden's. The customers served by plaintiff are only a fraction of the total number of ice cream retailers in the area.

DISCUSSION OF LAW

Customer lists are entitled to the protection accorded trade secrets if the names were built up over a period of time by substantial business effort, advertising, and expenditures of time and money. It is no defense to an action by an employer against an employee using such a trade secret that there was no contract or restrictive covenant in force between the employer and employee explicitly prohibiting this conduct. Nor does the fact that the employees are serving at the will of the employer justify a conspiracy to use an employer's trade secret in direct competition with the employer. It is not necessary that the trade secret or customer list be impossible to duplicate, only that the list be used by a former employee in violation of his responsibility not to use his employer's efforts to benefit himself at the employer's expense.

Employees cannot conspire to set up a competing business while they are still working for their employer.

Employees owe a fiduciary duty to their employer even though they may not be officers or directors.

In Tepfer & Sons, Inc. v. Zschaler, 25 A.D.2d 786, 269 N.Y.S.2d 552 (2d Dept. 1966), the court found that money damages were adequate, but here the defendants stepped so far over the line of loyalty owed by an employee to the firm which pays their salaries that monetary damages cannot repair the harm they have done.

It may well be that defendants could have compiled a list of customers similar to plaintiff's based on individual knowledge and access to pages in a telephone directory, but this does not appear to be the case here. The testimony before the court and the affidavits submitted by counsel indicate that defendants quickly and effectively solicited plaintiff's former customers, and that defendants did not compile a list of their own, but relied upon plaintiff's previous efforts.

Plaintiff has shown a reasonable probability of ultimate success on the merits, and of injury that would be irreparable.

This memorandum is intended to contain the court's findings of fact pursuant to F.R.Civ.P. 52(a).

A preliminary injunction will therefore be granted as requested.

Other Duties

In addition to fiduciary responsibility, and whatever special duties may be contained in the specific contract, the law of agency imposes other duties on an agent.

Duty of Care and Skill An agent is usually taken on because he has special knowledge or skills that the principal wishes to tap. The agent is under a legal duty to perform his work with the care and skill that is "standard in the locality for the kind of work which he is employed to perform" (Restatement, Section 379) and to exercise any special skills, if these are greater or more refined than those prevalent among those normally employed in the community. In short, the agent may not lawfully do a sloppy job.

Duty of Good Conduct In the absence of an agreement, a principal may not ordinarily dictate how an agent must live his private life. An overly fastidious florist may not instruct his truck driver to steer clear of the local bar on his way home from delivering flowers at the end of the day. But there are some jobs on which the personal habits of the agent may have an effect. The agent is not at liberty to act with impropriety or notoriety, so as to bring disrepute on the business in which the principal is engaged. A lecturer at an anti-alcohol clinic may be directed to refrain from frequenting bars. A bank cashier who becomes known as a gambler may be fired.

Duty to Keep and Render Accounts The agent must keep accurate financial records, take receipts, and otherwise act in conformity to standard business practices.

Duty to Act Only as Authorized This duty states a truism, but is one for which there are limits. A principal's wishes may have been stated ambiguously or may be broad enough to confer discretion on the agent. As long as the agent acts reasonably under the circumstances, he will not be liable for damages later if the principal ultimately repudiates what the agent has done. "Only conduct which is contrary to the principal's manifestations to him, interpreted in light of what he has reason to know at the time when he acts, . . . subjects the agent to liability to the principal." (Restatement, Section 383)

Duty Not to Attempt the Impossible or Impracticable Principal says to Agent: "Keep working until the job is done." Agent is not obligated to go without food or sleep because the principal misapprehended how long it would take to complete the job. Nor should the agent continue to expend the principal's funds in a quixotic attempt to gain business, sign up customers, or produce inventory when it is reasonably clear that such efforts would be in vain.

Duty to Obey As a general rule, the agent must obey reasonable directions concerning the manner of performance. What is reasonable depends on the customs of the industry or trade, prior dealings between agent and principal, and the nature of the agreement creating the agency. A principal may prescribe uniforms for various classes of employees, for instance, and a manufacturing company may tell its salesforce what sales pitch to use on customers. On the other hand, certain tasks entrusted to agents are not subject to the principal's control; for example, a lawyer may refuse to permit a client to dictate courtroom tactics.

Duty to Give Information Because the principal cannot be every place at once—that is why agents are hired, after all—much that is vital to the principal's business comes to the attention first of agents. If the agent has actual notice or reason to know of information that is relevant to matters entrusted to him, he has a duty to inform the principal. This duty is especially critical because information in the hands of an agent is, under most circumstances, imputed to the principal, whose legal liabilities to third persons may hinge on receiving information in timely fashion. Service of process, for example, requires a defendant to answer within a certain number of days; an agent's failure to communicate to the principal that a summons has been served may bar the principal's right to defend a lawsuit. The imputation to the principal of knowledge possessed by the agent is strict: even where the agent is acting adversely to the principal's interests—for example, by trying to defraud his employer—a third party may still rely on notification to the agent, unless the third party knows the agent is acting adversely.

"Shop Rights" Doctrine In *Grip Nut Co.* v. *Sharp,* 150 F.2d 192 (7th Cir. 1945), Sharp made a deal with Grip Nut Company that in return for a salary and bonuses as company president he would assign to the company

any inventions he made. When the five-year employment contract expired, Sharp continued to serve as chief executive officer, but no new contract was negotiated concerning either pay or rights to inventions. During the next ten years, Sharp invented a number of new products and developed new machinery to manufacture them; patent rights went to the company. However, he made one invention with two other employees and they assigned the patent to him. A third employee invented a safety device and also assigned the patent to Sharp. At one time Sharp's son invented a leak-proof bolt and a process to manufacture it; these, too, were assigned to Sharp. These inventions were developed in the company's plants at its expense.

When Sharp died, his family claimed the rights to the inventions on which Sharp held assignments and sued the company, which used the inventions, for patent infringement. The family reasoned that after the expiration of the employment contract, Sharp was employed only in a managerial capacity, not as an inventor. The court disagreed and invoked the "shop rights" doctrine, under which an invention "developed and perfected in [a company's] plant with its time, materials, and appliances, and wholly at its expense" may be used by the company without payment of royalties. "Because the servant uses his master's time, facilities and materials to attain a concrete result, the employer is entitled to use that which embodies his own property and to duplicate it as often as he may find occasion to employ similar appliances in his business." The company would have been given complete ownership of the patents had there been an express or implied (for example, the employee is hired to make inventions) contract to this effect between Sharp and the company.

Principal's Duties to Agent

Contract Duties

General Duties The fiduciary relationship of agent to principal does not run in reverse—that is, the principal is not the agent's fiduciary. Nevertheless, the principal has a number of contractually-related obligations toward his agent. In general, these are analogues of many of the agent's duties that we have just examined. In brief: a principal has a duty "to refrain from unreasonably interfering with [an agent's] work." (Restatement, Section 434) The principal is allowed, however, to compete with the agent, unless the agreement specifically prohibits it. The principal has a duty to inform his agent of risks of physical harm or pecuniary loss that inhere in the agent's performance of assigned tasks. Failure to warn an agent that travel in a particular neighborhood required by the job may be dangerous (a fact unknown to the agent but known to the principal) could under common law subject the principal to a suit for damages if the agent is injured while in the neighborhood performing his job. A principal is obliged to render accounts of monies due to agents; a principal's obligation to do so depends on a variety of factors, including the degree of independence of the agent, the method of compensation, and the customs of the particular business. An agent's reputation is no less valuable than a principal's, and so an agent is under no obligation to continue working for one who sullies it.

Employment at Will Under the traditional "employment-at-will" doctrine, an employee who is not hired for a specific period can be fired at any time. This doctrine, which has come under attack in recent years, is discussed on pp. 446–49.

Duty to Indemnify Agents commonly spend money pursuing the principal's business. Unless the agreement explicitly provides otherwise, the principal has a duty to indemnify or reimburse the agent. A familiar form of indemnity is the employee expense account. But the principal's obligation to indemnify is not limited to sums the agent expends on behalf of the principal, as illustrated by the following case.

SOUTHERN FARM BUREAU CASUALTY INSURANCE COMPANY v. GOODING
565 S.W.2d 421 (Ark. 1978)

GEORGE ROSE SMITH, JUSTICE. The principal question in this case is one of insurance coverage. In 1975 the appellant, Southern Farm Bureau, issued a $10,000/$20,000 policy of automobile liability insurance to the principal appellee, O. M. Gooding, a farmer. The policy specifically covered nine described automobiles and trucks, but it made no reference to a low-boy trailer owned by Gooding.

In November, 1975, Ivan Gooding, also an insured, was driving one of the described trucks on a highway. The truck, by means of its fifth wheel, was pulling the lowboy, upon which a bulldozer tractor was being transported. As Ivan allegedly drove too fast around a curve the chains holding the bulldozer gave way, so that the bulldozer was thrown into the path of an oncoming vehicle being driven by Donald B. Hawksley. Hawksley was injured.

Hawksley brought a $75,000 personal injury suit against the Goodings. Upon Southern Farm Bureau's denial of coverage, the Goodings filed a third-party complaint against Southern Farm Bureau and also against the insurance agent, Joe Rodman, who wrote the policy. It was alleged that Rodman had represented to the Goodings that trailers and lowboys would be covered when being pulled by an insured vehicle. Eventually Southern Farm Bureau and Rodman filed counterclaims against each other, each insisting that the other was liable for any possible recovery by Hawksley.

The two branches of the case were tried separately. At the first hearing, submitted largely on stipulations, the court determined that Southern Farm Bureau's policy protected the Goodings, up to $10,000, against liability for Hawksley's injuries. At the second trial, two weeks later, a jury returned a $10,000 verdict for Hawksley. The court's final judgment included the $10,000 award in favor of Hawksley against the Goodings, a similar award in favor of the Goodings against Southern Farm Bureau, plus penalty and attorney's fee, and a $3,538.97 award in favor of Rodman against Southern Farm Bureau, representing Rodman's expense and attorney's fee in defending the Goodings' claim against him.

* * *

It is argued that Southern Farm Bureau's agent, Rodman, should not have been allowed to recover the expenses and attorney's fee he incurred in defending the third-party complaint filed against him by the Goodings. We think the recovery was proper. A principal has a duty to indemnify his agent when the agent suffers a loss which, because of their relation, it is fair that the principal should bear. Restatement, 2d, Agency, § 438 (1958). In particular, the agent can recover the expenses of defending an action brought by a third person because of the agent's authorized conduct. If Rodman represented to the Goodings that the lowboy would be covered while being pulled by an insured vehicle, that representation was correct. Rodman, the agent, was subjected to the expense of litigation because his principal, Southern Farm Bureau, erroneously denied that the coverage existed. In the circumstances it is fair that the principal be required to indemnify the agent for his expenses, including his attorney's fee.

Rodman asks that a fee be allowed for the services of his attorneys on this appeal, but we can find no basis for such an allowance. In the trial court Rodman did not recover an attorney's fee for *this litigation with his principal*. He merely recovered the expenses to which he had been put by his principal, which happened to include an attorney's fee. The Goodings have not appealed from the judgment in favor of Rodman upon their complaint against him. Consequently, upon this appeal there has been no issue between Rodman and the Goodings, nor any possibility that a reversal would entail any liability on his part to them. As to Rodman, the only question on appeal has been whether he can recover his prior expenses from his principal. The situation presents no reason for a departure from the general rule that a successful litigant is not ordinarily entitled to attorney's fees.

Affirmed.

Tort Duties

Andy, who works in a dynamite factory, negligently stores dynamite in the wrong shed. Andy warns his fellow employee Bill that he has done so. Bill lights up a cigarette near the shed anyway, a spark lands on the ground, the dynamite explodes, and Bill is injured. May Bill sue his employer to recover damages? At common law, the answer would be no—three times no. First, the "fellow-servant" rule would bar recovery because the employer was held not to be responsible for torts committed by one employee against another. Second, Bill's failure to heed Andy's warning and his decision to smoke near the dynamite amounted to contributory negligence. Hence, even if the dynamite had been negligently stored by the employer, rather than by a fellow employee, the claim would have been dismissed. Third, the courts might have held that Bill had "assumed the risk": since he was aware of the dangers, it would not be fair to saddle the employer with the burden of Bill's actions.

The three common-law rules just mentioned ignited intense public fury by the turn of the twentieth century. In large numbers of cases, workers who were mutilated or killed on the job found themselves and their families without recompense. Union pressure and grass roots lobbying led to workers' (originally "workmen's") compensation acts—statutory enactments that dramatically overhauled the law of torts as it affected employees.

Table 13-1 Statutory Benefits (Texas) for Specific Injuries

MEMBER	*WEEKS*	*MEMBER*	*WEEKS*
Thumb	60	Foot	125
Index Finger	45	Leg at or above Knee	200
2d Finger	30	Eye	100
3d Finger	21	Hearing (Both Ears)	150
Little Finger	15	Eye and Leg above Knee	350
Hand	150	Eye and Arm above Elbow	350
Arm at or above Elbow	200	Eye and Hand	325
Great Toe	30	Eye and Foot	300
Any Other Toe	10		

NOTE: 2d joint of thumb equivalent to ½ thumb. More than ½ of thumb equivalent to whole thumb. 3d joint of any finger equivalent to ⅓ finger. More than middle and 3d joint of any finger equivalent to whole finger. For metacarpal bone (palm) add 10 weeks to number specified for corresponding thumb, finger or fingers. For all injuries to thumb, fingers and parts of one hand compensation limited to that allowed for hand.

Source: From *Employers' Handbook* of the Texas Employers' Insurance Association, 1975

Workers' compensation is a no-fault system. The employee gives up the right to sue the employer and receives in exchange predetermined compensation for a job-related injury, regardless of who caused it. This tradeoff was felt to be equitable to employer and employee: the employee loses the right to seek damages for pain and suffering—which can be a sizable portion of any jury award—but in return he can avoid the time-consuming and uncertain judicial process and assure himself that his medical costs and a portion of his salary will be paid—and paid promptly. The employer must pay for all injuries, even those for which he is blameless, but in return he avoids the risk of losing a big lawsuit, can calculate his costs actuarially, and can spread the risks through insurance.

Most workers' compensation acts provide 100 percent of the cost of a worker's hospitalization and medical care necessary to cure the injury and relieve him from its effects. They also provide for payment of lost wages and death benefits. Even an employee who is able to work may be eligible to receive compensation for specific injuries. Table 13-1 shows the table of benefits for specific injuries under the Texas statute. Assume a worker loses his arm above the elbow. He is entitled to two-thirds of his average weekly wage, not to exceed a specified maximum, for 200 weeks. If the loss is only partial (for example, partial loss of sight), the recovery is decreased by the percentage still usable. Thus a worker who loses half his sight in one eye would be limited to half the usual recovery.

Coverage Although workers' compensation laws are on the books of every state, in a few states they are not compulsory. In states where they are elective, the employer may decline to participate, in which event the employee must seek redress in court. But in most states permitting an employer election, the old common law defenses (fellow-servant rule, contributory negligence, and assumption of risk) have been statutorily eliminated, greatly enhancing an employee's chances of winning a suit. The incentive is therefore strong for employers to elect workers' compensation coverage.

Not all workers are covered. Those frequently excluded are farm and domestic laborers and public employees. But the trend has been to include more and more classes of workers. Approximately half the states now provide coverage for household workers, although the threshold of coverage varies widely fiom state to state. Some use an earnings test, the floor for coverage ranging from \$200 in annual earnings to \$10,000. Other states impose an hours threshold. People who fall within the domestics category include maids, babysitters, gardeners, and handymen, but generally do not include plumbers, electricians, and other independent contractors.

There are three general methods by which employers may comply with workers' compensation laws. First, they may purchase employer's liability and workers' compensation policies through private commercial insurance companies. These policies consist of two major provisions: payment by the insurer of all claims filed under workers' compensation and related laws (such as occupational disease benefits) and coverage of the costs of defending any suits filed against the employer, including any judgments awarded. Since workers' compensation statutes cut off the employee's right to sue, how can such a lawsuit be filed? The answer is that there are certain exceptions to the ban—for instance, a worker may sue if the employer deliberately injures an employee.

The second method of compliance with workers' compensation laws is to insure through a state fund established for the purpose. The third method is to self-insure. The laws specify conditions under which companies may resort to self-insurance and generally only the largest corporations qualify to do so.

Recurring Legal Issues Workers' compensation does not cover every accident or injury. It provides payments only to employees who are injured in some work-related activity. So three issues recur in the cases: (1) Is the injury work-related? (2) Is the injured person an employee? (3) How palpable must the "injury" be for compensation to be awarded?

Is the injury work-related? As a general rule, on-the-job injuries are covered no matter what their relationship to the employee's specific duties. Although injuries resulting from drunkenness or fighting are not generally covered, there are circumstances under which they will be, as the next case shows.

CHESTER v. WORLD FOOTBALL LEAGUE 75 Mich. App. 455, 255 N.W.2d 643 (1977)

V.J. Brennan, J. On September 27, 1974, plaintiffs Albert and Ardis Chester brought suit against defendants jointly and severally for injuries arising out of a dispute over wages between defendant Wyche and plaintiff Albert Chester while Chester was controller for defendant Detroit Wheels [hereafter Wheels]. Defendant World Football League [hereafter League] was joined as alleged co-employer of defendant Wyche. Motion for summary judgment was filed by defendants and granted by Wayne County Circuit Judge Benjamin D. Burdick on January 30, 1976. He found the claim against Wyche and the Wheels was barred by the exclusive remedy provisions of the Workmen's Compensation Act. He found for the League on the same basis or, alternatively, because Wyche acted outside the scope of any possible agency with the League. Plaintiffs appeal as of right.

The incident giving rise to this litigation occurred on September 20, 1974. Plaintiff had been employed as controller of the Wheels through Kelly Services, Inc [hereafter Kelly]. Part of the arrangement meant that the Wheels would pay Kelly and Kelly would then pay plaintiff. However, plaintiff's deposition indicated that Kelly maintained no control over his time, duties or conduct with the Wheels.

Plaintiff had been working for the Wheels since July, 1974. Prior to September 20, 1974, the Wheels became insolvent and unable to meet their payroll. Thereupon, the League seems to have agreed to pay Wyche's salary. The last paycheck Wyche received on September 20, 1974, came from the League.

On September 20, 1974, plaintiff was working at the offices of the Wheels. Wyche and some other football players entered and engaged plaintiff in discussion about back pay due the players. The conversation became heated and Wyche grabbed plaintiff by the arm, plaintiff claiming he was thereby injured.

* * *

Plaintiff first contends that the trial court erred by granting summary judgment for defendant Wheels. Plaintiff maintains that he was not, as a matter of law, an employee of defendant Wheels on September 20, 1974, and so was not precluded from bringing suit against them by the exclusive remedy provisions of the Workmen's Compensation Act.

Viewing the facts most favorably to plaintiff, we must disagree. Under the act, an employee is entitled to compensation if he receives a personal injury arising out of and in the course of his employment by an employer covered by the act. In this case, there is no dispute that Chester was injured in the course of his employment or that the Wheels were an employer covered by the act. What we must decide is the legal question of whether plaintiff was an employee of the Wheels within the meaning of the act.

The device used in Michigan to determine the existence of an employment relationship is the "economic reality" test. Generally, four factors are isolated: control, payment of wages, the right to hire and fire, and the right to discipline. Applying these factors to this case, we believe plaintiff was an employee of the Wheels.

* * *

The plaintiff in this case styles himself an independent contractor, removed from the control normally associated with an employee status. We see no distinction between the function plaintiff performed for the Wheels and similar high-level employees in other businesses who may have some control over the time, hours or duties of their employment. We believe summary judgment was properly granted in favor of defendant Wheels.

Plaintiff next argues that the trial court erred by granting summary judgment to defendant Wyche. He alleges that Wyche was not, as a matter of law, an employee of the Wheels on September 20, 1974, and so would not be protected by the exclusive remedy provisions of the Workmen's Compensation Act. We disagree.

We have determined that plaintiff was an employee of defendant Wheels for purposes of the Workmen's Compensation Act. We also recognize that defendant Wyche was an employee of the Wheels and that the act will bar suit against co-employees for injuries compensable under the act. This bar operates where the injury occurs in the regular course of employment. Therefore, the question we must decide is whether this incident developed within the course of their employment.

* * *

We find authority for the position that "injuries received in assault, either sportive or malicious, are not, by reason of such fact alone, beyond the realm of compensability". We do not believe even a favorable interpretation of the facts indicate defendant Wyche's assault "so gross and reprehensible . . . as to constitute intentional and wilful conduct". We feel the broad construction necessary and desirable for this provision justifies finding the assault within the course of the parties' employment. We perceive the incident as arising spontaneously from employee Wyche's attempt to collect salary from employee Chester. We find no error in granting summary judgment for defendant Wyche in this case.

* * *

Plaintiff's second amended complaint against the WFL asserted two separate theories of recovery. First, plaintiffs contended that the WFL was vicariously liable for Wyche's battery under the doctrine of *respondeat superior*. The second theory of liability articulated by plaintiff was that the WFL was negligent, among other reasons, in keeping Wyche, a man purportedly of known violent propensities, within the WFL organization, provoking Wyche to violence by failing to act to satisfy his grievances and failing to act to prevent those grievances from arising.

* * *

First, if there were undisputed facts below showing that Wyche did not act within any agency relationship with the WFL, summary judgment was warranted as to the first theory of recovery. Secondly, if the undisputed facts below show that Chester was an employee of the WFL, summary judgment was appropriate on both theories and the trial judge should be affirmed *in toto*. We will discuss each issue separately.

* * *

The proper test to determine an agency relationship, for purposes of *respondeat superior* liability, is the right to control. Examining the facts under the right-to-control test, there is clearly no agency between Wyche and the WFL. Wyche was under contract with the Wheels, not the WFL. Wyche was sent to see plaintiff to collect his money with permission of the Wheels, not the WFL. On the record before us, there is nothing to indicate that the WFL had the right to control Wyche. The only evidence adduced below of any relevance is that the WFL had voluntarily undertaken to meet the Wheels' payroll. In the instant case, this does not suffice to show that the WFL had the right to control Wyche; accordingly, summary judgment as to the first theory of liability was proper.

Plaintiffs' second theory, however, does not stand in the same position. In defendant WFL's brief, it is argued that Chester was an employee of the WFL. This view is premised upon the theory that if Wyche's salary was undertaken by the WFL, then Chester's salary was also taken over by the league. As we noted above, in the instant case the voluntary assumption of a salary obligation, by itself, does not meet the control test. Moreover, there is nothing in the record to indicate that Chester's salary was taken over by the league. In fact, it was never alleged below. We are now asked on appeal to infer this fact from the bankruptcy of the Wheels. We must decline this invitation.

As we previously noted, even were this true, the control test was not met. Furthermore, there is nothing in the record to indicate that the WFL had the right to control, hire or fire, or discipline Chester. Thus, there is nothing on the record to support the finding that Chester was an employee of the WFL. Accordingly, we reverse the summary judgment on plaintiffs' negligence theory.

Is the injured person an employee? Here, too, the courts are apt to be liberal in construing statutes to include those who might not seem to be employed. In *Betts* v. *Ann Arbor Public Schools,* 271 N.W.2d 498 (Mich. 1978), a University of Michigan student majoring in physical education was a student teacher in a junior high school. During a four-month period he taught two physical education courses. On the last day of his student teaching, he walked into the locker room and thirty of his students grabbed him and tossed him into the swimming pool. This was traditional, but he "didn't feel like going in that morning" and put up a struggle that ended with a whistle on an elastic band hitting him in the eye, which he subsequently lost as a result of the injury. He filed a workers' compensation claim. The school board argued that he could not be classified as an employee because he received no pay. Since he was injured by students—not considered agents of the school—he would probably have been unsuccessful in filing a tort suit; hence the workers' compensation claim was his only chance of recompense. The state workers' compensation appeal board ruled against the school on the ground that payment in money was not required. "Plaintiff was paid in the form of training, college credits towards graduation, and meeting of the prerequisites of a state provisional certificate." The state supreme court affirmed the award.

How palpable must the "injury" be? A difficult issue is whether a worker is entitled to compensation for psychological injury, including cumulative trauma. Until recently, insurance companies and compensation boards required physical injury before making an award. Claims that job stresses have led to nervous breakdowns or other mental disorders were rejected. But most courts have begun to liberalize the definition of injury and to recognize that psychological trauma can be real and that job stress can bring it on, as shown by the following case.

WOLFE v. SIBLEY, LINDSAY & CURR CO.
36 N.Y.2d 505, 369 N.Y.S.2d 637 (1975)

WACHTLER, JUDGE. This appeal involves a claim for workmen's compensation benefits for the period during which the claimant was incapacitated by severe depression caused by the discovery of her immediate supervisor's body after he had committed suicide.

The facts as adduced at a hearing before the Workmen's Compensation Board are uncontroverted. The claimant, Mrs. Diana Wolfe, began her employment with the respondent department store, Sibley, Lindsay & Curr Co. in February, 1968. After working for some time as an investigator in the security department of the store she became secretary to Mr. John Gorman, the security director. It appears from the record that as head of security, Mr. Gorman was subjected to intense pressure, especially during the Christmas holidays. Mrs. Wolfe testified that throughout the several years she worked at Sibley's Mr. Gorman reacted to this holiday pressure by becoming extremely agitated and nervous. She noted, however, that this anxiety usually disappeared when the holiday season was over. Unfortunately, Mr. Gorman's nervous condition failed to abate after the 1970 holidays.

The record indicates that Mr. Gorman remained agitated and "physically shakey" throughout the early part of 1971. According to Mrs. Wolfe, he was deeply concerned about his job performance and doubted his ability to measure up. These fears were exacerbated by the firing of a colleague in a neighboring department store. In reaction Mr. Gorman became more and more withdrawn and relied very heavily on Mrs. Wolfe who became his confidante on this subject and his "right hand" as to work matters. As he became more reclusive he began briefing her on details of the department functions so that she could handle more and varied situations. Mrs. Wolfe accepted this role and endeavored to ease his burden by assuming certain of his responsibilities and by trying to boost his morale.

Despite the fact that he followed Mrs. Wolfe's advice to see a doctor, Mr. Gorman's mental condition continued to deteriorate. On one occasion he left work at her suggestion because he appeared to be so nervous. This condition persisted until the morning of June 9, 1971 when according to the claimant, Mr. Gorman looked much better and even smiled and "tousled her hair" when she so remarked.

A short time later Mr. Gorman called her on the intercom and asked her to call the police to room 615. Mrs. Wolfe complied with this request and then tried unsuccessfully to reach Mr. Gorman on the intercom. She entered his office to find him lying in a pool of blood caused by a self-inflicted gunshot wound in the head. Mrs. Wolfe became extremely upset and was unable to continue working that day.

She returned to work for one week only to lock herself in her office to avoid the questions of her fellow workers. Her private physician perceiving that she was beset by feelings of guilt referred her to a psychiatrist and recommended that she leave work, which she did. While at home she ruminated about her guilt in failing to prevent the suicide and remained in bed for long periods of time staring at the ceiling. The result was that she became unresponsive to her husband and suffered a weight loss of 20 pounds. Her psychiatrist, Dr. Grinols diagnosed her condition as an acute depressive reaction.

After attempting to treat her in his office Dr. Grinols realized that the severity of her depression mandated hospitalization. Accordingly, the claimant was admitted to the hospital on July 9, 1971 where she remained for two months during which time she received psychotherapy and medication. After she was discharged, Dr. Grinols concluded that there had been no substantial remission in her depression and ruminative guilt and so had her readmitted for electroshock treatment. These treatments lasted for three weeks and were instrumental in her recovery. She was again discharged and, in mid-January, 1972, resumed her employment with Sibley, Lindsay, & Curr.

Mrs. Wolfe's claim for workmen's compensation was granted by the referee and affirmed by the Workmen's Compensation Board. On appeal the Appellate Division reversed citing its opinions in *Matter of Straws* v. *Fail* (17 A.D.2d 998, 233 N.Y.S.2d 893, mot for lv to app den 12 N.Y.2d 647, 238 N.Y.S.2d 1027, 188 N.E.2d 911); and *Matter of Chernin* v. *Progress Serv. Co.* (9 A.D.2d 170, 192 N.Y.S.2d 758, affd. 9 N.Y.2d 880, 216 N.Y.S.2d 697, 175 N.E.2d 827), for the proposition that mental injury precipitated solely by psychic trauma is not compensable as a matter of law. We do not agree with this conclusion.

Workmen's compensation, as distinguished from tort liability which is essentially based on fault, is designed to shift the risk of loss of earning capacity caused by industrial accidents from the worker to industry and ultimately the consumer. In light of its beneficial and remedial character the Workmen's Compensation Law should be construed liberally in favor of the employee (*Matter of Heitz* v. *Ruppert*, 218 N.Y. 148, 112 N.E. 750).

Liability under the act is predicated on accidental injury arising out of and in the course of employment (Workmen's Compensation Law, Consol.Laws, c. 69, § 2, subd. 7; § 10). Applying these concepts to the case at bar we note that there is no issue raised concerning the causal relationship between the occurrence and the injury. The only testimony on this matter was given by Dr. Grinols who stated unequivocally that the discovery of her superior's body was the competent producing cause of her condition. Nor is there any question as to the absence of physical impact. Accordingly, the focus of our inquiry is whether or not there has been an accidental injury within the meaning of the Workmen's Compensation Law.

Since there is no statutory definition of this term we turn to the relevant decisions. These may be divided into three categories: (1) psychic trauma which produces physical injury, (2) physical impact which produces psychological injury, and (3) psychic trauma which produces psychological injury. As to the first class our court has consistently recognized the principle that an injury caused by emotional stress or shock may be accidental within the purview of the compensation law. Cases falling into the second category have uniformly sustained awards to those incurring nervous or psychological disorders as a result of physical impact. As to those cases in the third category the decisions are not as clear.

* * *

We hold today that psychological or nervous injury precipitated by psychic trauma is compensable to the same extent as physical injury. This determination is based on two considerations. First, as noted in the psychiatric testimony there is nothing in the nature of a stress or shock situation which ordains physical as opposed to psychological injury. The determinative factor is the particular vulnerability of an individual by virtue of his physical makeup. In a given situation one person may be susceptible to a heart attack while another may suffer a depressive reaction. In either case the result is the same—the individual is incapable of functioning properly because of an accident and should be compensated under the Workmen's Compensation Law.

Secondly, having recognized the reliability of identifying psychic trauma as a causative factor of injury in some cases and the reliability by identifying psychological injury as a resultant factor in other cases, we see no reason for limiting recovery in the latter instance to cases involving physical impact. There is nothing talismanic about physical impact.

We would note in passing that this analysis reflects the view of the majority of jurisdictions in this country and England.

* * *

Accordingly, the order appealed from should be reversed and the award to the claimant reinstated, with costs.

Chapter Summary

An agent is one who acts on behalf of another. The law recognizes several types of agents, including (1) the general agent, one who possesses authority to carry out a broad range of transactions in the name and on behalf of the principal; (2) the special agent, one with authority to act only in a specifically designated instance or set of transactions; (3) the agent whose agency is coupled with an interest, one who has a property interest in addition to authority to act as an agent; (4) the subagent, one appointed by an agent with authority to do so; and (5) the servant, one whose physical conduct is subject to control of the principal.

A servant should be distinguished from an independent contractor, whose work is not subject to the control of the principal. The difference is important for purposes of taxation, workers' compensation, and liability insurance.

The agency relationship is usually created by contract, and sometimes governed by the Statute of Frauds, but some agencies are created by operation of law.

An agent owes his principal the highest duty of loyalty, that of a fiduciary. The agent must avoid self-dealing, preserve confidential information, perform with skill and care, conduct his personal life so as not to bring disrepute on the business for which he acts as agent, keep and render accounts, and give appropriate information to the principal.

Although the principal is not the agent's fiduciary, the principal does have certain obligations toward the agent—for example, to refrain from interfering with the agent's work and to indemnify. The employer's common law tort liability toward his employees has been replaced by the workers' compensation system, under which the employee gives up the right to sue for damages in return for prompt payment of medical and job-loss expenses. Injuries must have been work-related and the injured person must have been an employee. Courts today allow awards for psychological trauma in the absence of physical injury.

Problems

1. A woman was involved in an automobile accident which resulted in the death of a passenger in her car. After she was charged with manslaughter, her attorney agreed to work with the claims adjuster of her insurance company in handling the case. As a result of the agreement, the woman gave a statement about the accident to the claims adjuster. When the prosecuting attorney demanded to see the statement, the woman's attorney refused on the grounds that the claims adjuster was his agent. Is the attorney correct? Why?
2. A local hotel operated under a franchise agreement with a major hotel chain. Several customers charged the banquet director of the local hotel with misconduct and harassment. They sued the hotel chain (the franchisor) for acts committed by the local hotel (the franchisee), claiming that the franchisee was the agent of the franchisor. Is an agency created under these circumstances? Why?
3. A principal hired a mortgage banking firm to obtain a loan commitment of $10,000,000 from an insurance company for the construction of a shopping center. The firm was promised a fee of $50,000 for obtaining the commitment. The firm was successful in arranging for the loan, and the insurance company, without the principal's knowledge, agreed to pay the firm a finder's fee. The principal then refused to pay the firm the promised $50,000 and the firm brought suit to recover the fee. May the firm recover the fee? Why?
4. Based on his experience as a CIA agent, a former agent published a book about certain CIA activities in South Vietnam. The CIA did not approve publication of the book although, as a condition of his employment, the agent had agreed not to publish any information relating to the CIA without specific approval of the Agency. The government brought suit against the agent, claiming that all of the agent's profits from publishing the book should go to the government. Assuming that the government suffered only nominal damages because the agent published no classified information, will the government prevail? Why?
5. Upon graduation from college, Edison was hired by a major chemical company. During the time when he was employed by the company, Edison discovered a synthetic oil that could be manufactured at a very low cost. What rights, if any, does Edison's employer have to the discovery? Why?

6. An American company hired MacDonald to serve as its resident agent in Bolivia. MacDonald entered into a contract to sell cars to Bolivia and personally guaranteed performance of the contract as required by Bolivian law. The cars delivered to Bolivia were defective and Bolivia recovered a judgment of $83,000 from MacDonald. Must the American company reimburse MacDonald for this amount? Why?
7. According to the late Professor William L. Prosser, "The theory underlying the workmen's compensation acts never has been stated better than in the old campaign slogan, 'The cost of the product should bear the blood of the workman.' " What is meant by this statement?
8. An employee in a Rhode Island foundry inserted two coins in a coin-operated coffee machine in the company cafeteria. One coin stuck in the machine and the worker proceeded to "whack" the machine with his right arm. The arm struck a grate near the machine, rupturing the biceps muscle and causing a 10 percent loss in the use of the arm. Is the worker entitled to workers' compensation? Why?

14

Liability of Principal and Agent; Termination of Agency

In Chapter 13 we considered the relationship between agent and principal. Now we turn to relationships between third parties and the principal or agent. When the agent makes a contract for his principal or commits a tort in the course of his work, is the principal liable? What is the responsibility of the agent for torts committed and contracts entered into on behalf of his principal? How may the relationship be terminated, so that the principal or agent will no longer have responsibility toward or liability for the acts of the other? These are the questions addressed in this chapter.

Principal's Contract Liability

The key to determining whether a principal is liable for contracts made by his agent is **authority**: Was the agent authorized to negotiate the agreement and close the deal? Obviously, it would not be sensible to hold a contractor liable to pay for a ton of wood merely because a stranger wandered into the lumber yard claiming to represent the contractor. For there to be liability the principal must have authorized the agent in some manner to act in his behalf. There are three types of authority: *express, implied,* and *apparent*. We will consider each in turn.

Express Authority

The strongest form of authority is that which is expressly granted, often in written form. The principal consents to the agent's actions and the third party may then rely on the document attesting to the agent's authority to deal on behalf of the principal. One common form of express authority is the standard signature card on file with banks allowing corporate agents to write checks on the company's credit. The principal bears the risk of any wrongful action of his agent, as demonstrated in *Allen A. Funt Productions, Inc.* v. *Chemical Bank,* 405 N.Y.S.2d 94 (1978). Allen A. Funt submitted to his bank through his production company various certificates permitting his accountant to use the company's checking accounts. In fact, for several years the accountant embezzled money from the company by writing checks to himself and depositing them in his own account. The company sued its bank, charging it with negligence, apparently for failing to monitor the amount of money taken by the accountant. But the court dismissed the negligence complaint, citing a state statute based on the common law agency principle that a third party is entitled to rely on the express authorization given to an agent; in this case, the accountant drew checks on the account within the monetary limits contained in the signature cards on file with the bank.

Implied Authority

Not every detail on an agent's work can be spelled out. It is impossible to delineate step by step the duties of a general agent; at best, a principal can set forth only the general nature of the duties that the agent is to perform. Even a special agent's duties are difficult to describe in such detail as to leave him without discretion. If express authority were the only valid kind, there would be no efficient way to use an agent, both because the effort to describe the duties would be too great and because the third party would be reluctant to deal with him.

But the law permits authority to be "implied" by the relationship of the parties, by the nature and customs of the business, the circumstances surrounding the act in question, the wording of the agency contract, and the knowledge that the agent has of facts relevant to the assignment. The general rule is that the agent has implied or "incidental" authority to perform acts incidental to or reasonably necessary to carrying out the transaction. Thus, if a principal instructs his agent to "deposit a check in the bank today," the agent has authority to drive to the bank, unless the principal specifically prohibits the agent from doing so.

The theory of implied authority is especially important to business in the realm of the business manager, who may be charged with running the entire business operation or only a small part of it. In either event, the business manager has a relatively large domain of implied authority. He can buy goods and services; hire, supervise, and fire employees; sell or junk inventory; take in receipts and pay debts; and in general, direct the ordinary operations of the business. The full extent of the manager's authority depends on the circumstances—what is customary in the particular industry, the particular business, and among the individuals directly concerned.

On the other hand, a manager does not have implicit authority to undertake *unusual* or *extraordinary* actions on behalf of his principal. In the absence of express permission, an agent may not sell off part of the business, start a new business, change the nature of the business, incur debt (unless borrowing is integral to the business, as in banking, for example), or move the business premises. The owner of a hotel appoints Andy manager; Andy decides to rename the hotel and commissions an artist to prepare a new logo for the hotel's stationery. Andy has no implied authority to change the name or to commission the artist, though he does have implied authority to engage a printer to replenish the stationery supply—and possibly to make some design changes in the letterhead.

Even when there is no implied authority, in an emergency the agent may act in ways that would in the normal course require specific permission from the principal. If unforeseen circumstances arise and it is impracticable to communicate with the principal to find out what his wishes would be, the agent may do "what he reasonably believes to be necessary in order to prevent substantial loss to his principal." (*Restatement (Second) of Agency,* Section 47) During World War II, Eastern Wine Corporation marketed champagne in a bottle with a diagonal red stripe that infringed the trademark of a French producer. The French company had granted licenses to an American importer to market its champagne in the United States. The contract between producer and importer required the latter to notify the French company whenever a competitor appeared to be infringing its rights and to recommend steps by which the company could put a stop to the infringement. The authority to institute suit was not expressly conferred, and ordinarily the right to do so would not be inferred. Because France was under German occupation, however, the importer was unable to communicate with the producer, its principal. The court held that the importer could file suit to enjoin Eastern Wine from continuing to display the infringing red diagonal stripe, since legal action was "essential to the preservation of the principal's property." [G.H. Mumm Champagne v. Eastern Wine Corp., 52 F.Supp. 167 (S.D.N.Y. 1943)]

The rule that a person's position can carry with it implied authority is fundamental to American business practice. But outside the United States, this rule is not applicable, and the business executive traveling abroad should be aware that in civil-law countries, it is customary to present proof of authority to transact corporate business—usually in the form of a power of attorney. This is not always an easy task. Not only must the power of the traveling executive be shown, but the right of the corporate officer back in the United States to delegate authority must also be proven.

Apparent Authority

It is part and parcel of the agency relationship that through his actions in dealing with third parties the agent will affect the legal rights of the principal. What the third party knows about the agency agreement is irrelevant to the agent's legal authority to act. That authority runs from principal to agent. As long as an agent has authorization, either express or implied, he may bind the principal legally. Thus, the seller of a house may be ignorant of the buyer's true identity; the person he supposes to be the prospective purchaser actually might be the agent of an undisclosed principal. Nevertheless, if the agent is authorized to make the purchase, the seller's ignorance is not a ground for either seller or principal to void the deal.

But if a person has no authority to act as an agent, or an agent has no authority to act in a particular way, is the principal free from all consequences? The answer depends on whether or not the agent has "apparent authority"; that is, on whether or not the third person reasonably believes from the principal's words, written or spoken, or from his conduct, that he has in fact consented to the agent's actions. **Apparent authority** is a manifestation of authority communicated to the third person; it runs from principal to third party, not to the agent.

Apparent authority is sometimes said to be based on the principle of "estoppel." Estoppel is the doctrine that one should not profit from misrepresentation but should be bound by his assertions; the courts will not permit the deceitful party to deny what he has earlier said if someone else has relied to his detriment on the assertion.

Apparent authority can arise from prior business transactions. On July 10, Meggs sold his business, the right to use the trade name Rose City Sheet Metal Works, and a list of suppliers he had used. Three days later the buyer began ordering supplies from Central Supply Company, which was on Meggs's list but with which Meggs had last dealt four years previously. On September 3, Central received a letter from Meggs notifying it of the sale. The buyer failed to pay Central, which sued Meggs. The court held that Rose City Sheet Metal Works had apparent authority to buy on Meggs's credit; Meggs was liable for supplies purchased between July 10 and September 3. [Meggs v. Central Supply Co., 307 N.E.2d 288 (Ind.App. 1974)] In such cases, and in cases involving the firing of a general manager, actual notice should be given promptly to all customers. The following case illustrates other circumstances that may result in creation of apparent authority.

KANAVOS v. HANCOCK BANK & TRUST COMPANY
14 Mass. App. 326, 439 N.E.2d 311 (1982)

KASS, JUSTICE. At the close of the plaintiff's evidence, the defendant moved for a directed verdict, which the trial judge allowed. The judge's reason for so doing was that the plaintiff, in his contract action, failed to introduce sufficient evidence tending to prove that the bank officer who made the agreement with which the plaintiff sought to charge the bank had any authority to make it. Upon review of the record we are of opinion that there was evidence which, if believed, warranted a finding that the bank officer had the requisite authority or that the bank officer had apparent authority to make the agreement in controversy. We, therefore, reverse the judgment.

* * *

For approximately ten years prior to 1975, Harold Kanavos and his brother borrowed money on at least twenty occasions from the Hancock Bank & Trust Company (the Bank), and, during that period, the loan officer with whom Kanavos always dealt was James M. Brown. The aggregate loans made by the Bank to Kanavos at any given time went as high as $800,000.

Over that same decade, Brown's responsibilities at the Bank grew, and he had become executive vice-president. Brown was also the chief loan officer for the Bank, which had fourteen or fifteen branches in addition to its head office. Physically, Brown's office was at the head office, toward the rear of the main banking floor, opposite the office of the president—whose name was Kelley. Often Brown would tell Kanavos that he had to check an aspect of a loan transaction with Kelley, but Kelley always backed Brown up on those occasions.

* * *

[The plaintiff, Harold Kanavos, entered into an agreement with the defendant Bank whereby stock owned by the Kavanos brothers was sold to the Bank and the plaintiff was given an option to repurchase the stock. Kanavos' suit against the Bank was based on an amendment to the agreement offered by Brown.]

Kanavos was never permitted to introduce in evidence the terms of the offer Brown made. That offer was contained in a writing, dated July 16, 1976, on bank letterhead, which read as follows: "This letter is to confirm our conversation regarding your option to re-purchase the subject property. In lieu of your not exercising your option, we agree to pay you $40,000 representing a commission upon our sale of the subject property, and in addition, will give you the option to match the price of sale of said property to extend for a 60 day period from the time our offer is received." Brown signed the letter as executive vice-president. The basis of exclusion was that the plaintiff had not established the authority of Brown to make with Kanavos the arrangement memorialized in the July 16, 1976, letter.

* * *

Whether Brown's job description impliedly authorized the right of last refusal or cash payment modification is a question of how, in the circumstances, a person in Brown's position could reasonably interpret his authority. Whether Brown had *apparent authority* to make the July 16, 1976, modification is a question of how, in the circumstances, a third person, e.g., a customer of the Bank such as Kanavos, would reasonably interpret Brown's authority in light of the manifestations of his principal, the Bank.

Titles of office generally do not establish apparent authority. Brown's status as executive vice-president was not, therefore, a badge of apparent authority to modify agreements to which the Bank was a party.

Trappings of office, e.g., office and furnishing, private secretary, while they may have some tendency to suggest executive responsibility, do not without other evidence provide a basis for finding apparent authority. Apparent authority is drawn from a variety of circumstances. Thus in *Federal Natl. Bank* v. *O'Connell*, 305 Mass. 559, 562, 565–567, 26 N.E.2d 539 (1940), it was held apparent authority could be found because an officer who was a director, vice-president and treasurer took an active part in directing the affairs of the bank in question and was seen by third parties talking with customers and negotiating with them. In *Costonis* v.

Medford Housing Authy., 343 Mass. 108, 114–115, 176 N.E.2d 25 (1961) (but with Whittemore, Spalding and Cutter, JJ., dissenting), the executive director of a public housing authority was held to have apparent authority to vary specifications on the basis of the cumulative effect of what he had done and what the authority appeared to permit him to do.

In the instant case there was evidence of the following variety of circumstances: Brown's title of *executive* vice-president; the location of his office opposite the president; his frequent communications with the president; the long course of dealing and negotiations; the encouragement of Kanavos by the president to deal with Brown; the earlier amendment of the agreement by Brown on behalf of the Bank on material points, namely the price to be paid by the Bank for the shares and the repurchase price; the size of the Bank (fourteen or fifteen branches in addition to the main office); the secondary, rather than fundamental, nature of the change in the terms of the agreement now repudiated by the Bank, measured against the context of the overall transaction; and Brown's broad operating authority . . . all these added together would support a finding of apparent authority. When a corporate officer, as here, is allowed to exercise general executive responsibilities, the "public expectation is that the corporation should be bound to engagements made on its behalf by those who presume to have, and convincingly appear to have, the power to agree." Kempin, The Corporate Officer and the Law of Agency, 44 Va.L.Rev. 1273, 1280 (1958). This principle does not apply, of course, where in the business context, the requirement of specific authority is presumed, e.g., the sale of a major asset by a corporation or a transaction which by its nature commits the corporation to an obligation outside the scope of its usual activity. The modification agreement signed by Brown and dated July 16, 1976, should have been admitted in evidence, and a verdict should not have been directed.

Judgment reversed.

Ratification

Even if the agent possessed no actual authority, and there was no apparent authority on which the third person could rely, the principal may still be liable if he **ratifies** or adopts the agent's acts before the third person withdraws from the contract. Ratification usually relates back to the time of the undertaking, creating authority after the fact as though it had been established initially. Ratification is a voluntary act by the principal. Faced with the results of action purportedly done on his behalf but without authorization and through no fault of his own, he may affirm or disavow them as he chooses. To ratify, the principal may tell the parties concerned or by his conduct manifest that he is willing to accept the results as though the act were authorized. Or by his silence he may find under certain circumstances that he has ratified. Note that ratification does not require the usual consideration of contract law. The principal need be promised nothing extra for his decision to affirm to be binding on him. Nor does ratification depend on the position of the third party; for example, a loss stemming from his reliance on the "agent's" representations is not required.

In most situations, ratification leaves the parties where they expected to be, correcting "minor errors of agents without harm to any one," and giving "to the other party what he expected to get and to the principal what he was willing to receive" (Seavey, 1964, p. 58).

Principal's Tort Liability

When is the principal liable for injuries that the agent causes another to suffer? Here we may make a distinction between torts prompted by the principal himself and torts of which the principal was innocent. If the principal directed the agent to commit a tort or knew that the consequences of the agent's carrying out his instructions would bring harm to someone, the principal is liable. This is an application of the general common-law principle that one cannot escape liability by delegating an unlawful act to another. The syndicate that hires a contract-killer is as culpable of murder as the man who pulls the trigger. Similarly, a principal who is negligent in his use of agents will be held liable for their negligence. This rule comes into play when the principal fails to supervise employees adequately, gives faulty directions, or hires incompetent or unsuitable people for a particular job.

Imposing liability on the principal in these cases is readily justifiable since it is the principal's own conduct that is the underlying fault. But the principle of liability for one's agent is much broader, extending as it does to acts of which the principal had no knowledge, which he had no intention to commit nor involvement in, and which he may in fact have expressly prohibited the agent from engaging in. This is the principle of **respondeat superior** ("let the master answer") or **"vicarious liability,"** under which the principal is responsible for acts committed by the agent within the scope of the employment.

The modern basis for vicarious liability is sometimes termed the "deep pocket" theory: the principal (usually a corporation) has deeper pockets than the agent, meaning that it has the wherewithal to pay for the injuries traceable one way or another to events it set in motion. A million-dollar industrial accident is within the means of a company or its insurer; it is usually not within the means of the agent who caused it.

The "deep pocket" of the defendant-company is not always very deep, however. For many small businesses, in fact, the principle of *respondeat superior* is one of life or death. One example was the closing in San Francisco of the Larraburu Brothers Bakery—at the time, the world's second largest sourdough bread maker. The bakery was held liable for $2 million in damages after one of its delivery trucks injured a 6-year-old boy. The bakery's insurance policy had a limit of $1.25 million, and the bakery could not absorb the excess. The Larraburus had no choice but to cease operations.

Respondeat superior raises three difficult questions. (1) What type of agents can create tort liability for the principal? (2) Is the principal liable for the agent's intentional torts? (3) Was the agent acting within the scope of his employment? We will consider these questions in turn.

Agents for Whom Principals Are Vicariously Liable

In general, the broadest liability is imposed on the *master* in the case of tortious physical conduct by a *servant* (Chapter 13). If the servant acted within the scope of his employment—that is, if the servant's wrongful conduct occurred while performing his job—the master will be liable to the victim for damages, unless, as we have seen, the victim was another employee, in which event the workers' compensation system will be invoked. Physical injuries caused by non-servant agents are not generally chargeable to the principal. The distinction stems from the original difference between servant and agent: the servant was defined as one who did physical labor for a principal; those who were not subject to a master's control over their daily labor were non-servant agents. Because the master had an obligation to supervise those in his employ, liability was imposed when the supervision failed to prevent accidents—as, for example, when a salaried deliveryman drives too fast or runs a red light.

However, the principal is liable for nonphysical torts caused by agents other than servants—for example, a seller's agent who misrepresents the condition of goods can subject the seller to liability for damages. Whether or not the case involves physical injury, the legal analysis begins by determining whether the person who committed the tort is an agent, as the following case illustrates.

HANSON v. KYNAST
24 Ohio St. 3d 171 (1986)

On May 1, 1982, appellee, Brian K. Hanson, sustained a paralyzing injury while playing in a lacrosse game between Ohio State University ("OSU") and Ashland University, Inc. ("Ashland") at the Ashland lacrosse field. During the game Roger Allen, an OSU player, intercepted an Ashland player's pass and scored a goal. As Allen was scoring the goal, he was body-checked from behind by Ashland defender William D. Kynast. Allen fell and Kynast allegedly stood over Allen taunting him. Brian Hanson saw the contact and Kynast's subsequent behavior. Concerned for Allen's welfare, Hanson grabbed Kynast from the side or back and held him in a bear hug. Kynast immediately twisted and threw Hanson off his back. Hanson's head struck the ground and he sustained serious injuries.

The trainers for both teams came onto the field to attend Hanson. After discovering the seriousness of his injury (Hanson was numb and could not move), an assistant trainer for Ashland was sent to telephone the fire department for an ambulance.

Upon arriving on the scene, the ambulance driver discovered that the main entrance to the playing field was blocked by an illegally parked automobile. As a result, the ambulance driver had to find another entrance.

After immobilizing Hanson, the attendants transported him to Ashland Samaritan Hospital where he remained for almost an hour. He was then transferred to Mansfield General Hospital for surgery. The operation took place at approximately 11:00 p.m., more than five hours after he was taken from the first hospital. The surgery successfully relieved vascular compression thus preventing possible brain damage. Hanson, however, had sustained a serious spinal cord injury on impact. It was determined that he had suffered a compression fracture of his sixth vertebra and, as a result, Hanson is now an incomplete quadriplegic.

On December 13, 1983, Brian Hanson filed an amended complaint in the Court of Common Pleas of Ashland County against William Kynast and Ashland University, Inc. Hanson maintained, in relevant part, that because Kynast was acting as the agent of Ashland, the university was therefore liable for Kynast's alleged wrongful acts under the doctrine of *respondeat superior*. Hanson also alleged that Ashland was directly liable for negligently failing to have an ambulance or emergency vehicle present at the site of the game, and in permitting a motor vehicle to be parked in such a manner that the main entrance to the playing field was blocked. Ashland filed a timely answer denying the material allegations of the complaint.

On April 11, 1984, Ashland filed a motion for summary judgment. After obtaining a ninety-day continuance to complete discovery, Hanson filed a brief in opposition to Ashland's motion for summary judgment. Ashland attached documentary evidence to support its position. The trial court granted Ashland's motion on November 16, 1984. The court held that no agency relationship existed between Kynast and Ashland, and that Ashland did not have a legal duty to have an ambulance at the game. In a split decision, the court of appeals reversed the trial court's judgment, holding that genuine issues of fact existed on the question of agency and upon Ashland's duty to provide medical personnel at the game.

* * *

The first issue to be decided is whether the relationship of principal and agent existed between Kynast and Ashland. Because of the absence of proof as to the existence of a principal-agent relationship, the trial court essentially found as a matter of law that Ashland was not bound by Kynast's conduct under the doctrine of *respondeat superior*. We agree.

This court has held that the relationship of principal and agent or master and servant exists only when one party exercises the right of control over the actions of another, and those actions are directed toward the attainment of an objective which the former seeks. Therefore, a principal-agent relationship can be found in the instant case only if Kynast was under the control of Ashland, and if he took some action directed toward the attainment of Ashland's objective.

* * *

This court is of the opinion that this relationship between Kynast and Ashland is a relationship common to many students attending universities. A university offers a diversified educational experience which includes classroom instruction in a great variety of subjects as well as optional participation in events such as school clubs, and intramural and intercollegiate sports. All of these offerings are designed to expand and enrich a student's overall educational experience. Students evaluate and determine which university best meets their needs, and then pay a fee to attend that university. The relationship formed under these conditions has previously been characterized as contractual. The student pays a fee and agrees to abide by the university rules. In exchange, the university provides the student with a worthwhile education.

This relationship does not constitute a principal-agent relationship. The student is a buyer of education rather than an agent.

The appellee, however, maintains that Kynast's participation in lacrosse converted his status from the usual university-student relationship to that of principal-agent due to the control exercised by the lacrosse coach over Kynast, and because his participation in lacrosse resulted in beneficial publicity for Ashland. We disagree. In applying the law of agency to the facts of this case, we must conclude that Kynast was not controlled by Ashland, and that he was not playing the game for the school's benefit.

The degree of control necessary to establish agency has not been clearly defined. Instead, courts have generally examined various factors in determining whether the requisite amount of control exists. One such factor is whether the individual is performing in the course of the principal's business rather than in some ancillary capacity. In the case at bar, Kynast was not performing in the course of the principal's business, *i.e.*, he was not educating students. On the contrary, he was participating in one of the educationally related opportunities offered by the university. Another factor to be considered is whether the individual was receiving any compensation from the principal. It is undisputed that Kynast was never compensated for playing on the Ashland lacrosse team. A third factor is whether the principal supplied the tools and the place of work in the normal course of the relationship. Kynast supplied his own equipment in order to play lacrosse. The university did, however, provide the playing field.

*   *   *

To summarize, we conclude that a student who attends a university of his choice, receives no scholarship or compensation, voluntarily becomes a member of the university lacrosse team that engages in intercollegiate contests with other universities for which games no attendance fee is charged, who purchases his own equipment and who receives instructions from a coach while preparing for and playing such games, but is not otherwise controlled by the coach, and who participates in the game as a part of his total educational experience while attending school, is not the agent of the university at the time he is playing the game of lacrosse. Thus, appellee's claim that Ashland was liable for Kynast's wrongful acts through the doctrine of *respondeat superior* was properly rejected and the trial court properly entered summary judgment for appellant on this issue.

The second and final issue to be resolved is whether the trial court properly entered summary judgment for Ashland upon Hanson's claims that Ashland was negligent for failing to have an ambulance and medical personnel at the game, and for permitting an illegally parked car to block the playing field's entrance. The appellee maintains that such negligence resulted in the delay of his treatment.

In order to successfully establish negligence, the appellee must prove the existence of the following elements: (1) a duty owed by Ashland to Hanson, (2) a breach of this duty by Ashland, and (3) that Hanson's injuries were a proximate result of Ashland's conduct. It is unnecessary at this time to consider whether genuine issues of fact existed as to the first two elements of negligence for the reason that the uncontradicted evidence submitted by Ashland established that no damages proximately resulted from Ashland's alleged wrongdoing.

*   *   *

Accordingly, the judgment of the court of appeals is reversed.

Ordinarily, an individual or company is not vicariously liable for the tortious acts of independent contractors. The plumber who rushes to a home to repair a leak and causes a traffic accident does not subject the homeowner to liability. But there are exceptions to the rule. Generally, these exceptions fall into a category of duties that the law deems nondelegable. In some situations, one person is obligated to provide protection to or care for another. The failure to do so results in liability whether or not the harm befell the other because of an independent contractor's wrongdoing. Thus, a homeowner has a duty to ensure that physical conditions in and around the home are not unreasonably dangerous. If the owner hires an independent contracting firm to dig a sewer line and the contractor negligently fails to guard passersby against the danger of falling into an open trench, the homeowner is liable, because the duty of care in this instance cannot be delegated. (The contractor is, of course, liable to the homeowner for any damages paid to an injured passerby.)

Liability for Agents' Intentional Torts

In the nineteenth century, a principal was rarely held liable for intentional wrongdoing by the agent if the principal did not command the act complained of. The thought was that one could never infer authority to commit a willfully wrongful act. Today, liability for intentional torts is imputed to the principal whenever the agent is acting to further the principal's business. The following case illustrates, in the words of the court, the "outer bounds" of liability.

LYON v. CAREY
593 F.2d 649 (D.C. Cir. 1976)

McMillan, District Judge. Corene Antoinette Lyon, plaintiff, recovered a $33,000.00 verdict in the United States District Court for the District of Columbia before Judge Barrington T. Parker and a jury, against the corporate defendants, George's Radio and Television Company, Inc., and Pep Line Trucking Company, Inc. The suit, for damages, arose out of an assault, including rape, committed with a knife and other weapons upon the plaintiff on May 9, 1972, by Michael Carey, a nineteen-year-old deliveryman for Pep Line Trucking Company, Inc. Three months after the trial, Judge Parker set aside the verdict and rendered judgment for both defendants notwithstanding the verdict. Plaintiff appealed.

As to the defendant Pep Line Trucking Company, Inc., we reverse the district court's judgment and reinstate the verdict. Although the assault was perhaps at the outer bounds of *respondeat superior,* the case was properly one for the jury. It is within the enterprise liability of vendors like furniture stores and those who deliver for them that deliverymen, endeavoring to serve their masters, are likely to be in situations of friction with customers, and that when they secure entry into a customer's premises by means of a badge of employment, these foreseeable altercations may precipitate violence for which recovery may be had, even though the particular type of violence was not in itself anticipated or foreseeable. Whether the assault in this case was the outgrowth of a job-related controversy or simply a personal adventure of the deliveryman, was a question for the jury. This was the import of the trial judge's instructions. The verdict as to Pep Line should not have been disturbed.

Plaintiff was twenty-five years old, an employee of the D. C. Metropolitan Police Department. She is a twin sister of Irene Yvette Lyon, whose home was in an apartment at 5218 Fifth Street, S. E., in the District of Columbia. Irene Yvette Lyon had bought a mattress and springs for her bed from the defendant George's Radio and Television Company, Inc. The merchandise was to be delivered on May 9, 1972. Irene Lyon had to be at work and the plaintiff, Corene Lyon, had agreed to wait in her sister's apartment to receive the delivery.

A C.O.D. balance of $13.24 was due on the merchandise, and Irene Lyon had left a check for $13.24 to cover that balance. Plaintiff had been requested by her sister to "wait until the mattress and the springs came and to check and make sure they were okay."

Plaintiff, fully clothed, answered the door. Her description of what happened is sufficiently brief and unqualified that it will bear repeating in full. She testified, without objection, as follows:

> "A. I went to the door, and I looked in the peephole, and I asked who was there.
>
> The young man told me he was a delivery man from George's. He showed me a receipt, and it said, 'George's.' He said he couldn't take a COD, so I let him in, and I told him to bring the mattress upstairs and he said, 'No,' that he wasn't going to lug them upstairs, and he wanted the COD first, and I told him I wanted to see the mattress and boxsprings to

make sure they were okay and he said no, he wasn't going to lug them upstairs.

So this went back and forwards and so he was getting angry, and I told him to wait right here while I go get the COD.

* * *

"Q. Then what happened?

"A. And then he raped me."

Plaintiff's pre-trial deposition was a part of the record on appeal, and it shows that Carey raped plaintiff at knife point; that then he chased her all over the apartment with a knife and scissors and cut plaintiff in numerous places on her face and body, beat and otherwise attacked her. All of the physical injury other than the rape occurred after rather than before the rape had been accomplished.

Carey was tried for rape, pleaded guilty, and was sentenced to an active term in prison. Although he was named as a defendant, no one bothered to procure service of process upon him. Because Carey is not even a party, no question is presented on this appeal as to his liability.

Carey was an employee of the defendant Pep Line Trucking Company, Inc. Pep Line had an independent contract arrangement to make deliveries for George's Radio and Television Company, Inc. Carey was not an employee of George's. Carey was on the Lyon apartment premises for the purpose of delivering the mattress and springs which plaintiff's sister had bought from George's. Carey had the delivery receipt, and obtained entrance into the apartment upon the basis that he was making the delivery for George's. Plaintiff did not release the door chain until Carey displayed the George's delivery receipt.

As to the defendant Pep Line Trucking Company, Inc., the evidence will not support a finding that Pep Line knew or should have known that Carey had any proclivity or history more pronounced than that of any other nineteen-year-old boy for assaults, sexual or otherwise which would make Pep Line liable because of knowledge of a dangerous propensity.

The principal question, therefore, is whether the evidence discloses any other basis upon which a jury could reasonably find Pep Line, the employer of Carey, liable for the assault.

* * *

If, as in *Grimes v. Saul,* the assault was not motivated or triggered off by anything in the employment activity but was the result of only propinquity and lust, there should be no liability.

However, if the assault, sexual or otherwise, was triggered off or motivated or occasioned by a dispute over the conduct—then and there—of the employer's business, then the employer should be liable.

It is, then, a question of fact for the trier of fact, rather than a question of law for the court, whether the assault stemmed from purely and solely personal sources or arose out of the conduct of the employer's business; and the trial judge so instructed the jury.

It follows that, under existing decisions of the District of Columbia Circuit, plaintiff has made out a case for the jury against Pep Line Trucking, Inc.

* * *

As to the defendant George's, although the theory of independent contract as a defense is not totally consistent with the principles of liability which we follow here, we are not persuaded on these facts, including Pep Line's agreement to indemnify George's, that the trial judge erred in setting aside the verdict.

The judgment is affirmed as to the defendant George's and reversed as to the defendant Pep Line Trucking Company, Inc.

Deviations from Employment

It may be clear that the person causing an injury is the agent of another. But a principal cannot be responsible for every act of an agent. If an employee is following the letter of his instructions, it will be easy to determine liability. But suppose an agent deviates in some way from his job. The classic test of liability was set forth in an 1833 English case, *Joel* v. *Morison,* 6 Carrington & Payne 501. The plaintiff was run over on a highway by a speeding cart and horse. The driver was the employee of another, and inside was a fellow employee. There was no question that the driver had acted carelessly, but what they were doing on the road where the plaintiff was injured was disputed. For weeks before and after the accident, the cart had never been driven in the vicinity in which the plaintiff was walking, nor did it have any business there. The suggestion was that the employees might have gone out of their way for their own purposes. As the great English jurist, Baron Parke, put it in a famous statement: "If the servants, being on their master's business, took a detour to call upon a friend, the master will be responsible. . . . [B]ut if he was going on a frolic of his own, without being at all on his master's business, the master will not be liable." In applying this test, the court held the employer liable.

The test is thus one of degree, and it is not always easy to decide when a detour has become so great as to be transformed into a frolic. For a time, a rather mechanical rule was invoked to aid in making the decision. The courts looked to the servant's purposes in "detouring." If the servant's mind was fixed on accomplishing his own purposes, then the detour was held to be outside the scope of employment; hence the tort was not imputed to the master. But if the servant also intended to accomplish his master's purposes during his departure from the letter of his assignment, or if he committed the wrong while returning to his master's task after the completion of his frolic, then the tort was held to be within the scope of employment.

This test is not always easy to apply. If a hungry delivery man stops in at a restaurant outside the normal lunch hour, intending to continue to his next delivery after eating, he is within the scope of employment. But suppose he decides to take the truck home that evening, in violation of rules, in order to get an early start the next morning. Suppose he decides to stop by the beach, which is far away from his route. Does it make a difference if the employer knows that his truckers do this?

More recent court decisions have moved toward a different standard, one that looks to the foreseeability of the agent's conduct. By this standard, an employer may be held liable for his employee's conduct even when devoted entirely to the employee's own purposes, as long as it was foreseeable that the agent might act as he did. This is the "**zone of risk**," the place within which, if the master were to send out a search party to find a missing employee, it would be reasonable to look. The next case illustrates this standard.

O'BOYLE v. AVIS RENT-A-CAR SYSTEM, INC.
78 A.D.2d 431, 435 N.Y.S. 2d 296 (1981)

LAZER, JUSTICE. The tragic vehicular accident underlying this action occurred when a 16-year-old employee at a gasoline station from which an Avis car rental agency was being operated drove in a rental car to pick up lunch, tarried briefly with his girlfriend passenger, and during the return collided with another automobile, killing two of its occupants and seriously injuring two others. In their ensuing action, the victims or their representatives alleged, *inter alia,* that the collision was caused not only by the conduct of the employee, Robert Bruno, but also by the direct and vicarious negligence of the defendant G. Roland House, who owned the gas station and car rental agency, and the defendant Avis Rent-A-Car System, Inc., the owner of the car. At the conclusion of a trial on the issue of liability, the jury rendered a two-fold verdict [against the defendants].

* * *

On March 17, 1974 Sunday sales of gasoline were still banned due to the Arab oil embargo and the House station was open solely for the purpose of renting Avis cars. House arrived at 10:00 A.M., stayed for about an hour, and left Bruno alone and in charge for the balance of the day. At about 1:30 P.M., Greg Adams, another young House employee, appeared at the station to work on his own car and agreed to "watch the station" while Bruno and his girlfriend went to pick up a pizza which would provide lunch for Adams and Bruno. Although Adams was under the impression that Bruno was going to walk up the street to get the pizza, he saw the latter take a key off a rack and drive away in an Avis car.

After the pizza was purchased at Leonardi's, an establishment variously estimated as being one-eighth of a mile to two or three miles from the station, Bruno drove to a nursery in Armonk where he and his girlfriend "talked for about twenty minutes." When they left the nursery, it was Bruno's intention to drive the girl home and return to work, but about a mile from her house and a mile from the House station the car went out of control, entered the opposing lane of traffic, and crashed head-on with a car driven by Adele O'Boyle. Mrs. O'Boyle and her infant daughter perished while her husband and mother suffered serious injuries.

At the trial, conflicting evidence was adduced as to who was authorized to operate Avis vehicles and where and for what purpose they could be driven. House testified that he instructed Bruno "not to take an Avis car off the property under any conditions" but that he could drive Avis cars on the service station property. Although House said that this instruction was given to all employees, when asked whether he had ever authorized any licensed employee to take Avis cars off the premises, he replied that he had done so in certain emergency situations such as jump-starting a car or digging a customer out of a snow bank. House maintained that such occurrences were relatively rare and he usually would accompany his employee in rendering aid to the customer, after which the employee would drive the disabled car back to the station.

This testimony was supported by the deposition of Greg Adams, who was 14 years old and unlicensed when hired by House in 1972. Adams declared that his duties then were to "pump gas [and] rent Avis cars," that he had authority from House to drive Avis cars to and from gas pumps on the premises, and that this was observed on a number of occasions by Avis representatives. Adams asserted that on his first day on the job House advised him that there was to be "[n]o driving the Avis cars off the property" and that the direction was repeated to him at least once a week for a period of two years. Because Adams had recommended Bruno for the job, he was present during the latter's job interview and heard House say that Avis cars were not to be driven off the premises. Adams recalled only one occasion during his 22 months of employment preceding the accident when an Avis car was taken off the premises by a House employee in order to make a service call.

Countervailing evidence was offered by another part-time House employee, Perry Palazzetti, who testified at the trial. Palazzetti was 16 years old and unlicensed when hired in July, 1973, although he obtained a license shortly afterwards. In February, 1974, after closing the station, he drove an Avis car off the premises, and was apprehended in Connecticut for speeding. Palazzetti remembered some 10 to 15 instances when House had instructed him to drive Avis cars on service calls "for both purposes, Mr. House's purposes and Avis purposes" and about 10 other occasions when House directed a particular licensed employee to take an Avis car out for a service call. He was not asked, however, whether House had ever admonished him or anyone else never to take an Avis car off the premises.

Bruno's testimony, taken by deposition, tended to contradict House and Adams. Responding to a question as to whether House had ever told him not to drive an Avis car on a public highway, Bruno said that "he probably told me on the first day, but not after that." A few answers later, however, he asserted that House "never made any mention of my not taking any cars off the premises." Avis and House subsequently attacked Bruno's credibility by offering his admission that some three years after the accident he had told his psychiatrist that he did not have permission to take the car.

* * *

We have deferred for last, consideration of the most troublesome issue in the case—whether Bruno's negligent act fell within the scope of his employment. Foreseeability is the State's current criterion for measuring an employer's liability for conduct of employees whose behavior is alleged to have taken them beyond the scope of their employment. In a *respondeat superior* context, foreseeability differs significantly from the " 'foreseeably unreasonable risk of harm that spells negligence' " (*Bushey & Sons v. United States,* 398 F.2d 167, 171) (2 Cir.). It is a foresight which must impel the prudent man to " 'perceive the harm likely to flow from his long-run activity in spite of all reasonable precautions on his own part.' "

* * *

Plainly, then, the focus of our own inquiry must be upon the foreseeability of Bruno's conduct in taking a car to get his lunch. The jury knew that House was aware of Bruno's ability to drive and it was within the jury's discretion to believe testimony that Avis cars often had been utilized in the course of the service station business. An employer takes men and women "subject to the kind of conduct normal to such beings" (*Riviello v. Waldron,* 418 N.Y.S.2d 300, 391 N.E.2d 1278) and, obviously, young persons subject to the kind of conduct normal to them. Whether it was foreseeable over the long run of House's operation that in the course of activities in furtherance of his employer's interest an employee—even a young one—would take an Avis car to obtain lunch was a matter for the jury to decide. Considering the evidence and the inferences drawable from it, the jury's imposition of vicarious liability upon House cannot be deemed a defiance of rationality or contrary to the weight of the evidence.

* * *

Accordingly, there must be an affirmance.

Special Cases of Vicarious Liability

Vicarious liability is not limited to harm caused in the course of an agency relationship. It may also be imposed in other areas, including torts of family members, and other torts governed by statute or regulation. We will examine each in turn.

Use of Automobiles A problem commonly arises when an automobile owner lends his vehicle to a personal friend, someone who is not an agent, and the borrower injures a third person. Is the owner liable? In many states, the owner is not liable; in other states, however, two approaches impose liability on the owner.

The first approach is legislative: "owner's consent statutes" make the owner liable when the automobile is being driven with his consent or knowledge. The second approach to placing liability on the owner is judge-made and known as the "family purpose doctrine." Under this doctrine, a family member who negligently injures someone with the car subjects the owner to liability if the family member was furthering family purposes. These are loosely defined to include virtually every use to which a child, for example, might put a car. In a Georgia case, *Dixon* v. *Phillips* 217 S.E.2d

331 (Ga. 1975), the father allowed his minor son to drive the car, but expressly forbade him from letting anyone else do so. Nevertheless, the son gave the wheel to a friend and a collision occurred while both were in the car. The court held the father liable because he made the car available for the pleasure and convenience of his son and other family members.

Torts of Family Members At common law, the husband was liable for the torts of his wife, not because she was considered an agent but because she was considered to be an extension of him. "Husband and wife were only one person in law," says Holmes and any act of the wife was supposed to have been done at the husband's direction (to which Dickens's Mr. Bumble responded, in the memorable line, "if the law supposes that, the law is a ass—a idiot"). This ancient view has been abrogated by statute or by court ruling in all the states, so that now a wife is solely responsible for her own torts unless she in fact serves as her husband's agent.

Unlike wives, children were not presumed at common law to be agents or extensions of the father so that normally parents are not vicariously liable for their children's torts. However, as discussed in the following case, they can be held liable for failing to control children known to be dangerous.

GISSEN v. GOODWILL
80 So.2d 701 (Fla. 1955)

KANNER, ASSOCIATE JUSTICE. The trial court entered judgment against the appellant, Julius Gissen, for his failure to state a cause of actionable negligence against the appellee parents, Albert Goodwill and Mrs. Albert Goodwill, for injury inflicted by their minor child, Geraldine Goodwill, upon the appellant. The appeal is from this judgment.

This Court had dismissed the minor child as a party to this appeal for lack of jurisdiction.

It is averred in the second amended complaint that at the time of the appellant's injury, he was employed as a clerk at the Gaylord Hotel in the City of Miami Beach, Florida, and the appellees were residing as business invitees at the same hotel; that the minor child, Geraldine Goodwill, 8 years of age, "did wilfully, deliberately, intentionally and maliciously" swing a door "with such great force and violence against the plaintiff so that the middle finger on plaintiff's left hand was caught in the door and a portion of said finger was caused to be instantaneously severed and fell to the floor." It is further averred that

> owing to a lack of parental discipline and neglect in the exercise of needful paternal influence and authority, the defendants, Albert Goodwill and Mrs. Albert Goodwill carelessly and negligently failed to restrain the child, Geraldine Goodwill, whom they knew to have dangerous tendencies and propensities of a mischievous and wanton disposition. . . .

This is a case of first incidence in this Court's jurisdiction, posing as it does the problem of whether the specific set of circumstances here can render the parents of the minor child accountable at law for the tort alleged to have been committed by the child.

It is basic and established law that a parent is not liable for the tort of his minor child because of the mere fact of his paternity. However, there are certain broadly defined exceptions wherein a parent may incur liability: 1. Where he intrusts his child with an instrumentality which, because of the lack of age, judgment, or experience of the child, may become a source of danger to others. 2. Where a child, in the commission of a tortious act, is occupying the relationship of a servant or agent of its parents. 3. Where the parent knows of his child's wrongdoing and consents to it, directs or sanctions it. 4. Where he fails to exercise parental control over his minor child, although he knows or in the exercise of due care should have known that injury to another is a probable consequence.

Analyzing this problem in the light of the exceptions for parent liability enumerated, one may note that the exceptions relating to instrumentality intrusted to a child, to master and servant or agent relationship, and to parental consent or sanction of a tortious act by the child do not bear upon the circumstances here involved. It is only the fourth category which may be logically analyzed for the purpose of determining whether legal culpability might be attached to the parents of the child here concerned, and it is on this exception to the general rule that the appellant relies.

It is the position of the appellees that the appellant has not succeeded in alleging sufficiently that the appellee parents failed in the duty imposed upon them to exercise parental discipline and control over their 8 year old daughter with relation to a specific act which she was in the habit of doing and which caused the injury complained of; and that the failure so to do is fatal and thereby actionable negligence is not charged.

In the Restatement of the Law, sec. 316, pp. 858, 859, on the subject of Torts, dealing with the duty of the parent to control the conduct of his child, it is said, "A parent is under a duty to exercise reasonable care so to control his minor child as to prevent it from intentionally harming others or from so conducting itself as to create an unreasonable risk of bodily harm to them, if the parent

"(a) knows or has reason to know that he has the ability to control his child, and

"(b) knows or should know of the necessity and opportunity for exercising such control."

An analysis of cases related to or bearing upon the type of case that we have here is necessary in order to determine whether the second amended complaint states a cause of action or whether it is deficient for the reason urged by the appellees.

* * *

One common factor from the . . . cases appears salient in the assessment of liability to the parents, that the child had the habit of doing the particular type of wrongful act which resulted in the injury complained of. In the instant case, the cause of action sought to be established fails in that the negligence charged with relation to parental restraint is not claimed to flow from the commission of an act or course of conduct which the child habitually engaged in and which led to the appellant's injury. It is nowhere claimed that the child here involved had a propensity to swing or slam doors at the hazard of persons using such doors. The deed of a child, the enactment of which results in harm to another and which is unrelated to any previous act or acts of the child, cannot be laid at the door of the parents simply because the child happened to be born theirs. However, a wrongful act by an infant which climaxes a course of conduct involving similar acts may lead to the parents' accountability. A deed brought on by a totally unexpected reaction to a situation which is isolated of origin and provocation could not have been foretold or averted and hence could not render the parents responsible.

Therefore, from the allegations of the second amended complaint, it is not made to appear that the injury claimed to have been sustained by the appellant was a natural and probable consequence of negligence on the part of the appellee parents.

The judgment of the court below is affirmed.

Most states have statutorily changed the common law rule, making parents responsible for wilfull or malicious tortious acts of children whether or not they are known to be mischiefmakers. Thus the Illinois Parental Responsibility Law provides: "The parent or legal guardian of an unemancipated minor who resides with such parent or legal guardian is liable for actual damages for the wilful or malicious acts of such minor which cause injury to a person or property." (Ill.Rev.Stat. 1975, Chapter 70, paragraph 53) Several other states impose a monetary limit on such liability.

Other Torts Governed by Statute or Regulation There are certain types of conduct that statutes or regulation attempt to control by placing the burden of liability on those presumably in a position to prevent the unwanted conduct. An example is the "Dram Shop Act," which in many states subjects the owner of a bar to liability if the bar continues to serve an intoxicated patron who later is involved in an accident while intoxicated.

Principal's Criminal Liability

As a general proposition, a principal will not be held liable for an agent's unauthorized criminal acts, if the crimes are those requiring specific intent. Thus a department store proprietor who tells his chief buyer to get the "best deal possible" on next fall's fashions is not liable if the buyer steals clothes from the manufacturer.

There is a narrow exception to the broad policy of immunity. Courts have ruled that under certain regulatory statutes and regulations, an agent's criminality may be imputed to the principal, just as civil liability is imputed under Dram Shop Acts. These include pure food and drug acts, speeding ordinances, building regulations, child labor rules, and minimum wage and maximum hour legislation.

Agent's Personal Liability for Torts and Contracts

Tort Liability

That a principal is held vicariously liable and must pay damages to an injured third person does not excuse the agent, who actually committed the tortious acts. The agent is personally liable for his wrongful acts and must reimburse the principal for any damages he was forced to pay, as long as the principal did not authorize the wrongful conduct. The agent directed to commit a tort remains liable for his own conduct but is not obliged to repay the principal. Liability as an agent can be burdensome, sometimes perhaps more burdensome than as a principal. The latter normally purchases insurance to cover against wrongful acts of his agents, but liability insurance policies frequently do not cover the employee's personal liability if named in a lawsuit individually. Thus doctors' and hospitals' malpractice policies protect a doctor from both her own mistakes and those of nurses and others that the doctor would be responsible for; nurses, however, might need their own coverage. In the absence of insurance, an agent is at serious risk in this lawsuit-conscious age.

The risk is not total. The agent is not liable for torts of other agents unless he is personally at fault—for example, by negligently supervising a junior or by giving faulty instructions. Agent, general manager for Principal, hires Brown as subordinate. Brown is competent to do the job, but by failing to exercise proper control over a machine negligently injures Ted, a visitor to the premises. Principal and Brown are liable to Ted but Agent is not.

Contract Liability

In general, an agent is not personally liable for contracts he had negotiated on behalf of a principal. There is a major exception to the general rule in some countries. For example, English law provides that an agent of a principal who resides outside England is liable, even if it is clear that he is signing the contract as an agent.

In the United States, there are the following exceptions to the general rule: (1) when the agent is serving an undisclosed or partially-disclosed principal; (2) when the agent lacks authority or exceeds his authority; and (3) if the agent entered into the contract in a personal capacity. We will consider each exception in turn.

Agent for Undisclosed (or Partially Disclosed) Principal An agent need not, and frequently will not, inform the person with whom he is negotiating that he is acting on behalf of a principal. The secret principal is usually called an "**undisclosed principal.**" Or the agent may tell the other person that he is acting as an agent but not disclose the principal's name, in which event the principal is "**partially disclosed.**" To understand the difficulties that occur, consider the following hypothetical but common example. A real estate developer wants to acquire several parcels of land to put up an amusement park. He is anxious to keep his identity secret because he wants to hold the land cost down. If the landowners realized that a major building project was about to be launched, their asking price would be at least as high as the ferris wheel. So he obtains two options to purchase land by using two secret agents—Bonnie and Clyde. Bonnie does not mention to sellers that she is an agent (therefore to those sellers the developer is an undisclosed principal). Clyde tells those with whom he is dealing that he is an agent but refuses to divulge the developer's name or his business interest in the land. (Thus the developer is, to the latter sellers, a partially disclosed principal.) Suppose the sellers get wind of the impending construction and want to back out of the deal. Who may enforce the contracts against them?

The developer and the agents may sue to compel transfer of title. The undisclosed or partially disclosed principal may act to enforce his rights unless the contract specifically prohibits it or there is a representation that the signatories are not signing for an undisclosed principal. The agents may also bring suit to enforce the principal's contract rights because, as agents for an undisclosed or partially disclosed principal, they are considered parties to their contracts.

Now suppose the developer attempts to call off the deal. Whom may the sellers sue? Both the developer and the agents are liable. That the sellers had no knowledge of the developer's identity—or even that there was a developer—does not invalidate the contract. If the sellers first sue agent Bonnie (or Clyde), they may still recover the purchase price from the developer as long as they had no knowledge of his identity prior to winning the first lawsuit. The developer is discharged from liability if, knowing his identity, the plaintiffs persist in a suit against the agents and recover a judgment against them anyway. Similarly, if the seller sues the principal and recovers a judgment, the agents are relieved of liability. The seller thus has a "right of election" to sue either the agent or the undisclosed principal, a right that in many states may be exercised any time before the seller collects on the judgment. In the following case, the third party elected to sue an agent who failed to disclose the principal's name.

DETROIT PURE MILK CO. v. PATTERSON
128 Mich. App. 475, 360 N.W.2d 221 (1984)

MacKenzie, Presiding Judge. Plaintiff appeals as of right from a judgment of no cause of action entered in defendant's favor by the circuit court after a bench trial. Defendant stipulated that $13,316.29 was owed to plaintiff for dairy products sold on open account to two stores, Village Variety and Village Variety Food Market. However, defendant argued that he was not personally liable; rather, the corporation which owned the two stores was liable, and the circuit court agreed.

The background facts are as follows. Defendant first became a customer of plaintiff when he owned as sole proprietor the Village Variety store. Subsequently, defendant and a partner formed and became shareholders in a corporation named V.V.F.M., Inc., which in December of 1977 purchased the Village Variety Food Market store. In January of 1979 the Village Variety store was transferred to the corporation, and in June of that same year defendant and his wife became the sole shareholders of V.V.F.M., Inc.

Defendant testified that, when the Village Variety Food Market store opened, he conveyed to plaintiff's salesmen that the store was owned by a corporation and explained the need for separate accounts for Village Variety Food Market and Village Variety, which was still a sole proprietorship owned by defendant at that time. Defendant testified that separate accounts were maintained until the Village Variety store was transferred to the corporation. Defendant couldn't recall the names used on plaintiff's invoices, stating that they could have been Village Variety or Village Variety Food Market, or Village Variety #2. Defendant admitted that he could not recall whether he ever told plaintiff's salesmen of the name of the corporation. None of the checks used to pay plaintiff were in the name of V.V.F.M., Inc., or otherwise indicated incorporation. While neither store had a sign indicating ownership by V.V.F.M., Inc., defendant testified that the sales tax and liquor licenses displayed in the Village Variety Food Market store were in the name of V.V.F.M., Inc.

Plaintiff's testifying salesman stated that he had no recollection of defendant's ever mentioning anything about a corporation. He further testified that he never looked at the sales tax or liquor licenses in the Village Variety Food Market store.

The circuit court found for defendant on the basis that defendant did nothing to mislead plaintiff either directly or indirectly, and that it was plaintiff's duty as a seller extending credit to inquire into the business structure of its customers. We agree with plaintiff that the court incorrectly stated and applied the controlling law, and erred in finding for defendant.

In contracting with plaintiff for dairy products, defendant was acting as an agent for the corporation. Where the party transacting with an agent has notice that the agent is or may be acting for a principal, but has no notice of the principal's identity, the principal is partially disclosed. Unless otherwise agreed, an agent contracting with another for a partially disclosed principal is a party to and personally liable on the contract.

In *Harmon v. Parker,* 193 Mich. 542, 545–546, 160 N.W. 380 (1916), and *Stevens v. Graf.* 358 Mich. 122, 126, 99 N.W.2d 356 (1959), the Court quoted with approval the following from 1 Mechem on Agency (2d ed.), § 1413:

> The duty rests upon the agent, if he would avoid personal liability, to disclose his agency, and not upon others to discover it. It is not, therefore, enough that the other party has the means of ascertaining the name of the principal: the agent must either bring to him actual knowledge, or, what is the same thing, that which to a reasonable man is equivalent to knowledge or the agent will be bound. There is no hardship to the agent in this rule, as he always has it in his power to relieve himself from personal liability by fully disclosing his principal and contracting only in the latter's name. If he does not do this, it may well be presumed that he intended to make himself personally responsible.

We find it unnecessary to remand to the trial court for reconsideration under the applicable law as set forth above. Even viewing the evidence in a light most favorable to defendant, no rational trier of fact could find that plaintiff had knowledge of the corporate principal's identity. Although defendant testified that he informed plaintiff's salesmen of the corporation, there was no testimony by defendant to the effect that he informed plaintiff's salesmen of the corporation's name. Nor was there any evidence showing that defendant contracted only in the corporation's name; notably the invoices sent by plaintiff were not made out to V.V.F.M., Inc. Also, there was no evidence that defendant conveyed to plaintiff's salesmen that the contractual obligation to pay for the dairy products supplied be that of the corporation only, and plaintiff's salesmen may well have believed that, notwithstanding corporate ownership of the stores, defendant intended that his own credit, as well as that of the corporation, be relied on by plaintiff. It cannot reasonably be concluded that the licenses in the Village Variety Food Market store were alone sufficient to give plaintiff notice of the corporate principal's identity and relieve defendant of personal liability.

The trial court erred in granting a judgment for defendant, and should have granted judgment for plaintiff. We need not address the other issues raised by plaintiff on appeal.

Reversed and remanded for entry of judgment for plaintiff. Costs to plaintiff-appellant.

Lack of Authority in Agent An agent who purports to make a contract on behalf of a principal, but who in fact has no authority to do so, is liable to the other party. The theory is that the agent has warranted to the third party that he has the requisite authority. The principal is not liable in the absence of apparent authority or ratification.

But the agent does not warrant that the principal has capacity. Thus, an agent for a minor is not liable on a contract that the minor later disavows, unless the agent expressly warranted that the principal had attained his majority. In short, the implied warranty is that the agent has authority to make a deal, not that the principal will necessarily comply with the contract once the deal is made.

Agent Acting on His Own Account An agent will be liable on contracts made in a personal capacity as, for instance, when the agent personally guarantees repayment of a debt. The agent's intention to become personally liable is often difficult to determine on the basis of his signature on a contract. Generally, a person signing a contract can avoid personal liability only by showing that he was in fact signing as an agent. If the contract is signed "Jones, Agent," Jones can introduce evidence to show that there was never an intention to hold him personally liable. But if he signed "Jones" and neither his agency nor the principal's name is included, he will be personally liable.

Termination of Agency

The agency relationship is not permanent. Either by action of the parties or by law, the relationship will eventually terminate.

By Act of the Parties

Termination Inferred As with the creation of the relationship, it may be terminated either expressly or implicitly. Many agreements contain specified circumstances the occurrence of which signals the end of the agency. The most obvious of these circumstances is the expiration of a fixed period of time ("agency to terminate at the end of three months" or "on midnight, December 31"). It may also terminate on the accomplishment of a specified act ("on the sale of the house") or following a specific event ("at the conclusion of the last horse race"). But there are a number of other circumstances that will spell the end of the relationship by implication. Unspecified events or changes in business conditions or the value of the subject matter of the agency might lead to a reasonable inference that the agency should be terminated or suspended; for example, the principal desires the agent to buy silver but the silver market unexpectedly rises rapidly and overnight silver doubles in price. Other circumstances that end the agency include disloyalty of the agent (for example, he accepts an appointment that is adverse to his first principal or embezzles from the principal), bankruptcy of the agent or of the principal, the outbreak of war (if it is reasonable to infer that the principal, knowing of the war, would not want the agent to continue to exercise authority), and a change in the law that makes a continued carrying out of the task illegal or seriously interferes with it.

Mutual Consent The agent and principal may at any time mutually agree to end their relationship.

Revocation or Renunciation The decision to terminate need not be mutual, however. Unless the agency is coupled with an interest, neither principal nor agent can bind the other to continue the relationship nor compel the other to perform. A principal **revokes** the agency; an agent **renounces** it. Even a contract that states the agreement is irrevocable will not be binding, although it can be the basis for a damage suit against the one who breached the agreement by revoking or renouncing it. (Recent developments relating to the employment-at-will doctrine, which allows an employer to fire an employee at any time, are discussed in Chapter 16.) If the agency is coupled with an interest, however, so that the authority to act is given to secure an interest that the agent has in the subject matter of the agency, then the principal lacks the power to revoke.

By Operation of Law

Aside from the express agreements of the parties involved, or the necessary or reasonable inferences that can be drawn from their agreements, the law voids agencies under certain circumstances. The most frequent termination by operation of law is the death of principal or agent. The death of an agent also terminates the authority of subagents he has appointed, unless the principal has expressly consented to the continuing validity of their appointment. Similarly, if the agent or principal loses capacity to enter into an agency relationship, it is suspended or terminated.

Even though authority has terminated, whether by action of the parties or operation of law, the principal may still be subject to liability. Apparent authority in many instances will still exist. It is imperative for a principal on termination of authority to notify all those who may still be in a position to deal with the agent. The only exceptions to this requirement are when termination is effected by death, loss of the principal's capacity, or an event that would make it impossible to carry out the object of the agency.

Chapter Summary

A contract made by an agent on behalf of the principal legally binds the principal. Three types of authority may bind the principal: (1) express authority—that which is actually given and spelled out; (2) implied authority—that which may fairly be inferred from the parties' relationship and which is incidental to the agent's express authority; (3) apparent authority—that which reasonably appears to a third party under the circumstances to have been given by the principal. Even in the absence of authority, a principal may ratify the agent's acts.

The principal may be liable for tortious acts of the agent—but except under certain regulatory statutes, may not be held criminally liable for criminal acts of agents not prompted by the principal. Under the doctrine of *respondeat superior,* a principal is generally liable for acts by a servant within the scope of employment. A principal will not usually be held liable for acts of non-servant agents that cause physical damage, although he will be held liable for nonphysical torts, such as misrepresentation. The principal will not be held liable for tortious acts of independent contractors, although the principal may be liable for injuries resulting from his failure to act in situations in which he was not legally permitted to delegate a duty to act. Whenever an agent is acting to further the principal's business interests, the principal will be held vicariously liable for the agent's intentional torts. What constitutes scope of employment is not easy to determine; the modern trend is to hold a principal liable for the conduct of an agent if it was foreseeable that the agent might act as he did.

Most states have special rules of vicarious liability for special situations; for example, liability of an automobile owner for use by another. Spouses are not vicariously liable for each other, nor are parents for children, except for failing to control children known to be dangerous.

In general, an agent is not personally liable on contracts he has signed on behalf of a principal. This general rule has several exceptions recognized in most states: (1) when the agent is serving an undisclosed or partially disclosed principal; (2) when the agent lacks authority or exceeds his authority; and (3) if the agent entered into the contract in a personal capacity.

The agency relationship may be terminated by mutual consent, by express agreement of the parties that the agency will end at a certain time or on the occurrence of a certain event, or by an implied agreement arising out of the circumstances in each case. The agency may also be unilaterally revoked by the principal—unless the agency is coupled with an interest—or renounced by the agent. Finally, the agency will terminate by operation of law under certain circumstances, such as death of the principal or agent.

Problems

1. You are the loan officer at a local bank. Patterson wants to borrow $7,000 from the bank. Bank policy requires that you obtain a loan guaranty from Patterson's employer, a milk company. The manager of the company visits the bank and signs a guaranty on behalf of the company. The last paragraph of the guaranty states: "This guaranty is signed by an officer having legal right to bind the company thru authorization of the Board of Directors." Are you satisfied with this guaranty? Would you be satisfied if the president of the company, who was also a director, affirmed that the manager had authority to sign the guaranty? Why?
2. Ralph owned a retail meat market. Ralph's agent Sam, purporting to act on Ralph's behalf, borrowed $3,500 from Ted. Although he never received the money, Ralph repaid $200 of the alleged loan and promised to repay the rest. If Sam had no authority to make the loan, is Ralph liable? Why?

3. A guest arrived early one morning at the Hotel Ohio. Clemens, a person in the hotel office who appeared to be in charge, walked behind the counter, registered the guest, gave him a key, and took him to his room. The guest also checked valuables (a diamond pin and money) with Clemens, who signed a receipt on behalf of the hotel. Clemens in fact was a roomer at the hotel, not an employee, and had no actual authority to act on behalf of the hotel. When Clemens absconded with the valuables, the guest sued the hotel. Is the hotel liable? Why?
4. A basketball player, playing for a professional team, punched an opposing player in the face during the course of a game. The opponent, who was seriously injured, sued the owner of the team for damages. A jury awarded the player $222,000 for medical expenses, $200,000 for physical pain, $275,000 for mental anguish, $1,000,000 for lost earnings, and $1,500,000 in punitive damages (which was $500,000 more than requested by the player). The jury also awarded $50,000 to the player's wife for loss of companionship. If we assume that the player who threw the punch acted out of personal anger and had no intention to further the business, how could the damage award against his principal be legally justified?
5. A doctor in a University of Chicago hospital seriously assaulted a patient in an examining room. The patient sued the hospital on the theory that the doctor was an agent or employee of the hospital and the assault occurred within the hospital. Is the hospital liable for the acts of its agent? Why?
6. Hector was employed by a machine shop. One day, Hector made a delivery for his employer and then proceeded back to the shop. When he was four miles from the shop and on the road where the shop was located, he turned left onto another road to visit a friend, who lived five miles west of the turnoff. On the way to the friend's house, Hector caused an accident and a person injured in the accident sued Hector's employer. Is the employer liable? Why?
7. A fourteen-year-old boy, who had no driver's license, took his parents' car without permission and caused an automobile accident. A person injured in the accident sued the boy's parents under the Illinois Parental Responsibility Law cited in the text. Are the parents liable? Why?
8. Parke-Bernet Galleries, acting as agent for an undisclosed principal, sold a painting to Weisz. Weisz later discovered that the painting was a forgery and sued Parke-Bernet for breach of contract. In defense, Parke-Bernet argued that as a general rule, agents are not liable on contracts made for principals. Is this a good defense? Why?

15

Labor-Management Law

Over half a century, the federal law of labor relations has developed out of four basic statutes into an immense body of cases and precedent regulating the formation and governance of labor unions and the relationships among employers, unions, and union members. Like antitrust, labor law is a complex subject that has spawned a large class of specialized practitioners. Though specialized, it is a subject that no employer of any size can ignore, for labor law has a pervasive influence on how business is conducted throughout the United States. In this chapter we examine the basic statutory framework and the activities that it regulates.

A Brief History of Labor Legislation

In the Nineteenth Century

Labor unions appeared in modern form in America in the 1790s in Boston, New York, and Philadelphia. Early in the nineteenth century, employers began to seek injunctions against union organizing and other activities. Two doctrines were employed: (1) *common law conspiracy,* and (2) *common law restraints of trade.* The first doctrine held that workers who joined together were acting criminally as conspirators, regardless of the means chosen or the objectives sought.

The second doctrine—common law restraint of trade—was also a favorite theory of the courts to use in enjoining unionizing and other joint employee activities. Workers who banded together to seek better wages or working conditions were, according to this theory, engaged in concerted activity that restrained trade in their labor. This theory made sense in a day in which conventional wisdom held that an employer was entitled to buy labor as cheaply as possible—the price would obviously rise if workers were allowed to bargain jointly rather than if they were required to offer their services individually on the open market.

Under the Antitrust Laws

The Sherman Act did nothing to change this basic judicial attitude. A number of cases decided early in the act's history condemned labor activities as violations of the antitrust law. In particular, in the *Danbury Hatters' Case*, the Supreme Court held that a "secondary boycott" (see p. 422) against a non-unionized company violated the Sherman Act. The hatters instigated a boycott of retail stores that sold hats manufactured by a company whose workers had struck. The union was held liable for treble damages. [Loewe v. Lawlor, 208 U.S. 274 (1908)]

By 1912, labor had organized politically, and it played a pivotal role in electing Woodrow Wilson and giving him a Democratic Congress, which responded in 1914 with the Clayton Act's "labor exemption." Section 6 of the Clayton Act says that labor unions are not "illegal combinations or conspiracies in restraint of trade, under the antitrust laws." Section 20 forbids courts from issuing injunctions in cases involving strikes, boycotts, and other concerted union activities (which were declared to be lawful), as long as they arose out of disputes between employer and employees over the terms of employment.

But even the Clayton Act proved of little lasting value to the unions. In 1921 the Supreme Court again struck out against a secondary boycott that crippled the significance of the Clayton Act provisions. In the case, a machinists' union staged a boycott against an employer by whom the members were not employed in order to pressure the employer into permitting one of its factories to be unionized. The Court ruled that the Clayton Act exemptions applied only in cases involving an employer and his own employees. [Duplex Printing Press Co. v. Deering, 254 U.S. 443 (1921)] Without the ability to boycott under those circumstances free of antitrust prosecutions or treble-damage actions, labor would be hard-pressed to unionize many companies. More anti-union decisions followed.

Toward Modern Labor Legislation

Collective bargaining appeared on the national scene for the first time in 1918 with the creation of the War Labor Conference Board. A National

War Labor Board was empowered to mediate or reconcile labor disputes that affected industries essential to the war. But after the war, the board was abolished.

In 1926, Congress enacted the Railway Labor Act. This statute imposed a duty on railroads to bargain in good faith with their employees' elected representatives. The act also established the National Mediation Board to mediate disputes that were not resolved in contract negotiations. The stage was set for more comprehensive national labor laws. These would come with the Great Depression.

The Norris-LaGuardia Act The first labor law of the Great Depression was the Norris-LaGuardia Act of 1932. It dealt with the propensity of federal courts to issue preliminary injunctions, often *ex parte* (that is, after hearing only the plaintiff's argument), against union activities. Even though the permanent injunction might later have been denied, the effect of the vaguely worded preliminary injunction would have been sufficient to destroy the attempt to unionize. The Norris-LaGuardia Act forbids federal courts from temporarily or permanently enjoining certain union activities, such as peaceful picketing and strikes. The act is applicable to any "labor dispute," defined as embracing "any controversy concerning terms or conditions of employment, or concerning the association or representation of persons in negotiating, fixing, maintaining, changing, or seeking to arrange terms or conditions of employment, regardless of whether or not the disputants stand in the proximate relation of employer and employee." This language thus permitted the secondary boycott that had been held a violation of the antitrust laws in *Duplex*. The act also bars the courts from enforcing so-called "yellow-dog" contracts—agreements that employees made with their employer not to join unions.

The National Labor Relations Act (the Wagner Act) In 1935, Congress finally enacted a comprehensive labor statute. The National Labor Relations Act (NLRA), often called the Wagner Act after its sponsor, Senator Robert F. Wagner, declared in Section 7 that workers in interstate commerce "have the right to self-organization, to form, join or assist labor organizations, to bargain collectively through representatives of their own choosing, and to engage in concerted activities for the purpose of collective bargaining or other mutual aid or protection." Section 8 sets out five key "unfair labor practices." The five employer unfair labor practices are these:

1. Interference with the rights guaranteed by Section 7
2. Interference with the organization of unions, or dominance by the employer of union administration (this section thus outlaws "company unions")
3. Discrimination against employees who belong to unions

4. Discharging or otherwise discriminating against employees who seek relief under the act
5. Refusing to bargain collectively with union representatives.

The procedures for forming a union to represent employees in an appropriate "bargaining unit" are set out in Section 9. Finally, the Wagner Act established the National Labor Relations Board (NLRB) as an independent federal administrative agency, with power to investigate and remedy unfair labor practices.

The Supreme Court upheld the constitutionality of the act in 1937 in a series of five cases. In the first, *NLRB* v. *Jones & Laughlin Steel Corp.*, 301 U.S. 1 (1937), the Court ruled that congressional power under the Commerce Clause extends to activities that might affect the flow of interstate commerce, as labor relations certainly did. Through its elaborate mechanisms for establishing collective bargaining as a basic national policy, the Wagner Act has had a profound effect on interstate commerce during the last half-century.

The Taft-Hartley Act (Labor Management Relations Act) The Wagner Act did not attempt to restrict union activities in any way. For a dozen years, opponents of unions sought some means of curtailing the breadth of opportunity opened up to unions by the Wagner Act. After failing to obtain relief in the Supreme Court, they took their case to Congress and finally succeeded after World War II when, in 1947, Congress for the first time since 1930 had Republican majorities in both houses. Congress responded to critics of "Big Labor" with the Taft-Hartley Act, passed over President Truman's veto. Taft-Hartley—known formally as the Labor Management Relations Act—did not repeal the protections given employees and unions under the National Labor Relations Act. Instead, it balanced union power with a declaration of rights of employers. In particular, Taft-Hartley lists six unfair labor practices of unions, including secondary boycotts, strikes aimed at coercing an employer to fire an employee who refuses to join a union, and so-called "jurisdictional" strikes over which union should be entitled to do specified jobs at the worksite.

In addition to these provisions, Taft-Hartley contains several others that balance the rights of unions and employers. For example, the act guarantees both employers and unions the right to present their views on unionization and collective bargaining. Like employers, unions now became obligated to bargain in good faith. The act outlaws the "closed shop" (one in which a worker must belong to a union), gives federal courts the power to enforce collective bargaining agreements, and permits private parties to sue for damages arising out of a secondary boycott. The act also created the Federal Mediation and Conciliation Service to cope with strikes that create national emergencies, and it declared strikes by federal employees to be unlawful. It was this provision that President Reagan invoked in 1981 to fire air traffic controllers who walked off the job to get higher pay.

The Landrum-Griffin Act Congressional hearings in the 1950s brought to light union corruption and abuses and led in 1959 to the last of the major federal labor statutes, the Landrum-Griffin Act (Labor-Management Reporting and Disclosure Act). It established a series of controls on internal union procedures, including the method of electing union officers and the financial controls necessary to avoid the problems of corruption that had been encountered. Landrum-Griffin also restricted union picketing under various circumstances, narrowed the loopholes in Taft-Hartley's prohibitions against secondary boycotts, and banned "hot cargo" agreements (see p. 424).

The National Labor Relations Board—Organization and Functions

The National Labor Relations Board (NLRB) consists of five board members, appointed by the president and confirmed by the Senate, for five-year, staggered terms. The president designates one of the members as chairman. The president also appoints the general counsel, who is in charge of the board's investigatory and prosecutorial functions and who represents the NLRB when it goes (or is taken) to court. The general counsel also oversees the thirty-three regional offices scattered throughout the country, each of which is headed by a regional director.

The NLRB serves two primary functions: (1) It investigates allegations of unfair labor practices and provides remedies in appropriate cases. (2) It decides in contested cases which union should serve as the exclusive bargaining agent for a particular group of employees.

Unfair Labor Practice Cases

Unfair labor practice cases are voluminous—some 40,000 a year in the 1980s. A charge of an unfair labor practice must be presented to the board, which has no authority to initiate cases on its own. Charges are investigated at the regional level and may result in a complaint by the regional office. A regional director's failure to issue a complaint may be appealed to the general counsel, whose word is final and unappealable. A substantial number of charges are dismissed or withdrawn each year—sometimes as many as 70 percent. Once issued, the complaint is handled by an attorney from the regional office. Most cases, usually around 80 percent, are settled at this level. If not settled, the case will be tried before an administrative law judge, who will take evidence and recommend a decision and order.

If no one objects, the decision and order become final as the board's opinion and order. Any party may appeal the decision to the board in Washington. The board acts on written briefs, rarely on oral argument. The board's order may be appealed to the U.S. Courts of Appeals, although its findings of fact are not reviewable "if supported by substantial evidence on the record considered as a whole." The board may also go to the Court of Appeals to seek enforcement of its orders.

Representation Cases

The NLRB is empowered to oversee representative elections—that is, elections by employees to determine whether or not to be represented by a union. The board becomes involved if at least 30 percent of the members of a potential bargaining unit petition it to do so, or if an employer petitions on being faced with a claim by a union that it exclusively represents the employees. The board determines which bargaining unit is appropriate and which employees are eligible to vote. A representative of the regional office will conduct the election itself, which is by secret ballot. The regional director may hear challenges to the election procedure to determine whether the election was valid.

Labor and Management Rights Under the Federal Labor Laws

Choosing the Union as the Exclusive Bargaining Representative

Determining the Appropriate Unit As long as a union has a valid agreement with the employer, no rival union may seek an election to oust it except within sixty to ninety days before the contract expires. Nor may an election be held if an election has already been held in the bargaining unit during the preceding twelve months. To bar a new election under the valid contract rule, the agreement must be of no more than three years' duration.

Whom does the union represent? In companies of even moderate size, employees work at different tasks and have different interests. Must the secretaries, punch press operators, drivers, and clerical help all belong to the same union in a small factory? The NLRB has the authority to determine which group of employees will constitute the appropriate bargaining unit. To make its determination, the board must look at the history of collective bargaining among similar workers in the industry; the employees' duties, wages, skills, and working conditions; the relationship between the proposed unit and the structure of the employer's organization; and the desires of the employees themselves.

Two groups must be excluded from any bargaining unit—supervisory employees and independent contractors. Determining whether or not a particular employee is a supervisor is left to the discretion of the board.

Interfering with Employee Communications To conduct an organizing drive, a union must be able to communicate with the employees. But the employer has valid interests in seeing that employees and organizers do not interfere with plant operations or otherwise hinder the operation of the business. Several different problems arise from the need to balance these interests.

One problem is the protection of the employer's property rights. May nonemployee union organizers come onto the employer's property to distribute union literature—for example, by standing in the company's parking lots to hand out leaflets when employees go to and from work? May organizers, whether employees or not, picket or hand out literature in private shopping centers in order to reach the public—for example, to protest a company's policies toward its non-union employees? The interests of both employees and employers under the NLRA are twofold: (1) the right of the employees (a) to communicate with each other or the public and (b) to hear what union organizers have to say, and (2) the employer's (a) property rights, and (b) interest in managing the business efficiently and profitably.

The rules that govern in these situations are complex, but in general they appear to provide these answers: (1) If the persons doing the soliciting are not employees, the employer may bar them from entering his private property, even if they are attempting to reach employees—assuming that the employer does not discriminate and applies a rule against use of his property equally to everyone. [NLRB v. Babcock & Wilcox Co., 351 U.S. 105 (1956)] (2) If the solicitors are not employees and they are trying to reach the public, they have no right to enter the employer's private property. (3) If the solicitors are employees who are seeking to reach the public, they have the right to distribute on the employer's property—in a common case, in a shopping center—unless they have a convenient way to reach their audience on public property off the employer's premises. [Hudgens v. NLRB, 424 U.S. 507 (1976)] (4) If the solicitors are employees seeking to reach employees, the employer is permitted to limit the distribution of literature or other solicitations to avoid litter or the interruption of work, but he cannot prohibit solicitation on company property altogether.

In the leading case of *Republic Aviation Corp.* v. *NLRB*, 324 U.S. 793 (1945), the employer, a non-union plant, had a standing rule against any kind of solicitation on the premises. Thereafter, certain employees attempted to organize the plant. The employer fired one employee for soliciting on behalf of the union and three others for wearing union buttons. The Supreme Court upheld the board's determination that the discharges constituted an unfair labor practice under Section 8(a). It does not matter, the Court said, whether the employees had other means of communicating with each other or that the employer's rule against solicitation may have no effect on the union's attempt to organize the workers. In other words, the employer's intent or motive is irrelevant. The only question is whether the employer's actions might tend to interfere with the employees' exercise of their rights under the NLRA.

Regulating Campaign Statements A union election drive is not like a polite tea-party conversation; it is, like political campaigns, full of charges and countercharges. Employers who do not want their employees unionized may warn darkly of the effect of the union on profitability; organizers may exaggerate the company's financial position. Under a 1982 NLRB case, *Midland National Life Ins. Co.*, 263 N.L.R.B. 130, the board will not set aside an election if the parties misrepresent the issues or facts, but it will do so if the statements are made in a deceptive manner, e.g., through forged documents. The board also watches for threats and promises of rewards; for example, the employer might threaten to close the plant if the union succeeds. In *NLRB* v. *Gissel Packing Co.*, 395 U.S. 575 (1969), the employer stated his worries throughout the campaign that a union would prompt a strike and force the plant to close. The board ruled that the employer's statements were an impermissible threat. To the employer's claim that he was simply exercising his First Amendment rights, the Supreme Court held that although employers do enjoy freedom of speech, it is an unfair labor practice to threaten consequences that are not rooted in economic realities.

A union campaign has become an intricate legal duel, heavily dependent on strategic considerations of law and public relations. Neither management nor labor can afford to wage a union campaign without specialized advisers, who can guide the thrust and parry of the antagonists. Labor usually has such advisers because few organizational drives are begun without outside organizers who have access to union lawyers. A business person who attempts to fight a union, like a labor organizer or employee who attempts to organize one, takes a sizable risk when acting alone, without competent advice. For example, a simple statement like "We will get the heating fixed," in response to a seemingly innocent question about the "drafty old building" at a meeting with employees, can lead to a NLRB decision to set aside an election if the union loses, because the answer can easily be construed as a promise, and under Section 8(c) of the NLRA a promise of reward or benefit during an organization campaign is an unfair labor practice by management. Few union election campaigns occur without questions, meetings, and pamphleteering carefully worked out in advance.

The results of all the electioneering are worth noting. In the 1980s, some 20 percent of the total American workforce was unionized, the lowest percentage since the two major associations of unions—American Federation of Labor (AFL) and the Congress of Industrial Organizations (CIO)—merged in 1955. Unionism was clearly on the wane. Of the 7,000 elections held annually during the first half of the decade, labor won fewer than half (about 43 percent).

Exclusivity Once selected as the bargaining representative for an appropriate group of employees, the union has the **exclusive right to bargain.** Thereafter, individual employees may not enter into separate contracts with the employer, even if they voted against the particular union or against having a union at all. The principle of exclusivity is fundamental to the collective bargaining process. Just how basic it is can be seen in the following case, in which one group of employees protested what they thought were racially discriminatory work assignments, barred under the **collective bargaining agreement,** the contract between the union and the employer. Certain of the employees filed grievances with the union, which looked into the problem more slowly than the employees thought necessary. They urged that the union permit them to picket, but the union refused. They picketed anyway, calling for a consumer boycott. The employer warned them to desist, but they continued and were fired. The question was whether they were discharged for engaging in concerted activity protected under Section 7 of the National Labor Relations Act.

EMPORIUM CAPWELL CO. v. WESTERN ADDITION COMMUNITY ORGANIZATION
420 U.S. 50 (1975)

Opinion of the Court by MR. JUSTICE MARSHALL, announced by MR. CHIEF JUSTICE BURGER.

* * *

The Emporium Capwell Co. (Company) operates a department store in San Francisco. At all times relevant to this litigation it was a party to the collective-bargaining agreement negotiated by the San Francisco Retailer's Council, of which it was a member, and the Department Store Employees Union (Union) which represented all stock and marking area employees of the Company. The agreement, in which the Union was recognized as the sole collective-bargaining agency for all covered employees, prohibited employment discrimination by reason of race, color, creed, national origin, age, or sex, as well as union activity. It had a no-strike or lockout clause, and it established grievance and arbitration machinery for processing any claimed violation of the contract, including a violation of the anti-discrimination clause.

On April 3, 1968, a group of Company employees covered by the agreement met with the secretary-treasurer of the Union, Walter Johnson, to present a list of grievances including a claim that the Company was discriminating on the basis of race in making assignments and promotions. The Union official agreed to take certain of the grievances and to investigate the charge of racial discrimination. He appointed an investigating committee and prepared a report on the employees' grievances, which he submitted to the Retailer's Council and which the Council in turn referred to the Company. The report described "the possibility of racial discrimination" as perhaps the most important issue raised by the employees and termed the situation at the Company as potentially explosive if corrective action were not taken. It offered as an example of the problem the Company's failure to promote a Negro stock employee regarded by other employees as an outstanding candidate but a victim of racial discrimination.

Shortly after receiving the report, the Company's

labor relations director met with Union representatives and agreed to "look into the matter" of discrimination and see what needed to be done. Apparently unsatisfied with these representations, the Union held a meeting in September attended by Union officials, Company employees, and representatives of the California Fair Employment Practices Committee (FEPC) and the local anti-poverty agency. The secretary-treasurer of the Union announced that the Union had concluded that the Company was discriminating, and that it would process every such grievance through to arbitration if necessary. Testimony about the Company's practices was taken and transcribed by a court reporter, and the next day the Union notified the Company of its formal charge and demanded that the joint union-management Adjustment Board be convened "to hear the entire case."

At the September meeting some of the Company's employees had expressed their view that the contract procedures were inadequate to handle a systemic grievance of this sort; they suggested that the Union instead begin picketing the store in protest. Johnson explained that the collective agreement bound the Union to its processes and expressed his view that successful grievants would be helping not only themselves but all others who might be the victims of invidious discrimination as well. The FEPC and anti-poverty agency representatives offered the same advice. Nonetheless, when the Adjustment Board meeting convened on October 16, James Joseph Hollins, Tom Hawkins, and two other employees whose testimony the Union had intended to elicit refused to participate in the grievance procedure. Instead, Hollins read a statement objecting to reliance on correction of individual inequities as an approach to the problem of discrimination at the store and demanding that the president of the Company meet with the four protestants to work out a broader agreement for dealing with the issue as they saw it. The four employees then walked out of the hearing.

. . . On Saturday, November 2, Hollins, Hawkins, and at least two other employees picketed the store throughout the day and distributed at the entrance handbills urging consumers not to patronize the store. Johnson encountered the picketing employees, again urged them to rely on the grievance process, and warned that they might be fired for their activities. The pickets, however, were not dissuaded, and they continued to press their demand to deal directly with the Company president.

On November 7, Hollins and Hawkins were given written warnings that a repetition of the picketing or public statements about the Company could lead to their discharge. When the conduct was repeated the following Saturday, the two employees were fired.

. . . [T]he NLRB Trial Examiner found that the discharged employees had believed in good faith that the Company was discriminating against minority employees, and that they had resorted to concerted activity on the basis of that belief. He concluded, however, that their activity was not protected by § 7 of the Act and that their discharges did not, therefore, violate § 8(a)(1).

The Board, after oral argument, adopted the findings and conclusions of its Trial Examiner and dismissed the complaint. Among the findings adopted by the Board was that the discharged employees' course of conduct

> was no mere presentation of a grievance but nothing short of a demand that the [Company] bargain with the picketing employees for the entire group of minority employees.

The Board concluded that protection of such an attempt to bargain would undermine the statutory system of bargaining through an exclusive, elected representative, impede elected unions' efforts at bettering the working conditions of minority employees, "and place on the Employer an unreasonable burden of attempting to placate self-designated representatives of minority groups while abiding by the terms of a valid bargaining agreement and attempting in good faith to meet whatever demands the bargaining representative put forth under that agreement."

On respondent's petition for review the Court of Appeals reversed and remanded. The court was of the view that concerted activity directed against racial discrimination enjoys a "unique status" by virtue of the national labor policy against discrimination . . . The issue, then, is whether such attempts to engage in separate bargaining are protected by § 7 of the Act or proscribed by § 9(a).

* * *

Central to the policy of fostering collective bargaining, where the employees elect that course, is the principle of majority rule. If the majority of a unit chooses union representation, the NLRA permits it to bargain with its employer to make union membership a condition of employment, thereby imposing its choice upon the minority. . . .

* * *

In vesting the representatives of the majority with this broad power Congress did not, of course, authorize a tyranny of the majority over minority interests. First, it confined the exercise of these powers to the context of a " 'unit appropriate' for the purposes of collective bargaining," *i.e.*, a group of employees with a sufficient commonality of circumstances to ensure against the submergence of a minority with distinctively different interests in the terms and conditions of their employment. Second, it undertook in the 1959 Landrum-Griffin amendments, to assure that minority voices are heard as they are in the functioning of a democratic institution. Third, we have held, by the very nature of the exclusive bargaining representative's status as representative of *all* unit employees, Congress implicitly imposed upon it a duty fairly and in good faith to represent the interests of minorities within the unit. And the Board has taken the position that a union's refusal to process grievances against racial discrimination in violation of that duty, is an unfair labor practice. . . .

* * *

The decision by a handful of employees to bypass the grievance procedure in favor of attempting to bargain with their employer . . . may or may not be predicated upon the actual existence of discrimination. An employer confronted with bargaining demands from each of several minority groups would not necessarily, or even probably, be able to agree to remedial steps satisfactory to all at once. Competing claims on the employer's ability to accommodate each group's demands, *e.g.*, for reassignments and promotions to a limited number of positions, could only set one group against the other even if it is not the employer's intention to divide and overcome them. . . . In this instance we do not know precisely what form the demands advanced by Hollins, Hawkins, et al. would take, but the nature of the grievance that motivated them indicates that the demands would have included the transfer of some minority employees to sales areas in which higher commissions were paid. Yet the collective-bargaining agreement provided that no employee would be transferred from a higher-paying to a lower-paying classification except by consent or in the course of a layoff or reduction in force. The potential for conflict between the minority and other employees in this situation is manifest. With each group able to enforce its conflicting demands—the incumbent employees by resort to contractual processes and the minority employees by economic coercion—the probability of strife and deadlock, is high; the likelihood of making headway against discriminatory practices would be minimal.

* * *

Accordingly, we think neither aspect of respondent's contention in support of a right to short-circuit orderly, established processes for eliminating discrimination in employment is well-founded. The policy of industrial self-determination as expressed in § 7 does not require fragmentation of the bargaining unit along racial or other lines in order to consist with the national labor policy against discrimination. And in the face of such fragmentation, whatever its effect on discriminatory practices, the bargaining process that the principle of exclusive representation is meant to lubricate could not endure unhampered.

* * *

Reversed.

The Duty to Bargain

In Good Faith The NLRA requires both employer and union to bargain in good faith. What these words mean has long been the subject of controversy. Suppose Mr. Mardian, the company's chief negotiator, announces to Mr. Ulasewicz, the chief union negotiator, that "I will sit down and talk with you but I'll be damned if I will agree to a penny more an hour than the men are getting now." That is not a refusal to bargain: it is a statement of the company's position, and only Mardian's actual conduct during the negotiations will determine whether he was bargaining in good faith. Of course, if he refused to talk to Ulasewicz, he would have been guilty of a failure to bargain in good faith.

Suppose Mardian had steadily insisted during the bargaining sessions that the company must have complete control over every aspect of the labor relationship, including the right to hire and fire exactly as it saw fit, the right to raise or lower wages whenever it wanted, and the right to determine which employee was to do which job. The Supreme Court has said that an employer is not obligated to accept any particular term in a proposed collective bargaining agreement, and the NLRB may not second-guess any agreement eventually reached. [NLRB v. American National Insurance Co., 343 U.S. 395 (1962)] However, the employer must actually engage in bargaining, and a stubborn insistence on leaving everything entirely to the discretion of management has been construed as a failure to bargain. [NLRB v. Reed & Prince Manufacturing Co., 205 F.2d 131 (1st Cir. 1953)]

Suppose Mardian had responded to Ulasewicz's request for a ten-cent-an-hour raise: "If we do that, we'll go broke." Suppose further that Ulasewicz then demanded, on behalf of the union, that Mardian prove his contention but that Mardian refused. Under these circumstances, the Supreme Court has ruled, the Board is entitled to hold that management has failed to bargain in good faith, for once having raised the issue, the employer must in good faith demonstrate veracity. [NLRB v. Truitt Manufacturing Co., 351 U.S. 149 (1956)]

Mandatory Subjects of Bargaining The NLRB requires employers and unions to bargain over "terms and condition of employment." Wages, hours, and working conditions—whether workers must wear uniforms, when the lunch hour begins, the type of safety equipment on hand—are well understood terms and conditions of employment. But the statutory phrase is vague, and the cases abound with debates over whether a term insisted on by union or management is within the statutory phrase. No simple rule can be stated for determining whether a desire of union or management is mandatory or nonmandatory. The cases do suggest that management retains the right to determine the scope and direction of the enterprise, so that, for example, the decision to invest in labor-saving machinery is a nonmandatory subject—meaning that a union could not insist that an employer bargain over it, although the employer may negotiate it if he desires. Once a subject is incorporated in a collective bargaining agreement, neither side may demand that it be renegotiated during the term of the agreement.

The Board's Power to Compel an Agreement A mere refusal to agree, without more, is not evidence of bad-faith bargaining. That may seem a difficult conclusion to reach in view of what has just been said. Nevertheless, the law is clear that a company may refuse to accede to a union's demand for any reason other than an unwillingness to consider the matter in the first place. If a union negotiator cannot talk management into accepting his demand, then the union may take other actions—including strikes—to try to force management to bow. As Justice Black explains in the following case, it follows from this conclusion that the NLRB has no power to *compel* agreement—even if management is guilty of negotiating in bad faith. The federal labor laws are premised on the fundamental principle that the parties are free to bargain.

H. K. PORTER CO. v. NLRB
397 U.S. 99 (1970)

MR. JUSTICE BLACK delivered the opinion of the Court.

After an election respondent United Steelworkers Union was, on October 5, 1961, certified by the National Labor Relations Board as the bargaining agent for certain employees at the Danville, Virginia, plant of the petitioner, H. K. Porter Co. Thereafter negotiations commenced for a collective-bargaining agreement. Since that time the controversy has seesawed between the Board, the Court of Appeals for the District of Columbia Circuit, and this Court. This delay of over eight years is not because the case is exceedingly complex, but appears to have occurred chiefly because of the skill of the company's negotiators in taking advantage of every opportunity for delay in an act more noticeable for its generality than for its precise prescriptions. The entire lengthy dispute mainly revolves around the union's desire to have the company agree to "check off" the dues owed to the union by its members, that is, to deduct those dues periodically from the company's wage payments to the employees. The record shows, as the Board found, that the company's objection to a checkoff was not due to any general principle or policy against making deductions from employees' wages. The company does deduct charges for things like insurance, taxes, and contributions to charities, and at some other plants it has a checkoff arrangement for union dues. The evidence shows, and the court below found, that the company's objection was not because of inconvenience, but solely on the ground that the company was "not going to aid and comfort the union." Efforts by the union to obtain some kind of compromise on the checkoff request were all met with the same staccato response to the effect that the collection of union dues was the "union's business" and the company was not going to provide any assistance. Based on this and other evidence the Board found, and the Court of Appeals approved the finding, that the refusal of the company to bargain about the checkoff was not made in good faith, but was done solely to frustrate the making of any collective-bargaining agreement. In May 1966, the Court of Appeals upheld the Board's order requiring the company to cease and desist from refusing to bargain in good faith and directing it to engage in further collective bargaining, if requested by the union to do so, over the checkoff.

In the course of that opinion, the Court of Appeals intimated that the Board conceivably might have required petitioner to agree to a checkoff provision as a remedy for the prior bad-faith bargaining, although the order enforced at that time did not contain any such provision. In the ensuing negotiations the company offered to discuss alternative arrangements for collecting the union's dues, but the union insisted that the company was required to agree to the checkoff proposal without modification. . . . The union then filed in the Court of Appeals a motion for reconsideration of the earlier motion to clarify the 1966 opinion. The court granted that motion and issued a new opinion in which it held that in certain circumstances a "checkoff may be imposed as a remedy for bad faith bargaining." The case was then remanded to the Board and on July 3, 1968, the Board issued a supplemental order requiring the petitioner to "[g]rant to the Union a contract clause providing for the checkoff of union dues." The Court of Appeals affirmed this order. We granted certiorari to consider whether the Board in these circumstances has the power to remedy the unfair labor practice by requiring the company to agree to check off the dues of the workers. For reasons to be stated we hold that while the Board does have power under the National Labor Relations Act to require employers and employees to negotiate, it is without power to compel a company or a union to agree to any substantive contractual provision of a collective-bargaining agreement.

* * *

The object of this Act was not to allow governmental regulation of the terms and conditions of employment, but rather to ensure that employers and their employees could work together to establish mutually satisfactory conditions. The basic theme of the Act was that through collective bargaining the passions, arguments, and struggles of prior years would be channeled into constructive, open discussions leading, it was hoped, to mutual agreement. But it was recognized from the beginning that agreement might in some cases be impossible, and it was never intended that the Government would in such cases step in, become a party to the negotiations and impose its own views of a desirable settlement. This fundamental limitation was made abundantly clear in the legislative reports accompanying the 1935 Act. The Senate Committee on Education and Labor stated:

> The committee wishes to dispel any possible false impression that this bill is designed to compel the making of agreements or to permit governmental supervision of their terms. It must be stressed that the duty to bargain collectively does not carry with it the duty to reach an agreement, because the essence of collective bargaining is that either party shall be free to decide whether proposals made to it are satisfactory.

The discussions on the floor of Congress consistently reflected this same understanding.

* * *

. . . The parties to the instant case are agreed that this is the first time in the 35-year history of the Act that the Board has ordered either an employer or a union to agree to a substantive term of a collective-bargaining agreement.

Recognizing the fundamental principle "that the National Labor Relations Act is grounded on the premise of freedom of contract," the Court of Appeals in this case concluded that nevertheless in the circumstances presented here the Board could properly compel the employer to agree to a proposed checkoff clause. The Board had found that the refusal was based on a desire to frustrate agreement and not on any legitimate business reason. On the basis of that finding the Court of Appeals approved the further finding that the employer had not bargained in good faith, and the validity of that finding is not now before us. Where the record thus revealed repeated refusals by the employer to bargain in good faith on this issue, the Court of Appeals concluded that ordering agreement to the checkoff clause "may be the only means of assuring the Board, and the court, that [the employer] no longer harbors an illegal intent."

. . . It is implicit in the entire structure of the Act that the Board acts to oversee and referee the process of collective bargaining, leaving the results of the contest to the bargaining strengths of the parties. It would be anomalous indeed to hold that while § 8(d) prohibits the Board from relying on a refusal to agree as the sole evidence of bad-faith bargaining, the Act permits the Board to compel agreement in that same dispute. The Board's remedial powers under § 10 of the Act are broad, but they are limited to carrying out the policies of the Act itself. One of these fundamental policies is freedom of contract. While the parties' freedom of contract is not absolute under the Act, allowing the Board to compel agreement when the parties themselves are unable to agree would violate the fundamental premise on which the Act is based—private bargaining under governmental supervision of the procedure alone, without any official compulsion over the actual terms of the contract.

* * *

The judgment is reversed and the case is remanded to the Court of Appeals for further action consistent with this opinion.

Interference and Discrimination by the Employer

Union Activity on Company Property The employer may not issue a rule flatly prohibiting solicitation or distribution of literature during "working time" or "working hours"—a valid rule against solicitation or distribution must permit these activities during employees' free time, such as on breaks and at meals. A rule that barred solicitation on the plant floor during actual work would be presumptively valid. However, the board has the power to enjoin its enforcement if the employer used the rule to stop union soliciting but permitted employees during the forbidden times to solicit for charitable and other causes.

"Runaway Shops" A business may lawfully decide to move a factory for economic reasons, but it may not do so to discourage a union or break it apart. The removal of a plant from one location to another is known as a **runaway shop.** An employer's representative who conceals from union representatives that a move is contemplated commits an unfair labor practice because the union is deprived of the opportunity to negotiate over an important part of its members' working conditions. If a company moves a plant and it is later determined that the move was to interfere with union activity, the board may order the employer to offer affected workers employment at the new site and the cost of transportation.

Other Types of Interference Since "interference" is not a precise term but descriptive of a purpose embodied in the law, many activities fall within its scope. These include hiring professional strikebreakers to disrupt a strike, favoritism toward a particular union to discourage another one, awarding or withholding benefits to encourage or discourage unionization, misrepresentations and other acts during election campaigns, espionage and surveillance of workers, employment contracts with individual members of a union, blacklisting workers, physical or verbal attacks on union activists, and various forms of anti-union propaganda.

Discrimination against Union Members Under Section 8(a)(3), an employer may not discriminate against employees in hiring or tenure to encourage or discourage membership in a labor organization. Thus, an employer may not refuse to hire a union activist, or fire an employee who is actively supporting the union or an organizational effort, if the employee is otherwise performing adequately on the job. Nor may an employer discriminate among employees seeking reinstatement after a strike or discriminatory layoff or *lockout* (a closing of the job site to prevent employees from coming to work), hiring only those who were less vocal in their support of the union.

The provision against employer discrimination in hiring prohibits certain types of **compulsory** unionism. Four basic types of compulsory unionism are possible: the closed shop, the union shop, maintenance-of-membership agreements, and preferential hiring agreements. In addition, a fifth arrangement—the agency shop—while not strictly compulsory unionism, has characteristics similar to it. Section 8(a)(3) prohibits the closed shop and preferential hiring. But Section 14 permits states to enact more stringent standards and thus to outlaw the union shop, agency shop, and maintenance of membership as well.

1. *Closed shop* This requires a potential employee to belong to the union before being hired and to remain a member during employment. It is unlawful, because it would require an employer to discriminate on the basis of membership in deciding whether to hire.
2. *Union shop* An employer who enters into a union shop agreement with the union may hire a non-union employee, but all employees who are hired must then become members of the union and remain members so long as they work at the job. Because the employer may hire anyone, union or non-union member, the union shop is lawful, unless barred by state law.
3. *Maintenance-of-membership agreements* These require all employees who are members of the union before being hired to remain as members once they are hired, unless they take advantage of an "escape clause" to resign within a time fixed in the collective bargaining agreement. Workers who were not members of the union before being hired are not required to join once they are on the job. This type of agreement is lawful, again unless barred by state law.
4. *Preferential hiring* An employer who accepts a preferential hiring clause agrees to hire only union members as long as the union can supply him with a sufficient number of qualified workers. These clauses are unlawful.
5. *Agency shop* The agency shop is not true compulsory unionism, for it specifically permits an employee not to belong to the union. However, it does require the employee to pay into the union the same amount required as dues of members. The legality of an agency shop is determined by state law. If permissible under state law, it is permissible under federal law.

The Right to Strike

Section 13 of the NLRA says that "nothing in this Act, except as specifically provided for herein, shall be construed so as either to interfere with or impede or diminish in any way the right to strike, or to affect the limitations or qualifications on that right." The labor statutes distinguish between two types of strikes: the **economic** strike and the **unfair labor practice** strike. In the former, employees go out on strike to try to force the employer to give in to the workers' demands. In the latter, the strikes are protesting the employer's committing an unfair labor practice. The importance of the distinction lies in whether the employees are entitled to regain their jobs after it is over. In either type of strike, an employer may hire substitute employees during the strike itself. When it concludes, however, a difference arises. In *NLRB* v. *International Van Lines,* 409 U.S. 48 (1972), the Supreme Court said that an employer may hire permanent employees to take over during an economic strike, and he need not discharge the substitute employees when it is done. That is not true for unfair labor practice strikes: an employee who makes an unconditional offer to return to his job is entitled to it, even though in the meantime the employer may have replaced him.

These rules do not apply to unlawful strikes. Not every walkout by workers is permissible. Their collective bargaining agreement may contain a "no-strike" clause barring strikes during the life of the contract. Most public employees—that is, those who work for the government—are prohibited from striking. "Sitdown" strikes, in which the employees stay on the worksite, precluding the employer from using the facility, are unlawful. So are "wildcat" strikes, when a faction within the union walks out without authorization. Likewise unlawful are violent strikes, jurisdictional strikes, secondary strikes and boycotts, and strikes intended to force the employer to sign "hot cargo" agreements (p. 424).

To combat strikes, especially when many employers are involved with a single union trying to bargain for better conditions throughout an industry, an employer may resort to a lockout. Typically the union will call a **whipsaw strike,** striking some of the employers but not all. The whipsaw strike puts pressure on the struck employers because their competitors are still in business. The employers who are not struck may lawfully respond by locking out all employees who belong to the multi-employer union. This is known as a **defensive lockout.** In several cases, the Supreme Court has ruled that an **offensive lockout,** which occurs when the employer, anticipating a strike, locks the employees out, is likewise permissible.

Secondary Boycotts

Section 8(b)(4), added to the NLRA by the Taft-Hartley Act, prohibits workers from engaging in **secondary boycotts**—strikes, refusals to handle goods, threats, coercion, restraints, and other actions aimed at forcing any person to refrain from performing services for or handling products of any producer other than the employer, or to stop doing business with any other person. Like the Robinson-Patman Act (Chapter 19), this section of the NLRA is extremely difficult to parse and has led to many convoluted interpretations. However, its essence is to prevent workers from picketing employers not involved in the primary labor dispute.

Suppose that the Amalgamated Widget Workers of America puts up a picket line around the Ace Widget Company to force the company to recognize the union as the exclusive bargaining agent for Ace's employees. The employees themselves do not join in the picketing, but when a delivery truck shows up at the plant gates and discovers the pickets, it turns back because the driver's policy is never to cross a picket line. This activity falls within the literal terms of Section (8)(b)(4): it seeks to prevent the employees of Ace's suppliers from doing business with Ace. But in *NLRB v. International Rice Milling Co.*, 341 U.S. 665 (1951), the Supreme Court declared that this sort of **primary** activity—aimed directly at the employer involved in the primary dispute—is not unlawful. So it is permissible to throw up a picket line to attempt to stop anyone from doing business with the employer—whether suppliers, customers, or even the employer's other employees (for example, those belonging to other unions). That is why a single striking union is so often successful in closing down an entire plant: when the striking union goes out, the other unions "honor the picket line" by refusing to cross it and thus stay out of work as well. The employer might have been able to replace the striking workers if they comprised a small enough part of his labor force, but it becomes nearly impossible to replace all the workers within a dozen or more unions.

Suppose the United Sanders Union strikes the Ace Widget factory. Nonunion sanders refuse to cross the picket line. So Ace sends out its unsanded widgets to Acme Sanders, a job shop across town, to do the sanding job. When the strikers learn what Ace has done, they begin to picket Acme, at which point Acme's sanders honor the picket line and refuse to enter the premises. Acme goes to court to enjoin the pickets—an exception to the Norris-LaGuardia Act permits the federal courts to enjoin picketing in cases of unlawful secondary boycotts. Should the court grant the injunction? It might seem so, but under the so-called **ally doctrine**, the court will not. Since Acme is joined with Ace to help it finish the work, the courts deem the second employer an ally (or extension) of the first. The second picket line, therefore, is not secondary.

Suppose that despite the strike Ace Widget manages to ship its finished product to the Dime Store, which sells a variety of goods, including widgets. The union puts up a picket around the store; the picketers bear signs that urge shoppers to refrain from buying any Ace widgets at the Dime Store. Is this an unlawful secondary boycott? Again, the answer is no. A proviso to Section 8(b)(4) permits publicity aimed at truthfully advising the public that products of a primary employer with whom the union is on strike are being distributed by a secondary employer.

Now suppose that the picketers carried signs and orally urged shoppers not to enter the Dime Store at all until it stopped carrying Ace's widgets. That would be unlawful: a union may not picket a secondary site to persuade consumers to refrain from purchasing any of the secondary employer's products. Likewise, the union may not picket in order to cause the secondary employees (the sales clerks at the Dime Store) to refuse to go to work at the secondary employer. The latter is a classic example of inducing a secondary work stoppage, and it is barred by Section 8(b)(4).

"Hot Cargo" Agreements

A union might find it advantageous to include in a collective bargaining agreement a provision under which the employer agrees to refrain from dealing with certain people or from purchasing their products. For example, suppose the Teamsters Union negotiates a contract with its employers that permits truckers to refuse to carry goods to an employer being struck by the Teamsters or any other union. The struck employer is the primary employer; the employer who has agreed to the clause—known as a **hot cargo** clause—is the secondary employer. The Supreme Court upheld these clauses in *United Brotherhood of Carpenters and Joiners, Local 1976* v. *NLRB,* 357 U.S. 93 (1958), but the following year, Congress outlawed them in Section 8(e) with a partial exemption for the construction industry and a full exemption for garment and apparel workers.

Discrimination by Unions

A union certified as the exclusive bargaining representative in the appropriate bargaining unit is obligated to represent all employees within that unit, even those who are not members of the union. Various provisions of the labor statutes prohibit unions from entering into agreements with employers to discriminate against nonmembers. The laws also prohibit unions from treating employees unfairly on the basis of race, creed, color, or national origin.

Jurisdictional Disputes

Ace Widget, a peaceful employer, has a distinguished labor history. It did not resist the first union, which came calling in 1936, just after the NLRA was enacted, and by 1987 it had twenty-three different unions representing 7,200 workers at forty-eight sites throughout the United States. Then, because of increasingly more powerful and efficient machinery, United Widget Workers realized that it was losing jobs throughout the industry. It decided to attempt to bring within its purview jobs currently performed by members of other unions. United Widget Workers asked Ace to assign all sanding work to its members. Since sanding work was already being done by members of the United Sanders, Ace management refused. United Widget Workers decided to go on strike over the issue. Is the strike lawful? Under Section 8(b)(4)(D), regulating jurisdictional disputes, it is not. It is an unfair labor practice for a union to strike or engage in other concerted actions to pressure an employer to assign or reassign work to one union rather than another.

Bankruptcy and the Collective Bargaining Agreement

An employer is bound by a collective bargaining agreement to pay the wages of unionized workers specified in the agreement. But obviously no paper agreement can guarantee wages when an insolvent company goes out of business. Suppose a company files for reorganization under the bankruptcy laws (see Chapter 12). May it then ignore its contractual obligation to pay wages previously bargained for? In the early 1980s, several major companies—for example, Continental Airlines and Oklahoma-based Wilson Foods Corp.—sought the protection of federal bankruptcy law in part to cut union wages. Alarmed, Congress in 1984 amended the bankruptcy code to require companies to attempt to negotiate a modification of their contracts in good faith. If negotiations fail, a bankruptcy judge may approve only wage cuts that are necessary to a company's reorganization plan. In 1986, the U.S. Court of Appeals for the Third Circuit substantially reduced the power of companies to avoid their collective bargaining agreements. The court ruled that Wheeling-Pittsburgh Steel Corp. could not modify its contract with the United Steelworkers simply because it was financially distressed. The court pointed to the company's failure to provide a "snap-back" clause in its new agreement. Such a clause would restore wages to the higher levels of the original contract if the company made a comeback faster than anticipated. [Wheeling-Pittsburgh Steel Corp. v. United Steelworkers of America, 791 F.2d 1071 (3d Cir. 1986)] If followed in other circuits, or upheld by the Supreme Court, the ruling will probably cool the enthusiasm of some companies to seek voluntary reorganization under the bankruptcy laws to escape their union commitments.

Chapter Summary

Federal labor law is grounded in the National Labor Relations Act, which permits unions to organize and prohibits employers from engaging in unfair labor practices. Amendments to the NLRA, such as the Taft-Hartley Act and the Landrum-Griffin Act, declare certain acts of unions and employees also to be unfair labor practices.

The National Labor Relations Board supervises union elections and decides in contested cases which union should serve as the exclusive bargaining unit, and it also investigates allegations of unfair labor practices and provides remedies in appropriate cases.

Once elected or certified, the union is the exclusive bargaining unit for the employees it represents. Because the employer is barred from interfering with employee communications when the union is organizing for an election, he may not prohibit employees from soliciting fellow employees on company property but may limit the hours or spaces in which this may be done. The election campaign itself is an intricate legal duel; rewards, threats, and misrepresentations that affect the election are unfair labor practices.

The basic policy of the labor laws is to foster good-faith collective bargaining over wages, hours, and working conditions. The Board may not compel agreement: it may not order the employer or the union to adopt particular provisions, but it may compel a recalcitrant company or union to bargain in the first place.

Among the unfair labor practices committed by employers are

1. Discrimination against workers or prospective workers for belonging to or joining unions. Under federal law, the closed shop and preferential hiring are unlawful. Some states outlaw also the union shop, agency shop, and maintenance-of-membership agreements.
2. Interference with strikes. Employers may hire replacement workers during a strike, but in an unfair labor practice strike, as opposed to an economic strike, the replacement workers may be temporary only; workers are entitled to their jobs back at the strike's end.

Among the unfair labor practices committed by unions are

1. Secondary boycotts. Workers may not picket employers not involved in the primary labor dispute.
2. Hot cargo agreements. An employer's agreement, under union pressure, to refrain from dealing with certain people or purchasing their products is unlawful.

Problems

1. After years of working without a union, employees of Argenta Associates began organizing for a representation election. Management did not try to prevent the employees from passing out leaflets or making speeches on company property, but the company president did send out a notice to all employees stating that in his opinion they would be better off without a union. A week before the election, he sent another notice stating that effective immediately, each employee would be entitled to a twenty-five-cents-an-hour raise. The employees voted the union down. The following day, several employees began agitating for another election. This time management threatened to fire anyone who continued talking about an election on the ground that the union had lost and the employees would have to wait a year. The employees'

organizing committee filed an unfair labor practice complaint with the NLRB. What result?

2. Palooka Industries sat down with Local 308, which represented its telephone operators, to discuss renewal of the collective bargaining agreement. Palooka pressed its case for a nonstrike clause in the next contract, but Local 308 refused to discuss it at all. Exasperated, Palooka finally filed an unfair labor practice claim with the NLRB. What result?
3. Union organizers sought to organize the punch press operators at Dan's Machine Shop. The shop was located on a lot surrounded by heavily forested land from which access to employees was impossible. The only practical method of reaching employees on the site was in the company parking lot. When the organizers arrived to distribute handbills, the shop foreman, under instructions from Dan, ordered them to leave. At a hearing before the NLRB, the company said that it was not anti-union but that its policy, which it had always strictly adhered to, forbade non-employees from being on the property if not on company business. Moreover, company policy barred any activities that would lead to littering. The company noted that the organizers could reach the employees in many other ways—meeting the employees personally in town after hours, calling them at home, writing them letters, or advertising a public meeting. The organizers responded that these methods were far less effective means of reaching the employees. What result? Why?

16

Employment Law

In the previous chapter we examined the legal relationship between the employer and the employee who belongs, or wants to belong, to a union. Although federal labor law is confined to that relationship, laws dealing with the employment relationship—both state and federal—are far broader than that. Because most employees do not belong to unions, a host of laws dealing with the many faces of discrimination shapes employers' power over and duties to their employees. Beyond discrimination, the law also controls the extent to which an employer may terminate the relationship itself—by discharging the employee. We examine these issues in this chapter.

Employment Discrimination

In this section we consider laws that prohibit discrimination in employment. Until the 1960s, Congress had intruded but little in the affairs of employers except in union relationships. A company could refuse to hire members of racial minorities, prefer men over women in its promotion policies, or pay men more than women for the same work. But with the rise of the civil rights movement in the early 1960s, Congress (and many states) began to legislate away the employer's frequently exercised power to discriminate. The most important statutes are Title VII of the Civil Rights

Act of 1964, the Equal Pay Act of 1963, and the Age Discrimination Act of 1975.

Racial, Religious, Sex, and Nationality Discrimination

In Title VII of the Civil Rights Act of 1964, Congress for the first time outlawed discrimination in employment based on race, religion, sex, or national origin. The law applies to any employer whose business affects interstate commerce and who employs at least fifteen workers. Title VII declares:

> It shall be an unlawful employment practice for an employer to fail or refuse to hire or to discharge any individual, or otherwise to discriminate against any individual with respect to his compensation, terms, conditions, or privileges of employment, because of such individual's race, color, religion, sex, or national origin.

And in 1984 the Supreme Court said that Title VII applies to partnerships as well as corporations when ruling that it is illegal to discriminatorily refuse to promote a female lawyer to partnership status in a law firm. This applies, by implication, in other fields, such as accounting. [Hishon v. King & Spalding, 467 U.S. 69 (1984)] The remedy for unlawful discrimination is back pay and hiring, reinstatement, or promotion.

Title VII established the Equal Employment Opportunity Commission (EEOC) to investigate violations of the act. A victim of discrimination who wishes to file suit must first file a complaint with the EEOC to permit that agency to attempt to conciliate the dispute. The EEOC has filed a number of lawsuits to prove statistically that a company has systematically discriminated on one of the forbidden bases. The EEOC has received perennial criticism for its extreme slowness in filing suits and for failure to handle the huge backlog of complaints with which it has had to wrestle.

The courts have come to recognize two major types of Title VII cases:

1. *Disparate treatment* In this type of suit, the plaintiff asserts that because of race, sex, religion, or national origin, he or she has been treated less favorably within the organization than others. To prevail in a disparate treatment suit, the plaintiff must show that the company *intended* to discriminate because of one of the factors the law forbids to be considered. Thus, in *McDonnell Douglas Corp.* v. *Green,* 411 U.S. 792 (1973), the Supreme Court held that the plaintiff had shown the company intended to discriminate by refusing to rehire him because of his race. In general there are two types of disparate treatment cases—(a) pattern-and-practice cases, in which the employee asserts that the employer systematically discriminates on the grounds of race, religion, sex, or national origins, and (b) reprisal or retaliation cases, in which the employee must show that the employer discriminated against her because she asserted her Title VII rights.

2. *Disparate impact* In this second type of case, the employee need not show that the employer intended to discriminate but only that the effect or impact of the employer's action was discriminatory. However, to overcome the usual requirement of intent, the plaintiff must demonstrate that the reason for the employer's conduct (such as refusal to promote) was not job-related. Troublesome cases arise out of practices that appear to be neutral on the surface, such as educational requirements and tests administered to help the employer choose the most qualified candidate. In a seminal case, set out below, the Supreme Court held that an employer is not free to use any test he pleases; the test must bear a genuine relationship to job performance.

GRIGGS v. DUKE POWER CO.
401 U.S. 424 (1971).

MR. CHIEF JUSTICE BURGER delivered the opinion of the Court.

We granted the writ in this case to resolve the question whether an employer is prohibited by the Civil Rights Act of 1964, Title VII, from requiring a high school education or passing of a standardized general intelligence test as a condition of employment in or transfer to jobs when (a) neither standard is shown to be significantly related to successful job performance, (b) both requirements operate to disqualify Negroes at a substantially higher rate than white applicants, and (c) the jobs in question formerly had been filled only by white employees as part of a longstanding practice of giving preference to whites.

Congress provided, in Title VII of the Civil Rights Act of 1964, for class actions for enforcement of provisions of the Act and this proceeding was brought by a group of incumbent Negro employees against Duke Power Company. All the petitioners are employed at the Company's Dan River Steam Station, a power generating facility located at Draper, North Carolina. At the time this action was instituted, the Company had 95 employees at the Dan River Station, 14 of whom were Negroes; 13 of these are petitioners here.

The District Court found that prior to July 2, 1965, the effective date of the Civil Rights Act of 1964, the Company openly discriminated on the basis of race in the hiring and assigning of employees at its Dan River plant. The plant was organized into five operating departments: (1) Labor, (2) Coal Handling, (3) Operations, (4) Maintenance, and (5) Laboratory and Test. Negroes were employed only in the Labor Department where the highest paying jobs paid less than the lowest paying jobs in the other four "operating" departments in which only whites were employed. Promotions were normally made within each department on the basis of job seniority. Transferees into a department usually began in the lowest position.

In 1955 the Company instituted a policy of requiring a high school education for initial assignment to any department except Labor, and for transfer from the Coal Handling to any "inside" department (Operations, Maintenance, or Laboratory). When the Company abandoned its policy of restricting Negroes to the Labor Department in 1965, completion of high school also was made a prerequisite to transfer from Labor to any other department. . . .

The Company added a further requirement for new employees on July 2, 1965, the date on which Title VII became effective. To qualify for placement in any but the Labor Department it became necessary to register satisfactory scores on two professionally prepared aptitude tests, as well as to have a high school education. Completion of high school alone continued to render employees eligible for transfer to the four desirable departments from which Negroes had been excluded if the incumbent had been employed prior to the time of the new requirement. In September 1965 the Company began to permit incumbent employees who lacked a high school education to qualify for transfer from Labor or Coal Handling to an "inside" job by passing two tests— the Wonderlic Personnel Test, which purports to measure general intelligence, and the Bennett Mechanical Comprehension Test. Neither was directed or intended to measure the ability to learn or perform a particular job or category of jobs. The requisite scores used for both initial hiring and transfer approximated the national median for high school graduates.

* * *

The Court of Appeals reversed the District Court in part, rejecting the holding that residual discrimination arising from prior employment practices was insulated from remedial action. The Court of Appeals [held] . . . that there was no showing of a racial purpose of invidious intent in the adoption of the high school diploma requirement or general intelligence test and that these standards had been applied fairly to whites and Negroes alike. It held that, in the absence of a discriminatory purpose, use of such requirements was permitted by the Act. In so doing, the Court of Appeals rejected the claim that because these two requirements operated to render ineligible a markedly disproportionate number of Negroes, they were unlawful under Title VII unless shown to be job related.

The objective of Congress in the enactment of Title VII is plain from the language of the statute. It was to achieve equality of employment opportunities and remove barriers that have operated in the past to favor an identifiable group of white employees over other employees. Under the Act, practices, procedures, or tests neutral on their face, and even neutral in terms of intent, cannot be maintained if they operate to "freeze" the status quo of prior discriminatory employment practices.

. . . Congress did not intend by Title VII, however, to guarantee a job to every person regardless of qualifications. In short, the Act does not command that any person be hired simply because he was formerly the subject of discrimination, or because he is a member of a minority group. Discriminatory preference for any group, minority or majority, is precisely and only what Congress has proscribed. What is required by Congress is the removal of artificial, arbitrary, and unnecessary barriers to employment when the barriers operate invidiously to discriminate on the basis of racial or other impermissible classification.

. . . The touchstone is business necessity. If an employment practice which operates to exclude Negroes cannot be shown to be related to job performance, the practice is prohibited.

On the record before us, neither the high school completion requirement nor the general intelligence test is shown to bear a demonstrable relationship to successful performance of the jobs for which it was used. Both were adopted, as the Court of Appeals noted, without meaningful study of their relationship to job-performance ability. Rather, a vice president of the Company testified, the requirements were instituted on the Company's judgment that they generally would improve the overall quality of the work force.

The evidence, however, shows that employees who have not completed high school or taken the tests have continued to perform satisfactorily and make progress in departments for which the high school and test criteria are now used.

The Court of Appeals held that the Company had adopted the diploma and test requirements without any "intention to discriminate against Negro employees." . . .

The Company's lack of discriminatory intent is suggested by special efforts to help the undereducated employees through Company financing of two-thirds the cost of tuition for high school training. But Congress directed the thrust of the Act to the *consequences* of employment practices, not simply the motivation. More than that, Congress has placed on the employer the burden of showing that any given requirement must have a manifest relationship to the employment in question.

* * *

Nothing in the Act precludes the use of testing or measuring procedures; obviously they are useful. What Congress has forbidden is giving these devices and mechanisms controlling force unless they are demonstrably a reasonable measure of job performance. Congress has not commanded that the less qualified be preferred over the better qualified simply because of minority origins. Far from disparaging job qualifications as such, Congress has made such qualifications the controlling factor, so that race, religion, nationality, and sex become irrelevant. What Congress has commanded is that any tests used must measure the person for the job and not the person in the abstract.

The judgment of the Court of Appeals is, as to that portion of the judgment appealed from, reversed.

Discrimination Based on Religion

An employer who systematically refuses to hire Catholics, Jews, Buddhists, or members of any other religious group is obviously guilty of disparate treatment under Title VII. But refusal to deal with someone because of his religion is not the only type of violation under the law. Title VII defines religion as including religious observances and practices as well as belief and requires the employer to "reasonably accommodate to an employee's or prospective employee's religious observance or practice" unless the employer can demonstrate that a reasonable accommodation would work an "undue hardship on the conduct of the employer's business." Thus a company that refused even to consider permitting a devout Sikh to wear his religiously prescribed turban on the job would violate Title VII. But the company need not make an accommodation that would impose more than a minimal cost. For example, an employee in an airline maintenance department, open 24 hours a day, wished to avoid working on his sabbath. The employee belonged to a union, and, under the collective bargaining agreement, a rotation system determined by seniority would have put the worker into a work shift that fell on his sabbath. The Supreme Court held that the employer was not required to pay premium wages to someone whom the seniority system would not require to work on that day and could discharge the employee if he refused the assignment. [Trans World Airlines v. Hardison, 432 U.S. 63 (1977)]

Sex Discrimination

A refusal to hire or promote a woman simply because she is female is a clear violation of Title VII. Under the Pregnancy Discrimination Act of 1978 Congress declared that discrimination because of pregnancy is a form of sex discrimination. Congress is also debating a bill that would require employers to grant new parents as much as eighteen weeks of unpaid leave (see Box 16-1).

But the late 1970s brought another problem of sex discrimination to the fore: sexual harassment. The courts recognize that the age-old penchant of men to use their power to gain sexual favors is unlawful. Not only do individual supervisors violate the law if they explicitly or implicitly suggest to a woman that by submitting to sexual advances she might be hired,

Box 16-1 Social Traditions as Discrimination

Laboring for Maternity Leave Policy

By Karen Diegmueller

In the 1950s, life seemed so simple for women. They worked, wed, got pregnant and remained a part of the work force until shortly before the delivery date. With babes in arms, they abandoned their jobs usually until the children were safely tucked away in school. Such signs of simplicity are long past. Now women work, get pregnant, deliver their children and return to their jobs soon after—if they have jobs to return to.

. . . [A] parental leave bill guaranteeing job security for the mother (and father) of newborn or newly adopted children could [soon] be federal law. The legislation requires employers with 15 or more employees to allow a parent as much as 18 weeks of unpaid leave.

"It's a first step in some kind of national policy that puts guts into what has been a lot of talk about the family," says Ann Pauley, director of public information for the Women's Legal Defense Fund.

Despite the momentum that has been building for the bill's passage, there are those who are willing to risk being labeled enemies of motherhood, baseball and apple pie in order to halt the measure. Rep. Richard K. Armey is one.

"It's such an unnecessary intrusion by the public sector into the private sector," says the Texas Republican. "They've taken an isolated statistic and made a federal case out of it."

The issue has materialized with the shifting of demographics. A dozen years ago, 4[illegible].9 percent of married women with children younger than 18 worked outside the home. Today that group is rapidly nearing two-thirds: 61.4 percent worked in 1986, according to the Bureau of Labor Statistics. During that same period, women in the labor force with babies a year old or younger also rose dramatically—from 30.8 percent to 49.8 percent.

While more mothers work outside the home, their presence is not reflected in company maternity leave policies. Studies indicate that only 40 percent of working women are protected from losing their jobs in the event they take time off in conjunction with pregnancy.

Patricia Schroeder, a Colorado Democrat, introduced the legislation in the House, while Christopher J. Dodd, a Connecticut Democrat, introduced a similar measure in the Senate during the 99th Congress. But a vigorous lobbying campaign led by the U.S. Chamber of Commerce helped prevent the measure from reaching the floor of either chamber.

The bill also would require employers to give their workers time off to care for seriously ill children, and the House version provides for leave to care for dependent parents who are seriously ill.

Although the legislation retains its opponents, a variety of factors has changed the balance. . . . Not only does it enjoy a broad base of support, including women's groups, unions, religious organizations, the American Association of Retired Persons and the American Academy of Pediatrics, but the legislation also faces a less hostile Senate since the Democrats regained the majority.

Support also comes from child development experts and physicians. Studies suggest that for the mental and emotional well-being of the mother and child, they should be together for the first few months of the child's life. Also, many physicians believe that mothers need several months to recover physically from childbirth.

A favorable ruling . . . by the Supreme Court is also persuading policymakers to take another look at parental leave. After taking a couple of months off for the birth of her daughter, Lillian Garland was barred from returning to her job at the California Federal Savings and Loan Association in 1982, even though a state law protected her position.

After California ordered her rehired, the financial institution sued the state, arguing that its law

(continues on next page)

Box 16-1. *continued*

violated the federal Pregnancy Discrimination Act of 1978. The federal law requires companies to treat pregnant women the same as other disabled workers; if a company offers benefits for any disability, it must for pregnancy as well.

Writing for the majority in the 6–3 ruling, Justice Thurgood Marshall found the law promoted equal employment opportunity because it put women on the same footing as men in their ability to have children without losing their jobs. The dissenters, however, viewed the law as preferential treatment for pregnant women.

Since that ruling in January, two states have passed family and medical leave statutes, says Pauley. State employees in Connecticut will be allowed up to 24 weeks of unpaid leave for the birth or adoption of a child or the care of a seriously ill child or dependent parent. In Minnesota, firms with at least 21 workers must provide six weeks of unpaid leave to employees for the birth or adoption of a child.

They join a growing number of states that have taken the initiative on unpaid leave. Massachusetts, Montana and Wisconsin have statutes requiring maternity leave. Hawaii, Illinois, Kansas, New Hampshire, Oregon and Washington have authorized maternity leave via regulation.

A handful of states—New Jersey, California, Rhode Island, Hawaii and New York—and Puerto Rico mandate temporary disability insurance that includes pregnancy. Similar to unemployment compensation, worker and employer alike contribute to the pool that pays roughly half the pregnant worker's wages while she is on leave for some eight to ten weeks.

Some major employers have long given parental leave to their workers. A portion of the leave that such corporate giants as General Foods Corp., International Business Machines Corp. and Procter & Gamble Co. offer is paid, according to a report by a southern business group. The Southern Corporate Coalition, in fact, recommended in its report to the Southern Governors' Association that the business community upgrade maternity benefits and adopt policies supportive of the family. Such policies, the report noted, alleviate stress and foster worker productivity.

That report, along with a study of paid maternity leave programs conducted by the Conference Board, gives credence to supporters' claims that the benefits of parental leave outweigh the costs. According to the Conference Board analysis, there was no significant increase in the number of maternity claims filed nor in the cost of claims in New York and California after they mandated maternity leave.

given a raise, promoted, or assigned to more desirable work, but a company itself is liable for back pay and reinstatement or promotion if it knows or should have known that such practices were being carried on and did nothing to stop them. The company will also be liable to a qualified person denied a raise or promotion because someone else got it by submitting to sexual advances. The law applies equally to men who are propositioned by female supervisors.

In the next case, the Supreme Court held that Title VII's ban on sexual harassment encompassses more than the trading of sexual favors for employment benefits. Unlawful sexual harassment also includes the creation of a hostile or offensive working environment, subjecting both the offending employee and the company to damage suits even if the victim was in no danger of being fired or of losing a promotion or raise.

Low cost analyses conflict with estimates by the U.S. Chamber of Commerce. The chamber, which initially estimated the cost of the parental leave bill at $16 billion, revised its estimate downward to $2.6 billion after women's groups and the General Accounting Office, the investigative arm of Congress, criticized the original figure.

Opponents of the legislation are concerned primarily that small businesses will suffer. "It's not that small business doesn't want to provide this kind of benefit for their employees. It simply is a function of their ability to pay," says John S. Satagaj, president of the Small Business Legislative Council, a coalition of ninety small business trade associations.

Unlike larger businesses where employees can absorb a coworker's duties for short periods, small businesses lack that flexibility. Typically, says Satagaj, a temporary replacement has to be hired. But after the regular employee returns to work, "What do you do with the person you've trained?" he asks. "I can't quarrel with the goal [of taking time off to care for newborns]. That doesn't mean we can just go out to a business and say, 'You pay for it.' "

How affordable the legislation will be to the women targeted is also questionable. "For the average pregnant worker, there's another pressing problem: money. Is she going to receive a weekly benefit while on maternity leave?" wrote Melissa A. Berman in her Conference Board analysis. "Thus far, there are no proposals before the 100th Congress to mandate income for women on maternity leave, although [the legislation] would establish a commission to study policy options, and the subject of paid leave would certainly be high on the list of considerations."

Aside from any financial losses, there is a concern (posed principally by opponents) that women, particularly those in their child-bearing years, may jeopardize their careers if the Schroeder-Dodd legislation passes. Some argue that progress against discriminatory policies during the past two decades will deteriorate as employers become reluctant to hire women because it would cost more to employ them.

"The small business [operates] on the very narrow margin of investment," says Armey. Any additional cost will push it over the edge, he says, so "firms will naturally try to avoid these costs."

* * *

Source: Insight, June 15, 1987, p. 22

MERITOR SAVINGS BANK. v. VINSON
106 S.Ct. 2399 (1986)

Justice Rehnquist delivered the opinion of the Court.

This case presents important questions concerning claims of workplace "sexual harassment" brought under Title VII of the Civil Rights Act of 1964.

In 1974, respondent Mechelle Vinson met Sidney Taylor, a vice president of what is now petitioner Meritor Savings Bank (the bank) and manager of one of its branch offices. When respondent asked whether she might obtain employment at the bank, Taylor gave her an application, which she completed and returned the next day; later that same day Taylor called her to say that she had been hired. With Taylor as her supervisor, respondent started as a teller-trainee, and thereafter was promoted to teller, head teller, and assistant branch manager. She worked at the same branch for four years, and it is undisputed that her advancement there was based on merit alone. In September 1978, respondent notified Taylor that she was taking sick leave for an indefinite period. On November 1, 1978, the bank discharged her for excessive use of that leave.

Respondent brought this action against Taylor and the bank, claiming that during her four years at the bank she had "constantly been subjected to sexual harassment" by Taylor in violation of Title VII. She sought injunctive relief, compensatory and punitive damages against Taylor and the bank, and attorney's fees.

At the 11-day bench trial, the parties presented conflicting testimony about Taylor's behavior during respondent's employment. Respondent testified that during her probationary period as a teller-trainee, Taylor treated her in a fatherly way and made no sexual advances. Shortly thereafter, however, he invited her out to dinner and, during the course of the meal, suggested that they go to a motel to have sexual relations. At first she refused, but out of what she described as fear of losing her job she eventually agreed. According to respondent, Taylor thereafter made repeated demands upon her for sexual favors, usually at the branch, both during and after business hours; she estimated that over the next several years she had intercourse with him some 40 to 50 times. In addition, respondent testified that Taylor fondled her in front of other employees, followed her into the women's restroom when she went there alone, exposed himself to her, and even forcibly raped her on several occasions. These activities ceased after 1977, respondent stated, when she started going with a steady boyfriend.

* * *

Finally, respondent testified that because she was afraid of Taylor she never reported his harassment to any of his supervisors and never attempted to use the bank's complaint procedure.

Taylor denied respondent's allegations of sexual activity, testifying that he never fondled her, never made suggestive remarks to her, never engaged in sexual intercourse with her and never asked her to do so. He contended instead that respondent made her accusations in response to a business-related dispute. The bank also denied respondent's allegations and asserted that any sexual harassment by Taylor was unknown to the bank and engaged in without its consent or approval.

The District Court denied relief, but did not resolve the conflicting testimony about the existence of a sexual relationship between respondent and Taylor. It found instead that

> If [respondent] and Taylor did engage in an intimate or sexual relationship during the time of [respondent's] employment with [the bank], that relationship was a voluntary one having nothing to do with her continued employment at [the bank] or her advancement or promotions at that institution.

The court ultimately found that respondent "was not the victim of sexual harassment and was not the victim of sexual discrimination" while employed at the bank.

* * *

The Court of Appeals for the District of Columbia Circuit reversed. . . . The court stated that a violation of Title VII may be predicated on either of two types of sexual harassment: harassment that involves the conditioning of concrete employment benefits on sexual favors, and harassment that, while not affecting economic benefits, creates a hostile or offensive working environment. . . .

* * *

Respondent argues, and the Court of Appeals held, that unwelcome sexual advances that create an offensive or hostile working environment violate Title VII. Without question, when a supervisor sexually harasses a subordinate because of the subordinate's sex, that supervisor "discriminate[s]" on the basis of sex. Petitioner apparently does not challenge this proposition. It contends instead that in prohibiting discrimination with respect to "compensation, terms, conditions, or privileges" of employment, Congress was concerned with what petitioner describes as "tangible loss" of "an economic character," not "purely psychological aspects of the workplace environment." In support of this claim petitioner observes that in both the legislative history of Title VII and this Court's Title VII decisions, the focus has been on tangible, economic barriers erected by discrimination.

We reject petitioner's view. First, the language of Title VII is not limited to "economic" or "tangible" discrimination. The phrase "terms, conditions, or privileges of employment" evinces a congressional intent " 'to strike at the entire spectrum of disparate treatment of men and women' " in employment. Petitioner has pointed to nothing in the Act to suggest that Congress contemplated the limitation urged here.

Second, in 1980 the EEOC issued guidelines specifying that "sexual harassment," as there defined, is a form of sex discrimination prohibited by Title VII. As an "administrative interpretation of the Act by the enforcing agency," these guidelines, " 'while not controlling upon the courts by reason of their authority, do constitute a body of experience and informed judgment to which courts and litigants may properly resort for guidance.' " The EEOC guidelines fully support the view that harassment leading to noneconomic injury can violate Title VII.

In defining "sexual harassment," the guidelines first describe the kinds of workplace conduct that may be actionable under Title VII. These include "[u]nwelcome sexual advances, requests for sexual favors, and other verbal or physical conduct of a sexual nature." Relevant to the charges at issue in this case, the guidelines provide that such sexual misconduct constitutes prohibited "sexual harassment," whether or not it is directly linked to the grant or denial of an economic *quid pro quo,* where "such conduct has the purpose or effect of unreasonably interfering with an individual's work performance or creating an intimidating, hostile, or offensive working environment."

* * *

The District Court's conclusion that no actionable harassment occurred might have rested on its earlier "finding" that "[i]f [respondent] and Taylor did engage in an intimate or sexual relationship . . . , that relationship was a voluntary one." But the fact that sex-related conduct was "voluntary," in the sense that the complainant was not forced to participate against her will, is not a defense to a sexual harassment suit brought under Title VII. The gravamen of any sexual harassment claim is that the alleged sexual advances were "unwelcome." While the question whether particular conduct was indeed unwelcome presents difficult problems of proof and turns largely on credibility determinations committed to the trier of fact, the District Court in this case erroneously focused on the "voluntariness" of respondent's participation in the claimed sexual episodes. The correct inquiry is whether respondent by her conduct indicated that the alleged sexual advances were unwelcome, not whether her actual participation in sexual intercourse was voluntary.

* * *

Reversed and remanded.

Another sex-based problem that has been occupying the courts stems from a related law, the Equal Pay Act. This federal statute prohibits pay differentials between men and women if they are assigned to equal jobs: work requiring equal skill, effort, and responsibility. The statute seems to mean only that a woman may not be paid less than a man in the same job—flight attendant, telephone operator, sales manager. But some women have recently filed suit on a theory of **comparable worth**—a woman should be paid as much as a man if she is doing work that is comparable, even if the job is different. As Box 16-2 suggests, the economic theory has made certain inroads, even if its precise legal breadth remains in doubt.

Exceptions to Title VII

Although the language of Title VII is broad, the courts have allowed certain exceptions. For example, a practice or test that has a disparate impact on

Box 16-2 Comparable Worth: It's Already Happening

Companies Are Quietly Evening Up Pay Scales

BY AARON BERNSTEIN

Ever since the concept of comparable worth surfaced a few years ago, Corporate America has derided the idea—which holds that women should be paid the same as men for comparable jobs as well as for the same jobs. Destroys the free market, said the National Association of Manufacturers. Opens the door to unending litigation, worried the U.S. Chamber of Commerce.

Now, very quietly, major companies such as AT&T, BankAmerica, Chase Manhattan, IBM, Motorola, and Tektronix are trying forms of comparable worth. These experiments may be the first steps in a movement to raise women's pay, which averages 64¢ for each dollar men earn. Some experts say that stopping discrimination—which they say includes paying women less than men for comparable jobs—would erase half this gap. "In 10 years we'll probably have comparable worth, even though businesses will still be saying we don't," says George P. Sape of Organization Resources Counselors (ORC), a management consulting group.

SCARED TO DEATH

The latest moves have hardly ended the philosophical debate. Women's groups contend that secretaries earn less than janitors, even though the skills needed for the two jobs are comparable, simply because the secretaries are women. Opponents argue that a more plentiful supply of secretaries has kept their pay down.

But pragmatism is pushing companies toward comparable worth anyway. The doctrine was dealt a blow last year when a U.S. appeals court turned down the first major case brought to trial, against the state of Washington. However, proponents are keeping up the legal pressure with dozens of suits. Some 13 states already have laws that require public and private employers to pay equally for "comparable" work. Nurses in Alaska are claiming in a test case that this means comparable worth.

Corporations fear developments in the legislative arena as well. Some 30 states have comparable worth bills pending or have commissions studying the issue. Minnesota has applied the idea to state workers since 1983. Despite its court victory, Washington State is spending $482 million to raise the pay of women. The House of Representatives passed a bill in October that would require a comparable worth study of federal workers.

Such actions worry companies. "The bill in Congress scares employers to death: They fear it will put a stamp of approval on comparable worth," says Virginia R. Lamp, a labor relations attorney at the U.S. Chamber of Commerce.

For years many big companies have been doing the job comparisons necessary to make judgments on comparable worth, mostly for white-collar staffs. They evaluate jobs according to factors such as responsibility, skill, and physical labor. The factors are given points, and jobs are ranked by total points. "We call this method internal equity, which can be used to do comparable worth," says Lance A. Berger, a vice-president at Hay Associates Inc., a compensation firm.

EYE STRAIN

Now some companies, such as Tektronix Inc. and Motorola Inc., have started to adhere closely to internal comparisons—even when it means paying more than the market demands. "Many companies go through the exercise of doing the internal equity analysis, but then they upset these relationships if the market tells them to," says Richard A. Baker, Tektronix' corporate compensation manager. "We look at the market, but that's secondary to us." Both companies say it hasn't cost them much because their high-tech jobs don't have a history of being dominated by one gender.

Tektronix took another step when it put in a new pay system in the 1970s: It put all workers on the same evaluation system. Blue-collar pay rates tend to follow patterns set by unions, even in unorganized companies. Many female clericals are paid less because they're lumped in at the bottom of management evaluation systems, where there are no high-paying blue-collar jobs for comparison.

Other companies are trying to ensure that the factors used to evaluate jobs aren't biased against work usually done by women. After General Electric Co. was hit by a wage discrimination lawsuit in the 1970s, it overhauled its job evaluation methods, which now reflect comparable worth concepts.

BankAmerica Corp. went further in its new pay system by expanding the definition of physical labor used by most evaluation systems to include eye strain. This helps to measure work on video display terminals, which is usually done by women. The bank also looks at muscle strain, which lets it assess work done by tellers—also often female—who stand at bank windows all day. "This isn't the traditional evaluation method, which thinks of physical demands as lifting a box or something, as men usually do," says Dan C. Rowland, BankAmerica's director of compensation.

CATCHING DEVIATIONS

Other companies, such as International Business Machines Corp. and Control Data Corp., are looking directly at pay disparities between men and women. One approach is to find an average pay level for a series of jobs. Each employee's pay is then compared with the average. At the same time, a mathematical analysis is done to see if factors such as sex are significant predictors of pay levels. "You look to see if anybody is two or more standard deviations below the norm and hope they're not women," says one consultant. If they are, the company may raise the pay of women below the average.

Industry sources say Chase Manhattan Bank Corp. compared vice-presidents' jobs. It found that those in commercial banking, where women predominate, were paid less than those in male-dominated investment banking, although the jobs weren't that different. The bank narrowed the salary gap, in part by giving commercial bankers more responsibility and paying them more.

Some unionized companies are unwilling converts to comparable worth. The St. Louis Newspaper Guild alleged in a suit last year that the *St. Louis Post-Dispatch*'s largely female staff of in-house sales representatives, who sell ads over the phone, should be paid the same as its outside representatives, who are usually male. On Mar. 27, management agreed to raise in-house sales salaries by about 4.5%. "Our lawyers said the case had no merit, but we settled because of the legal fees we were running up," says Nicolas G. Penniman, publisher and general manager.

In 1980, pushed by its union, AT&T developed an evaluation system for comparing all the company's jobs with each other. The two sides didn't agree on how to implement the plan. But it's part of current bargaining aimed at reaching a new pact for 255,000 workers by May 31.

Northwestern Bell Telephone Co., which was spun off as part of U.S. West Inc. in AT&T's breakup, has gone further. Together with its unions, it developed a job evaluation system that reflects comparable worth. The two sides will use it to help set wages when they bargain over a new contract in August.

The pay gap between men and women won't shrink overnight. But as long as it persists, companies' subterranean efforts to close it will probably continue.

Source: *Business Week*, April 28, 1986, pp. 52–56

a racial group is allowable if the employer can prove that the practice is a business necessity or that the test is job related. Likewise, an employer may assign jobs, promotions, and benefits under a bona fide seniority system, even if it produces a discriminatory effect, as long as the employer has not designed or intended the seniority system to produce a discriminatory effect.

The courts have also allowed exceptions in cases in which religion, national origin, or sex is a **bona fide occupational qualification**—usually referred to as a BFOQ. For example, a gymnasium may legitimately hire only men to work in a men's locker room. A religious organization may lawfully employ, at least in certain positions, only those of the requisite faith. Race, however, can never be a BFOQ under Title VII.

Nor is discrimination permitted merely because the public might have certain preconceptions about the type of person who ideally should hold a certain job. For example, a person cannot be denied a job as a bank teller simply because he has an accent although that might be a disqualification if he were applying for a position as a telephone operator. Similarly, guidelines issued by the EEOC in 1978 specify that sex may be a BFOQ only when "necessary for the purpose of authenticity or genuineness." A playwright may specify a woman for a certain part in a play, but "stereotyped characterizations of the sexes" are an insufficient basis on which to rest a hiring decision. And so, although society has the notion that women generally are not adept at lifting weights, an employer may not routinely exclude women from jobs requiring this ability. He must test each individual applicant to determine whether the particular person can lift the proper amount.

Affirmative Action

Two exceedingly difficult problems, still not fully resolved, are the impact of Title VII on employment seniority and on affirmative action programs. Many union contracts require employers to rehire on the basis of seniority workers laid off for economic reasons. Those who have long been discriminated against and who only lately have been hired will obviously have far less seniority. In times of recession, they will be the ones to suffer most. Courts have been able in some cases to remedy this discriminatory effect by ordering employers to backdate the seniority to the time of the injury—that is, from the dates on which the employer first refused to hire or promote. Likewise, courts can order employers to figure seniority on a plantwide or companywide basis to alleviate the problem of the worker who was discriminatorily placed in a relatively menial position and who cannot transfer to a better job because of the limited number of openings determined by seniority.

Beginning in the 1960s, *affirmative action* programs were established in many industries, sometimes voluntarily but more often by statute or regulation. These seek to put a person where he would have been had he not been discriminated against. Because these programs use race as a criterion, they appear to violate Title VII insofar as they give preferential treatment to one race over another. Although the final chapter in this perplexing area of law is far from having been written, the Supreme Court, in *United Steelworkers* v. *Weber,* 443 U.S. 193 (1979), appeared to sanction agreements between private employers and unions that provide for voluntary affirmative action plans. The case arose when a white production worker at Kaiser Aluminum's Grammercy, Louisiana, plant sued to enjoin an affirmative action plan that provided that blacks would be accepted as craft trainees in equal numbers with whites until such time as their proportion to the company work force equaled the proportion of blacks to whites in the total workforce. Up to that time, blacks had been systematically excluded from the higher-paying craft positions. Weber, the white employee, had more seniority than many of the black workers selected for craft training, and he argued that Title VII barred the plant from adhering to a plan that discriminated against him on the basis of race. Said Justice Brennan for the five-to-two majority:

> We cannot agree with [Weber] that Congress intended to prohibit the private sector from taking effective steps to accomplish the goal that Congress designed Title VII to achieve. . . . It would be ironic indeed if a law triggered by a Nation's concern over centuries of racial injustice and intended to improve the lot of those who had 'been excluded from the American dream for so long,' constituted the first legislative prohibition of all voluntary, private, race-conscious efforts to abolish traditional patterns of racial segregation and hierarchy.

And in 1986, the Court rejected the Reagan Administration's argument that racial preferences may never be used except to redress actual victims of discrimination. In *Local 28, Sheet Metal Workers International Assn.* v. *Equal Employment Opportunity Commission,* 106 S.Ct. 3019 (1986), a six-to-three majority held that race-conscious remedies "may be appropriate where an employer or labor union has engaged in persistent or egregious discrimination, or where necessary to dissipate the lingering effects of pervasive discrimination," even when the benefits are for members of minority groups who were not personally discriminated against. But the Court unanimously held that racial preferences could not be an automatic remedy and that courts should be sparing in approving such preferences for those who were not themselves victims of discrimination.

The Court followed *Sheet Metal Workers* in 1987 in ruling that an affirmative action plan may give preference to women over men without violating Title VII. In *Johnson* v. *Transportation Agency,* 107 S.Ct. 1442 (1987), the Santa Clara County (California) Transportation Agency implemented a county-wide affirmative action plan designed to redress the effects of past practices in areas in which women had traditionally been underemployed or not hired at all. The plan permitted the agency to consider sex as one of many factors in hiring. Another factor was the ranking given job applicants by interviewers. The suit arose when a male applicant who scored two points higher at an interview than a female applicant lost a promotion to road dispatcher to her. The Court held that an employer is not bound strictly to rankings and test scores as long as applicants are qualified for the job. In upholding the woman's promotion, the Court stressed the flexibility of the plan:

> The Agency . . . has undertaken such a voluntary effort, and has done so in full recognition of both the difficulties and the potential for intrusion on males and non-minorities. The Agency has identified a conspicuous imbalance in job categories traditionally segregated by race and sex. It has made clear from the outset, however, that employment decisions may not be justified solely by reference to this imbalance, but must rest on a multitude of practical, realistic factors. . . . The decision [to take sex into account] was made pursuant to an affirmative action plan that represents a moderate, flexible, case-by-case approach to effecting a gradual improvement in the representation of minorities and women in the Agency's work force.

Age Discrimination

The Age Discrimination in Employment Act of 1967 (amended in 1978 and again in 1986) prohibits discrimination based on age, and recourse to this law has been growing at a faster rate than any other federal anti-bias employment law (Box 16-3). In particular the act protects workers over forty and prohibits forced retirement in most jobs because of age. Until 1987, federal law had permitted mandatory retirement at age seventy, but the 1986 amendments that took effect January 1, 1987, abolished the age ceiling, except for a few jobs such as firefighters, police officers, tenured university professors, and executives with annual pensions exceeding $44,000. Like Title VII, the law has a BFOQ exception—employers may set reasonable age limitations on certain high-stress jobs requiring peak physical condition, for example.

Discrimination against the Handicapped

The federal Rehabilitation Act of 1973, while not as broad as Title VII in its coverage of employers, nevertheless broadly bans discrimination against handicapped persons who are otherwise qualified to hold the job. The Supreme Court has said that "otherwise qualified" means a person "who is able to meet all of a program's requirements in spite of his handicap." In one particular case, a deaf woman was held not to be otherwise qualified for a job in a nursing program because hearing was a necessary requirement to carry out the duties of the job. (Southeastern Community College v. Davis, 442 U.S. 397 (1979)]

The act applies to businesses receiving federal financial assistance and to those entering into certain kinds of contracts (such as procurement contracts) with the federal government. Among other handicaps, the following

Box 16-3 Never Too Old to Sue

Forced Exits? Companies Confront Wave of Age-discrimination Suits
By Sydney P. Freedberg

A jury in Dade City, Fla., recently found Lykes Pasco Inc., a juice processor, guilty of age discrimination when it fired Malcolm Anderson, a 59-year-old worker with 30 years of service. The jurors awarded Mr. Anderson $196,940—about 10 times his final annual salary.

Whatever the merits of Mr. Anderson's case (the company is appealing), the outcome was typical in one respect: When juries hear age-discrimination lawsuits, the odds favor the worker.

"It's very hard to convince a jury that a nice, white-haired man who lost his job after 20 years doesn't deserve something against the big, bad corporation," says Larry Besnoff, a management lawyer in Philadelphia.

Age discrimination is the fastest-growing type of bias charge in the workplace. Last year, almost 27,000 complaints were lodged with federal and state agencies—more than twice the number filed in 1980. Although many cases never reach court, the occasional blockbuster settlement "puts the fear of God in lots of managers," says J. Robert Kirk, a Washington-based management lawyer.

While some areas of the law are still being mapped, enough cases have moved through the courts to give lawyers and personnel specialists a good idea of what constitutes age discrimination—and what does and doesn't work in pursuing or fighting such charges.

An individual who is pressing a lawsuit, for example, probably wants a jury trial; a company defending against such a suit probably wants a judge. Companies can still fire older workers, as long as age itself isn't a reason. But even casual asides—such as a boss referring to an employee as "the old man"—can be proof of discrimination. Companies sometimes lose suits because they can't document that an employee's work justified dismissal. But even with good personnel records, cases often boil down to credibility contests.

"You can trot out every statistic and business explanation in the book, but if a jury thinks an older worker has been treated unfairly, they won't listen," says Jack G. Knebel, a lawyer for Miles Inc. . . . [A] San Francisco jury [recently] ordered the company to pay $1.63 million to nine older workers who had been dismissed in a company-wide layoff. Miles, maker of Alka Seltzer, is asking for a new trial.

THE LAW

In the area of civil rights, the Age Discrimination in Employment Act is a "favored statute" among employees and their lawyers, says Paul Brenner, a staff lawyer for the Equal Employment Opportunity Commission. That's because the age act, unlike most other civil-rights statutes, allows jury trials as well as double damages for workers who prove "willful" discrimination by an employer.

Congress passed the law in 1967, preventing employers from using age as a basis for hiring or firing people ages 40 to 65. In 1978, the age cap was lifted to 70. . . . [Later] Congress eliminated the cap for most occupations. About one-third of the states have passed companion measures that restrict mandatory retirement.

Litigants typically start by filing a charge with the Equal Employment Opportunity Commission or its state counterpart. Such agencies can file a lawsuit on behalf of an employee, but their staffs are often bogged down. Thus, most workers simply go to court themselves.

WHO SUES?

The typical age-bias litigant is a white male supervisor in his 50s who was discharged in a corporate belt-tightening. A recent study by Syracuse University School of Management, which reviewed more than 10,000 age-discrimination claims, says the average litigant sees a lawsuit as his only refuge; he has no union to represent him and can't qualify for racial or sexual discrimination.

A majority of the complaints, the study says, originate in right-to-work states outside the

(continues on next page)

Box 16-3, *continued*

Northeast, where employers "may be more aggressive in discharging or forcing the retirement of older workers."

Last year, a fourth of the court actions filed by the Equal Employment Opportunity Commission fell under the age act. Raymond C. Fay, a Washington lawyer specializing in discrimination cases, attributes the rise in complaints to heightened public awareness of the law and the growing numbers of workers covered by it.

IN COURT

Only about one age-discrimination case in five makes it to a jury. "A lot of these complaints ought not to be in court," says Christopher S. Miller, an Atlanta lawyer who co-authored the Syracuse study. "They're straight grievance claims by older workers who were the unfortunate victims of companies that were forced to cut back."

The Syracuse study says judges rule for companies about two-thirds of the time, not including those cases decided on procedural issues. Conversely, Mr. Miller says, juries side with older workers about two-thirds of the time. Says San Francisco management lawyer Victor Schachter, "Juries are inherently biased in favor of long-term employees who work for deep-pocket companies."

RAVE REVIEWS

To avoid age-bias lawsuits, management specialists caution companies to avoid inflating performance appraisals and to ensure a thorough, accurate paper trail for each employee.

Such reviews played a role in the recent judgment against Miles, which merged with Cutter Laboratories Inc. in 1983 and inherited age-bias charges. At the trial in August, Miles argued that $60 million in losses prompted Cutter to lay off 1,200 workers in 1982 and that it picked the least productive employees with the worst sales records. But the nine workers who sued claimed that the company's standards were biased against workers over 40, and their lawyer produced records showing that they had received glowing performance evaluations over the years.

The six-member District Court jury—all but one over 40 years old—believed the salespeople. What's more, the jury found the discrimination "willful" and awarded double damages—$1.63 million.

WHAT TO DO?

Any hiring or firing decision in which age has crept into the process is suspect under the law.

A company can be held liable, for instance, if an age-neutral layoff policy ends up having a disproportionate effect on older workers. An employer could also have trouble in court for involuntarily transferring an older worker who performs at a minimally acceptable level. And a company can lose a lawsuit simply on the basis of a seemingly harmless aside. In the case of Lykes Pasco, a subsidiary of Tampa, Fla.-based Lykes Bros. Inc., two secretaries testified that two executives called Mr. Anderson "the old man" and "too darned old." (The executives denied it.) In

have been held to be covered by the law: blindness, congenital back problem, epilepsy, carrying a potentially contagious disease, former drug addiction, and former alcoholism. But the law excludes current alcohol or drug abuse that would hinder the performance of the employee's duties or would constitute a threat to property or safety.

Two emerging issues, far from settled, are (1) whether the Rehabilitation Act precludes drug testing on the job to determine whether an employee has a drug habit that would prevent performance of the job, and (2) whether victims of AIDS (acquired immune deficiency syndrome) are handicapped the Miles-Cutter case, a manager allegedly commented that he preferred salespeople in their 20s. (The manager denied it.)

"Remarks like, 'We need new blood,' can be the kiss of death for a company defending against an age-bias claim," says Mr. Miller, the Atlanta lawyer.

Even a company's manuals and forms can cause trouble if they reflect any age bias. Some businesses, for example, have decided to remove the "Date of Birth" box from their job-application forms and have stopped asking what year an applicant graduated from high school or college.

GOLDEN HANDCUFFS

To thwart lawsuits, some companies are starting to ask retiring employees to sign notarized releases waiving all age-discrimination claims. Some lawyers, however, debate the validity of such releases. . . . [I]n Cincinnati, a federal appeals court overturned a decision that had declared such a release illegal. The employee who had signed the release was a lawyer for NCR Corp.

COMING ATTRACTIONS

The current interest in age discrimination, lawyers say, may be nothing compared to what lies ahead. By the year 2010, people age 40 or over—those protected by the law—are expected to make up half the work force. More older people with medical handicaps are likely to file suit, alleging both age and handicap bias. "More older women and more older blacks will be contending for the same jobs held by older white men," says Mr. Miller.

As more companies seek ways to streamline aging work forces, new age-discrimination issues are likely to crop up in court: When does a "voluntary" early-retirement plan become subtly coercive? Can a company fire an older, higher-salaried worker to save money? And is the fast-track method of management—in which younger "bright stars" are transferred from department to department to broaden their experience—legal?

Source: *Wall Street Journal,* October 13, 1987, p. 37

A Profile of Litigation

An analysis of 280 federal court cases involving claims under the Age Discrimination in Employment Act showed that:

- 84% were filed by white males
- 68% dealt with an employee's dismissal or involuntary retirement
- 59% were filed by managerial and professional employees
- 54% were filed by employees between the ages of 50 and 59

Sources: Syracuse University; American Association of Retired Persons

under the law's definition. If they are not, then employers are within their rights to discharge or refuse to hire AIDS victims. As this text went to press, no federal court had yet considered whether AIDS victims or those who test positive for the AIDS virus fall within the definition. But such cases are sure to arise. In a controversial opinion in 1986, the Justice Department stated that the ability to transmit AIDS is not a handicap and, therefore, that an employer's reaction to fear that an employee or prospective employee might transmit AIDS does not violate the law. Whether this opinion will stand up in court remains to be seen. In 1987, the Supreme

Court ruled that a person afflicted with tuberculosis, a contagious disease, may be a handicapped person within the meaning of the Rehabilitation Act; contagion, by itself, is not sufficient to remove a person from the coverage of the law. The Court said that the trial court must conduct an individualized inquiry first to assess (a) the nature of the risk, (b) the duration of the risk, (c) the severity of the risk (the potential harm to third persons), and (d) the probabilities that the victim will transmit the disease to others, and then to determine whether the employer could make a reasonable accommodation in view of the risks. If the Court adheres to this position, it is likely that it will eventually find AIDS victims to be similarly protected. [Arline v. School Board, 107 S.Ct. 1123 (1987)]

Erosion of the Employment-at-Will Doctrine

At common law, an employee without a contract guaranteeing a job for a specific period was an "employee at will" and could be fired at any time and for any reason, or even for no reason at all. The various federal statutes we have just examined have made inroads on the at-will doctrine. Another federal statute, the Occupational Safety and Health Act, prohibits employers from discharging employees who exercise their rights under that law.

In recent years, many states also have begun to whittle away at the common law rule. Several states forbid retaliatory discharge against employees who file workers' compensation claims or who refuse to take lie detector tests. In some cases, these new rules have been enacted in statutory form. For example, some states have begun to enact so-called **whistle-blower** statutes, which protect the jobs of employees who "blow the whistle" on corrupt or otherwise illegal conduct of their employers. In other states, the courts have begun to recognize a "public policy" exception to the at-will doctrine. Thus, in *Palmateer* v. *International Harvester Co.*, 421 N.E.2d 876 (Ill. 1981), the Supreme Court of Illinois declared that an employee may not lawfully be fired for going to the authorities with information that a fellow employee might be involved in criminal actions.

Discharges motivated by special employee acts covered by statutory provisions or public policy are, relatively speaking, not a large class of cases. In any event, the emerging statutory and public policy exceptions do not cover firings unrelated to specific employee actions such as blowing the whistle or refusing to take a lie detector test. In many cases, personality conflicts or bad management practices may lead to employees' being fired without good cause. As long as the at-will doctrine remains, the employer's right to do so will be lawful. But beginning in the late 1970s, this long-standing doctrine came to be questioned at its roots.

The courts have found various ways to attack it. For example, courts in Massachusetts and New Hampshire declared that every employment agreement implicitly requires the employer to deal fairly with the employee, so that a discharge without good cause—such as incompetence, corruption, or habitual tardiness—is actionable. But that rule provides protection only if a contract exists. The New York Court of Appeals, in *Weiner* v. *McGraw-Hill, Inc.*, 433 N.E.2d 441 (N.Y. 1983), found something in the factual circumstances that implied a contract with the employee to treat him fairly and to discharge him only for cause. In this particular case, the implied contract was in the company's employment handbook.

In response to judicial attacks on the employment-at-will rule, companies have rewritten employee handbooks and required employees to sign disclaimers acknowledging that they serve at the will of the company. The validity of one such disclaimer was tested in the following case.

REID v. SEARS, ROEBUCK AND CO.
790 F.2d 453 (6th Cir. 1986)

LIVELY, CHIEF JUDGE. These three appeals were argued separately, but have been consolidated for opinion since all require application of the same body of Michigan law. The three plaintiffs are former employees of Sears who were discharged without a showing of good cause. The plaintiffs brought separate suits in Michigan courts, claiming that their employment contracts with Sears, though for indefinite terms, required Sears to show good cause before they could be discharged. All relied on the seminal decision of the Supreme Court of Michigan in *Toussaint v. Blue Cross & Blue Shield of Michigan,* 408 Mich. 579, 292 N.W.2d 880 (1980). The cases were removed to the United States District Court for the Eastern District of Michigan on the basis of diversity of citizenship. Three judges of the District heard the cases, 588 F.Supp. 558, and each granted summary judgment in favor of Sears.

In *Toussaint* the Supreme Court of Michigan recognized the general rule that "in the absence of distinguishing features or provisions or a consideration in addition to the services to be rendered, . . . contracts [for permanent employment] are indefinite hirings, terminable at the will of either party." The court held, however, that the general rule does not apply when the contract of employment provides that the employee may not be discharged except for cause. Though such a contract is indefinite, the requirement of cause is enforceable. A provision requiring cause for the discharge of an indefinite term employee "may become part of the contract either by express agreement, oral or written, or as a result of an employee's legitimate expectations grounded in an employer's policy statements." The court further held that the jury properly could have found that Toussaint had a legitimate expectation of continued employment on the basis of his employer's written policy statement set forth in a manual of personnel policies.

* * *

We state briefly the circumstances surrounding the three discharges:

Mary Ann Reid had been employed by Sears for 17 years. In January 1981, the battery was stolen from a car which her son had borrowed from his grandmother, plaintiff's mother. When the son called his father for advice, Mr. Reid agreed to buy a new battery to replace the stolen one, and he did so using his wife's 10% employee discount at Sears. When Mrs. Reid's mother consulted her insurance company, she was told that she could not recover without receipts for the purchase both of the stolen battery and of the replacement. She no longer had the first receipt, and the insurance company would not accept the second because it was in Mr. Reid's name, not hers. To substantiate her mother's insurance claim, Mrs. Reid asked Tom Dunaj, a non-supervisory employee in the automotive department, to make out two new invoices. He did so, although the new invoice for the replacement battery failed to take the employee discount into account.

Mr. Everest, the manager of the Grosse Pointe store where Mrs. Reid worked, was contacted by the insurance company when they noticed that the two invoices, though dated two months apart, were numbered consecutively. Upon being questioned, Dunaj and Reid admitted their actions, and both were fired for willful misconduct.

John Serra asserts that, during the year before he was fired, he was under pressure to give older salespeople working under him lower performance evaluations than they deserved. Because of this, he had arranged to transfer to sales. Before the transfer, however, a "bookcheck audit" was performed on the two divisions he was responsible for. A number of items were questioned, and Mr. Serra submitted explanations. One of the questionable bookchecks was for the sale of a lawnmower to Gary Redfern, one of Serra's salesmen. The lawnmower was sold at a sale price after the sale had ended. Mr. Serra's version of the story is that while the lawnmower was on sale, Redfern's father-in-law had received a "raincheck" on the lawnmower, which he intended to buy for Gary. Mr. Serra says that Gary, on questioning, told him that when the lawnmower came in, his father-in-law suggested that he instead give Gary the money so that he could use his 10% discount. Mr. Redfern, however, told company officials investigating the matter that this story was a complete fabrication and that Mr. Serra had simply given him a sale price on the mower. The sale came into question initially because a raincheck sale is supposed to be rung up on the original bookcheck with the sale date on it; this one was recorded on a new bookcheck. Mr. Serra notes that this deviation from policy required his authorization, and that the bookcheck does not bear his signature; the clerk who made the sale said he had Serra's oral authorization. Redfern also told the investigators that Serra had repeatedly authorized the sale of regular merchandise at sale prices. Mr. Serra was fired, and told that he was being discharged for a violation of company policy on "category 57 miscellaneous markdown," *i.e.*, for allowing the sale of merchandise at a promotional price when it was not on sale.

On March 20, 1982, while on break, Mary Batchelor went to the cosmetics department of Sears and made some purchases. While she was there, she dropped a bottle of nail polish into her purse. Sears asserts that she intended to steal it; she maintains that the polish must have fallen into her purse inadvertently after she checked its color against her own make-up. She says that when she discovered that she still had the polish she intended to pay for it, but decided to wait until later because her co-worker was so rushed. She went into the locker room, placed her purse in her locker, and put the polish in a separate locker, intending to pay for it later. She contends that employees customarily used the locker for that purpose, though she knew she wasn't supposed to. (A written directive forbidding this practice was sent around to some employees after Ms. Batchelor was fired.) Shortly after leaving the polish in the locker room, Ms. Batchelor was approached and questioned by two security guards. When she returned to work the following Monday morning, she was questioned. Ms. Batchelor maintains that she was badly intimidated by the interrogation. That morning, she wrote out a signed statement which reads:

> I went and paid for three items [D]rop[ed] nail polish in pocket book [G]ot [b]ack to my dept. and I took it out put it in locker. I had star[te]d not to pay for it. But could not do so. I was going to get Ann to [ri]ng it up [b]ut there was a lot of customers at the time.
>
> Mary Batchelor

At her deposition, Ms. Batchelor stated that she never meant to steal anything. Shortly after the statement was signed, Ms. Batchelor was fired. She alleges that she suffered severe depression.

Each of the three contends he or she was actually fired for reasons other than those which Sears gave. Mrs. Reid asserts that the cash office, where she worked, was soon to need fewer employees, and that her firing fits in with a general pattern at Sears of replacing higher paid full-time employees with lower paid part-timers. Mr. Serra claims he was fired in retaliation for his unwillingness to adjust his employee evaluations to further this policy. Ms. Batchelor maintains that the store was in the midst of a record-setting shoplifting campaign and that catching her redounded to the credit of the store manager.

* * *

The feature that distinguishes the present cases from *Toussaint* and all other Michigan decisions relied upon by the plaintiffs is the unequivocal language contained in the application for employment that each of the plaintiffs signed. *Toussaint* makes it clear that an employer can defeat claims that an employee could be discharged only for good cause by "requiring *prospective employees* to acknowledge that they serve at the will or pleasure of the company. . . ." 408 Mich. at 612, 292 N.W.2d 880 (emphasis added). Since the acknowledgement should be obtained from prospective employees, Sears properly included this provision of employment in the application form rather than in some documents to be signed by the employee after he or she was hired.

* * *

The employment contract with the three plaintiffs clearly included the terms of the application. *Toussaint* held that employers can avoid misunderstanding over the term of employment by "requiring prospective employees to acknowledge that they serve at the will or pleasure of the company. . . ." 408 Mich. at 612, 292 N.W.2d 880. Having obtained such an acknowledgement from each of the plaintiffs when they were prospective employees, Sears had done all that was required to create contracts for employment at will. Though *Toussaint* holds that there may be an implied contract that employment may be terminated only for good cause, it does not hold that this may be the case where an express contract makes the term of employment at will. It is well settled in Michigan that there cannot be an implied contract covering the same subject as an express one.

[Judgments affirmed.]

The employer's power to discharge employees is constrained not only by the anti-discrimination provisions of Title VII and by erosion of the employment-will-doctrine but also by the increasing resort to common-law suits for defamation. The basic charge in most such suits by former employees is that employers have libeled or slandered them when giving references to new or prospective employers. Like plaintiffs in age discrimination suits, discharged employees find sympathetic juries when their cases eventually get that far. Although the law is different from state to state, the national statistics show that more lawyers have been getting more such cases to the juries (see Box 16-4).

Chapter Summary

For the past twenty-five years, Title VII of the Civil Rights Act of 1964 has prohibited employment discrimination based on race, religion, sex, or national origins. Any employment decision, including hiring, promotion, and discharge, based on one of these factors is unlawful and subjects the employer to an award of back pay, promotion, or reinstatement. The EEOC may file suits as may the employee—after the commission screens the complaint.

Two major types of discrimination suits are those for disparate treatment (in which the employer intended to discriminate) and disparate impact (in which, regardless of intent, the impact of a particular non-job-related practice has a discriminatory effect. In matters of religion, the employer is bound not only to refrain from discrimination based on an employee's religious

Box 16-4 New Legal Peril for Employers Who Fire Workers

Fired Employees Turn the Reason for Dismissal into a Legal Weapon

By Gregory Stricharchuk

Companies that fire people are discovering they have to choose their final words very carefully.

Employees are turning the reason for their firing into a legal weapon: a libel charge. Because such individuals frequently are dismissed for poor performance or some form of misconduct that isn't well-documented they are able to claim that any report about their performance to others—such as from their former employer to a prospective employer—constitutes defamation.

The result is that libel suits filed by discharged employees against their former bosses today account for about a third of all defamation actions, according to Jury Verdict Research Inc. in Solon, Ohio. "These suits are the new workhorse in termination litigation," says Rodney A. Smolla, a University of Arkansas law professor and libel specialist.

THE SILENT TREATMENT

The trend is prompting many companies to refrain from making any negative statements about former employees. But even the very act of dismissing someone can still land a company in court. If a fired worker is forced to disclose in a job interview the reason he was let go, such "compelled self-publication," as the courts define it, can also constitute defamation.

"There's no such thing as just firing someone anymore," a corporate lawyer says.

Defending such actions can take years and cost employers tens of thousands of dollars. Former workers who won their cases collected an average of almost $112,000 in 1982, the latest year for which statistics are available.

"Juries don't have a lot of sympathy for big companies putting someone on the street," says John B. Lewis, a Cleveland lawyer who defends corporations against employment-related litigation. "Juries also have a high regard for a person's reputation."

Harshly criticizing a former employee to others is perhaps the easiest way a company can make itself vulnerable to a defamation suit. Consider Larry W. Buck, who was abruptly fired from his insurance broker's job at a Frank B. Hall & Co. office in Texas. When he couldn't find new employment, he hired a private detective to find out why he had been dismissed.

According to transcripts of testimony in Harris County court in Houston, Mr. Buck's former boss told the detective (who explained that Mr. Buck was being considered for a position of trust) that Mr. Buck was ruthless, disliked by his co-workers and a failure as a businessman. The boss described Mr. Buck as a "classical sociopath, a zero, a Jekyll-and-Hyde person who was lacking in . . . scruples."

Armed with the detective's tape-recorded interviews, Mr. Buck sued Frank B. Hall for defamation. In court, Hall executives said Mr. Buck was fired for failing to produce sufficient income, and they argued that he shouldn't recover damages because he invited their comments through hiring the investigator. But a jury agreed he had been libeled and slandered and awarded him $1.9 million. The U.S. Supreme Court upheld the award last year.

In other cases, fired employees are seeking libel damages simply because their performance was judged unsatisfactory—and that judgment was disseminated outside the company.

American Standard Corp., for example, found itself the target of a libel suit because of a letter it distributed to a state employment agency in 1978, noting that a manager had been fired for "unsatisfactory performance." The manager, Gerald F. Adler, maintained that he was dismissed for reporting alleged misdeeds at the company. (A spokesman for American Standard says the misdeeds were "vague and . . . never substantiated.")

Last January, Mr. Adler was awarded $2.8 million by a Baltimore federal jury. The judge who heard the case, however, threw out the jury's finding that Mr. Adler had been defamed and left damages related to "abusive discharge." Mr. Adler has appealed the decision; American Standard says it plans to appeal.

Anxious to avoid the high costs and aggravation of libel suits, many companies are sharply restricting information they will provide about former employees. Some refuse to offer anything more than a former worker's name, rank and dates of employment. But this tight-lipped approach can come back to haunt companies as they attempt to screen out incompetent and dishonest job applicants.

Arthur Silbergeld, a California lawyer, blames inadequate reference information for the high turnover of employees in that state's financial institutions. "Once on the job," he says, "the companies find that the employees can't do the job—that the skills aren't there."

An executive in TRW Inc.'s electronics and defense division recently told a U.S. Senate subcommittee that workers are able to cover up problems in their pasts and still land jobs in the defense industry because companies are wary of becoming involved in libel suits. Cleveland-based TRW, he said, would rather reject job applicants outright than confront them with negative information. Defending defamation suits, the company estimates, costs between $140,000 and $250,000 each.

Personnel consultants say one of the best ways companies can defend themselves against defamation litigation is to help discharged employees find new jobs through outplacement counseling. "People who find new jobs don't sue, while many who don't find jobs blame it on the previous employer," says Paul Thompson, a Virginia lawyer.

Companies can also help themselves by conducting regular and comprehensive performance appraisals and exit interviews. Such "progressive discipline," says John Donovan, a Buffalo, N.Y., lawyer, leaves no doubts why an employee was dismissed.

Even if a company refrains from releasing negative information about a fired employee, the company still may be vulnerable to a libel suit if the dismissal came with little warning and the reasons for the firing were unclear. If the discharged worker is forced to tell a new employer the reason he was let go, such "compelled self-publication" can constitute defamation if the reason for the firing can't be fully documented.

DISCLOSING THE FACTS

Four dental claims processors fired by Equitable Life Assurance Society in St. Paul, Minn., won a defamation suit against Equitable even though they—and not the company—disclosed they were dismissed for "gross insubordination." The four were fired after supervisors questioned expense vouchers they had submitted and ordered the women to change the vouchers.

Equitable's lawyers "laughed at us" when the suit was filed, says James W. Kenney, an attorney for the discharged employees. But a Ramsey County jury awarded the women more than $1 million.

The verdict was upheld last July by the Minnesota Supreme Court, which eliminated about $600,000 in punitive damages. Nonetheless, the ruling established in Minnesota the concept of compelled self-publication, which Georgia, Michigan and California also recognize.

Although it is unclear whether the verdict will result in a flood of similar suits, the Minnesota Supreme Court expressed such concerns in its ruling. The court said it disallowed the punitive damages because that award might stop employers from disclosing the reasons for discharging employees, which the court felt wouldn't be in the public interest.

A dissenting judge wrote, "Now the only way an employer can avoid litigation and the possible liability for substantial damages, is to cease communicating the reason (for) the termination, not only to third persons, but even to the employee."

Source: *Wall Street Journal,* October 2, 1986, p. 31

beliefs or preferences but also to accommodate the employee's religious practices, to the extent that the accommodation does not impose an undue hardship on the business.

Sex discrimination, besides refusal to hire a person solely on the basis of sex, includes discrimination based on pregnancy. Sexual harassment is a form of sex discrimination, and the term includes creation of a hostile or offensive working environment. A separate statute, the Equal Pay Act, mandates equal pay for men and women assigned to the same job. Comparable worth, a legal theory that surfaced in the early 1980s, would require employers to pay the sexes equally if they are working at comparable jobs, even if different; the theory is not yet established law.

One major exception to Title VII permits hiring people of a particular religion, sex, or nationality if that feature is a bona fide occupational qualification. There is no BFOQ exception for race. Nor is a public stereotype a legitimate basis for a BFOQ.

Affirmative action plans, permitting or requiring employers to hire on the basis of race to make up for past discrimination or to bring up the level of minority workers, have been approved even though the plans may seem to conflict with Title VII. But affirmative-action plans have not been permitted to overcome bona fide seniority systems.

The Age Discrimination in Employment Act protects workers over forty from discharge solely on the basis of age. Amendments to the law have abolished the age ceiling for retirement so that most people working for employers covered by the law cannot be forced to retire.

The Rehabilitation Act prohibits discrimination based on a handicap, as long as the prospective employee is otherwise qualified to perform the job. One major question yet to be settled is whether people suffering from AIDS, or carrying the AIDS virus, are handicapped and thus within the protection of the law.

At common law, an employer was free to fire an employee for any reason, or for no reason at all. In recent years, the employment-at-will doctrine has been eroded, and many state courts have found against employers on the basis of implied contracts, to which employers have responded with explicit disclaimers in employee handbooks and elsewhere.

Problems

1. Rainbow Airlines, a new air carrier headquartered in Chicago with routes from Nome to Canberra, extensively studied the psychology of passengers and determined that more than 93 percent of its passengers felt most comfortable with female flight attendants between the ages of twenty-one and thirty-four. To increase its profitability, the company issued a policy of hiring only such people for jobs in the air but opened all ground jobs to anyone who could otherwise qualify. The policy

made no racial distinction and, in fact, nearly 30 percent of the stewardesses hired were black. What violations of federal law has Rainbow committed, if any?

2. Tex Olafson worked for five years as a messenger for Pressure Sell Advertising Agency, a company without a unionized work force. On his fifth anniversary with the company, Tex was called in to the president's office, given a 10 percent raise, and was complimented on his diligence. The following week, a new head of the messenger department was hired. He wanted to appoint his nephew to a messenger job, but discovered that a company-wide hiring freeze prevented him from adding another employee to the messenger ranks. So he fired Tex and hired his nephew. What remedy, if any, does Tex have? What additional facts might change the result?
3. Ernest lost both his legs in combat in Vietnam. He has applied for a job with Excelsior Products in the company's quality control lab. The job requires inspectors to randomly check products coming off the assembly line for defects. Historically, all inspectors have stood two-hour shifts. Ernest proposes to sit in his wheelchair. The company refuses to hire him because it says he will be less efficient. Ernest's previous employment record shows him to be a diligent, serious worker. Does Ernest have a legal right to be hired? What additional facts might you want to know in deciding?
4. Marlene works for Frenzied Traders, a stock-brokerage with a seat on the New York Stock Exchange. For several years Marlene has been a floor trader, spending all day in the hurly-burly of stock trading, yelling herself hoarse. Each year she has received a large bonus from the company. She was just told the company that she is pregnant. Citing a company policy, she is told she can no longer engage in trading because it is too tiring for pregnant women. Instead, she may take a backroom job, though the company cannot guarantee that the floor job will be open after she delivers. Marlene also wants to take six months off after her child is born. The company says it cannot afford to give her that time. It has a policy of granting paid leave to anyone recuperating from a stay in the hospital and unpaid leave for four months thereafter. What legal rights does Marlene have, and what remedies is she entitled to?
5. Charlie Goodfellow works for Yum-Burger and has always commanded respect at the local franchise for being the fastest server. One day he undergoes a profound religious experience, converts to Sikhism, and changes his name to Sanjay Singh. The tenets of his religion require him to wear a beard and a turban. He lets his beard grow, puts on a turban, and his fellow workers tease him. One day a regional vice president arrives, sees that Sanjay is not wearing the prescribed Yum-Burger uniform, and fires him. What rights of Sanjay, if any, has Yum-Burger violated? What remedies are available to him?

PART FIVE

THE INVESTOR

17

Forms of Business Organization

It would be difficult to conceive of a complex society that did not operate its businesses through organizations. In this chapter we will explore in some detail the two most common forms of organization—partnerships and corporations. We also examine other, related forms, notably limited partnerships and business trusts.

Although their individual characteristics differ, most business organizations share a common feature: They are subject to securities regulation. In Chapter 18, we review the general nature of securities regulation—including the broad test used to determine the types of investments that are subject to regulation—and then focus on the impact of securities regulation on corporate governance.

Partnership

History of Partnership Law

Partnership is an ancient form of business enterprise, and special laws governing partnerships date as far back as 2300 B.C., when the Code of Hammurabi explicitly regulated the relations between partners. Partnership was an important part of Roman law, and it played a significant role in the law merchant, the international commercial law of the Middle Ages.

In the nineteenth century, both in England and the United States, partnership was a popular vehicle for business enterprise. But the law governing it was jumbled. Common-law principles were mixed with equitable standards, and the result was considerable confusion. Parliament moved to reduce the uncertainty by adopting the Partnership Act of 1890. Codification took longer in the United States. The Commissioners on Uniform State Laws undertook the task at the turn of the twentieth century, and the Uniform Partnership Act (UPA), completed in 1914, and the Uniform Limited Partnership Act (ULPA), completed in 1916, are the basis of our modern law. The UPA has been adopted by all states except for Louisiana, and only Louisiana has not enacted the ULPA or a revised version of the ULPA. Despite its name, the UPA has not been enacted uniformly among the states, however. Some states have adhered to theory that partnerships are discrete legal entities apart from the partners who comprise them.

Entity Theory

A **legal entity** is a person or group that the law recognizes as having legal rights, such as the right to own and dispose of property, to sue and be sued, and to enter into contracts. When individuals carry out a common enterprise as partners, a threshold legal question is whether the partnership is a legal entity. The common law said no. In other words, under the common-law theory, a partnership was but a convenient name for an aggregate of individuals, and the rights and duties recognized and imposed by law are those of the individual partners. By contrast, the mercantile theory of the law merchant held that a partnership is a legal entity that can have rights and duties independent of those of its members.

During the drafting of the UPA a debate raged over which theory to adopt. The drafters resolved the debate through a compromise. In Section 6(1), the UPA provides a neutral definition of partnership ("an association of two or more persons to carry on as co-owners a business for profit") and retained the common-law theory that a partnership is an aggregation of individuals. However, a partnership does have certain entity characteristics:

For Accounting Purposes The partnership may keep business records as if it were a separate entity, and its accountants may treat it as such for purposes of preparing income statements and balance sheets.

For Purposes of Taxation Federal tax law requires every partnership to file an informational tax return, but because partnerships are not taxable entities, they do not pay income taxes. Instead, each partner's **distributive share** which includes income or other gain, loss, deductions, and credits must be included in the partner's personal income tax return, whether or not the share is actually distributed.

For Purposes of Suing Because the UPA conceives of a partnership as an aggregation, suits to enforce a partnership contract or some other right must be filed in the name of all the partners. Similarly, to sue a partnership the plaintiff must name and sue each of the partners. This cumbersome procedure has been modified in many states, which have enacted special statutes expressly permitting suits by and against partnerships in the firm name. In suits on a claim in federal court, a partnership may sue and be sued in its common name.

For Purposes of Bankruptcy Under federal bankruptcy law, a partnership is an entity that may voluntarily seek the haven of a bankruptcy court or that may involuntarily be thrust into a bankruptcy proceeding by its creditors. The partnership cannot discharge its debts in a liquidation proceeding under Chapter 7 of the bankruptcy law, but it can be rehabilitated under Chapter 11 (see p. 343).

For Purposes of Owning Real Estate Like a corporation, a partnership may buy, sell, and hold real property in the partnership name. (UPA Sections 8(3) and 10(1).) Real estate bought in the partnership name can be sold only in its name. The UPA provisions are permissive, not mandatory, and partnership real estate is often held in the names of one or more partners.

Tests of Partnership Existence

Partnerships can come into existence quite informally. In contrast to the corporation, which is the creature of statute, partnership is a catch-all term for a large variety of working relationships, and frequently uncertainties arise about whether or not a particular relationship is that of partnership. The law can reduce the uncertainty in advance only at the price of severely restricting the flexibility of people to associate. As the chief drafter of the UPA explained: "All other business associations are statutory in origin. They are formed by the happening of an event designated in a statute as necessary to their formation. In corporations this act may be the issuing of a charter by the proper officer of the state; in limited partnerships, the filing by the associates of a specified document in a public office. On the other hand, an infinite number of combinations of circumstances may result in co-ownership of a business. Partnership is the residuum, including all forms of co-ownership, of a business except those business associations organized under a specific statute" (Lewis, 1915, p. 622). Nevertheless, a number of tests have been established that are clues to the existence of a partnership.

Co-ownership of a Business Recall the UPA's definition of a partnership: "an association of two or more persons to carry on as co-owners a business for profit." If what two or more people own is clearly a *business*—including capital assets, contracts with employees or agents, an income stream, debts incurred on behalf of the operation—a partnership exists. A tougher question arises when two or more persons co-own *property*. Do they automatically become partners? The answer can be important: if one of the owners, while doing business pertinent to the property, chances to injure a stranger, the latter could sue the other owners if there is a partnership.

Co-ownership comes in many guises. The three most common are *joint tenancy, tenancy in common,* and *tenancy by the entireties.* In **joint tenancy**, the owners hold the property under a single instrument, such as a deed, and if one dies the others automatically become owners of the deceased's share, which does not descend to his heirs. **Tenancy in common** has the reverse rule: the survivor tenants do not take the deceased's share. Each tenant in common has a distinct estate in the property. The **tenancy by the entirety** form of ownership is limited to spouses and its effects are similar to that of joint tenancy.

Suppose a husband and wife who own their home as tenants by the entirety decide to spend the summer at the seashore and rent their home for three months. Is their co-ownership sufficient to establish that they are partners? The answer is no. By UPA Section 7(2), the various forms of joint ownership by themselves do not establish partnership, whether or not the co-owners share profits made by the use of the property. To establish a partnership, the ownership must be of a business, not merely of property.

Sharing of Profits While co-ownership does not establish a partnership unless there is a business, a business, by itself, is not a partnership unless co-ownership is present. Of the tests used by courts to determine co-ownership, perhaps the most important is sharing of profits. UPA Section 7(4) provides that: "The receipt by a person of a share of the profits of a business is prima facie evidence that he is a partner in the business. . . ." That conclusion can be contradicted, however, by one of five explanations for the receipt of the money. No partnership exists if someone draws money from a business: (1) to repay a debt; (2) as wages or rent; (3) as an annuity to a representative of a deceased partner; (4) as interest on a loan; or (5) as consideration for the sale of good will of a business or other property.

Other Factors Courts are not limited to the profit-sharing test; they also look at these factors, among others: the right to participate in decision-making, the duty to share liabilities, and the manner in which the business is operated. The following case illustrates how these factors are weighed in court.

CHAIKEN v. EMPLOYMENT SECURITY COMMISSION
274 A.2d 707 (Del. Super. Ct. 1971)

STOREY, JUDGE. Pursuant to 19 Del.C. § 3359, the Employment Security Commission; hereinafter referred to as the Commission, levied an involuntary assessment against Richard K. Chaiken, complainant, hereinafter referred to as Chaiken, for not filing his unemployment security assessment report. Pursuant to the same statutory section, a hearing was held and a determination made by the Commission that Chaiken was the employer of two barbers in his barber shop and that he should be assessed as an employer for his share of unemployment compensation contributions. Chaiken appealed the Commission's decision pursuant to 19 Del.C. § 3344(c). This Court may not set aside a decision of the Commission unless there is either no substantial evidence to reasonably support the finding or error of law.

In this case there is sufficient evidence to support the finding, and no error of law.

Both in the administrative hearing and in his appeal brief Chaiken argues that he had entered into partnership agreements with each of his barbers and, therefore, was and is not subject to unemployment compensation assessment. Under 19 Del.C. § 3302(10) (D), the burden is upon the individual assessed to show that he is outside the ambit of the statutory sections requiring assessment. If Chaiken's partnership argument fails he has no secondary position and he fails to meet his burden.

Chaiken contends that he and his "partners":

1. properly registered the partnership name and names of partners in the Prothonotary's office, in accordance with 6 Del.C. § 3101,
2. properly filed federal partnership information returns and paid federal taxes quarterly on an estimated basis, and
3. duly executed partnership agreements.

Of the three factors, the last is most important. Agreements of "partnership" were executed between Chaiken and Mr. Strazella, a barber in the shop, and between Chaiken and Mr. Spitzer, similarly situated. The agreements were nearly identical. The first paragraph declared the creation of a partnership and the location of business. The second provided that Chaiken would provide barber chair, supplies, and licenses, while the other partner would provide tools of the trade. The paragraph also declared that upon dissolution of the partnership, ownership of items would revert to the party providing them. The third paragraph declared that the income of the partnership would be divided 30% for Chaiken, 70% for Strazella; 20% for Chaiken and 80% for Spitzer. The fourth paragraph declared that all partnership policy would be decided by Chaiken, whose decision was final. The fifth paragraph forbade assignment of the agreement without permission of Chaiken. The sixth paragraph required Chaiken to hold and distribute all receipts. The final paragraph stated hours of work for Strazella and Spitzer and holidays.

The mere existence of an agreement labelled "partnership" agreement and the characterization of signatories as "partners" does not conclusively prove the existence of a partnership. Rather, the intention of the parties, as explained by the wording of the agreement, is paramount.

A partnership is defined as an association of two or more persons to carry on as co-owners a business for profit. As co-owners of a business, partners have an equal right in the decision making process. But this right may be abrogated by agreement of the parties without destroying the partnership concept, provided other partnership elements are present.

Thus, while paragraph four reserves for Chaiken all right to determine partnership policy, it is not standing alone, fatal to the partnership concept. Co-owners should also contribute valuable consideration for the creation of the business. Under paragraph two, however, Chaiken provides the barber chair (and implicitly the barber shop itself), mirror, licenses and linen, while the other partners merely provide their tools and labor—nothing more than any barber-employee would furnish. Standing alone, however, mere contribution of work and skill can be valuable consideration for a partnership agreement.

Partnership interests may be assignable, although it is not a violation of partnership law to prohibit assignment in a partnership agreement. Therefore, paragraph five on assignment of partnership interests does not violate the partnership concept. On the other hand, distribution of partnership assets to the partners upon dissolution is only allowed after all partnership liabilities are satisfied. But paragraph two of the agreement, in stating the ground rules for dissolution, makes no declaration that the partnership assets will be utilized to pay partnership expenses before reversion to their original owners. This deficiency militates against a finding in favor of partnership intent since it is assumed Chaiken would have inserted such provision had he thought his lesser partners would accept such liability. Partners do accept such liability, employees do not.

Most importantly, co-owners carry on "a business for profit." The phrase has been interpreted to mean that partners share in the profits and the losses of the business. The intent to divide the profits is an indispensable requisite of partnership. Paragraph three of the agreement declares that each partner shall share in the income of the business. There is no sharing of the profits, and as the agreement is drafted, there are no profits. Merely sharing the gross returns does not establish a partnership. Nor is the sharing of profits prima facie evidence of a partnership where the profits received are in payment of wages.

The failure to share profits therefore, is fatal to the partnership concept here.

Evaluating Chaiken's agreement in the light of the elements implicit in a partnership, no partnership intent can be found. The absence of the important right of decision making or the important duty to share liabilities upon dissolution individually may not be fatal to a partnership. But when both are absent, coupled with the absence of profit sharing, they become strong factors in discrediting the partnership argument. Such weighing of the elements against a partnership finding compares favorably with Fenwick v. Unemployment Compensation Commission, which decided against the partnership theory on similar facts, including the filing of partnership income tax forms.

In addition, the total circumstances of the case taken together indicate the employer-employee relationship between Chaiken and his barbers. The agreement set forth the hours of work and days off—unusual subjects for partnership agreements. The barbers brought into the relationship only the equipment required of all barber shop operators. And each barber had his own individual "partnership" with Chaiken. Furthermore, Chaiken conducted all transactions with suppliers, and purchased licenses, insurance, and the lease for the business property in his own name. Finally, the name "Richard's Barber Shop" continued to be used after the execution of the so-called partnership agreements.

It is the conclusion of this Court that Chaiken did not carry the burden of proving the existence of partnerships with Spitzer and Strazella. The [Employment Security] Commission should have made this determination first rather than merely have tested the facts of the case under 19 Del.C. § 3302(10) (D). Since, however, no partnership at law exists, the facts support the Commission's finding that Chaiken did come within the provisions of 19 Del.C. § 3302(10) (D). The Commission's decision is affirmed.

It is so ordered.

Liability

All partners are entitled to share equally in the management and conduct of the business. Partners also serve as agents of the partnership for the purpose of its business. As a result, a partnership and its partners are bound by contracts made by a partner who has express, implied, or apparent authority. Likewise, the partnership and partners are liable for the tortious acts of any partner acting "in the ordinary course of the business of the partnership or with the authority of his co-partners." (UPA Section 13) Liability for an agent's contracts and torts is explored further in Chapter

14. The following case, however, illustrates the application of agency theory in a partnership setting.

HAASE v. MORTON & MORTON
115 N.W. 921 (Ia. 1908)

SHERWIN, J. The defendants, Wm. M. Morton and L. B. Morton, are physicians practicing their profession under the firm name of Morton & Morton in Iowa Falls and vicinity. Early in January, 1905, Dr. W. M. Morton, the senior member of the firm, was called to the plaintiff's home in Iowa Falls for the purpose of treating the plaintiff professionally. He made a thorough examination of her condition, and determined that a surgical operation was necessary. He also suggested that it would be safer and more convenient to perform the operation at the hospital located near the plaintiff's home, and undertook to and did make the necessary arrangements for performing it there. Soon thereafter the plaintiff was taken to the hospital by Dr. W. M. Morton. She was given a room where she dressed for the operating table, and was then taken to the operating room in the story above by one of the attendants who was fitting herself for a nurse. The plaintiff was then laid on the operating table, and the defendant Dr. L. B. Morton administered the anæsthetic, and the defendant Dr. Wm. M. Morton performed the operation. After the operation, the plaintiff was taken from the operating table and placed on a car or stretcher for the purpose of taking her to her room on the floor below. Both of the defendants assisted in placing her on the car. The car was about six feet long and had six rubber-tired wheels, two large wheels in the center, and two smaller ones at each end. When either set of end wheels was resting on the floor, the car inclined in that direction. After the plaintiff had been placed on the car, Dr. Wm. M. Morton left the operating room for the surgeon's dressing room, and Dr. L. B. Morton and Miss Klein, the nurse who had shown the plaintiff to the operating room, rolled the car into the elevator room for the purpose of taking it to the room below on the elevator, the doctor being in front of the car and the nurse behind it. When they reached the elevator room, they found the elevator door wide open and the elevator below. The elevator room was only six or seven feet square, and the car on which the plaintiff rested was stopped with the front end thereof resting on the wheels and only a foot from the elevator door. After the car had been stopped, Dr. L. B. Morton left it, and stepped to the side of the elevator shaft for the purpose of bringing the elevator to their floor. The machinery did not at once respond to his efforts, whereupon Miss Klein, the nurse, told the defendant that she would go and call the janitor. She then left the car, and, after she had gotten some seven or eight feet therefrom, the defendant said to her, "Never mind, I can get it from here." When Miss Klein turned to go back into the elevator room, the car was just rolling into the elevator shaft. She reached it, but too late to save the plaintiff, who was still unconscious, and they were both precipitated to the floor below some 15 feet. For injuries received in the fall, the plaintiff brings this suit.

At the close of the evidence the defendants moved for a directed verdict, and the motion was overruled. It is now urged that the evidence is not sufficient to support a verdict against either of the defendants, and that the court erred in denying the motion.

* * *

The appellant Wm. M. Morton denies liability on the ground that whatever liability exists must rest on the act of his partner L. B. Morton while he was assisting in the removal of the plaintiff from the operating room to her own room, and insists that the removal to her private room was not within the scope of the ordinary business of the firm. We are unable to agree with this contention, however. The defendants were partners in the general practice, and the partnership, acting through Dr. Wm. M. Morton, undertook to perform the operation and did in fact perform it.

* * *

It is very clear that plaintiff could not be left in the operating room during the period necessary for her recovery, and it was the duty of some one to see that she was safely removed therefrom and placed in a room suitable for such further treatment as her case might require. While it is shown that neither of the defendants owned or controlled the hospital, it does appear that they made all arrangements for plaintiff's stay there, and a jury would be justified in finding that defendants as part of their employment undertook to care for plaintiff from the time she entered the hospital until she was ready for discharge therefrom. And while this might not ordinarily include the work of the hospital employees, the doctors might assume the duty of returning the patient to his room, and in such event each member of the firm would be the agent of the other in carrying on the work. It is fundamental that each partner is the agent of the firm while engaged in the prosecution of the partnership business, and that the firm is liable for the torts of each, if committed within the scope of the agency. The trial court gave an instruction which embodied correct law on this subject and it was for the jury to say whether Lewis Morton was acting for the firm when the accident occurred. It surely should not be said as matter of law in all cases that after a serious surgical operation and while the patient is still unconscious, the physician may leave the patient on the operating table to find his way to his own room the best he may. Furthermore, the evidence shows that in this hospital the doctors accompanied their patients up and down the elevator.

* * *

The judgment should be, and it is, affirmed.

The practical impact of the rules making partners personally liable for partnership contracts and torts can be huge. In *Economics* (1973, p. 106), Professor Paul Samuelson says that unlimited liability

> reveals why partnerships tend to be confined to small, personal enterprises. . . . When it becomes a question of placing their personal fortunes in jeopardy, people are reluctant to put their capital into complex ventures over which they can exercise little control. . . . In the field of investment banking, concerns like J. P. Morgan & Company used to advertise proudly "not incorporated" so that their creditors could have extra assurance. But even these concerns have converted themselves into corporate entities. Comparatively recently, the giant brokerage concern Merrill Lynch, Pierce, Fenner & Smith incorporated itself. For a long time it had many major partners and scores of junior partners, illustrating that the barriers to running a large enterprise put up by the partnership form are not insuperable. Still, giant partnerships are now rare.

The last sentence is plainly incorrect. Many accounting and law firms boast of hundreds of partners. But it is clear that they do worry about liability, and for good cause (see Box 17-1).

Corporations

Historical Background

Like partnership, the corporation is an ancient concept, recognized in the Code of Hammurabi, and to some degree a fixture in every other major legal system since then. The first corporations were not business enterprises; instead, they were associations for religious and governmental ends

Box 17-1 Personal Liability of Accounting Firm Partners

Grant Thornton Finds Itself in Disarray

BY LEE BERTON

When Steve L. Hipp was invited early last year to join Alexander Grant & Co., he jumped at the chance. Mr. Hipp had been a partner at the troubled accounting firm of Fox & Co., which was being absorbed by Grant. Chicago-based Grant, now known as Grant Thornton, was a bigger firm and long regarded as the Mr. Clean of the accounting profession.

But a few months later, Mr. Hipp received a rude shock. Jose Gomez, Grant's managing partner for southern Florida, was accused of taking a $125,000 bribe from E.S.M. Government Securities Inc. in return for certifying false financial statements for at least four years. Mr. Gomez later pleaded guilty. Grant was sued for $300 million in actual damages and as much as $1 billion in punitive damages by parties that said they lost money in transactions with the now-collapsed Fort Lauderdale securities firm.

The total damages sought are more than five times Grant's malpractice insurance coverage and almost 50 times partners' capital.

Aware that a partner in a professional firm can be held liable for frauds proven against other partners, Mr. Hipp chose to become a manager in Grant rather than a partner. While he won't disclose the loss in potential income, he acknowledges the step-down is a "big sacrifice." But he adds, "It will save me a lot of liability worries."

TURMOIL AT FIRM

Grant itself is in turmoil. The nation's 11th-largest accounting firm is having problems obtaining new clients and partners, retaining current clients and keeping its executive suite intact. Recently, Grant's top partner said he will step down, and the No. 2 partner already left. "It's been rough times," says Peter Skomorowsky, regional managing partner in New York and the firm's official spokesman.

The firm's travail illustrates the pressures on a professional firm—whether it be in accounting, law, architecture or another field—when its reputation is threatened by a major liability suit. The problem is particularly significant for an accounting firm because, as an auditor, it is expected to be its clients' financial conscience.

"The E.S.M. case is the most dramatic example of how vulnerable professional partners are to mistakes made by colleagues in their firm," says Newton Minow, a partner in the Chicago law firm of Sidley & Austin and a former adviser to Arthur Andersen & Co., the biggest U.S. accounting firm. "This suit could be severely damaging to the firm."

To add to Grant's woes, the plaintiffs are suing more than 400 Grant partners who were served with court papers saying that their personal assets could be attached by the court in any settlement of the E.S.M. case. Some Grant partners considered shifting personal assets to wives or relatives, but Grant told them this isn't necessary.

"As far as I'm concerned, there's a better chance their wives will file for divorce than that they will lose their shirts because of E.S.M.," says Alvin Stein, a New York lawyer representing Grant.

Source: *The Wall Street Journal,* April 4, 1986

in which **perpetual life** was a practical requirement. It is difficult, if not impossible, to contemplate a city or church or university as an institution without legal status separate from that of its members. Some device is necessary for permitting an ongoing activity to carry on despite the death of one or more of its principals. If the mayor dies, must the city dissolve? Corporate status does the trick.

Until relatively late in legal history, kings, popes, and jurists assumed that corporations could be created only by political or ecclesiastical authority—that corporations were creatures of the state or church. By the seventeenth century, with feudalism on the wane and business enterprise becoming a growing force, kings extracted greater taxes and intervened more directly in the affairs of businesses by refusing to permit them to operate in corporate form except by royal grant. This came to be known as the "concession theory," because incorporation was a concession from the sovereign.

The most important concessions or charters were those given to the giant foreign trading companies, including the Russia Company (1554), British East India Company (1600), Hudson's Bay Company (1670, and still operating in Canada under the name "The Bay"), the South Sea Company (1711), and others. These were "joint stock" companies; that is, individuals contributed capital to the enterprise, which traded on behalf of all the stockholders. Originally, trading companies were formed for single voyages, but the advantages in a continuing fund of capital soon became apparent. Also apparent was the legal characteristic that above all led shareholders to subscribe to the stock: limited liability. They risked only the cash they put in, not their personal fortunes.

Some companies were wildly successful. The British East India Company paid its original investors a fourfold return between 1683 and 1692. But perhaps nothing excited the imagination of the British more than the discovery of a Spanish shipwreck carrying gold bullion; 150 companies were quickly formed to salvage sunken Spanish treasure. Though most of these were outright frauds, they ignited the search for easy wealth by a public unwary of the risks. In particular, the South Sea Company promised the sun and moon: in return for a monopoly over the slave trade to the West Indies, it told a delirious public that it would retire the public debt and make every person rich. Other promoters offered schemes, among many others, "to get oil from sunflower seeds, to build ships to proceed against pirates, to cultivate silkworms in Surrey, to make a *perpetuum mobile*" (Beard, 1962, p. 437).

In 1720, a fever gripped London that sent stock prices soaring. Beggars and earls alike speculated from January to August with the enthusiasm of a child giving away play money—and then the bubble burst. Without considering the ramifications, Parliament had enacted a highly restrictive Bubble Act, which was supposed to do away with unchartered joint-stock companies. When the government prosecuted four companies under the act for having fraudulently obtained charters, the public panicked and stock prices came tumbling down, resulting in one of history's worst financial collapses.

As a consequence, corporate development was severely retarded in England. Distrustful of the chartered company, Parliament issued few corporate charters, and then only for public or quasi-public undertakings, such as transportation, insurance, and banking enterprises. Corporation law languished: William Blackstone devoted less than 1 percent of his immensely influential *Commentaries on the Law of England* (1765) to corporations and omitted altogether any discussion of limited liability. In *The Wealth of Nations* (1776), Adam Smith doubted that the use of corporations would spread. England did not repeal the Bubble Act until 1825, and then because the value of true incorporation had become apparent from the experience of her former colonies.

The United States remained largely unaffected by the Bubble Act. Incorporation was granted only by special acts of state legislatures, even well into the nineteenth century, but many such acts were passed. Before the Revolution, perhaps fewer than a dozen business corporations existed throughout the thirteen colonies. During the 1790s alone, 200 businesses were incorporated, and their numbers swelled thereafter. The theory that incorporation should not be accomplished except through special legislation began to give way. As industrial development hastened in the mid-1800s, it was possible in many states to incorporate by adhering to the requirements of a general statute. Indeed, by the late nineteenth century, all but three states constitutionally *forbade* their legislatures from chartering companies through special enactments.

The U.S. Supreme Court contributed importantly to the development of corporate law. In *Paul* v. *Virginia,* 75 U.S. 168 (1868), the Court said that a state could prevent corporations not chartered there—**foreign** corporations, meaning from out-of-state—from coming in to engage in purely local business. The clear inference was that the states could not bar foreign corporations engaged in *interstate* business from their borders.

That decision brought about a competition in corporation laws. The early general laws had imposed numerous restrictions. The breadth of corporate enterprise was limited, ceilings were placed on total capital and indebtedness, incorporators were required to have residence in the state, often the duration of the company was not perpetual but was limited to a term of years or until a particular undertaking was completed, and the powers of management were circumscribed. These restrictions and limitations were thought to be necessary to protect the citizenry of the chartering legislature's own state. But once it became clear that companies chartered in one state could operate in others, states began in effect to "sell" incorporation for tax revenues, thus exporting the worst features of their laws. New Jersey led the way in 1875 with a general incorporation statute that greatly liberalized the powers of management and lifted many of the former restrictions. The Garden State was ultimately eclipsed by Delaware, which in 1899 enacted the most liberal corporation statute in the country, so that to the present day there are thousands of "Delaware corporations" that maintain no presence in the state other than an address on file with the secretary of state in Dover.

During the 1920s, the National Conference of Commissioners on Uniform State Laws drafted a Uniform Business Corporation Act, the final version of which was released in 1928. It was not widely adopted, but it did provide the basis during the 1930s for revisions of some state laws, including those in California, Illinois, Michigan, Minnesota, and Pennsylvania. By that time, in the midst of the Great Depression, the federal government for the first time intruded into corporate law in a major way by creating federal agencies—most notably the Securities and Exchange Commission, with power to regulate the interstate issuance of corporate stock.

Corporation Law Today

Following World War II, most states revised their general corporation laws. The most significant development was the preparation of the Model Business Corporation Act by the American Bar Association Committee on Corporate Laws. More than two-thirds of the states have adopted the Model Act in substance and major portions of the Model Act are followed in other states. The latest version of the act, the Revised Model Business Corporation Act of 1984 (RMBCA), will be referred to in our discussion of corporation law.

Partnerships Compared with Corporations

In deciding between a partnership or corporate form of business organization, investors consider several key factors.

Ease of Formation Partnerships are easy to form. If the business is simple enough and the partners few, the agreement need not even be written down. Creating a corporation is more complicated because formal documents must be placed on file with public authorities.

Ownership and Control All general partners have equal rights in the management and conduct of the business. By contrast, ownership and control of corporations are, in theory, separated. In *publicly held* corporations, which have many shareholders, the separation is real. Ownership is widely dispersed because millions of shares are outstanding and it is rare that any single shareholder will own more than a tiny percentage of stock. It is difficult under the best of circumstances for shareholders to exert any form of control over corporate operations. However, in the *closely held* corporation, which has few shareholders, the officers or senior managers are usually also the shareholders, so the separation of ownership and control is less pronounced or even non-existent.

Transferability of Interests Transferability of an interest in a partnership is a problem because a transferee cannot become a member unless all partners consent. The problem can be addressed and overcome in the partnership agreement. Transfer of interest in a corporation through a sale of stock is much easier, but for the stock of a small corporation there might be no market or there might be contractual restrictions on transfer.

Financing Partners have considerable flexibility in financing. They can lure potential investors by offering interests in profits and, in the case of general partnerships, control. Corporations can finance by selling freely transferable stock to the public.

Taxation The partnership is a conduit for income and is not taxed as a separate entity. Individual partners are taxed and, subject to limitations in the 1986 Tax Reform Act, can deduct partnership losses. Corporate earnings, on the other hand, are subject to double taxation. The corporation is first taxed as an entity on its own earnings. Then, when profits are distributed to shareholders in the form of dividends, the shareholders are taxed again. (A small corporation, with no more than thirty-five shareholders, can elect, under Subchapter S of the Internal Revenue Code, to be taxed as a partnership, to avoid this double taxation.) However, incorporating brings several tax benefits. For example, the corporation can take deductions for life, medical, and disability insurance coverage for its employees, whereas partners or sole proprietors cannot.

The Corporate Veil: The Corporation as Legal Entity

One last factor to be added to the list—and the one that ordinarily tips the balance in favor of incorporating—is this: the corporation is a legal entity in its own right, one that can provide a veil that protects its shareholders from personal liability. As satirized by attorney William Gilbert and his partner Arthur Sullivan in the operetta *Utopia, Ltd.*:

> Though a Rothschild you may be in your own capacity,
> As a company you've come to utter sorrow—
> But the liquidators say, "Never mind, you needn't pay ,
> So you start another company tomorrow.

This crucial factor accounts for the development of much of corporate law. Unlike the individual actor in the legal system, the corporation is difficult to deal with in conventional legal terms. As discussed in Chapter 2, corporations lack certain constitutional rights that natural persons possess. Furthermore, the business of the sole proprietor and the sole proprietor herself are one and the same. When a sole proprietor makes a decision, she risks her own capital. When the managers of a corporation take a corporate action, they are risking the capital of others—the shareholders. Thus, accountability is a major theme in the system of law constructed to cope with legal entities other than natural persons.

Given the importance of the corporate entity as a veil that limits shareholder liability, it is important to note that in two sets of circumstances the courts will pierce the veil: (1) when the corporation is used to commit a fraud or injustice, and (2) when the corporation does not act as if it were one.

Fraud The Felsenthal Company burned to the ground. Its president, one of the company's largest creditors and also virtually its sole owner, instigated the fire. The corporation sued the insurance company to recover the amount for which it was insured. The general rule of law is that "the willful burning of property by a stockholder in a corporation is not a defense against the collection of the insurance by the corporation, and that the corporation cannot be prevented from collecting the insurance because its agents willfully set fire to the property without the participation or authority of the corporation or of all of the stockholders." But because the fire was caused by the beneficial owner of "practically all" the stock, who also "has the absolute management of [the corporation's] affairs and its property, and is its president," the court refused to allow the company to recover the insurance money; allowing the company to recover would reward fraud. [Felsenthal Co. v. Northern Assurance Co., Ltd., 120 N.E. 268 (Ill. 1918)]

Failure to Act as a Corporation Failure to follow corporate formalities may subject stockholders to personal liability. This is a special risk that small—especially one-person—corporations run. Particular factors that bring this rule into play include inadequate capitalization, omission of regular meetings, failure to record minutes of meetings, failure to file annual reports, and commingling of corporate and personal assets. Where these factors exist, the courts may look through the corporate veil and pluck out the individual stockholder or stockholders to answer for a tort, contract breach, or the like. The classic case is the taxicab operator who incorporates several of his cabs separately and services them through still another corporation. If one of the cabs causes an accident, the corporation is usually "judgment proof" because the corporation will have few assets (practically worthless cab, minimum insurance). The courts frequently permit plaintiffs to proceed against the common owner on the grounds that the particular corporation was inadequately financed.

When a corporation owns a subsidiary corporation, the question frequently arises whether the subsidiary is acting as an independent entity. In answering this question, courts have developed the **instrumentality rule**, which is applied in the following case.

DANIA JAI-ALAI PALACE, INC. v. SYKES
425 So.2d 594 (Fla. 1983)

HURLEY, JUDGE. This appeal follows a plaintiff's verdict in a personal injury action. The principal question presented is whether a parent corporation may be held liable for torts committed by an employee of a wholly-owned subsidiary corporation. We answer in the affirmative since the record in this case contains substantial competent evidence to support findings that the subsidiary was a mere instrumentality of the parent and that the employee was acting within the course and scope of his employment. Therefore, for this and other reasons enumerated herein, we affirm in part and reverse in part.

On December 15, 1977, Gladys Sykes attempted to patronize the Dania Jai-Alai fronton. She arrived in her car and was directed into the valet parking area by a security guard employed by Dania Jai-Alai Palace, Inc. She purchased a parking ticket and turned the car over to the ticket seller who was employed by another corporation, Carrousel Concessions, Inc. Then she began to walk forward in front of her car toward the main gate of the fronton.

Ms. Sykes' car was the last in a short line of cars which were temporarily stopped near the fronton entrance waiting to be moved by parking attendants. There was about a four foot space between the Sykes' car and the one ahead. Since parking attendants were about to move the other cars in the line, the ticket seller, who was in overall charge of keeping things moving, got into Ms. Sykes' car and prepared to drive it. He looked at the gear shift indicator and moved it from "park" to "drive." As he did so, he took his foot from the brake pedal and placed it on the accelerator pedal. The car began to move forward and, at this point, he looked up and saw Ms. Sykes in front of the car, near its center. He attempted to brake, but his foot slipped and hit the accelerator. Ms. Sykes was propelled forward and crushed into the stationary car ahead; she was seriously injured.

Initially, Ms. Sykes sued Dania Jai-Alai Palace, Inc. (Dania). Later, when her attorneys discovered that Carrousel Concessions, Inc. (Carrousel) was running the valet parking, she amended her complaint to include Carrousel and to include Saturday Corporation (Saturday), the parent corporation of Dania and Carrousel. [The jury returned a verdict against all three corporate defendants for $775,000.]

* * *

LIABILITY OF DANIA

After both sides rested, the trial court ruled that Dania was liable for the negligence of Carrousel's parking attendant. The court reasoned that this "is a special factual situation . . . where someone is injured in the confines of the whole operation." Thus, the court concluded that Dania was liable because of the close knit nature of the operation in which both corporations combined forces to engage in a single business and held themselves out to the public as a single enterprise. We agree.

The uncontroverted evidence shows that Dania owns the entire premises. The operational aspect of business, however, has been divided between Dania and its sister corporation, Carrousel, which Dania financed. Dania handles the betting, the players, and the admission. Dania also handles maintenance and the hiring of security personnel. Carrousel, on the other hand, handles food, beverages, program sales, and parking. Notwithstanding this division of labor, the two corporations present a public image of a single enterprise. They advertise themselves simply as Dania Jai-Alai and the public has no reason to suspect that there is more than one entity involved.

When two corporations engage in a common enterprise that involves an inherent risk to members of the public, and hold themselves out to the public as a single enterprise, then both corporations will incur tort liability for the torts of the enterprise. We find that the trial court correctly applied this principle in the case at bar.

LIABILITY OF SATURDAY

Next, we consider the question of Saturday's liability. May a parent corporation be held liable for torts committed by an employee of a wholly-owned subsidiary? In this instance, the answer is "yes." Here, the jury applied the long-established principle of Florida law that, when one corporation controls and dominates another corporation to the extent that the second corporation becomes the "mere instrumentality" of the first, the dominant corporation is liable for the torts of the subservient corporation. In light of the jury's affirmative finding, our responsibility is not to re-weigh the evidence, *Levenstein v. Sapiro,* but only to determine whether the verdict is supported by competent substantial evidence.

At the outset, we reject appellants' contention that, in order to utilize the instrumentality doctrine, the plaintiff had to establish fraud or other wrongdoing on the part of Saturday. Although there are conflicting lines of cases on this point, we took a definitive position in *Vantage View, Inc. v. Bali East Development Corp.,* 421 So.2d 728 (Fla. 4th DCA 1982), and said that we intend to "follow the decision of the supreme court in *Barnes, Mayer, Aztec* and *Levenstein* which have held it sufficient to allege domination and control without the necessity of alleging improper purpose or unjust loss."

Whether a subsidiary is a mere instrumentality is normally a question of fact for the jury. "The central factual issue is control, *i.e.,* whether the parent corporation dominates the activities of the subsidiary." *Japan Petroleum Co. (Nigeria) Ltd. v. Ashland Oil, Inc.,* 456 F.Supp. 831, 841 (D.Del. 1978). The degree of control necessary to sustain liability under the instrumentality rule has been characterized as "total domination of the subservient corporation, to the extent that the subservient corporation manifests no separate corporate interests of its own and functions solely to achieve the purposes of the dominant corporation." *Krivo Industrial Supply Co. v. National Distillers & Chemical Corp.,* 483 F.2d 1098, 1106 (5th Cir. 1973), *modified per curiam,* 490 F.2d 916 (5th Cir. 1974). On the other hand, courts generally agree that the application of the instrumentality rule demands a case-by-case analysis. Because the instrumentality rule is "essentially equitable in character, the conditions under which a corporate entity may be disregarded vary, depending upon the circumstances in each case. It is therefore inappropriate to attempt to apply any verbalization of the test in a mechanical manner." *FMC Finance Corp. v. Murphree,* 632 F.2d 413, 422 (5th Cir. 1980).

A number of courts have suggested that the following factors are relevant in determining the applicability of the instrumentality rule. (1) The parent corporation owns all or majority of the capital stock of the subsidiary. (2) The parent and subsidiary corporations have common directors or officers. (3) The parent corporation finances the subsidiary. (4) The parent corporation subscribes to all the capital stock of the subsidiary or otherwise causes its incorporation. (5) The subsidiary has grossly inadequate capital. (6) The parent corporation pays the salaries or expenses or losses of the subsidiary. (7) The subsidiary has substantially no business except with the parent corporation or no assets except those conveyed to it by the parent corporation. (8) In the papers of the parent corporation, and in the statements of its officers, "the subsidiary" is referred to as such or as a department or division. (9) The directors or executives of the subsidiary do not act independently in the interest of the subsidiary but take direction from the parent corporation. (10) The formal legal requirements of the subsidiary as a separate and independent corporation are not observed.

Turning to the evidence in the case at bar and viewing it in the light most favorable to the plaintiff/appellee, we find that Carrousel was wholly owned by Saturday and that they shared common officers. Furthermore, although there was testimony that the day-to-day operation of Carrousel was placed in the hands of an independent general manager, there was other testimony that the general manager regularly reported to one of the common officers and thereafter implemented his directions. Testimony also indicated that the common officer was present on the premises of the fronton and had the ability to hire and fire employees of Carrousel. The proof further demonstrated that Saturday created Carrousel and initially funded it through Dania, its other subsidiary.

A highly relevant factor in evaluating the application of the instrumentality rule is whether there is proof that the subservient corporation was being used to further the purposes of the dominant corporation to the extent that the subservient corporation in reality had no separate, independent existence of its own. In the case at bar, there was substantial proof that Carrousel existed only to serve the needs of Saturday. For example, Carrousel only operated at two frontons, both of which were owned either directly or indirectly by Saturday. Carrousel maintained its offices within the fronton and gave all outward appearances of being part of an integrated operation. In this respect, it is noteworthy that Saturday and its two subsidiary corporations filed a consolidated federal income tax return and were jointly insured. The evidence suggests that Saturday maintained a pervasive control over all aspects of the fronton's operations and, given such evidence, we cannot say that the jury's finding that Carrousel was the mere instrumentality of Saturday is clearly erroneous. Therefore, we affirm the verdict finding Saturday liable for the acts of Carrousel. [The court remanded the case for further proceedings to determine whether Ms. Sykes had been negligent.]

Piercing the veil of a foreign subsidiary is especially important to plaintiffs in that it often results in access to the U.S. court system, as illustrated by Box 17-2.

Other Types of Personal Liability

Even when a corporation is formed for a proper purpose and is operated as a corporation, there are instances in which individual shareholders will be personally liable. For example, if a shareholder involved in company management commits a tort or enters into a contract in a personal capacity, he will remain personally liable for the consequences of his actions. In some states, statutes give employees special rights against shareholders. For example, a New York statute permits employees to recover wages, salaries, and debts owed them by the company from the ten largest shareholders of the corporation. (Shareholders of public companies whose stock is traded on a national exchange or over the counter are exempt.) Likewise, federal law permits the IRS to recover from the "responsible persons" any withholding taxes collected by a corporation but not actually paid over to the U.S. Treasury.

Classifications of Corporations

Nonprofit Corporations The term "corporation" embraces a variety of types. One common type is the nonprofit or not-for-profit corporation. This is defined in the American Bar Association Model Non-Profit Corporation Act as "a corporation no part of the income of which is distributable to its members, directors or officers." Nonprofit corporations may be formed under this law for charitable, educational, civil, religious, social, and cultural purposes, among others.

Public Corporation The public corporation is a governmental entity. It is also called a municipal corporation, to distinguish it from the publicly *held* corporation, which is sometimes also referred to as a "public" corporation—although it is in fact private; that is, not governmental. Major cities and counties, and many towns, villages, and special governmental units, such as sewer, transportation, and public utility authorities, are incorporated. The United States Postal Service, once a cabinet-level department, is

Box 17-2 Piercing the Veil of a Foreign Subsidiary

Peeking beneath the Corporate Veil
BY RICHARD GREENE

In 1975 Mark Donohue, a world-class driver, was killed when a tire blew out in a racing accident. His estate sued Goodyear Tire & Rubber Co., and a jury recently decided the company should fork over $9.6 million, plus interest. That is a total award of about $19.6 million, one of the largest wrongful death payments in history.

As you might expect, Goodyear's attorneys claimed a poorly made tire wasn't the cause of the accident. But they made another, more interesting argument. They said the tire that blew out wasn't really a Goodyear product even though it had the company's name. No, they argued, this tire was manufactured by a wholly owned subsidiary situated in the U.K., which meant Donohue's attorneys should go to England and sue there.

When buying a product from a well-known company, you probably don't care where it was manufactured or which subsidiary was involved. But the courts do. One of the reasons companies set up subsidiaries, in fact, is to use the corporate form to limit legal liability. For the same reason that you can't sue GM shareholders if a Chevrolet's brakes fail, you can't sue Goodyear if a tire made by its subsidiary has a blowout.

Naturally, plaintiffs want to get around this legal rule, which can force them to sue a thinly capitalized subsidiary instead of a rich parent. The Donohue litigation had a different focus. Unless the driver's estate could sue Goodyear directly—"piercing the corporate veil," in lawyers' terms—the case would have been tried in England. "That would have been much more difficult," explains Leonard Decof, the white-haired attorney who won the case. "The law is different there. They don't have jury trials in most civil cases. They don't have the discovery process. There's no subpoena power, so I couldn't force people to come into court to testify."

The law is clear on questions of subsidiary liability, at least to a point. "The general rule is that the separate incorporation of a subsidiary will be recognized as long as records are not intermingled, formalities of separate procedures are observed, and the parent and the sub are held out to the public as separate enterprises," says William Roberts, a partner with Blank, Rome, Comisky & McCauley.

This can present problems for smaller firms,

now a public corporation. These corporations are not organized for profit, do not have shareholders, and operate under different statutes than do business corporations.

Professional Corporations Until the 1960s, lawyers, doctors, accountants, and other professionals could not practice their professions in corporate form. This inability, based on a fear of professionals' being subject to the direction of the corporate owners, was financially disadvantageous. Under the federal income tax laws then in effect, corporations could establish far better pension plans than could the self-employed. During the 1960s the states began to let professionals incorporate, but the IRS balked, denying them many tax benefits. In 1969, the IRS finally conceded that it would tax professional corporations just as it would any other corporations, so that professionals could from that time on place a much higher proportion which don't have the resources to set up separate boards and financial arrangements for every subsidiary. But for giants like Goodyear, that's not where the difficulties arise. Big companies get into trouble over the question of whether they have dominated subsidiaries to the extent that they are indistinguishable from the parent. If a plaintiff's lawyer can prove that, he's well on his way to suing the parent directly.

Doing this in the Donohue litigation led to courtroom scenes worthy of Perry Mason. Goodyear's former chief executive, Charles Pilliod, was asked to comment about old press releases and annual reports in which the company talked about moving the British operation to the U.S. Pilliod argued that headquarters had no real control over the subsidiary, and even claimed that some of the company's earlier written statements were lies. "When [Mr. Pilliod] was being examined . . . he began to perspire, and well he might have," wrote the judge in the case.

Pilliod's perspiration helped Donohue's lawyer pierce Goodyear's corporate veil and go on to win in court. Now the tiremaker is appealing, and, unfortunately for it, the issue here stemmed from a personal injury claim. Goodyear's luck would probably have been better if the matter involved a more straightforward contract litigation. "In the contract area, the courts are going to be much more willing to maintain the corporate veil, unless there is fraud or some reason to think people were being misled," says William Steinbrink, a partner with Jones Day Reavis & Pogue. "With personal injury liability, there will be more concern about whether somebody ought to be compensated for an injury and less concern about who did it."

Corporations don't always take a hand's off attitude toward their subsidiaries in the courtroom. Consider the situation with workers' compensation claims. Injured workers can't sue an employer directly. Instead they automatically collect relatively small insurance claims from a state fund. But suing the parent separately can bring really big bucks. So defendants are often quick to argue that parent and sub are one and the same.

In this area of law, the answer to a question depends on who's asking.

Source: *Forbes,* August 13, 1984, p. 58

of tax-deductible income into a tax-deferred pension. That decision led to a burgeoning number of "professional corporations." The Model Professional Corporation Supplement (1984), developed by the American Bar Association, serves as a model for states in the development of professional corporation statutes.

Business Corporations There are two broad types of business corporations: *publicly held* (or *public*) and *closely held* (or *close* or *private*) corporations. Note that both types are private in the sense that they are not governmental.

The **publicly held** corporation is one in which stock is widely held or available for wide public distribution through such means as trading on a national or regional stock exchange. Its managers, if they are also owners of stock, usually constitute a small percentage of the total number of shareholders and hold a small amount of stock relative to the total shares outstanding. Few if any shareholders of public corporations know who their fellow shareholders are.

By contrast, the shareholders of the **closely held** corporation are few: perhaps only one and usually no more than thirty. Shareholders of the closely held corporation almost always share family ties or have some other association that permits each to know the others.

Though most closely held corporations are small, no economic or legal reason prevents them from being large. Some are huge, having annual sales of several billion dollars each. Roughly 95 percent of the some 2 million corporations in the United States are closely held.

The giant, publicly held companies with more than $1 billion in assets and sales—with initials such as IBM and GM—constitute an exclusive group of probably no more than 200. Publicly held corporations outside this elite class fall into two broad (nonlegal) categories: those that are quoted on stock exchanges (perhaps 1 percent of all corporations) and others whose stock is too widely dispersed to be called closely held but which are not traded on exchanges (perhaps 4 percent of the total).

General principles of corporation law apply to both publicly held and closely held corporations. In addition many states have adopted specific close corporation provisions. In some states these provisions are spread throughout the corporation act; in others, a separate chapter in the act is devoted to close corporations. The Model Statutory Close Corporation Supplement (1984), developed by the American Bar Association, takes the latter approach. The supplement provides that a corporation may elect close corporation status simply by so stating in the articles of incorporation.

Other Forms

Two types of business organization—the limited partnership and business trust—have aspects of both the partnership and the corporate form.

Limited Partnerships

Source The **limited partnership** is a business form that provides limited liability to an investor, much as a corporate stockholder has limited liability, while continuing to provide the tax benefits of partnership. Limited partnerships have been popular investments for those seeking tax shelters. However, the Tax Reform Act of 1986 diminished the tax benefits—for example, by placing restrictions on the ability of limited partners to take tax deductions for partnership losses.

The original source of limited partnership law is the Uniform Limited Partnership Act (ULPA), which was drafted in 1916. A revised version, the Revised Uniform Limited Partnership Act (RULPA), was adopted by the

National Conference of Commissioners on Uniform State Laws in 1976 and is now the law in most states. Only Louisiana has adopted neither of the acts. The following discussion is based on RULPA. The Uniform Partnership Act also applies to limited partnerships except where it is inconsistent with the limited partnership statutes.

Form of Partnership A limited partnership has two categories of partners: general and limited. The general partner has the powers and liability of partners under the UPA. The limited partner is not bound by the obligations of the partnership. With few exceptions the limited partner—which may be a corporation or another partnership—is strictly an investor. The limited partner has no say in the business. However, without consent of the limited partners, the general partners have no authority to undertake any action contrary to the certificate, or that would make it impossible to carry on the business.

A limited partner may assign his interest to anyone. The assignee may or may not become a new partner. Unless the assignee becomes a new partner, known as a "substituted limited partner," his only right is to collect the assignor's share of profits or other compensation or return of capital. An assignee becomes a substituted limited partner, with all the rights of a limited partner, if all the members—limited and general—consent or if the certificate explicitly gives the assignee the right to become one.

A person may be simultaneously a general and limited partner of the same partnership. In form he is a general partner. The only distinction between him and other general partners is that for purposes of right to a return of his capital contribution, he is treated as a limited partner.

Formation Unlike a regular partnership, a limited partnership comes into existence only when a certificate of partnership is filed with the secretary of state. The certificate must set forth certain information, including the name of the partnership and character and location of the business, the name and residence of each partner (general and limited partners must be designated as such), the value and description of each partner's contribution and the right of an assignee to become a substitute limited partner. The name of the partnership must include the word "limited." Each general and limited partner must sign the certificate and swear under penalties of perjury to the truth of the statements it contains.

Control Limited partners can encounter pitfalls that could jeopardize their claim to limited liability and burden them instead with unlimited liability. These pitfalls are noted in this and the next two headings.

Under RULPA Section 303(a) a limited partner will forfeit his right to limited liability if he takes part in the control of the business in a manner that is "substantially the same as the exercise of the powers of a general partner." If he exercises some but not substantial control, he is liable "only to persons who transact business with the limited partnership with actual knowledge of his participation in control." Moreover, Section 303(b) lists several "safe harbor" provisions that exclude certain acts from being construed as participation in control. These include being a contractor for, or an agent or employee of, the limited partnership or of a general partner, and consulting with and advising a general partner concerning the business. When an act falls outside the safe harbors, however, RULPA provides little guidance on what constitutes control. As a result, courts must review closely the facts in each case to resolve the control issue, as discussed in the following opinion.

FRIGIDAIRE SALES CORP. v. UNION PROPERTIES, INC.
88 Wash.2d 400, 562 P.2d 244 (1977)

HAMILTON, ASSOCIATE JUSTICE. Petitioner, Frigidaire Sales Corporation, sought review of a Court of Appeals decision which held that limited partners do not incur general liability for the limited partnership's obligations simply because they are officers, directors, or shareholders of the corporate general partner. We granted review, and now affirm the decision of the Court of Appeals.

The facts of the case are adequately set out in the Court of Appeals opinion, and only a cursory summation need be repeated here. Petitioner entered into a contract with Commercial Investors (Commercial), a limited partnership. Respondents, Leonard Mannon and Raleigh Baxter, were limited partners of Commercial. Respondents were also officers, directors, and shareholders of Union Properties, Inc., the only general partner of Commercial. Respondents controlled Union Properties, and through their control of Union Properties they exercised the day-to-day control and management of Commercial. Commercial breached the contract, and petitioner brought suit against Union Properties and respondents. The trial court concluded that respondents did not incur general liability for Commercial's obligations by reason of their control of Commercial, and the Court of Appeals affirmed.

We first note that petitioner does not contend that respondents acted improperly by setting up the limited partnership with a corporation as the sole general partner. Limited partnerships are a statutory form of business organization, and parties creating a limited partnership must follow the statutory requirements. In Washington, parties may form a limited partnership with a corporation as the sole general partner.

Petitioner's sole contention is that respondents should incur general liability for the limited partnership's obligations under RCW 25.08.070, because they exercised the day-to-day control and management of Commercial. Respondents, on the other hand, argue that Commercial was controlled by Union Properties, a separate legal entity, and not by respondents in their individual capacities.

* * *

Petitioner was never led to believe that respondents were acting in any capacity other than in their corporate capacities. The parties stipulated at the trial that respondents never acted in any direct, personal capacity. When the shareholders of a corporation, who are also the corporation's officers and directors, conscientiously keep the affairs of the corporation separate from their personal affairs, and no fraud or manifest injustice is perpetrated upon third persons who deal with the corporation, the corporation's separate entity should be respected.

For us to find that respondents incurred general liability for the limited partnership's obligations under RCW 25.08.070 would require us to apply a literal interpretation of the statute and totally ignore the corporate entity of Union Properties, when petitioner knew it was dealing with that corporate entity. There can be no doubt that respondents, in fact, controlled the corporation. However, they did so only in their capacities as agents for their principal, the corporate general partner. Although the corporation was a separate entity, it could act only through its board of directors, officers, and agents. Petitioner entered into the contract with Commercial. Respondents signed the contract in their capacities as president and secretary-treasurer of Union Properties, the general partner of Commercial. In the eyes of the law it was Union Properties, as a separate corporate entity, which entered into the contract with petitioner and controlled the limited partnership.

Further, because respondents scrupulously separated their actions on behalf of the corporation from their personal actions, petitioner never mistakenly assumed that respondents were general partners with general liability. Petitioner knew Union Properties was the sole general partner and did not rely on respondents' control by assuming that they were also general partners. If petitioner had not wished to rely on the solvency of Union Properties as the only general partner, it could have insisted that respondents personally guarantee contractual performance. Because petitioner entered into the contract knowing that Union Properties was the only party with general liability, and because in the eyes of the law it was Union Properties, a separate entity, which controlled the limited partnership, there is no reason for us to find that respondents incurred general liability for their acts done as officers of the corporate general partner.

The decision of the Court of Appeals is affirmed.

Use of Name If a limited partner knowingly permits her name to be used in the limited partnership name, she will be liable the same as a general partner to any creditor who does not have actual knowledge that she is a limited partner.

False Statements in Certificate A false statement in the certificate will make limited partners fully liable to anyone who suffers loss by reliance on the false statement, unless the limited partner(s) had no actual knowledge that the statement was false.

Business Trusts

Principles and History When a trust is created, property is given to the trustee, who holds it for the benefit of a third party. The trustee has "legal title," and the beneficiary has "equitable title," since the courts of equity would enforce the obligations of the trustee to honor the terms by which the property was conveyed to the trustee. The use of trusts for business purposes was a way around nineteenth century restrictions on use of the corporate form. The business trust flourished particularly in Massachusetts—hence is often called the Massachusetts trust—because that state's law imposed restrictions on corporate dealing in real estate, and the trust device was a handy way around those restrictions.

After the 1920s, the popularity of the business trust declined considerably, both because corporations were given in every state, including Massachusetts, the same power to deal in real property as natural persons and partnerships, and also because state and federal law began to regulate and tax business trusts in substantially the same manner as corporations. Many investment companies remain organized as trusts, however, and since the

1960s, with a change in federal and state tax laws permitting conduit treatment of income, many *real estate investment trusts* **(REITs)** were organized. Money market funds today often use the Massachusetts business trust form because it avoids the necessity of issuing stock certificates whenever a dividend is paid.

Formation Typically, the business trust is formed when its contributors place legal title to capital in the hands of trustees through a written declaration of trust. The document sets forth the powers and duties of the trustees and interests of the beneficiaries. Many states now require business trust declarations to be filed in an appropriate public office. Beneficiaries usually receive certificates that are freely transferable and that act in most respects like shares of corporate stock, but certificates are not required.

Operation Management is in the hands of the trustees, who are frequently self-perpetuating, although this is not a legal requirement. Trustees usually delegate day-to-day operations, if the company is at all sizable, to employed officers. In many states, beneficiaries bear the same relationship to the trustees as do limited partners to the partnership: participating in business control causes a forfeiture of limited liability. Some states—New York is one—view strictly the beneficiary's exercise of control: even a minor attempt to control might suffice to convert the trust into a partnership or joint venture. The trustee is a fiduciary, and generally cannot enter into contracts with the trust in his private capacity.

Liability Unless beneficiaries are in a position to control, their liability in most states is limited to their capital contribution. The trustees remain liable, although in most states trustees can limit their liability by contract with outside creditors. This they can do usually by making clear that they are entering into contracts "as trustees serving in a representative capacity only and not individually." If a trustee is held personally liable for a trust's debts, he is usually entitled to indemnification from the trust estate.

Taxation Federal income tax law and many state income tax laws treat the business trust as a corporation. Trust earnings are thus taxed before dividends or other distributions are made to the beneficiaries, unlike the method of taxing partnerships. By contrast, REITs are analogous to partnerships, and serve as a conduit for income to their beneficiaries, who are taxed directly on the distribution.

Transferability of Interests Unlike the rule of *delectus personae* in partnerships, no legal impediment prevents the free transfer of trust certificates. Hence beneficiaries can sell their certificates freely on the open market. Since beneficiaries have little or no power to control the affairs of the trust, their identity is usually of no consequence to the business.

Chapter Summary

The basic law of partnership is found in two statutes, the Uniform Partnership Act and the Uniform Limited Partnership Act. At common law, a partnership was not a legal entity and could not sue or be sued in the partnership name. The UPA defines a partnership as "an association of two or more persons to carry on as co-owners a business for profit" and, although it assumes that a partnership is an aggregation of individuals, it applies a number of rules characteristic of the legal entity theory. Thus, a partnership may keep business records as if it were a legal entity, may hold real estate in the partnership name, and may sue and be sued in federal court and in many state courts in the partnership name.

Partnerships may be created informally. Among the clues to the existence of a partnership are (1) co-ownership of a business, (2) sharing of profits, (3) right to participate in decision making, (4) duty to share liabilities, and (5) manner in which the business is operated. The hallmark of the corporate form of business enterprise is limited liability for its owners. Other features of corporations are separation of ownership and management, perpetual existence, and easy transferability of interests. In the early years of the common law, corporations were thought to be creatures of sovereign power and could be created only by state grant. But by the late nineteenth century, corporations could be formed by complying with the requirements of general corporation statutes in virtually every state. Today the standard is the Revised Model Business Corporation Act.

The corporation, as a legal entity, has many of the usual rights accorded natural persons. The principle of limited liability is broad but not absolute: when the corporation is used to commit a fraud or injustice or when the corporation does not act as if it were one, the courts will pierce the corporate veil and pin liability on stockholders.

Besides the usual business corporation, there are many other forms, including not-for-profit corporations and professional corporations. Business corporations are classified into two types: publicly held and closely held corporations.

Between partnerships and corporations lie a variety of the other types of association, notably limited partnerships and business trusts. The limited partnership provides limited liability to an investor; this type of entity is governed in most states by the RULPA. The limited partner has no say in the daily operation of the business. A limited partnership comes into existence only when a certificate of partnership is filed with the secretary of state. A limited partner may forfeit his limited liability if he takes part in control, uses his name in the partnership name, or if the certificate contains false statements on which someone has relied to his detriment—unless the limited partner has no knowledge of the falsity.

A business trust is operated by trustees who hold legal title to the business assets and who operate the business for the beneficiaries, who hold equitable title. Although the popularity of business trusts has declined considerably, many investment companies and real estate investment trusts are business trusts. Trust certificates held by the beneficiaries may be transferred like corporate stock. Management is usually delegated to paid officers.

Problems

1. Jimmy, Billy, and Lillian own, as partners, a warehouse. The income from the warehouse during the current year is $180,000, two-thirds of which goes to Jimmy. Who must file a tax return listing this income—the partnership or Jimmy? Who pays the tax—the partnership or Jimmy?
2. Larry and Curly, as partners, operate a small business. They fail to pay certain state taxes. Larry dies and, there being no partnership assets, the state demands payment from the personal assets in his estate. Must the estate pay? Why?
3. Popeye, a business student, decided to lease and operate an ice cream stand during his summer vacation. Because Popeye could not afford rent payments, his landlord agreed to take 30 percent of Popeye's profits as rent. As a result of this arrangement, are the landlord and Popeye partners? Why?
4. Trish lent $20,000 to Dick. They agreed that Dick would invest the money in real estate and, when the real estate was sold, he would pay back the $20,000 plus 40 percent of the profits as interest. Does this arrangement make Trish and Dick partners? Why?
5. Alpha and Beta, who are neighbors, decide to purchase an acre of land together as tenants in common. Does this purchase make them partners? Explain.
6. Two young business school graduates, LaVerne and Shirley, form a consulting firm. In deciding between the partnership and corporation form of organization, they are especially concerned about personal liability for giving bad advice to their clients; that is, in the event they are sued they want to prevent plaintiffs from taking their personal assets to satisfy judgments against the firm. Which form of organization would you recommend? Why?
7. Assume that LaVerne and Shirley (see problem 6) must negotiate a large loan from a local bank in order to finance their firm. A friend advises them that they should incorporate in order to avoid personal liability for the loan. Is this good advice? Why?
8. Assume that LaVerne and Shirley (see problem 6) have incorporated their business. One afternoon an old college friend visits Shirley at the office. Shirley and her friend decide to go out for dinner to discuss old

times. Shirley, being short of cash, takes money from a petty cash box to pay for dinner. (She first obtains permission from LaVerne, who has done the same thing many times in the past.) Over dinner, Shirley learns that her friend is now an IRS agent and is investigating Shirley's corporation. What problems does Shirley face in the investigation? Why?

18

Securities Regulation and Corporate Governance

Nature of Securities Regulation

What we commonly consider securities are essentially worthless pieces of paper. Their inherent value lies in the interest in property or an ongoing enterprise that they represent. This disparity between the tangible property—the stock certificate, for example—and the intangible interest it represents gives rise to several reasons for regulation. First, there is need for a mechanism to inform the buyer accurately what it is he is buying. Recall the South Sea Bubble and related schemes (see p. 466); unwary buyers discovered too late that they were investing mainly in empty air. Second, laws are necessary to prevent, and provide remedies for, deceptive and manipulative acts designed to defraud buyers and sellers. Third and finally, the evolution of stock trading on a massive scale has led to the development of numerous types of specialists and professionals, in dealings with whom the public can be at a severe disadvantage, and so the law undertakes to ensure that they do not take unfair advantage of their customers.

In this section we focus on the nature of securities regulation under two federal statutes: the Securities Act of 1933 and the Securities Exchange Act of 1934. We also look at state "Blue Sky" laws, intended to deter the kind of activity that led to the South Sea Bubble disaster. In the next section, we examine the relationship between corporate governance and securities regulation.

The Securities Act of 1933 and the Securities Exchange Act of 1934 are vitally important, having virtually refashioned the law governing corporations during the past half century. Indeed, it is not too much to say that although they deal with securities, they have become a general federal law of corporations. This body of federal law has assumed special importance in recent years as the states have engaged in a "race to the bottom" in attempting to compete with Delaware's permissive corporation law.

What Is a Security?

Securities law questions are technical and complex and usually require professional counsel. For the nonlawyer, the critical question on which all else turns is whether the particular investment or document is a security. If it is, anyone attempting any transaction beyond the routine purchase or sale through a broker should consult legal counsel to avoid the various civil and criminal minefields that the law has strewn about.

The definition of a security under Article 8 of the Uniform Commercial Code is not dispositive for purposes of federal securities law. The technical definition in the Securities Act of 1933, set out immediately below, is comprehensive, but it does not on its face answer all questions that financiers in a dynamic market can raise. Under Section 2(1), "security" includes

> any note, stock, treasury stock, bond, debenture, evidence of indebtedness, certificate of interest or participation in any profit-sharing agreement, collateral-trust certificate, preorganization certificate or subscription, transferable share, investment contract, voting-trust certificate, certificate of deposit for a security, fractional undivided interest in oil, gas, or other mineral rights, or, in general, any interest or instrument commonly known as a "security," or any certificate of interest or participation in, temporary or interim certificate for, receipt for, guarantee of, or warrant or right to subscribe to or purchase, any of the foregoing.

Under this definition, an investment may not be a security even though it is so labeled, and may be a security even though it is called something else. For example, does a service contract that obligates the seller to cultivate, harvest, and market an orange crop involve a security subject to regulation under federal law when the buyer has purchased an individual row of orange trees in an orchard? Yes, said the Supreme Court in *Securities & Exchange Commission* v. *W. J. Howey Co.*, 328 U.S. 293 (1946). The Court said the test is whether "the person invests his money in a common enterprise and is led to expect profits solely from the efforts of the promoter or a third party." Under this test, courts have liberally interpreted "investment contract" and "certificate of interest or participation in any profit-sharing agreement" to hold as securities interests in such property as real estate condominiums and cooperatives, commodity option contracts, and farm animals.

Note that the Supreme Court said that the investment must be in an enterprise from which profits are expected to come *solely* from the efforts of the promoter or a third party but not from the efforts of the investor himself. Can the promoters avoid liability under the federal securities laws if the investor is contractually required to undertake certain activities? The argument has been made, but the courts have held in several cases that the security aspects of an investment are not defeated when the lion's share of the effort is not to be undertaken by the investor. The reasons for this interpretation are set forth in what is probably the most celebrated of such cases, the SEC's action against Glenn W. Turner, who touted what for a time was a highly successful pyramid scheme.

S.E.C. v. GLENN W. TURNER ENTERPRISES INC.
474 F.2d 476 (9th Cir. 1973)

DUNIWAY, CIRCUIT JUDGE. This is an appeal from an order, 348 F.Supp. 766, granting the Securities and Exchange Commission a preliminary injunction. The injunction prohibits offering and selling by appellants of certain of their "Adventures" and "Plans", and also any withdrawal by appellants of funds from the assets of the corporate defendants other than in the regular course of business. Dare To Be Great, Inc. (Dare), a Florida corporation, is a wholly owned subsidiary of Glenn W. Turner Enterprises, Inc. The individual defendants are, or were, officers, directors, or employees of the defendant corporations.

The trial court's findings, which are fully supported by the record, demonstrate that defendants' scheme is a gigantic and successful fraud. The question presented is whether the "Adventures" or "Plan" enjoined are "securities" within the meaning of the federal securities laws. Of the five that Dare offers—Adventures I, II, III, and IV, and the $1,000 Plan—the court held that Adventures III and IV and the $1,000 Plan are securities. We affirm.

I. THE ADVENTURES AND THE $1000 PLAN—THE FACADE.

The five courses offered by Dare ostensibly involve two elements. In return for his money, the purchaser is privileged to attend seminar sessions and receives tapes, records, and other material, all aimed at improving self-motivation and sales ability. He also receives, if he purchases either Adventure III or IV or the $1,000 Plan, the opportunity to help to sell the courses to others; if successful he receives part of the purchase price as his commission. There is no doubt that this latter aspect of the purchase is in all respects the significant one.

Adventure I costs $300. The purchaser receives one portable tape recorder, twelve tape recorded lessons, and certain written material in notebooks. He is entitled to attend a 12–16 hour group session.

Adventure II includes Adventure I, and costs $700. The purchaser receives twelve more tape recorded lessons. He is offered approximately 80 hours of group sessions.

Adventure III includes Adventures I and II, and costs $2,000. The purchaser receives six more tape recordings, one notebook of written material called "The Fun of Selling," and a limited amount of written instructions and material, as well as thirty more hours of group sessions. The purchaser also receives a different sort of benefit. After fulfilling a few nominal requirements he becomes an "independent sales trainee," empowered to sell the Adventures. He receives $100 for each Adventure I, $300 for each Adventure II, and $900 for each Adventure III that he sells.

Adventure IV costs $5,000, and includes Adventure I, II and III. The purchaser receives six more tapes, the opportunity for thirty more hours of group sessions, the opportunity to attend two other week-long courses in Florida, at his own expense, and he may or may not receive a movie projector with six cartridge-type films. He also is now empowered to sell all the Adventures to others. For selling Adventure IV he gets $2,500.

Finally, there is the $1,000 Plan. For this sum the purchaser receives the tape cassettes sold in Adventure II, but not the accompanying written material. He also receives some additional sales instruction, and may be entitled to a 24-hour group session. He may also sell the Plan, if he brings two individuals to the person who sold him the Plan, and if these two also purchase the Plan from the first seller. If that occurs, he may then sell the Plan on his own, receiving $400 for each additional sale that he makes. If one brings three people into the scheme, he may sell the $1,000 Plan without buying it himself, and would earn the same $400 commission for each additional sale that he makes.

II. THE ADVENTURES AND THE PLAN IN OPERATION.

It is apparent from the record that what is sold is not of the usual "business motivation" type of courses. Rather, the purchaser is really buying the possibility of deriving money from the sale of the plans by Dare to individuals whom the purchaser has brought to Dare. The promotional aspects of the plan, such as seminars, films, and records, are aimed at interesting others in the Plans. Their value for any other purpose, is, to put it mildly, minimal.

Once an individual has purchased a Plan, he turns his efforts toward bringing others into the organization, for which he will receive a part of what they pay. His task is to bring prospective purchasers to "Adventure Meetings."

These meetings are like an old time revival meeting, but directed toward the joys of making easy money rather than salvation. Their purpose is to convince prospective purchasers, or "prospects," that Dare is a sure route to great riches. At the meetings are employees, officers, and speakers from Dare, as well as purchasers (now "salesmen") and their prospects. The Dare people, not the purchaser-"salesmen", run the meetings and do the selling. They exude great enthusiasm, cheering and chanting, there is exuberant handshaking, standing on chairs, shouting, and "money-humming".

* * *

While no express guarantee of success is made at the meetings, and the statement is made that the purchaser must expect to work, the impression which is fostered is of the near inevitability of success to be achieved by anyone who purchases a plan and follows Dare's instructions.

* * *

III. THE ADVENTURES AND PLANS AS SECURITIES.

The district court held that Adventures III and IV, and the $1,000 Plan were securities under the Securities Act of 1933, 15 U.S.C. § 77a et seq. and the Securities Exchange Act of 1934, 15 U.S.C. § 78a et seq. The definitions of security that are found in each Act are almost identical. Both definitions include the terms "investment contract," "certificate of interest or participation in any profit-sharing agreement," or any "instrument commonly known as a 'security'." The district court held that the plans in question fell into all three categories of securities. Because we find them to be investment contracts, we need not decide whether the other definitions are applicable as well.

* * *

In *SEC v. W. J. Howey Co.,* the Supreme Court set out its by now familiar definition of an investment contract:

> The test is whether the scheme involves an investment of money in a common enterprise with profits to come solely from the efforts of others. *Id.* at 301, 66 S.Ct. at 1104.

In *Howey* the Court held that a land sales contract for units of a citrus grove, together with a service contract for . . . cultivating and marketing the crops, was an investment contract and hence a security. The Court held that what was in essence being offered was "an opportunity to contribute money and to share in the profits of a large citrus fruit enterprise managed and partly owned by respondents." *Id.* at 299, 66 S.Ct. at 1103. The purchasers had no intention themselves of either occupying the land or developing it; they were attracted only "by the prospects of a return on their investment." *Id.* at 300, 66 S.Ct. at 1103. It was clear that the profits were to come "solely" from the efforts of others.

For purposes of the present case, the sticking point in the *Howey* definition is the word "soley," a qualification which of course exactly fitted the circumstances in *Howey*. All the other elements of the *Howey* test have been met here. There is an investment of money, a common enterprise, and the expectation of profits to come from the efforts of others. Here, however, the investor, or purchaser, must himself exert some efforts if he is to realize a return on his initial cash outlay. He must find prospects and persuade them to attend Dare Adventure Meetings, and at least some of them must then purchase a plan if he is to realize that return. Thus it can be said that the returns or profits are not coming "solely" from the efforts of others.

We hold, however, that in light of the remedial nature of the legislation, the statutory policy of affording broad protection to the public, and the Supreme Court's admonitions that the definition of securities should be a flexible one, the word "solely" should not be read as a strict or literal limitation on the definition of an investment contract, but rather must be construed realistically, so as to include within the definition those schemes which involve in substance, if not form, securities. Within this context, we hold that Adventures III and IV, and the $1,000 Plan, are investment contracts . . . within the meaning of the 1933 and 1934 Acts.

Strict interpretation of the requirement that profits to be earned must come "solely" from the efforts of others has been subject to criticism. Adherence to such an interpretation could result in a mechanical, unduly restrictive view of what is and what is not an investment contract. It would be easy to evade by adding a requirement that the buyer contribute a modicum of effort. Thus the fact that the investors here were required to exert some efforts if a return were to be achieved should not automatically preclude a finding that the Plan or Adventure is an investment contract. To do so would not serve the purpose of the legislation. Rather we adopt a more realistic test, whether the efforts made by those other than the investor are the undeniably significant ones, those essential managerial efforts which affect the failure or success of the enterprise.

In this case, Dare's source of income is from selling the Adventures and the Plan. The purchaser is sold the idea that he will get a fixed part of the proceeds of the sales. In essence, to get that share, he invests three things: his money, his efforts to find prospects and bring them to the meetings, and whatever it costs him to create an illusion of his own affluence. He invests them in Dare's get-rich-quick scheme. What he buys is a share in the proceeds of the selling efforts of Dare. Those efforts are the *sine qua non* of the scheme; those efforts are what keeps it going; those efforts are what produces the money which is to make him rich. In essence, it is the right to share in the proceeds of those efforts that he buys. In our view, the scheme is no less an investment contract merely because he contributes some effort as well as money to get into it. [Affirmed.]

The Securities & Exchange Commission

Functions The Securities & Exchange Commission is over half a century old, having been created by Congress in the Securities Exchange Act of 1934. It is an independent regulatory agency, subject to the rules of the Administrative Procedure Act (see Chapter 5). The commission is composed of five members, who have staggered five-year terms. Every June 5 the term of one of the commissioners expires. Although the president cannot remove commissioners during their term of office, he does have the power to designate the chairman from among the sitting members. The SEC is bipartisan: no more than three commissioners may be from the same political party.

The SEC's primary task is to investigate complaints or other possible violations of the law in securities transactions, and to bring enforcement proceedings when it believes that violations have occurred. It is empowered to conduct information inquiries, interview witnesses, examine brokerage records, and review trading data. If its requests are refused, it can issue subpoenas and seek compliance in federal court. Its usual leads come from complaints of investors and the general public, but it has authority to conduct surprise inspections of the books and records of brokers and dealers. Another source of leads is price fluctuations that seem to have been caused by manipulation rather than regular market forces.

Among the violations the SEC searches out are these: unregistered sale of securities subject to the registration requirement of the 1933 act, fraudulent acts and practices, manipulation of market prices, carrying out of a securities business while insolvent, misappropriation of customers' funds by brokers and dealers, and other unfair dealings by broker-dealers.

When the SEC believes that a violation has occurred, it can take one of three courses. It can seek a civil injunction in an appropriate U.S. District Court against further violations. It can refer the case to the Justice Department with a recommendation for criminal prosecution in cases of fraud or other willful violation of law. Or the SEC can proceed administratively, that is, hold its own hearing, with the usual due process rights, before an administrative law judge. If the commissioners by majority vote accept the findings of the administrative law judge, after reading briefs and hearing oral argument, they can impose a variety of sanctions: suspend or expel members of exchanges; deny, suspend, or revoke the registrations of broker-dealers; censure individuals for misconduct; and bar censured individuals (temporarily or permanently) from employment with a registered firm. The respondent in an administrative action may appeal these sanctions to a U.S. Court of Appeals.

Fundamental Mission of the SEC The SEC's fundamental mission is to ensure adequate disclosure in order to facilitate informed investment decisions by the public. Whether a particular security offering is worthwhile or worthless is a decision for the public, not for the SEC, which has no legal authority to pass on the merits of an offering or to bar the sale of securities if proper disclosures are made. One example was the 1981 sale of $274 million in limited partnership interests in a company called Petrogene Oil & Gas Associates, New York. The Petrogene offering was designed as a tax shelter. The company's filing with the SEC stated that the offering involved "a high degree of risk" and only those "who can afford the complete loss of their investment" should contemplate investing. Other disclosures: one member of the controlling group spent four months in prison for conspiracy to commit securities fraud; he and another principal were the subject of a New Mexico cease-and-desist order involving allegedly unregistered tax-shelter securities; the general partner, brother-in-law of one of the principals, had no experience in the company's proposed oil and gas operations (Petrogene planned to extract oil from plants by using radio frequencies); one of the oils to be produced was potentially carcinogenic; and the principals "stand to benefit substantially" whether or not the company fails and whether or not purchasers of shares recovered any of their investment. The prospectus went on to list specific risks. Despite this daunting compilation of troublesome details, the SEC permitted the offering because all disclosures were made (*Wall Street Journal,* December 29, 1981). It is the business of the marketplace, not the SEC, to determine whether the risk is worth taking.

Securities Act of 1933

Goals The Securities Act of 1933 is the fundamental "truth in securities" law. Its two basic objectives, in the words of its preamble: "to provide full and fair disclosure of the character of securities sold in interstate and foreign commerce and through the mails, and to prevent frauds in the sale thereof."

Registration The primary means for realizing these goals is the requirement of registration. Before securities subject to the act can be offered to the public, the issuer must file a registration statement and prospectus with the SEC, laying out in detail relevant and material information about the offering, as set forth in various schedules to the act. If the SEC approves the registration statement, the issuer must then provide any prospective purchaser with the prospectus. Since the SEC does not pass on the fairness of price or other terms of the offering, it is unlawful to state or imply in the prospectus that the commission has the power to disapprove securities for lack of merit, thereby suggesting that the offering is meritorious.

The SEC has prepared special forms for registering different types of issuing companies. All call for a description of the registrant's business and properties and of the significant provisions of the security to be offered, facts about how the issuing company is managed, and detailed financial statements certified by independent public accountants.

Once filed, the registration and prospectus become public and are open for public inspection. Ordinarily, the effective date of the registration statement is twenty days after filing. Until then, the offering may not be made to the public. Section 2(10) defines prospectus as any "notice, circular, advertisement, letter, or communication, written or by radio or television, which offers any security for sale or confirms the sale of any security." (An exception: brief notes advising the public of the availability of the formal prospectus.) The import of this definition is that any communication to the public about the offering of a security is unlawful unless it contains the requisite information.

SEC staff examine the registration statement and prospectus and if they appear to be materially incomplete or inaccurate, the commission may suspend or refuse the effectiveness of the registration statement until the deficiencies are corrected. Even after the securities have gone on sale, the agency has the power to issue a **stop order** that halts trading in the stock.

Section 5(c) of the act bars any person from making any sale of any security unless it is first registered. Nevertheless, there are certain classes of exemptions from the registration requirement. Perhaps the most important of these is Section 4(3), which exempts "transactions by any person other than an issuer, underwriter or dealer." Section 4(3) also exempts most transactions of dealers. So the net is that trading in outstanding securities (the secondary market) is exempt from registration under the 1933 act: you need not file a registration statement with the SEC every time you decide to buy or sell securities through a broker or dealer, for example. Other exemptions, in the words of an SEC summary, include: "(1) Private offerings to a limited number of persons or institutions who have access to the kind of information registration would disclose and who do not propose to redistribute the securities, (2) offerings restricted to the residents of the State in which the issuing company is organized and doing business, (3) securities of municipal, State, Federal and other government instrumentalities, of charitable institutions, of banks, and of carriers subject to the Interstate Commerce Act, (4) offerings not in excess of certain specified amounts made in compliance with regulations of the Commission . . . , and (5) offerings of 'small business investment companies' made in accordance with rules and regulations of the Commission" (*The Work of the SEC,* 1981, p. 6).

Penalties Section 24 provides for fines not to exceed $10,000 and a prison term not to exceed five years, or both, for willful violations of any provisions of the 1933 act. This section makes these criminal penalties specifically applicable to anyone who "willfully, in a registration statement filed under this title, makes any untrue statement of a material fact or omits to state any material fact required to be stated therein or necessary to make the statements therein not misleading." Sections 11 and 12 also provide that anyone injured by false declarations in registration statements, prospectuses, or oral communications concerning the sale of the security—as well as anyone injured by the unlawful failure of an issuer to register—may file a civil suit to recover the net consideration paid for the security or for damages if the security has been sold. Although these civil penalty provisions apply only to false statements in connection with the registration statement, prospectus, or oral communication, the Supreme Court has held that there is an "implied private right of action" for damages resulting from a violation of SEC rules under the act. [J. I. Case v. Borak, 377 U.S. 426 (1964)] The SEC has no authority to collect damages on behalf of injured investors, but the Court's ruling in the *Borak* case opened the courthouse doors to many who had been defrauded but were previously without a practical remedy.

Securities Exchange Act of 1934

Companies Covered The 1933 act is limited, as we have just seen, to new securities issues. The trading that takes place in the secondary market is far more significant, however. In a normal year trading in outstanding stock totals some twenty times the value of new stock issues. Because of this gap in coverage, Congress enacted the Securities Exchange Act of 1934. This law, which created the SEC, extended the disclosure rationale to securities listed and registered for public trading on the national securities exchanges. Amendments to the act have brought within its ambit every corporation whose equity securities are traded over the counter if the company has at least $5 million in assets and 500 or more shareholders.

Reporting Any company seeking listing and registration of its stock for public trading on a national exchange—or over the counter, if the company meets the size test—must first submit a registration application to both the exchange and the SEC. The registration statement is akin to that filed by companies under the 1933 act, although the 1934 act calls for somewhat fewer disclosures. Thereafter, companies must file annual and certain other periodic reports to update information in the original filing.

Proxies A proxy is the representative of the shareholder. A proxy may be a person who stands in for the shareholder or may be a written instrument by which the shareholder casts his votes before the meeting. Proxies are usually solicited by and given to management, either to vote for proposals or people named in the proxy, or to vote however the proxy holder wishes. Through the proxy device, management of large companies can maintain control over the election of directors. Proxies must be signed by the shareholder and are valid for eleven months from the time they are received by the corporation, unless the proxy explicitly states otherwise. Management may use reasonable corporate funds to solicit proxies if corporate policy issues are involved, but misrepresentations in the solicitation can lead a court to nullify the proxies and to deny reimbursement for the solicitation cost. Proxies may be revoked, unless "coupled with an interest" or "given as security." Only the last proxy given by a particular shareholder can be counted.

Proxy solicitations are regulated by the Securities and Exchange Commission. For instance, SEC rules require companies subject to the 1934 act to file proxy materials with the SEC at least ten days before proxies are mailed to shareholders. Proxy statements must disclose all material facts and companies must use a proxy form on which shareholders can indicate whether they approve or disapprove of the proposals (see Figure 18-1).

Figure 18-1 Sample Proxy Forms

UNIVERSAL BUSINESS CORPORATION **Proxy**

270 Universal Center, Horizon, California 91770

This Proxy is Solicited on Behalf of the Board of Directors

The undersigned hereby appoints John Red, Mary Blue, and Lee White as Proxies, each with the power to appoint his or her substitute, and hereby authorizes them to represent and to vote, as designated below, all the shares of common stock of Universal Business held on record by the undersigned on October 23, 1980, at the annual meeting of shareholders to be held on December 20, 1980 or any adjournment thereof.

1. ELECTION OF DIRECTORS FOR all nominees listed below (except as marked to the contrary below) ☐ WITHHOLD AUTHORITY to vote for all nominees listed below ☐

(INSTRUCTION: *To withhold authority to vote for any individual nominee strike a line through the nominee's name in the list below.*)

J. Allen, S. Brown, J. Doe, J. Green, G. Johansen, A. Jones, M. Roe, J. Smith and M. Stanton

2. PROPOSAL TO APPROVE THE APPOINTMENT OF DOLLAR AND CENTS as the independent public accountants of the corporation

☐ FOR ☐ AGAINST ☐ ABSTAIN

3. STOCKHOLDER PROPOSAL RELATING TO FORM AND CONTENT OF POST-MEETING REPORTS:

☐ FOR ☐ AGAINST ☐ ABSTAIN

4. In their discretion, the Proxies are authorized to vote upon such other business as may properly come before the meeting.

This proxy when properly executed will be voted in the manner directed herein by the undersigned stockholder. If no direction is made, this proxy will be voted for Proposals 1, 2 and 3.

Please sign exactly as name appears below. When shares are held by joint tenants, both should sign. When signing as attorney, as executor, administrator, trustee or guardian, please give full title as such. If a corporation, please sign in full corporate name by President or other authorized officer. If a partnership, please sign in partnership name by authorized person.

DATED: ________________, 1980

Signature

PLEASE MARK, SIGN, DATE AND RETURN THE PROXY CARD PROMPTLY USING THE ENCLOSED ENVELOPE.

Signature if held jointly

Source: *Federal Register,* November 29, 1979

Dissident groups opposed to management's position are entitled to solicit their own proxies at their own expense. The company must either furnish the dissidents with a list of all shareholders and addresses or mail the proxies at corporate expense. Since management usually prefers to keep the shareholder list private, dissidents can usually count on the corporation to foot the mailing bill.

Tender Offers In the case of closely held corporations, it is possible for a company bent on takeover to negotiate with each stockholder individually. That is impossible in the case of large publicly held companies. To reach all shareholders, the acquiring company must make a **tender offer.** In fact, the tender "offer" is not really an offer at all in the technical sense; it is an invitation to shareholders to tender their shares for sale at a stipulated price. The tender offer might express the price in cash or in shares of the acquiring company. Ordinarily the tender offeror will want to purchase only a controlling interest, so it will limit the tender to a specified number of shares and reserve the right not to purchase any above that number. It will also condition the tender offer on receiving a minimum number of shares so that it need buy none if stockholders do not offer a threshold number of shares for purchase.

One of the principal advantages of the tender offer as a means of gaining control is that it is less expensive than outright purchase of all assets or merger. If those routes are followed, the acquiring company must pay a fair market value for the whole company. The tender offeror, by comparison, can gain control for considerably less than the total value of the target company. Thereafter, if desired, the acquiring company can merge with the acquired company. Once the stock is purchased, the tender offeror will have gained control and can presumably win any matter put to shareholder vote, just as it thereafter can put friendly directors on the board of the target company.

Under the federal Williams Act, upon commencement of a tender offer for more than 5 percent of the target's stock, the offeror must file a statement with the Securities and Exchange Commission stating the source of funds used in making the purchase, the purpose of the purchase, and the extent of its holdings in the target company. Even when a tender offer has not been made, any person who acquires more than 5 percent ownership must file a statement with the SEC within ten days.

Penalties The logic of the *Borak* case also applies to this act, so that private investors may bring suit in federal court for violations of the statute that led to financial injury. Violations of any provision and the making of false statements in any of the required disclosures subject the defendant to a maximum fine of $100,000 and a maximum five-year prison sentence, but a defendant who can show that he had no knowledge of the particular rule he was convicted of violating may not be imprisoned. The maximum fine for a violation of the act by an exchange itself is $500,000. Any issuer omitting to file requisite documents and reports is liable to pay a fine of $100 for each day the failure continues.

The Foreign Corrupt Practices Act

One of many statutes enacted in the aftermath of Watergate, the Foreign Corrupt Practices Act (FCPA), is incorporated into the 1934 act. Investigations by the SEC and the Watergate Special Prosecutor turned up evidence that hundreds of companies had misused corporate funds, mainly by bribing foreign officials to induce them to enter into contracts with or grant licenses to American companies. Because revealing the bribe would normally be self-defeating, and in any event could be expected to stir up immense criticism, companies paying bribes routinely hid the payments in various accounts. The SEC's legal interest in the matter was not the morality of bribery but the falsity of the financial statements that were being filed.

Congress' response, the FCPA, was much broader than necessary to treat the abuses uncovered. The FCPA prohibits an issuer (that is, any U.S. business enterprise), a stockholder acting on behalf of an issuer, and "any officer, director, employee, or agent" of an issuer from using the mails, or interstate commerce corruptly to offer, pay, or promise to pay, anything of value to foreign officials, foreign political parties, or candidates, if the purpose is to gain business by inducing the foreign official to influence an act of the government to render a decision favorable to the American corporation. But, more important than the foreign-bribe provisions, the act includes accounting provisions which broaden considerably the authority of the SEC. These provisions are discussed in the following case—the first accounting provisions case brought to trial.

S.E.C. v. WORLD-WIDE COIN INVESTMENTS, LTD.
567 F.Supp. 724 (N.D. Ga. 1983)

VINING, DISTRICT JUDGE. This is a securities fraud action in which the Securities and Exchange Commission (SEC) seeks a permanent injunction against World-Wide Coin Investments, Ltd. (World-Wide) and the individual defendants as well as an order for a full accounting and disclosure of wrongfully received benefits. In an order entered March 29, 1983, this court directed the clerk to enter judgment for the SEC on all counts of the complaint and further directed defendants Hale and Seibert to (1) retain an independent auditor to perform a full accounting of World-Wide of all receipts and disbursements of cash and all purchases and sales and other acquisitions and dispositions of inventory and assets since July 1, 1979, and (2) return whatever shares of World-Wide stock they might hold to World-Wide. Finally, the court ordered World-Wide to make a full disclosure to its present shareholders with respect to all material information relating to its operations since July 1, 1979. The following memorandum opinion will constitute this court's findings of fact and conclusions of law as required by Fed.R.Civ.P. 52(a).

FACTUAL BACKGROUND

World-Wide Coin Investments, Ltd., is a Delaware corporation with its principal offices in Atlanta, Georgia, and is engaged primarily in the wholesale and retail sale of rare coins, precious metals, gold and silver coins, bullion, and, until 1979, in the retail sale of camera equipment. Its operations also include the sale of Coca-Cola collector items and certain commemorative items. Its inventory of rare coins comes from its purchases of collections from estates and private individuals, purchases from dealers, purchases on domestic commodities exchanges, and purchases at coin shows. Sales are transacted at the Atlanta office and at many major coin shows held in the United States. For some time it published a trade journal, *The Coin Wholesaler,* which carried both news and feature stories of special interest to coin collectors and investors, who comprised the majority of subscribers. Until August 1979, through its subsidiary World-Wide Camera Fair, Inc., World-Wide operated retail stores in Augusta, Athens, Savannah, Columbus, Georgia, and Jacksonville, Florida, selling camera and photographic equipment. All five stores were sold during the first quarter of fiscal year 1980.

World-Wide's common stock is registered with the SEC pursuant to the Securities Exchange Act of 1934, 15 U.S.C. § 78*l*(b), and until late 1981 was listed on the Boston Stock Exchange. Prior to July 1979, the company's assets totaled over $2,000,000, and it had over 40 employees. In August 1981, the time of the filing of this lawsuit, the company's assets amounted to less than $500,000, and it had only three employees.

Defendant Joseph H. Hale took over the management and control of World-Wide on July 24, 1979, as the controlling shareholder, chairman of the board, chief executive officer, and president. He was formerly a national bank examiner with the United States Treasury Department and was employed as an accountant and auditor for General Motors and the Glidden Company, where he obtained an understanding of the importance of internal controls and the concept of "GAAP" (generally accepted accounting principles). Following these experiences, he became a broker-dealer and is registered with the National Association of Securities Dealers (NASD) and the New York Stock Exchange.

Defendant Floyd Seibert is an employee of Health-Care International, Inc., a member of the board of directors of Florafax, Inc., and in September 1979 became a member of World-Wide's board of directors; he also constitutes World-Wide's one-man audit committee.

* * *

The Foreign Corrupt Practices Act, 15 U.S.C. § 78m(b)(2) (Amend.1977) ("FCPA") was enacted by Congress as an amendment to the 1934 Securities Exchange Act and was the legislative response to numerous questionable and illegal foreign payments by United States corporations in the 1970's. Although one of the major substantive provisions of the FCPA is to require corporate disclosure of assets as a deterrent to foreign bribes, the more significant addition of the FCPA is the accounting controls or "books and records" provision, which gives the SEC authority over the entire financial management and reporting requirements of publicly held United States corporations.

The FCPA was enacted on the principle that accurate recordkeeping is an essential ingredient in promoting management responsibility and is an affirmative requirement for publicly held American corporations to strengthen the accuracy of corporate books and records, which are "the bedrock elements of our system of corporate disclosure and accountability."

* * *

The FCPA reflects a congressional determination that the scope of the federal securities laws and the SEC's authority should be expanded beyond the traditional ambit of disclosure requirements. The consequence of adding these substantive requirements governing accounting control to the federal securities laws will significantly augment the degree of federal involvement in the internal management of public corporations.

* * *

Section 13(b)(2) contains two separate requirements for issuers in complying with the FCPA's accounting provisions: (1) a company must keep accurate books and records reflecting the transactions and dispositions of the assets of the issuer, and (2) a company must maintain a reliable and adequate system of internal accounting controls. In applying these two separate requirements to the instant case, the court will examine the requirements of each provision and the problems inherent in their interpretation.

The "books and records" provision, contained in section 13(b)(2)(A) of the FCPA has three basic objectives: (1) books and records should reflect transactions in conformity with accepted methods of reporting economic events, (2) misrepresentation, concealment, falsification, circumvention, and other deliberate acts resulting in inaccurate financial books and records are unlawful, and (3) transactions should be properly reflected on books and records in such a manner as to permit the preparation of financial statements in conformity with GAAP and other criteria applicable to such statements.

* * *

The second branch of the accounting provisions—the requirement that issuers maintain a system of internal accounting controls—appears in section 13(b)(2)(B). Like the recordkeeping provisions of the Act, the internal controls provision is not limited to material transactions or to those above a specific dollar amount. While this requirement is supportive of accuracy and reliability in the auditor's review and financial disclosure process, this provision should not be analyzed solely from that point of view. The internal controls requirement is primarily designed to give statutory content to an aspect of management stewardship responsibility, that of providing shareholders with reasonable assurances that the business is adequately controlled.

* * *

The evidence in this case reveals that World-Wide, aided and abetted by Hale and Seibert, violated the provisions of section 13(b)(2) of the FCPA. As set forth in the factual background portion of this order, the internal recordkeeping and accounting controls of World-Wide has been sheer chaos since Hale took over control of the company. For example, there has been no procedure implemented with respect to writing checks: employees have had access to presigned checks; source documents were not required to be prepared when a check was drawn; employees have not been required to obtain approval before writing a check, and, even when a check was drawn to "cash," supporting documentation was usually not prepared to explain the purpose for which the check was drawn. In addition to extremely lax security measures such as leaving the vault unguarded, there has been no separation of duties in the areas of purchase and sales transactions, and valuation procedures for ending inventory. Furthermore, no promissory notes or other supporting documentation has been prepared to evidence purported loans to World-Wide by Hale or by his affiliate companies.

Since Hale obtained control of World-Wide, employees have not been required to write source documents relating to the purchase and sale of coins, bullion, or other inventory. Because of this total lack of an audit trail with respect to these transactions and the disposition of World-Wide's assets, it has been virtually impossible to determine if an item has been sold at a profit or at a loss. Furthermore, there are more than $1,700,000 worth of checks drawn to Hale or to Hale's affiliates, or to cash, for which no adequate source documentation exists. Furthermore, Hale and Seibert knew that the medallions that were sold to World-Wide by Hale in 1979 were overvalued and unmarketable. Even so, they allowed the incorrect value of the medallions to be entered on the books of World-Wide. They also knew that the company's books and records were neither accurate nor complete. Pursuant to their directives, source documents were not prepared with respect to the transfer of funds; additionally, no audit trail was maintained for the acquisition and disposition of inventory. Furthermore, it appears that there were numerous false and misleading statements and omissions in the company's numerous reports to the SEC, many of which were filed late or not at all.

Individually, the acts of these defendants do not appear so egregious as to warrant the full panoply of relief requested by the SEC nor to impose complete liability under the FCPA. However the court cannot ignore the all-pervasive effect of the combined failure to act, failure to keep accurate records, failure to maintain any type of inventory control, material omissions and misrepresentation, and other activities which caused World-Wide to decrease from a company of 40 employees and assets over $2,000,000 to a company of only three employees and assets of less than $500,000. It is evident that World-Wide, Hale, and Seibert violated all provisions contained in section 13(b)(2)(A) and (B) and the SEC's rules promulgated thereunder.

Blue Sky Laws

Long before congressional enactment of the securities laws in the 1930s, the states had legislated securities regulations. Today, every state has enacted a "Blue Sky Law"—so called because their purpose is to prevent "speculative schemes which have no more basis than so many feet of 'blue sky'." [Hall v. Geiger-Jones Co., 242 U.S. 539 (1917)] The federal Securities Act of 1933 specifically preserves the jurisdiction of states over securities.

Blue sky laws divide into three basic types. The simplest is that which prohibits fraud in the sale of securities. Thus, at a minimum, issuers cannot mislead investors about the purpose of the investment. All blue sky laws have antifraud provisions; some have no other provisions. The second type calls for registration of broker-dealers; the third type for registration of securities. Some state laws parallel the federal laws in intent and form of proceeding, so that they overlap; other blue sky laws empower state officials (unlike the SEC) to judge the merits of the offerings. As part of a movement toward deregulation, several states have recently modified or eliminated "merit" laws.

Many of the blue sky laws are inconsistent with each other, making national uniformity difficult. In 1956, the National Conference of Commissioners on Uniform State Laws approved the Uniform Securities Act. It has not been designed to reconcile the conflicting philosophies of state regulation, but to take them into account and to make the various forms of regulation as consistent as possible. States adopt various portions of the law, depending on their regulatory philosophies. The Uniform Securities Act has antifraud, broker-dealer registration, and securities registration provisions.

Securities Regulation and Corporate Governance

The governance of a corporation rests with the board of directors. Section 8.01 of the Revised Model Business Corporation Act (RMBCA) states that "all corporate powers shall be exercised by or under the authority of, and the business and affairs of the corporation managed under the direction of, its board of directors." A director is a fiduciary, and, as the RMBCA puts it, must perform his duties "in good faith, with the care an ordinarily prudent person in a like position would exercise under similar circumstances." (Section 8.30) Among the director's responsibilities: determining the mix of products and services to be offered, wages of employees and compensation of executives, prices to be charged, dividends; selection and removal of officers; delegation of operating authority to the managers; and supervising the company as a whole.

These specific responsibilities are fairly clear. A problem arises, however, in defining the broader functions and responsibilities of the board of directors. Box 18-1 represents an attempt by the Business Roundtable to de-

Box 18-1 The Social Impact of Corporate Actions

Corporate Social Responsibility

[A] major board responsibility is the consideration of significant social impacts of corporate activities and relatedly the consideration of views of substantial groups (other than share owners) significantly affected by such activity.

The board's responsibility is to direct the enterprise in the interest of the owners, subject to the constraints imposed by law. However, the interest of share owners cannot be conceived solely in terms of short-range profit maximizaiton. The owners have an interest in balancing short-range and long-range profitability, in considering the political and social viability of the enterprise over time and in adjusting to the global environment in which it operates. Moreover, share owners and directors alike have an interest in assuring that entities with which they are identified behave ethically and as good citizens. It is the board's duty to consider the overall impact of the activities of the corporation on (1) the society of which it is a part, and on (2) the interests and views of groups other than those immediately identified with the corporation. This obligation arises out of the responsibility to act primarily in the interest of the share owners—particularly their long-range interest.

But if it is important to recognize the social responsibility of the owners of the enterprise and of its directors, it is also important to be clear about the boundaries of that responsibility.

First, the private business corporation is recognized and utilized in a free society not as an instrument to accomplish some ill-defined social objectives, but to perform specific economic functions—to provide particular goods and services, and to do so efficiently. This is not the sole mission, but it is the primary and indispensable one.

To perform this task successfully in a competitive market economy, the corporation has to have some control over its costs and has to earn enough to survive and to attract new investment. If the enterprise cannot do this, it cannot provide continued employment. The first corporate obligation therefore—an obligation to both owners and employees—is profitable operation.

Second, other groups affected by corporate activities cannot be placed on a plane with owners, and some of them are not clearly identifiable. More fundamentally, an economic system based on economic decentralization and therefore on private savings and investment has to provide opportunities (not guarantees) for profitable operation. The viability of the system depends on the continued willingness of private persons and institutions to invest and this in turn requires permitting (again not guaranteeing) a return on investment.

Third, there has been a tendency through the proxy proposal mechanisms of the Securities and Exchange Commission to try to make the corporation an arena for debate about issues which should be decided through the political and legislative process. Corporations, corporate boards and corporate share owners, are not the right bodies to resolve on their own, for example, issues involving relations with other countries or U.S. military policy.

Fourth, many of the social causes pursued by activist groups represent minority views rather than a prevailing consensus. The political process by which law is enacted provides an opportunity—although an imperfect one—to weigh the costs and benefits of complying with new social demands.

Fifth, just as the board cannot review every particular aspect of business operations, it cannot be expected to consider every question no matter how minor as to the social or public effect of those operations. However, major environmental impacts, equal employment opportunity, important relationships with communities or governmental authorities, issues such as foreign trade or investment activities affecting this country's international relations, and matters of comparable magnitude are part of the operation of a business and proper for board consideration.

Source: The Business Roundtable, *The Role and Composition of the Board of Directors of the Large Publicly Owned Corporation*, 1978 scribe a key board function—the duty to consider the social impact of corporate actions. We discussed corporate social responsibility in depth in Chapter 6.

Not so long ago, boards of directors of large companies were quiescent bodies, virtual "rubber stamps" for their friends among management who put them there. By the late 1970s, with the general increase in the climate of litigiousness, one out of every nine companies on the Fortune list saw its directors or officers hit with claims for violation of their legal responsibilities (*Business Insurance,* 1979, p. 18). Serving as a director or officer was never free of business risks. Today the task is fraught with legal risk as well.

Two broad categories of obligations apply to both directors and officers. One is a *duty of loyalty,* the other the *duty of care.* After examining these obligations we turn to the impact of securities regulation, as illustrated by insider trading restrictions, on management decision making.

Duty of Loyalty

As a fiduciary of the corporation, the director, as well as officers and majority shareholders, owes her primary loyalty to the corporation and its stockholders. When there is a conflict between her personal interest and the interest of the corporation, she is legally bound to put the corporation's interest above her own.

Two situations commonly arise implicating the director's or officer's duty of loyalty: (1) contracts with the corporation; and (2) corporate opportunity.

Contracts with the Corporation The law does not bar a director from contracting with the corporation she serves. However, unless the contract or transaction is "fair to the corporation," RMBCA Section 8.31 imposes on her a stringent duty of disclosure. In the absence of a fair transaction, any contracts between the corporation and one of its directors, or another corporation or entity in which she has an interest, are voidable, unless the director has made full disclosure of her personal relationship or interest in the contract either to the board or to the shareholders, and they approve the contract (without counting the director's vote).

Corporate Opportunity Whenever a director or officer learns of an opportunity to engage in a variety of activities or transactions that might be beneficial to the corporation, her first obligation is to present the opportunity to the corporation. The rule encompasses the chance of acquiring another corporation, purchasing property, and licensing or marketing patents or products. Whether a particular opportunity is a *corporate* opportunity can be a delicate question. The next case shows the kind of analysis that is required.

FARBER v. SERVAN LAND COMPANY, INC.
393 F.Supp. 633 (S.D. Fla. 1974)

ROETTGER, DISTRICT JUDGE.

[A minority shareholder brought suit against certain directors and majority shareholders alleging that they breached their fiduciary duty by purchasing real estate adjacent to a golf course owned by the corporation. The golf course and the adjoining acreage were later sold as a package to outside investors.]

* * *

Both as directors and majority stockholders of Servan Land Corporation, defendants Seriani and Savin stood in a fiduciary relationship to the corporation and to the minority shareholders as beneficiaries and by virtue of this position, defendants have the burden of proving fairness and good faith in their dealings with the corporation. As a fiduciary, an officer, director or dominant shareholder cannot use his power for his personal advantage to the detriment of the stockholders.

This court in no way takes lightly the principle that a director has an obligation to his corporation of "absolute and most scrupulous good faith." It would be easy to move from such a pious pronouncement to entering a decree in favor of plaintiff but sitting as a court of equity, this court cannot do so.

Plaintiff invokes the court's equitable powers by seeking restitution and an accounting to remedy the claimed breach of fiduciary duty occasioned by defendants' appropriation of a corporate opportunity and wrongful allocation of purchase price. Plaintiff urges that Perlman v. Feldman, 219 F.2d 173 (2nd Cir. 1955) compels a decision in his favor so that the profit personally enjoyed by defendants Seriani and Savin on the sale of the 160 acres adjacent to the corporate property be considered a corporate asset and distributed among the shareholders.

In Perlman v. Feldman the majority stockholders, in selling their controlling interest in the corporation had also sold a corporate asset—the ability to control the product. The consideration received for the sale of corporate stock included the value of the stockholders' controlling interest in the corporation which the court of appeals found to be a corporate asset. The court of appeals, in approving the intervention of equity, found that the sale of stock for excessive consideration directly harmed the corporate interests and constituted a breach of fiduciary duty.

Although this court has determined that defendants Seriani and Savin should have offered the 160 acres to the corporation before purchasing the property for themselves, the purchase of this property worked to the distinct advantage of the corporation and not to its detriment because it enhanced the value of the major corporate asset—the golf course. In fact, unlike *Perlman* where the sale of the stock for excessive consideration harmed the corporation, Servan Land Company and its stockholders, Farber included, profited from the joint sales of the 160 acres and the golf course, not only because of the increased value of the golf course but because of the defendants' overvaluation of the corporate land to the detriment of the defendants' individual land.

This case is in marked contrast to other Florida cases where courts have seen fit to invoke equitable powers and impress a trust on individual property. In Newspaper Journal Corp. v. Gore, 147 Fla. 217, 2 So.2d 741 (1941) the corporate officer purchased land of the "utmost importance" to the corporation—the very land on which the property of the corporation was situated—and thereafter rented the property back to the corporation at an increased rental! Not only did the increased rental fee charged by the individual corporate officers to the corporation directly harm the corporation, but the acquisition of both tracts of land by the corporation, which could have financed the purchases, would have been valuable in carrying out the business of the corporation.

Where there is a duty on the part of officers to acquire property for the corporation and in violation of the obligation they purchase it individually, as in *Gore Newspapers,* Florida law is established that the individuals cannot retain the benefit of their self-serving actions. Similarly, in Pan American Trading & Trapping v. Crown Paint, 99 So.2d 705 (Fla.1957) although the land might not have been of the utmost importance to the corporation's welfare as in *Gore* the evidence established that the land was to be acquired as a site for expansion of corporate operations, a valid and significant corporate purpose of the corporation. The equitable powers of the court were properly invoked to impress a trust upon the property purchased by the individual officer in his own name instead of for the corporation.

Not only did the corporation actually profit from the personal actions of Seriani and Savin, but the 160 acres did not constitute a corporate opportunity nor was its acquisition adverse to the interests of the corporation. The mere fact that the land was adjacent to the corporate land in itself does not support a conclusion that therefore the acreage was a corporate opportunity. The property had no substantial relation to the corporation's primary purpose of operating a golf course and the individual purpose was not antagonistic to any significant corporate purpose and thus the facts do not fall within the general proposition that an officer of a corporation cannot acquire title to or an interest in property prejudicial to the corporation.

Plaintiff seeks for himself and, however involuntarily, for the other stockholders the results of Seriani and Savin's risk in purchasing the property. The argument that a corporation does not have sufficient funds to undertake the venture will not normally absolve fiduciaries of accountability for profiting from a corporate opportunity. In Irving Trust Company v. Deutsch, 73 F.2d 121 (2nd Cir. 1934) the court held that directors could not take over a corporate contract for the purchase of patent rights essential to a corporate purpose for their own profit by a claim of corporate financial inability and thereby divert corporate gains from the transaction. However, not only might Servan Land Company have been financially unable to purchase the 160 acres, but less than a year before the purchase by Seriani and Savin, the directors and stockholders declined to pursue the possibility of purchasing this very same land. . . .

The court concludes the 160 acres was not a corporate opportunity requiring that defendants must account for their profit on the risk they, but not the corporation eleven months earlier, were willing to take.

In addition, the court concludes that defendants Seriani and Savin have satisfactorily sustained the burden of explaining this transaction and establishing its propriety because of the benefit to the corporation by their holding the abutting property and being willing to aggregate it with the corporate property at the time of sale. It must be noted that the sale of the corporate property had been contemplated by the stockholders for some years.

* * *

Judgment is hereby entered for defendants.

When a director serves on more than one board, the problem of corporate opportunity becomes even more complex, because he may be caught in a situation of conflicting loyalties. Moreover, multiple board memberships pose another serious problem. A major study of overlapping memberships, published in 1978 following an investigation by the staff of the Senate Governmental Affairs Subcommitee on Reports, Accounting, and Management, reported that among 130 of the nation's largest companies, there were 530 direct and 12,193 indirect interlocking directors (*The Economist,* 1978, p. 129). The thirteen largest companies had 240 direct and 5,547 indirect interlocks. A **direct interlock** occurs when one person sits on the boards of two different companies; an **indirect interlock**, when directors of two different companies serve jointly on the board of a third company. The Clayton Act prohibits interlocking directorates between direct competitors. No violations of that law were uncovered in the 1978 study, but the potential for conflict of loyalties remains. For example,

Citicorp, the bank holding company, had eighteen indirect links on twelve boards with its arch-rival Chase Manhattan. Citicorp also had thirty indirect ties on nineteen boards to J. P. Morgan (parent company of J. P. Morgan Trust Co.), twenty-six links on fifteen boards with Manufacturers Hanover, twenty-four on sixteen boards with Chemical New York, and fourteen on nine boards with Bankers Trust.

Duty of Care

The second major aspect of the director's responsibility is that of due care. RMBCA Section 8.30 calls on the director to perform his duties "with the care an ordinarily prudent person in a like position would exercise under similar circumstances." An "ordinarily prudent person" means one who directs his intelligence in a thoughtful way to the task at hand. The director is not held to the higher standard required of a specialist (finance, marketing) unless he is one. A director of a small, closely held corporation will not necessarily be held to the same standard as a director who is given a staff by a large, complex, diversified company. The standard of care is that which an ordinarily prudent person would use who is in "a like position" to the director in question. Moreover, the standard is not an objective, timeless one for all people in the same position. It also depends on the circumstances: a fast-moving situation calling for a snap decision will be treated differently later, if there are recriminations because it was the wrong decision, than a situation in which time was not of the essence.

What of the care itself? What kind of care would an ordinarily prudent person in *any* situation, regardless of the circumstances, be obligated to give? At a minimum, the director must *pay attention*. He must attend meetings, receive and digest information adequate to inform him about matters requiring board action, and monitor the performance of those to whom he has delegated the task of operating the corporation. Of course, documents can be misleading, reports can be slanted, information coming from self-interested management can be distorted. To what heights must suspicion be raised? To what degree must the director assume the role of Sherlock Holmes? RMBCA Section 8.30 forgives directors the necessity of playing detective whenever information, including financial data, is received in an apparently reliable manner from corporate officers or employees, or from experts such as attorneys and public accountants.

A director does not spend all his time on corporate affairs, is not omnipotent, and must be permitted to rely on the word of others. Nor can directors be infallible in making decisions. Managers work in a business environment, in which risk is a substantial factor. No decision, no matter how rigorously arrived at, is guaranteed. Accordingly, the law forgives mistakes made on the basis of good faith judgment, if the director has exercised due care. This is the so-called **business judgment rule.** The business judgment rule is part of the fabric of the case law in every state. Assuming that no conflicts of interest or other breaches of any duty of loyalty or due care were present, the courts will not substitute their own judgment for that of the directors. In the words of the Delaware Supreme Court:

> The business judgment rule is an acknowledgment of the managerial prerogatives of Delaware directors. . . . It is a presumption that in making a business decision the directors of a corporation acted on an informed basis, in good faith and in the honest belief that the action taken was in the best interests of the company. [Aronson v. Lewis, 473 A.2d 805, 812 (Del. 1984)]

In a battle for control of a corporation, directors have an inherent self-interest in their decisions, and these decisions also have a major impact on shareholders. As a result Delaware courts have modified the usual business judgment presumption by placing an initial burden on directors to show that their investigations and actions were reasonable. The Delaware approach is illustrated by the following case involving a Preferred Share Purchase Rights Plan—commonly known as a "poison pill."

MORAN v. HOUSEHOLD INTERNATIONAL, INC.
500 A.2d 1346 (Del. 1985)

McNeilly, Justice This case presents to this Court for review the most recent defense mechanism in the arsenal of corporate takeover weaponry—the Preferred Share Purchase Rights Plan ("Rights Plan" or "Plan"). The validity of this mechanism has attracted national attention. *Amici curiae* briefs have been filed in support of appellants by the Securities and Exchange Commission ("SEC") and the Investment Company Institute. An *amicus curiae* brief has been filed in support of appellees ("Household") by the United Food and Commercial Workers International Union.

In a detailed opinion, the Court of Chancery upheld the Rights Plan as a legitimate exercise of business judgment by Household. We agree, and therefore, affirm the judgment below.

* * *

On August 14, 1984, the Board of Directors of Household International, Inc. adopted the Rights Plan by a fourteen to two vote. The intricacies of the Rights Plan are contained in a 48-page document entitled "Rights Agreement". Basically, the Plan provides that Household common stockholders are entitled to the issuance of one Right per common share under certain triggering conditions. There are two triggering events that can activate the Rights. The first is the announcement of a tender offer for 30 percent of Household's shares ("30% trigger") and the second is the acquisition of 20 percent of Household's shares by any single entity or group ("20% trigger").

If an announcement of a tender offer for 30 percent of Household's shares is made, the Rights are issued and are immediately exercisable to purchase 1/100 share of new preferred stock for $100 and are redeemable by the Board for $.50 per Right. If 20 percent of Household's shares are acquired by anyone, the Rights are issued and become non-redeemable and are exercisable to purchase 1/100 of a share of preferred. If a Right is not exercised for preferred, and thereafter, a merger or consolidation occurs, the Rights holder can exercise each Right to purchase $200 of the common stock of the tender offeror for $100. This "flip-over" provision of the Rights Plan is at the heart of this controversy.

Household is a diversified holding company with its principal subsidiaries engaged in financial services, transportation and merchandising. HFC, National Car Rental and Vons Grocery are three of its wholly-owned entities.

Household did not adopt its Rights Plan during a battle with a corporate raider, but as a preventive mechanism to ward off future advances. The Vice-Chancellor found that as early as February 1984, Household's management became concerned about the company's vulnerability as a takeover target and began considering amending its charter to render a takeover more difficult. . . .

In the meantime, appellant Moran, one of Household's own Directors and also Chairman of the Dyson-Kissner-Moran Corporation, ("D-K-M") which is the largest single stockholder of Household, began discussions concerning a possible leveraged buyout of Household by D-K-M. D-K-M's financial studies showed that Household's stock was significantly undervalued in relation to the company's break-up value. It is uncontradicted that Moran's suggestion of a leveraged buy-out never progressed beyond the discussion stage.

Concerned about Household's vulnerability to a raider in light of the current takeover climate, Household secured the services of Wachtell, Lipton, Rosen and Katz ("Wachtell, Lipton") and Goldman, Sachs & Co. ("Goldman, Sachs") to formulate a takeover policy for recommendation to the Household Board at its August 14 meeting. After a July 31 meeting with a Household Board member and a pre-meeting distribution of material on the potential takeover problem and the proposed Rights Plan, the Board met on August 14, 1984.

Representatives of Wachtell, Lipton and Goldman, Sachs attended the August 14 meeting. The minutes reflect that Mr. Lipton explained to the Board that his recommendation of the Plan was based on his understanding that the Board was concerned about the increasing frequency of "bust-up" takeovers, the increasing takeover activity in the financial service industry, such as Leucadia's attempt to take over Arco, and the possible adverse effect this type of activity could have on employees and others concerned with and vital to the continuing successful operation of Household even in the absence of any actual bust-up takeover attempt. Against this factual background, the Plan was approved.

Thereafter, Moran and the company of which he is Chairman, D-K-M, filed this suit. On the eve of trial, Gretle Golter, the holder of 500 shares of Household, was permitted to intervene as an additional plaintiff. The trial was held, and the Court of Chancery ruled in favor of Household. Appellants now appeal from that ruling to this Court.

* * *

The business judgment rule is a "presumption that in making a business decision the directors of a corporation acted on an informed basis, in good faith and in the honest belief that the action taken was in the best interests of the company." *Aronson v. Lewis,* Del.Supr., 473 A.2d 805, 812 (1984) (citations omitted). Notwithstanding, in *Unocal* we held that when the business judgment rule applies to adoption of a defensive mechanism, the initial burden will lie with the directors. The "directors must show that they had reasonable grounds for believing that a danger to corporate policy and effectiveness existed. . . . [T]hey satisfy that burden 'by showing good faith and reasonable investigation. . . .' " *Unocal,* 493 A.2d at 955 (citing *Cheff v. Mathes,* 199 A.2d at 554–55). In addition, the directors must show that the defensive mechanism was "reasonable in relation to the threat posed." Moreover, that proof is materially enhanced, as we noted in *Unocal,* where, as here, a majority of the board favoring the proposal consisted of outside independent directors who have acted in accordance with the foregoing standards. Then, the burden shifts back to the plaintiffs who have the ultimate burden of persuasion to show a breach of the directors' fiduciary duties.

There are no allegations here of any bad faith on the part of the Directors' action in the adoption of the Rights Plan. There is no allegation that the Directors' action was taken for entrenchment purposes. Household has adequately demonstrated, as explained above, that the adoption of the Rights Plan was in reaction to what it perceived to be the threat in the market place of coercive two-tier tender offers.

* * *

In addition, to meet their burden, the Directors must show that the defensive mechanism was "reasonable in relation to the threat posed". The record reflects a concern on the part of the Directors over the increasing frequency in the financial services industry of "boot-strap" and "bust-up" takeovers. The Directors were also concerned that such takeovers may take the form of two-tier offers. In addition, on August 14, the Household Board was aware of Moran's overture on behalf of D-K-M. In sum, the Directors reasonably believed Household was vulnerable to coercive acquisition techniques and adopted a reasonable defensive mechanism to protect itself.

In conclusion, the Household Directors receive the benefit of the business judgment rule in their adoption of the Rights Plan.

* * *

The Directors adopted the Plan in the good faith belief that it was necessary to protect Household from coercive acquisition techniques. The Board was informed as to the details of the Plan. In addition, Household has demonstrated that the Plan is reasonable in relation to that threat posed. Appellants, on the other hand, have failed to convince us that the Directors breached any fiduciary duty in their adoption of the Rights Plan.

While we conclude for present purposes that the Household Directors are protected by the business judgment rule, that does not end the matter. The ultimate response to an actual takeover bid must be judged by the Directors' actions at that time, and nothing we say here relieves them of their basic fundamental duties to the corporation and its stockholders. Their use of the Plan will be evaluated when and if the issue arises.

Affirmed.

Insider Trading

Corporate insiders—directors, officers, important shareholders—can have a substantial trading advantage if they are privy to important confidential information. Learning bad news (such as financial loss, cancellation of key contracts) in advance of all other stockholders will permit the privileged few to sell shares before the price falls. Discovering good news (major oil find, unexpected profits), conversely, gives the insider a decided incentive to purchase shares before the price rises.

Because of the unfairness to those who are ignorant of inside information, federal law for half a century has regulated insider trading, beginning with the enactment of the Securities Exchange Act of 1934. Since then, insider trading has become a considerable legal hazard, regulated in the main by federal law. Two provisions of the 1934 Securities Exchange Act are paramount.

Recapture of Short-Swing Profits: Section 16(b) The Securities Exchange Act assumes that any director, officer, or shareholder owning 10 percent or more of the stock is using inside information if he or any family member makes a profit from trading activities, either buying and selling, or selling and buying, during a six-month period. Section 16(b) penalizes any such person by permitting the corporation, or a shareholder suing on its behalf, to recover the profits. The law applies to any company with more than $5 million in assets and at least 500 or more shareholders of any class of stock.

Suppose on January 1, Bob (a company officer) purchases 100 shares of BCT stock for $60 a share. On September 1, he sells them for $100 a share. What result? Bob is in the clear, because his $4,000 profit was not realized during a six-month period. Now suppose that the price falls, and one month later, on October 1, he repurchases 100 shares at $30 a share and holds them for two years. What result? He will be forced to pay back $7,000 in profits even if he had no inside information. Why? In August, Bob held 100 shares of stock, and again on October 1—within a six-month period. His net gain on these transactions was $7,000 ($10,000 realized on the sale, less $3,000 cost of the purchase).

As a consequence of Section 16(b) and certain other provisions, trading in securities by directors, officers, and large stockholders presents numerous complexities; see Box 18-2. For instance, the law requires people in this position to make periodic reports to the SEC about their trades. As a practical matter, directors, officers, and large shareholders should not trade in their own company stock in the short run without legal advice. As the following case indicates, if Section 16(b) is violated, they will be held liable even though they did not use inside information.

ARROW DISTRIBUTING CORP. v. BAUMGARTNER
783 F.2d 1274 (5th Cir. 1986)

ALVIN B. RUBIN, CIRCUIT JUDGE. A shareholder sued under § 16(b) of the Securities Exchange Act of 1934, on behalf of a corporation whose stock has been registered in accordance with the Act, to recover profits realized by the corporation's officers on the sale of corporation stock. The officers sold stock before the registration, then, after the registration and within six months of the date of sale, exercised a stock option to purchase a greater number of shares at a price lower than the amount for which they had sold their shares.

* * *

Congress adopted § 16(b) of the Act, which Professor Louis Loss characterizes as a "nice example of 'native American radicalism,' " to prevent insiders of publicly-held corporations, who had advance knowledge of facts that, upon public disclosure, would produce either a rise or fall in the market price of the stock, from realizing a personal profit by buying or selling the corporation's shares before the good or bad news was made public. The exploitation by insiders of information not available to the public was considered unfair to the public investors who were not privy to the information. Moreover, the profit potential prompted some insiders to manipulate the market price of their corporation's shares by causing the corporation to inaugurate and follow financial policies calculated to produce sudden fluctuations in that price.

Considering any case-by-case rule impracticable, Congress adopted "a flat rule taking the profits out of a class of transactions in which the possibility of abuse was believed to be intolerably great." The general rule used to compute recoverable profits under § 16(b) is to match the shares bought at the lowest price against an equal number of shares sold at the highest price within six months of such purchase. It was described to Congress by the spokesman for the Roosevelt administration who advocated its adoption as a "crude rule of thumb." The rule is frequently and properly referred to as prophylactic because it is designed to preserve the health of the securities market and prevent the disease of insider trading.

The corporate officers first urge that § 16(b) is not applicable because two crucial events occurred before the security was registered: the sale was made and the option agreement was granted.

When a security is not registered under the 1934 Act at the time stock is purchased but is registered before it is sold, § 16(b) has been held applicable. It is, however, a nonsequitur to reason that, if the sale precedes both registration and purchase, the section is inapplicable. The sequence of purchase and sale is in no way restricted by the language of § 16(b).

While they acknowledge that the courts have subjected insiders' short-swing transactions to § 16(b) even though the issuer's shares were not registered at the time of the purchases involved, the officers argue that the absence of any decisions involving pre-registration sales proves that such transactions were not intended to be subject to the purview of § 16(b). As Professor Loss has observed in another connection, the lack of jurisprudence concerning some applications of § 16(b) proves little. Because of the simplicity of its provisions, "the number of reported decisions is probably no criterion of the total amount of short-term profits recaptured or, once the section became well known, simply foregone."

This conclusion is supported by another portion of the same section of the statute pertaining to a "beneficial owner," that is, a shareholder of at least 10 percent of the issuer's stock. That clause provides that § 16(b) is applicable only if the 10-percent-shareholder status obtains both at the time of the purchase and the sale involved in the short-swing transaction. The statute contains no similar requirement with respect to a short-swing transaction effected by a director or officer of an issuer. The express requirement that a beneficial owner have that status at both ends of the transaction implies that an officer or director need not.

Accordingly, an insider's short-swing transaction is subject to § 16(b) if the insider has held his corporate position at either the time of his purchase or the time of his sale. Analogously, short-swing transactions effected by a director or officer are subject to § 16(b) even though the issuer's securities were registered under § 12(g) of the Act only at the time of purchase or of sale. As Professor Loss states: "The courts have also imposed liability in the cognate situation in which an equity security of the issuer first becomes registered between the dates of the two transactions."

* * *

The insiders contend, in a last-ditch defense, that § 16(b) should not be applied to them because in this case there was no possibility of speculative abuse. The existence of that possibility is irrelevant, for neither actual use of inside information nor intention to exploit such information is required to establish § 16(b) liability. In the "garden variety" insider purchase and sale, or sale and purchase, of securities within a period of less than six months, proof of the possibility of speculative abuse is wholly immaterial.

* * *

The insiders' companion economic-reality argument points to no specific direction. "[T]he economists are not of one persuasion." The strictly economic arguments, moreover, display "apparent scorn for the moral or public opinion factor." "Why should the public enter the market," Professor Loss writes, "if the rules of the game make it perfectly legitimate for insiders (and their friends and business associates) to play with marked cards?" Section 16(b) is a strict-liability rule. It was enacted precisely because of the difficulty of establishing whether an insider did indeed benefit from the information available to him in his strategic position. It adopts a purely objective test: if a sale and a purchase or a purchase and a sale result in net gain, the gain is recoverable.

The argument that the officers might have avoided any possibility of liability to the corporation by postponing the exercise of their option ignores the fact that § 16(b) may always be escaped by waiting at least six months between the two transactions. As Professor Loss has pointed out, the " 'crude rule of thumb' works two ways. An insider who holds for six months or more before selling does not become liable under § 16(b), no matter how much proof is adduced of unfair resort to nonpublic information." That the insider ignorantly or illadvisedly made a sale or a purchase within the period, when he might have avoided the statute by waiting, does not obviate its application.

For these reasons, the judgment in favor of the defendant-officers is reversed and judgment is rendered on behalf of the plaintiff-stockholder. The case is remanded for computation of the recoverable gain consistent with this opinion.

Box 18-2 Insider Trading and the Crash of 1987

Corporate Insiders May Find Buying Stock after the Crash Broke "Short-swing" Rule

By Jill Bettner

Many corporate insiders who sold company stock earlier this year, then bought back shares at lower prices after the October stock market crash, may have violated a longstanding federal securities law barring "short-swing" profits by insiders.

Already, shareholders' lawyers have notified at least a dozen companies that corporate officials may have engaged in illegal short-swing trades. These companies could wind up in court if they don't collect the profits from those trades, and they will have to pay shareholders' lawyers hefty fees for discovering any violations.

"What we're seeing is probably just the tip of the iceberg," says Jesse Brill, a securities lawyer with Dean Witter Reynolds Inc. in San Francisco. A former Securities and Exchange Commission lawyer, Mr. Brill tracks legal developments affecting corporate insiders for a monthly newsletter.

Most insiders whose situations have recently come to light bought company stock in the week following the Oct. 19 plunge, after selling shares at much higher prices in the preceding six months.

But the short-swing profit rule, contained in seciton 16(b) of the 1934 Securities and Exchange Act, works two ways: It prohibits insiders—officers, directors, and owners of 10% or more of a company's stock—not only from buying low and selling high within six months, but also from first selling high and then buying low.

"It's a profit even if the sale comes first," Mr. Brill says.

Many insiders say they learned this, to their chagrin, only after the fact, Roland C. Baer Jr., a director of Charleston, W.Va.-based Allegheny & Western Energy Corp. and president of its Mountaineer Gas Co. unit, bought 3,000 Allegheny & Western shares Oct 26, when the oil and natural gas company's stock stood at $10. But in July he had sold 5,000 shares at $28.50 and another 3,000 at $27.25, giving him a short-swing profit of about $55,000 before commissions.

"It was an honest mistake," he says. He plans to return his profit by year's end.

Some executives say institutional investors hurried them into buying back their companies' shares when everybody else was selling. David Downey, chairman of Downey Designs International Inc. in Indianapolis, which remounts diamonds and other gems as a while-you-wait service in department stores, says many institutional investors were "calling up in October wanting to unload, and others were saying, 'Do something,' " he says. "I started this company 24 years ago. It's my baby. I wasn't about to sit by and do nothing."

Mr. Downey blames his company's "high-priced New York lawyers for not warning me I could be doing something illegal. 'You screwed up,' they told me (afterward)," he says.

A week after the crash, when Mr. Downey bought 50,000 shares, the stock was at $3.50, well below its initial offering price of $6 on June 17. As part of the offering, Mr. Downey had sold 187,500 shares. His short-swing profit from the two transactions amounted to about $94,000 after underwriting fees and brokerage commissions.

"It seems like I am in violation of the rule," he says, "but I haven't taken any action yet. I'm waiting to hear back from my attorneys."

That he remains the company's largest stockholder "isn't much solace," he says, adding that the stock has fallen further, to $3.125, "and I can't do anything with (the shares) for another six months."

Although the short-swing rule may appear simple, securities lawyers say it has many gray areas. For example, they say court decisions haven't established a clear precedent for cases involving stock purchases by or for members of an insider's immediate family. James Moore, a vice president of California Energy Co., bought company stock in late October for his children's saving accounts. He says it could cost him $24,300.

On Sept. 9, Mr. Moore sold 7,000 shares at $6.90 in California Energy, a Santa Clara, Calif.,

(continues on next page)

Box 18-2, *continued*

company that is developing geothermal power plants. On Oct. 23, he bought 5,000 shares at $3.75 and four days later another 2,000 shares at $2.625.

Some federal courts have ruled that an insider has to prove that only the children benefited from such transacitons, but in one case "an insider who had trusts for his kids wasn't held liable even though he was a co-trustee," says Peter Romeo, a partner in the Washington law firm of Hogan & Hartson.

Mr. Moore says, "I'm a geologist, not a lawyer, but I've learned a lot about rule 16(b) in the past month." He says preliminary responses from his own lawyer and the company's counsel hold that he didn't violate the rule. "Whatever I'm advised, I'll do," he says.

In all of these cases, the possible infractions were uncovered by lawyers who specialize in pursuing short-swing violators. In fact, enforcement of the short-swing rule effectively rests with these lawyers. That's because the 1934 law makes the courts, rather than the SEC, responsible for seeing that short-swing profits go back to the companies. But only shareholders can initiate any action against short-swing traders.

The information that leads these lawyers to possible violations is contained in Form 4 filings, required of insiders on any company stock transaction. But lawyers in the field maintain that many short-swing trades go undetected, either because they get lost in the mountain of filings or because insiders simply ignore the filing requirement and get away with it.

Typically, a lawyer first uncovers a possible case of short-swing profits, then finds a shareholder on whose behalf to act. The lawyer next notifies the company involved, which contacts the insider. Most cases involving a violation get settled without going to court: The insider simply returns the money.

The incentive for these lawyers: Companies must pay them fees of up to one-third of the amounts recovered. (When more than one lawyer finds the same violation, the fee goes to the first to notify the company.) Company shareholders, meanwhile, receive no direct payment; they gain only indirectly, through an enriched corporate treasury.

Source: *Wall Street Journal*, December 21, 1987, p. 21

Insider Trading: Section 10(b) and Rule 10b-5 Section 10(b) of the Securities Exchange Act of 1934 prohibits any person from using the mails or facilities of interstate commerce "to use or employ, in connection with the purchase or sale of any security . . . any manipulative or deceptive device or contrivance in contravention of such rules and regulations as the Commission may prescribe as necessary or appropriate in the public interest or for the protection of investors." In 1942, the SEC learned of a company president who misrepresented the company's financial condition in order to buy shares at a low price from current stockholders. So the SEC adopted a rule under the authority of Section 10(b). Rule 10b-5, as it was dubbed, has remained unchanged for more than forty years and spawned thousands of lawsuits and SEC proceedings. It reads as follows:

> It shall be unlawful for any person, directly or indirectly, by the use of any means or instrumentality of interstate commerce, or of the mails, or of any facility of any national securities exchange,

(1) to employ any device, scheme, or artifice to defraud,

(2) to make any untrue statement of a material fact or to omit to state a material fact necessary in order to make the statements made, in the light of circumstances under which they were made, not misleading, or

(3) to engage in any act, practice, or course of business which operates or would operate as a fraud or deceit upon any person, in connection with the purchase or sale of any security.

Rule 10b-5 applies to *any* person who purchases or sells any security. It is not limited to securities registered under the 1934 act. It is not limited to publicly held companies. It applies to any security issued by any company, including the smallest closely held company. In substance, it is an antifraud rule, enforcement of which seems, on its face, to be limited to action by the SEC. But over the years the courts have permitted people injured by those who violate the statute to file private damage suits. This sweeping rule has at times been referred to as the "federal law of corporations" or the "catch everybody" rule.

Insider trading ran headlong into Rule 10b-5 beginning in 1964, in a series of cases involving Texas Gulf Sulphur Company (TGS). On November 12, 1963, the company discovered a rich deposit of copper and zinc while drilling for oil near Timmins, Ontario. Keeping the discovery quiet, it proceeded to acquire mineral rights in adjacent lands. By April 1964, word began to circulate about Texas Gulf's find. Newspapers printed rumors, and the Toronto Stock Exchange experienced a wild speculative spree. On April 12, Charles F. Fogarty, executive vice president of TGS, issued a press release downplaying the discovery, asserting that the rumors greatly exaggerated the find, and stating that more drilling would be necessary before coming to any conclusions. Four days later, on April 16, TGS publicly announced that it had uncovered a strike of 25 million tons of ore. In the months following this announcement, TGS stock doubled in value.

The SEC charged several TGS officers and directors with having purchased or told their friends (so-called "tippees") to purchase TGS stock from November 12, 1963 through April 16, 1964 on the basis of material inside information. The SEC also alleged that the April 12, 1964 press release was deceptive. The U.S. Court of Appeals, in *SEC* v. *Texas Gulf Sulphur Co.*, 401 F.2d 833 (2d Cir. 1968), decided that the defendants who purchased the stock before the public announcement had violated Rule 10b-5. According to the court, ". . . anyone in possession of material inside information must either disclose it to the investing public, or, if he is disabled from disclosing to protect a corporate confidence, or he chooses not to do so, must abstain from trading in or recommending the securities concerned while such inside information remains undisclosed." On remand the District Court ordered certain defendants to pay $148,000 into an escrow account to be used to compensate parties injured by the insider trading.

The Court of Appeals also concluded that the press release violated Rule 10b-5 if "misleading to the reasonable investor." On remand, the District Court held that TGS failed to exercise "due diligence" in issuing the release. Sixty-nine private damage actions were subsequently filed against TGS by shareholders who claimed they sold their stock in reliance on the release. TGS settled most of these suits in late 1971 for $2.7 million.

Following the TGS episode, the Supreme Court has refined Rule 10b-5 on two major fronts. First, the Court, in *Ernst & Ernst* v. *Hochfelder*, 425 U.S. 185 (1976), decided that proof of scienter—defined as "mental state embracing intent to deceive, manipulate, or defraud"—is required in private damage actions under rule 10b-5. In other words, negligence alone will not result in Rule 10b-5 liability. The Supreme Court has also held that scienter must be established in SEC injunctive actions. [Aaron v. SEC, 446 U.S. 680 (1980)]

Second, the Supreme Court has placed limitations on the liability of tippees under Rule 10b-5. In 1980, the Court reversed the conviction of an employee of a company that printed tender offer and merger prospectuses. Using information obtained at work, the employee had purchased stock in target companies and later sold it for a profit when takeover attempts were publicly announced. The Court held that the employee was not an insider or fiduciary, and "a duty to disclose under Section 10(b) does not arise from the mere possession of nonpublic market information." [Chiarella v. United States, 445 U.S. 222 (1980)] This case set the stage for the following decision, which is the leading case on tippee liability.

DIRKS v. SECURITIES AND EXCHANGE COMMISSION
463 U.S. 646 (1983)

JUSTICE POWELL delivered the opinion of the Court.

Petitioner Raymond Dirks received material nonpublic information from "insiders" of a corporation with which he had no connection. He disclosed this information to investors who relied on it in trading in the shares of the corporation. The question is whether Dirks violated the antifraud provisions of the federal securities laws by this disclosure.

In 1973, Dirks was an officer of a New York broker-dealer firm who specialized in providing investment analysis of insurance company securities to institutional investors. On March 6, Dirks received information from Ronald Secrist, a former officer of Equity Funding of America. Secrist alleged that the assets of Equity Funding, a diversified corporation primarily engaged in selling life insurance and mutual funds, were vastly overstated as the result of fraudulent corporate practices. Secrist also stated that various regulatory agencies had failed to act on similar charges made by Equity Funding employees. He urged Dirks to verify the fraud and disclose it publicly.

Dirks decided to investigate the allegations. He visited Equity Funding's headquarters in Los Angeles and interviewed several officers and employees of the corporation. The senior management denied any wrongdoing, but certain corporation employees corroborated the charges of fraud. Neither Dirks nor his firm owned or traded any Equity Funding stock, but throughout his investigation he openly discussed the information he had obtained with a number of clients and investors. Some of these persons sold their holdings of Equity Funding securities, including five investment advisers who liquidated holdings of more than $16 million.

While Dirks was in Los Angeles, he was in touch regularly with William Blundell, the *Wall Street Journal*'s Los Angeles bureau chief. Dirks urged Blundell to write a story on the fraud allegations. Blundell did not believe, however, that such a massive fraud could go undetected and declined to write the story. He feared that publishing such damaging hearsay might be libelous.

During the two-week period in which Dirks pursued his investigation and spread word of Secrist's charges, the price of Equity Funding stock fell from $26 per share to less than $15 per share. This led the New York Stock Exchange to halt trading on March 27. Shortly thereafter California insurance authorities impounded Equity Funding's records and uncovered evidence of the fraud. Only then did the Securities and Exchange Commission (SEC) file a complaint against Equity Funding and only then, on April 2, did the *Wall Street Journal* publish a front-page story based largely on information assembled by Dirks. Equity Funding immediately went into receivership.

The SEC began an investigation into Dirks' role in the exposure of the fraud. The SEC concluded: "Where 'tippees'—regardless of their motivation or occupation—come into possession of material 'information that they know is confidential and know or should know came from a corporate insider,' they must either publicly disclose that information or refrain from trading." 21 S. E. C. Docket 1401, 1407 (1981) (footnote omitted) (quoting *Chiarella* v. *United States,* 445 U.S. 222, 230 n. 12 (1980)). Recognizing, however, that Dirks "played an important role in bringing [Equity Funding's] massive fraud to light," 21 S. E. C. Docket, at 1412, the SEC only censured him.

Dirks sought review in the Court of Appeals for the District of Columbia Circuit. The court entered judgment against Dirks "for the reasons stated by the Commission in its opinion."

* * *

In the seminal case of *In re Cady, Roberts & Co.,* 40 S. E. C. 907 (1961), the SEC recognized that the common law in some jurisdictions imposes on "corporate 'insiders,' particularly officers, directors, or controlling stockholders" an "affirmative duty of disclosure . . . when dealing in securities." The SEC found that not only did breach of this common-law duty also establish the elements of a Rule 10b-5 violation, but that individuals other than corporate insiders could be obligated either to disclose material nonpublic information before trading or to abstain from trading altogether. In *Chiarella,* we accepted the two elements set out in *Cady Roberts* for establishing a Rule 10b-5 violation: "(i) the existence of a relationship affording access to inside information intended to be available only for a corporate purpose and (ii) the unfairness of allowing a corporate insider to take advantage of that information by trading without disclosure." In examining whether Chiarella had an obligation to disclose or abstain, the Court found that there is no general duty to disclose before trading on material nonpublic information, and held that "a duty to disclose under § 10(b) does not arise from the mere possession of nonpublic market information." Such a duty arises rather from the existence of a fiduciary relationship.

Not "all breaches of fiduciary duty in connection with a securities transaction," however, come within the ambit of Rule 10b-5. There must also be "manipulation or deception." In an inside-trading case this fraud derives from the "inherent unfairness involved where one takes advantage" of "information intended to be available only for a corporate purpose and not for the personal benefit of anyone." *In re Merrill Lynch, Pierce, Fenner & Smith, Inc.,* 43 S. E. C. 933, 936 (1968). Thus, an insider will be liable under Rule 10b-5 for inside trading only where he fails to disclose material nonpublic information before trading on it and thus makes "secret profits." *Cady, Roberts,* 40 S. E. C., at 916, n. 31.

We were explicit in *Chiarella* in saying that there can be no duty to disclose where the person who has traded on inside information "was not [the corporation's] agent, . . . was not a fiduciary, [or] was not a person in whom the sellers [of securities] had placed their trust and confidence." Not to require such a fiduciary relationship, we recognized, would "depar[t] radically from the established doctrine that duty arises from a specific relationship between two parties" and would amount to "recognizing a general duty between all participants in market transactions to forgo actions based on material, nonpublic information." This requirement of a specific relationship between the shareholders and the individual trading on inside information has created analytical difficulties for the SEC and courts in policing tippees who trade on inside information. Unlike insiders who have independent fiduciary duties to both the corporation and its shareholders, the typical tippee has no such relationships. In view of this absence, it has been unclear how a tippee acquires the *Cady, Roberts* duty to refrain from trading on inside information.

* * *

[A] tippee assumes a fiduciary duty to the shareholders of a corporation not to trade on material nonpublic information only when the insider has breached his fiduciary duty to the shareholders by disclosing the information to the tippee and the tippee knows or should know that there has been a breach.

* * *

In determining whether a tippee is under an obligation to disclose or abstain, it thus is necessary to determine whether the insider's "tip" constituted a breach of the insider's fiduciary duty. All disclosures of confidential corporate information are not inconsistent with the duty insiders owe to shareholders. In contrast to the extraordinary facts of this case, the more typical situation in which there will be a question whether disclosure violates the insider's *Cady, Roberts* duty is when insiders disclose information to analysts. In some situations, the insider will act consistently with his fiduciary duty to shareholders, and yet release of the information may affect the market. For example, it may not be clear—either to the corporate insider or to the recipient analyst—whether the information will be viewed as material nonpublic information. Corporate officials may mistakenly think the information already has been disclosed or that it is not material enough to affect the market. Whether disclosure is a breach of duty therefore depends in large part on the purpose of the disclosure. This standard was identified by the SEC itself in *Cady, Roberts:* a purpose of the securities laws was to eliminate "use of inside information for personal advantage." Thus, the test is whether the insider personally will benefit, directly or indirectly, from his disclosure. Absent some personal gain, there has been no breach of duty to stockholders. And absent a breach by the insider, there is no derivative breach.

* * *

Determining whether an insider personally benefits from a particular disclosure, a question of fact, will not always be easy for courts. But it is essential, we think, to have a guiding principle for those whose daily activities must be limited and instructed by the SEC's inside-trading rules, and we believe that there must be a breach of the insider's fiduciary duty before the tippee inherits the duty to disclose or abstain. In contrast, the rule adopted by the SEC in this case would have no limiting principle.

Under the inside-trading and tipping rules set forth above, we find that there was no actionable violation by Dirks. It is undisputed that Dirks himself was a stranger to Equity Funding, with no preexisting fiduciary duty to its shareholders. He took no action, directly, or indirectly, that induced the shareholders or officers of Equity Funding to repose trust or confidence in him. There was no expectation by Dirk's sources that he would keep their information in confidence. Nor did Dirks misappropriate or illegally obtain the information about Equity Funding. Unless the insiders breached their *Cady, Roberts* duty to shareholders in disclosing the nonpublic information to Dirks, he breached no duty when he passed it on to investors as well as to the *Wall Street Journal.*

It is clear that neither Secrist nor the other Equity Funding employees violated their *Cady, Roberts* duty to the corporation's shareholders by providing information to Dirks. The tippers received no monetary or personal benefit for revealing Equity Funding's secrets, nor was their purpose to make a gift of valuable information to Dirks. As the facts of this case clearly indicate, the tippers were motivated by a desire to expose the fraud. In the absence of a breach of duty to shareholders by the insiders, there was no derivative breach by Dirks. Dirks therefore could not have been "a participant after the fact in [an] insider's breach of a fiduciary duty." *Chiarella,* 445 U.S., at 230, n. 12.

We conclude that Dirks, in the circumstances of this case, had no duty to abstain from the use of the inside information that he obtained. The judgment of the Court of Appeals therefore is reversed.

Box 18-3 The Fuzzy Definition of Insider Trading

What's Legal—and What's Not
BY MONCI JO WILLIAMS

Ivan Boesky broke the law when he bought stocks of takeover targets on tips from an investment banker, Dennis Levine of Drexel Burnham Lambert. But Boesky did no wrong when he sold $440 million worth of securities before the Securities and Exchange Commission revealed its insider trading charges against him, knowing full well that the prices almost certainly would fall after the revelation. How could Boesky be guilty of a crime in the first case and innocent in the second? Because the SEC says so.

* * *

Insider trading used to be fairly simple: A person violated the law if he bought or sold stock on the basis of material non-public information about his company. Information is material if it is something a reasonable investor would want to know before he buys or sells. That basic definition was affirmed by the Supreme Court in a landmark 1968 decision on an SEC case against executives of Texas Gulf Sulphur. The company discovered a couple of huge mineral deposits, and Texas Gulf officers loaded up on the stock before they broke the news to the public.

The Supreme Court has held in other cases that an outsider violates the law when he trades on information from an inside tipster. The tipster is a lawbreaker as well, even if he doesn't trade himself. That was the case with former LTV chairman Paul Thayer, who was convicted of feeding inside information to a lady friend.

The rules have become considerably more complicated as the SEC has expanded the definition of insider trading to include investors who are not insiders and who trade on information that may not be material to the ongoing business of a company. Ever the champion of the small investor, the SEC worries about what lawyers call the informational advantage that the big boys—company officers, security analysts, arbitragers—have because they are closer to the action.

The SEC has been fretting most in recent years about the informational advantage that stock market professionals sometimes have in takeover fights. In 1980 it adopted Rule 14e-3, which makes it illegal for *anyone* with inside information about a takeover to trade the target company's stock. An investor is in violation of the rule even if he doesn't get the information directly from an insider. He simply has to "know or have reason to know" that the information came from an insider.

Rule 14e-3 and Ivan Boesky were made for each other. Dennis Levine gave him advance word of takeovers and Boesky took big positions in the stocks of target companies, reaping enormous profits when the prices of the stocks subsequently shot up. Boesky sealed his guilt by agreeing to share his winnings with Levine, making it undeniable that he believed Levine was furnishing him with bona fide information and not just Wall Street scuttlebutt.

By almost any logic, Boesky's big sell-off in advance of the SEC's announcement of the charges against him should be illegal too. In both cases Boesky came out ahead by virtue of inside information that was material to the prices of the securities he traded. But the SEC's logic is unlike any other, and it has different rules when the inside information does not involve a takeover. Part of its reasoning seems to be that the charges against Ivan may have been material to him and his investment partnership, but not to the companies whose stocks he sold.

What's more, it apparently is legal in many cases for an outsider to trade on material nonpublic information, provided he did not get it from an inside tipster and the information is about anything other than a tender offer. The SEC would prefer otherwise. It would like to prosecute anyone trading on undisclosed news. But the U.S. Supreme Court tied its hands in a case involving Raymond Dirks, the security analyst who uncovered the Equity Funding scandal in 1973.

(continues on next page)

Box 18-3, *continued*

* * *

The SEC, meanwhile, is trying to free its hands to go after outsiders. It has expanded the scope of insider trading with something called the misappropriation theory, which holds that it is illegal to trade on stolen information. That's the argument the SEC used in its charges against Foster Winans, the *Wall Street Journal* reporter who passed on the names of stocks about to be mentioned in the newspaper's Heard on the Street column. Winans was not an insider and didn't even have material information about the companies involved. The SEC got a conviction against Winans by arguing that what he did was illegal because he stole the information from his employer. Winans is appealing and some legal experts think he could win.

What Winans did was plainly unfair to other investors—and unethical—even if it ultimately proves to have been legal. If the SEC loses the Winans appeal, it will figure out another way to go after similar actions in the future. Indeed, it seems safe to assume the commission will find some rationale to prosecute people for any kind of trading that it regards as unfair to investors in general.

The SEC's refusal to come up with a clear definition of insider trading makes life precarious for arbitragers. Though many, like Boesky, are lawyers who know the regulations cold, they spend their lives working in the gray areas of the law. They trade information as furiously as they trade stocks, forever calling raiders, investment bankers, and takeover lawyers to get the slightest informational edge on their competitors. They walk up to the legal line the SEC has drawn and then lean as far over it as they can. Problem is, the SEC keeps moving the line.

That's a problem for ordinary corporate folks as well. Many people think the term insider applies just to officers and directors, the ones who have to file disclosure forms whenever they buy or sell their company's stock. In fact, anyone who is privy to important information about his or her employer can be an insider. If you find out someone has made a secret bid for your company and buy some shares, you have violated Rule 14e-3. The rules are more vague for other kinds of news. But all executives should keep a couple of thoughts in mind. Since they know more about their company than outsiders, they always are in possession of some inside information. And the Texas Gulf decision still stands. Whether information is "material" is a judgment call, and the SEC is the judge. So if you have any doubts about where you stand, don't trade before you consult your company's lawyer.

Source: *Fortune,* December 22, 1986, pp. 36–37

Several lower courts have used the misappropriation theory in insider trading cases in addition to the tests of liability set forth in *Dirks*. Under this theory, a person who is not an insider faces potential liability for misappropriating information from her employer. In a leading case involving the misappropriation theory, the Second Circuit Court of Appeals reinstated an indictment against employees who traded on the basis of inside information obtained through their work at investment banking firms. The court concluded that the employees' violation of their fiduciary duty to the firms violated securities law. [United States v. Newman, 664 F.2d 12 (1981)] The SEC has also adopted Rule 14e-3, which provides that a person who has inside information about a tender offer (see p. 494) must either disclose the information or refrain from trading.

In 1987, the Supreme Court affirmed the conviction of a *Wall Street Journal* reporter who leaked advanced information about the contents of his "Heard on the Street" column (see Box 18-3). The reporter, who was sentenced to eighteen months in prison, had been convicted on both mail and wire fraud (see p. 171) and securities law charges for misappropriating information. The Court upheld the mail and wire fraud conviction by an 8–0 vote and the securities law conviction by a 4–4 vote. (In effect, the tie vote affirmed the conviction.) [Winans v. United States, 56 U.S.L.W. 4007 (1987)]

In 1984, Congress substantially increased the penalties for insider trading. The maximum criminal penalty for violating the 1934 act was raised from $10,000 to $100,000. A civil penalty of up to three times the profit made (or loss avoided) by insider trading can also be imposed. The maximum five-year prison term (see p. 494) was not changed. In 1987, one of the defendants mentioned in Box 18-3, Dennis Levine, settled insider-trading charges by agreeing to forfeit $10.6 million in illegal profits; he also was sentenced to two years in prison. Another defendant, Ivan Boesky, reached a settlement in which he agreed to pay $100 million. Boesky was sentenced to a three-year prison term.

Chapter Summary

Beyond state corporation laws, federal statutes—most importantly, the Securities Act of 1933 and the Securities Exchange Act of 1934—regulate the issuance of corporate securities. The federal definition of security is broad, encompassing most investments even though called by other names.

The law does not prohibit risky stock offerings; it bans only those lacking adequate disclosure of risks. The primary means for realizing this goal is the registration requirement: registration statements, prospectuses, and proxy solicitations must be filed with the SEC. A 1968 amendment to the 1934 act requires disclosure whenever anyone seeks control of a company by making a tender offer for or other acquisition of more than 5 percent of the target company's outstanding stock. Penalties for violation of securities law include criminal fines and jail terms, as well as civil suits by both the SEC and by private individuals injured by the violation of SEC rules.

One recent amendment to the 1934 act is the Foreign Corrupt Practices Act, which prohibits an issuer from paying a bribe or making any other payment to foreign officials in order to gain business by inducing the foreign official to influence his government in favor of the American company. This law requires issuers to keep accurate sets of books to record the dispositions of their assets and to maintain internal accounting controls to ensure that transactions comport with management's authorization.

The Securities Exchange Act of 1934 presents special hazards to those trading in public stock on the basis of inside information. One provision requires reimbursement to the company of any profits made from selling and buying stock during any six-month period by directors, officers, or shareholders owning 10 percent or more of the company's stock. Under Rule 10b-5, the SEC and private parties may sue insiders who traded on information not available to the general public, thus gaining an advantage either in selling or buying the stock. Insiders include directors, officers, and current shareholders, as well as outside lawyers, accountants, and investment advisers who gained confidential information through their work for the company. But the mere possession of nonpublic market information does not convert someone unconnected with the company into an insider.

Problems

1. Anne operated a clothing store called Anne's Rags, Inc. She owned all of the stock in the company. After several years in the clothing business, Anne sold her store to Louise, who personally managed the business. Is the sale governed by the anti-fraud provisions of federal securities law? Why?
2. While waiting tables at a campus-area restaurant, you overhear a conversation between two corporate executives, who indicate that their company has developed a new product that will revolutionize the computer industry. The product is to be announced in three weeks. If you purchase stock in the company before the announcement, will you be liable under federal securities law? Why?
3. Eric was hired as a management consultant by a major corporation to conduct a study, which took him three months to complete. While working on the study Eric learned that someone working in research and development for the company had recently made an important discovery. Before the discovery was announced publicly, Eric purchased stock in the company. Did he violate federal securities law? Why?
4. While working for the company, Eric also learned that it was planning a takeover of another corporation. Before announcement of a tender offer, Eric purchased stock in the target company. Did he violate securities law? Why?
5. The commercial lending department of First Bank made a substantial loan to Alpha Company after obtaining a favorable confidential earnings report from Alpha. Over lunch, Heidi, the loan officer who handled the loan, mentioned the earnings report to a friend who worked in the bank's trust department. The friend proceeded to purchase stock in Alpha for several of the bank's trusts. Discuss the legal implications.
6. In problem 5, assume that a week after the loan to Alpha, First Bank financed Beta Company's takeover of Alpha. During the financing negotiations, Heidi mentioned the Alpha earnings report to Beta officials;

furthermore, the report was an important factor in Heidi's decision to finance the takeover. Discuss the legal implications.

7. In problem 6, assume that after work one day, Heidi told her friend in the trust department that Alpha was Beta's takeover target. The friend proceeded to purchase additional stock in Alpha for a bank trust he administered. Discuss the legal implications.
8. A corporation called Co-op City ran a 200-acre housing project in New York City. In order to rent housing in the project, tenants had to purchase stock in the corporation for $25 per share. Upon expiration of their leases, tenants were required to sell the stock back to the corporation for $25. Does the stock fall within the definition of a security for purposes of federal securities law? Why?

PART SIX

GOVERNMENT REGULATION OF BUSINESS

19

Antitrust 1: Restraints of Trade

> Democracy is the recurrent suspicion that more than half the people are right more than half the time.
>
> E. B. WHITE

Introduction to Government Regulation

In a sense, all law is government regulation, since it is ultimately interpreted by and enforced in a court, a branch of government. But as we intend the term, government regulation differs from much of the law that we have studied to this point. The common law of torts, for example, spells out legal duties, but it tells us much more about what we should not do than about how we must act. Even the Uniform Commercial Code, a complex statute, regulates by spelling out rights and duties that, for the most part, operate only in the absence of private agreement.

Government regulation, then, refers to those sets of rules outside the common law that instruct businesses how to act or prohibit them from acting. It also refers to *federal* law primarily, for the history of business regulation during the past quarter century and more is the sometimes steady, sometimes explosive, growth of federal law and regulations in the private sector. Many state and federal regulations apply to certain types of businesses—manufacturers, for instance, or makers and sellers of flammable fabrics. But the antitrust laws apply—with some exceptions to be noted—to every business in the United States that operates in interstate commerce. Although these laws are the preserve of specialists, a general knowledge of their content and application is crucial for anyone in business.

In this chapter, we take up the origins of the federal antitrust laws and the basic rules governing restraints of trade (Section 1 of the Sherman Act and Section 3 of the Clayton Act). In Chapter 20, we turn to concentrations of market power: monopoly (Section 2 of the Sherman Act) and acquisitions and mergers (Section 7 of the Clayton Act). In Chapter 21, we explore the law of deceptive acts and unfair trade practices, both as administered by the FTC and as regulated at common law. In Chapter 22, we survey briefly how antitrust and other laws serve to shape and regulate a major form of modern business enterprise–franchising.

History and Basic Framework of the Antitrust Laws

Why Antitrust Laws?

The antitrust laws are aimed at maintaining competition as the motive force of the U.S. economy. The very word "antitrust" implies opposition to the giant *trusts* that began to develop after the Civil War. Until then, the economy was largely local; manufacturers, distributors, and retailers were generally small. The Civil War demonstrated the utility of large-scale enterprise in meeting the military's ferocious production demands, and business owners were quick to understand the advantage of size in attracting capital. For the first time, immense fortunes could be made in industry, and adventurous entrepreneurs were quick to do so in an age that lauded the acquisitive spirit.

The first great business combinations were the railroads. To avoid ruinous price wars, railroad owners made private agreements known as "pools" through which they divided markets and offered discounts to favored shippers who agreed to ship goods on certain lines. The pools discriminated against particular shippers and certain geographic regions, and public resentment grew.

Farmers felt the effects first and hardest, and they organized politically to express their opposition. In time they succeeded in lobbying railroad regulation laws through many state houses. In *Munn* v. *Illinois,* 94 U.S. 113 (1877), the Supreme Court rejected a constitutional attack on a state law regulating the transportation and warehousing of grain; the Court declared that the "police powers" of the states permit the regulation of property put to public uses. But in time many state railroad laws were struck down because they interfered with interstate commerce, which only Congress may regulate constitutionally. The consequence was federal legislation: the

Interstate Commerce Act of 1887, establishing the first federal administrative agency, the Interstate Commerce Commission.

In the meantime, the railroads had discovered that their pools lacked enforcement power. Those who nominally agreed to be bound by the pooling arrangement could and often did cheat. Ultimately, the corporate form of business enterprise would permit immense accumulations of capital to be placed under the control of a small number of managers, but in the 1870s and 1880s the corporation was not yet established as the best legal form of operation. To overcome these disadvantages, clever lawyers for John D. Rockefeller organized his Standard Oil of Ohio as a common-law *trust*. Trustees were given corporate stock certificates of various companies; by combining numerous corporations into the trust, the trustees could effectively manage and control an entire industry. Within a decade, the Cotton-oil Trust, Lead Trust, Sugar Trust, and Whiskey Trust, along with oil, telephone, steel, tobacco, and others, had become or were in the process of becoming monopolies.

Consumers howled. The political parties got the message: In 1888, both Republicans and Democrats put an antitrust plank in their platforms. In 1889, the new president, Republican Benjamin Harrison, damned monopolies as "dangerous conspiracies," and called for legislation to remedy the tendency of monopolies to "crush out" competition.

The result of all this commotion was the Sherman Antitrust Act of 1890, sponsored by Senator John Sherman of Ohio. Its two key sections forbade combinations in restraint of trade and monopolizing. Senator Sherman and its other sponsors declared that the act had roots in a common-law policy that frowned on monopolies. To an extent it had, but it added something quite important for the future of business and the American economy: the power of the federal government to enforce a national policy against monopoly and restraints of trade. Nevertheless, passage of the Sherman Act did not still the public clamor because it took fifteen years or so before a national administration began to enforce it, when President Theodore Roosevelt—the "trust buster"—sent his attorney general after the Northern Securities Corporation, a transportation holding company.

During its seven years, the Roosevelt Administration initiated fifty-four antitrust suits. The pace picked up under the Taft Administration, which in only four years filed ninety antitrust suits. But the pressure for further reform did not abate, especially when the Supreme Court, in the Standard Oil Case of 1911 (see p. 531), declared that the Sherman Act forbids only "unreasonable" restraints of trade. A congressional investigation of U.S. Steel Corporation brought to light several practices that had gone unrestrained by the Sherman Act. It also sparked an important debate, which echoes into our own time, about the nature of national economic policy. Should it encourage competition or regulate business?

Big Business was firmly on the side of regulation, but Congress opted for the policy followed waveringly to the present: competition enforced by government, not a partnership of government and industry, must be the engine of the economy. Accordingly, in 1914 at the urging of President Woodrow Wilson, Congress enacted two more antitrust laws, the Clayton Act and the Federal Trade Commission Act. The Clayton Act outlawed specific practices, such as price discrimination, exclusive dealing and tying contracts, acquisition of a company's competitors, and interlocking directorates. The Federal Trade Commission Act outlawed "unfair methods" of competition, established the FTC as an independent administrative agency, and gave it power to enforce the antitrust laws alongside the Department of Justice.

The Sherman, Clayton, and FTC acts remain the basic texts of antitrust law. Over the years, many states have enacted antitrust laws as well; these laws govern intrastate competition and for the most part are modeled on the federal laws. The state antitrust laws are beyond the scope of this textbook.

Two additional federal statutes were adopted during the next third of a century, though both were, in form, amendments to the Clayton Act. Enacted in the midst of the Depression in 1936, the Robinson-Patman Act prohibits various forms of price discrimination. The Celler-Kefauver Act, strengthening the Clayton Act's prohibition against the acquisition of competing companies, was enacted in 1950 in the hopes of stemming what seemed to be a tide of corporate mergers and acquisitions. We examine these laws in turn.

The Basic Statutes

The Sherman Act Section 1 of the Sherman Act declares: "Every contract, combination in the form of trust or otherwise, or conspiracy, in restraint of trade or commerce among the several states, or with foreign nations, is declared to be illegal." This is sweeping language. What it embraces seems to depend entirely on the meaning of the words "restraint of trade or commerce." Whatever they might mean, *every* such restraint is declared unlawful. But in fact, as we will see, the proposition cannot be stated so baldly, for in 1911 the Supreme Court limited the reach of this section to *unreasonable* restraints of trade.

What does "restraint of trade" mean? The Sherman Act's drafters based the act on a common-law policy against monopolies and other infringements on competition. But the common law of trade restraints had been developed in only rudimentary form, and the words have come to mean whatever the courts say they mean, following the general principles described below. In short, the antitrust laws, and the Sherman Act in particular, authorize the courts to create a federal "common law" of competition.

Section 2 of the Sherman Act proscribes monopolization: "Every person who shall monopolize, or attempt to monopolize, or combine or conspire with any other person or persons, to monopolize any part of the trade or commerce among the several states, or with foreign nations, shall be deemed guilty of a misdemeanor." In 1976, Congress upped the ante: violations of the Sherman Act are now felonies. We examine Section 2 in greater detail in the next chapter. For now, suffice it to say that unlike Section 1, this section does not require a combination between two or more people. A single company acting on its own can be guilty of monopolizing or attempting to monopolize.

The Clayton Act The Clayton Act was enacted in 1914 to plug what many in Congress saw as loopholes in the Sherman Act. Passage of the Clayton Act was closely linked to that of the Federal Trade Commission Act. Unlike the Sherman Act, the Clayton Act is not a criminal statute; it merely declares certain defined practices as unlawful, and leaves it to the government or to private litigants to seek to enjoin them. But unlike the FTC Act, the Clayton Act does spell out undesirable practices—principally, four. Violations of the Sherman Act require an *actual* adverse impact on competition, whereas violation of the Clayton Act requires merely a *probable* adverse impact. Thus, the enforcement of the Clayton Act involves a prophecy which the defendant must rebut to escape an adverse judgment.

The four types of proscribed behavior are these:

1. Discrimination in prices charged different purchasers of the same commodities (Section 2); see pp. 548–56 of this chapter.
2. Conditioning the sale of one commodity on the purchaser's refraining from using or dealing in commodities of the seller's competitors (Section 3); see pp. 543–48 of this chapter.
3. Acquiring the stock of a competing corporation (Section 7). Because the original language did not prohibit various types of acquisitions and mergers that had grown up with modern corporate law and finance, Congress amended this section in 1950 (the Celler-Kefauver Act) to extend its prohibition to a wide variety of acquisitions and mergers. We consider the impact of this section in the next chapter.
4. Membership by a single person on more than one corporate board of directors if the companies are or were competitors (Section 8).

The Federal Trade Commission Act Like the Clayton Act, the FTC Act is a civil statute, involving no criminal penalties. Unlike the Clayton Act, its prohibitions are broadly worded. Its centerpiece is Section 5, which forbids "unfair methods of competition in commerce, and unfair or deceptive acts or practices in commerce." We examine Section 5 in Chapter 21.

Enforcement and Penalties

Enforcement Four different means of enforcing the antitrust laws are available.

1. The U.S. Department of Justice may bring civil actions to enjoin violations of any section of the Sherman and Clayton Acts and may institute criminal prosecutions for violations of the Sherman Act. Both civil

and criminal actions are filed by the offices of the U.S. Attorney in the appropriate federal district, under the direction of the Attorney General. In practice, the Justice Department's guidance comes through its Antitrust Division in Washington, headed by an Assistant Attorney General. With several hundred lawyers and dozens of economists and other professionals, the Antitrust Division annually files fewer than 100 civil and criminal actions, although some of the cases—*U.S.* v. *American Telephone & Telegraph* and *U.S.* v. *IBM* for example—were immensely complicated, took years to dispose of, and consumed tens of thousands of hours of staff time and tens of millions of dollars in government and defense costs.

2. The FTC hears cases under the Administrative Procedure Act, as described in Chapter 5. The Commission's decisions may be appealed to the U.S. Courts of Appeals. The FTC may also promulgate "trade regulation rules," which define fair practices in specific industries. The agency has some 500 lawyers in Washington and a dozen field offices, but only about half the lawyers are directly involved in antitrust enforcement.
3. In the Antitrust Improvements Act of 1976, Congress authorized state attorneys general to file antitrust suits in federal court for damages on behalf of its citizens; this is known as a *parens patriae* claim. Any citizen of the state who might have been injured by the defendant's actions may opt out of the suit and bring his own private action. The states have long had the authority to file antitrust suits seeking injunctive relief on behalf of their citizens.
4. Private individuals and companies may file suits for damages or injunctions if they have been directly injured by a violation of the Sherman or Clayton Acts. Private individuals or companies may not sue under the FTC Act, no matter how unfair or deceptive the behavior complained of; only the FTC may do so. In 1983, more than 1,500 private antitrust suits were filed in the federal courts, compared to fewer than 100 suits filed by the Department of Justice.

Enforcement in International Trade The Sherman and Clayton acts apply when a company's activities affect American commerce. As discussed further on pp. 703–07, this means that these laws apply to American companies that agree to fix the price of goods to be shipped abroad and to the acts of an American subsidiary of a foreign company.

Sanctions and Penalties for Violating the Antitrust Laws

Criminal sanctions Until 1976, violations of the Sherman Act were misdemeanors. The maximum fine was $50,000 for each count on which the defendant was convicted (only $5,000 until 1955), and the maximum jail sentence was one year. In 1976, the sanctions were increased. Today, the maximum sentence for each count is $1 million for corporations and $100,000 for individuals, and the maximum jail term is three years.

Forfeitures One provision in the Sherman Act, not much used, permits the government to seize any property in transit in either interstate or foreign commerce if it was the subject of a contract, combination, or conspiracy outlawed under Section 1.

Injunctions and consent decrees The Justice Department may enforce violations of the Sherman and Clayton Acts by seeking injunctions in federal district court. The injunction can be a complex set of instructions, listing in some detail the practices that a defendant is to avoid and even the way in which it will be required to conduct its business thereafter. Once an injunction is issued and affirmed on appeal, or the time for appeal has passed, it confers continuing jurisdiction on the court to hear complaints by those who say the defendant is violating it. In a few instances, the injunction or consent decree (see below) is in effect the basic "statute" by which an industry operates. A 1956 decree against American Telephone & Telegraph Company kept the company out of the computer business for a quarter-century until the government's monopoly suit against AT&T was settled and a new decree issued in 1983. The federal courts also have the power to break up a company convicted of monopolizing or to order divestiture when the violation consists of unlawful mergers and acquisitions.

The FTC may issue "cease and desist orders" against practices condemned under Section 5 of the FTC Act—which includes violations of the Sherman and Clayton Acts—and these orders may be appealed to the courts.

Rather than litigate a case fully, defendants may agree to **consent decrees**, in which, without admitting guilt, they agree not to carry on the activity complained of. Violations of injunctions, cease and desist orders, and consent decrees subject companies to a fine of $10,000 a day for every day the violation continues.

Use of judgment in private suit Companies frequently enter into consent decrees, not just because they wish to avoid the expense and trouble of trial. Section 5 of the Clayton Act says that whenever an antitrust case brought by the federal government under either the Clayton Act or the Sherman Act goes to final judgment, the judgment can be used, in a private suit in which the same facts are at issue, as *prima facie* evidence that the violation was committed. This is a powerful provision, because it means that a private plaintiff need prove only that the violation in fact injured him. He need not prove that the defendant committed the acts that amount to antitrust violations. Since this provision makes it relatively easy for private plaintiffs to prevail in subsequent suits, defendants in government suits have a strong inducement to enter into consent decrees, because these are not considered judgments. Likewise, a guilty plea in a criminal case gives the plaintiff in a later private civil suit *prima facie* evidence of the defendant's liability. However, a plea of *nolo contendere* (see p. 185) will avoid this result. This provision has been the spur for a considerable proportion of all private antitrust suits. For example, the government's price-fixing case against the electric equipment industry that sent certain executives of General Electric to jail in the 1950s led to more than 2,200 private suits.

Treble damages The crux of the private suit is its unique damage award: any successful plaintiff is entitled to collect *three times* the amount of damages actually suffered—**treble damages**, as they are known—and to be paid the cost of his attorneys. These fees can be huge: defendants have had to pay out millions of dollars for attorneys' fees alone in single cases during the 1970s. The theory of treble damages is that they will serve as an incentive to private parties to police industry for antitrust violations, thus saving the federal government the immense expense of maintaining an adequate staff for that job.

Class actions One of the most important developments in antitrust law during the 1970s was the rise of the **class action**. Under liberalized rules of federal procedure, a single plaintiff may sue on behalf of the entire class of people injured by an antitrust violation. This device makes it possible to bring numerous suits that would otherwise never have been contemplated. A single individual who has paid one dollar more than he would have been charged in a competitive market obviously will not file suit. But if there are 10 million consumers like him, then in a class action he may seek—on behalf of the entire class, of course—$30 million ($10 million trebled), plus attorneys' fees. Critics charge that the class action is a device that in the antitrust field benefits only the lawyers, who have a large incentive to find a few plaintiffs willing to have their names used in a suit run entirely by the lawyers. Nevertheless, it is true that the class action permits antitrust violations to be rooted out that could not otherwise be attacked privately. During the 1970s, suits against drug companies and the wallboard manufacturing industry were among the many large-scale antitrust class actions.

Interpreting the Laws

Vagueness It does not take a very attentive reader to notice that the antitrust laws, and especially Section 1 of the Sherman Act, are exceedingly vague. As Chief Justice Charles Evans Hughes once put it: "The Sherman Act, as a charter of freedom, has a generality and adaptability comparable to that found to be desirable in constitutional provisions." [Appalachian Coals v. United States, 288 U.S. 344, 359 (1933)] Without the sweeping but vague language, the antitrust laws might quickly have become outdated. As written, they permit courts to adapt the law to changing circumstances.

The "Rule of Reason" Section 1 of the Sherman Act says that "every" restraint of trade is illegal. But is a literal interpretation really possible? No, for as Justice Brandeis noted in 1918 in one of the early price-fixing cases: "Every agreement concerning trade, every regulation of trade restrains. To bind, to restrain, is of their very essence." [Chicago Board of Trade v. United States, 246 U.S. 231 (1918)] When a manufacturing company contracts to buy raw materials, trade in those goods is restrained: no one else will have access to them. But to interpret the Sherman Act to include such a contract is an absurdity. Common sense says that "every" cannot really mean *every* restraint.

Throughout this century, the courts have been occupied with this question. With the hindsight of thousands of cases, the broad outlines of the answer can be confidently stated. Beginning with *Standard Oil Co. of New Jersey* v. *United States,* 221 U.S. 1 (1911), the Supreme Court has held that only *unreasonable* restraints of trade are unlawful.

Often called the "rule of reason," the interpretation of Section 1 made in *Standard Oil* itself has two possible meanings, and they have been confused over the years. The rule of reason could mean that a restraint is permissible only if it is *ancillary* to a legitimate business purpose. The standard example is a covenant not to compete. Suppose you decide to purchase a well-regarded bookstore in town. The proprietor is well-liked and has developed loyal patrons. He says he is going to retire in another state. You realize that if he changed his mind and stayed in town to open another bookstore, your new business would suffer considerably. So you negotiate as a condition of sale that he agree not to open another bookstore within ten miles of the town for the next three years. Since your intent is not to prevent him from going into business—as it would be if he had agreed never to open a bookstore anywhere—but merely to protect the value of your purchase, this restraint of trade is ancillary to your business purpose. The rule of reason holds that this is not an unlawful restraint of trade.

Another interpretation of the rule of reason is even broader. It holds that agreements that might directly impair competition are not unlawful unless the particular impairment itself is unreasonable. For example, several retailers of computer software are distraught at a burgeoning "price war" that will possibly reduce prices so low that they will not be able to offer their customers proper service. To avert this "cut-throat competition," the retailers agree to set a price floor—a floor which, under the circumstances, is reasonable. Chief Justice White, who wrote the *Standard Oil* opinion, might have found that such an agreement was reasonable because, in view of its purposes, it was not *unduly* restrictive and did not unduly restrain trade.

This latter view is not the law. "The true test of legality," Justice Brandeis wrote in 1918 in *Chicago Board of Trade,* "is whether the restraint imposed is such as merely regulates and perhaps thereby promotes competition or whether it is such as may suppress or even destroy competition." In short, the rule of reason does not attempt to distinguish between justifiable and unjustifiable impairments of competition. Rather, it requires that the courts examine whether under the circumstances it makes sense to brand the act complained of as an impairment at all.

"Per Se" Rules Not every act or commercial practice needs to be weighed by the rule of reason. Some acts have come to be regarded as intrinsically impairing competition, so that no further analysis need be made if the plaintiff can prove that the defendant carried them out, or attempted or conspired to do so. Price-fixing is an example. Price-fixing is said to be *per se* illegal under the Sherman Act—that is, unlawful on its face. The question in a case alleging price-fixing is not whether the price was reasonable or whether it impaired or enhanced competition but whether the price in fact *was* fixed. Only the latter question can be at issue.

Under the Clayton Act The rule of reason and the *per se* rules apply to the Sherman Act. The Clayton Act has a different standard. It speaks in terms of acts that may tend substantially to lessen competition. The courts must construe these terms too, and in the sections that follow we will see how they have done so.

"Horizontal" Restraints of Trade

Classification of antitrust cases and principles is not self-evident because so many cases turn on complex factual circumstances. One convenient way to group the cases is to look to the relationship of those who have agreed or conspired. If the parties are competitors—whether competing manufacturers, wholesalers, retailers, or others—the resulting restraint of trade is said to be **horizontal.** If the parties are at different levels of the distribution chain—for example, manufacturer and retailer—their agreement is said to involve a **vertical** restraint of trade. These categories are not airtight: a retailer might get competing manufacturers to agree not to supply a competitor of the retailer. This is a vertical restraint with horizontal effects.

Price-fixing

Directly Agreements to fix prices are *per se* violations of Section 1 of the Sherman Act. The *per se* rule was announced explicitly in *United States* v. *Trenton Potteries,* 273 U.S. 392 (1927). In that case, twenty individuals and twenty-three corporations, makers and distributors of 82 percent of the vitreous pottery bathroom fixtures used in the United States, were found guilty of having agreed to establish and adhere to a price schedule. On appeal they did not dispute that they had combined to fix prices. They did argue that the jury should have been permitted to decide whether what they had done was reasonable. The Supreme Court disagreed, holding that any fixing of prices is a clear violation of the Sherman Act.

Twenty-four years later, the Court underscored this no-nonsense *per se* rule in *Kiefer-Stewart Co.* v. *Joseph E. Seagram & Sons,* 340 U.S. 211 (1951). The defendants were distillers who had agreed to sell liquor only to those wholesalers who agreed to resell for no more than a *maximum* price set by the distillers. The defendants argued that setting maximum prices did not violate the Sherman Act because such prices promoted rather than restrained competition. Again the Supreme Court disagreed: "[S]uch agreements, no less than those to fix minimum prices, cripple the freedom of traders and thereby restrain their ability to sell in accordance with their own judgment."

The *per se* prohibition against price-fixing is not limited to agreements that directly fix prices. Hundreds of schemes that have the effect of controlling prices have been tested in court and found wanting—some because they were *per se* restraints of trade, others because their effects were unreasonable—that is, because they impaired competition—under the circumstances. In the following sections, we examine some of these cases briefly.

Exchanging Price Information Knowledge of competitors' prices can be an effective means of controlling prices throughout an industry. Members of a trade association of hardwood manufacturers adopted a voluntary "open competition" plan. About 90 percent of the members adhered to the plan. They accounted for one-third of the production of hardwood in the United States. Under the plan, members reported daily on sales and deliveries and monthly on production, inventory, and prices. The association in turn sent out price, sales, and production reports to the participating members. Additionally, members met from time to time to discuss these matters, and they were exhorted to refrain from excessive production in order to keep prices at profitable levels. In *American Column and Lumber Company* v. *United States,* 257 U.S. 377 (1921), the Court condemned this plan as a *per se* violation of Section 1.

Not every exchange of information is necessarily a violation, however. In the later *Maple Flooring Manufacturers' Association* v. *United States,* 268 U.S. 563 (1925), the Court refused to find a violation in the practice of an association of twenty-two hardwood floor manufacturers in circulating a list to all members of average costs and freight rates, as well as summaries of sales, prices, and inventories. The apparent difference between *American Column and Lumber* and *Maple Flooring* was that in the latter the members did not discuss prices at their meetings and their rules permitted them to charge individually whatever they wished. It is not unlawful, therefore, for members of an industry to meet to discuss common problems or to develop statistical information about the industry through a common association, as long as the discussions do not border on price or on techniques of controlling prices, such as by restricting output. Usually it takes evidence of collusion to condemn the exchange of prices or other data.

Controlling Output Competitors also fix prices by controlling an industry's output—for example, by agreeing to limit the amount of goods each company makes or by otherwise limiting the amount that comes to market. This latter technique was condemned in *United States* v. *Socony-Vacuum Oil Co.,* 310 U.S. 150 (1940). To prevent oil prices from dropping, dominant oil companies agreed to and did purchase from independent refiners surplus gasoline which the market was forcing them to sell at distress prices. By buying up this gasoline, the large companies created a price floor for their own product. This conduct, said the Court, is a *per se* violation.

Regulating Competitive Methods Many companies may wish to eliminate certain business practices—such as offering discounts or trading stamps on purchase of goods. But they are afraid or powerless to do so unless their competitors also stop. The temptation is strong to agree with one's competitors to jointly end these noxious habits; doing so in most instances is unlawful when the result would be to affect the price at which the product is sold. Not every regulation of a business practice is necessarily unlawful, however. Companies might decide that it would serve their customers' interests as well as their own if the product could be standardized, so that certain names or marks signify a grade or quality of product. When no restriction is placed on what grades are to be sold or at what prices, no restraint of trade has occurred.

In the case that follows, the question is whether the practice that is the subject of the agreement violates Section 1. The practice was competitive bidding. A canon of ethics of the National Society of Professional Engineers prohibited members from making competitive bids. This type of prohibition has been common in the codes of ethics of dozens—perhaps hundreds—of occupational groups claiming professional status. These groups justify the ban by citing public benefits, though not necessarily price benefits, that flow from observance of the "ethical" rule. Note that the commerce in question was sale of a service, not of a product.

NATIONAL SOCIETY OF PROFESSIONAL ENGINEERS v. UNITED STATES
435 U.S. 679 (1978)

MR. JUSTICE STEVENS delivered the opinion of the Court.

This is a civil antitrust case brought by the United States to nullify an association's canon of ethics prohibiting competitive bidding by its members. The question is whether the canon may be justified under the Sherman Act, 15 U.S.C. § 1 *et seq.* (1976 ed.), because it was adopted by members of a learned profession for the purpose of minimizing the risk that competition would produce inferior engineering work endangering the public safety. The District Court rejected this justification without making any findings on the likelihood that competition would produce the dire consequences foreseen by the association. The Court of Appeals affirmed. We granted certiorari to decide whether the District Court should have considered the factual basis for the proffered justification before rejecting it. Because we are satisfied that the asserted defense rests on a fundamental misunderstanding of the Rule of Reason frequently applied in antitrust litigation, we affirm.

Engineering is an important and learned profession. There are over 750,000 graduate engineers in the United States, of whom about 325,000 are registered as professional engineers. Registration requirements vary from State to State, but usually require the applicant to be a graduate engineer with at least four years of practical experience and to pass a written examination. About half of those who are registered engage in consulting engineering on a fee basis. They perform services in connection with the study, design, and construction of all types of improvements to real property—bridges, office buildings, airports, and factories are examples. Engineering fees, amounting to well over $2 billion each year, constitute about 5% of total construction costs. In any given facility, approximately 50% to 80% of the cost of construction is the direct result of work performed by an engineer concerning the systems and equipment to be incorporated in the structure.

The National Society of Professional Engineers (Society) was organized in 1935 to deal with the nontechnical aspects of engineering practice, including the promotion of the professional, social, and economic interests of its members. Its present membership of 69,000 resides throughout the United States and in some foreign countries. Approximately 12,000 members are consulting engineers who offer their services to governmental, industrial, and private clients. Some Society members are principals or chief executive officers of some of the largest engineering firms in the country.

The charges of a consulting engineer may be computed in different ways. He may charge the client a percentage of the cost of the project, may set his fee at his actual cost plus overhead plus a reasonable profit, may charge fixed rates per hour for different types of work, may perform an assignment for a specific sum, or he may combine one or more of these approaches. . . . This case . . . involves a charge that the members of the Society have unlawfully agreed to refuse to negotiate or even to discuss the question of fees until after a prospective client has selected the engineer for a particular project. Evidence of this agreement is found in § 11(c) of the Society's Code of Ethics, adopted in July 1964.

The District Court found that the Society's Board of Ethical Review has uniformly interpreted the "ethical rules against competitive bidding for engineering services as prohibiting the submission of any form of price information to a prospective customer which would enable that customer to make a price comparison on engineering services." If the client requires that such information be provided, then § 11(c) imposes an obligation upon the engineering firm to withdraw from consideration for that job.

* * *

In *Goldfarb v. Virginia State Bar,* 421 U.S. 773, 95 S.Ct. 2004, 44 L.Ed.2d 572, the Court held that a bar association's rule prescribing minimum fees for legal services violated § 1 of the Sherman Act. In that opinion the Court noted that certain practices by members of a learned profession might survive scrutiny under the Rule of Reason even though they would be viewed as a violation of the Sherman Act in another context.

* * *

[P]etitioner argues that its attempt to preserve the profession's traditional method of setting fees for engineering services is a reasonable method of forestalling the public harm which might be produced by unrestrained competitive bidding. To evaluate this argument it is necessary to identify the contours of the Rule of Reason and to discuss its application to the kind of justification asserted by petitioner.

* * *

The test prescribed in *Standard Oil* is whether the challenged contracts or acts "were unreasonably restrictive of competitive conditions." Unreasonableness under that test could be based either (1) on the nature or character of the contracts, or (2) on surrounding circumstances giving rise to the inference or presumption that they were intended to restrain trade and enhance prices. Under either branch of the test, the inquiry is confined to a consideration of impact on competitive conditions.

* * *

Price is the "central nervous system of the economy," *United States v. Socony-Vacuum Oil Co.,* 310 U.S. 150, 226 n. 59, and an agreement that "interfere[s] with the setting of price by free market forces" is illegal on its face. *United States v. Container Corp.,* 393 U.S. 333, 337. In this case we are presented with an agreement among competitors to refuse to discuss prices with potential customers until after negotiations have resulted in the initial selection of an engineer. While this is not price fixing as such, no elaborate industry analysis is required to demonstrate the anticompetitive character of such an agreement. It operates as an absolute ban on competitive bidding, applying with equal force to both complicated and simple projects and to both inexperienced and sophisticated customers. As the District Court found, the ban "impedes the ordinary give and take of the market place," and substantially deprives the customer of "the ability to utilize and compare prices in selecting engineering services." On its face, this agreement restrains trade within the meaning of § 1 of the Sherman Act.

The Society's affirmative defense confirms rather than refutes the anticompetitive purpose and effect of its agreement. The Society argues that the restraint is justified because bidding on engineering services is inherently imprecise, would lead to deceptively low bids, and would thereby tempt individual engineers to do inferior work with consequent risk to public safety and health. The logic of this argument rests on the assumption that the agreement will tend to maintain the price level; if it had no such effect, it would not serve its intended purpose. The Society nonetheless invokes the Rule of Reason, arguing that its restraint on price competition ultimately inures to the public benefit by preventing the production of inferior work and by insuring ethical behavior. As the preceding discussion of the Rule of Reason reveals, this Court has never accepted such an argument.

It may be, as petitioner argues, that competition tends to force prices down and that an inexpensive item may be inferior to one that is more costly. There is some risk, therefore, that competition will cause some suppliers to market a defective product. Similarly, competitive bidding for engineering projects may be inherently imprecise and incapable of taking into account all the variables which will be involved in the actual performance of the project. Based on these considerations, a purchaser might conclude that his interest in quality—which may embrace the safety of the end product—outweighs the advantages of achieving cost savings by pitting one competitor against another. Or an individual vendor might independently refrain from price negotiation until he has satisfied himself that he fully understands the scope of his customers' needs. These decisions might be reasonable; indeed, petitioner has provided ample documentation for that thesis. But these are not reasons that satisfy the Rule; nor are such individual decisions subject to antitrust attack.

The Sherman Act does not require competitive bidding; it prohibits unreasonable restraints on competition. Petitioner's ban on competitive bidding prevents all customers from making price comparisons in the initial selection of an engineer, and imposes the Society's views of the costs and benefits of competition on the entire marketplace. It is this restraint that must be justified under the Rule of Reason, and petitioner's attempt to do so on the basis of the potential threat that competition poses to the public safety and the ethics of its profession is nothing less than a frontal assault on the basic policy of the Sherman Act.

The Sherman Act reflects a legislative judgment that ultimately competition will produce not only lower prices, but also better goods and services. "The heart of our national economic policy long has been faith in the value of competition." *Standard Oil Co. v. FTC,* 340 U.S. 231, 248, 71 S.Ct. 240, 249, 95 L.Ed. 239. The assumption that competition is the best method of allocating resources in a free market recognizes that all elements of a bargain—quality service, safety, and durability—and not just the immediate cost, are favorably affected by the free opportunity to select among alternative offers. Even assuming occasional exceptions to the presumed consequences of competition, the statutory policy precludes inquiry into the question whether competition is good or bad.

The fact that engineers are often involved in large-scale projects significantly affecting the public safety does not alter our analysis. Exceptions to the Sherman Act for potentially dangerous goods and services would be tantamount to a repeal of the statute. In our complex economy the number of items that may cause serious harm is almost endless—automobiles, drugs, foods, aircraft components, heavy equipment, and countless others, cause serious harm to individuals or to the public at large if defectively made. The judiciary cannot indirectly protect the public against this harm by conferring monopoly privileges on the manufacturers.

* * *

In sum, the Rule of Reason does not support a defense based on the assumption that competition itself is unreasonable. Such a view of the Rule would create the "sea of doubt" on which Judge Taft refused to embark in *Addyston,* 85 F., at 284, and which this Court has firmly avoided ever since.

The judgment entered by the District Court, as modified by the Court of Appeals, prohibits the Society from adopting any official opinion, policy statement, or guideline stating or implying that competitive bidding is unethical. Petitioner argues that this judgment abridges its First Amendment rights. We find no merit in this contention.

* * *

The judgment of the Court of Appeals is affirmed.

Non-price Restraints of Trade

Allocating Territories Suppose four ice cream manufacturers decided one day that their efforts to compete in all four corners of the city were costly and destructive. Why not simply strike a bargain: each will sell ice cream to retail shops in only one quadrant of the city. This is not a pricing arrangement; they are each free to sell at whatever price they desire. But it is a restraint of trade, for in carving up the territory in which each may sell, they make it impossible for grocery stores to obtain their products except in the favored quadrant. The point becomes obvious when examined on a national scale: suppose Ford and General Motors agreed that Ford would not sell its cars in New York and GM would not sell them in California?

Most cases of territorial allocation are examples of vertical restraints in which manufacturers and distributors, say, strike a bargain. But some cases deal with horizontal allocation of territories. In *United States* v. *Sealy,* 388 U.S. 350 (1967), the defendant company licensed manufacturers to use the Sealy trademark on beds and mattresses and restricted the territories in which the manufacturers could sell. The evidence showed that the licensees, some thirty small bedding manufacturers, actually owned the licensor and were using the arrangement to allocate the territory. It was held to be unlawful *per se.*

Exclusionary Agreements We said earlier that it might be permissible for manufacturers through a trade association to establish certain quality standards for the convenience of the public. As long as these standards are not exclusionary and do not reflect any control over price, they might not inhibit competition. The "UL" mark on electrical and other equipment—a mark to show that the product conforms to specifications of the private Underwriters' Laboratory—is an example. But suppose that certain widget producers establish the Scientific Safety Council, a membership association whose staff ostensibly assigns quality labels to those manufacturers who meet certain engineering and safety standards. In fact, however, the manufacturers are using the widespread public acceptance of the SSC mark to keep the market to themselves, by refusing to let nonmembers join and by refusing to let nonmembers use the SSC mark, even if their widgets conform to the announced standards. This subterfuge would be a violation of Section 1.

Boycotts Agreements by competitors to **boycott** (refuse to deal with) those who engage in undesirable practices are unlawful. In an early case, a retailers' trade association circulated a list of wholesale distributors who sold directly to the public. The intent was to warn member retailers not to buy from those wholesalers. Although each member was free to act however he wanted, the Court saw in this blacklist a plan to promote a boycott. [Eastern State Lumber Dealers' Association v. United States, 234 U.S. 600 (1914)]

This policy remains true even if the object of the boycott is to prevent unethical or even illegal activities. Members of a garment manufacturers association agreed with a textile manufacturers association not to use any textiles that had been "pirated" from designs made by members of the textile association. The garment manufacturers also each pledged, among other things, not to sell their goods to any retailer who did not refrain from using pirated designs. The argument that this was the only way to prevent unscrupulous design pirates from operating fell on deaf judicial ears; the Supreme Court held the policy unlawful under Section 5 of the FTC Act, the case having been brought by the FTC. [Fashion Originators' Guild of America v. Federal Trade Commission, 312 U.S. 457 (1941)]

Proof of Agreement

It is vital for business managers to realize that once an agreement or conspiracy is shown to have existed, they or their companies can be convicted of violating the law even if neither agreement nor conspiracy led to concrete results. Suppose the sales manager of Extremis Widget Company sits down over a plate of fettucine with the sales manager of De Minimis Widget Company and says, "Why are we working so hard? I have a plan that will let us both relax." He explains that their companies can put into operation a data exchange program that will stabilize prices. The latter does not immediately commit himself, but after lunch he goes to the stationery store and purchases a notebook in which to record the information he will get from a telephone test of the plan. That action is probably enough to establish a conspiracy to fix prices, and the government could file criminal charges at that point. Discussion with your competitors of prices, discounts, production quotas, rebates, bid rigging, trade-in allowances, commission rates, salaries, advertising, and the like is exceedingly dangerous—and can lead to criminal conduct, and potential jail terms.

Proof of Harm

It is unnecessary to show that the public is substantially harmed by a restraint of trade, as long as the plaintiff can show that the restraint injured him. In *Klor's, Inc.* v. *Broadway-Hale Stores,* 359 U.S. 207 (1959), the plaintiff was a small retail appliance shop in San Francisco. Next door to it was a competing appliance store, one of a chain of stores run by Broadway-Hale. Klor's alleged that Broadway-Hale, using its "monopolistic buying power," persuaded ten national manufacturers and their distributors, including GE, RCA, Admiral, Zenith, and Emerson, to cease selling to Klor's or to sell at discriminatory prices. The defendants did not dispute the allegations. Instead, they moved for summary judgment on the ground that even if true, the allegations did not give rise to a legal claim because the public could not conceivably have been injured as a result of their concerted refusal to deal. As evidence, they cited the uncontradicted fact that within blocks of Klor's, hundreds of household appliance retailers stood ready to sell the public the very brands Klor's was unable to stock as a result of the boycott. The district court granted the motion and dismissed Klor's complaint. The Court of Appeals affirmed. But the Supreme Court reversed:

> This combination takes from Klor's its freedom to buy appliances in an open competitive market and drives it out of business as a dealer in the defendants' products. It deprives the manufacturers and distributors of their freedom to sell to Klor's. . . . It interferes with the natural flow of interstate commerce. It clearly has, by its "nature" and "character," a "monopolistic tendency." As such it is not to be tolerated merely because the victim is just one merchant whose business is so small that his destruction makes little difference to the economy. Monopoly can surely thrive by the elimination of such small businessmen, one at a time, as it can by driving them out in large groups.

"Vertical" Restraints of Trade

We have been exploring the Sherman Act as it applies to horizontal restraints of trade—that is, restraints of trade between competitors. We now turn our attention to vertical restraints—those that are the result of agreements or conspiracies between different levels of the chain of distribution, such as manufacturer and wholesaler or wholesaler and retailer.

Resale Price Maintenance

Generally Is it permissible for a manufacturer to require his distributors or retailers to sell his products at a set price? The general answer is that he may not.

Why, though, would the manufacturer want to fix the price at which the retailer sells his goods? Many reasons have been advanced. For instance, long-run sales of many branded appliances and other goods depend on service by the retailer. Unless the retailer can get a fair price, it will not provide adequate service. Shoddy service will ultimately hurt the brand name and lead to fewer sales. Another argument is that unless all retailers must abide by a certain price, some goods will not be stocked at all. For instance, the argument runs, bookstores will not stock slow-selling books if they cannot be guaranteed a good price on bestsellers. Stores free to discount bestsellers will not have the profit margin to stock other types of books. To guarantee sales of bestsellers to bookstores carrying many lines of books, it is necessary to put a floor under the price of books. Still another argument is that brand-name goods are inviting targets for "loss leader" sales; if one merchant drastically discounts "Extremis" Widgets, other merchants may not want to carry the line, and the manufacturer may experience unwanted fluctuations in sales.

None of these reasons appease the critics of price fixing, including the most important critics—the federal judges. As long ago as 1910, the Supreme Court declared vertical price fixing—what has come to be called **resale price maintenance**—unlawful under the Sherman Act. Dr. Miles Medical Company required wholesalers that bought its proprietary medicines to sign an agreement in which they agreed not to sell to retailers who did not have a "retail agency contract" with Dr. Miles, and not to sell below a certain price. The retail agency contract similarly contained a price floor. Dr. Miles argued that since it was free to make or not make the medicines, it should be free to dictate the prices at which purchasers could sell it. The Supreme Court said that Dr. Miles's arrangements with more than 400 jobbers and 25,000 retailers was no different than if the wholesalers or retailers agreed among themselves to fix the price. Dr. Miles "having sold its product at prices satisfactory to itself, the public is entitled to whatever advantage may be derived from a competition in the subsequent traffic." [Dr. Miles Medical Co. v. John D. Park & Sons Co., 220 U.S. 373 (1910)]

Refusal to Deal Nine years later, in *United States* v. *Colgate & Co.*, 250 U.S. 300 (1919), the Supreme Court held that a producer may announce a price at which he wants retailers to resell his product and may tell the retailers that he will refuse to deal with any who do not sell at the established price—as long as the retailers do not enter an agreement with the producer or with each other. This holding was curious because it seemed to promise an easy way to maintain resale prices. But almost from the start the Court showed that the decision was a narrow one. *Colgate* does not mean that the courts will no longer infer from the circumstances an agreement, combination, or conspiracy. All it meant was that a naked refusal to deal, even if announced in advance, is not enough by itself to violate Section 1. In a series of later cases, the Court held that surrounding circumstances may amount to an agreement. Finally, it issued the following opinion, which, though it did not overturn *Colgate,* demonstrated that the early case meant just what it said, nothing more.

UNITED STATES v. PARKE, DAVIS & CO. 362 U.S. 29 (1960)

BRENNAN, J. The Government sought an injunction under § 4 of the Sherman Act against the appellee, Parke, Davis & Company on a complaint alleging that Parke Davis conspired and combined, in violation of §§ 1 and 3 of the Act, with retail and wholesale druggists in Washington, D.C., and Richmond, Virginia, to maintain the wholesale and retail prices of Parke Davis pharmaceutical products. . . . After the Government completed the presentation of its evidence at the trial, and without hearing Parke Davis in defense, the District Court for the District of Columbia dismissed the complaint . . . on the ground that upon the facts and the law the Government had not shown a right to relief. . . .

Parke Davis makes some 600 pharmaceutical products which it markets nationally through drug wholesalers and drug retailers. The retailers buy these products from the drug wholesalers or may make large quantity purchases directly from Parke Davis. Some time before 1956 Parke Davis announced a resale price maintenance policy in its wholesalers' and retailers' catalogues. The wholesalers' catalogue contained a Net Price Selling Schedule listing suggested minimum resale prices of Parke Davis products sold by wholesalers to retailers. The catalogue stated that it was Parke Davis' continuing policy to deal only with drug wholesalers who observed that schedule and who sold only to drug retailers authorized by law to fill prescriptions. Parke Davis, when selling directly to retailers, quoted the same prices listed in the wholesalers' Net Price Selling Schedule but granted retailers discounts for volume purchases. Wholesalers were not authorized to grant similar discounts. The retailers' catalogue contained a schedule of minimum retail prices applicable in States with Fair Trade Laws and stated that this schedule was suggested for use also in States not having such laws. These suggested minimum retail prices usually provided a 50% mark-up over cost on Parke Davis products purchased by retailers from wholesalers but, because of the volume discount, often in excess of 100% mark-up over cost on products purchased in large quantities directly from Parke Davis.

There are some 260 drugstores in Washington, D.C., and some 100 in Richmond, Virginia. Many of the stores are units of Peoples' Drug Stores, a large retail drug chain. There are five drug wholesalers handling Parke Davis products in the locality who do business with the drug retailers. The wholesalers observed the resale prices suggested by Parke Davis. However, during the spring and early summer of 1956 drug retailers in the two cities advertised and sold several Parke Davis vitamin products at prices substantially below the suggested minimum retail prices; in some instances the prices apparently reflected the volume discounts on direct purchases from Parke Davis since the products sold below the prices listed in the wholesalers' Net Price Selling Schedule. The Baltimore office manager of Parke Davis in charge of the sales district which included the two cities sought advice from his head office how to handle this situation. The Parke Davis attorney advised that the company could legally "enforce an adopted policy arrived at unilaterally" to sell only to customers who observed the suggested minimum resale prices. He further advised that this meant that "we can lawfully say 'we will sell you only so long as you observe such minimum retail prices' but cannot say 'we will sell you only if you agree to observe such minimum retail prices,' since except as permitted by Fair Trade legislations [sic] agreements as to resale price maintenance are invalid." Thereafter in July the branch manager put into effect a program for promoting observance of the suggested minimum retail prices by the retailers involved. The program contemplated the participation of the five drug wholesalers. In order to insure that retailers who did not comply would be cut off from sources of supply, representatives of Parke Davis visited the wholesalers and told them, in effect, that not only would Parke Davis refuse to sell to wholesalers who did not adhere to the policy announced in their catalogue, but also that it would refuse to sell to wholesalers who sold Parke Davis products to retailers who did not observe the suggested minimum retail prices. Each wholesaler was interviewed individually but each was informed that his competitors were also being apprised of this. The wholesalers without exception indicated a willingness to go along.

Representatives called contemporaneously upon the retailers involved, individually, and told each that if he did not observe the suggested minimum retail prices, Parke Davis would refuse to deal with him, and that furthermore he would be unable to purchase any Parke Davis products from the wholesalers. Each of the retailers was also told that his competitors were being similarly informed.

Several retailers refused to give any assurances of compliance and continued after these July interviews to advertise and sell Parke Davis products at prices below the suggested minimum retail prices. Their names were furnished by Parke Davis to the wholesalers. Thereafter Parke Davis refused to fill direct orders from such retailers and the wholesalers likewise refused to fill their orders. This ban was not limited to the Parke Davis products being sold below the suggested minimum prices but included all the company's products, even those necessary to fill prescriptions.

* * *

The District Court held that the Government's proofs did not establish a violation of the Sherman Act because "the actions of [Parke Davis] were properly unilateral and sanctioned by law under the doctrine laid down in the case of United States v. Colgate & Co., 250 U.S. 300, 39 S.Ct. 465, 63 L.Ed. 992. . . ."

* * *

The Government concedes for the purposes of this case that under the *Colgate* doctrine a manufacturer, having announced a price maintenance policy, may bring about adherence to it by refusing the deal with customers who do not observe that policy. The Government contends, however, that subsequent decisions of this Court compel the holding that what Parke Davis did here by entwining the wholesalers and retailers in a program to promote general compliance with its price maintenance policy went beyond mere customer selection and created combinations or conspiracies to enforce resale price maintenance in violation of §§ 1 and 3 of the Sherman Act.

* * *

The program upon which Parke Davis embarked to promote general compliance with its suggested resale prices plainly exceeded the limitations of the *Colgate* doctrine and . . . effected arrangements which violated the Sherman Act. Parke Davis did not content itself with announcing its policy regarding retail prices and following this with a simple refusal to have business relations with any retailers who disregarded that policy. Instead Parke Davis used the refusal to deal with the wholesalers in order to elicit their willingness to deny Parke Davis products to retailers and thereby help gain the retailers' adherence to its suggested minimum retail prices. The retailers who disregarded the price policy were promptly cut off when Parke Davis supplied the wholesalers with their names. The large retailer who said he would "abide" by the price policy, the multiunit Peoples' Drug chain, was not cut off. In thus involving the wholesalers to stop the flow of Parke Davis products to the retailers, thereby inducing retailers' adherence to its suggested retail price, Parke Davis created a combination with the retailers and the wholesalers to maintain retail prices and violated the Sherman Act. . . .

. . . With regard to the retailers' suspension of advertising Parke Davis did not rest with the simple announcement to the trade of its policy in that regard followed by a refusal to sell to the retailers who would not observe it. First it discussed the subject with Dart Drug. When Dart indicated willingness to go along the other retailers were approached and Dart's apparent willingness to cooperate was used as the lever to gain their acquiescence in the program. Having secured those acquiescences Parke Davis returned to Dart Drug with the report of that accomplishment. Not until all this was done was the advertising suspended and sales to all the retailers resumed. In this manner Parke Davis sought assurances of compliance and got them, as well as the compliance itself. It was only by actively bringing about substantial unanimity among the competitors that Parke Davis was able to gain adherence to its policy.

* * *

The judgment is reversed and the case remanded to the District Court with directions to enter on appropriate judgment enjoining Parke Davis from further violations of the Sherman Act unless the company elects to submit evidence in defense and refutes the Government's right to injunctive relief established by the present record.

Other Restrictions on Resale

Resale price maintenance is not the only kind of restriction that producers desire to place on the resale of goods. Another important class of restrictions is **territorial.** To encourage its dealers—especially franchised dealers—to exert maximum effort to sell its products, a producer might wish to assign the dealer an exclusive area within which to sell the product.

The question is whether these restrictions are lawful, given that *horizontal* allocations of territory among competitors are *per se* violations of Section 1 (*Sealy;* see p. 537). As we will see in Chapter 22, the courts follow the rule of reason—it is not a *per se* violation to allocate distributors' territory if there are sound business reasons for doing so apart from a desire to restrain trade.

Tying and Exclusive Dealing Contracts

We move now to a non-price vertical form of restraint. Suppose you went to the grocery store intent on purchasing a bag of potato chips to satisfy a late night craving. Imagine your surprise—and indignation—if the store manager waved a paper in your face and said: "I'll sell you this bag only on the condition that you sign this agreement to buy all of your potato chips in the next five years from me." Or if he said: "I'll sell only if you promise never to buy potato chips from my rival across the street." These are **exclusive dealing contracts**, and if the effect may be substantially to lessen competition they are unlawful under Section 3 of the Clayton Act. They also may be unlawful under Section 1 of the Sherman Act and Section 5 of the FTC Act. Another form of exclusive dealing, known as **tying,** is also prohibited under Section 3 and the other statutes. A tying contract results when you are forced to take a certain product in order to get the product you are really after: "I'll sell you the potato chips you crave, but only if you purchase five pounds of my Grade B liver."

Section 3 of the Clayton Act declares it unlawful for any person engaged in commerce

> in the course of such commerce, to lease or make a sale or contract for sale of goods, wares, merchandise, machinery, supplies or other commodities, whether patented or unpatented, for use, consumption or resale . . . or fix a price charged therefor, or discount from or rebate upon, such price, *on the condition . . . that the lessee or purchaser . . . shall not use or deal in the goods, wares, merchandise, machinery, supplies, or other commodities of a competitor or competitors of the lessor or seller,* where the effect of such lease, sale, or contract for sale or such condition . . . may be to substantially lessen competition or tend to create a monopoly in any line of commerce [emphasis added by authors].

Tying Under Section 3, the potato chip example is not unlawful, for you would not have much of an effect on competition nor tend to create a monopoly if you signed with your corner grocery. But the Clayton Act has serious ramifications for a producer who might wish to require a dealer to sell only its products—such as a fast-food franchisee that can carry cooking ingredients bought only from the franchisor (Chapter 22), an appliance store that can carry only one national brand of refrigerators, or an ice cream parlor that must buy ice cream supplies from the supplier of its machinery.

This latter situation came under review in *International Salt Co.* v. *United States*, 332 U.S. 392 (1947). International Salt was the largest American producer of salt for industrial uses. It held patents on two machines necessary for using salt products; one injected salt into foodstuffs during canning. It leased most of these machines to canners, and the lease required the lessees to purchase from International all salt to be used in the machines. The case was decided on summary judgment; the company did not have the chance to prove the reasonableness of its conduct. The Court held that it was not entitled to. International's valid patent on the machines did not confer on it the right to restrain trade in unpatented salt. Doing so was a violation of both Section 1 of the Sherman Act and Section 3 of the Clayton Act:

> Not only is price-fixing unreasonable, *per se,* but also it is unreasonable, *per se,* to foreclose competitors from any substantial market. The volume of business affected by these contracts cannot be said to be insignificant or insubstantial, and the tendency of the arrangement to accomplishment of monopoly seems obvious. Under the law, agreements are forbidden which "tend to create a monopoly," and it is immaterial that the tendency is a creeping one rather than one that proceeds at full gallop; nor does the law await arrival at the goal before condemning the direction of the movement.

The Clayton Act applies only to "commodities." In a case involving the sale of newspaper advertising space (to purchase space in the morning paper an advertiser would have to take space in the company's afternoon paper), the government lost because it could not use the narrower standards of Section 3 and could not prove that the defendant had monopoly power over the sale of advertising space. (Another afternoon newspaper carried advertisements and its sales did not suffer.) In the course of his opinion, Justice Clark set forth the rule for determining legality of tying arrangements under both the Clayton and Sherman Acts:

> When the seller enjoys a monopolistic position in the market for the "tying" product [*i.e.,* the product that the buyer wants] or if a substantial volume of commerce in the "tied" product [*i.e.,* the product that the buyer does not want] is restrained, a tying arrangement violates the narrower standards expressed in section 3 of the Clayton Act because from either factor the requisite potential lessening of competition is inferred. And because for even a lawful monopolist it is "unreasonable *per se* to foreclose competitors from any substantial market" a tying arrangement is banned by section 1 of the Sherman Act wherever both conditions are met. [Times-Picayune Publishing Co. v. United States, 345 U.S. 594 (1953)]

This rule was broadened in 1958 in a Sherman Act case involving the Northern Pacific Railroad Company, which had received 40 million acres of land from Congress in the late nineteenth century in return for building a rail line from the Great Lakes to the Pacific. For decades Northern Pacific leased or sold the land on condition that the buyer or lessee use Northern Pacific to ship any crops grown on the land or goods manufactured there. To no avail the railroad argued that unlike International Salt's machines, the railroad's "tying product" (its land) was not patented, and that the land users were free to ship on other lines if they could find cheaper rates. Wrote Justice Black:

> [A] tying arrangement may be defined as an agreement by a party to sell one product but only on the condition that the buyer also purchases a different (or tied) product, or at least agrees that he will not purchase that product from any other supplier. Where such conditions are successfully exacted competition on the merits with respect to the tied product is inevitably curbed. . . . They deny competitors free access to the market for the tied product, not because the party imposing the tying requirements has a better product or a lower price but because of his power or leverage in another market. At the same time buyers are forced to forego their free choice between competing products. . . . *They are unreasonable in and of themselves whenever a party has sufficient economic power with respect to the tying product to appreciably restrain free competition in the market for the tied product and a "not insubstantial" amount of interstate commerce is affected.* . . . In this case . . . the undisputed facts established beyond any genuine question that the defendant possessed substantial economic power by virtue of its extensive landholdings which it used as leverage to induce large numbers of purchasers and lessees to give it preference. [Northern Pacific Railway Co. v. United States, 356 U.S. 1 (1958) (emphasis added by authors)]

Taken together, the tying cases suggest that anyone with certain market power over a commodity or other valuable (such as a trademark) runs a serious risk of violating the Clayton Act or Sherman Act or both if he insists that the buyer must also take some other product as part of the bargain.

Exclusive Dealing and Requirements Contracts Pre-Clayton Act cases upheld many exclusive dealing arrangements under the Sherman Act rule of reason. And although after 1914 the courts took a dim view of tying arrangements, they appeared to take a more relaxed view of exclusive dealing arrangements. But in 1949, the Supreme Court rewrote the ground rules in the famous *Standard Stations* case [Standard Oil of California v. United States, 337 U.S. 293 (1949)]. In previous cases, the Supreme Court had struck down an exclusive dealership in a situation in which the seller had 40 percent of the national markets; it had upheld such an arrangement where the seller had only 1 percent. In *Standard Stations,* Standard Oil had 23 percent of the market for gasoline sales in nine Western states—7 percent was sold to its own filling stations, 7 percent to independent stations, and 9 percent to commercial users. Its 14 percent of the retail sales market compared to 42 percent shared by six major competitors. The remaining 44 percent of the market was divided by some seventy smaller refiners. Standard entered into exclusive supply contracts with the filling stations to which it sold gasoline, as did all of Standard's competitors. Under these contracts, the independent stations agreed to purchase all their requirements for gasoline and certain other products (oil, tires, tubes, batteries, and other accessories) from Standard. The company had about 8,000 supply contracts with independents. The exclusive supply contracts certainly seemed to fall within the terms of Section 3. (Reread the language of the section on p. 546.) But the government faced one problem. Section 3 requires that the effect of the exclusivity be to substantially lessen competition or tend to create a monopoly. At most, only 14 percent of the market was involved. Certainly there was no monopoly nor likely to be. What about lessening of competition?

The Standard contracts involved some $60 million worth of gasoline. In *International Salt,* the sales totaled only some $500,000, and that was held to be a substantial enough market from which competitors were foreclosed. So the Standard arrangement must fall unless there is some logical distinction to be made between a *tying* contract and a *requirements* contract. Justice Frankfurter said that there is indeed a distinction—but as it turned out, not one that led very far. A *tying contract* has practically no justification, so the courts don't have to look very hard for evidence of a probable impact on competition. On the other hand, said Justice Frankfurter, *requirements contracts*

> may well be of economic advantage to buyers as well as to sellers, and thus indirectly of advantage to the consuming public. In the case of the buyer they may assure supply, afford protection against rises in price, enable long-term planning on the basis of known costs, and obviate the expense and risk of storage in the quantity necessary for a commodity having a fluctuating demand. From the seller's point of view, requirements contracts may make possible a substantial reduction of selling expenses, give protection against price fluctuations, and—of particular advantage to a newcomer to the field to whom it is important to know what capital expenditures are justified—offer the possibility of a predictable market. . . . They may be useful, moreover, to a seller trying to establish a foothold against the counterattacks of entrenched competitors. . . . Since these advantages of requirements contracts may often be sufficient to account for their use, the coverage by such contracts of a substantial amount of business affords a weaker basis for the inference that competition may be lessened than would similar coverage by tying clauses, especially where the latter is combined with market control of the tying device.

That language might seem to point the way toward approving Standard's exclusive supply contracts. But it did not. For one thing, even if Standard had not improved its competitive position during the period it used these supply contracts, who could say that its position might not have deteriorated if it had not used them? Since all the major sellers used exclusive supply contracts, the effect might have been to entrench them all at the expense of the small refiners. It is not the judges' job, the Court was saying, to balance the exclusive dealing arrangement against other possible methods of distribution, for the Clayton Act says that exclusive dealing is not permissible whenever substantial competition "may be" lessened. Reasonableness of the practice does not count when the circumstances suggest, as they did here, that substantial competition may be lessened. Hence, Justice Frankfurter concluded, "the qualifying clause of Section 3 ["where the effect . . . may be substantially to lessen competition . . ."] is satisfied by *proof that competition has been foreclosed in a substantial share of the line of commerce affected* [emphasis added by authors]. . . . [E]vidence that competitive activity has not actually declined is inconclusive."

Standard Stations appeared to put the kibosh on requirements contracts, but the Supreme Court resurrected them twelve years later in *Tampa Electric Co.* v. *Nashville Coal Co.,* 365 U.S. 320 (1961). Tampa Electric is a Florida electric utility. It built two new plants designed to generate electricity by burning coal. To secure a supply, it made a deal with Nashville Coal to supply both plants with all the coal they could use during their first two years of operation and thereafter to supply each plant with not less than 250,000 tons each year for the succeeding twenty years. Without delivering any coal, Nashville breached the contract, claiming that it violated the antitrust laws. The district court ruled that the amount of coal consumed within "peninsular Florida" amounted to 700,000 tons, the amount that Tampa Electric would require at the end of the second year. Although some 700 coal producers served the area, the court concluded that the supply contract excluded competitors from a substantial amount of trade. The Court of Appeals affirmed. The Supreme Court reversed, holding that the lower courts had used too small a marketplace to measure the impact of the contract.

The proper "relevant competitive market" was the entire area in which Nashville competed with the other 700 producers. That area included ten states. In that market, the amount of coal tied up in the Tampa-Nashville contract was only 1 percent. Although the total contract sales amounted to $128 million, dollar volume is not the test. The question is "whether the pre-emption of competition to the extent of the tonnage involved tends to substantially foreclose competition in the relevant coal market." Measured against the 250 million tons of coal sold in the entire area. Tampa's requirement was small.

The effect of *Tampa Electric* seems to be that when the amount of commerce involved is small, requirements contracts are permissible. But that is not the end of the story, for nothing is ever simple in the field of antitrust. The marketing executive must also bear in mind Section 5 of the FTC Act, which has no clause linking the exclusive dealing to the effect on commerce. Section 5 speaks only in terms of "unfair methods of competition and unfair or deceptive acts or practices in commerce." Can Section 5 reach exclusive dealing arrangements? Yes, said the Supreme Court in a 1966 FTC case.

Brown Shoe is one of the largest shoe makers in the world and was then second largest in the United States. The company launched a Brown Franchise Stores' Program, under which it sold its shoes to 659 independent retail shoe stores on condition that they refrain from selling any competing line of shoes. In return, the stores received valuable services, including architectural plans, costly merchandising records, services of a Brown field representative, and right to participate in cheap group insurance. In an administrative proceeding under Section 5, the FTC held that the franchise program effectively foreclosed Brown's competitors from selling to a substantial number of retail outlets. The Court of Appeals set aside the Commission's cease and desist order. In *Federal Trade Commission* v. *Brown Shoe Co.*, 384 U.S. 316 (1966), the Supreme Court reversed, reinstating the order, even though the affected retailers accounted for only about 1 percent of the shoe dealers in the United States—the same percentage that was held permissible in *Tampa Electric*. Justice Black explained:

> [T]he Commission has broad powers to declare trade practices unfair. The broad power of the Commission is particularly well established with regard to trade practices which conflict with the basic policies of the Sherman and Clayton Acts even though such practices may not actually violate these laws. The record in this case shows beyond doubt that Brown, the country's second largest manufacturer of shoes, has a program, which requires shoe retailers, unless faithless to their contractual obligations with Brown, substantially to limit their trade with Brown's competitors. This program obviously conflicts with the central policy of both § 1 of the Sherman Act and § 3 of the Clayton Act against contracts which take away freedom of purchasers to buy in an open market. Brown nevertheless contends that the Commission has no power to declare the franchise program unfair without proof that its effect "may be to substantially lessen competition or tend to create a monopoly" which of course would have to be proved if the Government were proceeding against Brown under § 3 of the Clayton Act or other provisions of the antitrust laws. This power of the Commission was emphatically stated in F.T.C. v. Motion Picture Advertising Service Co., 344 U.S. 392, at pp. 394–95: "It is . . . clear that the Federal Trade Commission Act was designed to supplement and bolster the Sherman Act and the Clayton Act . . . to stop in their incipience acts and practices which, when full blown, would violate those Acts . . . as well as to condemn as 'unfair methods of competition' existing violations of them." We hold that the Commission acted well within its authority in declaring the Brown franchise program unfair whether it was completely full blown or not.

Price Discrimination

Historical Background

If the relatively simple and straightforward language of the Sherman Act can provide litigants and courts with interpretive headaches, the law against price discrimination—the Robinson-Patman Act—can strike the student with a crippling migraine. Technically, Section 2 of the Clayton Act, the Robinson-Patman Act, has been verbally abused almost since its enactment in 1936. It has been called the "Typhoid Mary of Antitrust," a "grotesque manifestation of the scissors and paste-pot method" of draftsmanship. Critics carp at more than its language; many have asserted over the years that the act is anticompetitive because it prevents many firms from lowering their prices to attract more customers.

Despite this rhetoric, the Robinson-Patman Act has withstood numerous attempts to modify or repeal it, and it can come into play in many everyday situations. Although in recent years the Justice Department has declined to enforce it, leaving government enforcement efforts to the Federal Trade Commission, *private* plaintiffs are actively seeking treble damages in numerous cases. So whether it makes economic sense or not, the act is a living reality for marketers. This next section introduces certain problems that lurk in deciding how to price goods and how to respond to competitors' prices.

The original Section 2, enacted in 1914, was aimed at the price-cutting practice of the large trusts, which would reduce the price of products below cost where necessary in a particular location, to wipe out smaller competitors who could not long sustain such losses. But the original Clayton Act exempted from its terms any "discrimination in price . . . on account of differences in the quantity of the commodity sold." This was a gaping loophole, that made it exceedingly difficult to prove a case of price discrimination.

Not until the Depression in the 1930s did sufficient cries of alarm over price discrimination force Congress to act. The alarm was centered on the practices of large grocery chains. Their immense buying power was used as a lever to pry out price discounts from food processors and wholesalers. Unable to extract similar price concessions, the small "mom and pop" grocery stores found that they could not offer the retail customer the lower food prices set by the chains. The small shops began to fail. In 1936, Congress strengthened Section 2 by enacting the Robinson-Patman Act. Although prompted by concern about how large buyers could use their purchasing power, the act in fact places most of its restrictions on the pricing decisions of sellers.

Statutory Framework

The heart of the act is Section 2(a), which reads in pertinent part as follows:

> [I]t shall be unlawful for any person engaged in commerce . . . to discriminate in price between different purchasers of commodities of like grade and quality . . . where the effect of such discrimination may be substantially to lessen competition or tend to create a monopoly in any line of commerce, or to injure, destroy or prevent competition with any person who either grants or knowingly receives the benefit of such discrimination, or with customers of either of them.

This section provides certain defenses to a charge of price discrimination. For example, differentials in price are permissible whenever they "make only due allowances for differences in the cost of manufacture, sale, or delivery resulting from the differing methods or quantities in which such commodities are to such purchasers sold or delivered." This section also permits sellers to change prices in response to changing marketing conditions or the marketability of the goods—for example, if perishable goods begin to deteriorate, the seller may drop the price in order to move the goods quickly.

Section 2(b) provides the major defense to price discrimination: any price is lawful if made in good faith to meet competition.

Discrimination by the Seller

Preliminary Matters

Simultaneous Sales To be discriminatory, the different prices must have been charged in sales made at the same time or reasonably close in time. What constitutes a reasonably close time depends on the industry and the circumstances of the marketplace. The time span for dairy sales would be considerably shorter than for sales of mainframe computers, given the nature of the product, the frequency of sales, the unit cost, and the volatility of the markets.

Identity of Purchaser Another preliminary issue is the identity of the actual purchaser. A supplier who deals through a dummy wholesaler might be charged with price discrimination even though on paper only one sale appears to have been made. Under the "indirect purchaser" doctrine, a seller who deals with two or more retail customers, but passes their orders on to a single wholesaler and sells the total quantity to the wholesaler in one transaction, can be held to have violated the act. The retailers are treated as indirect purchasers of the supplier.

Sale of Commodities The act applies only to *sales of commodities*. A lease, rental, or license to use a product does not constitute a sale; hence price differentials under one of those arrangements cannot be unlawful under Robinson-Patman. Likewise, since the act applies only to commodities, tangible things, the courts have held that it does not apply to the sale of intangibles, such as rights to license or use patents, shares in a mutual fund, newspaper or television advertising, or title insurance.

Of Like Grade and Quality Only those sales involving goods of "like grade and quality" can be tested under the act for discriminatory pricing. What do these terms mean? The leading case is *FTC* v. *Borden Co.*, 383 U.S. 637 (1966), in which the Supreme Court ruled that trademarks and labels do not, for Robinson-Patman purposes, distinguish products that are otherwise the same. Grade and quality must be determined "by the characteristics of the product itself." When the products are physically or chemically identical, they are of like grade and quality, regardless of how imaginative marketing executives attempt to distinguish them. But physical differences that affect marketability can serve to denote products as being of different grade and quality, even if the differences are slight and do not affect the seller's cost in manufacturing or marketing.

Competitive Injury

To violate the Robinson-Patman Act, the seller's price discrimination must have an anticompetitive effect. The usual Clayton Act standard for measuring injury applies to Robinson-Patman violations—that is, a violation occurs when the effect may be substantially to lessen competition or tend to create a monopoly in any line of commerce. But because the Robinson-Patman Act has a more specific test of competitive injury, the general standard is rarely cited.

The more specific test measures the impact on particular persons affected. Section 2(a) says that it is unlawful to discriminate in price where the effect is "to injure, destroy, or prevent competition with any person who grants or knowingly receives the benefit of such discrimination or to customers of either of them." The effect—injury, destruction, or prevention of competition—is measured against three types of those suffering it: (1) competitors of the seller or supplier (that is, competitors of the person who "grants" the price discrimination); (2) competitors of the buyer (that is, competitors of the buyer who "knowingly receives the benefit" of the price differential); and (3) customers of either of the two types of competitors. As we will see, the third category presents many difficulties.

For purposes of our discussion, assume the following scenario. Ace Brothers Widget Company manufactures the usual sizes and styles of American domestic widgets. It competes primarily with National Widget Corporation, although several smaller companies make widgets in various parts of the country. Ace Brothers is the largest manufacturer and sells throughout the United States. National sells primarily in the western states. The industry has several forms of distribution. Many retailers buy directly from Ace and National, but several regional and national wholesalers also operate, including Widget Jobbers, Ltd. and Widget Pushers & Sons. The retailers in any particular city compete directly against each other to sell to the general public. Jobbers and Pushers are in direct competition. Jobbers also sells directly to the public, so that it is in direct competition with retailers as well as Widget Pushers. As everyone knows, widgets are extremely price sensitive, being virtually identical physically.

Primary-line Injury Now consider the situation in California, Oregon, and Wisconsin. The competing manufacturers, Ace Brothers and National Widgets, both sell to wholesalers in California and Oregon, but only Ace has a sales arm in Wisconsin. Seeing an opportunity, Ace drops its prices to wholesalers in California and Oregon and raises them in Wisconsin, putting National at a competitive disadvantage. This situation, illustrated below, is an example of **primary-line injury**—the injury is done directly to a competitor of the company that differentiates its prices. This is price discrimination, and it is prohibited under Section 2(a).

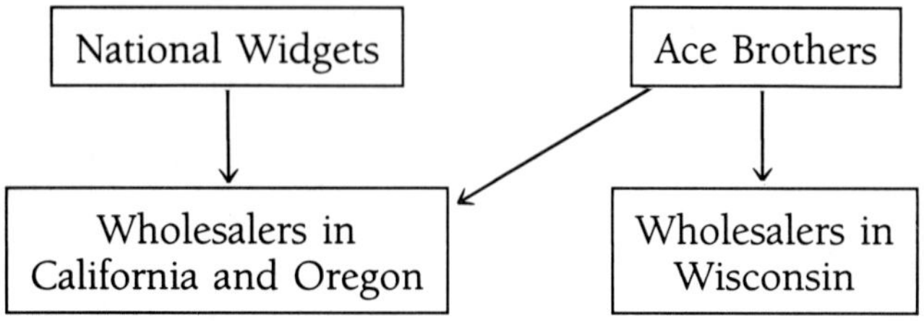

Most forms of primary-line injury have a geographical basis, but they need not. Suppose National sells exclusively to Jobbers in Northern California, and Ace Brothers sells both to Jobbers and several other wholesalers. If Ace cuts its prices to Jobbers, while charging higher prices to the other wholesalers, the effect is also primary-line injury to National. Jobbers will obviously want to buy more from Ace at lower prices, and National's reduced business is therefore a direct injury. If Ace intends to drive National out of business, this violation of Section 2(a) could also be an attempt to monopolize in violation of Section 2 of the Sherman Act.

Secondary-line Injury Next we consider injury done to competing buyers. Suppose that Ace Brothers favors Jobbers—or that Jobbers, a powerful and giant wholesaler, induces Ace to act favorably by threatening not to carry Ace's line of widgets otherwise. Although Ace continues to supply both Jobbers and Widget Pushers, it cuts its prices to Jobbers. As a result, Jobbers can charge its retail customers lower prices than can Pushers, so that Pushers' business begins to slack off. This is **secondary-line injury** at the buyer's level. Jobbers and Pushers are in direct competition, and by impairing Pushers' ability to compete, the requisite injury has been committed. This situation can be illustrated as follows:

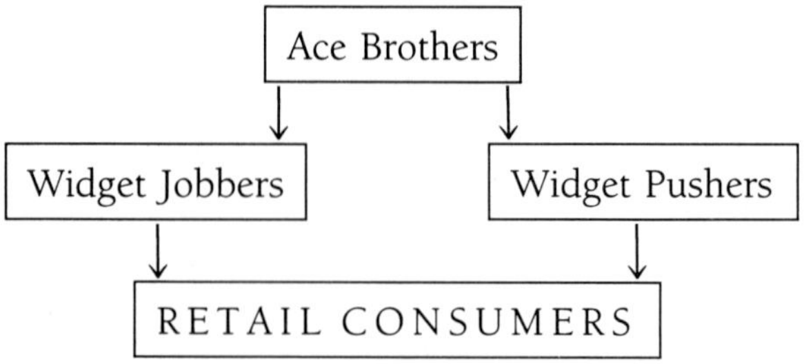

Variations on this secondary-line injury are possible. Assume Ace Brothers sells directly to Fast Widgets, a retail shop, and also to Jobbers. Jobbers sells to retail shops that compete with Fast Widgets and also directly to consumers. The situation looks like this:

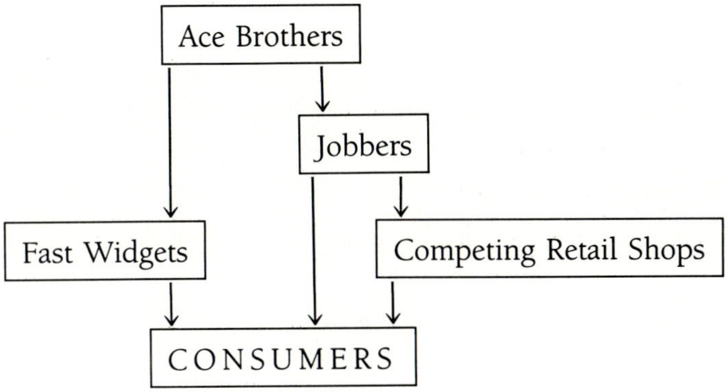

If Ace favors Jobbers by cutting its prices, discriminating against Fast Widgets, the transaction is unlawful, even though Jobbers and Fast Widgets do not compete for sales to other retailers. Their competition for the business of ultimate consumers is sufficient to establish the illegality of the discrimination. A variation on this situation was at issue in the first important case to test Section 2(a) as it affects buyers. Morton Salt sold to both wholesalers and retailers, offering quantity discounts. Its pricing policy was structured to give large buyers great savings, computed on a yearly total, not on shipments made at any one time. Only five retail chains could take advantage of the higher discounts, and as a result, these chains could sell salt to grocery shoppers at a price below that at which the chains' retail competitors could buy it from their wholesalers. Here is a schematic illustration:

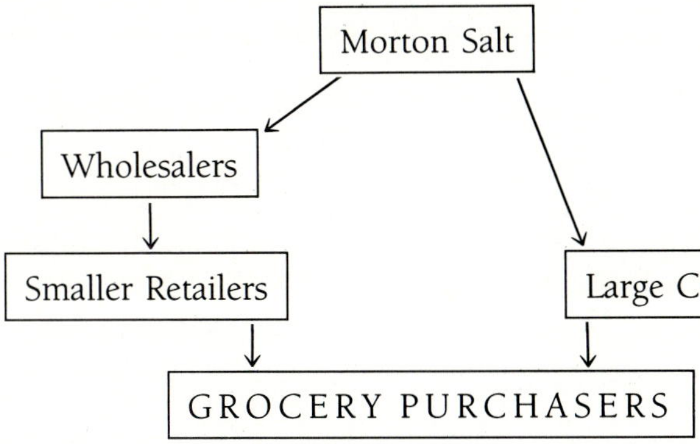

In this case for the first time, the Supreme Court in *FTC* v. *Morton Salt Co.*, 334 U.S. 37 (1948), declared that the impact of the discrimination does not have to be actual; it is enough if there is a "reasonable *possibility*" of competitive injury.

In order to make out a case of secondary-line injury, it is necessary to show that the buyers purchasing at different prices are in fact competitors. Suppose that Ace Brothers sells to Fast Widgets, the retailer, and also to Boron Enterprises, a manufacturer that incorporates widgets in most of its products. Boron does not compete against Fast Widgets, and therefore Ace Brothers may charge different prices to Boron and Fast without fearing Robinson-Patman repercussions. Here is the Boron-Fast schematic:

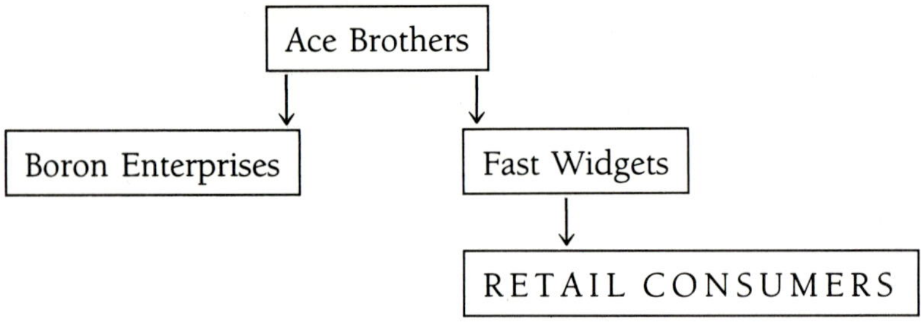

Third-line Injury Second-line injury to buyers does not exhaust the possibilities. Robinson-Patman also works against so-called **third-line** or *tertiary-line* injury. At stake here is injury another rung down the chain of distribution. Ace Brothers sells to Pushers, which processes unfinished widgets in its own factory and sells them in turn directly to retail customers. Ace also sells to Jobbers, a wholesaler without processing facilities. Jobbers sells to retail shops that can process the goods and sell directly to consumers, thus competing with Pushers for the retail business. Schematically, that distribution chain looks like this:

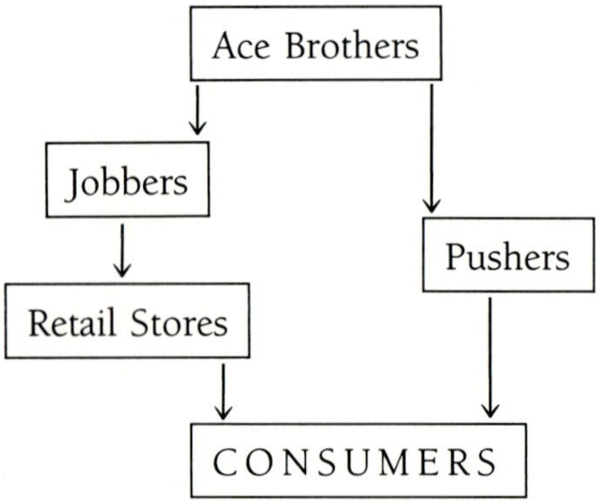

If Ace's price differs between Pushers and Jobbers, so that Jobbers is able to sell at a lower price to the ultimate consumers than Pushers, a Robinson-Patman violation has occurred.

Fourth-line Injury In a complex economy, the distribution chain can go on and on. So far, we have examined discrimination on the level of competing supplier-sellers, on the level of competing customers of the supplier-seller, and on the level of competing customers of customers of the supplier-seller. Does the vigilant spotlight of Robinson-Patman penetrate below this level? The Supreme Court has said yes. In *Perkins* v. *Standard Oil Co.*, 395 U.S. 642 (1969), the Supreme Court said that "customer" in Section 2(a) means any person who distributes the supplier-seller's product, regardless of how many intermediaries are involved in getting the product to him.

Seller's Defenses

Cost Justification

Price discrimination is not *per se* unlawful. The Robinson-Patman Act allows the seller two general defenses: (1) cost justification; and (2) meeting competition. If the seller can demonstrate that sales to one particular buyer are cheaper than sales to others, a price differential is permitted, if it is based entirely on the cost differences. For example, if one buyer is willing to have the goods packed in cheaper containers or larger crates that save money, that cost can be passed along to the buyer. Similarly, a buyer who takes over a warehousing function formerly undertaken by the seller is entitled to have the cost saving reflected in the selling price. Suppose the buyer orders his entire requirements for the year from the manufacturer, a quantity many times greater than that taken by any other customer. This large order permits the manufacturer to make the goods at a considerably reduced unit cost. May the manufacturer pass those savings along to the quantity buyer? He may, as long as he does not pass along the entire savings but only that attributable to the particular buyer. For other buyers add to his total production run, and they thus contribute to the final unit production cost. The marketing manager should be aware that the courts strictly construe cost-justification claims, and few companies have succeeded with this defense.

Meeting Competition

Lowering a price to meet competition is a complete defense to a charge of price discrimination. Assume Ace Brothers is selling widgets to retailers in Indiana and Kentucky at $100 per dozen. National Widgets suddenly enters the Kentucky market and, because it has lower manufacturing costs than Ace, sells widgets to the four Kentucky widget retailers at $85 per dozen. Ace may lower its price to that amount in Kentucky without lowering its Indiana price. However, if National's price violated the Robinson-Patman Act and Ace knew or should have known that it did, Ace may not reduce its prices. The defense of meeting competition has certain limitations. For example, the seller may not use this defense as an excuse to charge different customers a price differential over the long run. Moreover, if National's lower prices result from quantity orders, Ace may reduce its prices only for like quantities. Ace may not reduce its price for lesser quantities if National charges more for smaller orders. And, although Ace may meet National's price to a given customer, Ace may not legally charge less.

Other Prohibitions

Unlawful Brokerage Payments

Section 2(c) prohibits payment of commissions by one party in a transaction to the opposite party (or to the opposite party's agent) in a sale of goods, unless services are actually rendered for them. Suppose the buyer's broker warehouses the goods. May the seller pass along this cost to the broker in the form of a rebate? Isn't that "services rendered"? Although it might seem so, the courts have said no, because they refuse to concede that a buyer's broker or agent can perform services for the seller. Because Section 2(c) of the Robinson-Patman Act stands on its own, the plaintiff need prove only that a single payment was made. Further proof of competitive impact is unnecessary. Hence, Section 2(c) cases are relatively easy to win once the fact of a brokerage commission is uncovered.

Allowances for Merchandising and Other Services

Sections 2(d) and 2(e) prohibit sellers from granting discriminatory allowances for merchandising and from performing other services for buyers on a discriminatory basis. These sections are necessary because price alone is far from the only way to offer discounts to favored buyers. Allowances and services covered by these sections include advertising allowances, floor and window displays, warehousing, return privileges, and special packaging.

Exemptions from the Antitrust Laws

Regulated Industries

Congress has subjected several industries to oversight by specific regulatory agencies. These include banking, securities and commodities exchanges, communications, transportation, and fuel and energy. The question often arises whether companies within those industries are immune to antitrust attack. No simple answer can be given. As a general rule, activities that fall directly within the authority of the regulatory agency are immune. The agency is said to have exclusive jurisdiction over the conduct—for example, the rate structure of the national stock exchanges, which are supervised by the Securities & Exchange Commission. But determining whether a particular case falls within a specific power of an agency is still up to the courts, and judges tend to read the antitrust laws broadly and the regulatory laws narrowly when they seem to clash. A doctrine known as "primary jurisdiction" often dictates that the question of regulatory propriety must first be submitted to the agency before the courts will rule on an antitrust question. If the agency decides the activity complained of is otherwise impermissible, the antitrust question becomes moot.

Organized Labor

In the Clayton Act, Congress explicitly exempted labor unions from the antitrust laws in order to permit workers to band together. Section 6 says that "the labor of a human being is not a commodity or article of commerce. Nothing contained in the antitrust laws shall be construed to forbid the existence and operation of labor . . . organizations, . . . nor shall such organizations, or the members thereof, be held or construed to be illegal combinations or conspiracies in restraint of trade, under the antitrust laws." This provision was included to reverse earlier decisions of the courts that had applied the Sherman Act more against labor than business. Nevertheless, the immunity is not total, and unions have run afoul of the laws when they have combined with non-labor groups to achieve a purpose unlawful under the antitrust laws. Thus, a union could not bargain with an employer to sell its products above a certain price floor.

Insurance

Under the McCarran-Ferguson Act of 1945, insurance companies are not covered by the antitrust laws to the extent that the states regulate the business of insurance. Whether or not the states adequately regulate insurance and the degree to which the exemption applies is a complex business.

State Action

In 1943, the Supreme Court ruled in *Parker* v. *Brown,* 317 U.S. 341 (1943), that when a valid state law regulates a particular industry practice, which the industry members are bound to follow, then they are exempt from the federal antitrust laws. Such laws include regulation of public power and licensing and regulation of the professions. This exemption for "state action" has proved troublesome and, like the other exemptions, a complex matter to apply. But it is clear that the state law must require or compel the action, and not merely permit it. No state law would be valid if it simply said: "Bakers in the state may jointly establish tariffs for the sale of cookies."

The recent trend of Supreme Court decisions is to construe the exemption as narrowly as possible. A city, county, or other subordinate unit of a state is not immune under the *Parker* doctrine. A municipality can escape the consequences of antitrust violations—for example, in its operation of utilities—only if it is carrying out express policy of the state. Even then, a state mandated price-fixing scheme may not survive a federal antitrust attack, as the next case shows. New York law required liquor retailers to charge a certain minimum price, but because the state itself did not actively supervise the policy it had established, it fell to the Supreme Court's antitrust axe.

324 LIQUOR CORP. v. DUFFY
107 S.Ct. 720 (1987)

JUSTICE POWELL delivered the opinion of the Court.

The State of New York requires retailers to charge at least 112 percent of the "posted" wholesale price for liquor, but permits wholesalers to sell to retailers at less than the "posted" price. The question presented is whether this pricing system is valid under . . . the state-action exemption from the antitrust laws. . . .

Wholesalers of liquor in the State of New York must file, or "post," monthly price schedules with the State Liquor Authority (SLA). The schedules must report, "with respect to each item," "the bottle and case price to retailers." The ABC Law itself does not require that the posted case price of an item bear any relation to its posted bottle price. The SLA, however, has promulgated a rule stating that for cases containing 48 or fewer bottles, the posted bottle price multiplied by the number of bottles in a case must exceed the posted case price by a "breakage" surcharge of $1.92.

Retailers of liquor may not sell below "cost." The statute defines "cost" as "the price of such item of liquor to the retailer plus twelve percentum of such price." "Price," in turn, is defined as the posted bottle price in effect at the time the retailer sells or offers to sell the item. Although the statute defines retail cost in terms of the wholesaler's posted bottle price, retailers generally purchase liquor by the case. The SLA expressly has authorized wholesalers to reduce, or "post off," the case price of an item without reducing the posted bottle price of the item. By reducing the case price without reducing the bottle price, wholesalers can compel retailers to charge more than 112 percent of the actual wholesale cost. Similarly, because § 101–bb(2)(b) defines "cost" in terms of the posted bottle price in effect when the retailer sells or offers to sell the item, wholesalers can sell retailers large quantities in a month when prices are low and then require the retailers to sell at an abnormally high markup by raising the bottle price in succeeding months. The New York retail pricing system thus permits wholesalers to set retail prices, and retail markups, without regard to actual retail costs. New York wholesalers advertise in trade publications that their "post offs" will guarantee retailers large markups, sometimes in excess of 30 percent. Wholesalers also advertise that buying large quantities while wholesale prices are low will result in extra retail profits after wholesale prices are raised. The effect of this complex of statutory provisions and regulations is to permit wholesalers to maintain retail prices at artificially high levels.

Appellant 324 Liquor Corporation sold two bottles of liquor to SLA investigators in June 1981 for less than 112 percent of the posted bottle price.

Because the wholesalers had "posted off" their June 1981 case prices without reducing the posted bottle prices, appellant's retail prices represented an 18 percent markup over its actual wholesale cost. As a result of this violation, appellant's license was suspended for 10 days and it forfeited a $1,000 bond. Appellant sought relief from the penalties on the ground that § 101–bb violates § 1 of the Sherman Act, 15 U. S. C. § 1.

* * *

In *Parker* v. *Brown,* 317 U.S. 341 (1943), the Court held that the Sherman Act does not apply "to the anticompetitive conduct of a State acting through its legislature." *Town of Hallie* v. *City of Eau Claire,* 471 U.S. 34, 38 (1985). *Parker* v. *Brown* rests on principles of federalism and state sovereignty. Under those principles, "an unexpressed purpose to nullify a state's control over its officers and agents is not lightly to be attributed to Congress." *Parker* v. *Brown,* 317 U.S., at 351. At the same time, "a state does not give immunity to those who violate the Sherman Act by authorizing them to violate it, or by declaring that their action is lawful." Our decisions have established a two-part test for determining immunity under *Parker* v. *Brown.* "First, the challenged restraint must be 'one clearly articulated and affirmatively expressed as state policy'; second, the policy must be 'actively supervised' by the State itself." *California Retail Liquor Dealers Assn.* v. *Midcal Aluminum, Inc.,* at 105. New York's liquor pricing system meets the first requirement. The state legislature clearly has adopted a policy of resale price maintenance. Just as clearly, however, New York's liquor pricing system is not actively supervised by the State. As in *Midcal,* the State "simply authorizes price setting and enforces the prices established by private parties." New York "neither establishes prices nor reviews the reasonableness of the price schedules." New York "does not monitor market conditions or engage in any 'pointed reexamination' of the program." Each wholesaler sets its own "posted" prices; the State does not control month-to-month variations in posted prices. Nor does the State supervise the wholesaler's decision to "post off," the amount of the "post off," the corresponding decrease, if any, in the bottle price, or the frequency with which a wholesaler posts off. The State has displaced competition among liquor retailers without substituting an adequate system of regulation. "The national policy in favor of competition cannot be thwarted by casting such a gauzy cloak of state involvement over what is essentially a private price-fixing arrangement."

Reversed and remanded.

Group Solicitation of Government Action

Suppose representatives of the railroad industry lobby extensively and eventually successfully for state legislation that hampers truckers, the railroads' deadly enemies. Is this a combination or conspiracy to restrain trade? In *Eastern Railroad President's Conference* v. *Noerr Motor Freight, Inc..* 365 U.S. 127 (1961), the Supreme Court said no. What has come to be known as the *Noerr* doctrine holds that applying the antitrust laws to such activities would violate First Amendment rights to petition the government. One exception to this rule of immunity for soliciting action by the government comes when certain groups seek to harass competitors by instituting state or federal proceedings against them if the claims are baseless or known to be false.

Baseball

Baseball, the Supreme Court said back in 1923, is not "in commerce." Congress has never seen fit to overturn this doctrine. Although some inroads have been made in the way that the leagues and clubs may exercise their power, the basic decision stands. Some things are sacred.

Chapter Summary

Four basic antitrust laws regulate the competitive activities of American business: the Sherman Act, the Clayton Act, the Federal Trade Commission Act, and the Robinson-Patman Act. The Sherman Act prohibits restraints of trade and monopolizing. The Clayton Act prohibits a variety of anticompetitive acts, including mergers and acquisitions that might tend to lessen competition. The Federal Trade Commission Act prohibits unfair methods of competition and unfair and deceptive acts or practices in commerce. The Robinson-Patman Act—actually an amendment to the Clayton Act—prohibits a variety of price discriminations. These laws are enforced in four ways: (1) by the U.S. Department of Justice, (2) by the Federal Trade Commission, (3) by state attorneys general, and (4) by private suits.

The courts have interpreted Section 1 of the Sherman Act, prohibiting every contract, combination, or conspiracy in restraint of trade, by the lights of a rule of reason, so that reasonable restraints ancillary to a legitimate business practice are lawful. But the courts will not ask whether an act is reasonable if it is carried out in order to restrain trade; such acts necessarily violate Section 1. Some acts—price fixing, for example—are illegal *per se*.

One broad class of acts that violate Section 1 are horizontal restraints of trade: agreements or conspiracies among competitors to restrain trade in their business or industry. Condemned acts include price fixing, exchanging price information when doing so permits industry members to control prices, controlling output, regulating competitive methods, allocating territories, exclusionary agreements, and boycotts.

Vertical restraints of trade are another unlawful class of acts under Section 1. These include resale price maintenance, refusals to deal, and unreasonable territorial restrictions on distributors.

Exclusive dealing contracts and tying contracts whose effect may be to substantially lessen competition violate Section 3 of the Clayton Act and may also violate both Section 1 of the Sherman Act and Section 5 of the Federal Trade Commission Act. Requirements and supply contracts are unlawful if they tie up so much of a commodity that they tend substantially to lessen competition or might tend to do so.

The Robinson-Patman Act (Section 2 of the Clayton Act) prohibits discrimination in price for different purchasers of commodities of like grade and quality, if the effect may be substantially to (1) lessen competition or tend to create a monopoly in any line of commerce, or (2) impair competition with (a) any person who grants or (b) knowingly receives the benefit of the discrimination, or (c) with customers of either of them.

Some industries are insulated from the direct reach of the antitrust laws. These include industries separately regulated under federal law, organized labor, insurance, activities mandated under state law, group solicitation of government action, and baseball.

Problems

1. To protect its businesses against ruinous price wars, the state legislature has passed a law permitting manufacturers to set a "suggested resale price" on all goods that they make and sell direct to retailers. Retailers are forbidden to undercut the resale price by more than 10 percent. A retailer who violates the law may be sued by the manufacturer for treble damages: three times the difference between the suggested resale price and the actual selling price. But out-of-state retailers are bound by no such law and are regularly discounting the goods between 35 and 40 percent. As the general manager of a large discount store located within a few miles of a city across the state line, you wish to offer the public a price of only 60 percent of the suggested retail price on items covered by the law in order to compete with the out-of-state retailers to which your customers have easy access. May you lower your price in order to compete? How would you defend yourself if sued by a manufacturer whose goods you discounted in violation of the law?
2. The DiForio Motor Car Company is a small manufacturer of automobiles and sells to three distributors in Peoria. The largest distributor, Hugh's Autos, tells DiForio that it is losing money on its dealership and will quit selling the cars unless DiForio agrees to give it an exclusive contract. DiForio tells the other distributors, whose contracts were renewed from year to year, that it will no longer sell them cars at the end of the contract year. Smith Autos, one of the other dealers, protests, but DiForio refuses to resupply it. Smith Autos sues DiForio and Hugh's. What result? Why?
3. The widget industry consists of six large manufacturers who together account for 62 percent of output, which in 1985 amounted to $2.1 billion in domestic U.S. sales. The remaining 38 percent is supplied by more than forty manufacturers. All six of the large manufacturers and thirty-one of the forty small manufacturers belong to the Widget Manufacturers Trade Association (WMTA). An officer from at least two of the six manufacturers always serves on the WMTA executive committee, which consists of seven members. The full WMTA board of directors consists of one member from each manufacturer. The executive committee meets once a month for dinner at the Widgeters Club; the full board meets semiannually at the Widget Show. The executive committee, which always meets with the association's lawyer in attendance, discusses a wide range of matters, including industry conditions, economic trends, customer relations, technological developments,

and the like, but scrupulously refrains from discussing price, territories, or output. However, after dinner at the bar, five of the seven members meet for drinks and discuss prices in an informal manner. The chairman of the executive committee concludes the discussion with the following statement: "If I had to guess, I'd guess that the unit price will increase by 5 percent the first of next month." On the first of the month, his prediction is proven to be correct among the five companies whose officers had a drink, and within a week, most of the other manufacturers likewise increase their prices. At the semiannual meeting of the full board, the WMTA chairman notes that prices have been climbing steadily and he ventures the hope that they will not continue to do so because otherwise they will face stiff competition from the Gidget industry. However, following the next several meetings of the executive committee, the price continues to rise as before. The Justice Department gets wind of these discussions and sues the companies whose officers are members of the board of directors and also sues individually the members of the executive committee and the chairman of the full board. What laws have they violated, if any, and who has violated them? What remedies or sanctions may the department seek?

4 Twenty-five local supermarket chains banded together as Topco Associates Incorporated to sell groceries under a private label. Topco was formed in 1940 to compete with the giant chains, which had the economic clout to sell private-label merchandise unavailable to the smaller chains. Topco acted as a purchasing agent for the members. By the late 1960s, Topco's members were doing a booming business: $1.3 billion in retail sales, with market share ranging from 1.5 percent to 16 percent in the markets that members served. Topco-brand groceries comprised no more than 10 percent of any store's total merchandise. Under Topco's rules, members were assigned exclusive territories in which to sell Topco-brand goods. A member chain with stores located in another member's exclusive territory could not sell Topco-brand goods in those stores. Topco argued that the market division was necessary to give each chain the economic incentive to advertise and develop brand consciousness, and thus to be able to compete more effectively against the large nonmember supermarkets' private labels. If other stores in the locality could also carry the Topco brand, then it would not be a truly "private" label and there would be no reason to tout it, since it would be like any national brand foodstuff, and Topco members did not have the funds to advertise the brand nationally. Which, if any, antitrust laws has Topco violated? Why?

5. Illinois Brick Company manufactures concrete blocks, which it sells to masons, who in turn work on the blocks and resell them to general contractors. In the 1970s, general contractors used the enhanced blocks to fulfill state building contracts. Illinois Brick Company has a

price-fixing agreement with other manufacturers of concrete block. The State of Illinois discovers the agreement and sues Illinois Brick for treble damages. How can the company defend itself? Suppose the masons also sue the company? What result in each case? Why?

6. In 1983, Panda Bears Incorporated, a small manufacturer, began to sell its patented panda bear robot dolls (they walk, smile, and eat bamboo shoots) to retail toy shops. The public took an immediate fancy to panda bears and the company found it difficult to meet the demand. Retail shops sold out even before their orders arrived. In order to allocate the limited supply fairly, while it tooled up to increase production runs, the company announced to its distributors that it would not sell to any retailers that did not also purchase its trademarked Panda Bear's Bambino Bamboos. It also announced that it would refuse to supply any retailer that sold the robots for less than $59.95. Finally, it said that it would refuse to sell unless the retailer agreed to use exclusively the company's repair services when customers brought the bears back to repair malfunctions in its delicate, patented computerized nervous system. By the following year, with demand still rising, inferior competitive products began to appear of both the robots and the bamboo shoots. Some retailers began to lower the Panda Bear price to meet the competition. The company refused to resupply them. Panda Bears Incorporated also decreed that it would refuse to sell to retailers who carried any other type of bamboo. What antitrust violations, if any, has Panda Bear Incorporated committed? What additional information might be useful in helping you to decide?
7. Sampson Company sells car tires to automotive parts stores for resale to consumers. The manager of Ace Auto Supplies is the brother of Sampson's sales manager. Ace competes with Tyler Auto Supplies. Sampson's sales manager wants to give a break to Ace by charging it 20 percent less for the same quantity of tires than the price to Tyler. But Sampson's sales manager has heard of the Robinson-Patman Act and knows that price discrimination is probably unlawful if it is not cost justified. So he calls up Fred's Tire Wholesalers and says he will be referring a substantial amount of business to the wholesaler in the future. All sales to Ace and Tyler will be made by Sampson but will be processed through Fred's, which need do nothing but fill the order. In this way, Sampson hopes to avoid charges of price discrimination, because it is only making one sale—namely, to Fred's. Is Sampson vulnerable to a price discrimination charge by Tyler? Why?

20

Antitrust 2: Concentrations of Power

Monopolies and other concentrations of economic power can thwart competition. Indeed, in a pure sense, a monopoly means the lack of competition, or at least of effective competition. As the Supreme Court has long defined it, monopoly is "the power to control market prices or exclude competition." [United States v. Grinnell Corp., 384 U.S. 563, 571 (1966)] Public concern about the economic and political power of the large trusts, which tended to become monopolies in the late nineteenth century, led to Section 2 of the Sherman Act in 1890 and to Section 7 of the Clayton Act in 1914. These statutes are not limited to the behemoths of American industry such as IBM or American Telephone & Telegraph Company. A far smaller company that dominates a relatively small geographic area, or merges with another company in an area where few others compete, can be in for trouble under Sections 2 or 7. These laws, therefore, should be of concern to all businesses, not just those on the Fortune 500 list. In this chapter, we will consider how the courts have interpreted both the Section 2 prohibition against monopolizing and the Section 7 prohibition against mergers and acquisitions that tend to lessen competition or to create monopolies.

Section 2 of the Sherman Act: The Law Against Monopolizing

Introduction

Section 2 of the Sherman Act reads as follows:

> Every person who shall monopolize, or attempt to monopolize, or combine or conspire with any other person or persons, to monopolize any part of the trade or commerce among the several states, or with foreign nations, shall be deemed guilty of a [felony].

We begin the analysis of Section 2 with the fundamental proposition that a monopoly is not *per se* unlawful. Section 2 itself makes this proposition inescapable: it forbids the act of *monopolizing*, not the condition or attribute of *monopoly*. Why should that be so? If monopoly power is detrimental to a functioning competitive market system, why should not the law ban the very existence of a monopoly?

The answer is that we cannot hope to have "perfect competition" but only "workable competition." Any number of circumstances might lead to monopolies that we would not want to eliminate. Demand for a product might be limited to what one company could produce, there thus being no incentive for any competitor to come into the market. A small town may be able to support only one supermarket, newspaper, or computer outlet. If a company is operating efficiently through economies of scale, we would not want to split it apart and watch the resulting companies fail. An innovator may have a field all to himself, yet we would not want to penalize the inventor for his very act of invention. Or a company might simply be smarter and more efficient, finally coming to stand alone through the very operation of competitive pressures. It would be an irony indeed if the law were to condemn a company that was forged in the fires of competition itself. As the Supreme Court has said, the Sherman Act was designed to protect competition, not competitors.

A company that has had a monopoly position "thrust upon it" is perfectly lawful. The law penalizes not the monopolist as such, but the competitor who gains his monopoly power through illegitimate means with an intent to become a monopolist, or who after having become a monopolist acts illegitimately to maintain his power.

A Section 2 case involves three essential factors:

1. What is the **relevant market** for determining dominance? The question of relevant market has two aspects, a **geographic** dimension and a **product** dimension. As we saw in the *Tampa Electric* case (Chapter 19), it makes a considerable difference whether the company is thought to be a competitor in ten states or only one. A large company in one

state may appear tiny matched against competitors operating in many states. Likewise, if the product itself has real substitutes, it makes little sense to brand its maker a monopolist. For instance, Coca-Cola is made by only one company, but that does not make the Coca-Cola Company a monopoly, for its soft drink competes with many in the marketplace.

2. How much **monopoly power** is too much? What share of the market must a company have to be labeled a monopoly? Is a company with 50 percent of the market a monopoly? 75 percent? 90 percent?
3. What constitutes an **illegitimate means** of gaining or maintaining monopoly power?

These factors are often closely intertwined, especially the first two. This makes it difficult to examine each separately, but to the extent possible we will address each factor in the order given.

Relevant Market

Product Market The monopolist never exercises power in the abstract. When exercised, monopoly power is used to set prices or exclude competition in the market for a particular product or products. Therefore it is essential in any Section 2 case to determine what products to include in the relevant market.

In the *duPont* case below, the Court phrased the test in terms of "cross-elasticity of demand"—to what degree can a substitute be found for the product in question if the producer sets the price too high? If consumers stay with the product as its price rises, moving to a substitute only at a very high price, then the product is probably in a market by itself. If consumers shift to another product with slight rises in price, then the product market must include all such substitutes.

UNITED STATES v. E. I. DU PONT DE NEMOURS & CO.
351 U.S. 377 (1956)

MR. JUSTICE REED delivered the opinion of the Court.

The United States . . . charged du Pont with monopolizing, attempting to monopolize and conspiracy to monopolize interstate commerce in cellophane . . . in violation of Section 2 of the Sherman Act.

* * *

During the period that is relevant to this action, du Pont produced almost 75 percent of the cellophane sold in the United States, and cellophane constituted less than 20 percent of all "flexible packaging material" sales. This was the designation accepted at the trial. . . .

The Government contends that, by so dominating cellophane production, du Pont monopolized a "part of the trade or commerce" in violation of Section 2. Respondent agrees that cellophane is a product which constitutes "a 'part' of commerce within the meaning of Section 2." But it contends that the prohibition of Section 2 against monopolization is not violated because it does not have the power to control the price of cellophane or to exclude competitors from the market in which cellophane is sold. The court below found that the "relevant market for determining the extent of du Pont's market control is the market for flexible packaging materials," and that competition from those other materials prevented du Pont from possessing monopoly powers in its sales of cellophane.

The Government asserts that cellophane and other wrapping materials are neither substantially fungible nor like priced. For these reasons, it argues that the market for other wrappings is distinct from the market for cellophane and that the competition afforded cellophane by other wrappings is not strong enough to be considered in determining whether du Pont has monopoly powers. Market delimitation is necessary under du Pont's theory to determine whether an alleged monopolist violates Section 2. The ultimate consideration in such a determination is whether the defendants control the price and competition in the market for such part of trade or commerce as they are charged with monopolizing. Every manufacturer is the sole producer of the particular commodity it makes but its control in the above sense of the relevant market depends upon the availability of alternative commodities for buyers: i.e., whether there is a cross-elasticity of demand between cellophane and the other wrappings. This interchangeability is largely gauged by the purchase of competing products for similar uses considering the price, characteristics and adaptability of the competing commodities. The court below found that the flexible wrappings afforded such alternatives. This Court must determine whether the trial court erred in its estimate of the competition afforded cellophane by other materials. . . .

If cellophane is the "market" that du Pont is found to dominate, it may be assumed it does have monopoly power over that "market." Monopoly power is the power to control prices or exclude competition. It seems apparent that du Pont's power to set the price of cellophane has been limited only by the competition afforded by other flexible packaging materials. Moreover, it may be practically impossible for anyone to commence manufacturing cellophane without full access to du Pont's technique. However, du Pont has no power to prevent competition from other wrapping materials. The trial court consequently had to determine whether competition from the other wrappings prevented du Pont from possessing monopoly power in violation of Section 2. Price and competition are so intimately entwined that any discussion of theory must treat them as one. It is inconceivable that price could be controlled without power over competition or vice versa. This approach to the determination of monopoly power is strengthened by this Court's conclusion in prior cases, that, when an alleged monopolist has power over price and competition, an intention to monopolize in a proper case may be assumed.

* * *

Determination of the competitive market for commodities depends on how different from one another are the offered commodities in character for use, how far buyers will go to substitute one commodity for another. For example, one can think of building materials as in commodity competition but one could hardly say that brick competed with steel or wood or cement or stone in the meaning of Sherman Act litigation; the products are too different. This is the interindustry competition emphasized by some economists. On the other hand, there are certain differences in the formulae for soft drinks but one can hardly say that each one is an illegal monopoly. Whatever the market may be, we hold that control of price or competition established the existence of monopoly power under Section 2.

* * *

The Government argues:

> We do not here urge that in no circumstances may competition of substitutes negative possession of monopolistic power over trade in a product. The decisions make it clear at the least that the courts will not consider substitutes other than those which are substantially fungible with the monopolized product and sell at substantially the same price.

But where there are market alternatives that buyers may readily use for their purposes, illegal monopoly does not exist merely because the product said to be monopolized differs from others. If it were not so, only physically identical products would be a part of the market. To accept the Government's argument, we would have to conclude that the manufacturers of plain as well as moisture-proof cellophane were monopolists, and so with films such as Pliofilm, foil, glassine, polyethylene, and Saran, for each of these wrapping materials is distinguishable. These were all exhibits in the case. New wrappings appear, generally similar to cellophane; is each a monopoly? What is called for is an appraisal of the "cross-elasticity" of demand in the trade. . . . The varying circumstances of each case determine the result. In considering what is the relevant market for determining the control of price and competition, no more definite rule can be declared than that commodities reasonably interchangeable by consumers for the same purposes make up that "part of the trade or commerce," monopolization of which may be illegal. As respects flexible packaging materials, the market geographically is nationwide.

Cellophane differs from other flexible packaging materials. From some it differs more than from others. The basic materials from which the wrappings are made . . . are aluminum, cellulose, acetate, chlorides, wood pulp, rubber hydrochloride, and ethylene gas. . . .

It may be admitted that cellophane combines the desirable elements of transparency, strength and cheapness more definitely than any of the others. . . .

But despite cellophane's advantages, it has to meet competition from other materials in every one of its uses. . . . Food products are the chief outlet, with cigarettes next. The Government makes no challenge to Finding 283 that cellophane furnishes less than 7 percent of wrappings for bakery products, 25 percent for candy, 32 percent for snacks, 35 percent for meats and poultry, 27 percent for crackers and biscuits, 47 percent for fresh produce, and 34 percent for frozen foods. Seventy-five to eighty percent of cigarettes are wrapped in cellophane. . . . Thus cellophane shares the packaging market with others. The over-all result is that cellophane accounts for 17.9 percent of flexible wrapping materials, measured by the wrapping surface. . . .

Moreover a very considerable degree of functional interchangeability exists between these products . . . It will be noted . . . that except as to permeability to gases, cellophane has no qualities that are not possessed by a number of other materials. Meat will do as an example of interchangeability. . . . Although du Pont's sales to the meat industry have reached 19,000,000 pounds annually, nearly 35 percent, this volume is attributed "to the rise of self-service retailing of fresh meat." . . . In fact, since the popularity of self-service meats, du Pont has lost "a considerable proportion" of this packaging business to Pliofilm. . . . Pliofilm is more expensive than cellophane, but its superior physical characteristics apparently offset cellophane's price advantage. While retailers shift continually between the two, the trial court found that Pliofilm is increasing its share of the business. . . .

An element for consideration as to cross-elasticity of demand between products is the responsiveness of the sales of one product to price changes of the other. If a slight decrease in the price of cellophane causes a considerable number of customers of other flexible wrappings to switch to cellophane, it would be an indication that a high cross-elasticity of demand exists between them; that the products compete in the same market. The court below held that the "[g]reat sensitivity of customers in the flexible packaging markets to price or quality changes" prevented du Pont from possessing monopoly control over price. . . . The record sustains these findings. . . .

We conclude that cellophane's interchangeability with the other materials mentioned suffices to make it a part of this flexible packaging market.

* * *

The "market" which one must study to determine when a producer has monopoly power will vary with the part of commerce under consideration. The tests are constant. That market is composed of products that have reasonable interchangeability for the purposes for which they are produced—price, use and qualities considered. While the application of the tests remains uncertain, it seems to us that du Pont should not be found to monopolize cellophane when that product has the competition and interchangeability with other wrappings that this record shows.

On the findings of the District Court, its judgment is affirmed.

Geographic Market A company need not dominate the worldwide market for a particular product or service to be held a monopolist. The Sherman Act speaks of "any part" of the trade or commerce—the "area of effective competition," as the Supreme Court has defined it. It may appear that the smaller the part the government can point to, the greater its chances of prevailing, since a company usually will have greater control over a single marketplace than a regional or national market. Hence, alleged monopolists usually argue for a broad geographic market, while the government tries to narrow it, by pointing to such factors as transportation costs and the degree to which consumers will shop outside the defined area. But this rule is not invariable. Sometimes the government will argue for a broad market because in any given regional or small market the defendant may face determined local competition or because the local market will sustain only one producer or supplier.

Monopoly Power

After the relevant product and geographic markets are defined, the next question is whether the defendant has sufficient power within them to constitute a monopoly. The usual test is the market share the putative monopolist enjoys, although no rigid rule or mathematical formula is possible. In *United States* v. *Aluminum Co. of America,* 148 F.2d 416 (2d Cir. 1945), Judge Learned Hand said that Alcoa's 90 percent share of the ingot market was enough to constitute a monopoly but that 64 percent would have been doubtful. In the *Cellophane* case, the Court seemed to suggest that du Pont's 75 percent share of the cellophane market would have made the company a monopoly had the relevant market been restricted to cellophane.

Monopolization: Acquiring and Maintaining a Monopoly

As noted, possessing a monopoly is not *per se* unlawful. Once a company has been found to have monopoly power in a relevant market, the final question is whether it either acquired its monopoly power in an unlawful way or has acted unlawfully to maintain it. This additional element of "deliberateness" does not mean that the government must prove that the defendant *intended* to monopolize, in the sense that what he *desired* was the complete exclusion of all competitors. It is enough to show that the monopoly would probably result from his actions, for as Judge Hand put it: "No monopolist monopolizes unconscious of what he is doing."

What constitutes proof of unlawful acquisition or maintenance of a monopoly? In general, it consists of showing that the defendant's acts were aimed at or had the probable effect of excluding competitors from the market. Violations of Section 1 or other provisions of the antitrust laws are examples. "Predatory pricing"—charging less than cost—can be evidence that the defendant's purpose was monopolistic, for small companies cannot compete with large manufacturers, which are capable of sustaining continued losses until the competition folds up and ceases operations.

In *United States* v. *Lorain Journal Company,* 342 U.S. 143 (1951), the town of Lorain, Ohio, could support only one newspaper. With a circulation of 20,000, the *Lorain Journal* reached more than 99 percent of the town's families. The *Journal* had thus lawfully become a monopoly. But when a radio station was set up, the paper found itself competing directly for local and national advertising. To retaliate, the *Journal* refused to accept advertisements unless the advertiser agreed not to advertise on the local station. The Court agreed that this was an unlawful attempt to boycott, and hence was a violation of Section 2 because the paper was using its monopoly power to exclude a competitor. (Where was the *interstate* commerce? The Court said that the radio station was in interstate commerce because it broadcast national news supported by national advertising.)

Practices that help a company acquire or maintain its monopoly position need not be unlawful in themselves. In the *Aluminum* case below, Alcoa claimed its monopoly power was the result of superior business skills and techniques, which led it constantly to build plant capacity and expand output at every opportunity. But Judge Hand thought otherwise, given that for a quarter of a century other producers could not break into the market because Alcoa acted at every turn to make it impossible for them to compete, even as Alcoa increased its output by some 800 percent. Judge Hand's explanation remains the classic exposition.

UNITED STATES v. ALUMINUM COMPANY OF AMERICA
148 F.2d 416 (2d. Cir. 1945)

JUDGE LEARNED HAND.

*   *   *

It does not follow because "Alcoa" had such a monopoly that it "monopolized" the ingot market: it may not have achieved monopoly; monopoly may have been thrust upon it. If it had been a combination of existing smelters which united the whole industry and controlled the production of all aluminum ingot, it would certainly have "monopolized" the market. . . . We may start therefore with the premise that to have combined ninety percent of the producers of ingot would have been to "monopolize" the ingot market; and, so far as concerns the public interest, it can make no difference whether an existing competition is put an end to, or whether prospective competition is prevented. . . . Nevertheless, it is unquestionably true that from the very outset the courts have at least kept in reserve the possibility that the origin of a monopoly may be critical in determining its legality; and for this they had warrant in some of the congressional debates which accompanied the passage of the Act. . . . This notion has usually been expressed by saying that size does not determine guilt; that there must be some "exclusion" of competitors; that the growth must be something else than "natural" or "normal"; that there must be a "wrongful intent," or some other specific intent; or that some "unduly" coercive means must be used. At times there has been emphasis upon the use of the active verb, "monopolize," as the judge noted in the case at bar.

. . . A market may, for example, be so limited that it is impossible to produce at all and meet the cost of production except by a plant large enough to supply the whole demand. Or there may be changes in taste or in cost which drive out all but one purveyor. A single producer may be the survivor out of a group of active competitors, merely by virtue of his superior skill, foresight, and industry. In such cases a strong argument can be made that, although, the result may expose the public to the evils of monopoly, the Act does not mean to condemn the resultant of those very forces which it is its prime object to foster: finis opus coronat. The successful competitor, having been urged to compete, must not be turned upon when he wins.

*   *   *

[As] Cardozo, J., in United States v. Swift & Co., 286 U.S. 106, p. 116, 52 S. Ct. 460, 463, 76 L.Ed. 999, . . . said, "Mere size . . . is not an offense against the Sherman Act unless magnified to the point at which it amounts to a monopoly . . . but size carries with it an opportunity for abuse that is not to be ignored when the opportunity is proved to have been utilized in the past." "Alcoa's" size was "magnified" to make it a "monopoly"; indeed, it has never been anything else; and its size not only offered it an "opportunity for abuse," but it "utilized" its size for "abuse," as can easily be shown.

It would completely misconstrue "Alcoa's" position in 1940 to hold that it was the passive beneficiary of a monopoly, following upon an involuntary elimination of competitors by automatically operative economic forces. Already in 1909, when its last lawful monopoly ended, it sought to strengthen its position by unlawful practices, and these concededly continued until 1912. In that year it had two plants in New York, at which it produced less than 42 million pounds of ingot; in 1934 it had five plants (the original two, enlarged; one in Tennessee; one in North Carolina; one in Washington), and its production had risen to about 327 million pounds, an increase of almost eight-fold. Meanwhile not a pound of ingot had been produced by anyone else in the United States. This increase and this continued and undisturbed control did not fall undesigned into "Alcoa's" lap; obviously it could not have done so. It could only have resulted, as it did result, from a persistent determination to maintain the control, with which it found itself vested in 1912. There were at least one or two abortive attempts to enter the industry, but "Alcoa" effectively anticipated and forestalled all competition, and succeeded in holding the field alone. True, it stimulated demand and opened new uses for the metal, but not without making sure that it could supply what it had evoked. There is no dispute as to this; "Alcoa" avows it as evidence of the skill, energy and initiative with which it has always conducted its business: as a reason why, having won its way by fair means, it should be commended, and not dismembered. We need charge it with no moral derelictions after 1912; we may assume that all its claims for itself is true. The only question is whether it falls within the exception established in favor of those who do not seek, but cannot avoid, the control of a market. It seems to us that that question scarcely survives its statement. It was not inevitable that it should always anticipate increases in the demand for ingot and be prepared to supply them. Nothing compelled it to keep doubling and redoubling its capacity before others entered the field. It insists that it never excluded competitors; but we can think of no more effective exclusion than progressively to embrace each new opportunity as it opened, and to face every newcomer with new capacity already geared into a great organization, having the advantage of experience, trade connections and the elite of personnel. Only in case we interpret "exclusion" as limited to manoeuvres not honestly industrial, but actuated solely by a desire to prevent competition, can such a course, indefatigably pursued, be deemed not "exclusionary." So to limit it would in our judgment emasculate the Act; would permit just such consolidations as it was designed to prevent.

*   *   *

We disregard any question of "intent." Relatively early in the history of the Act—1905—Holmes, J., in Swift & Co. v. United States, explained this aspect of the Act in a passage often quoted. Although the primary evil was monopoly, the Act also covered preliminary steps, which, if continued, would lead to it. These may do no harm of themselves; but if they are initial moves in a plan or scheme which, carried out, will result in monopoly, they are dangerous and the law will nip them in the bud. . . . In order to fall within § 2, the monopolist must have both the power to monopolize, and the intent to monopolize. To read the passage as demanding any "specific" intent, makes nonsense of it, for no monopolist monopolizes unconscious of what he is doing. So here, "Alcoa" meant to keep, and did keep, that complete and exclusive hold upon the ingot market with which it started. That was to "monopolize" that market, however innocently it otherwise proceeded. So far as the judgment held that it was not within § 2, it must be reversed.

Innovation as Evidence of Intent to Monopolize During the 1970s, several monopolization cases seeking huge damages were filed against a number of well-known companies, including Xerox, IBM, and Eastman Kodak. In particular, IBM was hit with several suits as an outgrowth of the Justice Department's lawsuit against the computer maker. (*United States* v. *IBM* was filed in 1969 and did not terminate until 1982, when the government agreed to drop all charges, a complete victory for the company.) The plaintiffs in many of these suits—SCM Corporation against Xerox, California Computer Products Incorporated against IBM (the *Calcomp* case), Berkey Photo Incorporated against Kodak—charged that the defendants had maintained their alleged monopolies by strategically introducing key product innovations that rendered competitive products obsolete. For example, hundreds of computer companies manufacture peripheral equipment "plug-compatible" with IBM computers. Likewise, Berkey manufactured film usable in Kodak cameras. When the underlying products are changed—mainframe computers, new types of cameras—the existing manufacturers are left with unusable inventory and face a considerable time lag in designing new peripheral equipment. In some of these cases, the plaintiffs managed to obtain sizable treble damage awards—SCM won more than $110 million, IBM initially lost one case in the amount of $260 million, and Berkey bested Kodak to the tune of $87 million. Had these cases been sustained on appeal, a radical new doctrine would have been imported into the antitrust laws: that innovation for the sake of competing is unlawful.

As it happened, however, none of these cases withstood appellate scrutiny, though to date the Supreme Court has refused to hear appeals in any of the major cases, so the law has emerged entirely from decisions of the federal courts of appeals. Thus, in *ILC Peripherals Leasing Corp.* v. *International Business Machines* (the *Memorex* case), 458 F.Supp. 423 (N.D. Cal. 1978), Memorex argued that, among other things, IBM's tactic of introducing a new generation of computer technology at lower prices constituted monopolization. The court disagreed, noting that other companies could "reverse engineer" IBM equipment much more cheaply than IBM could originally design it and that IBM computers and related products were subject to intense competition to the benefit of plug-compatible equipment users. IBM's actions undoubtedly hurt Memorex, but they were part and parcel of the competitive system, the very essence of competition. "This kind of conduct by IBM," the court said, "is precisely what the antitrust laws were meant to encourage. . . . Memorex sought to use the antitrust laws to make time stand still and preserve its very profitable position. This court will not assist it and the others who would follow after in this endeavor."

The various strands of the innovation debate are perhaps best summed up in the *Berkey* case as follows.

BERKEY PHOTO, INC. v. EASTMAN KODAK COMPANY
603 F.2d 263 (2d. Cir. 1979)

IRVING R. KAUFMAN, CHIEF JUDGE. To millions of Americans, the name Kodak is virtually synonymous with photography. . . . It is one of the giants of American enterprise, with international sales of nearly $6 billion in 1977 and pre-tax profits in excess of $1.2 billion.

This action, one of the largest and most significant private antitrust suits in history, was brought by Berkey Photo, Inc., a far smaller but still prominent participant in the industry. Berkey competes with Kodak in providing photofinishing services—the conversion of exposed film into finished prints, slides, or movies. Until 1978, Berkey sold cameras as well. It does not manufacture film, but it does purchase Kodak film for resale to its customers, and it also buys photofinishing equipment and supplies, including color print paper, from Kodak.

The two firms thus stand in a complex, multifaceted relationship, for Kodak has been Berkey's competitor in some markets and its supplier in others. In this action, Berkey claims that every aspect of the association has been infected by Kodak's monopoly power in the film, color print paper, and camera markets, willfully acquired, maintained, and exercised in violation of § 2 of the Sherman Act, 15 U.S.C. § 2. . . . Berkey alleges that these violations caused it to lose sales in the camera and photofinishing markets and to pay excessive prices to Kodak for film, color print paper, and photofinishing equipment.

* * *

. . . [T]he jury found for Berkey on virtually every point, awarding damages totalling $37,620,130. Judge Frankel upheld verdicts aggregating $27,154,700 for lost camera and photofinishing sales and for excessive prices on film and photofinishing equipment. . . . Trebled and supplemented by attorneys' fees and costs pursuant to § 4 of the Clayton Act, 15 U.S.C. § 15, Berkey's judgment reached a grand total of $87,091,309.47, with interest, of course, continuing to accrue.

Kodak now appeals this judgment.

* * *

The principal markets relevant here, each nationwide in scope, are amateur conventional still cameras, conventional photographic film, photofinishing services, photofinishing equipment, and color print paper.

* * *

The "amateur conventional still camera" market now consists almost entirely of the so-called 110 and 126 instant-loading cameras. These are the direct descendants of the popular "box" cameras, the best-known of which was Kodak's so-called "Brownie." Small, simple, and relatively inexpensive, cameras of this type are designed for the mass market rather than for the serious photographer.

Kodak has long been the dominant firm in the market thus defined. Between 1954 and 1973 it never enjoyed less than 61% of the annual unit sales, nor less than 64% of the dollar volume, and in the peak year of 1964, Kodak cameras accounted for 90% of market revenues. Much of this success is no doubt due to the firm's history of innovation.

* * *

Berkey has been a camera manufacturer since its 1966 acquisition of the Keystone Camera Company, a producer of movie cameras and equipment. In 1968 Berkey began to sell amateur still cameras made by other firms, and the following year the Keystone Division commenced manufacturing such cameras itself. From 1970 to 1977, Berkey accounted for 8.2% of the sales in the camera market in the United States, reaching a peak of 10.2% in 1976. In 1978, Berkey sold its camera division and thus abandoned this market.

* * *

Despite the generally recognized evils of monopoly power, it is "well settled," that § 2 does not prohibit monopoly *simpliciter*—or, as the Supreme Court phrased it in the early landmark case of *Standard Oil Co. of New Jersey,* 221 U.S. at 62, 31 S.Ct. 502, "monopoly in the concrete."

Thus, while proclaiming vigorously that monopoly power is the evil at which § 2 is aimed, courts have declined to take what would have appeared to be the next logical step—declaring monopolies unlawful *per se* unless specifically authorized by law. To understand the reason for this, one must comprehend the fundamental tension—one might almost say the paradox—that is near the heart of § 2. . . .

The conundrum was indicated in characteristically striking pose by Judge Hand, who was not able to resolve it. Having stated that Congress "did not condone 'good trusts' and condemn 'bad' ones; it forbad all," he declared with equal force. "The successful competitor, having been urged to compete, must not be turned upon when he wins." . . . We must always be mindful lest the Sherman Act be invoked perversely in favor of those who seek protection against the rigors of competition.

* * *

In sum, although the principles announced by the § 2 cases often appear to conflict, this much is clear. The mere possession of monopoly power does not *ipso facto* condemn a market participant. But, to avoid the proscriptions of § 2, the firm must refrain at all times from conduct directed at smothering competition. This doctrine has two branches. Unlawfully acquired power remains anathema even when kept dormant. And it is no less true that a firm with a legitimately achieved monopoly may not wield the resulting power to tighten its hold on the market.

* * *

As Kodak had hoped, the 110 system proved to be a dramatic success. In 1972—the system's first year—the company sold 2,984,000 Pocket Instamatics, more than 50% of its sales in the amateur conventional still camera market. The new camera thus accounted in large part for a sharp increase in total market sales, from 6.2 million units in 1971 to 8.2 million in 1972. . . .

Berkey's Keystone division was a late entrant in the 110 sweepstakes, joining the competition only in late 1973. Moreover, because of hasty design, the original models suffered from latent defects, and sales that year were a paltry 42,000. With interest in the 126 dwindling, Keystone thus suffered a net decline of 118,000 unit sales in 1973. The following year, however, it recovered strongly, in large part because improvements in its pocket cameras helped it sell 406,000 units, 7% of all 110s sold that year.

Berkey contends that the introduction of the 110 system was both an attempt to monopolize and actual monopolization of the camera market.

* * *

It will be useful at the outset to present the arguments on which Berkey asks us to uphold its verdict:

Kodak, a film and camera monopolist, was in a position to set industry standards. Rivals could not compete effectively without offering products similar to Kodak's. Moreover, Kodak persistently refused to make film available for most formats other than those in which it made cameras. Since cameras are worthless without film, this policy effectively prevented other manufacturers from introducing cameras in new formats. Because of its dominant position astride two markets, and by use of its film monopoly to distort the camera market, Kodak forfeited its own right to reap profits from such innovations without providing its rivals with sufficient advance information to enable them to enter the market with copies of the new product on the day of Kodak's introduction. This is one of several "predisclosure" arguments Berkey has advanced in the course of this litigation.

* * *

Through the 1960s, Kodak followed a checkered pattern of predisclosing innovations to various segments of the industry. Its purpose on these occasions evidently was to ensure that the industry would be able to meet consumers' demand for the complementary goods and services they would need to enjoy the new Kodak products. But predisclosure would quite obviously also diminish Kodak's share of the auxiliary markets. It was therefore, in the words of Walter Fallon, Kodak's chief executive officer, "a matter of judgment on each and every occasion" whether predisclosure would be for or against Kodak's self-interest.

* * *

. . . Kodak decided not to release advance information about the new film and format. The decision was evidently based on the perception of Dr. Louis K. Eilers, Kodak's chief executive officer at that time, that Kodak would gain more from being first on the market for the sale of all goods and services related to the 110 system than it would lose from the inability of other photofinishers to process Kodacolor II.

* * *

Judge Frankel did not decide that Kodak should have disclosed the details of the 110 to other camera manufacturers prior to introduction. Instead, he left the matter to the jury. . . . We hold that this instruction was error and that, as a matter of law, Kodak did not have a duty to predisclose information about the 110 system to competing camera manufacturers.

As Judge Frankel indicated, and as Berkey concedes, a firm may normally keep its innovations secret from its rivals as long as it wishes, forcing them to catch up on the strength of their own efforts after the new product is introduced. It is the possibility of success in the marketplace, attributable to superior performance, that provides the incentives on which the proper functioning of our competitive economy rests. . . .

Withholding from others advance knowledge of one's new products, therefore, ordinarily constitutes valid competitive conduct. Because, as we have already indicated, a monopolist is permitted, and indeed encouraged, by § 2 to compete aggressively on the merits, any success that it may achieve through "the process of invention and innovation" is clearly tolerated by the antitrust laws.

* * *

Moreover, enforced predisclosure would cause undesirable consequences beyond merely encouraging the sluggishness the Sherman Act was designed to prevent. A significant vice of the theory propounded by Berkey lies in the uncertainty of its application. Berkey does not contend, in the colorful phrase of Judge Frankel, that "Kodak has to live in a goldfish bowl," disclosing every innovation to the world at large. However predictable in its application, such an extreme rule would be insupportable. Rather, Berkey postulates that Kodak had a duty to disclose limited types of information to certain competitors under specific circumstances. But it is difficult to comprehend how a major corporation, accustomed though it is to making business decisions with antitrust considerations in mind, could possess the omniscience to anticipate all the instances in which a jury might one day in the future retrospectively conclude that predisclosure was warranted. And it is equally difficult to discern workable guidelines that a court might set forth to aid the firm's decision. For example, how detailed must the information conveyed be? And how far must research have progressed before it is "ripe" for disclosure? These inherent uncertainties would have an inevitable chilling effect on innovation. They go far, we believe, towards explaining why no court has ever imposed the duty Berkey seeks to create here.

* * *

We do not perceive, however, how Kodak's introduction of a new format was rendered an unlawful act of monopolization in the camera market because the firm also manufactured film to fit the cameras. The 110 system was in substantial part a camera development. . . .

Clearly, then, the policy considerations militating against predisclosure requirements for monolithic monopolists are equally applicable here. The first firm, even a monopolist, to design a new camera format has a right to the lead time that follows from its success. The mere fact that Kodak manufactured film in the new format as well, so that its customers would not be offered worthless cameras, could not deprive it of that reward. Nor is this conclusion altered because Kodak not only participated in but dominated the film market. Kodak's ability to pioneer formats does not depend on it possessing a film monopoly. Had the firm possessed a much smaller share of the film market, it would nevertheless have been able to manufacture sufficient quantities of 110-size film—either Kodacolor X or Kodacolor II—to bring the new camera to market. It is apparent, therefore, that the ability to introduce the new format without predisclosure was solely a benefit of integration and not, without more, a use of Kodak's power in the film market to gain a competitive advantage in cameras.

* * *

Conclusion. We have held that Kodak did not have an obligation, merely because it introduced film and camera in a new format, to make any predisclosure to its camera-making competitors. Nor did the earlier use of its film monopoly to foreclose format innovation by those competitors create of its own force such a duty where none had existed before. In awarding Berkey $15,250,000, just $828,000 short of the maximum amount demanded, the jury clearly based its calculation of lost camera profits on Berkey's central argument that it had a right to be "at the starting line when the whistle blew" for the new system. The verdict, therefore, cannot stand.

* * *

Attempts to Monopolize

Section 2 prohibits not only actual monopolization but also attempts to monopolize. An attempt need not succeed to be unlawful; a defendant who tries to exercise sway over a relevant market can take no legal comfort from failure. Of course, some people attempt the impossible, and a new company with virtually no market share can scarcely be accused of attempting to monopolize simply because it adopts market practices that would be unlawful in the hands of a company with a huge market share. In any event, the plaintiff must show a specific intent to monopolize, not merely an intent to commit the act or acts that constitute the attempt.

Remedies

Since many of the defendant's acts that constitute Section 2 monopolizing are also violations of Section 1 or of the Clayton Act, why should plaintiffs resort to Section 2 at all? What practical difference does Section 2 make? One answer is that not every act of monopolizing is a violation of another law. Leasing and pricing practices that are perfectly lawful for an ordinary competitor may be unlawful only because of Section 2. But the more important reason is the remedy provided by the Sherman Act: **divestiture.** In the right case, the courts may order the company broken up.

In the *Standard Oil* decision of 1911 (see p. 531), the Supreme Court held that the Standard Oil Company constituted a monopoly and ordered it split apart into separate companies. Several other trusts were similarly dealt with. In many of the early cases, doing so posed no insuperable difficulties, because the companies themselves essentially consisted of separate manufacturing plants knit together by financial controls. But not every company is a loose confederation of potentially separate operating companies.

The *Alcoa* case (p. 570) was fraught with difficult remedial issues. Judge Hand's opinion came down in 1945, but the remedial side of the case did not come up until 1950. By then the industry had changed radically, with the entrance of Reynolds and Kaiser as effective competitors, reducing Alcoa's share of the market to 50 percent. Because any aluminum producer needs considerable resources to succeed and because aluminum production is crucial to national security, the later court refused to order the company broken apart. The court ordered Alcoa to take a series of measures that would boost competition in the industry—for example, Alcoa stockholders had to divest themselves of the stock of a closely related Canadian producer in order to remove Alcoa's control of that company; and the court rendered unenforceable a patent-licensing agreement with Reynolds and Kaiser that required them to share their inventions with Alcoa, even though neither the Canadian tie nor the patent agreements were in themselves unlawful.

Although the trend has been away from breaking up the monopolist, it is still employed as a potent remedy. In perhaps the largest monopolization case ever brought—*United States* v. *American Telephone & Telegraph Company*—the government sought divestiture of several of AT&T's constituent companies, including Western Electric and the various local operating companies. To avoid prolonged litigation, AT&T agreed in 1982 to a consent decree that required it to spin off all its operating companies, companies which had been central to AT&T's decades-long monopoly.

Acquisitions and Mergers under Section 7 of the Clayton Act

Neither Section 1 nor Section 2 of the Sherman Act proved particularly apt in barring mergers between companies or acquisition by one company of another. As originally written, neither did the Clayton Act, which prohibited only mergers accomplished through the sale of stock, not mergers or acquisitions carried out through acquisition of assets. In 1950 Congress amended the Clayton Act to cover the loophole concerning acquisition of assets. It also narrowed the search for relevant market; henceforth, if competition might be lessened *in any line of commerce in any section of the country,* the merger is unlawful.

As amended, the pertinent part of Section 7 of the Clayton Act read as follows:

> [N]o corporation engaged in commerce shall acquire, directly or indirectly, the whole or any part of the stock or other share capital and no corporation subject to the jurisdiction of the Federal Trade Commission shall acquire the whole or any part of the assets of another corporation engaged also in commerce,

where in any line of commerce in any section of the country, the effect of such acquisition may be substantially to lessen competition, or to tend to create a monopoly.

No corporation shall acquire, directly or indirectly, the whole or any part of the stock or other share capital and no corporation subject to the jurisdiction of the Federal Trade Commission shall acquire the whole or any part of the assets of one or more corporations engaged in commerce, where in any line of commerce in any section of the country, the effect of such acquisition, of such stock or assets, or of the use of such stock by the voting or granting of proxies or otherwise, may be substantially to lessen competition, or to tend to create a monopoly.

Definitions

Mergers and acquisitions—for the sake of brevity, we will refer to both throughout the rest of this chapter as mergers—are usually classified into three types: *horizontal, vertical,* and *conglomerate.*

Horizontal Mergers A horizontal merger is one between competitors—for example, between two bread manufacturers or two grocery chains competing in the same locale.

Vertical Mergers A vertical merger is that of a supplier and customer. If the customer acquires the supplier, it is known as **backward vertical integration**; if the supplier acquires the customer, it is **forward vertical integration.** For example, a book publisher that buys a paper manufacturer has engaged in backward vertical integration. Its purchase of a bookstore chain would be forward vertical integration.

Conglomerate Mergers Conglomerate mergers do not have a standard definition, but generally are taken to be mergers between companies whose businesses are not directly related. Many commentators have subdivided this category into three types. In a "**pure**" conglomerate merger, the businesses are not related—as when a steel manufacturer acquires a movie distributor. In a **product-extension merger**, the manufacturer of one product acquires the manufacturer of a related product—for instance, a producer of household cleansers, but not of liquid bleach, acquires a producer of liquid bleach. In a **market-extension merger**, a company in one geographic market acquires a company in the same business in a different location—as when a bakery operating only in San Francisco buys a bakery operating only in Palo Alto. Since they had not competed, this would not be a horizontal merger.

General Principles

As in monopolization cases, a relevant product and geographic market must first be marked out to test the effect of the merger. But Section 7 has a market definition different from that of Section 2. Section 7 speaks of "*any line* of commerce in any *section* of the country" (emphasis added). And its test for the effect of the merger is the same as that we have already seen for exclusive dealing cases governed by Section 3: "may be substantially to lessen competition or to tend to create a monopoly." Taken together, this language makes it easier to condemn an unlawful merger than an unlawful monopoly. The relevant product market is any *line* of commerce, and the courts have taken this language to permit the plaintiff to prove the existence of "submarkets" in which the relative effect of the merger is greater. The relevant geographic market is any *section of the country,* which means that the plaintiff can show the appropriate effect in a city or a particular region and not worry about having to show the effect in a national market. Moreover, as we have seen, the effect is one of probability, not actuality. *Might* competition be substantially lessened?—not: Was it in fact substantially lessened? Or, did the merger *tend* to create a monopoly?—not: Did it in fact create one?

In *United States* v. *du Pont,* 353 U.S. 586 (1957), the government charged that du Pont's "commanding position as General Motors' supplier of automotive finishes and fabrics" was not achieved on competitive merit alone but because du Pont had acquired a sizable block of GM stock, and the "consequent close intercompany relationship led to the insulation of most of the General Motors' market from free competition," in violation of Section 7. Between 1917 and 1919, du Pont took a 23 percent stock interest in GM. The district court dismissed the complaint, partly on the grounds that at least before the 1950 amendment to Section 7, the Clayton Act did not condemn vertical mergers and partly on the grounds that du Pont had not dominated GM's decision to purchase millions of dollars' worth of automotive finishes and fabrics. The Supreme Court disagreed and sent the case back to trial. The Court specifically held that even though the stock acquisition had occurred some thirty-five years earlier, the government can resort to Section 7 whenever it appears that the result of the acquisition will violate the competitive tests set forth in the section.

Defining the Market In the seminal *Brown Shoe* case, 380 U.S. 294 (1962), the Supreme Court said that the outer boundaries of broad markets "are determined by the reasonable interchangeability of use or the cross-elasticity of demand between the product itself and substitutes for it" but that narrower "well defined submarkets" might also be appropriate lines of commerce. In drawing market boundaries, the Court said, courts should realistically reflect "[c]ompetition where, in fact, it exists." Among the factors to consider are "industry or public recognition of the submarket as a separate economic entity, the product's peculiar characteristics and uses, unique production facilities, distinct customers, distinct prices, sensitivity to price changes and specialized vendors." To select the geographic market, the court must consider both "the commercial realities" of the industry and the economic significance of the market.

The "Failing Company" Doctrine One defense to a Section 7 case is that one of the merging companies is "failing." In *Citizen Publishing Company* v. *United States,* 394 U.S. 131 (1969), the Supreme Court said that the defense is applicable if two conditions are satisfied. First, a company must be staring bankruptcy in the face; it must have virtually no chance of being resuscitated without the merger. Second, the acquiring company must be the only available purchaser, and the failing company must have made bona fide efforts to search for another purchaser.

Beneficial Effects That a merger might produce beneficial effects is not a defense to a Section 7 case. As the Supreme Court said in *United States* v. *Philadelphia National Bank,* 374 U.S. 321, 371 (1963): "[A] merger, the effect of which 'may be substantially to lessen competition' is not saved because, on some ultimate reckoning of social or economic debits or credits, it may be deemed beneficial." And in *FTC* v. *Procter & Gamble Company,* 386 U.S. 568, 580 (1967), the Court said: "Possible economies cannot be used as a defense to illegality. Congress was also aware that some mergers which lessen competition may also result in economies but it struck the balance in favor of protecting competition."

Tests of Competitive Effect

Horizontal Mergers Three factors are critical in assessing whether a horizontal merger may substantially lessen competition: the (1) market shares of the merging companies, (2) concentration ratios, and (3) trends in the industry toward concentration.

The first factor is self-evident. A company with 10 percent or even 5 percent of the market is in a different position from one with less than 1 percent. A **concentration ratio** refers to the number of firms that constitute an industry. An industry with only four firms is obviously much more concentrated than one with ten or seventy firms. **Concentration trends** refer to the frequency with which firms in the relevant market have been merging. The first merger in an industry with a low concentration ratio might be predicted to have no likely effect on competition, but a merger of two firms in a four-firm industry would obviously have a pronounced effect.

In the *Philadelphia Bank* case just quoted, the Court announced this test of legality in assessing the legality of a horizontal merger. "[A] merger which produces a firm controlling an undue percentage share of the relevant market, and results in a significant increase in the concentration of firms in that market is so inherently likely to lessen competition substantially that it must be enjoined in the absence of evidence clearly showing that the merger is not likely to have such anticompetitive effects." In this case, the merger led to a 30 percent share of the commercial banking market in a four-county region around Philadelphia and an increase in concentration by more than one-third, and the Court held that those numbers amounted to a violation of Section 7. The Court also said in *Philadelphia Bank* that "if concentration is already great, the importance of preventing even slight increases in concentration and so preserving the possibility of eventual deconcentration is correspondingly great."

In 1976, Congress enacted the Hart-Scott-Rodino Antitrust Improvements Act. Among other things, that law requires certain companies to notify the Justice Department before actually completing mergers or acquisitions, whether by private negotiation or by public tender offer. When one of the companies has sales or assets of $100 million or more and the other company $10 million or more, pre-merger notification must be provided at least thirty days prior to completion of the deal—or fifteen days in the case of a tender offer of cash for publicly traded shares—if the resulting merger would give the acquiring company $50 million worth or 15 percent of assets or voting securities in the acquired company. The rules are complex, but they are designed to give the department time to react to a merger before it has been secretly accomplished and then announced. The 1976 act gives the department the authority to seek an injunction against the completion of any such merger, which of course greatly simplifies the remedial phase of the case should the courts ultimately hold that the merger would be unlawful. (Note: Section 7 is one of the "tools" in the kit of the lawyer who defends companies against unwelcomed takeover attempts: if the target company can point to lines of its business in which it competes with the acquiring company, it can threaten antitrust action in order to block the merger.)

Vertical Mergers To prove a Section 7 case involving a vertical merger, the plaintiff must show that the merger forecloses competition "in a substantial share of" a substantial market. But statistical factors alone do not govern in a vertical merger. Thus in *Ford Motor Co.* v. *United States,* 405 U.S. 562 (1972), the merger between Ford and Autolite, a manufacturer of spark plugs, was held unlawful because it eliminated Ford's potential entry into the market as an independent manufacturer of spark plugs and because it foreclosed Ford "as a purchaser of about ten percent of total industry output" of spark plugs. This decision underscores the principle that a company may serve to enhance competition simply by waiting in the wings as a potential entrant to a market. If other companies feel threatened by a company the size of Ford undertaking to compete where it had not done so before, the existing manufacturers will likely keep their prices low so as not to tempt the giant in. Of course, had Ford entered the market on its own by independently manufacturing spark plugs, it might ultimately have caused weak competitors to fold. As the Court said: "Had Ford taken the internal-expansion route, there would have been no illegality; not, however, because the result necessarily would have been commendable, but simply because that course has not been proscribed."

Conglomerate Mergers Recall the definition of a conglomerate merger (p. 582). None of the three types listed has a direct impact on competition, so the test for illegality is more difficult to state and apply than for horizontal or vertical mergers. But they are nonetheless within the reach of Section 7. In the late 1960s and early 1970s, the government filed a number of divestiture suits against conglomerate mergers. It did not win them all, and none reached the Supreme Court; most were settled by consent decree, leading in several instances to divestiture either of the acquired company or another division of the acquiring company. Thus International Telephone & Telegraph Company agreed to divest itself of Canteen Corporation and either of the following two groups: (1) Avis, Levitt & Sons, and Hamilton Life Insurance Company or (2) Hartford Fire Insurance Company. Ling-Temco-Vought agreed to divest itself of either Jones & Laughlin Steel or Braniff Airways and Okinite Corporation. In these and other cases, the courts have looked to specific potential effects, such as raising the barriers to entry into a market and eliminating potential competition, but they have rejected the more general claim of "the rising tide of economic concentration in American industry."

Entrenching oligopoly One way to attack conglomerate mergers is to demonstrate that by taking over a dominant company in an oligopolistic industry, a large and strong acquiring company will further entrench the oligopoly. In *FTC* v. *Procter & Gamble Co.,* 386 U.S. 568 (1967), the government challenged P & G's acquisition of Clorox. P & G was the leading seller of household cleansers, with annual sales of more than $1 billion. In addition, it was the "nation's largest advertiser," promoting its products so heavily that it was able to take advantage of substantial advertising discounts from the media. Clorox had more than 48 percent of national sales for liquid bleach in a heavily concentrated industry. Since all liquid bleach is chemically identical, advertising and promotion plays the dominant role in selling the product. P & G did not make or sell liquid bleach prior to the merger—hence it was a "product-extension" merger rather than a horizontal one.

The Court concluded that smaller firms would fear retaliation from P & G if they tried to compete in the liquid bleach market and that "a new entrant would be much more reluctant to face the giant Procter than it would have been to face the smaller Clorox." Hence, "the substitution of the powerful acquiring firm for the smaller, but already dominant firm may substantially reduce the competitive structure of the industry by raising entry barriers and by dissuading the smaller firms from aggressively competing." The entrenchment theory probably applies only to highly concentrated industries and dominant firms, however. Many subsequent cases have come out in favor of the defendants on a variety of grounds—that the merger led simply to a more efficient acquired firm, that the existing competitors were strong and able to compete, or even that the acquiring firm merely gives the acquired company a "deep pocket" the better to finance its operations.

Eliminating potential competition This theory holds that but for the merger the acquiring company might have competed in the acquired company's market. In *Procter & Gamble,* for example, P & G might have entered the liquid bleach market itself, and thus given Clorox a "run for its money." An additional strong company would then have been in the market. When P & G bought Clorox, however, it foreclosed that possibility. This theory depends on proof of some probability that the acquiring company would have entered the market. When the acquired company is small, however, a Section 7 violation is unlikely; these so-called "toe-hold" mergers permit the acquiring company to become a competitive force in an industry without necessarily sacrificing any pre-existing competition.

Reciprocity Many companies are both heavy buyers and sellers of products. A company may buy from its customers as well as sell to them. This practice is known in antitrust jargon as **reciprocity.** Reciprocity means the practice of a seller who uses his volume of purchases from the buyer to induce the buyer to purchase from the seller. The clearest example arose in *FTC* v. *Consolidated Foods Corp.*, 380 U.S. 592 (1965). Consolidated owned wholesale grocery outlets and retail food stores. Gentry made dehydrated onions and garlic. The Court agreed that the merger of these companies violated Section 7 because of the possibility of reciprocity: Consolidated made bulk purchases from several food processors, which were purchasers of dehydrated onions and garlic from Gentry and others. Processors who did not buy from Gentry might feel pressured to do so in order to keep Consolidated as a customer for their food supplies. If so, other onion and garlic manufacturers would be foreclosed from competing for sales. A merger that raises the mere possibility of reciprocity is not *per se* unlawful, however. The plaintiff must demonstrate that it was probable the acquiring company would adopt the practice—for example, by conditioning future orders for supplies on the receipt of orders for onions and garlic—and that doing so would have an anticompetitive effect given the size of the reciprocating companies and their positions in the market.

Joint Ventures Section 7 can also apply to joint ventures, a rule first announced in 1964. Two companies, Hooker and American Potash, dominated sales of sodium chlorate in the southeast, with 90 percent of the market. Pennsalt Chemicals Corporation produced the rest in the west and sold it in the southeast through Olin-Mathieson Chemical Corporation. The latter two decided to team up, the better to compete with the giants, and so they formed Penn-Olin, which they jointly owned. The district court dismissed the government's suit, but the Supreme Court reinstated it, saying that a joint venture can serve to blunt competition, or at least potential competition, between the parent companies. The Court said that the lower court must look to a number of criteria to determine whether the joint venture was likely to lessen competition substantially. These factors include:

> The number and power of the competitors in the relevant market; the background of their growth; the power of the joint venturers; the relationship of their lines of commerce; competition existing between them and the power of each in dealing with the competitors of the other; the setting in which the joint venture was created; the reasons and necessities for its existence; the joint venture's line of commerce and the relationship thereof to that of its parents; the adaptability of its line of commerce to non-competitive practices; the potential power of the joint venture in the relevant market; and appraisal of what the competition in the relevant market would have been if one of the joint venturers had entered it alone instead of through Penn-Olin; the effect, in the event of this occurrence, of the other joint venturer's potential competition; and such other factors as might indicate potential risk to competition in the relevant market. [United States v. Penn-Olin Chemical Co., 378 U.S. 158 (1964)]

These numerous factors illustrate how the entire economic environment surrounding the joint venture—and mergers in general—must be assessed to determine the legalities.

Chapter Summary

Section 2 of the Sherman Act prohibits monopolizing or attempting to monopolize any part of interstate or foreign trade or commerce. The law does not forbid monopoly as such, but acts or attempts or conspiracies to monopolize. The prohibition includes the monopolist who has acquired his monopoly through illegitimate means.

Three factors are essential in a Section 2 case: (1) relevant market for determining dominance, (2) the degree of monopoly power, and (3) the particular acts claimed to be illegitimate.

Relevant market has two dimensions: product and geographic. Since many goods have close substitutes, the courts look to the degree to which consumers will shift to other goods or suppliers if the price of the commodity or service in question is priced monopolistically. This test is known as cross-elasticity of demand. If the cross-elasticity is high—meaning that consumers will readily shift—then the other goods or services must be included in the product market definition, thus reducing the share of the market that the defendant will be found to have. The geographic market is not the country as a whole, because Section 2 speaks in terms of "any part" of trade or commerce. Usually the government or private plaintiff will try to show that the geographic market is small, since that will tend to give the alleged monopolist a larger share of it.

Market power in general means the share of the relevant market that the alleged monopolist enjoys. The law does not lay down fixed percentages, but various decisions seem to suggest that two-thirds of a market might be too low but three-quarters high enough to constitute monopoly power.

Acts that were aimed at or had the probable effect of excluding competitors from the market are acts of monopolizing. Examples are predatory pricing and boycotts. Despite repeated claims during the 1970s and 1980s by smaller competitors, large companies have prevailed in court against the argument that innovations suddenly sprung on the market without notice are *per se* evidence of intent to monopolize.

Remedies for Section 2 violations include damages, injunction, and divestiture. These remedies are also available in Clayton Act Section 7 cases.

Section 7 prohibits mergers or acquisitions that might tend to lessen competition in any line of commerce in any section of the country. Mergers and acquisitions are usually classified in one of three ways: horizontal (between competitors), vertical (between different levels of the distribution chain), or conglomerate (between businesses that are not directly related). The latter may be divided into product-extension and market-extension mergers. The relevant market test is different than in monopolization cases; in a Section 7 action, a relevant submarket may be proved.

In assessing horizontal mergers, the courts will look to the market shares of the merging companies, industry concentration ratios, and trends toward concentration in the industry. To prove a Section 7 vertical merger case, the plaintiff must show that the merger forecloses competition "in a substantial share of" a substantial market. Conglomerate merger cases are harder to prove, and require a showing of specific potential effects, such as raising barriers to entry into an industry, thus entrenching monopoly, or eliminating potential competition. Joint ventures may also be condemned by Section 7. The Antitrust Improvements Act of 1976 requires certain companies to give pre-merger notice to the Justice Department.

Problems

1. National Widget Company is the dominant manufacturer of widgets in the United States, with 72 percent of the market for low-priced widgets, and 89 percent of the market for high-priced widgets. Dozens of companies compete with National in the manufacture and sale of compatible peripheral equipment for use with National's widgets, including countertops, holders, sprockets and gear assemblies, instruction booklets, computer software, and several hundred replacements parts. Revenues of these peripherals run upwards of $100 million annually. Beginning with the 1981 model year, National Widget sprang a surprise: a completely redesigned widget that made most of the peripheral equipment obsolete. Moreover, National set the price for its peripherals below that which would make economic sense for competitors to invest in new plants to tool up for producing redesigned peripherals.

Five of the largest peripheral-equipment competitors sued National under Section 2 of the Sherman Act. One of these, American Widget Peripherals Inc., had an additional complaint: on making inquiries in early 1980, National's general manager assured American that it would not be redesigning any widgets until late 1985 at the earliest. On the basis of this statement, American invested $50 million in a new plant to manufacture the now obsolescent peripheral equipment and as a result will probably be forced into bankruptcy. What result? Why?

2. In 1959, The Aluminum Company of America (Alcoa) acquired the stock and assets of the Rome Cable Corporation. Alcoa and Rome both manufactured bare and insulated aluminum wire and cable, used for overhead electric power transmission lines. Rome, but not Alcoa, manufactured copper conductor, used for underground transmissions. Insulated aluminum wire and cable is quite inferior to copper, but it can be used effectively in overhead transmission, and Alcoa increased its share of annual installations from 6.5 percent in 1950 to 77.2 percent in 1959. During that time copper lost out to aluminum for overhead transmission. Aluminum and copper conductor prices do not respond to one another.

   In 1958—the year prior to the merger—Alcoa was the leading producer of aluminum conductor, with 27.8% of the market; in bare aluminum conductor, it also led the industry with 32.5%. Alcoa plus Kaiser controlled 50% of the aluminum conductor market and, with its three leading competitors, more than 76%. Only nine concerns (including Rome with 1.3%) accounted for 95.7% of the output of aluminum conductor, Alcoa was third with 11.6% and Rome was eighth with 4.7%. Five companies controlled 65.4% and four smaller ones, including Rome, added another 22.8%.

   The Justice Department sued Alcoa-Rome for violation of Section 7 of the Clayton Act. What is the government's argument? What result?

3. Quality GraPhics has been buying up the stock of companies that manufacture billboards. Quality now owns or controls 23 of the 129 companies that make billboards, and their sales account for 3.2 percent of the total national market of $72 million. In Texas, Quality has acquired 27 percent of the billboard market and, in the Dallas–Ft. Worth area alone, about 25 percent. Billboard advertising accounts for only 0.001 percent of total national advertising sales—the majority goes to newspaper, magazines, television, and radio advertising. What claims could the Justice Department assert in a suit against Quality? What is Quality's defense? What result?

21

Unfair and Deceptive Trade Practices

General Powers of the Federal Trade Commission

Traditionally, common law prohibited a variety of trade practices unfair either to competitors or to consumers. These included "passing off" one's products as though they were made by someone else, using a trade name confusingly similar to that of another, stealing trade secrets, and various forms of misrepresentation. In the Federal Trade Commission Act, Congress empowered a federal agency for the first time to investigate and deter acts of unfair competition.

Section 5 gave the FTC power to enforce a provision stating that "unfair methods of competition in commerce are hereby declared unlawful." By "unfair methods of competition," Congress originally intended acts that constituted violations of the Sherman and Clayton antitrust acts. Nevertheless, from the outset the commissioners of the FTC took a broader view of their mandate. Specifically, they were concerned about the problem of false and deceptive advertising and promotional schemes. But the original Section 5 was confining; it seemed to authorize FTC action only when the deceptive advertising injured a competitor of the company. In 1931, the Supreme Court ruled that this was indeed the case: an advertisement that deceived the public was not within the FTC's jurisdiction unless a competitor was injured by the misrepresentation also. Congress responded in 1938 with the Wheeler-Lea amendments to the FTC Act. To the words "unfair methods of competition" were added these words: "unfair or deceptive acts or practices in commerce." Now it became clear that the FTC had a broader role to play than as a second agency enforcing the antitrust laws. Henceforth, the FTC would be the guardian also of consumers.

Deceptive practices that the FTC has prosecuted are also amenable to suit at common law. A tire manufacturer who advertises that his "special tire" is "new" when it is actually a retread has committed a common law misrepresentation, and the buyer could sue for rescission or damages. But it should be apparent that this approach is piecemeal. A lawsuit or two will not stop the determined fraud. Moreover, lawsuits such as these are expensive to bring and the amount of damages awarded is usually small, so the incentive is usually lacking to police fraudulent business practices through a common law action. Through Section 5, however, the FTC can seek far-reaching remedies against the sham and the phony; it is not limited to proving damages to individual customers case by case. So the FTC—and analogous state and municipal agencies created in many states—can serve far more effectively to regulate deceptive and unfair business practices.

As an administrative agency, the FTC has broader powers than those vested in the ordinary prosecutorial authority, such as the Department of Justice. It can initiate administrative proceedings in accordance with the Administrative Procedure Act to enforce the several statutes that it administers. It may issue cease and desist orders and enforce them in court, seek temporary and permanent injunctions, fines, and monetary damages, and promulgate *trade regulation rules* (TRRs). Although the FTC's authority to issue TRRs had long been assumed (and was approved by the U.S. Court of Appeals in Washington in 1973), Congress formalized it in 1975 in the FTC Improvement Act (part of the Magnuson-Moss Warranty Act), which gives the FTC explicit authority to prescribe rules defining unfair or deceptive acts or practices.

A **trade regulation rule** is like a statute. It is a detailed statement of procedures and substantive dos and don'ts. Before promulgating a TRR, the commission must publish its intention to do so in the Federal Register and must hold open hearings on its proposals. Draft versions of a TRR must be published to allow the public to comment. Once issued, the final version is published as part of the Code of Federal Regulations and becomes a permanent part of the law, unless modified or repealed by the FTC itself or by Congress—or overturned by a court on grounds of arbitrariness, lack of procedural regularity, or the like. A violation of a TRR is treated exactly like a violation of a federal statute. Once the FTC proves that a defendant violated a TRR no further proof is necessary that the act was unfair or deceptive. Examples of TRRs include the Retail Food Store

Advertising and Marketing Practices Rule, Games of Chance in the Food Retailing and Gasoline Industries Rule, Care Labeling of Textile Wearing Apparel Rule, Mail Order Merchandise Rule, Cooling-Off Period for Door-to-Door Sales Rule, and Use of Negative Option Plans by Sellers in Commerce.

General Principles of Law Governing Deceptive Acts and Practices

With a staff of 1,600 and ten regional offices, the Federal Trade Commission is, at least from time to time, an active regulatory agency. Its energy and efficiency vary with the political climate in Washington and the strength and energy of the consumer movement. Critics have often charged that what the FTC chooses to investigate defies common sense because so many of the cases seem to involve trivial or at least relatively unimportant offenses: Does the nation really need a federal agency to guard us against pronouncements by singer Pat Boone on the efficacy of acne medication or the provenance of certain ostensibly native crafts sold to tourists in Alaska? One answer is that through such cases, important principles of law are declared and ratified.

To be sure, most readers of this book, unlikely to be gulled by false claims, may see a certain Alice-in-Wonderland quality to FTC enforcement. But the first principle of FTC action is that it gauges deceptive acts and practices as interpreted by the general public, not of the more sophisticated. As a U.S. Court of Appeals once said, the FTC Act was not "made for the protection of experts, but for the public—that vast multitude which includes the ignorant, the unthinking, and the credulous."

The deceptive statement or act need not actually deceive. Before 1983, it was sufficient that the statement had a "capacity to deceive." According to a standard adopted in 1983, however, the FTC will take action against deceptive advertising "if there is a representation, omission or practice that is likely to mislead the consumer acting reasonably in the circumstances, to the consumer's detriment." Critics of the new standard have charged that it will be harder to prove deception because an advertisement must be "likely to mislead" rather than merely have a "capacity to deceive." The FTC might also be put to the burden of showing that consumers reasonably interpreted the ad and that they relied on the ad. Whether the standard will reduce the volume of FTC actions against deceptive advertising remains to be seen.

The FTC also has the authority to proceed against "unfair . . . acts or practices." These need not be deceptive, but instead are of such a character that they offend a common sense of propriety, justice, or honest way of comporting oneself.

Deceptive Acts and Practices

Failure to Disclose Pertinent Facts

The business community is under no general obligation to disclose everything. Advertisers may put a bright face on their products as long as they do not make a direct material misrepresentation or misstatement. But under certain circumstances, an advertiser may be required to disclose more than it did in order not to be misleading. For example, if a fact not disclosed might have a material bearing on a consumer's decision whether to purchase the product, its omission might be tantamount to deception, as the following case suggests.

J. B. WILLIAMS CO. v. FTC
381 F.2d 884 (6th Cir. 1967)

CELEBREZZE, CIRCUIT JUDGE. The question presented by this appeal is whether Petitioners' advertising of a product, Geritol, for the relief of iron deficiency anemia, is false and misleading so as to violate Sections 5 and 12 of the Federal Trade Commission Act.

* * *

The J. B. Williams Company, Inc. is a New York corporation engaged in the sale and distribution of two products known as Geritol liquid and Geritol tablets. Geritol liquid was first marketed in August, 1950; Geritol tablets in February, 1952. Geritol is sold throughout the United States and advertisements for Geritol have appeared in newspapers and on television in all the States of the United States.

Parkson Advertising Agency, Inc. has been the advertising agency for Williams since 1957. Most of the advertising money for Geritol is spent on television advertising. . . .

The Commission's Order requires that not only must the Geritol advertisements be expressly limited to those persons whose symptoms are due to an existing deficiency of one or more of the vitamins contained in the preparation, or due to an existing deficiency of iron, but also the Geritol advertisements must affirmatively disclose the negative fact that a great majority of persons who experience these symptoms do not experience them because they have a vitamin or iron deficiency; that for the great majority of people experiencing these symptoms, Geritol will be of no benefit. Closely related to this requirement is the further requirement of the Order that the Geritol advertisements refrain from representing that the symptoms are generally reliable indications of iron deficiency.

* * *

The main thrust of the Commission's Order is that the Geritol advertising must affirmatively disclose the negative fact that a great majority of persons who experience these symptoms do not experience them because there is a vitamin or iron deficiency.

The medical evidence on this issue is conflicting and the question is not one which is susceptible to precise statistical analysis.

* * *

While the advertising does not make the affirmative representation that the majority of people who are tired and rundown are so because of iron deficiency anemia and the product Geritol will be an effective cure, there is substantial evidence to support the finding of the Commission that most tired people are not so because of iron deficiency anemia, and the failure to disclose this fact is false and misleading because the advertisement creates the impression that the tired feeling is caused by something which Geritol can cure.

* * *

Here the advertisements emphasize the fact that if you are often tired and run-down you will feel stronger fast by taking Geritol. The Commission, in looking at the overall impression created by the advertisements on the general public, could reasonably find these advertisements were false and misleading. The finding that the advertisements link common, non-specific symptoms with iron deficiency anemia, and thereby create a false impression because most people with these symptoms are not suffering from iron deficiency anemia, is both reasonable and supported by substantial evidence. The Commission is not bound to the literal meaning of the words, nor must the Commission take a random sample to determine the meaning and impact of the advertisements.

Petitioners argue vigorously that the Commission does not have the legal power to require them to state the negative fact that "in the great majority of persons who experience such symptoms, these symptoms are not caused by a deficiency of one or more of the vitamins contained in the preparation or by iron deficiency or iron deficiency anemia;" and "for such persons the preparation will be of no benefit."

We believe the evidence is clear that Geritol is of no benefit in the treatment of tiredness except in those cases where tiredness has been caused by a deficiency of the ingredients contained in Geritol. The fact that the great majority of people who experience tiredness symptoms do not suffer from any deficiency of the ingredients in Geritol is a "material fact" under the meaning of that term as used in Section 15 of the Federal Trade Commission Act and Petitioners' failure to reveal this fact in this day when the consumer is influenced by mass advertising utilizing highly developed arts of persuasion, renders it difficult for the typical consumer to know whether the product will in fact meet his needs unless he is told what the product will or will not do. . . .

* * *

The Commission forbids the Petitioners' representation that the presence of iron deficiency anemia can be self-diagnosed or can be determined without a medical test. The danger to be remedied here has been fully and adequately taken care of in the other requirements of the Order. We can find no Congressional policy against self-medication on a trial and error basis where the consumer is fully informed and the product is safe as Geritol is conceded to be. In fact, Congressional policy is to encourage such self-help. In effect the Commission's Order 1(f) tends to place Geritol in the prescription drug field. We do not consider it within the power of the Federal Trade Commission to remove Geritol from the area of proprietary drugs and place it in the area of prescription drugs. This requirement of the Order will not be enforced. We also find this Order is not unduly vague and fairly apprises the Petitioners of what is required of them. Petition denied and, except for 1(f) of the Commission's Order, enforcement of the Order will be granted.

* * *

Descriptions of Products

Although certain words are considered mere puffing ("greatest," "best"), at least under certain circumstances, other words, which have more precise connotations, can cause trouble if they are misused. One example is the word "new." In most cases, the FTC has held that if a product is more than six months old, it is not new and may not lawfully be advertised as such.

The efficacy of products is perhaps their most often advertised aspect. An ad that states a product will do more than it can is almost always deceptive if the claim is specific. Common examples that the FTC continues to do battle over are claims that a cream, pill, or other substance will "rejuvenate" the body, "cure baldness," "permanently" remove wrinkles, or restore the vitality of hair.

The composition of goods is another common category of deceptive claims. For example, a product advertised as "wool" had better be 100 percent wool; a mixture of wool and synthetic fabrics cannot be advertised as "wool." The FTC has lists of dozens of descriptive words with appropriate definitions.

Labeling of certain products is strictly regulated by specific statutes. Under the Food, Drug, and Cosmetic Act, artificial colors and flavors must be disclosed. Other specific federal statutes include the Wool Products Labeling Act, the Textile Fiber Products Identification Act, the Fur Products Labeling Act, and the Flammable Fabrics Act, the enforcement of which is entrusted to the FTC. In 1966, Congress enacted the Fair Packaging and Labeling Act. It governs most consumer products and gives the FTC authority to issue regulations for proper labeling of most of them. In particular, the statute is designed to help standardize quantity descriptions ("small," "medium," and "large") and to facilitate shoppers who wish to compare the value of competing goods in the stores.

Misleading Price and Savings Claims

"Buy one, get another for half price." "Suggested retail price: $25. Our price: $5.95." "Yours for only $95. You save $50." Claims such as these assault the eye and ear daily. Unless these ads are strictly true, they are violations of Section 5. To regulate deceptive price and savings claims, the FTC has issued a series of *Guides Against Deceptive Pricing* that set forth certain principles by which the commission will judge the merits of price claims. These guides are not themselves law, but they are important clues to how the FTC will act when faced with a price-claim case.

In general, the guides deal with five claims, as follows:

1. *Comparisons of the sale price to a former price* The former price must have been offered for a substantial period of time in the near past for a seller to be justified in referring to it. A product that once had a price tag of $50, but which never actually sold for more than $40, cannot be hawked at the "former price of $50."
2. *Comparable products* "This same mattress and box springs would cost you $450 at retail." The advertisement is true only if the seller is in fact offering the same merchandise and if the price he quoted is genuine.
3. *"Suggested" retail price* The same rules apply as those just mentioned. But in the case of a "manufacturer's suggested" price, an additional wrinkle can occur: the manufacturer might help the retailer deceive by listing a "suggested" price that is in fact considerably above the going price in the retailer's trading area. Whether it is the manufacturer who is doing his own selling, or the retailer who takes advantage of the "list

price" ticket on the goods, the resulting claim of a bargain is deceptive if the product does not sell for the list price in any market or in the market of the retailer.

4. *Bargain based on purchase of something else* The usual statement in these cases is "buy one, get one free" (or at some percentage of the usual selling price). Again, the watchwords are *literal accuracy*. If the package of batteries normally sells in the advertiser's store for 99 cents, and two packages are now selling for that price, then the advertisement is unexceptionable. But advertisers are often tempted to raise the original selling price or reduce the size or quantity of the bargain product; doing so is deceptive.
5. *False claims to explain a "sale" price* "Giant clearance sale" or "going out of business" or "limited offer" are common advertising gimmicks. If true, they are legitimate, but it takes very little to make them deceptive. A "limited offer" that goes on forever (or a sale price charged beyond the date on which a sale is said to end) is deceptive. Likewise, false claims that imply the manufacturer is charging the customer a small price are illegitimate. These include claims like "wholesale price," "manufacturer's close-outs," "irregulars," or "seconds."

"Bait and Switch" Advertisements

A common sales pitch in retail is the "bait and switch." The retailer "baits" the prospective customer by dangling an alluring sale before his eyes. "Steinway Grand—only $1,000." But when the customer arrives at the store he finds that the advertised product has sold out. The retailer then tries to sell the disappointed customer a much higher priced product. Or the salesman may have the product, but he will disparage it—privately pointing out that it does not really live up to the advertised expectations—and will exhort the customer to buy the "better," more expensive model. These and related tactics are all violations of Section 5. In its *Guides Against Bait Advertising,* the FTC lists several such unfair practices. These include: (1) refusing to demonstrate the advertised product, (2) disparaging the product (for example, by exhibiting a visibly inferior grade of product next to higher-priced merchandise), (3) failing to stock enough of the advertised product to meet anticipated demand (although the advertiser may say "supplies limited," if that is the case), (4) stating that delivery of the advertised product will take an inordinate amount of time, (5) demonstrating a defective product, and (6) deliberately discouraging the would-be buyer from purchasing the advertised product.

Free Offers

Careless advertisers will discover that "free," perhaps the most powerful word in advertising, comes at a cost. As just noted, a product is not free if it is conditional on buying another product and the price of the "free" product is included in the purchased product ("buy one tube and get another tube free"). Just how far the commission is prepared to take this rule is clear from *F.T.C.* v. *Mary Carter Paint Co.,* 382 U.S. 46 (1965). In that case, the company offered from the time it began business to sell on a two-for-one basis: "every second can FREE, gallon or quart." The problem was that it had never priced and sold single cans of paint, so the FTC assumed that the price of the second can was included in the first, even though Mary Carter established single can prices which were comparable, it claimed, to those for paint of comparable quality sold by competing manufacturers. The Supreme Court sustained the commission's finding of deception.

Product Comparisons and Disparagements

Product disparagement—saying defamatory things about a competitor's product—is a common law tort, redressable under state law. It is also actionable under Section 5 of the FTC Act. The FTC brands as disparagement the making of specific untrue statements about a competitor's product. The agency labels an indirect form of disparagement "comparative misrepresentation"—making false claims of superiority of one's own product. Again, the common law puffing rule would permit the manufacturer of an over-the-counter pain reliever to make the general statement: "Our pill is the best." But the claim that a pill "works three times as fast as the leading competitor" violates Section 5 if untrue.

Truth has always been a defense to claims of product disparagement, but even that common law rule has been eroded in recent years with the application of the *significance* doctrine. A statement may be technically true but insignificant and made in such a way as to be misleading. The leading case, set out below, concerned a comparative study published in *Reader's Digest* of tar and nicotine in cigarettes. The article suggested that the differences were inconsequential to health, but the company making the cigarette with the smallest amount of tar and nicotine touted the fact anyway.

P. LORILLARD CO. v. FEDERAL TRADE COMMISSION
186 F.2d 52 (4th Cir. 1950)

PARKER, CHIEF JUDGE. This is a petition to set aside an order of the Federal Trade Commission which directed that the P. Lorillard Company cease and desist from making certain representations found to be false in the advertising of its tobacco products. The Commission has filed answer asking that its order be enforced. The company was ordered to cease and desist "from representing by any means directly or indirectly:

* * *

> . . . That Old Gold cigarettes or the smoke therefrom contains less nicotine, or less tars and resins, or is less irritating to the throat than the cigarettes or the smoke therefrom of any of the six other leading brands of cigarettes."

* * *

Laboratory tests introduced in evidence show that the difference in nicotine, tars and resins of the different leading brands of cigarettes is insignificant in amount; and there is abundant testimony of medical experts that such difference as there is could result in no difference in the physiological effect upon the smoker. There is expert evidence, also, that the slight difference in the nicotine, tar and resin content of cigarettes is not constant between different brands, but varies from place to place and from time to time, and that it is a practical impossibility for the manufacturer of cigarettes to determine or to remove or substantially reduce such content or to maintain constancy of such content in the finished cigarette. This testimony gives ample support to the Commission's findings.

* * *

The company relies upon the truth of the advertisements complained of, saying that they merely state what had been truthfully stated in an article in the Reader's Digest. An examination of the advertisements, however, shows a perversion of the meaning of the Reader's Digest article which does little credit to the company's advertising department—a perversion which results in the use of the truth in such a way as to cause the reader to believe the exact opposite of what was intended by the writer of the article. A comparison of the advertisements with the article makes this very plain. The article, after referring to laboratory tests that had been made on cigarettes of the leading brands, says:

"The laboratory's general conclusion will be sad news for the advertising copy writers, but good news for the smoker, who need no longer worry as to which cigarette can most effectively nail down his coffin. For one nail is just about as good as another. Says the laboratory report: 'The differences between brands are, practically speaking, small, and no single brand is so superior to its competitors as to justify its selection on the ground that it is less harmful.' How small the variations are may be seen from the data tabulated on page 7."

The table referred to in the article was inserted for the express purpose of showing the insignificance of the difference in the nicotine and tar content of the smoke from the various brands of cigarettes. It appears therefrom that the Old Gold cigarettes examined in the test contained less nicotine, tars and resins than the others examined, although the difference, according to the uncontradicted expert evidence, was so small as to be entirely insignificant and utterly without meaning so far as effect upon the smoker is concerned. The company proceeded to advertise this difference as though it had received a citation for public service instead of a castigation from the Reader's Digest. In the leading newspapers of the country and over the radio it advertised that the Reader's Digest had had experiments conducted and had found that Old Gold cigarettes were lowest in nicotine and lowest in irritating tars and resins, just as though a substantial difference in such content had been found. The following advertisement may be taken as typical:

"OLD GOLDS FOUND
LOWEST IN NICOTINE
OLD GOLDS FOUND
LOWEST IN THROAT-IRRITATING
TARS AND RESINS

"See Impartial Test by Reader's Digest July Issue.

"See How Your Brand Compares with Old Gold.

"Reader's Digest assigned a scientific testing laboratory to find out about cigarettes. They tested seven leading cigarettes and Reader's Digest published the results.

"The cigarette whose smoke was lowest in nicotine was Old Gold. The cigarette with the least throat-irritating tars and resins was Old Gold.

"On both these major counts Old Gold was best among all seven cigarettes tested.

"Get July Reader's Digest. Turn to Page 5. See what this highly respected magazine reports.

"You'll say, 'From now on, my cigarette is Old Gold.' Light one? Note the mild, *interesting* flavor. Easier on the throat? Sure: And *more* smoking pleasure: Yes, it's the *new* Old Gold—finer yet, since 'something new has been added'."

The fault with this advertising was not that it did not print all that the Reader's Digest article said, but that it printed a small part thereof in such a way as to create an entirely false and misleading impression, not only as to what was said in the article, but also as to the quality of the company's cigarettes. Almost anyone reading the advertisements or listening to the radio broadcasts would have gained the very definite impression that Old Gold cigarettes were less irritating to the throat and less harmful than other leading brands of cigarettes because they contained substantially less nicotine, tars and resins, and that the Reader's Digest had established this fact in impartial laboratory tests; and few would have troubled to look up the Reader's Digest to see what it really had said. The truth was exactly the opposite. There was no substantial difference in Old Gold cigarettes and the other leading brands with respect to their content of nicotine, tars and resins and this was what the Reader's Digest article plainly said. The table whose meaning the advertisements distorted for the purpose of misleading and deceiving the public was intended to prove that there was no practical difference and did prove it when properly understood. To tell less than the whole truth is a well known method of deception; and he who deceives by resorting to such method cannot excuse the deception by relying upon the truthfulness per se of the partial truth by which it has been accomplished.

In determining whether or not advertising is false or misleading within the meaning of the statute regard must be had, not to fine spun distinctions and arguments that may be made in excuse, but to the effect which it might reasonably be expected to have upon the general public. "The important criterion is the net impression which the advertisement is likely to make upon the general populace." As was well said by Judge Coxe in Florence Manufacturing Co. v. J. C. Dowd & Co., 2 Cir., 178 F. 73, 75, with reference to the law relating to trademarks: "The law is not made for the protection of experts, but for the public—that vast multitude which includes the ignorant, the unthinking and the credulous, who, in making purchases, do not stop to analyze, but are governed by appearances and general impressions."

* * *

For the reasons stated, the petition to set aside the order will be denied and the order will be enforced.

During the 1970s, to help enforce its rules against comparative misrepresentations, the FTC began to insist that advertisers fully document any quantitative claims that their products were superior to others. This meant that the advertiser should have proof of accuracy not only if the commission comes calling; the advertiser should collect the information beforehand, otherwise the claim will be held presumptively deceptive.

Endorsements

How wonderful to have a superstar (or maybe yesterday's superstar) appear on television drooling over your product. Presumably, millions of people would buy a throat spray if Beverly Sills swore by it, or a pair of jeans if Brooke Shields wore them, or a face cream if Catherine Deneuve blessed it. In more subtle ways, numerous products are touted every day with one form of testimonial or another: "three out of four doctors recommend . . ." or "drivers across the country use. . . ." In this area, the opportunities for deception are rife.

It is not a deception for a well-known personality to endorse a product without disclosing that she is being paid to do so. But the person giving the testimonial must in fact use the product; if she does not, the endorsement is deceptive. Suppose an astronaut just returned to earth is talked into endorsing suspenders ("they keep your pants from floating away") that he was seen to be wearing on televised shots of the orbital mission. If he has customarily worn them, he may properly endorse them. But if he stops wearing them for another brand or because he has decided to go back to wearing belts, reruns of the TV commercials must be pulled from the air.

That a particular consumer is in fact ecstatically happy about how a product helped him does not save a false statement: it is deceptive to present this glowing testimonial to the public if there are no facts to back up his claim. The assertion "I was cured by apricot pits" to market a cancer remedy would not pass FTC muster. Nor may an endorser give a testimonial involving subjects known only to experts if he is not himself that kind of expert, as shown in the following consent decree, negotiated by the FTC with singer Pat Boone.

COOGA MOOGA, INC.
Trade Reg. Rep. (CCH) ¶21,417
(FTC 1978) [1976-1979 Transfer Binder]

The FTC issued a complaint alleging that Karr Preventative Medical Products, Inc. (KPMP), Beverly Hills, Calif., and its controlling officer, Atida H. Karr, M.D., have made false and unsubstantiated claims for Acne-Statin, a mail order preparation advertised for the treatment of acne. . . .

The FTC also accepted an agreement containing a consent order entered into by Charles E. "Pat" Boone and Cooga Mooga, Inc., Los Angeles, Calif., of which Mr. Boone is president. Mr. Boone appeared in print and television advertisements for Acne-Statin in which he provided an endorsement for the product. Key provisions of the consent agreement require that Mr. Boone make a reasonable inquiry before endorsing products in the future and that he pay part of any restitution that may be ordered in this matter.

The Commission's administrative complaint against KPMP and Dr. Karr alleges in part that: (1) Acne-Statin neither will cure acne nor can eliminate its cause, as claimed; (2) they have falsely advertised that Acne-Statin is superior to all other acne preparations and to soap in the anti-bacterial treatment of acne; (3) contrary to other claims, there are time and quantity limitations on the money-back guarantee for Acne-Statin; and (4) there was no reasonable basis for claims that Acne-Statin will cure acne and result in skin free of acne blemishes or for various other performance claims.

*   *   *

Under their agreed-to order, Mr. Boone and Cooga Mooga, Inc. must have a reasonable basis when making any claim relating to the efficacy, performance, any characteristic or property, or the result of use of any product. Also, they must make a reasonable inquiry into the truthfulness of any proposed endorsement of this nature.

Mr. Boone must also pay his pro rata share of any restitution which might be ordered by the Commission or by a court.

The consent agreement, among other things, prohibits misrepresentations of—(a) the benefits Boone family members have derived from any product; (b) product tests or product test results; and (c) the efficacy, use or performance of any product where the use or misuse could affect the user's health and safety.

According to Albert H. Kramer, Director, Bureau of Consumer Protection, the negotiated order, while not a binding legal precedent, stands for the principle that an endorser must verify the claims made about the advertised product before the first commercial goes on the air or appears in print, or else risk FTC action. Unless the endorser is an expert on the subject, the endorser must look to independent reliable sources to validate claims, tests, or studies supplied by the advertiser. Failure to make a reasonable effort at independent evaluation could result in personal liability for the endorser.

*   *   *

Pictorial and Television Advertising

Pictorial representations create special problems because the picture can belie the caption or the announcer's words. A picture showing an expensive car may be deceptive if the dealer does not stock those cars or if the only readily available cars are different models. The ways of deceiving by creating false inferences through pictures are limited only by imagination. White-coated "doctors," seals of the British monarchy, and plush offices can connote various things about a product, even if the advertisement never says that the man in the white coat was a doctor, that the product was related to the British crown, or that the company had its operations in the building depicted.

Television demonstrations may also suggest nonexistent properties or qualities in a product. In one case, the commission ordered the manufacturer of a liquid cleaner to cease showing it in use near hot stoves and candles, implying falsely that it was nonflammable. A commercial showing a knife cutting through nails is deceptive if the nails were pre-cut and different knives were used for the before and after shots.

Unfair Trade Practices

We turn now to certain practices that, while they have deceptive elements, also operate unfairly in ways beyond mere deception. In general, these types of unfair practices will be attacked: (1) failing to substantiate material representations in advertisements before publishing them or putting them on the air; (2) failing to disclose certain material information necessary for consumers to make rational comparisons of price and quality of products; and (3) taking unconscionable advantage or exploiting the weakness of certain consumers. The FTC has enjoined many such ads of the first type. The second type of unfairness has led the commission to issue a number of TRRs setting forth what must be disclosed—for example, octane ratings of gasoline. In this section we focus briefly on the third category.

Contests and Sweepstakes

In 1971, the FTC obtained a consent order from *Reader's Digest,* barring it from promoting a mail order sweepstakes in which those responding had a chance to win large monetary or other prizes by returning numbered tickets, unless the magazine expressly disclosed how many prizes would be awarded and unless all such prizes were in fact awarded. *Reader's Digest* had heavily promoted the size and number of prizes, but few of the winning tickets were ever returned and consequently few of the prizes were ever actually awarded. [Reader's Digest Assoc., 79 F.T.C. 599 (1971)]

Beginning in the 1960s, the retail food and gasoline industries began to heavily promote games of chance. Investigations by the FTC and a House Small Business subcommittee showed that the games were rigged: winners were "picked" early by planting the winning cards early on in the distribution; winning cards were sent to geographic areas most in need of the promotional benefits of announcing winners; not all prizes were awarded before many games terminated; and local retailers could spot winning cards and cash them in or give them to favored customers. As a result of these investigations, the FTC in 1969 issued its Trade Regulation Rule for Games of Chance in the Food Retailing and Gasoline Industries, strictly regulating how the games may operate and be promoted.

Many marketers use "contests," as opposed to sweepstakes, in merchandising their products. In a contest, the consumer must actually do something other than return a ticket, such as fill in a Bingo card or come up with certain words. It is an unfair practice for the sponsoring company not to abide by its own rules in determining winners.

Door-to-door and Mail-order Selling

In 1974 the FTC promulgated a TRR requiring a three-day "cooling off" period, within which any door-to-door sales can be cancelled. The contract must state the buyer's right to the cooling-off period.

For many years, certain unscrupulous distributors would mail unsolicited merchandise and demand payment through a series of dunning letters and bills. In 1970, Congress enacted legislation that declares any unsolicited mailing and subsequent dunning to be an unfair trade practice under Section 5. Under this law, if you receive an unsolicited product in the mail, you may treat it as a gift and use it; you are under no obligation to return it or pay for it.

Another regulation of mail-order sales is the FTC's Mail-order Merchandise TRR. Any direct-mail merchandiser must deliver the promised goods within thirty days or give the consumer an option to accept delayed delivery or a prompt refund of his money—or cancellation of the order if it has not been prepaid.

Negative Option Plans

The "negative option" was devised in the 1920s by the Book-of-the-Month Club. It is a marketing device through which the consumer responds to the seller only if he wishes *not* to receive the product. As used by book clubs and other distributors of goods that are sent out periodically, the customer agrees when "joining" to accept and pay for all items, unless in advance of their arrival he specifically indicates he wishes to reject them. If he does nothing, he must pay. Difficulties arise when the negative option notice is late arriving in the mail or when a member quits and continues to receive the monthly notices.

In 1974, the FTC issued a TRR governing use of negative option plans by sellers. The TRR laid down specific notice requirements. Among other things, a subscriber is entitled to ten days in which to notify sellers that he has rejected the particular item about to be sent. If a customer has cancelled his membership, the seller must take back and pay the former member's mailing expenses for any merchandise mailed after cancellation. The former member may treat any shipments beyond one after cancellation as unsolicited merchandise and keep it without having to pay for it or return it.

Remedies

The Federal Trade Commission has a host of weapons in its remedial arsenal. It may issue cease and desist orders against unfair and deceptive acts and practices, and "let the punishment fit the crime." For instance, the FTC can order a company to remove or modify a deceptive trade name. It may order companies to substantiate their advertising. Or, if a company fails to disclose facts about a product, the commission may order the company to affirmatively disclose the facts in future advertising. In the *J. B. Williams* case, for example (p. 590), the court upheld the commission's order that the company tell consumers in future advertising that the condition Geritol is supposed to treat—iron-poor blood—is only rarely the cause of symptoms of tiredness that Geritol would help cure.

The FTC has often exercised its power to order affirmative disclosures during the past decade, but its power to correct advertising deceptions is even broader. In *Warner-Lambert Co.* v. *Federal Trade Commission,* 562 F.2d 749 (D.C. Cir. 1977), *cert. denied,* 435 U.S. 950 (1978), the U.S. Court of Appeals in Washington approved the commission's power to order a company in future advertisements to *correct* its former misleading and deceptive statements regarding Listerine mouthwash, should it choose to continue to advertise the product. The court also approved the FTC's formula for determining how much the company must spend: an amount equal to the average annual expenditure on advertising the mouthwash during the ten years preceding the case.

In addition to its injunctive powers, the FTC may seek civil penalties of $10,000 for violation of final cease and desist orders, and if the violation is a continuing one—an advertising campaign that lasts for weeks or months—each day is considered a separate violation. The commission may also sue for up to $10,000 per violation, as above, for violations of its TRRs. Under the FTC Improvement Act of 1975, the commission is authorized to seek injunctions and collect monetary damages on behalf of injured consumers in cases involving violations of TRRs. It may also seek restitution for consumers in cases involving cease and desist orders, if the party continuing to commit the unfair or deceptive practice should have known that it would be dishonest or fraudulent to continue doing so. The exact reach of this power to seek restitution, which generally had not been available before 1975, remains to be tested in the courts. Unlike their rights under the antitrust statutes, however, *private* parties have no right to sue under Section 5 of the FTC Act.

Little FTC Acts

Even when consumers have no direct remedy under federal law for unfair or deceptive acts and practices, they may have recourse under state laws modeled on the FTC Act, known as Little FTC Acts. These acts are more liberal than the federal unfair trade rules, and permit consumers—and in several states, even aggrieved businesses—to sue when injured by a host of "immoral, unethical, oppressive, or unscrupulous" commercial acts. Often a successful plaintiff can recover treble damages and attorneys' fees. Unlike the current federal standard for defining deceptive acts, the state standards rest on capacity to deceive. Use of Little FTC Acts is expected to rise.

Chapter Summary

Section 5 of the Federal Trade Commission Act gives the Federal Trade Commission the power to enforce a provision prohibiting "unfair methods of competition and unfair or deceptive acts or practices in commerce." In doing so the FTC may bring enforcement proceedings against companies on a case-by-case basis or may promulgate trade regulation rules.

A deceptive act or practice need not actually deceive, as long as it is "likely to mislead." An unfair act or practice need not deceive at all but must offend a common sense of propriety, justice, or an honest way of acting. Among the proscribed acts or practices are these: failure to disclose pertinent facts, false or misleading description of products, misleading price and savings claims, bait and switch advertisements, free offer claims, false product comparisons and disparagements, and endorsements by those who do not use the product or who have no reasonable basis for making the claims. Among the unfair trade practices that the FTC has sought to deter are certain types of contests and sweepstakes, high-pressure door-to-door and mail-order selling, and certain types of negative option plans.

The FTC has a number of remedial weapons: cease and desist orders tailored to the particular deception or unfair act (including affirmative disclosure in advertising and corrections in future advertising), civil monetary penalties, and injunctions, damages, and restitution on behalf of injured consumers. Only the FTC may sue to correct violations of Section 5; private parties have no right to sue under Section 5.

Problems

1. Door-to-door salespersons of an encyclopedia company offer a complete set of encyclopedias to "selected" customers. They tell customers that their only obligation is to pay for a ten-year updating service. In fact the price of the updating service includes the cost of the encyclopedias. The Federal Trade Commission sues, charging deception under Section 5 of the FTC Act. The encyclopedia company defends on the ground that no one could possibly have been misled because everyone must have understood that no company could afford to give away a twenty-volume set of books for free. What result?
2. Vanessa Cosmetics takes out full-page advertisements in the local newspaper stating that "this Sunday only" the Vanessa Makeup Kit will be "reduced to only $25." In fact, the regular price has been $25.50. Does this constitute deceptive advertising? Why?
3. Lilliputian Department Stores advertises a "special" on an electric carrot slicer, priced "this week only at $10." When customers come to the store, they find the carrot slicer in frayed boxes, and the advertised special is clearly inferior to a higher-grade carrot slicer priced at $25. When customers ask about the difference, the store clerk tells them that "you wouldn't want to buy the cheaper one; it wears out much too fast." What grounds, if any, exist to charge Lilliputian with violations of the FTC Act?
4. A toothpaste manufacturer advertises that special tests demonstrate that its toothpaste shows fewer cavities than a "regular toothpaste." In fact the "regular" toothpaste was not marketed, but was merely the advertiser's brand stripped of its fluoride. Various studies over the years have demonstrated, however, that fluoride in toothpaste will reduce the number of cavities a user will get. Is this advertisement deceptive under Section 5 of the FTC Act?
5. McDonald's advertises a sweepstakes through a mailing that says prizes are to be reserved for 15,610 "lucky winners." The mailing further states that "You may be [a winner] but you will never know if you don't claim your prize. All prizes not claimed will never be given away, so hurry." The mailing does not give the odds of winning. The Federal Trade Commission sues to enjoin the mailing as deceptive. What result?

22

Franchising Law

To facilitate the study of law and its relation to the business community, we have examined particular forms of enterprise and business activities one at a time. That has allowed us to focus on a single cluster of problems, like matters affecting consumers or employees. It has also simplified the discussion because many forms of business operations, such as partnerships and corporations, are subject to well-defined bodies of law—for example, the Uniform Partnership Act and the Revised Model Business Corporation Act. Likewise, certain business activities are directly regulated by particular laws. For example, a variety of state and federal securities laws regulate the sale of stock, and both the common law of contracts and such statutes as the Uniform Commercial Code regulate contractual activities.

But business operations and activities are rarely so simple that we can understand their legal relations by reference to a particular law. Indeed, only by examining a host of laws can we understand the full range of legal relations of entities such as corporations. We need to look at more than the Revised Model Business Corporation Act, but also virtually the entire range of the common law (torts, contracts, agency, and many other branches) and dozens of state and federal statutes (including environmental and labor laws).

To see how business must operate in the full legal environment, we explore in this chapter an important method of business operation:

franchising. Familiar to all Americans chiefly in the form of fast-food outlets but also in dozens of other industries as well, the franchise is not a business entity as such, like a partnership or corporation. Indeed, both franchisor and franchisee may, themselves, individually be organized as partnerships or corporations. It is, rather, a relationship between manufacturers or other suppliers and distributors—one that permits regional or even national brand identification without the huge capital accumulation required for companies that not only own central manufacturing and marketing facilities but also retail distribution outlets.

Defining the Franchise Relationship

The term "franchise" has varied meanings in different state and federal statutes. In general, a franchise has four elements. It is (1) a contract by which in return for (2) the payment of a fee, a franchisee is granted the (3) right to sell or distribute the franchisor's goods or services in a manner substantially prescribed by the franchisor, and in which the business method involves (4) substantial use of the franchisor's trademark, trade name, or commercial symbol. The franchise is used principally in three categories of business operations:

- *Distributorships* or *Product Franchises* (through which a manufacturer licenses a distributor to sell its products). Typically, automobile dealerships and gasoline stations operate under product franchises.
- *Business-format Franchises* (under which the franchisee is closely identified as part of a "family" belonging to the franchisor). Fast-food chains, real estate brokerages, and many accounting firms operate under business-format franchises.
- *Manufacturing Plants* (under which the franchisor permits the franchisee actually to manufacture and market its products under standards prescribed by the franchisor). Many electronic goods are manufactured and sold under this arrangement.

Beginning in the 1960s, franchising became a popular method of business operation, and the federal and state governments promulgated many laws and regulations to cope with problems and abuses. These include the Automobile Dealers Franchise Act, the earliest federal franchise law; the Federal Trade Commission's Franchising Rule (a trade regulation rule, see p. 588); the Petroleum Marketing Practices Act, and a host of state laws, such as the California Franchise Investment Law (1970) and the New York Franchise Disclosure Law (1980). Beyond these specific laws and regulations aimed at protecting franchisees, other federal and state laws, including those dealing with antitrust, trademarks, and consumer protection, are significant aspects of the entire body of law governing franchise operations.

Not every business relationship involving suppliers and sellers is necessarily a franchise. As opposed to franchisees, sellers may be employees of the manufacturer or independent contractors, distributors, consignees, or independent retail dealers. Three factors are crucial to the distinction between franchise and these other relationships: (1) the degree of control exercised by the supplier over the methods by which the seller conducts its business, (2) the use of the supplier's trademarks, and (3) the nature of the payment for the goods ultimately sold. For example, a person operating a perfume counter in a department store may be an independent contractor; although using the store's name on sales receipts and conforming to certain standards laid down by the store in hiring sales personnel, the operator is in reality a lessee of space, not a franchisee of the store. The operator buys products from someone else, and the store maintains no control over the operator's use of the manufacturer's trademarks. In contrast, a popcorn stand at a movie theater is usually described as a concessionaire, rather than a franchisee, because the operator merely rents space to conduct his or her own business, different from that of the lessor. Also the franchisee differs from other similar types of business relationships, such as business cooperatives, joint ventures, partnerships, merchandise brokerages, and sales agencies.

The Franchisor's Intangible Property Rights

The heart of the franchise system is the identity of the products or services offered by disparate outlets. As one court has said: "Success of this new merchandising concept [franchising] and for each Midas dealer necessitated that the American motorist recognize the Midas name and have confidence that each dealer was an exhaust specialist who handled the same quality product, provided the same clean and comfortable surroundings, gave the same prompt and dependable service and honored the same unique Midas guarantee." [Perma Life Mufflers, Inc. v. International Parts Corp., 376 F.2d 692 (7th Cir. 1967)] This means that a central concern to the franchisor is protection of the trademarks, copyrights, patents, trade secrets, or commercial symbols that tie all his distributors together into a network distinguishable from all others. We examine intangible (or intellectual) property rights in more detail in Chapter 24. Here we look briefly at those aspects of the law that gave control to the franchisor.

It would do a franchisor little good to create a network of identically named products or distributors if he could not control the ingredients being used in the manufacture or sale of the final product or the method of retail operations. Subject to certain antitrust difficulties discussed on page 606, the franchisor may, in licensing trademarks, trade secrets, or other intangible property rights, dictate how franchisees will use those rights. For example, a fast-food franchisor may instruct its myriad outlets what type of meat they may use in their hamburgers and how they may cook them.

Several distinct problems may arise depending on the type of property interest at stake. For example, a franchisor may license the use of patents but cannot demand royalty payments for use of the patented product or manufacturing process beyond the term of the patent itself. Patented products or processes, by definition, are open to public inspection, because the federal patent law requires that they be described in detail in the application filed in the U.S. Patent Office. By contrast, a trade secret (p. 662) is valuable only as long as it is actually kept secret. Since trade secrets (a soft-drink formula, for instance) are frequently crucial in the franchisor's business, the law permits the franchisor to control how the secrets are used to prevent public disclosure. Thus, a franchisor may by contract forbid the franchisee from disclosing the secrets publicly and may even bar the franchisee from competing in the product after the franchise term has expired.

Antitrust Considerations

Selecting the Franchisee

In general, the franchisor is free to grant or deny franchises to whomoever it chooses. But that freedom is subject to particular legal limitations—for example, state and federal laws that prohibit choices made solely on the basis of race, sex, or national origin. Discriminatory motives are not the only limitation. Although a franchisor may determine in its own business interests how many (or how few) franchises to grant, it may not hide unlawful business actions behind the general rule. Thus, a franchisor cannot obtain immunity in a conspiracy with other companies to drive a particular company out of business by pointing to a general freedom to restrict the number of franchises. Such a conspiracy violates Section 1 of the Sherman Act (p. 526), as do agreements between a franchisor and its franchisees to deny a license to an outsider to carry its goods. That was the situation in *Klor's, Inc.* v. *Broadway-Hale Stores, Inc.*, 359 U.S. 207 (1959), discussed on p. 539. A manufacturer and various retail outlets agreed that Klors, a discount appliance store, should not be allowed to sell the manufacturer's goods. The Supreme Court held that the agreement was a direct violation of the Sherman Act.

Territorial Restrictions

As we noted in Chapter 19, a major issue under the antitrust laws is the right of producers to assign exclusive territories to their distributors to give them the maximum incentive to sell the goods. To maintain the exclusivity, a franchise agreement might specify that a Chicago dealership may not move outside its assigned territory to sell the product—for example, by opening up a new retail store in Peoria if some other retailer has been assigned that territory. This policy sacrifices maximum "intra-brand" competition for maximum "inter-brand" competition. Sellers of the Wonder-Chop Food Processor may not be allowed to compete against each other in each city, but they will feel much freer to compete against Cuisinart and other manufacturers of food processing machines. An agreement among *competing producers* or food processors to divide the selling market (e.g., Wonder-Chop to sell exclusively in Chicago, Miracle-Chop to sell exclusively in Kansas City), clearly violates the Sherman Act. As competitors, they have engaged in forbidden *horizontal* allocations of territory. But are *vertical* allocations of selling territory (that is, those decreed by a single producer for its distributors) likewise illegal *per se* (see p. 531)?

In 1963, in *United States* v. *White Motor Co.,* 372 U.S. 253 (1963), the Supreme Court reversed a court of appeals decision holding that a *customer* allocation scheme was *per se* unlawful. White Motor struck a bargain with its dealers requiring them to sell White trucks only to those companies with offices or purchasing headquarters within the dealer's territory. The Court said that the allocation scheme was not *per se* unlawful and that the rule of reason should be applied and sent the case back for trial to determine the effect of this restriction on competition.

Four years later, however, the Supreme Court reversed itself, and held in favor of a *per se* rule. In *United States* v. *Arnold Schwinn & Co.,* 388 U.S. 365 (1967), the Court declared vertical territorial restrictions unlawful. Schwinn's franchised retailers were allowed to sell only within their assigned territories and could not sell Schwinn bicycles to unfranchised retailers anywhere. However, the franchisees could stock bicycles other than Schwinns. Although the Court said it was following the rule of reason, the decision had the effect of a *per se* rule, because the Court reasoned that by parting with title to the Schwinn bicycles when it sold them to its franchisees, Schwinn lost the legal right to tell its purchasers how or where to sell them, regardless of the effects.

Ten years later, the Court dramatically reversed itself again, reverting to the rule of reason to analyze all vertical territorial restriction cases. The reasons for so doing and the current state of the law are set forth in the following case.

CONTINENTAL T.V., INC. v. GTE SYLVANIA INC.
433 U.S. 36 (1977)

MR. JUSTICE POWELL delivered the opinion of the Court.

Franchise agreements between manufacturers and retailers frequently include provisions barring the retailers from selling franchised products from locations other than those specified in the agreements. This case presents important questions concerning the appropriate antitrust analysis of these restrictions under § 1 of the Sherman Act.

Respondent GTE Sylvania Inc. (Sylvania) manufactures and sells television sets through its Home Entertainment Products Division. Prior to 1962, like most other television manufacturers, Sylvania sold its televisions to independent or company-owned distributors who in turn resold to a large and diverse group of retailers. Prompted by a decline in its market share to a relatively insignificant 1% to 2% of national television sales, Sylvania conducted an intensive reassessment of its marketing strategy, and in 1962 adopted the franchise plan challenged here. Sylvania phased out its wholesale distributors and began to sell its televisions directly to a smaller and more select group of franchised retailers. An acknowledged purpose of the change was to decrease the number of competing Sylvania retailers in the hope of attracting the more aggressive and competent retailers thought necessary to the improvement of the company's market position. To this end, Sylvania limited the number of franchises granted for any given area and required each franchisee to sell his Sylvania products only from the location or locations at which he was franchised. A franchise did not constitute an exclusive territory, and Sylvania retained sole discretion to increase the number of retailers in an area in light of the success or failure of existing retailers in developing their market. The revised marketing strategy appears to have been successful during the period at issue here, for by 1965 Sylvania's share of national television sales had increased to approximately 5%, and the company ranked as the Nation's eighth largest manufacturer of color television sets.

This suit is the result of the rupture of a franchiser-franchisee relationship that had previously prospered under the revised Sylvania plan. Dissatisfied with its sales in the city of San Francisco, Sylvania decided in the spring of 1965 to franchise Young Brothers, an established San Francisco retailer of televisions, as an additional San Francisco retailer. The proposed location of the new franchise was approximately a mile from a retail outlet operated by petitioner Continental T.V., Inc. (Continental), one of the most successful Sylvania franchisees. Continental protested that the location of the new franchise violated Sylvania's marketing policy but Sylvania persisted in its plans. Continental then canceled a large Sylvania order and placed a large order with Phillips, one of Sylvania's competitors.

During this same period, Continental expressed a desire to open a store in Sacramento, Cal., a desire Sylvania attributed at least in part to Continental's displeasure over the Young Brothers decision. Sylvania believed that the Sacramento market was adequately served by the existing Sylvania retailers and denied the request. In the face of this denial, Continental advised Sylvania in early September 1965, that it was in the process of moving Sylvania merchandise from its San Jose, Cal., warehouse to a new retail location that it had leased in Sacramento. Two weeks later, allegedly for unrelated reasons, Sylvania's credit department reduced Continental's credit line from $300,000 to $50,000. In response to the reduction in credit and the generally deteriorating relations with Sylvania, Continental withheld all payments owed to John P. Maguire & Co. Inc. (Maguire), the finance company that handled the credit arrangements between Sylvania and its retailers. Shortly thereafter, Sylvania terminated Continental's franchises, and Maguire filed this diversity action in the United States District Court for the Northern District of California seeking recovery of money owed and of secured merchandise held by Continental.

The antitrust issues before us originated in cross-claims brought by Continental against Sylvania and Maguire. Most important for our purposes was the claim that Sylvania had violated § 1 of the Sherman Act by entering into and enforcing franchise agreements that prohibited the sale of Sylvania products other than from specified locations. At the close of evidence in the jury trial of Continental's claims, Sylvania requested the District Court to instruct the jury that its location restriction was illegal only if it unreasonably restrained or suppressed competition. Relying on this Court's decision in *United States* v. *Arnold, Schwinn & Co.*, the District Court rejected the proffered instruction in favor of the following one:

> Therefore, if you find by a preponderance of the evidence that Sylvania entered into a contract, combination or conspiracy with one or more of its dealers pursuant to which Sylvania exercised dominion or control over the products sold to the dealer, after having parted with title and risk to the products, you must find any effort thereafter to restrict outlets or store locations from which its dealers resold the merchandise which they had purchased from Sylvania to be a violation of Section 1 of the Sherman Act, regardless of the reasonableness of the location restrictions.

In answers to special interrogatories, the jury found that Sylvania had engaged "in a contract, combination or conspiracy in restraint of trade in violation of the antitrust laws with respect to location restrictions alone," and assessed Continental's damages at $591,505, which was trebled pursuant to 15 U.S.C. § 15 to produce an award of $1,774,515.

On appeal, the Court of Appeals for the Ninth Circuit, sitting en banc, reversed by a divided vote.

* * *

In the present case, it is undisputed that title to the television sets passed from Sylvania to Continental. Thus, the *Schwinn per se* rule applies unless Sylvania's restriction on locations falls outside *Schwinn's* prohibition against a manufacturer's attempting to restrict a "retailer's freedom as to where and to whom it will resell the products." As the Court of Appeals conceded, the language of *Schwinn* is clearly broad enough to apply to the present case. Unlike the Court of Appeals, however, we are unable to find a principled basis for distinguishing *Schwinn* from the case now before us.

Both Schwinn and Sylvania sought to reduce but not to eliminate competition among their respective retailers through the adoption of a franchise system. Although it was not one of the issues addressed by the District Court or presented on appeal by the Government, the Schwinn franchise plan included a location restriction similar to the one challenged here. These restrictions allowed Schwinn and Sylvania to regulate the amount of competition among their retailers by preventing a franchisee from selling franchised products from outlets other than the one covered by the franchise agreement. To exactly the same end, the Schwinn franchise plan included a companion restriction, apparently not found in the Sylvania plan, that prohibited franchised retailers from selling Schwinn products to nonfranchised retailers. In *Schwinn* the Court expressly held that this restriction was impermissible under the broad principle stated there. In intent and competitive impact, the retail-customer restriction in *Schwinn* is indistinguishable from the location restriction in the present case. In both cases the restrictions limited the freedom of the retailer to dispose of the purchased products as he desired. The fact that one restriction was addressed to territory and the other to customers is irrelevant to functional anti-trust analysis, and indeed, to the language and broad thrust of the opinion in *Schwinn*.

* * *

Vertical restrictions reduce intrabrand competition by limiting the number of sellers of a particular product competing for the business of a given group of buyers. Location restrictions have this effect because of practical constraints on the effective marketing area of retail outlets. Although intrabrand competition may be reduced, the ability of retailers to exploit the resulting market may be limited both by the ability of consumers to travel to other franchised locations and, perhaps more importantly, to purchase the competing products of other manufacturers. None of these key variables, however, is affected by the form of the transaction by which a manufacturer conveys his products to the retailers.

Vertical restrictions promote interbrand competition by allowing the manufacturer to achieve certain efficiencies in the distribution of his products. These "redeeming virtues" are implicit in every decision sustaining vertical restrictions under the rule of reason. Economists have identified a number of ways in which manufacturers can use such restrictions to compete more effectively against other manufacturers. For example, new manufacturers and manufacturers entering new markets can use the restrictions in order to induce competent and aggressive retailers to make the kind of investment of capital and labor that is often required in the distribution of products unknown to the consumer. Established manufacturers can use them to induce retailers to engage in promotional activities or to provide service and repair facilities necessary to the efficient marketing of their products. Service and repair are vital for many products, such as automobiles and major household appliances. The availability and quality of such services affect a manufacturer's goodwill and the competitiveness of his product. Because of market imperfections such as the so-called "free rider" effect, these services might not be provided by retailers in a purely competitive situation, despite the fact that each retailer's benefit would be greater if all provided the services than if none did.

Economists also have argued that manufacturers have an economic interest in maintaining as much intrabrand competition as is consistent with the efficient distribution of their products. Although the view that the manufacturer's interest necessarily corresponds with that of the public is not universally shared, even the leading critic of vertical restrictions concedes that *Schwinn's* distinction between sale and nonsale transactions is essentially unrelated to any relevant economic impact. Indeed, to the extent that the form of the transaction is related to interbrand benefits, the Court's distinction is inconsistent with its articulated concern for the ability of smaller firms to compete effectively with larger ones. Capital requirements and administrative expenses may prevent smaller firms from using the exception for nonsale transactions.

We conclude that the distinction drawn in *Schwinn* between sale and nonsale transactions is not sufficient to justify the application of a *per se* rule in one situation and a rule of reason in the other. The question remains whether the *per se* rule stated in *Schwinn* should be expanded to include non-sale transactions or abandoned in favor of a return to the rule of reason. We have found no persuasive support for expanding the *per se* rule. As noted above, the *Schwinn* Court recognized the undesirability of "prohibit[ing] all vertical restrictions of territory and all franchising. . . ." And even Continental does not urge us to hold that all such restrictions are *per se* illegal.

* * *

In sum, we conclude that the appropriate decision is to return to the rule of reason that governed vertical restrictions prior to *Schwinn*. When anticompetitive effects are shown to result from particular vertical restrictions they can be adequately policed under the rule of reason, the standard traditionally applied for the majority of anticompetitive practices challenged under § 1 of the Act. Accordingly, the decision of the Court of Appeals is

Affirmed.

Restricting Purchases and Sales of Non-franchisor Products

To assure uniformity and consistent quality, the franchisor will insist that its franchisees adhere to certain standards. In food franchising, for example, the franchisor will want to assure customers that the ingredients conform to the same grade throughout all selling areas. In automobile dealerships, the manufacturer will wish to exhibit only its brand. To accomplish these objectives, the franchisor will attempt to restrict its franchisees' options in purchasing raw materials and supplies or in selling products made by someone other than the franchisor.

Such restrictions are not *per se* violations of the antitrust laws. A fast-food franchisor may lawfully demand that its outlets purchase only Grade A milk or meat. The automobile manufacturer may lawfully tell its dealers that they may not sell competitors' cars. But the ways in which franchisors may seek to assure such quality and brand identification are nearly infinite, and not every such scheme is legal. For instance, as we saw in Chapter 19, many forms of tying agreements are unlawful: An agreement between a tire company and a gasoline company through which the gasoline company will require its gas stations, on pain of losing their franchises if they refuse, to sell only one brand of tires violates the antitrust laws. [Federal Trade Commission v. Texaco, 393 U.S. 223 (1968)]

In the next two cases, the courts had to wrestle with these issues. In the first case, the question was whether a take-out chicken franchisor could require its outlets to purchase food supplies from the franchisor only. In the second case, the question was whether an ice-cream franchisor could prohibit its outlets from selling such foodstuffs as hot dogs and hamburgers.

SIEGEL v. CHICKEN DELIGHT, INC.
448 F.2d 43 (9th Cir. 1971)

MERRILL, Circuit Judge: This antitrust suit is a class action in which certain franchisees of Chicken Delight seek treble damages for injuries allegedly resulting from illegal restraints imposed by Chicken Delight's standard form franchise agreements. The restraints in question are Chicken Delight's contractual requirements that franchisees purchase certain essential cooking equipment, dry-mix food items, and trade-mark bearing packaging exclusively from Chicken Delight as a condition of obtaining a Chicken Delight trade-mark license. These requirements are asserted to constitute a tying arrangement, unlawful per se under § 1 of the Sherman Act, 15 U.S.C. § 1.

After five weeks of trial to a jury in the District Court, plaintiffs moved for a directed verdict, requesting the court to rule upon four propositions of law: (1) That the contractual requirements constituted a tying arrangement as a matter of law; (2) that the alleged tying products—the Chicken Delight name, symbols, and system of operation—possessed sufficient economic power to condemn the tying arrangement as a matter of law; (3) that the tying arrangement had not, as a matter of law, been justified; and (4) that, as a matter of law, plaintiffs as a class had been injured by the arrangement.

The court ruled in favor of plaintiffs on all issues except part of the justification defense, which it submitted to the jury. On the question submitted to it, the jury rendered special verdicts in favor of plaintiffs. . . . Chicken Delight has taken this interlocutory appeal from the trial court rulings and verdicts.

Over its eighteen years existence, Chicken Delight has licensed several hundred franchisees to operate home delivery and pick-up food stores. It charged its franchisees no franchise fees or royalties. Instead, in exchange for the license granting the franchisees the right to assume its identity and adopt its business methods and to prepare and market certain food products under its trade-mark, Chicken Delight required its franchisees to purchase a specified number of cookers and fryers and to purchase certain packaging supplies and mixes exclusively from Chicken Delight. The prices fixed for these purchases were higher than, and included a percentage markup which exceeded that of, comparable products sold by competing suppliers.

In order to establish that there exists an unlawful tying arrangement plaintiffs must demonstrate *First,* that the scheme in question involves two distinct items and provides that one (the tying product) may not be obtained unless the other (the tied product) is also purchased. *Second,* that the tying product possesses sufficient economic power appreciably to restrain competition in the tied product market. *Third,* that a "not insubstantial" amount of commerce is affected by the arrangement. Chicken Delight concedes that the third requirement has been satisfied. It disputes the existence of the first two. Further it asserts that, even if plaintiffs should prevail with respect to the first two requirements, there is a *fourth* issue: whether there exists a special justification for the particular tying arrangement in question.

The District Court ruled that the license to use the Chicken Delight name, trade-mark, and method of operations was "a tying item in the traditional sense," the tied items being the cookers and fryers, packaging products, and mixes.

* * *

The hallmark of a tie-in is that it denies competitors free access to the tied product market, not because the party imposing the arrangement has a superior product in that market, but because of the power or leverage exerted by the tying product. . . .

Chicken Delight urges us to hold that its trade-mark and franchise licenses are not items separate and distinct from the packaging, mixes, and equipment, which it says are essential components of the franchise system. To treat the combined sale of all these items as a tie-in for antitrust purposes, Chicken Delight maintains, would be like applying the antitrust rules to the sale of a car with its tires or a left shoe with the right. Therefore, concludes Chicken Delight, the lawfulness of the arrangement should not be measured by the rules governing tie-ins. We disagree.

In determining whether an aggregation of separable items should be regarded as one or more items for tie-in purposes in the normal cases of sales of products the courts must look to the function of the aggregation. Consideration is given to such questions as whether the amalgamation of products resulted in cost savings apart from those reductions in sales expenses and the like normally attendant upon any tie-in, and whether the items are normally sold or used as a unit with fixed proportions.

Where one of the products sold as part of an aggregation is a trade-mark or franchise license, new questions are injected. In determining whether the license and the remaining ("tied") items in the aggregation are to be regarded as distinct items which can be traded in distinct markets consideration must be given to the function of trade-marks.

The historical conception of a trade-mark as a strict emblem of source of the product to which it attaches has largely been abandoned. The burgeoning business of franchising has made trade-mark licensing a widespread commercial practice and has resulted in the development of a new rationale for trade-marks as representations of product quality. This is particularly true in the case of a franchise system set up not to distribute the trade-marked goods of the franchisor, but, as here, to conduct a certain business under a common trade-mark or trade name. Under such a type of franchise, the trade-mark simply reflects the goodwill and quality standards of the enterprise which it identifies. As long as the system of operation of the franchisees lives up to those quality standards and remains as represented by the mark so that the public is not misled, neither the protection afforded the trade-mark by law nor the value of the trade-mark to the licensee depends upon the source of the components.

This being so, it is apparent that the goodwill of the Chicken Delight trade-mark does not attach to the multitude of separate articles used in the operation of the licensed system or in the production of its end product. It is not what is used, but how it is used and what results that have given the system and its end product their entitlement to trade-mark protection. It is to the system and the end product that the public looks with the confidence that established goodwill has created.

* * *

[A]ttempts by tie-in to extend the trade-mark protection to common articles (which the public does not and has no reason to connect with the trade-mark) simply because they are said to be essential to production of that which is the subject of the trade-mark, cannot escape antitrust scrutiny.

Chicken Delight's assertions that only a few essential items were involved in the arrangement does not give us cause to reach a different conclusion. The relevant question is not whether the items are essential to the franchise, but whether it is essential to the franchise that the items be purchased from Chicken Delight. That raises not the issue of whether there is a tie-in but rather the issue of whether the tie-in is justifiable, a subject to be discussed below.

We conclude that the District Court was not in error in ruling as matter of law that the arrangement involved distinct tying and tied products.

Under the per se theory of illegality, plaintiffs are required to establish not only the existence of a tying arrangement but also that the tying product possesses sufficient economic power to appreciably restrain free competition in the tied product markets.

Chicken Delight points out that while it was an early pioneer in the fast food franchising field, the record establishes that there has recently been a dramatic expansion in this area, with the advent of numerous firms, including many chicken franchising systems, all competing vigorously with each other. Under the circumstances, it contends that the existence of the requisite market dominance remained a jury question.

The District Court ruled, however, that Chicken Delight's unique registered trade-mark, in combination with its demonstrated power to impose a tie-in, established as matter of law the existence of sufficient market power to bring the case within the Sherman Act.

We agree. . . .

It can hardly be denied that the Chicken Delight trade-mark is distinctive; that it possesses goodwill and public acceptance unique to it and not enjoyed by other fast food chains.

It is now clear that sufficient economic power is to be presumed where the tying product is patented or copyrighted.

* * *

Chicken Delight maintains that, even if its contractual arrangements are held to constitute a tying arrangement, it was not an unreasonable restraint under the Sherman Act. Three different bases for justification are urged.

First, Chicken Delight contends that the arrangement was a reasonable device for measuring and collecting revenue. There is no authority for justifying a tying arrangement on this ground. Unquestionably, there exist feasible alternative methods of compensation for the franchise licenses, including royalties based on sales volume or fees computed per unit of time, which would neither involve tie-ins nor have undesirable anticompetitive consequences.

Second, Chicken Delight advances as justification the fact that when it first entered the fast food field in 1952 it was a new business. . . . As to the period here involved—1963 to 1970—it contends that transition to a different arrangement would be difficult if not economically impossible.

We find no merit in this contention. Whatever claim Chicken Delight might have had to a new business defense in 1952—a question we need not decide—the defense cannot apply to the 1963–70 period. To accept Chicken Delight's argument would convert the new business justification into a perpetual license to operate in restraint of trade.

The third justification Chicken Delight offers is the "marketing identity" purpose, the franchisor's preservation of the distinctiveness, uniformity and quality of its product.

In the case of a trade-mark this purpose cannot be lightly dismissed. Not only protection of the franchisor's goodwill is involved. The licensor owes an affirmative duty to the public to assure that in the hands of his licensee the trade-mark continues to represent that which it purports to represent. For a licensor, through relaxation of quality control, to permit inferior products to be presented to the public under his licensed mark might well constitute a misuse of the mark.

However, to recognize that such a duty exists is not to say that every means of meeting it is justified. Restraint of trade can be justified only in the absence of less restrictive alternatives. In cases such as this, where the alternative of specification is available, the language used in Standard Oil Co v. United States, 337 U.S. at 306, 69 S.Ct at 1058, 93 L.Ed. 1371, in our view states the proper test, applicable in the case of trade-marks as well as in other cases:

> "* * * the protection of the good will of the manufacturer of the tying device—fails in the usual situation because specification of the type and quality of the product to be used in connection with the tying device is protection enough. * * * The only situation, indeed, in which the protection of good will may necessitate the use of tying clauses is where specifications for a substitute would be so detailed that they could not practicably be supplied."

The District Court found factual issues to exist as to whether effective quality control could be achieved by specification in the case of the cooking machinery and the dip and spice mixes. These questions were given to the jury under instructions; and the jury, in response to special interrogatories, found against Chicken Delight.

As to the paper packaging, the court ruled as matter of law that no justification existed.

> "Defendants' showing on paper packaging is nothing more than a recitation of the need for distinctive packaging to be used uniformly by all franchisees in identifying the hot foods. This was not contested. However, the admissions in evidence clearly demonstrate that the tied packaging was easily specifiable. In fact, the only specifications required were printing and color. Moreover, defendants have admitted that any competent manufacturer of like products could consistently and satisfactorily manufacture the packaging products if defendants furnished specifications. Those suppliers could have sold to the franchisees through normal channels of distribution."

We agree. One cannot immunize a tie-in from the antitrust laws by simply stamping a trade-mark symbol on the tied product—at least where the tied product is not itself the product represented by the mark.

We conclude that the District Court was not in error in holding as matter of law (and upon the limited jury verdict) that Chicken Delight's contractual requirements constituted a tying arrangement in violation of § 1 of the Sherman Act. . . . [J]udgment is affirmed.

SUSSER v. CARVEL CORPORATION
322 F.2d 505 (2nd Cir. 1964)

LUMBARD, Chief Judge (writing for the majority in part and dissenting in part).

The plaintiffs in nine actions which were tried together in the Southern District of New York appeal from the dismissal of their complaints which alleged violations of the antitrust laws and sought treble damages from the Carvel Corporation, a New York corporation which manufactures dairy and primarily soft ice cream products, its subsidiary organizations, certain of its individual officers and attorneys, and a number of its suppliers. The plaintiffs, former and present individual operators of Carvel franchise outlets in Massachusetts, Connecticut and Pennsylvania, also charged the Carvel defendants with fraudulent misrepresentations in the franchise negotiations.

. . . The plaintiffs alleged that Carvel had unlawfully fixed the prices of the retail products sold at the franchise stores and that the franchise agreements embodied tying and exclusive dealing arrangements violative of the Sherman and Clayton acts. The complaints also charged that the contracts between Carvel and the supplier defendants embodied concerted refusals to deal with the plaintiffs violative of the antitrust laws. In a pretrial order the plaintiffs stipulated that they would rely solely upon "per se" violations of the antitrust laws as shown in certain written agreements and other documents. From a judgment which, with one exception, dismissed the complaints against all the defendants on the ground that the plaintiffs had failed to prove violations of the antitrust laws, the plaintiffs appeal.

THE CARVEL FRANCHISE SYSTEM

Although the franchise operators conduct their stores as independent businessmen, through provisions in the franchise agreement Carvel is able to maintain a chain of 400 stores uniform in appearance as well as in operation. The dealer is obligated to conduct his business in accordance with a Standard Operating Procedure Manual (Manual) which governs in great detail the general operation of the store, including the types of products which may be offered for sale, the recipes for their preparation, the nature and placement of advertising displays in the store, the color of the employees' uniforms, and the hours when the store lights must be turned on. The stores are identical in design, each featuring the Carvel crown and cone trademark on a flat slanting roof, glass walls at its front, and the name "Carvel" on its sides in neon lights. This distinctive design is protected by a design patent. The ice cream, which is processed from a mix prepared from a secret formula, is dispensed from a patented machine which bears the Carvel name or trademark. The paper containers, ice cream cones, and spoons all bear the Carvel name and in some instances are unique in design.

* * *

The appellants maintain that the franchise agreements embody violations of the Sherman and Clayton acts insofar as they require the dealer to refrain from selling any non-Carvel product. . . .

* * *

We do not agree.

In Tampa Electric Co. v. Nashville Co., 365 U.S. 320, 81 S.Ct. 623, 5 L.Ed.2d 580 (1961), the Supreme Court held valid a contract between Tampa, a public utility, and Nashville, a medium sized coal company, which obligated Nashville to supply Tampa's entire requirements of coal over a twenty-year period—one form of an exclusive dealing arrangement. After discussing the necessity of delineating the relevant line of commerce and the geographical market, the Court noted that requirements contracts "have not been declared illegal *per se*" and. . . . further emphasized the significance of the possible economic justification for the accused arrangement, in light of the legitimate reasons for employing such a device.

. . . Instead of introducing evidence to establish the economic effects of the Carvel franchise structure, [plaintiffs] merely protest that anti-competitive effects may be inferred solely from the existence of such a network of exclusive dealerships. But the whole tenor of Tampa Electric does not permit adherence to such a stringent standard of legality.

In any event, we need not rely solely upon the appellants' failure to adduce concrete evidence concerning the relevant line of commerce and geographical market and the probable anticompetitive effects of the Carvel arrangement. For in terms of at least one factor which the Supreme Court deemed significant in Tampa Electric—that of economic justification—the Carvel exclusive dealership arrangement withstands any attack on its legality.

As Judge Dawson found, "the cornerstone of a franchise system must be the trademark or trade name of a product." The fundamental device in the Carvel franchise agreement itself is the licensing to the individual dealer of the right to employ the Carvel name in his advertising displays, on the products he sells, and on the store itself. The stores are uniform in design as well as in the public display of the ice cream machinery employed, the placement of advertising displays, and the products offered for sale. The requirement that only Carvel products be sold at Carvel outlets derives from the desirability that the public identify each Carvel outlet as one of a chain which offers identical products at a uniform standard of quality. The antitrust laws certainly do not require that the licensor of a trademark permit his licensees to associate with that trademark other products unrelated to those customarily sold under the mark. It is in the public interest that products sold under one particular trademark should be subject to the control of the trademark owner. Carvel was not required to accede to the requests of one or another of the dealers that they be permitted to sell Christmas trees or hamburgers, for example, which would have thrust upon Carvel the obligation to acquaint itself with the production and sale of these items so as to establish reasonable quality controls.

Nor do the antitrust laws proscribe a trademark owner from establishing a chain of outlets uniform in appearance and operation. Trademark licensing agreements requiring the sole use of the trademarked items have withstood attack under the antitrust laws where deemed reasonably necessary to protect the goodwill interest of the trademark owner, and such agreements certainly are not unlawful *per se* under the antitrust laws. Judge Dawson was fully warranted in concluding that in the context of the entire Carvel franchise system the requirement that no non-Carvel products be sold at the retail level is reasonably necessary for the protection of Carvel's goodwill.

* * *

Accordingly, the judgments of the district court are affirmed.

Termination

A great deal of litigation has arisen over termination of franchises. A franchisor is as free to terminate its franchisee-distributors as it is to franchise them initially, which is to say that when the franchisor decides to terminate for business reasons, the law will not stand in the way. The franchisee who fails to meet sales quotas, to invest sufficient funds in the business, or to uphold quality standards will have no legal recourse if terminated for those reasons. Standard clauses in franchise agreements that permit franchisors to terminate at the end of a stated period will pass muster; in several cases, the courts have ruled that a franchisor may even terminate all its franchises and offer the franchisees employment. [Bushie v. Stenocord Corp., 460 F.2d 116 (9th Cir. 1972)]

But it sometimes happens that franchisors have terminated their franchisees for reasons that run afoul of the antitrust laws: as part of an agreement with other franchisees, for example, to divide the territory, to raise prices, or for some other unlawful objective. Because franchisees have often sunk their life savings into their business, the courts scrutinize especially carefully cases in which it is alleged that franchisors have unfairly terminated. Many federal and state laws provide additional protection to franchisees by restricting the allowable reasons for terminating or by providing a procedure by which a franchisor must act if it intends to terminate.

In the next case, the Supreme Court discusses the distinctions—such as the difference between concerted and independent actions—that are important in termination cases in which antitrust issues are raised.

MONSANTO CO. v. SPRAY-RITE SERVICE CORP.
465 U.S. 752 (1984)

Justice Powell delivered the opinion of the Court.

This case presents a question as to the standard of proof required to find a vertical price-fixing conspiracy in violation of § 1 of the Sherman Act.

Petitioner Monsanto Co. manufactures chemical products, including agricultural herbicides. By the late 1960's, the time at issue in this case, its sales accounted for approximately 15% of the corn herbicide market and 3% of the soybean herbicide market. In the corn herbicide market, the market leader commanded a 70% share. In the soybean herbicide market, two other competitors each had between 30% and 40% of the market. Respondent Spray-Rite Service Corp. was engaged in the wholesale distribution of agricultural chemicals from 1955 to 1972. Spray-Rite was essentially a family business, whose owner and president, Donald Yapp, was also its sole salaried salesman. Spray-Rite was a discount operation, buying in large quantities and selling at a low margin.

Spray-Rite was an authorized distributor of Monsanto herbicides from 1957 to 1968. In October 1967, Monsanto announced that it would appoint distributors for 1-year terms, and that it would renew distributorships according to several new criteria. Among the criteria were: (i) whether the distributor's primary activity was soliciting sales to retail dealers; (ii) whether the distributor employed trained salesmen capable of educating its customers on the technical aspects of Monsanto's herbicides; and (iii) whether the distributor could be expected "to exploit fully" the market in its geographical area of primary responsibility. Shortly thereafter, Monsanto also introduced a number of incentive programs such as making cash payments to distributors that sent salesmen to training classes, and providing free deliveries of products to customers within a distributor's area of primary responsibility.

In October 1968, Monsanto declined to renew Spray-Rite's distributorship. At that time, Spray-Rite was the 10th largest out of approximately 100 distributors of Monsanto's primary corn herbicide. Ninety percent of Spray-Rite's sales volume was devoted to herbicide sales, and 16% of its sales were of Monsanto products. After Monsanto's termination, Spray-Rite continued as a herbicide dealer until 1972. It was able to purchase some of Monsanto's products from other distributors, but not as much as it desired or as early in the season as it needed. Monsanto introduced a new corn herbicide in 1969. By 1972, its share of the corn herbicide market had increased to approximately 28%. Its share of the soybean herbicide market had grown to approximately 19%.

Spray-Rite brought this action under § 1 of the Sherman Act. It alleged that Monsanto and some of its distributors conspired to fix the resale prices of

Monsanto herbicides. Its complaint further alleged that Monsanto terminated Spray-Rite's distributorship, adopted compensation programs and shipping policies, and encourged distributors to boycott Spray-Rite in furtherance of this conspiracy. Monsanto denied the allegations of conspiracy, and asserted that Spray-Rite's distributorship had been terminated because of its failure to hire trained salesmen and promote sales to dealers adequately.

The case was tried to a jury. The District Court instructed the jury that Monsanto's conduct was *per se* unlawful if it was in furtherance of a conspiracy to fix prices. In answers to special interrogatories, the jury found that (i) the termination of Spray-Rite was pursuant to a conspiracy between Monsanto and one or more of its distributors to set resale prices, (ii) the compensation programs, areas of primary responsibility, and/or shipping policies were created by Monsanto pursuant to such a conspiracy, and (iii) Monsanto conspired with one or more distributors to limit Spray-Rite's access to Monsanto herbicides after 1968. The jury awarded $3.5 million in damages, which was trebled to $10.5 million. Only the first of the jury's findings is before us today.

The Court of Appeals for the Seventh Circuit affirmed. It held that there was sufficient evidence to satisfy Spray-Rite's burden of proving a conspiracy to set resale prices. The court stated that "proof of termination following competitor complaints is sufficient to support an inference of concerted action."

. . . We reject the statement by the Court of Appeals for the Seventh Circuit of the standard of proof required to submit a case to the jury in distributor-termination litigation, but affirm the judgment under the standard we announce today.

This Court has drawn two important distinctions that are at the center of this and any other distributor-termination case. First, there is the basic distinction between concerted and independent action—a distinction not always clearly drawn by parties and courts. Section 1 of the Sherman Act requires that there be a "contract, combination . . . or conspiracy" between the manufacturer and other distributors in order to establish a violation. Independent action is not proscribed. A manufacturer of course generally has a right to deal, or refuse to deal, with whomever it likes, as long as it does so independently. *United States v. Colgate & Co.,* 250 U.S. 300, 307 (1919). . . .

The second important distinction in distributor-termination cases is that between concerted action to set prices and concerted action on nonprice restrictions. The former have been *per se* illegal since the early years of national antitrust enforcement. The latter are judged under the rule of reason, which requires a weighing of the relevant circumstances of a case to decide whether a restrictive practice constitutes an unreasonable restraint on competition. See *Continental T.V., Inc., v. GTE Sylvania Inc.,* 433 U.S. 36 (1977).

* * *

. . . On a claim of concerted price fixing, the antitrust plaintiff must present evidence sufficient to carry its burden of proving that there was such an agreement. If an inference of such an agreement may be drawn from highly ambiguous evidence, there is a considerable danger that the doctrines enunciated in *Sylvania* and *Colgate* will be seriously eroded.

The flaw in the evidentiary standard adopted by the Court of Appeals in this case is that it disregards this danger. Permitting an agreement to be inferred merely from the existence of complaints, or even from the fact that termination came about "in response to" complaints, could deter or penalize perfectly legitimate conduct. As Monsanto points out, complaints about price cutters "are natural—and from the manufacturer's perspective, unavoidable—reactions by distributors to the activities of their rivals." Such complaints, particularly where the manufacturer has imposed a costly set of nonprice restrictions, "arise in the normal course of business and do not indicate illegal concerted action." *Roesch, Inc., v. Star Cooler Corp.,* 671 F.2d 1168, 1172 (CA8 1982). . . .

Thus, something more than evidence of complaints is needed. There must be evidence that tends to exclude the possibility that the manufacturer and nonterminated distributors were acting independently. . . .

Applying this standard to the facts of this case, we believe there was sufficient evidence for the jury reasonably to have concluded that Monsanto and some of its distributors were parties to an "agreement" or "conspiracy" to maintain resale prices and terminate price cutters. In fact there was substantial *direct* evidence of agreements to maintain prices. There was testimony from a Monsanto district manager, for example, that Monsanto on at least two occasions in early 1969, about five months after Spray-Rite was terminated, approached price-cutting distributors and advised that if they did not maintain the suggested resale price, they would not receive adequate supplies of Monsanto's new corn herbicide. When one of the distributors did not assent, this information was referred to the Monsanto regional office, and it complained to the distributor's parent company. There was evidence that the parent instructed its subsidiary to comply, and the distributor informed Monsanto that it would charge the suggested price. Evidence of this kind plainly is relevant and persuasive as to a meeting of minds.

* * *

If, as the courts below reasonably could have found, there was evidence of an agreement with one or more distributors to maintain prices, the remaining question is whether the termination of Spray-Rite was of or pursuant to that agreement. It would be reasonable to find that it was, since it is necessary for competing distributors contemplating compliance with suggested prices to know that those who do not comply will be terminated. Moreover, there is some circumstantial evidence of such a link. Following the termination, there was a meeting between Spray-Rite's president and a Monsanto official. There was testimony that the first thing the official mentioned was the many complaints Monsanto had received about Spray-Rite's prices. In addition, there was reliable testimony that Monsanto never discussed with Spray-Rite prior to the termination the distributorship criteria that were the alleged basis for the action. By contrast, a former Monsanto salesman for Spray-Rite's area testified that Monsanto representatives on several occasions in 1965–1966 approached Spray-Rite, informed the distributor of complaints from other distributors—including one major and influential one—and requested that prices be maintained. Later that same year, Spray-Rite's president testified. Monsanto officials made explicit threats to terminate Spray-Rite unless it raised its prices.

We conclude that the Court of Appeals applied an incorrect standard to the evidence in this case. The correct standard is that there must be evidence that tends to exclude the possibility of independent action by the manufacturer and distributor. That is, there must be direct or circumstantial evidence that reasonably tends to prove that the manufacturer and others had a conscious commitment to a common scheme designed to achieve an unlawful objective. Under this standard, the evidence in this case created a jury issue as to whether Spray-Rite was terminated pursuant to a price-fixing conspiracy between Monsanto and its distributors.

The judgment of the court below is affirmed.

Disclosure Requirements

With the growth of franchising in the 1960s, the incidence of fraud, bad faith, and unfair dealing rose dramatically. Competition grew intense, poorly informed investors signed franchise agreements with unfair or deceptive terms that could not possibly have allowed them to become profitable, celebrities agreed to lend their names to product endorsements but—unbeknownst to many franchisees—not personally to support the product or to assure its quality. As a consequence, several states enacted franchise disclosure laws, and the Federal Trade Commission adopted the Franchise Disclosure Rule in 1978. Although differing in detail, the state laws and the federal rule in general require franchisors to make a variety of disclosures about the product or service it is franchising, the nature of the business, and the type and amount of financial investment required of the franchisee. Often franchisors must make these disclosures in the form of registration statements similar to prospectuses for stock offerings filed with the SEC. In some states, registration authorities must first screen advertising of franchise opportunities. To avoid needless duplication, most states permit the filing of a Uniform Franchising Offering Circular, which calls for a host of financial and other disclosures. The FTC rule establishes minimum federal standards for disclosure, but it does not preempt tougher state laws. The federal rule is broad in coverage: the rule governs offers of "business opportunities," even if not labeled "franchise," whenever the distributor must pay the franchisor to start the business. Like the securities laws, the state and federal franchise disclosure rules are complex. The days of amateurs creating instant businesses through franchising schemes are now past; no one should attempt to establish a franchise without a thorough review by lawyers. Indeed, so complex is the system of regulation that there has begun to be talk of a federal takeover of all franchise regulation (see Box 22-1).

Product Liability

As we saw in Chapter 10, the old law of privity of contract, which insulated a manufacturer from legal liability to the ultimate consumer of its product, has now almost completely disappeared. Strict liability theory has given product liability law a powerful impact on all who manufacture goods. For franchisors in particular, the development of strict liability has meant that the franchisor cannot, through agreements with its franchisees, automatically disclaim liability when something goes wrong with the product—whether it is defective meat sold in a fast-food outlet or a defective automobile sold by a dealer. Whether a franchisor will be held liable depends in large part on the degree of control it exercises over how the product is manufactured and sold. In the next case, involving an exploding soda bottle, the question was whether the Seven-Up Company, the franchisor, was liable because its agreement gave it control over the design of the carton in which the bottle was sold.

KOSTERS v. SEVEN-UP CO.
595 F.2d 347 (6th Cir. 1979)

MERRITT, Circuit Judge.

* * *

The defendant, the Seven-Up Company, appeals from a $150,000 jury verdict awarded for injuries caused by an exploding 7-Up bottle. The plaintiff removed a cardboard carton containing six bottles of 7-Up from a grocery shelf, put it under her arm and headed for the check-out counter of the grocery store. She was blinded in one eye when a bottle slipped out of the carton, fell on the floor and exploded, causing a piece of glass to strike her eye

Box 22-1 A Federal Takeover of Franchise Regulations

Franchise Rules: An F.T.C. View
BY BARNABY J. FEDER

After years of grumbling, franchisers and their attorneys have gained a sympathetic ear within the Federal Trade Commission for their complaints about the "patchwork quilt" of state and Federal regulations they face.

"Maybe everything is just wonderful but I have had people come to me and say Ray Kroc couldn't get started today," said Terry Calvani, a commission member, referring to the late founder of the McDonald's Corporation. "If that's true, we have a problem."

Mr. Calvani recently began pressing state regulators to look more closely at the costs of the lack of uniformity in their laws. To the astonishment of some experts, he also raised the possibility that the F.T.C. might pre-empt state law altogether.

"The notion of Federal pre-emption is a bombshell," said David J. Kaufman, a partner at the New York law firm of Kaufman, Caffey, Gildin, Rosenblum & Schaeffer. Mr. Kaufman helped write New York State's franchising rules while a special deputy attorney general. The state's rules, along with those of California and Illinois, are considered to be the most stringent in the nation.

Franchising regulation grew up in response to shady franchising schemes that flourished in the 1960's and early 1970's, costing many investors their life savings. California passed the first laws in 1971. Today, 15 states have rules governing the information that must be disclosed in a prospectus before selling a franchise, 19 states have rules covering the termination of franchises and 23 states have "business opportunity" laws that cover the sale of all new businesses.

The Federal Trade Commission has its own disclosure regulations, adopted in 1979. However, unlike many state regulations, they do not require the disclosure statement to be reviewed before a sale is made and do not give franchisees the right to file a lawsuit if the disclosure statement is defective. State regulators are scornful of the Federal commitment to enforcement in the area.

"We clean things up when they come across our desk," said Sheldon Horowitz, the special deputy attorney general who is New York State's franchise section chief. "The F.T.C waits until the horse is stolen," he said in comments made after Mr. Calvani presented his views to franchise lawyers in New York last month.

By some estimates, more than one-third of the nation's retailing sector is affected by this welter of regulations. Franchising traces its legal roots in

as she looked down. The 7-Up carton was a so-called "over-the-crown" or "neck-thru" carton designed to be held from the top and made without a strip on the sides of the carton which would prevent a bottle from slipping out if held underneath.

The carton was designed and manufactured by Olinkraft, Inc. Olinkraft sold it to the Brooks Bottling Company, a franchisee of the defendant, Seven-Up Company. Seven-Up retains the right to approve the design of articles used by the bottler, including cartons. The franchise agreement between Seven-Up and the Brooks Bottling Company requires that "cases, bottles, and crowns used for 7-Up will be of a type . . . and design approved by the 7-Up Company," and "any advertising . . . material . . . must be approved by the 7-Up Company before its use by the bottler."

Using an extract provided by Seven-Up, Brooks produced the beverage and poured it into bottles. After securing Seven-Up's approval of the design under the franchise agreement, Brooks packaged the bottles in cartons selected and purchased by Brooks from various carton manufacturers, including Olinkraft. Brooks then sold cartons of 7-Up to stores in some 52 Michigan counties, including Meijers Thrifty Acres Store in Holland, Michigan, where the plaintiff the United States to the efforts of I. M. Singer & Company to sell more sewing machines in the 1850's. It became deeply established in the automobile, gasoline and soft-drink bottling businesses before World War II but did not explode as a retailing method until the rapid expansion of the service sector in the 1950's and 1960's.

The franchisers say that the varying laws covering the sale of new franchises and the varying treatment of franchise law from state to state pile needless costs on established companies while forming costly and even prohibitive barriers to newcomers.

The burdens for large franchisers are limited in many states by exemptions based on their past performance and large capitalization. Start-up franchisers are not so lucky, according to Mr. Kaufman. "I don't know about Mr. Kroc, but Colonel Sanders certainly wouldn't have been able to get Kentucky Fried Chicken franchised today with his limited resources," Mr. Kaufman said.

The National Council of Commissioners on Uniform State Laws has proposed a "Uniform Franchise and Business Opportunities Act," but both regulators and attorneys representing franchisers agree that it would never be adopted without significant amendments.

The regulators' own trade group, the North American Security Administrators Association, has also been discussing ways to introduce more uniformity in the laws. But many are wary.

"There are different ideas about what's proper to protect franchisees in different parts of the country," said Mr. Horowitz. "Uniformity isn't necessarily the best thing."

The threat of Federal pre-emption is discounted by many franchising experts. They note that, even if Mr. Calvani and his four fellow commissioners became convinced pre-emption was a good idea, it would require rule-making procedures that could last years.

"This is a proposal that business would like but taking jurisdiction of any kind away from states is a highly charged political problem," said Louis G. Rudnick, a partner at Rudnick & Wolfe in Chicago, which is special counsel to the International Franchise Association, a Washington-based trade group.

Mr. Calvani has tried to minimize such concerns by emphasizing that his main goal is an exploration of the costs of "needless diversity." Moreover, he said, any pre-emption might well be partial. The F.T.C. might want, for instance, to leave power to enforce any national rules in the hands of the states, he added.

Source: *New York Times,* Monday, March 7, 1988

picked up the carton and carried it under her arm toward the checkout counter. Plaintiff settled her claims against the bottler, the carton manufacturer and the grocer for $30,000.

Seven-Up denied liability, insisting its approval of the cartons was only of the "graphics" and for the purpose of assuring that its trademark was properly displayed.

* * *

Seven-Up Company concedes that a franchisor, like a manufacturer or supplier, may be liable to the consumer for its own negligence, without regard to privity, under the doctrine of *MacPherson v. Buick Motor Co.* Seven-Up contends, however, that it does not carry the liabilities of a supplier when it did not supply the product and that other theories of strict tort liability do not apply. Liability may not be laid on the basis of implied warranty, it says, when the franchisor did not manufacture, handle, design or require the use of the particular product. The precise question before us here is whether Michigan's principles of "strict accountability" for breach of implied warranty extend to a franchisor who retains the right of control over the product (the carton) and specifically consents to its distribution in the form sold but does not actually manufacture, sell, handle, ship or require the use of the product.

Different questions may arise in other franchising contexts. In some instances, the franchisor may not retain the right of control or may not actually approve the form of the product. The franchisee may sell a product contrary to the instructions or without the knowledge of the franchisor. The consumer may attempt to hold the franchisor liable for the conduct of the franchisee under the agency doctrines of *respondeat superior* or apparent authority. We do not deal with these questions here.

In this case, the Seven-Up Company not only floated its franchisee and the bottles of its carbonated soft drink into the so-called "stream of commerce." The Company also assumed and exercised a degree of control over the "type, style, size and design" of the carton in which its product was to be marketed. The carton was submitted to Seven-Up for inspection. With knowledge of its design, Seven-Up consented to the entry in commerce of the carton from which the bottle fell, causing the injury. The franchisor's sponsorship, management and control of the system for distributing 7-Up, plus its specific consent to the use of the carton, in our view, places the franchisor in the position of a supplier of the product for purposes of tort liability.

We are not saying that the Seven-Up Company is absolutely liable as an insurer of the safety of the carton under the theory of implied warranty, simply by virtue of its status as a franchisor. In the first place, under Michigan's theory of implied warranty of fitness, the carton must be found to be "defective," or as the District Judge more accurately put it, "not reasonably safe." It must be harmful or unsafe because something is wrong with it, and the jury must so find. Moreover, here the franchisor inspected the carton and approved it. Thus, we need not reach the question whether the franchisor would carry the liabilities of a supplier if it had not been made aware of the product and given the opportunity to assess the risks.

When a franchisor consents to the distribution of a defective product bearing its name, the obligation of the franchisor to compensate the injured consumer for breach of implied warranty, we think, arises from several factors in combination: (1) the risk created by approving for distribution an unsafe product likely to cause injury, (2) the franchisor's ability and opportunity to eliminate the unsafe character of the product and prevent the loss, (3) the consumer's lack of knowledge of the danger, and (4) the consumer's reliance on the trade name which gives the intended impression that the franchisor is responsible for and stands behind the product. Liability is based on the franchisor's control and the public's assumption, induced by the franchisor's conduct, that it does in fact control and vouch for the product.

These are factors Michigan courts have relied on in the past in determining who may be held liable for breach of implied warranty of fitness in other products liability situations. We believe Michigan courts would apply these principles in the franchising situation presented by this case, and we therefore conclude that the case was correctly submitted to the jury to assess liability for breach of implied warranty.

[Reversed on other grounds and remanded.]

The *Kosters* case establishes that the franchisor can be liable for failure of the franchisee to assure a safe product. The reverse is also true: franchisees may be liable to some extent for failures of the franchisor. Suppose, for example, that an automobile manufacturer ships a batch of cars with defective steering wheels and that the defect is visible to the dealer on arrival. The dealer cannot avoid liability by pointing to the manufacturer's legal responsiblity to manufacture safe cars. Beginning in the late 1970s, however, many states have enacted statutes requiring franchisors to indemnify franchisees for defects that originated with the franchisor or that were produced because the franchisee was required to follow specific instructions from the franchisor in assembly or repair.

Liability of Franchisor for Franchisee's Acts

The franchisor may assume that its franchisee is simply a distributor of its products. But if the agreement is not carefully worded or if the franchisor controls too tightly how the franchisee is to operate the business, the franchisor may discover that the franchisee has become its agent for whose acts the franchisor is responsible in accordance with the agency principles covered in Chapter 14. If the franchisee is held to be an agent, the franchisor may wind up being held liable for the franchisee's debts, unpaid wages, and even, under certain circumstances, sales and other taxes. Whether a franchisee is an agent of the franchisor is ultimately a question of fact for the jury to decide, not a legal question that can be answered in the abstract by a court, as the next case shows.

RILEY v. FORD MOTOR CO.
442 F.2d 670 (5th Cir. 1971)

ALDISERT, Circuit Judge. A jury awarded the purchaser of a 1969 Lincoln Mark III automobile $30,000 in damages against Ford Motor Company for breach of warranty and negligent repair of certain defects. Appellant Ford insists that the district court erred in withdrawing from the jury the question whether the dealer acted as its agent, and argues that the damages were excessive as a matter of law. Having concluded that both contentions are correct, we must reverse and remand the cause for a new trial.

Appellee purchased his new automobile from a Florida dealer at a cost of $8,476.00, and Ford issued a self-styled "New Vehicle Warranty." Shortly thereafter he took the car to Robinson Brothers, an Alabama Ford dealer, for repair of a window and removal of a noise in the rear end. According to Riley these defects were not corrected. At trial he testified that in the weeks following the requested repairs, and before the car was returned to Robinson Brothers for further repairs, these additional malfunctions developed: air conditioning did not work, speed control did not function, power seats became inoperative, the radio aerial functioned spasmodically, the rear seat did not fit, headlight panels were not synchronized, the cigarette lighter was missing, windshield wipers were defective, engine knocked upon acceleration, the transmission did not function properly, gear shift lever would not function, and the left door would not close properly.

Dissatisfied with the car's condition, appellee wrote to Ford setting forth in detail his complaints, and requesting Ford "to direct me to a dealer employing trained service personnel, or furnish me with someone capable of overseeing service personnel available in order to insure that the defects in my automobile are properly corrected in an expert and dependable manner." Ford dispatched a Technical Service Representtive who road tested the automobile, agreed that it was not functioning properly, and offered to take it to Robinson Brothers where he would personally supervise its repair. The owner believed he had a better idea. Refusing to again leave his car with Robinson's, he brought this action against Ford seeking recovery on two theories: breach of warranty and negligent repair.

Because the negligence count is predicated on the alleged negligence of Robinson Brothers, recovery against Ford depends on a showing that the dealer was, in fact, an agent of the manufacturer. The evidence on this issue was conflicting. The contract between Ford and Robinson Brothers provided:

> The agreement does not, in any way, create a relationship of principal and agent between the company and the dealer and under no circumstances shall the dealer be considered to be the agent of the company. The dealer shall not act or attempt to act or represent himself directly or by implication as agent of the company or in any

> manner assume or create or attempt to assume or create any obligation on behalf of or in the name of the company.

Furthermore, Ford owned no stock in the dealership, paid no portion of its employees' salaries, paid no rental for the building it occupied, and had no employees stationed there for supervision or control. It is undisputed, however, that Robinson Brothers sent its mechanics to Ford's training school, received "factory campaign notices" relating to particular problems with certain models, and sold Lincoln-Mercury automobiles manufactured by Ford.

During the re-direct examination of William H. Robinson, the court interrupted testimony regarding the agency issue:

> I can't help what is in that contract. If Lincoln sells a car and says we warrant it, I don't care what is in the contract. They are acting for Ford Motor Company.

In this diversity action, we are referred to Alabama law for the relevant substantive law principles which will govern this case. It has long been the law of Alabama that "the question of agency is a matter of fact, which it is the province of the jury to determine upon, under the instructions of the court." That the district court, by its statement, "[t]hey are acting for Ford Motor Company," effectively removed the issue of agency from the jury is clear. It is equally evident that this amounted to reversible trial error.

* * *

Reversed and remanded for a new trial.

Chapter Summary

Although differing in legal consequences from state to state, in general a franchise is created when a contract calls for a franchisee to pay a fee for the right to sell trademarked goods in a manner the franchisor substantially prescribes. The principal types of franchises are distributorships, business-format franchises, and manufacturing plants. Not all supplier-distributor relations are necessarily franchises. Other types include consignment, independent contracting, independent retail dealershps, concessions, and leases.

The franchisor's control over its trademark, trade name, or commercial symbol lies at the heart of the franchise operation. In general, the franchisor has the right to dictate to its franchisees how the franchisor's intangible property rights will be used. The right to do so is subject to a large exception—one that the antitrust laws have laid down.

The franchisor may select or terminate franchisees at will unless its refusal to select a franchisee or its decision to terminate one was the consequence of an agreement violating the antitrust laws or other federal and state laws that protect franchisees.

Although allocations of territory among competitors (horizontal allocations) are *per se* violations of the Sherman Act, vertical allocations the franchisor imposes on its distributor network are not necessarily violations; the courts will follow the rule of reason before striking them down. Within antitrust limits, franchisors may also assure uniformity and consistent quality by insisting that its franchisees adhere to standards. These standards may, for example, prohibit franchisees from selling products not made by the franchisor. Again, the courts follow the rule of reason and will permit the franchise practice to stand if a sound business reason can justify it.

An increasing number of states and the Federal Trade Commission regulate the promotion and sale of franchise opportunities. These laws and the FTC's Franchise Disclosure Rule generally require filing of franchise disclosure statements akin to securities registration statements.

Franchisors will generally be liable for injuries stemming from defective products, unless the assembly, installation, or repair of the product is entirely within the control of the franchisee. Franchisees may also be held liable for product defects. Whether a franchisor is liable for acts of its franchisees beyond product safety concerns depends on whether the franchisees are in fact agents of the franchisor.

Problems

1. Tastee Tidbits, a national chain of snack foods, requires its distributors to buy all ingredients from a subsidiary of the parent franchisor. The franchisor also requires all 387 distributors to use the Tastee Tidbits logo and to sell Tastee's foodstuffs in distinctive huts built in the shape of a popcorn kernel. The franchise agreement specifies the cooking conditions and instructs the franchisees to build their kitchens to exacting specifications. The agreement also says that each franchisee is "an independent entity for purposes of paying all taxes, hiring all personnel, and establishing all lines of bank credit." Last month Tastee Tidbits introduced Cheesey-Spicearoma, a new snack food (consisting of garlic, onions, cinnamon, and pepperoni), that it advertised extensively nationwise. Several dozen people in fourteen states became violently ill after eating a portion of Cheesy-Spicearoma and have sued the local Tastee Tidbit outlets and the parent corporation. What legal defenses, if any, do the local outlets have? What defenses, if any, does the parent franchisor have?
2. Boomerang Brothers is a manufacturer of a toy that was once a hot item in stores nationally. But lately its appeal has been waning. Boomerang had been selling its product to wholesalers for resale to general department stores and also through a chain of distributors that stocked only Boomerang's products. As sales declined, one of Boomerang's distributors suggested to the national sales manager that Boomerang stop selling to the department stores and create a single franchise in each state to market the toys. Now the sales manager discusses the idea with the company's top executives, all of whom are enthusiastic about the idea. So they announce that effective January 1, they will stop selling to department stores and will terminate all but one distributor in each state. The remaining distributor in each state will have an exclusive territory within the state to market the toys. Distributors who

have been cut off file suit. With what legal violations, if any, can they charge Boomerang Brothers? What defenses, if any, does Boomerang have?

3. Ears-of-Plenty, Inc. sells juicy corn on the cob, fresh from farms daily. It requires its franchised outlets to purchase all their corn requirements from a subsidiary company organized to supply corn to all franchisees. Under the franchise agreement, the franchisees must have a variety of condiments, including butter and salt, available for customers. For more than ten years, Ears-of-Plenty has prospered selling only the delicious ears of corn. One day the Ears-of-Plenty franchise in Duluth, Minn., decides to enhance its profits by offering some other foodstuffs for sale, including fresh green vegetables, special sauces and dips, and ice cream and chocolate sauce. Ears, Inc., the franchisor, sends a letter to the Duluth franchisee, instructing it to stop selling all vegetables, sauces, dips, and ice cream. When the franchisee refuses, Ears, Inc. terminates the franchise. The Duluth outlet sues, charging the franchisor with antitrust violations. What result?

PART SEVEN

PROPERTY RIGHTS AND ENVIRONMENTAL PROTECTION

23

Regulation of Real Property and the Environment

In this chapter and the next we examine the impact of governmental regulation on real and personal property interests. In this chapter we first discuss the general nature of property rights, including the classification of property as tangible versus intangible and real versus personal. We then explore the regulation of **real property rights** by tort law and agreement, and public control of land use through eminent domain and zoning. The chapter concludes with an overview of environmental law, an area that has played a major role in shaping property rights in the United States. In Chapter 24 we turn to a discussion of government regulation and **personal property.** Nowhere has government regulation of personal property had a greater impact than on intellectual property, an intangible personal interest that we will explore in depth in the chapter.

The General Nature of Property Rights

Defined

Property, which seems so commonsense a concept, is difficult to define in an intelligible way, though philosophers have been striving to do so for the past 2,500 years. To say that property is what we own is to beg the question—or substitute a synonym for the word we are trying to define. Blackstone's famous definition is somewhat verbose: "The right of property is that sole and despotic dominion which one man claims and exercises over the external things of the world, in total exclusion of the right of any other individual in the universe. It consists in the free use, enjoyment, and disposal of all a person's acquisitions, without any control or diminution save only by the laws of the land." Attempting a more formal and concise definition, the *Restatement of the Law of Property,* Chapter 1 (Introductory Note), defines property as the "legal relationship between persons with respect to a thing."

The *Restatement's* definition makes an essential point: property is a *legal relationship,* not a listing. This relationship deals with the power of one person to use objects in ways that affect others, to exclude others from the property, and to acquire and transfer property. However, the definition does not contain within itself a list of those things capable of being expressed in that relationship. We all know that we can own personal objects like radios and coats and even more complex "objects" like homes and minerals under the ground. Property also embraces objects whose worth is not so much intrinsic as representative or symbolic: ownership of stock in a corporation is valued not for the piece of paper called a stock certificate but for dividends, the power to vote for directors, and the right to sell the stock on the open market. Wholly intangible "things," like copyrights and patents and bank accounts, are capable of being owned as property. But the list of things that can be property is not fixed. Our concept of property continues to evolve. In the United States, many jobs are considered a type of property—protection against being fired, claims on pension funds, and other employment rights are converting what was once simply a contractual claim into a more solid-sounding property right. Welfare payments also are regarded as property, at least for purposes of the due process clause of the Fourteenth Amendment. A state cannot deprive a person of such payments without first holding a hearing. Likewise, some courts have even begun to recognize a person's educational degree as a property right in divorce proceedings, although most courts—as the following leading case demonstrates—have not gone that far.

In re THE MARRIAGE OF GRAHAM
194 Colo. 429, 574 P.2d 75 (1978)

LEE, JUSTICE. This case presents the novel question of whether in a marriage dissolution proceeding a master's degree in business administration (M.B.A.) constitutes marital property which is subject to division by the court. In its opinion in *Graham v. Graham,* Colo. App., 555 P.2d 527, the Colorado Court of Appeals held that it was not. We affirm the judgment.

The Uniform Dissolution of Marriage Act requires that a court shall divide marital property, without regard to marital misconduct, in such proportions as the court deems just after considering all relevant factors. The Act defines marital property as follows:

> For purposes of this article only, "marital property" means all property acquired by either spouse subsequent to the marriage except:
>
> (a) Property acquired by gift, bequest, devise, or descent;
>
> (b) Property acquired in exchange for property acquired prior to the marriage or in exchange for property acquired by gift, bequest, devise, or descent;
>
> (c) Property acquired by a spouse after a decree of legal separation; and
>
> (d) Property excluded by valid agreement of the parties. (Section 14-10-113(2), C.R.S.1973.)

The parties to this proceeding were married on August 5, 1968, in Denver, Colorado. Throughout the six-year marriage, Anne P. Graham, wife and petitioner here, was employed full-time as an airline stewardess. She is still so employed. Her husband, Dennis J. Graham, respondent, worked part-time for most of the marriage, although his main pursuit was his education. He attended school for approximately three and one-half years of the marriage, acquiring both a bachelor of science degree in engineering physics and a master's degree in business administration at the University of Colorado. Following graduation, he obtained a job as an executive assistant with a large corporation at a starting salary of $14,000 per year.

The trial court determined that during the marriage petitioner contributed seventy percent of the financial support, which was used both for family expenses and for her husband's education. No marital assets were accumulated during the marriage. In addition, the Grahams together managed an apartment house and petitioner did the majority of housework and cooked most of the meals for the couple. No children were born during the marriage.

The parties jointly filed a petition for dissolution, on February 4, 1974, in the Boulder County District Court. Petitioner did not make a claim for maintenance or for attorney fees. After a hearing on October 24, 1974, the trial court found, as a matter of law, that an education obtained by one spouse during a marriage is jointly-owned property to which the other spouse has a property right. The future earnings value of the M.B.A. to respondent was evaluated at $82,836 and petitioner was awarded $33,134 of this amount, payable in monthly installments of $100.

The court of appeals reversed, holding that an education is not itself "property" subject to division under the Act, although it was one factor to be considered in determining maintenance or in arriving at an equitable property division.

The purpose of the division of marital property is to allocate to each spouse what equitably belongs to him or her. The division is committed to the sound discretion of the trial court and there is no rigid mathematical formula that the court must adhere to. An appellate court will alter a division of property only if the trial court abuses its discretion. This court, however, is empowered at all times to interpret Colorado statutes.

The legislature intended the term "property" to be broadly inclusive, as indicated by its use of the qualifying adjective "all" in section 14-10-113(2). Previous Colorado cases have given "property" a comprehensive meaning, as typified by the following definition: "In short it embraces anything and everything which may belong to a man and in the ownership of which he has a right to be protected by law." *Las Animas County High School District v. Raye,* 144 Colo. 367, 356 P.2d 237.

Nonetheless, there are necessary limits upon what may be considered "property," and we do not find any indication in the Act that the concept as used by the legislature is other than that usually understood to be embodied within the term. One helpful definition is "everything that has an exchangeable value or which goes to make up wealth or estate." *Black's Law Dictionary* 1382 (rev. 4th ed. 1968). In *Ellis v. Ellis,* Colo., 552 P.2d 506, this court held that military retirement pay was not property for the reason that it did not have any of the elements of cash surrender value, loan value, redemption value, lump sum value, or value realizable after death. The court of appeals has considered other factors as well in deciding whether something falls within the concept, particularly whether it can be assigned, sold, transferred, conveyed, or pledged, or whether it terminates on the death of the owner.

An educational degree, such as an M.B.A., is simply not encompassed even by the broad views of the concept of "property." It does not have an exchange value or any objective transferable value on an open market. It is personal to the holder. It terminates on death of the holder and is not inheritable. It cannot be assigned, sold, transferred, conveyed, or pledged. An advanced degree is a cumulative product of many years of previous education, combined with diligence and hard work. It may not be acquired by the mere expenditure of money. It is simply an intellectual achievement that may potentially assist in the future acquisition of property. In our view, it has none of the attributes of property in the usual sense of that term.

Our interpretation is in accord with cases in other jurisdictions. We have been unable to find any decision, even in community property states, which appears to have held that an education of one spouse is marital property to be divided on dissolution. This contention was dismissed in *Todd v. Todd,* 272 Cal.App.2d 786, 78 Cal.Rptr. 131 (Ct.App.), where it was held that a law degree is not a community property asset capable of division, partly because it "cannot have monetary value placed upon it." Similarly, it has been recently held that a person's earning capacity, even where enhanced by a law degree financed by the other spouse, "should not be recognized as a separate, particular item of property." *Stern v. Stern,* 66 N.J. 340, 331 A.2d 257.

Other cases cited have dealt only with related issues. For example, in awarding alimony, as opposed to dividing property, one court has found that an education is one factor to be considered. *Daniels v. Daniels,* 20 Ohio Op.2d 458, 185 N.E.2d 773 (Ct.App.). In another case, the wife supported the husband while he went to medical school. *Nail v. Nail,* 486 S.W.2d 761 (Tex.). The question was whether the accrued good will of his medical practice was marital property, and the court held it was not, inasmuch as good will was based on the husband's personal skill, reputation, and experience.

The trial court relied on *Greer v. Greer,* 32 Colo.App. 196, 510 P.2d 905, for its determination that an education is "property." In that case, a six-year marriage was dissolved in which the wife worked as a teacher while the husband obtained a medical degree. The parties had accumulated marital property. The trial court awarded the wife alimony of $150 per month for four years. The court of appeals found this to be proper, whether considered as an adjustment of property rights based upon the wife's financial contribution to the marriage, or as an award of alimony in gross. The court there stated that ". . . [i]t must be considered as a substitute for, or in lieu of, the wife's rights in the husband's property. . . ." We note that the court did not determine that the medical education itself was divisible property. The case is distinguishable from the instant case in that here there was no accumulation of marital property and the petitioner did not seek maintenance [alimony].

A spouse who provides financial support while the other spouse acquires an education is not without a remedy. Where there is marital property to be divided, such contribution to the education of the other spouse may be taken into consideration by the court. Here, we again note that no marital property had been accumulated by the parties. Further, if maintenance is sought and a need is demonstrated, the trial court may make an award based on all relevant factors. Certainly, among the relevant factors to be considered is the contribution of the spouse seeking maintenance to the education of the other spouse from whom the maintenance is sought. Again, we note that in this case petitioner sought no maintenance from respondent.

The judgment is affirmed.

The Economist's View

Property is not solely a legal concept, of course, and different disciplines express different philosophies about the purpose of property. To the jurist, property rights should be protected because it is just to do so. To the economist, "the legal protection of property rights has an important economic function: to create incentives to use resources efficiently" (Posner,

1973, p. 10). For a truly efficient system of property rights, the economist would require *universality* (everything is owned), *exclusivity* (the owners of each thing may exclude all others from using it), and *transferability* (owners may exchange their property). Together, these aspects of property would lead, under an appropriate economic model, to efficient production and distribution of goods. Because efficiency is a desideratum in a modern economy, the tendency may be to regard these features as necessary legal aspects of property as well. To do so would be mistaken. Rightly or wrongly, the law of property does not conform entirely to the economic conception of the ownership of productive property.

Classification of Property

Property can be classified in various ways, including tangible vs. intangible, private vs. public, and personal vs. real. **Tangible property** is that which physically exists, like a building, a ring, or a machine tool. **Intangible property** is something without physical reality that entitles the owner to certain benefits. **Public property** is that which is owned by the government; **private property** is that which is owned by anyone else, including a corporation.

Perhaps the most important distinction is between real and personal property. Essentially, **real property** is immovable; **personal property**, also known as *chattels,* is movable. Chattels that become affixed to personal property in a certain manner are called *fixtures* and are treated as real property.

Importance of the Distinction Between Real and Personal Property

In our legal system, the distinction between real and personal property is significant in several ways. For example, the sale of personal property, but not real property, is governed by Article 2 of the Uniform Commercial Code. Real estate transactions, by contrast, are governed by the general law of contracts. Suppose goods are exchanged for realty. UCC Section 2-304 says that the transfer of the goods and the seller's obligations with reference to them are subject to Article 2, but not the transfer of the interests in realty nor the transferor's obligations in connection with them.

The form of transfer depends on whether the property is real or personal. Real property is normally transferred by a deed, which must meet formal requirements. Transfer of personal property often can be done without any documents at all.

Another difference lies in the law that governs the transfer of property on death. A person's heirs must depend on the law of the state for distribution of his property if he dies *intestate*—without a will. Who the heirs are and what their share of the property will be may depend on whether it is real or personal. For example, widows may be entitled to a different percentage of real than personal property when their husbands die intestate.

Tax laws also differ in their approach to real and personal property. In particular, the rules of valuation, depreciation, and enforcement depend heavily on the character of the property. Thus, real property depreciates more slowly than personal property, and real property owners generally have a longer time than personal property owners to make good unpaid taxes before the state seizes the property.

Importance of the Distinction in Different Legal Systems

Another way to consider the importance of the distinction between real and personal property in American law is to view the distinctions made among the types of property in a fundamentally different legal system. In the Soviet Union, the distinction between real and personal property is virtually absent. Instead, law in the communist regime focuses on the distinction between property as a means of production and property used for consumption. Property used by the individual for his own personal needs and not for the generation of profits or investment is considered personal and subject to rules that are familiar to the common law. An individual may use, sell, and bequeath personal property as he sees fit. But this category of personal or private property is far smaller than it is in the United States. Under the common law, an automobile, whether used for business or pleasure, is personal property and may be transfered at will. Not so in the Soviet Union, where an automobile used in business—as say, a taxi—is not owned privately and, hence, is not personal property in our sense.

Virtually all property used to produce a profit or that could be used for investment—capital—is publicly owned, whether land and buildings (real property in our sense) or machines and other tools (personal property in our sense). This kind of property is public, owned either wholly by the state or by the agricultural cooperatives. The communist law worries far less about who the owner is than how particular people will be able to use this public property. Acquisition and transfer are far less important than the right to use and manage. Ownership under such a regime which dictates production quotas for virtually every enterprise is thus a radically different concept than it is in a common-law system.

Regulation of Land Use

Land use regulation falls into three broad categories: (1) restriction on the use of land through tort law; (2) private regulation by agreement; and (3) public ownership or regulation through the powers of eminent domain and zoning.

Regulation of Land Use by Tort Law

Tort law is used to regulate land use in two ways. (1) The owner may become liable for certain activities carried out on the real estate that affect others beyond the real estate. (2) The owner may be liable to persons who, upon entering the real estate, are injured.

Landowner's Activities The two most common torts in this area are *nuisance* and *trespass*. A common-law **nuisance** is an interference with the use and enjoyment of one's land. Examples of nuisances are excessive noise (especially late at night), polluting activities, and emissions of noxious odors. But the activity must produce substantial harm, not fleeting, minor injury, and it must produce those effects on the reasonable person, not on someone who is peculiarly allergic to the complained of activity. A person who suffered migraine headaches at the sight of croquet being played on a neighbor's lawn would not likely win a nuisance lawsuit. However, the meaning of nuisance is impossible to define with any precision. As Professor William Prosser has said: "There is perhaps no more impenetrable jungle in the entire law than that which surrounds the word 'nuisance.' It has meant all things to all men, and has been applied indiscriminately to everything from an alarming advertisement to a cockroach baked in a pie. There is general agreement that it is incapable of any exact or comprehensible definition" (1971, p. 571).

A **trespass** is the wrongful physical invasion of or entry upon land possessed by another. Loud noise blaring out of speakers in the house next door might be a nuisance but could not be a trespass, because noise is not a physical invasion. But spraying pesticides on your gladiolas could constitute a trespass on your neighbor's property if the pesticide drifts across the boundary.

Nuisance and trespass are complex theories, a full explanation of which would consume far more space than we have. What is important to remember is that these torts are two-edged swords. In many situations, the landowner himself will want to use these theories to sue trespassers or persons creating a nuisance, but in many others the landowner will be liable under these theories for his own activities. However, courts are often reluctant to use tort theories in private litigation against property owners in order to achieve public objectives—for the reasons stated in the following case.

BOOMER v. ATLANTIC CEMENT COMPANY
26 N.Y.2d 219, 257 N.E.2d 87. (1970)

BERGAN, JUDGE. Defendant operates a large cement plant near Albany. These are actions for injunction and damages by neighboring land owners alleging injury to property from dirt, smoke and vibration emanating from the plant. A nuisance has been found after trial, temporary damages have been allowed; but an injunction has been denied.

The public concern with air pollution arising from many sources in industry and in transportation is currently accorded ever wider recognition accompanied by a growing sense of responsibility in State and Federal Governments to control it. Cement plants are obvious sources of air pollution in the neighborhoods where they operate.

But there is now before the court private litigation in which individual property owners have sought specific relief from a single plant operation. The threshold question raised by the division of view on this appeal is whether the court should resolve the litigation between the parties now before it as equitably as seems possible; or whether, seeking promotion of the general public welfare, it should channel private litigation into broad public objectives.

A court performs its essential function when it decides the rights of parties before it. Its decision of private controversies may sometimes greatly affect public issues. Large questions of law are often resolved by the manner in which private litigation is decided. But this is normally an incident to the court's main function to settle controversy. It is a rare exercise of judicial power to use a decision in private litigation as a purposeful mechanism to achieve direct public objectives greatly beyond the rights and interests before the court.

Effective control of air pollution is a problem presently far from solution even with the full public and financial powers of government. In large measure adequate technical procedures are yet to be developed and some that appear possible may be economically impracticable.

It seems apparent that the amelioration of air pollution will depend on technical research in great depth; on a carefully balanced consideration of the economic impact of close regulation; and of the actual effect on public health. It is likely to require massive public expenditure and to demand more than any local community can accomplish and to depend on regional and interstate controls.

A court should not try to do this on its own as a by-product of private litigation and it seems manifest that the judicial establishment is neither equipped in the limited nature of any judgment it can pronounce nor prepared to lay down and implement an effective policy for the elimination of air pollution. This is an area beyond the circumference of one private lawsuit. It is a direct responsibility for government and should not thus be undertaken as an incident to solving a dispute between property owners and a single cement plant—one of many—in the Hudson River valley.

The cement making operations of defendant have been found by the court at Special Term to have damaged the nearby properties of plaintiffs in these two actions. That court, as it has been noted, accordingly found defendant maintained a nuisance and this has been affirmed at the Appellate Division. The total damage to plaintiffs' properties is, however, relatively small in comparison with the value of defendant's operation and with the consequences of the injunction which plaintiffs seek.

The ground for the denial of injunction, notwithstanding the finding both that there is a nuisance and that plaintiffs have been damaged substantially, is the large disparity in economic consequences of the nuisance and of the injunction. This theory cannot, however, be sustained without overruling a doctrine which has been consistently reaffirmed in several leading cases in this court and which has never been disavowed here, namely that where a nuisance has been found and where there has been any substantial damage shown by the party complaining an injunction will be granted.

*   *   *

This result at Special Term and at the Appellate Division is a departure from a rule that has become settled; but to follow the rule literally in these cases would be to close down the plant at once. This court is fully agreed to avoid that immediately drastic remedy; the difference in view is how best to avoid it.*

One alternative is to grant the injunction but postpone its effect to a specified future date to give opportunity for technical advances to permit defendant to eliminate the nuisance; another is to grant the injunction conditioned on the payment of permanent damages to plaintiffs which would compensate them for the total economic loss to their property

*Respondent's investment in the plant is in excess of $45,000,000. There are over 300 people employed there.

present and future caused by defendant's operations. For reasons which will be developed the court chooses the latter alternative.

If the injunction were to be granted unless within a short period—e.g., 18 months—the nuisance be abated by improved methods, there would be no assurance that any significant technical improvement would occur.

The parties could settle this private litigation at any time if defendant paid enough money and the imminent threat of closing the plant would build up the pressure on defendant. If there were no improved techniques found, there would inevitably be applications to the court at Special Term for extensions of time to perform on showing of good faith efforts to find such techniques.

Moreover, techniques to eliminate dust and other annoying by-products of cement making are unlikely to be developed by any research the defendant can undertake within any short period, but will depend on the total resources of the cement industry nationwide and throughout the world. The problem is universal wherever cement is made.

For obvious reasons the rate of the research is beyond control of defendant. If at the end of 18 months the whole industry has not found a technical solution a court would be hard put to close down this one cement plant if due regard be given to equitable principles.

On the other hand, to grant the injunction unless defendant pays plaintiffs such permanent damages as may be fixed by the court seems to do justice between the contending parties. All of the attributions of economic loss to the properties on which plaintiffs' complaints are based will have been redressed.

* * *

The orders should be reversed, without costs, and the cases remitted to Supreme Court, Albany County to grant an injunction which shall be vacated upon payment by defendant of such amounts of permanent damage to the respective plaintiffs as shall for this purpose be determined by the court.

Injury to Persons Entering the Real Estate Traditionally, liability for injury has depended on the status of the person who enters the real estate.

Trespassers If the person is an intruder without permission—a **trespasser**—the landowner owes him no duty of care unless he knows of the intruder's presence, in which case the owner must exercise reasonable care and warn of hidden dangers of which the landowner is aware. A known trespasser is someone whom the landowner actually sees on the property or whom he knows frequently intrudes on the property, as in the case of someone who habitually walks across the land. If a landowner knows that people frequently walk across his property and one day he puts a poisonous chemical on the ground to eliminate certain insects, he is obligated to warn those who continue to walk on the grounds. Intentional injury to known trespassers is not allowed, even if the trespasser is a criminal intent on robbery, for the law values human life above property rights. For the aftermath of one such incident, in which a farmer rigged a hidden spring-gun to prevent his farmhouse from being robbed, see Box 23-1.

Children If the trespasser is a child, a different rule applies in most states. This is the doctrine of **attractive nuisance.** Originally this rule was enunciated to deal with cases in which something on the land attracted the child to it, like a swimming pool. In recent years, most courts have dropped the requirement that the child must have been attracted to the danger.

Box 23-1 Intentional Injury to Trespasser

The Thief's Revenge

One summer night in 1967, a 27-year-old gas-station-mechanic-turned-thief broke into an abandoned farmhouse near the sleepy southern Iowa village of Eddyville (population: 1,000). As he opened the door to a front room, shotgun pellets ripped through the door—and tore a 2½-inch hole through the thief's right leg. The door-knob had been wired to the trigger of a 20-gauge shotgun fixed to a bedpost in the room.

Marvin Katko later pleaded guilty to petty larceny and received a 30-day suspended sentence plus a $50 fine. But Katko, who was crippled for life by the blast, thought house owner Edward Briney had been overzealous in protecting his property. He sued Briney. The judge instructed the jury that the law "placed a higher value upon human safety than upon mere rights in property." The jury awarded Katko $20,000 in actual damages and $10,000 in punitive damages. (The Iowa Supreme Court affirmed the landmark decision 8–1.)

RENT

Then a flood of sympathetic letters and contributions poured in to farmer Briney from 39 states and even Vietnam, where a U.S. soldier's wife wrote, "it makes me feel my husband is fighting for the wrong government." To help Briney pay the judgment, three of his neighbors purchased one-quarter of his land for a modest $10,000, allowing him to rent it for taxes and bank interest.

But as the value of good Iowa soil rose over the years, this particular flame of human kindness flickered lower. Last year, Briney's three neighbors first offered to sell the land back to him—but at a price he could not afford. They then kicked him off the land and sold it for a fat profit. Charging that his erstwhile benefactors held the land effectively in trust for him, Briney has now sued them. He wants either the right to buy the land back at the original price or to collect $14,000, which he claims represents the increase in value of the land. But since Briney still owes Katko for part of the judgment, he has assigned his rights to the convicted thief. Next fall, victim and robber will go to court hand in hand against the good Samaritans.

Source: *Newsweek,* June 9, 1975

Instead, the following elements of proof are necessary to make out a case of attractive nuisance:

1. The child must have been injured by a structure or other artificial condition.
2. The possessor of the land (not necessarily the owner) must have known or should have known that young children would be likely to trespass.
3. The possessor must have known or should have known that the artificial condition exists and that it posed an unreasonable risk of serious injury.
4. The child must have been too young to appreciate the danger that the artificial condition posed.
5. The risk to the child must have far outweighed the utility of the artificial condition to the possessor.

6. The possessor did not exercise reasonable care in protecting the children or eliminating the danger.

Suppose Farmer Brown keeps an old buggy on his front lawn, accessible from the street. A five-year-old boy clambers up the buggy one day, falls through a rotted floor board, and breaks his leg. Is Farmer Brown liable? Probably so. The child was too young to appreciate the danger posed by the buggy, a structure. The farmer should have appreciated that young children would be likely to come onto the land when they saw the buggy and that they would be likely to climb up onto the buggy. Moreover, he should have known, if he did not know in fact, that the buggy, left outside for years without being tended, would pose an unreasonable risk. The buggy's utility as a decoration was far overbalanced by the risk that it posed to children, and the farmer failed to exercise reasonable care.

Licensees A nontrespasser who comes onto the land without being invited, or, if invited, for purposes unconnected with any business conducted on the premises, is known as a **licensee.** This class of visitors to the land consists of (1) social guests (people you invite to your home for a party), (2) a salesman not invited by the owner who wishes to sell something to the owner or occupier of the property, and (3) persons visiting a building for a purpose not connected with the business on the land (for example, students who visit a factory to see how it works). The landowner owes the same duty of care to licensees that he owes to known trespassers. That is, he must warn them against hidden dangers of which he is aware, and he must exercise due care to ensure that they are not injured.

Invitees A final category of persons entering land is that of **invitee.** This is one who has been invited onto the land, usually, though not necessarily, for a business purpose of potential economic benefit to the owner or occupier of the premises. This category is confusing because it sounds as though it should include social guests (who clearly are invited onto the premises), but traditionally social guests are said to be licensees. Invitees include customers of stores, users of athletic and other clubs, customers of repair shops, strollers through public parks, restaurant and theater patrons, hotel guests, and the like. From the owner's perspective, the major difference between licensees and invitees is that he is liable for injuries resulting to the latter from hidden dangers that he *should have been aware of,* even if he is not actually aware of the dangers. How hidden the dangers and how broad the owner's liability depend on the circumstances, but liability sometimes can be quite broad; recall the case of the woman who recovered damages from a motel that provided inadequate security against her being raped (Chapter 9). Difficult questions arise in lawsuits brought by invitees (or *business invitees,* as they are sometimes called) when the actions of persons other than the landowner contribute to the injury, as illustrated by the following case.

KOLOSKY v. WINN DIXIE STORES, INC. 472 So.2d 891 (Fla. 1985)

HERSEY, CHIEF JUDGE. Helen and Kenneth Kolosky, plaintiffs below, appeal the trial court's final judgment directing a verdict in favor of Winn Dixie Stores, Inc. We reverse.

The Koloskys sued Winn Dixie, alleging negligence in failing to maintain its premises in a safe condition—specifically, in permitting three children to run unrestrained through the store—resulting in injury to Mrs. Kolosky. The complaint included a derivative claim by Mr. Kolosky.

The case was tried before a jury. Mrs. Kolosky testified that on December 4, 1980, she and her husband went shopping in a Winn Dixie store in Okeechobee, Florida. They were in the store thirty to forty-five minutes. When the Koloskys first entered the store, a woman carrying a baby and accompanied by three little boys (whom Mrs. Kolosky estimated were all under the age of six) entered just ahead of them. On several occasions over the course of the next half hour or more, she observed the three boys running through the store playing tag. She also saw a number of Winn Dixie employees stocking shelves in various aisles. This testimony was corroborated by Mr. Kolosky.

As the couple waited in the checkout line, Mrs. Kolosky realized she had forgotten to get coffee, proceeded to the coffee aisle, and started back to the checkout line. As she reached the end of the aisle, the three boys ran around the corner and knocked her down.

The store manager, James Addison, testified that there were six employees stocking the ten aisles of the store on the day in question. They all denied having observed the children running in the store.

The jury awarded $80,000 to Mrs. Kolosky and $20,000 to Mr. Kolosky, to be reduced fifty percent because of Mrs. Kolosky's own negligence. Winn Dixie renewed its motion for directed verdict on which the trial judge had previously reserved ruling. The trial court in its final judgment granted Winn Dixie's motion, finding in pertinent part, as follows:

> The injury sustained by Plaintiff was not the proximate cause of the purported negligent act of Defendant, and at most any such act amounted only to a remote cause of said injury; and further as to Plaintiff's injury, there is an independent intervening cause not foreseeable and the probable consequence of any wrongful actions of the Defendant.

* * *

The proprietor of a business owes a duty to invitees to protect them from reasonably foreseeable risks. "Foreseeability may be established . . . by proving that the proprietor had actual or constructive knowledge of a dangerous condition on his premises that was likely to cause harm to a patron." *Hall v. Billy Jack's, Inc.*, 458 So.2d 760, 761 (Fla.1984). A store may be held liable on the basis of constructive notice if "the condition is one which has existed for sufficient length of time that the owner should have known of it . . . ," regardless of whether it was created by a store employee or by an outsider.

* * *

In the instant case, evidence was adduced that the three children were observed running unsupervised through the store aisles several times over the course of approximately thirty to forty-five minutes. Winn Dixie had six employees stocking shelves at the time, and the store manager was present as well. This is sufficient to support a finding of constructive notice of the dangerous condition and a reasonable opportunity to correct it.

* * *

Appellee cites a number of cases in which a store or other business was found not to be liable for injuries inflicted on one patron or customer by another. These cases are distinguishable because each involves a sudden, unexpected action by the tortfeasor where there was no prior indication that the tortfeasor was engaging in the type of conduct which caused the injury. Under such circumstances the business does not have actual or constructive

A 8
B 9
C 0
D 1
E 2
F 3
G 4
H 5
I 6
J 7